DATE DUE

NOV 0 2 1996	
11/16/95	
DEC 1 1996	9863518
MAR 1 9 2005	2310167

GAYLORD

PRINTED IN U.S.A.

Research and Theory
in Family Science

Research and Theory in Family Science

Edited by

Randal D. Day
Washington State University

Kathleen R. Gilbert
Indiana University

Barbara H. Settles
University of Delaware

Wesley R. Burr
Brigham Young University

Brooks/Cole Publishing Company

I**T**P™ *An International Thomson Publishing Company*

Pacific Grove • Albany • Bonn • Boston • Cincinnati • Detroit • London • Madrid • Melbourne
Mexico City • New York • Paris • San Francisco • Singapore • Tokyo • Toronto • Washington

Sponsoring Editor: *Vicki Knight*
Marketing Representative: *Hester Winn*
Editorial Associate: *Lauri Banks Ataide*
Production Editor: *Kirk Bomont*
Manuscript Editor: *Bill Waller*
Permissions Editor: *Elaine Jones*
Marketing Team: *Carolyn Crockett and Jean Vevers Thompson*

Interior and Cover Design: *Roy R. Neuhaus*
Interior Illustration: *Susan H. Horovitz and Lisa Torri*
Art Coordinator: *Susan H. Horovitz*
Indexer: *Do Mi Stauber*
Typesetting: *Joan Mueller Cochrane*
Cover Printing: *Color Dot Graphics, Inc.*
Printing and Binding: *Quebecor Printing Fairfield*

HQ
518
.R43
1995

For more information, contact:

BROOKS/COLE PUBLISHING COMPANY
511 Forest Lodge Road
Pacific Grove, CA 93950
USA

International Thomson Publishing Europe
Berkshire House 168–173
High Holborn
London WC1V 7AA
England

Thomas Nelson Australia
102 Dodds Street
South Melbourne, 3205
Victoria, Australia

Nelson Canada
1120 Birchmount Road
Scarborough, Ontario
Canada M1K 5G4

International Thomson Editores
Campos Eliseos 385, Piso 7
Col. Polanco
11560 México D. F. México

International Thomson Publishing GmbH
Königswinterer Strasse 418
53227 Bonn
Germany

International Thomson Publishing Asia
221 Henderson Road
#05–10 Henderson Building
Singapore 0315

International Thomson Publishing Japan
Hirakawacho Kyowa Building, 3F
2-2-1 Hirakawacho
Chiyoda-ku, Tokyo 102
Japan

Printed in the United States of America

10   9   8   7   6   5   4   3   2   1

Library of Congress Cataloging-in-Publication Data

Research and theory in family science / edited by Randal D. Day . . .
    [et al.].
        p.   cm.
    Includes biliographical references and index.
    ISBN 0-534-21780-x
    1. Family, 2. Family—Research.   I. Day. Randal D., [date].
HQ518.R43 1995

306.85—dc20   94-30436
                                                    CIP

We dedicate this book to our families, who support and provide the important meanings of life; to our students, whom we serve and in whom resides the future; and to our colleagues, who provide the professional hope that what we do has purpose.

Contributors

Suzanne Bartle
Department of Family Relations and Human Development
The Ohio State University
Columbus, OH 43210

Denise Ann Bodman
Department of Family Resource and Human Development
Arizona State University
Tempe, AZ 85287

Wesley R. Burr
Department of Family Sciences
Brigham Young University
Provo, UT 84602

Karen Price Carver
Department of Human Development
Washington State University
Pullman, WA 99163

Marilyn Coleman
Department of Human Development and Family Studies
University of Missouri-Columbia
Columbia, MO 65211

Kerry Daly
Department of Family Studies
University of Guelph
Guelph, Ontario N1G 2W1

Randal D. Day
Department of Human Development
Washington State University
Pullman, WA 99163

Mark Fine
Department of Psychology
University of Dayton
Dayton, OH 45469

Larry Ganong
Department of Human Development and Family Studies
University of Missouri-Columbia
Columbia, MO 65211

Kathleen R. Gilbert
Department of Applied Health Science
Indiana University
Bloomington, IN 47405

Kip W. Jenkins
Institute of Religion
University of Idaho
Moscow, ID 83871

Robert Keim
Department of Human Family Resources
Northern Illinois University
DeKalb, IL 60115

Geoffrey K. Leigh
Department of Human Development and Family Studies
University of Nevada, Reno
Reno, NV 89557

Linda Matocha
College of Nursing
University of Delaware
Newark, DE 19716

Patrick C. McKenry
Department of Family Relations and Human Development
The Ohio State University
Columbus, OH 43210

D. Eugene Mead
Department of Family Sciences
Marriage and Family Therapy Graduate Program
Brigham Young University
Provo, UT 84602

Colleen I. Murray
Department of Human Development and Family Studies
University of Nevada, Reno
Reno, NV 89557

David H. Olson
Department of Family Social Science
University of Minnesota
St. Paul, MN 55108

Dennis Orthner
Human Services Research Laboratory
Department of Social Work
University of North Carolina at Chapel Hill
Chapel Hill, NC 27599

Gary W. Peterson
Department of Family Resources and Human Development
Arizona State University
Tempe, AZ 85287

Peggy Quinn
Department of Social Work
University of Texas at Arlington
Arlington, TX 76013

Barbara H. Settles
Department of Individual and Family Studies
University of Delaware
Newark, DE 19716

Suzanne K. Steinmetz
Department of Sociology
Indiana University
Indianapolis, IN 46202

Karen Schmid
College of Social Sciences
St. Cloud State University
St. Cloud, MN 56303

Jay D. Teachman
Department of Human Development
Washington State University
Pullman, WA 99163

Linda J. Wark
Department of Family Relations and Human Development
The Ohio State University
Columbus, OH 43210

Preface

As the study of the family continues to grow and mature, knowledge about family processes builds. This text is designed to provide advanced students with substantive information about those processes. It is written to target those students who are interested in further exploring the family realm. We assume that readers have had an introductory course in family science.

When we gave instructions to the authors about writing their chapters, we asked them to focus more on processes within the family realm than on larger issues or on individuals within the family. The text is written from the perspective that between the larger social world and the individual psychological world is a unique small group, the family. We assume that activities and processes occur within families that may not be found elsewhere. We also assume that by studying these activities and processes, students will better learn how to intervene in family problems as they make their way into the workforce.

This text was reorganized many times. As the editorial team struggled with how to present the material, it became clear that the usual ways of organizing a family text were not working. Family texts are usually organized along a developmental trajectory—beginning with engagement and proceeding to love, marriage, children, marital problems, and death. Instead, this book is organized around family *processes*, so that the advanced student can begin to explore the theories and research about the "interior" of families. These processes are presented within the larger contexts in which families

live and work. Additionally, these processes are explored in the context of a variety of family challenges.

In Part I, we explore four contexts within which families thrive—larger societal value systems, ideologies about connectedness, gender formulations, and cultural difference.

In Part II, we examine the theoretical and scientific approaches used by family scientists as they try to understand family interaction.

In Part III, we give the reader a more in-depth view of the processes families use as they move through their days, solve problems, and make life's decisions. We analyze how family members communicate, parent, and resolve sexual problems.

Part IV presents several topics relating to family changes. The authors were challenged not simply to make a compendium of all that is known about a topic, but instead to discuss the topics from a systemic viewpoint and to illuminate processes the families use in periods of crisis.

Finally, two chapters about the field of family science are included in Part V to stimulate discussion about what a person does when he or she wants to work in this field.

As you read and study about the family in this text, we invite you to comment directly to us about the issues we raise. It is our intention that there be a second edition of this text, and we would very much like to hear from you about topics not covered (and we know there are many), issues not raised, applications that can be made, and ways to improve this material. In a way, we are asking you (and teachers as well) to help think through what "ought" to be taught to upper-division students who are preparing for work in the family and human service arena. We would appreciate your ideas and feedback.

Acknowledgments

No project can be done in isolation. First, we wish to thank the authors who contributed to this volume. Without their hard work and patience, the project would have not succeeded. As this text took shape over the course of several years, it became clear to us that it was taking on a life of its own, becoming somewhat different from the image with which we began. That image changed, in many cases, as the result of reactions from reviewers and the chapter authors. We were pushed to make the product better and more usable than it originally would have been.

We are also in debt to the National Council on Family Relations, especially the Family Science section.

Over the course of the development of this text, chapters have been part of presentations at several NCFR meetings. The session format used by the council has been very useful in providing feedback.

The Teaching Family Science Conference also provided a forum in which aspects of this chapter were discussed and reworked. The chapters by Karen Schmid, Peggy Quinn, Philip Osborne, and Robert Keim emerged from discussions at this conference.

We are indebted to our departments, which have provided technical support and assistance. Brooks/Cole has also been a consistent and helpful sponsor of this project. We are appreciative of the work of Vicki Knight, who assisted us through this process.

Finally, we'd like to thank the reviewers who critiqued the manuscript: Douglas A. Abbott, University of Nebraska-Omaha; Bernita Quoss, University of Wyoming; and Jane Rysberg, California State University, Chico.

Randal D. Day
Kathleen R. Gilbert
Barbara H. Settles
Wesley R. Burr

Brief Contents

Contents

CHAPTER   8

The Science of Family Science
Karen Price Carver / Jay D. Teachman   113

PART   III

Understanding
Family Processes   129

CHAPTER   9

Family Systems:
Understanding Your Roots
David H. Olson   131

C H A P T E R   1 0

Families in Everyday Life
Barbara H. Settles   154

C H A P T E R   1 1

Communication in Families
Kip W. Jenkins   171

Research and Theory
in Family Science

PART I

Families in Contexts

The goal of this text (and each chapter) is to provide you with a better understanding of family processes within an ecological context. Urie Bronfennbrenner, a well-known researcher and specialist in human development, has suggested that the world of the individual is best understood when we think about the setting in which he or she lives. Writers who use this perspective often think of the metaphor of the Russian "nested" dolls. Each carved wooden doll fits inside the next larger one. The individual lives within a family, families flourish within communities, and communities form larger cultures. It is, however, important to remember that these *contexts* are not the only element of this puzzle. Within the context and "behind closed doors," families use *processes* to solve the problems of everyday life, meet crises, and negotiate the challenges that cross their paths. Part I considers the contexts, which are the frameworks, settings, and situations in which families succeed or falter. (The processes are taken up in Part III.)

In Chapter 1, Dennis Orthner presents the first context to be considered: the historical framework within which Western families have emerged and the transitions through which they are going. He limits his discussion to Western families and targets how those families have thrived in the United States. He uses in his discussion of "family values" a popular notion in North American culture. In the 1990s, many are asking what the role of the family is. Some suggest that it has no place in society (in its current form), and others wax nostalgic for days gone by when families were better or

stronger than now. Orthner asks us to consider the value of marriage versus independence. As you read this chapter, ask yourself if you believe that marriage is a "given." Perhaps there are other ways in which society should be handling close relationships. Another important theme, found in both Chapters 1 and 2, is the contrast between individualism and collectivism. As both authors remind us, how we resolve this matter has a substantial impact upon family policy and internal family functioning.

Chapter 2 asks us to take a hard look at the history of autonomy in American culture. The author, Gary W. Peterson, reminds us that a primary theme of American society is fierce independence. We must now consider how that context meshes with the idea of family connection. Peterson asks the important question "Can both exist simultaneously?" As he explores the issues of autonomy, he shows us how this idea has emerged as a major theme in a variety of disciplines. He also shows us that this concept is a critical one for family science. A primary objective for families and family researchers is to discover the optimal balance between connectedness and individualism.

Chapter 3 asks us to consider one important framework that defines the world in which we live: gender. Again, as an issue of historical significance, the author, Peggy Quinn, suggests that gender roles and assignments have changed dramatically over the past 50 years in the United States. Additionally, she shows how many of those changes have been different for men and women of different subcultures. One of her conclusions is that economic and cultural conditions have had a substantial impact on the context of family life.

Chapter 4 presents another setting. In this chapter Karen Schmid suggests that cultural diversity is something to embrace, not something that we casually tolerate. Some scholars are beginning to realize that it is diversity that makes us stronger. It is less useful in today's society to think about trying to get all families to be similar. Think of a lawn with its uniform blades of grass all cut to the same length. The contrasting view is the meadow, with tall grass as well as short weeds (troubling to some and delightful to others). We also see a variety of flowers and other plants whose names we may not even know. Some are suggesting that they like the feel and smell of the meadow better than the clipped lawn. So we must look at families from all over the world and from different cultures not as aberrational but as vital to the richness of the meadow.

Certainly, these are not the only contexts within which the family abides. Throughout the text you will see several other contextual chapters mixed in which those we are calling process chapters and even applied chapters, which appear at the end of the book. There are various ways in which one can arrange the cascading fountain of ideas we place under the rubric of family science. It may be the case that as you read this text your instructor will want to present these issues in his or her own order. Of course, we all bring to the study of the family our own unique world view and personal experience. Which, of course, is another one of the framing contexts used to view the family.

Families in Transition: Changing Values and Norms

Dennis Orthner
University of North Carolina

The American family has been changing. On that, most observers agree, no matter their vantage point. The politics of the 1990s have been dominated by concerns over family change and "family values" (Doherty, 1992). The fear that these undergirding values are eroding and that families are being left adrift on a sea of confusion has raised the specter of family decline and disorganization as the norm rather than the exception.

Any observer of the family will have noticed a seemingly negative picture of the family that has emerged in recent times: divorce rates have been rising, women have entered the labor force in record numbers, children are more likely to be left unattended or in group day-care arrangements, nonmarital cohabitation is increasingly common, and the number of single people in the population has been rising. These trends have been noted, examined, and speculated about for decades by social scientists and are now quite familiar to the public through an ever-increasing number of special reports in the media and often sensational debates in public-policy arenas.

The purpose of this chapter, as an introduction to this text, is to focus on the directions of change and, if possible, help draw attention to that which will (1) mitigate the negative impacts of change and (2) foster those emerging family patterns and values that help the family adapt to contemporary cultural drifts. The fundamental question is no longer (if it ever was) *how to stop* family changes from occurring but *how to shape* family changes in a direction that minimizes their disruptions on potentially vulnerable groups, such as children and the poor, and maximizes the effectiveness of other organizations in society, such as businesses and community services.

It is my position that these family changes are connected to and perhaps rooted in fundamental shifts in norms and values in North American society as well as in the world. Much of the discussion about the family centers on changes in family structures and functions. However, these are but behavioral manifestations (structural observations) and interpretations (functional observations) of what is occurring at the soul of society. The beliefs that once formed the basis for relational stability are being reexamined. No longer do people understand what is expected of them. The sanctions that used to enforce boundaries for inappropriate behaviors have been crumbling. We can no longer easily define the required duties and obligations associated with such critical roles as husband, wife, mother, father, grandparent, or neighbor.

Too much attention in the debate over family change has been focused on the *structural properties* of families today. Not enough attention is paid to the *underlying processes* of families, including their abilities to handle new stresses, reach out for assistance, adopt new roles, alter patterns of courtship and sexuality, and satisfactorily adapt to the changes that are occurring in other systems outside themselves. (For a more complete discussion of these types of processes see Chapters 6 and 9.) True, counting the number of divorces or determining whether a mother is employed is much easier, but these structural characteristics by themselves are quite weak predictors of the consequences that most of us really care about: personal and family well-being, economic mobility, educational attainment, children's health, and antisocial behavior (Cherlin, 1988; Edwards, 1987).

Norms of individual and family behaviors and the values that underlie those behaviors are in transition. This results in unstable and widely varying interpretations of appropriate and inappropriate behavior. During major transitions such as these, any organization (family, corporation, government) will find it difficult to establish firm rules for organizational formation, maintenance, and dissolution. The family system is not alone in this struggle: we can see similar organizational stresses and redefinitions being deliberated in businesses (Burrell & Morgan, 1982), in schools (U. S. National Commission on Excellence in Education, 1983), in governments (*perestroika*), and in communities (Bellah, Madsen, Sullivan, Swidler, & Tipton, 1985). Nearly all social systems are renegotiating their fundamental bases for order. The oft-noted "crisis" of reorganization is much broader than the family, but the seeds for new organizational patterns and the high costs of failing to achieve a new level of stability occur *within* the family.

Changing Family Values and Beliefs

Beliefs and values undergird any social organization or system. These values represent the vital cultural elements of a system, and they help chart the course for the behaviors of the system's members. The family system is no exception. It develops and maintains sets of beliefs and values that define the rules of behavior for family members. These rules vary between societies and also between subgroups within a society. Thus, it is not surprising that the values and expressed beliefs in the United States regarding premarital sexuality, for example, can be quite different from those in Sweden or China. Likewise, subcultures within the United States may also vary in their expectations of sexual expression.

It is commonly believed that the values that govern family goals and behavior have changed significantly over the last century. In his discourse on "new rules," Daniel Yankelovich (1981) refers to the "giant plates of the culture" that have been changing dramatically over this century. As in the geological theory of plate tectonics, these cultural plates sometimes shift position, grind

against each other, and promote instabilities in basic values and beliefs (the cultural equivalent of an earthquake). According to Yankelovich:

> We now need a new social ethic. Without one we are disoriented, lacking a firm basis for choice. We need new rules to define the epochal tasks that must be accomplished in our era to bring about that minimal harmony between individual and society that is the mark of a successful civilization. (p. 249)

Many of the core values that have been changing are related to fundamental processes of the family. To the extent that these have been radically changed, the bases for family organization may have changed. Some of the core values commonly assumed to have been altered include the high priority given to independence instead of marriage, to individual freedom over collective interests, to instrumental commitments instead of intrinsic commitments, and to personal pleasure instead of nurturance.

The Value of Marriage versus Independence

Those who speculate that the family system is declining contend that marriage as an ideal is less important today than it was earlier. They suggest that positive values associated with voluntary singleness have become more common, making marriage more of a choice than a necessity among those who have traditionally been in the marriage market. If this is true, marriage as a valued institution is indeed in trouble, and other forms of nonmarital living arrangements may replace it in the future.

Several sources provide evidence to support this thesis, including the increased proportion of unmarried people in the population and the rising number of nonmarital cohabitants. It is clear that a decision not to marry is no longer considered a disgrace, and delaying marriage for several years is less likely to foster predictions of spinsterhood. More adults in the United States today are ambivalent on the issue of whether it is better to be married than single for life (33%), and a minority (16%) even disagree with that assumption (Bumpass & Sweet, 1988). Likewise, there is growing acceptance of nonmarital cohabitation, with 33% of adults considering these relationships "OK" in 1989, compared with 22% in 1986 ("Attitudes toward Marriage," 1989). But concerns over a drift toward preferences for independent living arrangements appear to be overblown. A consistent 96% of the American public for 30 years has expressed a personal desire for marriage (Cherlin, 1988). Only 8% of adult women consider remaining single an ideal, and this has not changed for two decades (Gallup, 1987). More than 80% of the high school classes of 1972 and 1980 said it was "very important" to marry and have a happy family life, and these beliefs increased after graduation (Zill & Rogers, 1988). Surveys of college freshman have also remained consistent, with 70% of those surveyed in 1970 and 1985 expressing a strong desire for rearing a family (Zill & Rogers, 1988).

What these statistics suggest is a greater tolerance for independent living in the population but a stable personal preference for marriage among youths and adults. While the percentage of adults who are single and cohabitating has increased, this increase appears to be the result of marriage delays and the use of cohabitation as a testing phase in courtship rather than a rejection of marriage as a way of life. The overall marriage rate may decline from the 95% pinnacle of the 1970s to an 85 to 90% rate, but this is still high by worldwide standards. Somewhat more traditional societies, such as Ireland and Australia, have considerably lower marriage rates (McDonald, 1988), but they are not usually considered in "decline." If anything, the value of marriage as a preferable living arrangement appears to be holding its own during this time of institutional transition.

Individualism versus Collectivism

A second value-related concern is that individualism has become so strong that interest in the collectivities of family and community has substantially declined. This is not a question of the ability of adults to form commitments but of the centrality of personal interests over the interests of others. Bellah and his colleagues note that "individualism lies at the very core of American cultures. . . . We believe in the dignity, indeed the sacredness, of the individual. . . . Our highest and noblest aspirations, not only for ourselves but for those we care about, for our society and for the world, are closely

linked to our individualism" (Bellah et al., 1985, p. 142; see also Chapter 2 for an in-depth discussion of the nature of individualism versus collectivism). Popenoe (1988) worries, however, that "cultural trends associated with the growing importance placed on 'self-fulfillment' . . . could be regarded as another important contributor to the high family-dissolution rate" (p. 289).

Unlike marital preferences, the level of individualism in a society and the degree to which it is changing are difficult to assess. However, history generally regards American society as highly individualistic over its entire course. Early observers of American community and family patterns frequently commented on the strength of individualistic ethics, not just on the frontier but in cities as well (Tocqueville, 1898/1969). Carl Solberg (1973) has written, "The oldest dilemma that has afflicted American society from its founding in the New World has been the ceaseless conflict between its often unbridled individualism and its fitful and inadequate sense of community" (p. 259). Indeed, American communities have never been characterized by the sense of what the German sociologist Tönnies called *Gemeinschaft*, a collective sense of primary relationships that dominates all aspects of community and kin life.

If individualism has been such a dominant feature of American life, how has it manifested itself in the family? One way is through what has been called the development of "modified extended families" (Litwak, 1960). Without a strong tradition of extended family households in America (Goode, 1963), we created, from the very beginning, a pattern of relatively independent households with strong help networks with kin and friends. If these help networks have been eroding, we can assume that individualism has indeed triumphed over collective interests, at least in the family arena.

Studies conducted during the 1950s found that people felt a strong sense of obligation to help family members. To some researchers this came as a surprise, because they too had come to believe that family interests had declined in favor of individualism (Young & Willmot, 1957). These researchers instead discovered frequent visits among family members, financial help given to younger and older members, help with child care and other household tasks, and exchanges of advice on a variety of matters. In fact, even though most people admitted that they preferred to prove their independence by rarely seeking help, few refused help when it was offered (Sussman, 1965).

The situation today is not that different. Visits among relatives, especially with parents, have not declined significantly since the 1950s. Over half (53%) of the adults who have parents see them at least once a month, and a similar percentage (51%) agree that aging parents should live with their adult children. Among the sample of families participating in the National Survey of Families and Households (Bumpass & Sweet, 1988), the majority (55%) believe that they can call on their relatives in the middle of the night if they have an emergency, and two out of three (66%) say they can borrow $200 from a relative in an emergency. This is not a gloomy picture of rugged individualism. Rather, it suggests that collective interests and concerns remain strong in American families, even with the historical context of a culture that promotes individual interests. As Peterson suggests in Chapter 2, Americans are still attempting to find the best balance between individual and collective interests, but little evidence suggests that they are giving up on the family perspective in the process.

Commitment versus Autonomy

The tension between commitment and autonomy is experienced by both individuals and societies. Autonomy has often been prized because it reflects a level of competence that is typically associated with adulthood and maturity. While commitments imply reciprocal obligations, autonomy promises the freedom to enter and leave obligations based on self-defined interests alone. McDonald (1988) explains:

> The dilemma faced by families today is the same dilemma that occupied the minds of the Enlightenment philosophers: the reconciliation of the goal of personal autonomy with the conviction that man is irreducibly social. . . . In a heavily structured society, roles are prescribed and the individual has little scope for self-direction. The Enlightenment was a reaction to such structure, and for the past 250 years we have been following a topsy-turvy path towards the goal of individual autonomy. (p. 44)

From a developmental vantage point, childhood has been described in a similar fashion. Many of the developmental activities of children are associated with increased autonomy (Erikson, 1968), culminating in adolescence and young adulthood when this freedom reaches its hiatus. After that, adults seek, once again, a balance between the security of attachments and the freedom to pursue individual interests (Scanzoni, 1987). Indeed, an adult's level of maturity is often defined not by the ability to pursue personal gain but by the ability to sacrifice individual interests in favor of commitments to others.

One of the most commonly used frameworks in family theory and family therapy is built on the assumption of a balance between autonomy and commitments. In their "circumplex" model of family behavior, Olson and his colleagues (1983) assume that extremes in either family member autonomy (disengagement) or cohesion (enmeshment) have measurable negative consequences for relationships. Their research indicates that families whose members have balanced interests in separateness and togetherness are the most likely to report being satisfied and to stay married.

The inability of many couples to sustain lifelong commitments is often taken as evidence that family commitments have weakened. Furthermore, a large proportion of youths and adults worry that this trend will continue. In a recent survey, 45% of those polled believed that most people who got married would get divorced; only 39% believed that people got married and expected it to last forever ("Attitudes toward Marriage," 1989). Nevertheless, many people have difficulty sorting out this general sense of pessimism from a personal sense of optimism about their own relationships. The vast majority of adults (71%) believe that "marriage is a lifelong commitment that should not be ended except under extreme circumstances" (Bumpass & Sweet, 1988). Even more Americans (85%) say they would remarry their spouses if they had to do it all over again (D. Weiss, 1988). Even the divorced and separated hold positive ambitions: most who can do so will remarry, and 81% still believe that marriage is a commitment for life.

These statistics do not indicate that Americans are running headlong away from marriage and family commitments. Instead, they indicate a strong underlying search for meaningful commitments and a healthy fear of the negative consequences if their relationships do not last. Perhaps social scientists have been all too successful in pronouncing the decline in commitments, because the fear of marital failure continued to rise through the 1980s, even though divorce rates have stabilized and even declined in the past decade and a half.

What social scientists have not been as successful at marketing (to others or themselves) is the understanding that commitment is a process, not a stable product. Social-psychological research tells us that a commitment is inherently unstable, "something that grows and changes over time" (Brickman, 1987). Long-term commitments are more uncommon than common, and commitments have rarely been for life, unless there were external constraints that made no other option available. For example, even though divorce may have been uncommon in the 19th century, marital desertion was a serious problem.

Unfortunately, we know much less about the processes of commitment than we do the consequences of its absence. We understand much better its instrumental aspects, based on weighing expected costs and rewards, than its intrinsic aspects, which are more selfless and other-centered (Orthner, 1981). Bellah and his colleagues (1985) suggest that commitments themselves have not eroded during the 20th century; instead, we have shifted our bases for commitment toward intrinsic qualities, what they call "the therapeutic attitude." This type of commitment is inherently more satisfying but more fragile. Thus, the balance between autonomy and commitment continues to shift, not away from commitments but toward those types of commitment that provide mutual and balanced gratifications for all family members.

Nurturance versus Narcissism

Of all of the concerns about the contemporary family and its underlying values, none is perhaps more worrisome than the fear that men and women have lapsed into a narcissistic binge with little concern for anyone other than themselves. This fear reached epidemic proportions in the 1970s and early 1980s as an increasingly vocal humanistic psychology movement placed considerable emphasis on the reification of the self (Schnall, 1981). The search for intimacy, a basic human need, was intensely directed toward personal awareness and needs, where it had always begun, and away from lasting relationships, where intimacy usually matured (Orthner, 1981). A cultural drift toward narcissism was claimed by many observers (Nelson, 1977).

Elements of this concern have been raised earlier, but we now need to face it head on. Have we lost any of our capacity to nurture either other adults or children? Has the basic social value of supporting others been eroded? Does selfishness, caring, or some balance of the two characterize most relationships? These are critical questions that focus our attention on a core set of values for the contemporary family. If the modern family has shifted its primary functions away from meeting instrumental needs toward meeting expressive needs, its ability to provide nurturance for its members has become the mainstay of its existence.

About one fundamental maxim there is little debate: The human psychological need for nurturance is innate. Unlike lower animals, humans are born with the need to be dependent and with few, if any, instincts to guide their development. The earliest relationships formed by humans are based on the physiological processes, including feeding and body comfort. Although these forces transform themselves in adulthood, the needs for nurturance remain. The basic psychological need for interdependence is considered fundamental to personal well-being and is equally strong in both women and men. As Ashley Montague (1971) observes, "It is probable that sexual activity, indeed the frantic preoccupation with sex that characterizes Western culture, is in many cases not the expression of sexual interest at all, but rather a search for the satisfaction of the need for contact" (p. 167).

The evidence that modern men and women are no longer interested in nurturing others, only themselves, is scanty. The data supporting this claim are largely impressionistic and qualitative. On the contrary, expressed desires for intimate relationships have not decreased, nor have people who have left unsatisfactory relationships turned against the search for intimacy with others. Summarizing the results of their landmark study of divorced men and women, Hetherington, Cox, and Cox (1977) write:

> The divorced individuals wanted sustained, meaningful relationships and were not satisfied with a

series of superficial encounters. The formation of lasting intimate relations, involving deep concern and a willingness to make sacrifices for the partner, as well as a strong attachment and desire to be near the person, was a strong factor in happiness, self-esteem, and feelings of competence in sexual relations for both divorced men and women. (p. 42)

But what about the children? If the nurturance needs of adults are largely being met, are the needs of children being sacrificed? Yes, if public perceptions are any guide. Nearly three out of four adults (74%) believe that the problems affecting children have grown worse since they were young. This is especially true for women (79%) and African Americans (84%), and the perceptions of parents and nonparents are similar. Much of the blame for the problems of children are laid on parents; only 53% of adults believe that most children have loving parents. As for the larger society, 63% think that too little effort has been directed toward the problems of children (Harris, 1987).

Studies of children themselves present a much more mixed picture. Some indicators have improved over the past few decades, especially children's physical health; some have declined over this period, especially social misconduct and suicide; others have both risen and fallen, especially indicators of economic well-being and academic achievement; and still others have remained the same—notably, measures of psychological well-being (Zill & Rogers, 1988). On balance, the lives and circumstances of children have not declined to the extent that the public perceives. But there is little question that most adults feel collectively guilty about their lack of attention to the nurturance needs of children (Komarnicki, 1991). Still, when parents were asked if they wished they could be free from the responsibilities of childrearing, only 8% agreed and 71% disagreed (Bumpass & Sweet, 1988). Although this is not the picture of parental and societal neglect that some would like to paint, it does suggest that more attention to children's needs is needed.

Overall, the data reviewed suggest that needs for adult and child nurturance remain strong in U. S. society. The issues being raised over the rearing and nurturance of children reflect an undercurrent of concern that is now being transformed into more support services for parents and their children. The increased emphasis on narcissism and selfishness that has been suggested does

not appear to be a strong cultural value at this time, but it may reflect heightened opportunities for personal freedom during adolescence and young adulthood.

Values Revolution versus Evolution

The much-heralded values revolution that we hear so much about today is a bust. Even so, changes have occurred in some of the family-related values we have just examined. Most of these changes can be described as extensions of cultural drifts that have been occurring for decades, even centuries. Like the imagery of change in Yankelovich's (1981) "giant plates of culture," this so-called values revolution has been a slow and grinding process.

The notion of a values *evolution* appears to better account for the trends we have observed. Instead of Americans having transformed their culture in the last several decades toward individualism and autonomy and away from marriage and nurturance, the data suggest that few of the basic tenets of family organization have changed. Long-term trends away from family values have been overblown. There has been too much emphasis on changes since the 1950s; the relatively brief period since then represents a blip on the broad historical panorama we have examined.

There are warning signs, however, that we need to move cautiously in some value-related areas. The cultural drift toward increased autonomy and less understanding of the nurturance needs of children may have gone too far. Recent surveys suggest that the American public is concerned about this trend and wants to see renewed attention to fostering commitments and caring for children, both within the family and in public and private institutions. This concern of the public is echoed by a growing number of commentators who believe that we need to chart a new course. Nevertheless, the route of this new course must be bounded by the rather consistent values that have been evolving in America since its inception.

Changing Family Norms

Even though the basic family values embedded in our culture have not changed dramatically, the norms of family behavior have been undergoing significant transformations in the last few decades. Family norms, as I am defining them, refer to the expectations for those behaviors associated with the statuses and roles of family members. Whereas values are attached to beliefs, norms are guidelines for behavior and can emerge as a consequence of behavioral changes as well. Thus, norms guide our actions and tell us what are appropriate and inappropriate ways to behave in the circumstances in which we find ourselves.

Many of the problems associated with the contemporary family are not tied to value transitions as much as they are to norm transitions. To a large extent, the family system as a whole, as well as the processes occurring within many families, are confused by conflicting, incongruent, or absent family norms. Because the rules of family behavior have changed so dramatically in some areas, many men, women, and children do not know how to respond to the expectations of one another. With so many alternative cues to guide behavior, confusion is now more the rule than the exception in intimate relationships.

This concern over the rules that guide family behavior has been growing. Observers of family processes have noted that many of the more definitive guidelines for conduct in families have been relaxed or lost over the past several decades (Burr, Day, & Bahr, 1993). Family health is often clinically defined by the presence of well-understood and nondestructive rule systems that guide family interaction and personal conduct. But destructive rules or the absence of clear rules makes family interaction difficult and diminishes opportunities for establishing successful mutual adaptations to changing family conditions or needs (Reiss, 1981).

Family roles, in particular, are experiencing major rule transitions. The sociologist Joan Aldous (1978) refers to this as a period in which *role making* is dominating the process of *role taking*. During an earlier period of our history, the roles of men, women, and children were relatively well defined. The expectations for the socialization of boys and girls were quite clear, and the qualities one looked for in a mate were easily discernible. At that time, most women and men simply adopted the roles of their parents and got the cues for their behavior from relatively well-defined norms. This is not the case today. While traditional roles remain the norm in some subsets of society, most men and women are not sure of the expectations that others have for them or that they have for themselves.

This sense of normative ambiguity has led to considerable confusion and stress in many families. For example, several studies have found that couples with congruent expectations regarding the household roles of men and women are much more likely to be satisfied and stable in their marriages than couples with incongruent expectations (Bowen & Orthner, 1983; Levinger, 1986; Olson et al., 1983). Other research studies have shown that congruency between norms and behaviors can have important psychological consequences. For example, a study of depression in married women found that the least depressed women were those who were employed and preferred to be and those who were not employed and preferred not to be. The wives who were employed but not by their choice were significantly more depressed; the most depressed were those who were not employed but who wanted to be (Ross, Mirowski, & Huber, 1983).

Another contemporary problem associated with a normative change lies in the significant shift away from ascribed family roles toward achieved family roles. In other words, the roles in the family, be they mother, father, son, or daughter, are no longer defined by larger societal norms. Instead, each role has to be customized and defined within the context of the family system itself. My role as a father, for example, is defined more by the expectations of what my wife and children want of me than what society says a father should do for his family. While this gives me more freedom to develop a personally enjoyable father role, it also increases the level of anxiety associated with the role, since my success as a father is contingent on ever-changing reinforcements. Thus, family norms have become more fluid and subject to change as a result of interactions and changes in other social norms.

A brief review of norm changes in several areas of family development can illustrate this point. Norms associated with relational formation, relational maintenance, and relational disillusion will be examined.

Relational-formation norms.   The norms that guide dating, courtship, and mate selection have changed dramatically in recent decades. The guidelines for appropriate interpersonal and sexual behavior have changed so quickly that children and their parents now have major differences in the behaviors they expect to dominate adolescence and young adulthood. Dating, for example, has been largely replaced by "going out" and group events that have few of the rules traditionally associated with dating in the 1950s and 1960s.

The norms relating to sexual behavior have also changed. While the proportion of adolescents engaging in sexual intercourse has increased somewhat, even more revolutionary are the norms associated with this behavior. The proportion of adults who believed in total sexual abstinence before marriage dropped from 80% to only 30% between 1963 and 1975 (National Opinion Research Center, 1977). Among adults who responded to the national General Social Surveys, 68% in 1969 believed that premarital sex was wrong, compared with only 39% in 1985. This trend became somewhat more conservative between 1985 and 1987, when 46% reported that they believed premarital sex was wrong. However, the adults in the latter year were so split on the issue that 46% said it was wrong while 48% said it was all right (National Opinion Research Corporation, 1988).

Norms linking pregnancy and marriage have also changed. In the 1960s, youths who became pregnant were expected to get married, and over half of them did prior to the birth. In contrast, by the 1980s more babies were being conceived outside of marriage, but fewer than one-third of these conceptions resulted in the mother's marriage by the time of the birth (O'Connell & Rogers, 1984). Thus, even though children represent a sign of stability in marriage, they are less likely to precipitate a marriage than they were a decade or two ago.

Even norms associated with marriage itself have undergone some significant transformations. The legal event of marriage is less and less associated with the formal confirmation of commitment between partners. Nonmarital cohabitation has become so common that many observers now consider it a stage in the family life cycle, more of a choice than a deviation from normative family development patterns. A survey in 1989 found that 31% of American adults considered living together before marriage to be "OK," while 37% considered it "always wrong." However, age is a major factor in these attitudes. Among those under 30, 43% considered living together an acceptable arrangement, while only 11% of those over 60 agreed with this position ("Attitudes," 1989).

These and other data suggest that relational-formation norms have undergone significant change

and are continuing to do so. The level of confusion over courtship and sexual norms is extremely high, leaving open many avenues for interpretation for those who are developing relationships or observing these relationships, such as parents. Without adequate societal guidelines, considerable deviations are likely in what some consider to be acceptable behaviors. And the end of this confusion does not appear to be in sight.

Relational-maintenance norms.   The ambiguity of relational norms is also reflected in marriage and other adult relationships. So confusing are many of these expectations that most social and family scientists have given up their attempts to describe the traditional family life cycle. The researchers conducting a large longitudinal sample of adults (the Panel Study of Income Dynamics) were forced to abandon the traditional family-development approach of tracking families over time. They relinquished that strategy because "there were no consistent or acceptable definitions of what constitutes the same family over time" (Duncan & Morgan, 1985, p. 53).

Today, only a minority of families follow what was once the traditional pattern of the couple getting married and having children, mothers staying at home with the children, children leaving home, and the couple living into old age and death together. Glen Elder (1975) cautions that predictable development in the family is limited because our conceptions of development are tied to the "reproductive process . . . and [are] applicable . . . to a restrictive segment of the population that follows the script of a marriage which endures to old age and produces at least one child; variations in family form are excluded" (p. 178).

Nowhere is the ambiguity in family norms more apparent than in the emerging roles of mothers and fathers. The overwhelming majority of adults (78%) believe that couples should have children in order for their marriage to be happy (Komarnicki, 1991). However, not only has parenthood become more voluntary, but the role expectations of parents themselves are also much less clear that was true earlier. Women, in particular, are much less sure about how to incorporate parenting, marriage, and employment into their lives.

Data from recent surveys indicate considerable disagreement over emerging norms affecting the personal and family roles of American women. Only one out of four adults (23%) approve of mothers with preschool children working full time, and nearly half (46%) believe that a preschool child will suffer if the mother is employed (Bumpass & Sweet, 1988). These attitudes are in sharp contrast to the reality that over half of all mothers with preschool children are now in the labor force, and this figure continues to rise. Furthermore, 70% of the women under age 30 say they want a family *and* a career (D. Weiss, 1988). This figure is up from 52% who felt that way in 1964 (Harris, 1987).

Men too are experiencing pressure to change their roles and to accommodate new norms of working, fathering, and being a husband. Norms for fathering, for example, have begun to change dramatically. No longer are men encouraged to be completely absent from the home. But norms for new fathering and homemaking roles are not yet well entrenched (LaRossa, 1988). On the one hand, over half of American men (54%) say that the most satisfying accomplishment for men today is being a father (D. Weiss, 1988). This has resulted in a noticeable shift toward more participation of fathers in children's activities. On the other hand, Furstenberg (1988) refers to the development of a "good-dad, bad-dad complex" in which fathers now feel freer to be involved with their children, while also feeling freer to leave an unhappy home situation. And many indeed do just that. Not having been socialized into this emerging new family role, many men have problems with these confusing and often conflicting sets of expectations. To reduce this tension, many choose to leave these uncomfortable relationships. This has, without a doubt, contributed to increases in marital instability.

Relational-dissolution norms. Even though the divorce rate has been rising for several decades and has remained stable at a comparatively high level for 15 years, norms and expectations surrounding divorce also remain relatively unclear. Nearly all members of couples hope that they will stay married to their partner. But the acceptance of divorce as an alternative to marital unhappiness has certainly increased. The variations in expectations of divorce, however, were expressed by the couples participating in a national survey of families and households (Bumpass & Sweet, 1988). When asked whether they approved of unhappy couples divorcing

when their youngest child was under 5 years of age, the sample was equally divided between those who approved (33%) and those who disapproved (33%) of divorce in this situation. The remainder had mixed feelings. While we have no trend data on this question, the public tolerance of divorce has probably increased as the divorce rate has risen.

Furstenberg and Spanier (1984) contend that we are experiencing a paradigm shift in family norms in which "conjugal succession" is increasingly being accepted, although not preferred: "Divorce has become so commonplace that it represents, for much of the population, an optional stage in an increasingly variable conjugal career" (p. 47). This paradigm shift, according to Farber (1988), is largely the result of changes in family statuses and the lack of clear-cut norms associated with family statuses: "The ambiguity of status removes the labels or tags by which stability can be attained. . . . Loss of the distinctive hierarchical character of family and marital statuses increases the vulnerability of the family—and, by extension, all of society—to situational demands for change" (p. 432).

Since most divorced persons remarry, the ambiguity in family roles and norms continues into new relationships. Even though they are much more common, stepfamily patterns are not yet well defined. Epstein (1988) observes that "new step family ties are not institutionalized, and there are no established norms regarding 'proper' behavior in them" (p. 181). Thus, each new blended family must make up its own rules without adequate guidelines. As a result, all the parties involved—mothers, fathers, stepparents, and children—have to customize the norms for their families based on uniquely derived rules rather than well-established societal rules. Given this situation, it is little wonder that stepfamily relationships are often somewhat strained and that second marriages experience even higher divorce rates than first marriages.

The Revolution in Family Norms

It is apparent that a revolution in family norms is now confronting us. While the dominant values undergirding the family have been slowly shifting, norms of family behavior have moved more quickly to take advantage of the freedoms that greater independence and autonomy now permit. The family system that had once been called the "haven" and "respite" from the changes occurring in other organizations—notably, business and government—has become more vulnerable to the status and role confusion in the larger society. Neither inside nor outside the family do we now have clear-cut answers to the major issues influencing the roles of women, men, professionals, government leaders, or teachers.

The norms encompassing the family have become the new battleground in public debate. What is considered "profamily" can be interpreted as either ultraliberal, ultraconservative, or somewhere in between. While some family advocates argue about what they consider to be family "values," the real debate generally focuses on norms and expectations of family members, most often parents. Answers to James A. Levine's (1976) plaintive question *Who Will Raise the Children?* are not provided in terms of whether children should be taken care of. We all agree that the nurturance of children is a family and societal responsibility. Instead, we disagree over whether this responsibility, which until fairly recently was solely that of mothers, should now be shared by fathers and other caregivers. The data do not suggest that the value associated with children has diminished that much. What has changed are the expectations regarding people's responsibilities for their nurturance.

Likewise, the norms guiding marriage are increasingly similar to the norms in other intimate relationships. John Scanzoni (1987) refers to an emerging family paradigm involving norms that include what he calls "sexually bonded close relationships." Among couples without children, he finds the normative patterns of men and women to be very similar and the processes of relational development, maintenance, and disillusion to be increasingly indistinguishable. Robert Weiss (1987) observes that

> marriage is increasingly becoming like co-habitation. The woman may wear a wedding ring, but her name and, of course, her job will be unaffected.... For the woman who is a professional or executive, or on her way to becoming one of these, it is no longer possible to use the survey research rule that the social status of a married woman is that of her husband. (p. 465)

Thus, we appear to be moving toward a pattern of relational norms in which there is some confusion over expectations but in which more latitude for normative flexibility is permitted *childless couples*, whether married or not. When a third party such as a child enters the picture, some of this flexibility is removed. Many members of society are still trying to determine how the major relational transformation, which used to take place with marriage, can now be transferred to parenthood when there are no legal requirements for childbirth. Perhaps the greater attention now being given to child-custody arrangements instead of divorce is evidence of growing societal interest in and control over some of the freedom men and women have acquired, especially in the area of parental norms and responsibilities.

An Interpretation of Family Change

The changes in family norms that have just been described indicate that the fundamental social processes of the family are still unstable. When these normative changes are coupled with the structural changes occurring in the family and society, we get an overall picture of confusion that can be distressing to some family members as well as to outside observers of the family. Unfortunately, we cannot draw any clear-cut positive or negative interpretation from current events. It is possible to look at the direction of these changes positively, if one believes that new family patterns are necessary for the new societal conditions within which families find themselves. On the other hand, the disabling aspects of current changes are resulting in negative outcomes for some groups in our society. If one takes a short-range view, it is easy to be pessimistic.

Clearly, the pessimists are all around us today. In fact, the situation is not that different from the one Vincent (1966) wrote of over two decades ago: "Since the earliest writings available, changes occurring in the institution of the family have been used and interpreted to support either an optimistic or pessimistic premise concerning social change, and the pessimists have consistently outnumbered the optimists" (p. 31).

Nevertheless, even though the statistics on the well-being of American adults and children are well known, they can be interpreted very differently by equally competent scholars. For example, a review of data on American adolescents led Uhlenberg and Eggebeen (1986) to posit a very negative picture of the current situation of American teenagers. In a review and extension of the same data, however, Furstenberg and Condran (1988) suggest that the situation of American adolescents is not nearly as dire as suggested. Similar debates have been held over the consequences of day care for children, the effects of the mother's employment, the causes of declining SAT scores, and so on. After considering these kinds of debates, Schwartz (1987) notes:

> Most commentators dislike the new individualist and utilitarian ethic and blame its emergence on a generation (baby boomers), or on women (for leaving the home and wanting equality), on capitalism (for evaluating relationships according to goods and services distributed), or even psychiatry (for concentrating on the self as opposed to the community). This seems like a lot of tree counting to me when the obvious fact is we are now in a forest. (p. 456)

The major problem with most of the pessimists is the rather narrow period within which they define their frame of reference. Whether they publicly express their assumptions or not, there is an underlying current of nostalgia toward an earlier period of imagined family history when women were in the home, men worked outside for good wages, grandparents lived nearby, children went to good schools, marriages lasted for life, and communities were close. These commentators believe and propose that families today have drifted away from that ideal and that this change has harmful implications for individuals and society.

This tendency to create what Goode (1963) refers to as the "classical family of Western nostalgia" continues. Even though some writers deny their nostalgia, they follow Goode's prediction and "write of a period *still* more remote, *their* grandparents' generation when things were much better" (1963, p. 7). In his history of writings on family decline, Popenoe (1988) notes that this tendency to assert that the family is worse off than it was in an earlier period has been going on since the beginning of written history. For example, writing a century ago, Thwing and Thwing (1887) interpreted the family patterns they observed much as some family critics do today:

> The last fifty years have changed the marriage relation from a permanent lifelong state to a union existing for the pleasure of the parties. The change . . . is so revolutionary, involving the very foundation of human society, that we must not believe it to be the result of any temporary conditions. (p. 241)

How should we interpret these warnings? Should we ignore earlier dire predictions and pay attention only to recent ones? Has doomsday for the family finally arrived? We can interpret this pattern of contemporary pessimism in at least two ways. First, we can assume that the trends being observed are linear and that the family system has been declining (however defined) throughout recorded history. This would mean that there once was an optimal family pattern and that we have been drifting away from that utopia for centuries. Other than a few radical social evolutionists, such as Marx and Sorokin, almost no one seems to support this point of view.

A second but more likely explanation comes from the dominant position of equilibrium-oriented models of reality that have been used by most observers, even today. These models posit that stability in systems is the norm and that system change is inherently problematic. Until recently, nearly all sociocultural models were built on this assumption, including the dominant models in history, sociology, family science, anthropology, and psychology. While the names now attached to these models are relatively new, such as structural-functionalism, cognitive consistency theory, balance theory, and so on, the premises of stability/equilibrium models have dominated observations of human behavior for centuries.

These stability-oriented models have conditioned observers to be critical of current changes that suggest departures from the patterns of the immediate past. Thus, following the observation of Goode (1971), "We are all so emotionally involved in our own observations that we are not good observers. Our comments are all too likely to be self-justifications and rationalizations rather than cool attempts to find out how even our own family has operated" (p. 4). Since the family, especially "our family," is so important to us, interpretations of its change can rarely be looked at dispassionately. Our values and fears get intermingled with data, and thus we find equally competent social scientists using the same data to project quite different visions of the future.

Institutional Transition: The Fourth Wave

The family in Western society appears to be undergoing a major reorganization of its institutional parameters. In fact, we appear to be at the early stages of a new "wave" of institutional change, perhaps as significant as the major social reorganizations that have taken place in the past. As I see it, three major waves of family systems have sequentially dominated human history. The *first wave* was best represented by wandering family and communal units in the preagriculture period. In this system, community interests overshadowed family interests, since little to no property was controlled by individual families. The *second family wave* occurred after the domestication of agriculture. Extended families dominated this period, because property lines had to be much more clearly differentiated.

The *third wave* emerged after industrialization, and again, a major reorganization of the family took place. Property was no longer as important to family survival, so norms and values were built around independent family units with new, differentiated roles and responsibilities for family members. This transition into the industrial family, as reviewed by Shorter (1975), Aries (1962), and Bellah and his colleagues (1985), resulted both in a significant disorganization for those families and in concerns about the survivability of the family as an institution in society.

The *fourth wave* of institutional change is now upon us. The lack of defined family norms and adequate support systems to help us meet some of our basic needs is evidence of this significant transformation. This fourth wave, when it stabilizes, will represent a significant departure from the way in which families are viewed or have been viewed in the recent past. I suspect that this new wave will encourage more relationship testing in early adulthood and more coalescence around children in the lives of parents. Divorce rates will probably decrease somewhat, in part because formal marriages may not take place until later, but also because

the norms and guidelines for forming and maintaining these relationships will be clearer than they are today.

This suggestion that we are at the beginning of a major cultural transformation in relationships is not an isolated one. Many behavioral and social scientists who have attempted to describe marriage and family relationships in nonfunctionalist terms have had to struggle with redefining the concept of family in terms that are not proscribed by equilibrium-oriented assumptions. Three decades ago, for example, John Edwards (1967) tried to express a process theory of the family in his critique of Hobart's (1963) functionalist view of family norms and values. Edwards (1987) has continued to refine his thinking:

> We desperately need an alternative model of normal development, a model devoid of the present nuclear family bias. . . . It would focus, instead, on the processal nature of youthful development. Crucially, it would delineate the components of well-being and the patterns of "healthy" families, regardless of their structural configurations. (p. 28)

John Scanzoni and his colleagues (1989) have recently attempted to define the nature of this emerging institution. They replace the functionalist, equilibrium-oriented view, which is very resistant to change, with a nonfunctionalist process definition such as the one proposed by Giddens (1981): "By institutions I mean structured social practices that have a broad spatial and temporal extension . . . and which are followed or acknowledged by the majority of the members of a society" (p. 164). This new paradigm suggests that institutions are a social product, the accumulations of norms, rules, and roles that reflect contemporary thinking and are changed by current social processes. This is in contrast to the traditional, equilibrium-oriented paradigm in which institutions are considered outside the perimeter of the contemporary environment and resistant to current normative changes, even though widespread.

If, following this line of thinking, the family is indeed in the midst of a major institutional transformation, the current level of family instability is temporary, even though long by human-lifetime standards. As the attitude surveys reviewed earlier suggest, the hope for a new level of stability lies with the young. The older generations are very concerned about family changes, since they have witnessed a significant shaking of their traditional family roots. The current generation of parents is also anxious about these changes, but not nearly so much. The young are more hopeful. They see these changes as largely positive, but they worry that the rules and support they need are not there to comfortably guide their relationships. As Bellah and his colleagues (1985) observe:

> Perhaps most common today, however, is a note of uncertainty, not a desire to turn back to the past but an anxiety about where we seem to be headed. In this view, modernity seems to be a period of enormously rapid change, a transition from something relatively fixed toward something not yet clear. Many might still find applicable Matthew Arnold's assertion that "We are wandering between two worlds, one dead, the other powerless to be born." (p. 276–277)

Toward Family Adaptation

Many individuals and families have trouble coping with the changes that are occurring in the American family. To take the extreme position that the family is merely adapting is to seriously understate the current level of disequilibrium that many people are experiencing. Instead, I take the position that the family is changing and that this change is inevitable and potentially adaptive. Many families are experiencing severe distress. There are not enough industry and government supports to compensate for many of the services that family members used to provide one another; new roles for husbands, wives, and parents have not yet been well formulated; and potentially valuable informal support networks are not yet well established.

We need to keep in mind that much of the maladaptation that we observe is concentrated in selected pockets of society. Divorce rates are particularly high among those who marry young and those who are economically disadvantaged. Family violence is also concentrated in selected ethnic and poor families. Teenage pregnancies are much more common among the economically disadvantaged, and these young women are more likely to rear their children outside of marriage. This is not to say that some families are

immune to these and other problems, but it is important to keep in mind that the disabling effects of present changes are not cutting evenly across society. The majority of first marriages do not end in divorce, the overwhelming majority of families do not experience child or spouse abuse, the majority of teenage girls do not get pregnant, the majority of adolescents do graduate from high school, and the majority of youths and adults consider themselves very happy with their lives in this changing world.

We also have to keep in mind that family adaptation is more than a macro process. It is also a micro process in which change is a normal part of relational life. Family "health" is largely defined as the extent to which families are able to make constructive changes over time. In fact, families that resist making changes in their roles and norms are generally viewed as unhealthy or maladapted (Olson et al, 1983). In contrast, "strong families" are defined today as those who foster cohesion by adjusting to the needs of family members (Orthner & Bowen, 1992). Therefore, the healthy expression of marriage, parenthood, and childhood is one of an unfolding realization of adaptive processes, not one of continuity and resistance to change.

If the adaptation at the individual family level is normal, why should we expect the opposite at the macro family level? If resistance to change, such as the dominating husband not agreeing to let his wife take a job, is considered bad for families, how can we assume that women's entering the labor force in ever-increasing numbers is an indication of family decline, as some have suggested? A society, after all, is built upon the accumulated interchanges between its macro and micro environments. To expect individual families to adapt but family institutions to remain stable is a contradiction in terms and a major flaw in logic.

It appears to me that a case for cautious optimism can be well supported. The American public, particularly youths and young adults, are embracing with considerable fervor many of the normative changes that are occurring. Few people, either men or women, agree any longer that "a woman's place is in the home." Most people agree that women should be given equal opportunity in the job market. Almost no one expects women or children to stay at home with abusive husbands or parents, under the guise that what happens in the home is a "private family matter." Therefore, while many "values" are changing (as was mentioned earlier in this chapter), the value of the family *as* it changes remains steady. I feel some optimism about the changes *and* the notion that what happens behind closed doors remains important and essential to everyday life.

Fears over family change remain, but it is difficult to tell if these fears are the result of personal family experiences or the reification of rhetoric. So much alarm has been spread, some real and a lot of it unreal, that the public is much more concerned about change than it ought to be (Glenn, 1991). Statistics are quoted out of context, percentages are used inappropriately, and probabilities are thrown out as if they apply to everyone when they represent averages across many different groups, some of which throw the mean completely out of kilter.

Implications for Policy and Family Sciences

A new, systematic approach to family policy, research, and scholarship is needed. The old piecemeal strategy of limited government intervention, weak to uneven business concern, welfare-oriented support systems, value-free research, and a largely hands-off attitude on the part of schools and churches has contributed more to the problems of family change than to their solution. A new commitment to the value of the family to society must be made, not based on rhetoric or nostalgic visions of the past but oriented toward the future, with a clearer image of accurately describing what is happening today and where the family is headed. Daniel Yankelovich (1981) says it well:

> For a successful social ethic to take hold, people must form commitments that advance the well-being of society as well as themselves. For this to occur, people must receive clear and distinct signals from the larger society—from political leadership, from mass media, from institutional leadership (business, religion, education, labor, artists and scientists, intellectual community) and from informal interchanges of views with friends and neighbors. These signals should convey the terms of the new giving/getting compact communicating to Americans that we have now entered into a new age, offering new opportunities, tradeoffs, choices and

constraints. The signals must permit people to understand how they can link their personal aspirations to the new realities. (pp. 259–260)

What are some of these signals that should be sent? What priority should be given to different family issues? What organizations and systems should be involved in developing this agenda for the future? Who should lead this effort? These and a host of other questions must be answered. Based on this review, however, it would appear that priorities should be given to policies that meet two major objectives: (1) to increase the opportunity for families to develop stable relationships between husband and wives and parents and children and (2) to reduce the cost of instabilities that may occur because of institutional or family transitions. For these policies to be developed, careful research is needed to guide key decisions and formulate programs and services that strengthen families. In academia, we need programs and departments that have the courage to examine the tough family concerns that are often the core of social change. Too many disciplines view the family as a *context* for their central interests of individual development, education, poverty, or the like. Family science, on the other hand, views the family as its core interest, and that unique perspective must be strengthened.

At the community and societal levels, policies should be evaluated based upon whether they promote the adaptation of families to emerging social and economic conditions. If they cannot meet that test, these policies should be discarded and replaced. At the level of the family, we need to ask ourselves whether policies, programs, and services promote family cohesion and adaptation or whether they make it too easy for cohesion to be eroded and adaptability to be slowed. Families themselves need to be given the tools to assess their own progress toward meeting personal and family objectives through education, counseling, and training.

This promotion of family values must start at the top. In businesses where family policies have been effectively integrated, the leadership has almost always included a key company officer and his or her family. In the military services, significant advances have been made to promote positive family policies, and the leadership for these changes again started at the top (Bowen

& Orthner, 1989). This is no time for leaders to hide in the background, waiting for grass roots movements to emerge from below to carry them and their organizations along. Serious consideration needs to be given to family issues, and the time to begin is now. This plea is echoed by Peter McDonald (1988), an Australian sociologist:

> In the face of the enormous push toward competition, deregulation, and autonomy, so powerfully reinforced in this area of market forces, we need policies which promote the conviction that men and women are irreducively social and that we have a strong psychological need for companionship and intimacy. Education for both children and adults must extend beyond the utilitarian to a recognition that we are social beings who have intimate human relationships with others. We need to reinterate the undoubted value of family life; to emphasize the positive rather than rant and rave about the negative.

Chapter Summary

Discussion Questions

1. What are the differences between values and norms? Why is it important for us to understand this difference?
2. What kinds of research and reviews are necessary for an appropriate understanding of the directions that families are taking under the "fourth wave"?
3. Orthner asserts that the rules undergirding the family are inadequate. Give some examples of weak and strong rules from your own family. What assistance can we provide families that will help them build stronger rules?
4. Both Orthner and Peterson (see Chapter 2) note the tension in families between individualism and collectivism. Compare and contrast their ideas. How can Orthner's societal-level family concerns be understood in terms of Peterson's concerns for internal family processes?

Additional Resources

Popenoe, D. (1988). *Disturbing the nest: Family change and decline in modern societies.* New York: Aldine de Gruyter.

Brickman, P. (1987). *Commitment, conflict, and caring.* Englewood Cliffs, NJ: Prentice-Hall.

Doherty, W. J. (1992, May/June). Private lives, public values. *Psychology Today,* pp. 32–37.

Farber, B. (1988). The future of the American family: A dialectical account. *Journal of Family Issues, 8,* 431–433.

References

Aldous, J. (1978). *Family careers: Developmental change in families.* New York: Wiley.

Aries, P. (1962). *Centuries of childhood: A social history of family life.* New York: Vintage Books.

Attitudes toward marriage. (1989, February 13). CBS *News/New York Times Poll.*

Bellah, R. N., Madsen, R. Sullivan, W. M., Swidler, A., & Tipton, S. M. (1985). *Habits of the heart.* New York: Harper & Row.

Bowen, G. L., & Orthner, D. K. (1983). Sex role congruency and marital quality. *Journal of Marriage and the Family, 45,* 223–230.

Bowen, G. L., & Orthner, D. K. (1989). *The organization family.* New York: Praeger.

Brickman, P. (1987). *Commitment, conflict and caring.* Englewood Cliffs, NJ: Prentice-Hall.

Bumpass, L., & Sweet, J. (1988). *National survey of families and households.* Madison: University of Wisconsin.

Burr, W. R., Day, R. D., & Bahr, K. S. (1993). *Family science.* Pacific Grove, CA: Brooks/Cole.

Burrel, G., & Morgan, G. (1982). *Sociological paradigms and organizational analysis.* Exeter, NH: Heineman Educational Books.

Cherlin, A. J. (Ed.). (1988). *The changing American family and public policy.* Washington, DC: Urban Institute Press.

Doherty, W. J. (1992, May/June). Private lives, public values. *Psychology Today,* pp. 32–37.

Duncan, G., & Morgan, J. N. (1985). The panel study of income dynamics. In G.H. Elder, (Ed.), *Life course dynamics.* Ithaca, NY: Cornell University Press.

Edwards, J. N. (1967). Changing family structure and youthful well-being. *Journal of Family Issues, 8,* 355–372.

Edwards, J. N. (1987). The future of the family revisited. *Journal of Marriage and the Family, 29,* 505–511.

Elder, G. H., Jr. (1975). Age differentiation and the life course. In E.D. Macklin & R. H. Rubin (Eds.), *Contem-*

porary families and alternative lifestyles. Newbury Park, CA: Sage.

Epstein, C. F. (1988). Toward a family policy: Changes in mothers' lives. In A.J. Cherlin (Ed.), *The changing American family and public policy* (pp. 157–192). Washington, DC: The Urban Institute Press.

Erikson, E. (1968). Identity, youth, and crisis. New York: Norton.

Farber, B. (1988). The future of the American family: A dialectical account. *Journal of Family Issues, 8,* 431–433.

Furstenberg, F. F., Jr. (1988). Good dads–bad dads: Two faces of fatherhood. In A.J. Cherlin (Ed.), *The changing American family and public policy* (pp. 193–218). Washington, DC: Urban Institute Press.

Furstenberg, F. F., Jr., & Condran, G. A. (1988). Family change and adolescent well-being: A reexamination of U.S. trends. In A.J. Cherlin (Ed.), *The changing American family and public policy* (pp. 117–156). Washington, DC: Urban Institute Press.

Furstenberg, F. F., Jr., & Spanier, G. G. (1984). *Recycling the family: Remarriage after divorce.* Newbury Park, CA: Sage.

Gallup, G. (1987). U.S. women endorse jobs, marriage, and children. *Gallup Reports, 267,* 24–25.

Giddens, A. (1981). Agency, institution, and time-space analysis. In K. Knorr-Cetina & A.V. Cicourel (Eds.), *Advances in social theory and methodology.* Boston: Routledge & Kegan Paul.

Glenn, N. D. (1991). *The family values of Americans.* New York: Institute for American Values.

Goode, W. (1963). *World revolution and family patterns.* New York: Free Press.

Goode, W. (1971). *The contemporary American family.* Chicago: Quadrangle.

Harris, L. (1987). *Inside America.* New York: Vintage Books.

Hetherington, M., Cox, M., & Cox, R. (1977, April). Divorced fathers. *Psychology Today,* pp. 42–46.

Hobart, C. W. (1963). Commitment, value conflict, and the future of the American family. *Marriage and Family Living, 25,* 405–412.

Komarnicki, M. (1991). *Public attitudes toward the American family.* New York: Institute for American Values.

LaRossa, R. (1988). Fatherhood and social change. *Family Relations, 37,* 451–457.

Levine, J. A. (1976). *Who will raise the children?* New York: Bantam Books.

Levinger, G. (1986). Compatibility in relationships. *Social Science, 71,* 173–177.

Litwak, E. (1960). Geographic mobility and extended family cohesion. *American Sociological Review, 25,* 385–394.

McDonald, P. (1988). Families in the future: The pursuit of personal autonomy. *Family Matters, 22,* 40–44.

Meeting the challenge of a nation at risk. (1984). Cambridge, MA: USA Research.

Montague, A. (1971). *Touching: The human significance of skin.* New York: Columbia University Press.

National Opinion Research Center. (1977). *Cumulative codebook for the 1972–1977 general social surveys.* Chicago: University of Chicago Press.

National Opinion Research Corporation. (1988). *General social survey.* Chicago: Author.

Nelson, M. C. (Ed.). (1977). *The narcissistic condition.* New York: Columbia University Press.

O'Connell, M., & Rogers, C. C. (1984). Out-of-wedlock births, premarital pregnancies and their effect on family formation and dissolution. *Family Planning Perspectives, 16,* 157–162.

Olson, D. H., McCubbin, H. I., Barnes, H. L., Larsen, A. S., Muxen, M. J., & Wilson, M. A. (1983). *Families: What makes them work.* Newbury, Park, CA: Sage.

Orthner, D. K. (1981). *Intimate relationships: An introduction to marriage and the family.* Menlo Park, CA: Addison-Wesley.

Orthner, D.K., & Bowen, G.L. (1992). *Family adaptation in the military.* Ann Arbor, MI: Resources in Education.

Popenoe, D. (1988). *Disturbing the nest: Family change and decline in modern societies.* New York: Aldine de Gruyter.

Reiss, D. (1981). *The family's construction of reality.* Cambridge, MA: Harvard University Press.

Ross, C. E., Mirowsky, J., & Huber, J. (1983). Dividing work, sharing work and in-between: Marriage patterns and depression. *American Sociological Review, 48,* 809–823.

Scanzoni, J. (1987). Families in the 1980s: Time to refocus our thinking. *Journal of Family Issues, 8,* 394–421.

Scanzoni, J., Polonko, K., Teachman, J., & Thompson, L. (1989). *The sexual bond: Rethinking families and close relationships.* Newbury Park, CA: Sage.

Schnall, M. (1981). *Limits: A search for new values.* New York: Clarkson N. Potter.

Schwartz, P. (1987). The family as a changed institution. *Journal of Family Issues, 8,* 455–459.

Shorter, E. (1975). *The making of the modern family.* New York: Basic Books.

Solberg, C. (1973). *Riding high.* New York: Mason & Lipscomb.

Sussman, M. (1965). Relationships of adult children with their parents in the United States. In E. Shanas & G. F. Streib (Eds)., *Social structure and the family: Generational relations.* Englewood Cliffs, NJ: Prentice-Hall.

Thwing, C. F., & Thwing, C. F. B. (1887). *The family: An historical and social study.* Boston: Lee & Shepard.

Tocqueville, A. de (1969). *Democracy in America* (G. Lawrence, Trans., Ed.). New York: (Original work published 1898).

Uhlenberg, P., & Eggebeen, D. (1986). The declining well-being of American adolescents. *The Public Interest, 82,* 25–38.

U.S. National Commission on Excellence in Education. (1983). A nation at risk, the imperative for education reform: A report to the Nation and Secretary of Education, U. S. Department of Education. Washington, DC: The Commission of Superintendent of Documents, U.S. Government Printing Office.

Vincent, C. (1966). Familia spongia: The adaptive function. *The Family Coordinator, 21,* 143–150.

Weiss, D. (1988, October). 100% American. *Good Housekeeping,* p. 120.

Weiss, R. (1987). On the current state of the American family. *Journal of Family Issues, 8,* 464–467.

Yankelovich, D. (1981). *New rules: Searching for self-fulfillment in a world turned upside down.* New York: Random House.

Young, M., & Willmot, P. (1957). *Family and kinship in East London.* Glencoe, IL: Free Press.

Zill, N., & Rogers, C. C. (1988). Recent trends in the well-being of children in the United States and their implications for public policy. In A. Cherlin (Ed.), *The changing American family and public policy* (pp. 31–116). Washington, DC: Urban Institute Press.

Autonomy and Connectedness in Families

Gary W. Peterson
Arizona State University

Some of the most perceptive observations about American family and social life were those of the French historian and commentator Alexis de Tocqueville in his book *Democracy in America* over a century and a half ago (Tocqueville, 1835/1969). Many of Tocqueville's conclusions, as he toured the 19th-century United States, were so astute that even today family scientists and scholars from other disciplines can turn to this source for insights into enduring aspects of American social and familial life (Bellah, Madsen, Sullivan, Swidler, & Tipton, 1985).

One of Tocqueville's most thoughtful conclusions was that "individualism" and "self-interest" were the primary social forces that motivated the American people early in their national development. While he felt that excessive emphasis on the self-contained person separated Americans, made them selfish, and confined them to "the solitude of their own hearts," he also recognized that they enjoyed associating with others as a means of promoting social progress. Consistent with this tendency for "individualistic" Americans to seek "togetherness," Tocqueville saw marriage, love, and the family as important means of controlling the excesses of individualism. By making these observations, he expressed what the historian Page Smith (1987) refers to as the "prolonged contest in American history between the values of community and the code of individualism" (p. 849).

Such observations highlight the importance of the social forces of individuality on the one hand and the need for togetherness on the other. These aspects of social development are of particular importance within families, perhaps the most elementary forms of human association. As Hess and Handel (1959) proposed more

than three decades ago, families are composed of members who are both "connected to one another, and . . . separate from one another." Each family member "possesses an incredible psychobiological individuality" combined with the fact that the "connectedness of family members is equally basic" (pp. 4–5). This fundamental duality of family life guides individuals in becoming their own person while, at the same time, spurring efforts to find gratifying connections with other family members. Constantine (1986) contributes to this tradition of thought by arguing that "enabled families," or those that function effectively in a variety of circumstances, are especially effective in merging both individual and family interests.

Understanding Autonomy and Connectedness

Consistent with these ideas, the overall purpose of this chapter is to describe the forces of individuality and togetherness within families as important dimensions of study for the emerging discipline of family science. As mentioned in the introduction to Part I, contexts can be created from a number of sources. In this chapter, we will examine how a cultural ideal has had a significant impact on how we perceive the family. The basic issue (as introduced in Chapter 1) is the struggle between the needs, rights, and urges of the individual as those needs are juxtaposed to the needs and aspirations of a family group. Although many terms have been used to describe these forces, the concepts of autonomy and connectedness will be preferred when applied to family life. Specifically, *autonomy* refers to mechanisms within families that allow each person to assert his or her individuality in reference to family obligations, behavioral controls, rules, beliefs, and emotional processes. Correspondingly, *connectedness* is defined as a process that maintains family togetherness in the form of obligations, conformity to expectations, cooperative behavior, and emotional ties.

One objective is to show how autonomy and connectedness within families are partial derivatives of larger societal forces referred to as *individualism* and *collectivism*. A corresponding task will be to demonstrate how the unique qualities of families provide special meaning to the competing forces of autonomy and connectedness. A related topic will be how the family's hierarchical structure has an impact on the expression of autonomy and connectedness throughout the family system. Such distinctive family qualities and structural issues, in turn, are intended to inspire new ways of thinking about autonomy and connectedness that contribute to an emerging discipline of family science.

Perhaps this chapter's most important means of constructing a family-science viewpoint, however, will be to describe how the issues of autonomy and connectedness are addressed within a variety of social science perspectives. Because this knowledge is scattered, family scientists can play a leading role in synthesizing this information, defining the critical issues, and conducting systematic programs of research on autonomy and connectedness from a family perspective. As a means of exploring this objective, therefore, sections of this chapter will show how the forces of autonomy and connectedness are dealt with in traditional psychoanalytic theory, object-relations theory, self-identity literature, attachment theory, scholarship on social competence, various family-therapy approaches, and the emerging discipline of family science. Further efforts will be made to show how these perspectives enhance our understanding of the processes of autonomy and connectedness within different levels of the family system. Finally, a concluding section identifies how these diverse conceptions of autonomy and connectedness point to issues that family scientists might pursue in expanding our current knowledge about these issues.

Individualism and Collectivism in Society

Before exploring how families deal uniquely with autonomy and connectedness, it is important to recognize how these issues are partial reflections of individualism and collectivism, ideas that are central in Western civilization and American society. It is important for family scientists to understand this heritage so that respective contributions of families and the larger society can be more fully appreciated.

Although individualism has a long history in Western civilization, its modern form probably emerged in England during the 17th, 18th, and 19th centuries through the writings of such philosophers as Thomas Hobbes, John Locke, Adam Smith, and Jeremy Bentham. Specifically, individualism is an orientation emphasizing the self-directed, self-contained, and comparatively unrestrained person or ego. It involves values that are person-centered, with individual interests or goals being preeminent, rather than the interests of societal groups. In general, individualism includes the idea that society is best served by allowing all members to maximize their freedom, accept responsibility for choosing their own objectives, and acquire the means to pursue their own interests (Baumeister, 1987; Perloff, 1987; Spence, 1985).

Collectivism first emerged in the 18th-century philosophical works of Jean-Jacques Rousseau, G. W. F. Hegel, and Karl Marx. In reaction to individualism, collectivism emphasized the community and its rights, rather than the interests of the isolated person. According to Rousseau's version of collectivism in the *Social Contract*, individuals find their true being and freedom only in submission to the "general will of society," which "is always right and tends to the public advantage." A collectivist point of view is also expressed by Marx when he argues in *A Contribution to the Critique of Political Economy* that "it is not men's consciousness which determines their being, but their social being which determines their consciousness." Consequently, who each of us *is* as a person is greatly shaped by our group memberships and social experiences.

As the contemporary psychologist Janet Spence (1985) has proposed, every society, every social group, and every individual must deal with seemingly contradictory impulses of the human experience—individuality and collectivism. The particular balance established between these forces, however, varies widely across nationalities and even among the subcomponents of a single society. In the United States, for example, it is often argued that we have resolved this "contest" by tilting decidedly in favor of individualism (Bellah et al., 1985; Sampson, 1977, 1988; Spence, 1985). Whether we speak of individual rights recognized by America's founding fathers, the rugged individualism required to explore and settle the Western frontier, the economic autonomy enshrined in laissez-faire capitalism, or the solitude and self-reliance celebrated by the transcendentalist writers Henry David Thoreau and Ralph Waldo Emerson, America has a long history of promoting the self-contained individual.

Although *individualism* has seemed to dominate America, others have argued that too much emphasis on either person or community is costly, with the optimal solution being a balance between these forces (Bakan, 1966). From the beginnings of the American republic, the need for social *interdependence* became expressed through such developments as a plethora of voluntary associations, and the governmental assistance initiated by Franklin D. Roosevelt's New Deal and Lyndon B. Johnson's Great Society. While recognizing that both of these forces have been at work, various social critics have different opinions about which force they viewed as more problematic in American life. In the 1950s, for example, William H. Whyte, Jr. (1956) criticized the "collectivist" tendencies of corporations to value "team players" rather than the "rugged individualists" enshrined throughout our history. In another important work of the period, David Riesman and his associates (1950) were critical of the tendency of midcentury Americans to accommodate the requirements of social and economic institutions while failing to gain personal fulfillment—a circumstance he referred to as "other-directedness."

More recently, however, social commentators have voiced the opposite point of view by identifying the serious flaws of individualism and seeking to curb its more serious costs. Bellah and his colleagues (1985), for example, have argued that American individualism "may have grown cancerous" to the point of endanger-

ing freedoms by destroying essential forces of integration that moderate its more destructive potentialities (p. vii). These commentators highlight certain cultural traditions that limit the most problematic forms of individualism (without destroying it), while providing alternative models for Americans to consider. Even earlier, Garrett Hardin (1968) had anticipated this viewpoint by arguing that individual freedom had created the moral dilemma referred to as the "tragedy of the commons." In doing so, he challenged the central assumption that decisions reached individually will always contribute to the general welfare. Accordingly, Christopher Lasch (1978) extended this theme by arguing that competitive individualism had degenerated into a "culture of narcissism"—an unrelenting preoccupation with self, a condition of living for the moment without concern for posterity. All of these societal issues, of course, have considerable impact within families, but they do so in unique ways that reflect the special intensity, intimacy, and structure of family relationships.

The Special Qualities of Families

Although the requirements for autonomy (that is, individualism) and connectedness (that is, collectivism) exist in the larger society, these issues take on fundamentally different meanings and special intensities within families. In other words, the "family world" is composed of special qualities that differ greatly from other contexts within our society (Burr, Day, & Bahr, 1993; Walters, 1982). Furthermore, family members often relate to one another in ways that foster different expressions of autonomy and connectedness within distinct family subcomponents. Of all the various social disciplines, therefore, family science should pay special attention to the distinctive qualities and structure of families.

Families Are Unique

A unique family quality that modifies how autonomy and connectedness are expressed is the great diversity of ways in which families impinge on the lives of their members (Gelles & Straus, 1979, Peterson, 1986a;

Walters, 1982). Specifically, the family world may influence such diverse areas of our life as our educational goals, how we deal with conflict, the religious or secular philosophies that we choose, the issues about which we feel comfortable talking, and even how we squeeze the toothpaste tube. No other social setting influences so many aspects of our daily life and complicates both how we assert our individuality and maintain connections with others. In contrast, other social contexts such as religious, occupational, or educational institutions are "special-purpose groups" whose influences are confined within a more narrow range.

Another distinctive aspect of families is their *involuntary* membership and the assumption that family ties have greater permanence than those of other social groups (Gelles & Straus, 1979; Walters, 1982). Specifically, because we are born into and do not choose our first family membership, it is difficult if not impossible to resign from this intimate environment. Although leaving or divorcing one's spouse is a difficult but increasingly common event (Martin & Bumpass, 1988), an even more problematic development is for parents to sever their child-rearing responsibilities. It is certainly easier for most of us to change our jobs, educational programs, social organizations, or even friendships than it is to change our family relationships. Consequently, most other group associations have greater changes in membership, last for shorter periods in the human life cycle, and result in human relationships of less intensity (Peterson, 1986a).

The assumption, if not the reality, therefore, is that family ties *are intended* to have greater permanence than those of other social groups. These expectations for greater permanence are reinforced by interpersonal obligations, social sanctions, and legal arrangements (reflecting the presumption of permanence) that define the broad parameters for marital and parent/child relationships. One result of such formal arrangements is that a person's quest for autonomy (or individuality) is constrained by such forces, while connections with other family members are often complicated by assumptions of permanence and reinforced by legal requirements.

Families in Western societies also differ from other social groups in the extent to which their activities can be concealed from public view (Gelles & Strauss, 1979; Peterson, 1986a). One consequence of such privacy is

that families are more likely than other human associations to be arenas for expressing "backstage" behavior, intimacy, deeper self-revelations, and the darker side of our human experience (Burr et al., 1993; Peterson, 1986a). Although privacy can be a valuable resource for restoring ourselves psychologically, the irony of family life is that it also allows these "private domains" to hide the worst forms of neglect, deprivation, conflict, and violence from public view. This extensive ability to avoid external monitoring provides families with special mechanisms that control progress toward autonomy and maintain connections. Specifically, the "private world" that results allows families to construct unique views of reality and regulate how individuality and connectedness are managed with minimal intervention from outside forces.

Families are also different from other social groups in the intensity of feelings and emotions expressed within their boundaries (Bowen, 1978). Although strong emotions can be expressed within work settings or voluntary associations, the intensity, variety, and continuity of family emotions are unequaled within other relationships. As a result, family members are bound together by powerful expressions of love, attachment, loyalty, and sensitivity to one another's feelings that may even be rooted somewhat in biological tendencies (Bowen, 1978; Bowlby, 1988). The other side of the coin, however, is that families are crucibles for feelings of rejection, frustration, smoldering anger, and volcanic rage leading to violence.

Positive emotional experiences within families provide psychological support for members to assert their individuality and explore social environments outside family boundaries. The negative feelings found in some families, however, may foster "separation processes," or developments that result in members cutting themselves off from family ties. In contrast, expressions of love, attachment, and loyalty are among the strongest and most complicated connections that bind family members together. Another possibility, however, is the use of both positive and negative emotions by family members to foster unhealthy connections that are excessively close and subvert a person's progress toward autonomy.

Another special feature of families is the tendency for members of these social groups to jointly construct a "family paradigm," or "world view." Specifically, paradigms refer to assumptions about the nature of family relationships as well as the ways in which members should relate to and interpret their environment (Hess & Handel, 1959; Kantor & Lehr, 1975; Reiss, 1981). Although issues of autonomy and connectedness are prevalent in all families, great variation exists in the extent to which these forces are encouraged or tolerated within families having different paradigms (Constantine, 1986). For example, certain family paradigms deemphasize individuality, encourage members to remain connected, reinforce shared perceptions of the world, and demand adherence to family purposes. Members of other families, on the other hand, share world views that strongly encourage autonomy at the expense of common purposes and conformity to the group.

Finally, it is important to realize that biological or natural propensities may play a role in the expression of autonomy and connectedness within families. Although not strictly a unique feature of families, such phenomena as (1) attachment behavior between parents and children (Bowlby, 1988), (2) primitive emotional processes that govern autonomy and togetherness in family life (Bowen, 1978), and (3) biologically based forces within the personality that encourage both intimate connections and individuality (S. Freud, 1949; Mahler, Pine, & Bergman, 1975) may provide evidence that individuality and family bonds have roots in natural forces. (See the discussions of these issues in later sections of this chapter.) Any acknowledgment of such natural propensities, in turn, does not presume that specific types of family relationships or particular family structures are biologically inevitable. Instead, such conceptions simply recognize the possible existence of biological propensities, which are always subject to substantial alteration by social, cultural, and other environmental influences. It is probably wise, therefore, to consider the possibility that human development may include at least some tendencies both to form secure connections (perhaps familial in nature) and to assert one's individuality. An overall assessment is that families are environments in which biological propensities, multiple influences, assumptions of permanence, privacy, emotional intensities, and constructed paradigms combine to form unique contexts for the expression of connectedness and autonomy.

The Structure of Families

One of the most interesting paradoxes is that while autonomy and connectedness are *pervasive* throughout the family system, the *expression* of these processes may be quite different within various subcomponents of families. As is mentioned in Chapter 6, on family systems theory, the family system is more than structure and assigned roles. All aspects of families are interrelated through dynamic, mutual, and circular mechanisms (Bertalanffy, 1968; Buckley, 1967; Constantine, 1986; Skynner, 1976, 1981; Steinglass, 1987). Moreover, this idea from systems theory indicates that each element of a family operates as an integral component of the overall system, through which families consist of more than the sum of their parts. The result of this "wholistic" quality is that every element or phenomenon within the system may either have implications for or manifest itself throughout the family. Such a viewpoint contrasts sharply with the traditional "scientific" view of families as being reducible to isolated elements that are related through cause/effect links.

The other side of this paradox is that families are organized hierarchically, a condition that differentially specifies how autonomy and connectedness are expressed within various subcomponents of the system. Central to this quality of families is the idea that systems are organized in a series of levels (individual, dyadic, and whole-system levels), (Cromwell & Peterson, 1983; Kantor & Lehr, 1975; Skynner, 1976, 1981; Steinglass, 1987). While all subsystems of families are complex and different from other components, each level maintains boundaries that are variably permeable to (or interconnected with) input from the outside. As a result, the individual, dyadic, and systemic levels of families occur in hierarchical fashion and are simultaneously interdependent and distinct.

The *individual*, from this perspective, is a biological and psychological system conceptualized as a basic level of the larger system, having many possibilities for autonomy and connectedness in reference to others. Although partly explainable with biological and psychological models, individuals cannot be adequately understood without reference to the social context (the family) or without examining how their behavior has consequences for their interpersonal environment (part of which is the family) (Peterson, 1986a). Next, the more encompassing *dyadic* level consists of the marital, parent/child, and sibling subsystems. Finally, the *family unit* is the most general level, which circumscribes the marital, parent/child, and sibling subsystems (Cromwell & Peterson, 1983; Peterson & Cromwell, 1983). Each of these levels, in turn, has some elements that are unique and some that are held in common with other levels of the system. Because each level does *not determine* another but functions only within a system of *mutual influences*, autonomy and connectedness can be expressed in similar, but somewhat distinct, themes within the individual, dyadic, and systemic levels of families (Constantine, 1986).

Conceptions of Autonomy and Connectedness in the Social Sciences

As previously indicated, family scientists can profit from the insights of other disciplines in selecting critical issues upon which to focus. One means of accomplishing this objective is to examine a topic from different viewpoints and identify key issues to which a family perspective might provide additional understanding. Consequently, subsequent sections of this chapter provide different perspectives on autonomy and connectedness from traditional psychoanalytic theory, object-relations theory, self-identity literatures, attachment theory, scholarship on social competence, family-therapy approaches, and the emerging discipline of family science. All of these perspectives provide somewhat analogous emphases on autonomy and connectedness, but they often do so with different assumptions, with distinct conceptual metaphors, and from different levels of the family system.

The Psychoanalytic View

The psychoanalytic perspective deals with autonomy and connectedness primarily at the individual level, but it also recognizes how these forces operate within the dyadic level of family systems. In its traditional form, psychoanalytic theory provides a perspective on the nature of autonomy and connectedness within the parent/child relationship. Of particular importance is the belief that autonomy is achieved through a process in which the young must *separate* from early bonds with parents and form new connections beyond family boundaries (A. Freud, 1958; S. Freud, 1949).

According to classic perspectives provided by Sigmund and Anna Freud, both connectedness and autonomy are rooted in such individual-level phenomena as the sexual energies of the libido, the biological changes of puberty, and personality conflicts that result—all of which have implications for dyadic relationships within families (especially the parent-child level of the family system) (A. Freud, 1958, 1969; S. Freud, 1949, 1953). Family connectedness (or the bond between mother and child) originates in attachments that infants experience from having their hunger and oral drive gratified by mothers. Later, in early childhood, connectedness is fostered by the id's libidinal attachment initially to the opposite sex parent, and subsequently through identification with the parent of the same gender during resolution of oedipal and Electra issues. With the onset of puberty during early adolescence, however, the young experience a reemergence of oedipal and Electra issues that are stimulated, in part, by the hormonal and physiological changes of this period. During the phase of development referred to as the genital stage, adolescents are supposed to resolve these incestuous desires for the parent of the opposite gender by refocusing their libidinal energies on a love object (that is, a peer of the opposite sex) outside the family (A. Freud, 1958, 1969; S. Freud, 1949, 1953).

Progress toward greater individuality results from sublimation, a defense mechanism through which adolescents suppress their oedipal or Electra desires and *separate* from parents as a means of achieving acceptable relationships with a person of the opposite gender. Consequently, the psychoanalytic perspective conceptualizes autonomy as a product of the libido's tendencies to attain genital pleasure from a love object beyond family boundaries. The resulting separation process is accomplished, to a large extent, by transforming the parent/child relationship through the stress and anxiety created by unacceptable impulses from the id (A. Freud, 1958, 1969).

Proponents of the psychoanalytic perspective, therefore, contend that connectedness and autonomy (in the form of separateness) are rooted in biological mechanisms and psychological drives originating within the individual level of families. Despite this focus on the person, however, these forces are important for redefining parent/child relationships at the dyadic level and in linking individuals to associations beyond family boundaries (gaining autonomy from families).

The View of Object-Relations Theory

Although traditional psychoanalytic theory is concerned primarily with individuals and their elemental motives (drives and needs for attachment and separation), object-relations theory, a neopsychoanalytic approach, views "family connections" as resulting from internalized expectations and "images" of others that are acquired during early development (Friedman, 1980; Scharff & Scharff, 1987; Slipp, 1984, 1988). That is, residues of these early experiences in the form of "internalized objects"—mental images of self and others—lead to expectations for future relationships (Klein, 1946; Segal, 1964; Winnicott, 1965).

During childhood, the incorporation of object relations occurs initially through global *introjections* of self/other interactions, general images of the other person, and the affect associated with such conceptions. Later, as development proceeds, connectedness with others begins to occur through *identification*, a more sophisticated process than introjection, which involves clearer distinctions between one's self-image and other objects. Rather than internalizing global qualities (as occurs through introjection), identification involves the incorporation of complicated roles, specific role expectations, particular attributes, and more carefully defined behaviors that are associated with objects of choice (Mahler et al., 1975; Winnicott, 1965).

According to Mahler and her colleagues (1975), for example, infants initially become closely connected, or "symbiotically fused," with their mother through a process of internalizing object relations. Following this achievement, the infant moves toward autonomy through "separation-individuation" during the "first individuation process." Correspondingly, Blos (1979) has argued that a "second individuation process" occurs during adolescence, a period of preparation for mature, adult relationships by building further on the progress toward autonomy achieved during early childhood. Similar to classic versions of psychoanalytic theory, therefore, object-relations perspectives share the position that autonomy is attained through a *separation* process in reference to parents.

Failure to achieve separation/individuation, in turn, produces emotional attachments within families that undermine the development of differentiated and cohesive identities. Depending on the degree of failure to separate, severe crises may develop when children reach school age, become adolescents, or leave home as adults. That is, excessive attachments often handicap the ability of individuals to develop effective social, marital, and family lives when they become adults (Scharff & Scharff, 1987; Slipp, 1984, 1988).

In contrast, a key to successful relationship development is for children to receive care from parents who are consistently loving and reliably supportive. Thus, when early parent/child relationships are secure and loving, the young seem more capable of both separating from and retaining loving connections with their caretakers. Consequently, the well-nurtured child feels like a worthwhile person, with capacities to delay gratification, tolerate frustration, and achieve competent ego functioning.

Children with histories of effective object relations develop the ability to tolerate closeness as well as separateness. If a person's long-term experiences are constructive, his or her identity is more likely to be enriched and revised, especially at critical points of development during the oedipal, pubertal, adolescent, and adult periods. As a result, these individuals have greater abilities both to choose their family connections and to assert their autonomy (or separate).

Thus, while maintaining its base within the individual level, object-relations theory is more clearly focused on the dyadic level of families than are traditional psychoanalytic approaches. Rather than concentrating simply on inner drives, this perspective gives considerable attention to dyadic associations—and especially the mental representations of these relationships—as important mechanisms for the processes of autonomy and connectedness.

Identity, Self, and the Family

Scholarship on identity development is another area that illustrates how families play an important role in either fostering or hindering autonomy and connectedness. According to this work, the self, or identity, is one of the most common means of expressing autonomous development at the individual level of families. Traditionally, a person's identity has often been conceptualized as a bastion of one's individuality. Of special importance has been the tendency to view the self in terms of its separateness, or distinctiveness, from other individuals, relationships, and life contexts (Allport, 1955, 1960; Baumeister, 1987; Erikson, 1959, 1968; Maslow, 1968). Traditionally, "finding oneself" has been a process of becoming one's own person by discontinuing past traditions, choosing one's own values, pursuing one's own preferences, and breaking free of family ties (Bellah et al., 1985). The relationship between autonomy and identity, in turn, is complex; the two are interrelated and perhaps even indistinguishable at times. Some independence from family ties is probably necessary to acquire a sense of who one is, with autonomy being an aspect of one's self-concept throughout life.

Contrasting with this view of self as separated from others is the growing awareness that identity development involves both autonomy and connectedness (or intimacy) (Dyk & Adams, 1987; Sampson, 1985). Accordingly, the dyadic and overall systemic levels of families are prominent environments where relationship connectedness provides the context for the closely related processes of autonomy and self-concept development (Openshaw & Thomas, 1986). Such a conception of identity development coincides with the growing perspective that personality development takes place both in social contexts and as a direct outcome of social relations. Consequently, studying the origins of personality (or individuality) and studying the onset of social relations (or connectedness) are increasingly becoming two sides of the same coin (Mead, 1934; Sroufe & Fleeson, 1986).

Perhaps the most prominent theory of identity development, that of Erik Erikson (1968), has recently been criticized for focusing too extensively on individuation and insufficiently on the central role of attachment in self-definition. Contrasting with the centrality of autonomy and separation for the male identity, Gilligan (1982) argues that self-definition in women is rooted more extensively in the experiences of relationships, connections, and caring. According to this viewpoint, interdependence with family members and other close relationships form a contextual web through which women define themselves. Other commentators apply these newer ideas about identity formation to both genders by arguing that the self is an "ensemble of social relationships" involving a unity between the issues of individuality and connectedness (Lykes, 1985). According to Franz & White (1985), for example, healthy identity development involves processes of attachment, interpersonal connections, and caring orientations, on the one hand, and the processes of individuation and "agency" on the other. Such a conception recognizes that part of our self-discovery, our dignity, our personal worth, are products of interactions with others during close relationships (Bellah et al., 1985).

Corresponding with autonomy and connectedness issues at individual levels is the fact that families also provide relationship contexts at both the dyadic and overall system levels that foster identity development. For example, within the dyadic level, parents who foster identity development tend to use controlling, supportive, and communication behaviors that strike a balance between encouraging individuality and togetherness (Adams, Dyk, & Benion, 1987; Openshaw & Thomas, 1986). Specifically, rational control, two-way communication, reasonable standards for behavior, mutual acceptance of perspectives, and nurturance (through warmth, companionship, and acceptance) are dyadic-level behaviors that both foster a balance between autonomy and connectedness and encourage identity development (Adams et al., 1987; Baumrind, 1978; Grotevant, 1987; Grotevant & Cooper, 1986; Hauser, Powers, Noam, & Jacobson, 1984; Peterson & Rollins, 1987; Powers, Hauser, Schwartz, Noam, & Jacobsen, 1983; Rollins & Thomas, 1979).

Families also provide general climates at the overall systemic level that foster identity development. For example, moderate levels of emotional bonding among family members as well as moderate capacities for changing family roles and power relations seem to provide the most desirable context for identity development (Adams et al., 1987; Olson, McCubbin, Barnes, Maxen, Larsen, & Wilson, 1983; Olson, Russell, & Sprenkle, 1983). In short, moderate parental control, reasonable flexibility in family structure, and substantial levels of emotional support are system-level processes that provide (1) a secure structure for self-definition that is grounded in connections with others and (2) sufficient self-confidence to assert one's individuality.

The development of a family member's self, or identity, therefore, is fostered most effectively in relationships that balance autonomy and connectedness. Such development is promoted both by behaviors within the parent/child relationship (dyadic level) and processes at the overall system level of families.

Attachment Theory

Autonomy and connectedness are also central aspects of attachment theory, developed most prominently by John Bowlby (1969, 1973, 1980). This perspective identifies biological propensities of the young that, in turn, are greatly subject to environmental influences and lead to special kinds of relationships with attachment figures. Based, in part, on evolutionary theory, Bowlby proposes that attachment processes are rooted in genetic propensities of the young to seek and for parents to provide protection.

In general, attachment theory provides a prototypical model of socioemotional development from the cradle to the grave (Bowlby, 1988) that links the individual level of the family system to the dyadic level. Specifically, it postulates that infant ties with attachment objects (usually but not always the mother) become models for later relationships and give rise to expectations and assumptions about self and others. According to this perspective, family connectedness is provided by the development of the "attachment system," while adaptive forms of autonomy emerge out of and use healthy attachment as the basis from which physical and social environments are explored. Furthermore, as development proceeds from infancy through adulthood, both attachment (connectedness) and exploratory (autonomous) behavior take on quite different and successively more complex forms (Ainsworth, 1982, 1989; Bowlby 1988; Bretherton, 1985; Sroufe & Fleeson, 1986).

Drawing from ethological and objects-relations theories, Bowlby (1969, 1973, 1980) has argued that human nature includes the propensity to make strong emotional bonds with particular individuals. Specifically, the term *attachment system* refers to both a cognitive and behavioral organization hypothesized to exist within individuals. From an observer's perspective, the goal of a person's attachment system is the regulation of behavior to encourage proximity to and contact with an "attachment figure" or figures (Ainsworth, 1982; Bretherton, 1985; Sroufe & Fleeson, 1986). An individual's attachment consists, therefore, of internalized representations of relationships and complex but changing patterns of behavior that "connect" young children to their caretakers (dyadic level).

Although this elementary form of connectedness is most obvious when the attached person is frightened, fatigued, or ill, these behaviors are greatly diminished when the attachment figure provides protection, help, and soothing. The most adaptive forms of attachment behavior, in turn, are fostered by caretakers who are sensitive and responsive to infant signals. Simply the awareness that an attachment figure is available and responsive provides a strong feeling of security for the young (Bowlby, 1988; Bretherton, 1985).

During healthy adolescent and adult development, these attachments often persist in combination with newer bonds (commonly of a heterosexual nature) within dating, premarital, and marital relationships (Sroufe & Fleeson, 1986; Weiss, 1986). Specifically, Bowlby (1973) postulates that early mother/child relationships continue to influence interpersonal associations during the life course as internalized "working models," or representations of self and others. That is, securely attached children are more likely to experience healthy connectedness in the future because they have developed working models through which they view themselves as lovable and other people as trustworthy. Children who have experienced difficulties with early attachment, on the other hand, are likely to develop either pessimistic or hostile models of the social world and to believe themselves incapable of maintaining effective connections with others. Unfortunately, insecure children are more likely as adults to become immature, anxious, and clingy, on the one hand, or aloof, emotionally closed, and compulsively self-reliant on the other (Bowlby, 1988).

Besides connectedness, Bowlby (1988) proposes that healthy autonomy develops through ever-widening exploratory behavior that is based on attachment but ironically emerges and develops in contrast to it. As a basic component of their human nature, young children are viewed as motivated to explore the environment, engage in play activities, and take part in varied activities with peers. The most adaptive forms of autonomous exploration occur when the attachment figure is used as a "secure base." That is, provided the parents have been responsive and accessible when called upon, a healthy child will subsequently feel secure enough to explore the environment.

Initially, however, these explorations are of short duration and limited to the environment immediately surrounding the attachment figure. During the toddler period, however, a securely attached child becomes sufficiently self-assured to increase the time and distance of separation—first to half-days and later to whole days. With further maturation, in turn, their excursions become even more extensive. By adolescence, autonomous exploration may be frequent and last for hours, days, weeks, or even months as new attachment figures are sought.

Throughout our adult lives, therefore, we seem most contented when we attain autonomy through successively longer excursions from attachment figures serving as secure bases (Ainsworth, 1982; Bowlby, 1988). In fact, when applied to adult love relationships, attachment perspectives on secure forms of love seem to embody both connectedness and autonomy. Specifically, adults involved in such relationships are characterized as feeling involved in a "warm relationship" while experiencing "self-fulfillment" as well as "ready for love and its risks without being anxious." Participants in secure associations often seek a deep, pervasive rapport while sharing relationship control and without losing their individuality (Bartholomew & Horowitz, 1991; Shaver & Hazan, 1988; Weiss, 1986).

As a result, the work on attachment again illustrates how the processes of autonomy and connectedness become manifest within family relationships. Having its roots in biological propensities, attachment theory provides a model that defines how autonomy and connectedness are interdependent processes throughout the life span. Central concepts of this perspective are the attachment system, secure base, and exploratory behavior.

Social Competence

Another body of literature, focusing on family dyadic levels, deals with youthful social competence as a larger concept that encompasses autonomy and connectedness. Much of this work also examines how parents create a climate that influences the development of social competence in the young (the parent/child subsystem) (Baumrind, 1978, 1987; Peterson & Leigh, 1990; Rollins & Thomas, 1979). Although social competence is composed of several subdimensions, a general definition is the ability of children and adolescents to function adaptively in relationships with peers, parents, and other adults (Inkeles, 1968; Waters & Sroufe, 1983). Recent conceptions of social competence identify its subdimensions as (1) the establishment of a balance between autonomy and connectedness, (2) effective internal or cognitive resources (for example, high self-esteem), and (3) the development of effective social skills (Peterson & Leigh, 1990).

As part of the first subdimension, the balance between autonomy and connectedness, most conceptions of "competence" include the ability to form connections by conforming to social expectations (or "fitting in") and establishing positive bonds with others (Inkeles, 1968; Peterson & Leigh, 1990; Rollins & Thomas, 1979). Beyond togetherness with others, however, emphasis is also placed on the complementary (although seemingly contradictory) ability to assert one's individuality in circumstances where expectations for social responses lack clarity (Peterson & Leigh, 1990; Waters & Sroufe, 1983). Individuals who possess such autonomous qualities often demonstrate independent judgment in managing circumstances to benefit both themselves and others in a variety of situations. Of special relevance is the idea that many situations requiring social competence do not provide precise role expectations or scripts to follow. Instead, much reliance is placed on the abilities of youths to exercise autonomous judgment, creatively assess their circumstances, enact behavior that is socially meaningful, and make constant readjustments to changing circumstances.

Socially competent youths are neither passive recipients nor simply reactors to stimuli but are both active and reactive agents to their developmental and environmental circumstances (Dodge, Pettit, McClaskey, & Brown, 1986). As a result, social competence is a complex concept that combines seemingly contradictory processes in a complementary arrangement within a larger construct. Specific subdimensions of connectedness include the maintenance of emotional ties, formal obligations, shared values, and cooperative behavior (Bronfenbrenner, 1970, 1985; Peterson & Rollins, 1987; Rollins & Thomas, 1979). Specific components of autonomy include gaining emotional self-control, developing a personal value system, acquiring the ability to make one's own decisions, and achieving freedom of action in reference to authority figures (Douvan & Adelson, 1966; Frank, Avery, & Laman, 1988; Hill & Holmbeck, 1986; Hoffman, 1984).

This adaptive balance between autonomy and connectedness is further complemented by two additional dimensions of social competence referred to as (1) internal (or cognitive) resources and (2) social skills. The first of these dimensions, internal resources, refers to several attributes that bolster youth's self-confidence and assist them in asserting their autonomy (for example, high self-esteem and internal locus of control) and several other abilities that maintain connections with others (for example, social perspective-taking and interpersonal problem-solving abilities). In contrast, the second of these resources, social skills, refers to behavioral repertoires that adolescents develop in relations with peers, parents, and other adults. Some of these skills, in turn, are useful in developing one's autonomy (assertiveness skills or the expression of opinions), while others are used to foster connections with others (conversational skills and showing interest in others). Consequently, effective social skills consist of those behaviors that foster the ability of youths to achieve individual interpersonal goals and be accepted in social relationships (Armas & Kelley, 1989; Dodge et al., 1986; Felner, Lease, & Phillips, 1990; Peterson & Leigh, 1990).

Besides the specific attributes of social competence, the current literature also identifies qualities of the parent/child relationship (the dyadic level of families) that seem to foster dimensions of autonomy and connectedness (Baumrind, 1987; Peterson & Leigh, 1990; Peterson & Rollins, 1987; Rollins & Thomas, 1979). Parental support, for example, provides the interesting paradox of fostering both connectedness within the parent/child relationship and sufficient autonomy to engage in interpersonal associations beyond the family. Specifically, the supportive dimension of the parent-child relationship promotes togetherness, on the one hand, by encouraging the young to identify with parents and incorporate their attitudes, values, and role expectations. Furthermore, parental nurturance also fosters connectedness by contributing to compliance with parents, moral internalization, and voluntary responsiveness to parental expectations (for example, internalized conformity) (Henry, Wilson, & Peterson, 1989; Hoffman, 1980; Peterson & Leigh, 1990; Peterson & Rollins, 1987; Peterson, Rollins, & Thomas, 1985; Rohner, 1986; Staub, 1979). At the same time, however, parental support fosters youthful autonomy by providing a base of security from which to expand and the self-confidence to explore beyond family boundaries (Pardeck & Pardeck, 1990; Peterson & Stivers, 1986).

Research on parent/child relations also verifies that firm, rational control (authoritative, or inductive, control) by parents and two-way communication foster both autonomy and connectedness (Baumrind, 1978, 1987; Peterson & Leigh, 1990; Peterson & Rollins, 1987; Rollins & Thomas, 1979). Such forms of parental influence, in turn, often contribute to a firm but rational rule structure and mutual respect within relationships (forms of connectedness), while allowing for sufficient individuality to develop. In contrast to authoritarian (or coercive) parenting, which demands conformity at the expense of individuality, rational control combined with two-way communication allows for autonomy to emerge—but only within the context of moderate parental influence and togetherness (Baumrind, 1987; Peterson & Leigh, 1990). Parents who encourage such communication and rational control tend to foster voluntary commitment and personal choice in the young, rather than blind obedience or alienation from the parent (Peterson et al., 1985).

Much of the social-competence literature, therefore, proposes that a balance between autonomy and connectedness is a central aspect of this concept. Furthermore, a substantial body of this work examines how other dimensions of social competence and parent/child behavior foster both autonomy and connectedness within dyadic levels of families. It is also important to keep in mind that much of the information collected about this topic was done with white families from very restricted populations. Generalizations may not apply to families of different races or cultures. For an examination of how differences in culture may affect these issues, refer to Chapter 4, "Multicultural Family Science."

Family Therapy

The rapidly emerging field of family therapy also has several approaches dealing with autonomy and connectedness from an overall system level of analysis. Specifically, these approaches include the Bowenian (Bowen, 1978; Kerr & Bowen, 1988), structural (Minuchin, 1974), and family-paradigm (Constantine, 1986) perspectives which deal respectively with the emotional, structural, and cognitive (interpretive) aspects of family life.

The Bowenian approach.   One of these approaches, developed by the psychiatrist Murray Bowen, has its roots in psychoanalytic theory (the individual level) but also demonstrates how family emotional processes operate to govern degrees of autonomy and connectedness at the system level of analysis. Although Bowenian theory has changed over the years, it has always dealt with forces that encourage either "family togetherness" (connectedness) or the process of breaking free toward individuality (autonomy). Bowen is especially attentive to problems resulting from family emotional processes, conceptualized as primitive, biological forces that can impair the personal development of family members. According to this perspective, the ideal situation is for togetherness and individuality to be balanced, with an imbalance toward togetherness being referred to as "fusion," or "undifferentiation" (Bowen, 1978; Kerr & Bowen, 1988).

Differentiation of self, perhaps the central concept of Bowen's theory, refers to the ability of a person to function autonomously. It allows family members to avoid excessive emotional reactions to family circum-

stances. A differentiated (or autonomous) person is one who separates thinking from feeling and remains independent of, but not emotionally separated from, his or her family. Consequently, a person with such qualities is not an emotionally detached Mr. Spock of *Star Trek* fame but someone who balances thinking and feeling. Individuals who have this ability are capable of combining emotional responsiveness and spontaneity with sufficient rationality or objectivity to manage the pull of emotional forces within families (Bowen, 1978; Kerr & Bowen, 1988).

Any deficiencies in emotional autonomy, or emotional fusion, in Bowen's terms, involve the inability of family members to distinguish their thoughts from feelings. Under these circumstances, emotions flood our intellect, impair our rational capacities, and hinder our interpersonal, problem-solving abilities. Consequently, undifferentiated family members are governed by the ebbs and flows of feelings to which they blindly succumb or which they manage artificially through cutting themselves off from emotional experiences in a manner that fails to resolve fundamental issues. Consisting of intense attachments, emotional fusion can be prevalent either in dependent individuals who cling to others or in aloof persons who isolate themselves. The more that emotional fusion exists, the more that individuals become pawns to the emotional reactions of other family members. Specific problems resulting from emotional fusion often include emotional distance or cutoff, physical or emotional dysfunctions, and overt conflicts within families (Bowen, 1978).

The structural approach.   A second school of family therapy that deals with autonomy and connectedness is structural family therapy, developed by Salvador Minuchin (1974). Rather than addressing these issues from the perspective of emotional processes, however, Minuchin's approach concentrates on family structure—or the redundancies, organized patterns, rules, and coalitions that govern family interaction. Structure is the conceptual mechanism used to describe how families become organized to determine how, when, and with whom their members should relate (Colapinto, 1991).

Family structure is shaped, in part, by patterns in the larger society and by unique constraints within each family. Of special importance is the hierarchical structure of each family, or the mechanism through which the distribution of family authority is conceptualized. According to Minuchin, families are structurally differentiated into subsystems, each of which shares organization with the larger family but also has its own boundaries, distinct rules, and patterns of interaction (Colapinto, 1991; Minuchin, 1974).

Individuals, subsystems, and whole families have interpersonal boundaries that surround each component and regulate the extent to which information is exchanged throughout the family. That is, boundaries function to define the degree of separateness and connectedness within families and each of their subsystems. Varying on a continuum from "rigid" to "clear" to "diffuse," boundaries have a substantial impact on the nature of relationships within families and their subcomponents.

Boundary ridigity, for example, helps to structure relationships that permit little contact with outside systems, resulting in "disengagement," Minuchin's term for family mechanisms that foster extreme individual autonomy. On the positive side, disengaged individuals or subsystems tend to be autonomous and oriented toward mastery. In contrast, high amounts of disengagement limit the amount of nurturance provided and isolate family members and subsystems. At the other extreme are boundaries characterized as being *diffuse, or unclear,* one result of which are "enmeshed relationships" involving intrusive forms of mutual support that inhibit autonomy. Although members of enmeshed families are affectionate and considerate and spend a lot of time together, they also encourage dependency, are less comfortable by themselves, and have difficulty relating to people beyond the family boundaries. According to Minuchin (1974), the ideal circumstance occurs when *clear boundaries* are prevalent, within which normal relationships can develop. Specifically, boundaries of this kind allow sufficient autonomy for each person to pursue individual goals while simultaneously developing complementary patterns of mutual support (connectedness).

The family-paradigm approach. Contrasting with either emotional processes or structural arrangements, a third perspective from family therapy focuses on the cognitive or perceptual mechanisms within families that shape degrees of autonomy and connectedness among members. Specifically, the concept of a *family paradigm* refers to a perspective jointly held by family members and composed of basic assumptions about (1) how to view the world, (2) how to relate to one another, and (3) how to deal with the surrounding environment. That is, family paradigms provide a sense of meaning and order, which, in turn, provides a rationale for selecting goals, making decisions, governing behavior, and managing resources (Reiss, 1981). Furthermore, a complicating aspect of family paradigms is that most of these world views are constructed and maintained unconsciously.

Another basic feature of this perspective is that families vary widely in the type of paradigm that each constructs and maintains (Constantine, 1986; Reiss, 1981). Such paradigm variations, in turn, include very different conceptions about the nature of autonomy and connectedness within families. "Closed families," for example, maintain a "core image" that stability, security, and belonging are essential, with group interests and connectedness taking precedence over individuality (or autonomy). In contrast, the family type referred to as "random" has a guiding image that novelty, creativity, and individuality are needed for members to maintain relationships both with one another and their changing environments. Consequently, random families place more emphasis on autonomy than connectedness, because individual creativity is valued as the resource for devising various ways to encourage change. A third type, referred to as "open," seeks to balance autonomy and connectedness by resolving any conflicts between individual and group interests through the processes of open negotiation and collaboration. Finally, "synchronous" families, or those based on essential agreement and singularity of mind, often deny that the issues of individuality versus the group even exist. According to Constantine (1986), the ideal condition for such families occurs when each member transcends himself or herself and achieves identification with the group.

Finally, an important idea from the family-paradigm perspective is that value judgments should not be made about appropriate amounts of autonomy and connectedness that are needed for effective family functioning. Instead, Constantine (1986) cautions against such verdicts when the particular world view, specific objectives, and challenges faced by each family have not been considered. Although all families must satisfy individual and group needs to some extent, precisely how such issues are addressed may vary widely across family types. That is, any of the four family types, having very different combinations of autonomy and connectedness, can give rise to either "enabled" (functional) or "problematic" forms.

Three distinct family therapy perspectives, therefore, can be used to conceptualize autonomy and connectedness in terms of different aspects of family development, such as emotional, structural, and interpretive (cognitive) dimensions. The three therapy approaches also differ in identifying the optimal balances between autonomy and connectedness, with the structural and Bowenian perspectives recommending a fairly even balance and the family-paradigm orientation proposing that a variety of arrangements may work.

A Family-Science View of Autonomy and Connectedness

Perhaps the most prominent theoretical and research program in family science that deals with autonomy and connectedness is the circumplex model of family functioning by David Olson and his associates (1983) (see Chapter 9). Olson's goal is to examine dimensions of the entire family system, rather than either individual (intrapsychic) or dyadic (parent/child or husband/wife) levels of analysis. Because the circumplex model synthesizes a diverse array of social science scholarship in a unique way, the resulting model differs from those of older versions. Specifically, this model proposes that families differ in terms of two fundamental processes: *cohesion* and *adaptability*, with *communication* being a third dimension that influences the other two processes.

Cohesion refers to emotional bonding (closeness versus distance) that members experience with one another and the degree of emotional autonomy a person achieves within the family system (Olson, Sprenkle, & Russell, 1979). Several bipolar terms have often been used to convey similar concepts: separateness versus connectedness (Hess & Handel, 1959), emotional di-

vorce versus emotional fusion (Bowen, 1978), centrifugal versus centripetal (Stierlin, 1974), and disengagement versus enmeshment (Minuchin, 1974). Of special importance is the proposal by Olson and his associates that families vary along the cohesion dimension (from extreme low cohesion to extreme high cohesion) in terms of the categories "disengaged," "separated," "connected," and "enmeshed."

Adaptability refers to the capacity of family systems to change their power structures, role relationships, and rules in response to situational and developmental stress (Olson et al., 1979). It refers to diverse means through which family members deal with rules, roles, and hierarchical relationships that provide the structural context for various levels of autonomy and connectedness. The categories "rigid," "structured," "flexible," and "chaotic" are used to reflect variation in the family-adaptability concept.

As a means of conceptualizing the circumplex model, a diagram is used in which the cohesion and adaptability dimensions intersect at right angles (see Chapter 9). The resulting matrix forms a typology of 16 family types, which are further reducible to three major categories of family functioning: balanced, midrange, and extreme. Perhaps the central hypothesis of the circumplex model is that both cohesion and adaptability are expected to predict family functioning in a curvilinear manner. Specifically, this means that optimal functioning exists within family systems that achieve moderate levels of cohesion and adaptability, rather than extremely high or low levels.

However, the cumulative body of evidence on the hypothesized curvilinear relationships is mixed. Some of the studies comparing families that have identifiable problems with nonproblem families, for example, provide support for the curvilinear hypothesis by indicating that families with juvenile delinquents, schizophrenics, neurotics, alcoholics, and sex offenders are more prevalent in extreme rather than balanced family types (Carnes, 1989; Clarke, 1984; Olson, 1986; Olson & Killorin, 1984; Roderick, Henggler, & Hanson, 1987). In fact, some reviewers have concluded that studies with the best designs support Olson's proposal that balanced families provide the healthiest interpersonal environments (Burr & Lowe, 1987).

Contrasting evidence, however, also indicates that cohesion and adaptability are either linear predictors or are unrelated to various adaptive qualities of families (Beavers, Hampson, & Hulgas, 1985; Green, Kolevon, & Vosler, 1985; Miller, Epstein, Bishop, & Keitner, 1985; Thomas & Cierpka, 1989; Walker, McLaughlin, & Green, 1988). Specifically, some studies have reported divergent patterns of prediction for the cohesion and adaptability scales (Green, 1989; Hampson, Beavers, & Hulgas, 1988), with one study of special prominence (Green, Harris, Forte, & Robinson, 1991) finding that family well-being was unrelated to adaptability but was a linear function of cohesion. These investigators concluded, in turn, that while the circumplex model had provided a useful theory, the instrument developed to measure its constituent concepts (FACES III) had been less effective. Consequently, the authors of this article recommend that cohesion and adaptability might be measured more effectively through the use of bipolar items that fit curvilinear assumptions, rather than unipolar, Likert items that presuppose linearity.

The circumplex model, therefore, describes how various degrees of autonomy and connectedness are accommodated by different patterns of cohesion and adaptability at the overall system level of families. Viewing both of these dimensions simultaneously, cohesion and adaptability vary from accommodating high to low levels of autonomy and connectedness among family members. The difference is that cohesion represents the degree of emotional bonding, whereas adaptability deals with the structural and power relationships within families. An important conclusion based on the circumplex model is that families and their members function most effectively when moderate levels of cohesion and adaptability are prevalent, which fosters an atmosphere of balance between autonomy and connectedness. Although cohesion and adaptability are hypothesized to demonstrate curvilinear relationships, investigators who have tested this idea have reported inconsistent results.

Conclusions for Family Science

An overall assessment of the scholarship on autonomy and connectedness reveals that all of these varied perspectives share, in part, analogous concerns with autonomy and connectedness in families. Certainly, the widespread concern for these processes within so many perspectives illustrates how autonomy and connectedness are of such fundamental importance within families. Despite this pervasive quality, however, several additional issues are raised upon which family scientists might focus their efforts to increase our understanding of autonomy and connectedness.

One of the most obvious conclusions, for example, is that both autonomy and connectedness are multidimensional concepts, with subcomponents that are likely to be related but qualitatively different. That is, family members seem to become autonomous by developing independent behavior (making one's own decisions and acquiring freedom of action), defining a personal value system, constructing cognitive definitions that encourage independence (family paradigms), establishing family structural relations (boundaries, rules, and power relationships) that allow flexibility, and contributing to an emotional climate that fosters autonomy. The other, but complementary, side of the coin is that family members are connected to one another through expectations for cooperative behavior, shared values, cognitive paradigms that foster togetherness and common goals, family structural relations that maintain order, and emotional bonds that serve as psychological resources and provide security.

Although multidimensional conceptions of autonomy and connectedness have been anticipated elsewhere (Douvan & Adelson, 1966; Frank, Avery, & Laman, 1988; Hill & Holmbeck, 1986), family scientists are best suited to expand such efforts within the larger "family realm" and to explore subdimensions of these processes throughout the family system. Consequently, an appropriate research topic would be for family scientists to examine how different dimensions of autonomy and connectedness are interrelated across the family life cycle. Specifically, although behavioral, emotional, and cognitive conceptions of autonomy may be somewhat related, there is no guarantee, for example, that adolescents will achieve emotional autonomy from parents at the same time that they are achieving freedom to pursue leisure activities with peers (behavioral autonomy). Furthermore, how these subcomponents either predict or are predicted by other processes and circumstances within families (for example, marital quality, divorce, family stress, conflict, decision-making) will require much greater attention.

Closely related to the issue of multidimensionality is the idea that autonomy and connectedness may have both commonalities and distinct qualities across different levels of the family system. Although analogs of autonomy and connectedness seem to parallel each other across system levels, this does not ensure that exactly the same form, degree, or timing of these processes will occur within each component of family life. In fact, almost by definition, the boundaries that demarcate the special qualities of each subsystem are also likely to redefine how each component uniquely allows autonomy and connectedness to be expressed. For example, there is no guarantee that development will be the same for (1) identity development at the individual level, (2) behavioral autonomy that is fostered by parenting styles (a component of social competence) at the dyadic level, and (3) overall family rules that allow flexibility (adaptability) at the entire system level. Although research by Olson and his associates has begun to examine individuality and togetherness, this work has been restricted largely to the entire family system and has not been pursued with the same sophistication within the individual and dyadic levels.

An important focus for family scientists, therefore, is to examine the extent to which autonomy and connectedness have either similar or different patterns of development within each level of the family system. Perhaps the most common view is that each level of the family system engages in reciprocal relationships with other levels. Such an interpretation would suggest that analogous issues should mutually influence and parallel each other to some extent.

Despite the logic of this "parallel" perspective, however, the degree to which such correspondence actually occurs remains largely unexplored. If analogous developments parallel each other, for example, evidence would be provided about the extent to which family systems and subsystems are interdependent and place constraints on other levels. In contrast, the study of variation across system components may provide greater insight into the health and pathology of families by examining various patterns of interlevel congruence or incongruence in reference to autonomy and connectedness.

Another possibility is that interlevel incongruence may be greater during important transitional periods of family development. When families have teenage members, for example, pressures for greater autonomy at the individual level (each adolescent) may be greater than either the dyadic or overall system levels can accommodate, causing greater parent/youth conflict in which the adolescent's goals are at odds with those of parents and the larger family system.

A third major issue deals with the ability of family scientists to recommend optimal levels of autonomy and connectedness for families and their members. One possibility presented by several perspectives is that a "balanced," or moderate, level of both autonomy and connectedness is the most adaptive climate for individual and family development. Olson and his associates (1979, 1983, 1989), for example, take this position through their curvilinear proposal for the cohesion and adaptability dimensions of the circumplex model. Correspondingly, Bowen (1978) proposes that emotional connections in families must be tempered by balanced amounts of thoughtful objectivity (or cognitive autonomy) in reference to relationships. Finally, the scholarship on social competence also agrees that balanced levels of autonomy and connectedness are central aspects of this overall adaptive quality (Baumrind, 1987; Peterson & Leigh, 1990), while Minuchin (1974) adds that optimal families have clear boundaries and relationships characterized as falling somewhere within moderate ranges between disengaged and enmeshed.

Although this "balanced view" of autonomy and connectedness in families appears to be dominant, certain problems continue to exist, which makes this a potentially fruitful area of future work for family scientists. The first dilemma is that recent findings have provided only inconsistent support for the circumplex model's hypothesis that cohesion and adaptability are related to family well-being in a curvilinear manner (Green et al., 1991). In response to such confusing results, therefore, family scientists should continue to refine current forms of measurement and more accurately operationalize and test these relationships (Pratt & Hanson, 1987). One possibility is that cohesion and adaptability might actually be associated with effective functioning in a more complicated manner than either a simple linear or even a typical curvilinear relationship with a symmetrical shape. Instead, cohesion and adaptability might predict various adaptive qualities in a curvilinear manner only at extremely high levels of both variables (Burr & Lowe, 1987). That is, families would benefit from most levels of connectedness and autonomy, until their relationships become either very emotionally intrusive (extremely high in cohesion, or suffocating) or extensively chaotic as individuality is pursued without cooperation (extremely high in adaptability). Given such complexities, therefore, the examination of these issues can be important areas of future attention for family scientists.

Another weakness in the logic for balanced models as the optimal family condition is the lack of consideration given to ethnic and cultural differences. Specifically, scholars who accept such a viewpoint seem to imply that families from any culture or ethnicity who deviate from an equal balance between autonomy and connectedness are likely to develop problems. The difficulty with such speculations, however, is that families in our society vary greatly in the extent to which they encourage either togetherness or individuality. For example, a sizable minority of ethnic and religious groups such as Latino, Slovak-American, Puerto Rican, Chinese-American, Irish Catholic, Amish, and Mormon families place strong emphasis on family togetherness (Mindel & Habenstein, 1976; Peterson & Leigh, 1990). Although some authorities might view this as excessive closeness at the expense of individuality (that is, pathological enmeshment), an equally viable perspective is that such varieties of the American family are adaptive precisely because the norms within their subcultures encourage family bonds and cohesiveness (Olson, Russell, & Sprenkle, 1983).

Closely related to the cultural variability issue is Constantine's (1986) contention that we should not presume that balanced levels of togetherness and individuality are the only standard when we consider that families construct their own paradigms, each with unique features and special priorities. Instead, "enabled," or functional, families can take many different forms, with varied configurations of individuality and connectedness being either fostered or constrained. Consequently, family scientists should resist the tendency to portray balanced families as the optimal condition without first considering the possibility of paradigm variation across families.

Akin to the issue of balance is the question about how autonomy and connectedness develop in relation to each other. This issue is often posed as either (1) that growth in autonomy will occur only at the expense of connectedness or (2) that autonomy and connectedness are complementary (and compatible) concepts that develop together. In the first case, traditional conceptions of autonomy and connectedness often portray these developments as opposite ends of the same continuum—respective locations that make them mutually exclusive (see Figure 2.1a). Consequently, any movement up this continuum toward higher autonomy necessarily will mean that proportionate decreases will occur in connectedness (or that a negative relationship will exist between autonomy and connectedness). An illustration of such contradictory trends is found in traditional theories about the development of adolescents within families. Specifically, such viewpoints have long questioned the abilities of youth to succeed in

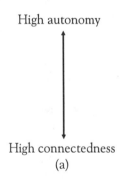

High autonomy

High connectedness
(a)

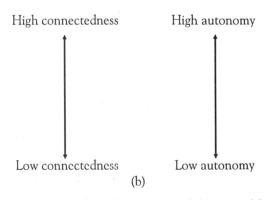

High connectedness   High autonomy

Low connectedness   Low autonomy
(b)

FIGURE 2.1   Traditional (a) and revised (b) views of the relationship between connectedness and autonomy.

establishing a difficult balance between achieving autonomy and maintaining ties with parents. Consequently, greater autonomy is acquired through a process of *separation* from the bonds of early childhood, with increased independence coming at the expense of connectedness with parents (Blos, 1979; A. Freud, 1969; Hall, 1904).

Standing in contrast to this traditional perspective, however, is another conceptualization that views autonomy and connectedness as separate dimensions, each of which varies from high amounts to low amounts (see Figure 2.1b). Such an interpretation allows autonomy and connectedness to vary independently of each other and creates the likelihood that a variety of relationships (for example, positive linear, curvilinear, or no relationship) can result between autonomy and connectedness. Corresponding with this viewpoint is more recent work on family and adolescent development indicating that moderate levels of adolescent autonomy and connectedness can coexist in reference to parents as complementary developments (Baumrind, 1987; Grotevant & Cooper, 1986; Hill, 1987; Peterson, 1986b; Youniss & Smollar, 1985). Consequently, results of this kind suggest that autonomy develops within the context of continuing togetherness, rather than through a process of separation.

Finally, when we consider how autonomy and connectedness develop in relation to each other, what immediately comes to mind is the Hegelian philosophical concept of the "dialectic," which originally meant a discourse, or discussion. For Hegel, all reality, concepts, and ideas are in constant evolution toward a more complex stage through a process involving the development and resolution of internal contradictions. Using the dialectical method of thesis, antithesis, and synthesis in discourse, an idea or phenomenon is initially posed, confronted, and interpreted in reference to its contrast, as well as ultimately united with its inverse to take another form. Despite initial contradictions, therefore, a phenomenon can eventually be conceptualized as part of a larger whole, involving a mutual relationship with its opposite.

Recent scholarship suggests that such a dialectical relationship may exist between autonomy and connectedness. Thus, when either of these processes is considered separately (thesis), each appears to contradict (antithesis) the other. Very early in development, however, these opposing forces become reconciled as connectedness becomes the mechanism or secure base from which autonomy arises. Subsequently, as development proceeds, it becomes clear that the two processes are both necessary and inextricably linked in variable amounts within well-functioning families. The result is that a new synthesis arises through which autonomy and connectedness are reconciled and incorporated into the concept of "interdependence"—a recognition that we may become both ourselves and connected to others as part of the same process. Family scientists can increase our understanding of these issues by exploring how autonomy and connectedness develop in relation to each other throughout the family system. An initial hypothesis, however, is that seemingly opposing processes rapidly become part of a larger phenomenon involving complementary sides of the same coin.

Chapter Summary

Discussion Questions

1. How do the processes of autonomy and connectedness in families reflect similar issues in the larger society?
2. Trace the use of the terms *autonomy* and *connectedness* as described by Peterson. Do you agree with his assessment that these terms are, for the most part, interchangeable?
3. Peterson builds upon the idea that families have special qualities. What are the consequences (with regard to these unique qualities) for the issues of autonomy and connectedness?
4. According to psychoanalytic theory, in what ways are autonomy and connectedness rooted in the individual level of a family system?
5. How do object relations in families play a role in the development of autonomy and connectedness?

Additional Resources

Constantine, L. L. (1986). *Family paradigms*. New York: Guilford Press.

Burr, W. R., Day, R. D., & Bahr, K. S. (1993). *Family science*. Pacific Grove, CA: Brooks/Cole. Of particular interest is Chap. 10.

Green, R. G., Kolevon, M. F., & Vosler, N. R. (1985). The Beavers-Timberlawn model of family competence and the circumplex model of family adaptability and cohesion: Separate, but equal? *Family Process, 24*, 385–398.

Peterson, G. W., & Leigh, G. K. (1990). The family and social competence in adolescence. In T. P. Gullotta, G. R. Adams, & R. Montemayor (Eds.), *Developing social competency in adolescence: Advances in adolescent development: Vol. 3* (pp. 97–138). Newbury Park, CA: Sage.

References

Adams, G. R., Dyk, P., & Bennion, L. D. (1987). Parent-adolescent relationships and identity formation. *Family Perspective, 21*(4), 249–260.

Ainsworth, M. D. S. (1982). Attachment: Retrospect and prospect. In C. M. Parkes & J. Stevenson-Hinde (Eds.), *The place of attachment in human behavior* (pp. 3–30). New York: Basic Books.

Ainsworth, M. D. S. (1989). Attachments beyond infancy. *American Psychologist, 44*, 709–716.

Allport, G. W. (1955). *Becoming*. New Haven, CT: Yale University Press.

Allport, G. W. (1960). The open system in personality theory. *Journal of Abnormal and Social Psychology, 61*, 301–310.

Armas, A. de, & Kelley, A. K. (1989). Social relationships in adolescence: Skill development and training. In J. Worrell & F. Danner (Eds.), *The adolescent as decision maker: Applications to development and education* (pp. 83–109). New York: Academic Press.

Bakan, D. (1966). *The duality of human existence: Isolation and communion in Western man*. Boston: Beacon.

Bartholomew, K., & Horowitz, L. M. (1991). Attachment styles among young adults: A test of a four-category model. *Journal of Personality and Social Psychology, 61*(2), 226–244.

Baumeister, R. F. (1987). How the self became a problem: A psychological review of historical research. *Journal of Personality and Social Psychology, 52*(1), 163–176.

Baumrind, D. (1978). Parental disciplinary patterns and social competence in children. *Youth and Society, 9*(3), 239–276.

Baumrind, D. (1987, June 2–6). *Effective parenting during the early adolescent transition*. Presentation at the Family Research Consortium, second annual Summer Institute, Santa Fe, NM.

Beavers, W. R., Hampson, R. B., & Hulgas, Y. F. (1985). Commentary: The Beavers systems approach to family assessment. *Family Process, 22*, 85–97.

Bellah, R. N., Madsen, R., Sullivan, W. M., Swidler, A., & Tipton, L. M. (1985). *Habits of the hearts: Individualization and commitment in American life*. New York: Harper & Row.

Bertalanffy, L. von. (1968). *General system theory*. New York: Braziller.

Blos, P. (1979). *The adolescent passage*. New York: International Universities Press.

Bowen, M. (1978). *Family therapy in clinical practice*. New York: Aronson.

Bowlby, J. (1969). *Attachment and loss: Vol. 1. Attachment*. New York: Basic Books.

Bowlby, J. (1973). *Attachment and loss: Vol. 2. Separation*. New York: Basic Books.

Bowlby, J. (1980). *Attachment and loss: Vol. 3. Loss, sadness and depression*. New York: Basic Books.

Bowlby, J. A. (1988). *A secure base: Parent-child attachment and healthy human development*. New York: Basic Books.

Bretherton, I. (1985). Attachment theory: Retrospect and prospect. In I. Bretherton & E. Waters (Eds.), *Monographs of the Society for Research in Child Development: Growing points of attachment theory and research, 50*(1–2, Serial No. 209), pp. 3–35.

Bronfenbrenner, U. (1970). *Two worlds of childhood: U.S. and U.S.S.R.* New York: Russell Sage Foundation.

Bronfenbrenner, U. (1985). Freedom and discipline across the decades. In H. Von Hentig (Ed.), *Ordnung und Unordnung* (pp. 326–339). Weinheim, Germany: Beltz.

Buckley, W. (1967). *Sociology and modern systems theory*. Englewood Cliffs, NJ: Prentice-Hall.

Burr, W. R., Day, R. D., & Bahr, K. S. (1993). *Family science*. Pacific Grove, CA: Brooks/Cole.

Burr, W. R., & Lowe, T. A. (1987). Olson's circumplex model: A review and extension. *Family Science Review, 1*, 5–22.

Carnes, P. J. (1989). Sexually addicted families: Clinical use of the circumplex model. In D. H. Olson, C. S. Russell, & D. H. Sprenkle (Eds.), *Circumplex model: Systemic assessment and treatment of families*. New York: Haworth Press.

Clarke, J. (1984). *The family types of schizophrenics, neurotics, and "normals."* Unpublished doctoral dissertation, Department of Family Social Science, University of Minnesota.

Colapinto, J. (1991). Structural family therapy. In A. S. Gurman & D. P. Kniskern (Eds.), *Handbook of family therapy, Vol. 2*. New York: Brunner/Mazel.

Constantine, L. L. (1986). *Family paradigms*. New York: Guilford Press.

Cromwell, R. E., & Peterson, G. W. (1983). Multisystem-multimethod family assessment in clinical contexts. *Family Process, 22,* 147–163.

Dodge, K. A., Pettit, G. L., McClaskey, C. L., & Brown, M. M. (1986). Social competence in children. *Monographs of the Society for Research in Child Development, 51*(2, Serial No. 213).

Douvan, E., & Adelson, J. (1966). *The adolescent experience.* New York: Wiley.

Dyk, P. A. H., & Adams, G. R. (1987). The association between identity development and intimacy during adolescence: A theoretical treatise. *Journal of Adolescent Research, 2*(3), 223–235.

Erikson, E. (1959). *Identity and the life cycle.* New York: International Universities Press.

Erikson, E. (1968). *Identity, youth and crisis.* New York: Norton.

Felner, R. D., Lease, A. M., & Phillips, R. S. C. (1990). Social competence and the language of adequacy as a subject matter of psychology: A quadripartite framework. In T. P. Gullotta, G. R. Adams, & R. Montemayor (Eds.), *Developing social competency in adolescence: Advances in adolescent development* (pp. 245–264). Newbury Park, CA: Sage.

Frank, S. J., Avery, C. B., & Laman, M. J. (1988). Young adults' perceptions of their relationships with their parents: Individual differences in connectedness, competence, and emotional autonomy. *Developmental Psychology, 24*(5), 729–737.

Franz, C. E., & White, K. M. (1985). Individuation and attachment in personality development: Extending Erikson's theory. *Journal of Personality, 53*(2), 224-256.

Freud, A. (1958). Adolescence. *Psychoanalytic Study of the Child, 13,* 255–287.

Freud, A. (1969). Adolescence as a developmental disturbance. In J. G. Caplan & S. Lebovici (Eds.), *Adolescence: Psychological perspectives.* New York: Basic Books.

Freud, S. (1949). *Outline of psychoanalysis.* New York: Norton.

Freud, S. (1953). *A general introduction to psychoanalysis.* New York: Permabooks.

Friedman, L. (1980). Integrating psychoanalytic object relations understanding with family systems interventions in couples therapy. In J. Pearce & L. Friedman (Eds.), *Family therapy: Combining psychodynamic and family systems approaches.* New York: Grune & Stratton.

Gelles, R. J., & Straus, M. A. (1979). Determinants of violence in the family: Toward a theoretical integration. In W. R. Burr, R. Hill, F. I. Nye, & I. L. Reiss (Eds.), *Contemporary theories about the family: Vol. 1* (pp. 549–581). New York: Free Press.

Gilligan, C. (1982). *In a different voice: Psychological theory and women's development.* Cambridge, MA: Harvard University Press.

Green, R. G. (1989). Choosing family measurement devices for practice and research: SFI and FACES III. *Social Service Review, 63,* 304–320.

Green, R. G., Harris, R. N., Forte, J. A., & Robinson, M. (1991). Evaluating FACES III and the circumplex model: 2,440 families. *Family Process, 30,* 55–73.

Green, R. G., Kolevon, M. F., & Vosler, N. R. (1985). The Beavers-Timberlawn model of family competence and the circumplex model of family adaptability and cohesion: Separate, but equal? *Family Process, 24,* 385–398.

Grotevant, H. (1987). Toward a process model of identity formation. *Journal of Adolescent Research, 2*(3), 203-222.

Grotevant, H. D., & Cooper, C. R. (1986). Individuation in family relationships: A perspective on individual differences in the development of identity and role-taking skill in adolescence. *Human Development, 29,* 82–100.

Hall, G. S. (1904). *Adolescence.* New York: Appleton.

Hampson, R. B., Beavers, W. R., & Hulgas, Y. F. (1988). Commentary: Comparing the Beavers and circumplex models of family functioning. *Family Process, 27,* 85–92.

Hardin, G. (1968). The tragedy of the commons. *Science, 162,* 1243–1248.

Hauser, S. T., Powers, S. I., Noam, G. G., & Jacobson, A. M. (1984). Familial contexts of adolescent ego development. *Child Development, 55,* 195–213.

Henry, C. L., Wilson, L. M., & Peterson, G. W. (1989). Parental power bases and processes as predictors of adolescent conformity. *Journal of Adolescent Research, 4,* 15–32.

Hess, R. D., & Handel, G. (1959). *Family worlds.* Chicago: University of Chicago Press.

Hill, J. P., (1987). Research on adolescents and their families: Past and prospect. In C. E. Irwin (Ed.), *New directions for child development: Adolescent social behavior and health,* (pp. 13–31). San Francisco: Jossey-Bass.

Hill, J. P., & Holmbeck, G. N. (1986). Attachment and autonomy during adolescence. *Annals of Child Development, 3,* 145–189.

Hoffman, J. A. (1984). Psychological separation of late adolescents from their parents. *Journal of Counseling Psychology, 31*(2), 170–178.

Hoffman, M. L. (1980). Moral development in adolescence. In J. Adelson (Ed.), *Handbook of adolescent psychology.* New York: Wiley.

Inkeles, A. (1968). Society, social structure, and child socialization. In J. A. Clausen (Ed.), *Socialization and society* (pp. 73–129). Boston: Little, Brown.

Kantor, D., & Lehr, W. (1975). *Inside the family.* San Francisco: Jossey-Bass.

Kerr, M., & Bowen, M. (1988). *Family evaluation*. New York: Norton.

Klein, M. (1946). Notes on some schizoid mechanisms. *International Journal of Psycho-Analysis*, 99–110.

Lasch, C. (1978). *The culture of narcissism*. New York: Norton.

Lykes, M. B. (1985). Gender and individualistic vs. collectivist bases for notions about the self. *Journal of Personality*, 53(2), 356–383.

Mahler, M., Pine, F., & Bergman, A. (1975). *The psychological birth of the human infant*. New York: Basic Books.

Martin, T. C., & Bumpass, L. (1988). Recent trends in marital disruption. *Demography*, 26, 37–51.

Maslow, A. H. (1968). *Toward a psychology of being*. New York: Van Nostrand.

Mead, G. H. (1934). *Mind, self and society*. Chicago: University of Chicago Press.

Miller, I. W., Epstein, N. B., Bishop, D. L., & Keitner, G. I. (1985). The McMaster Family Assessment Device: Reliability and validity. *Journal of Marital and Family Therapy*, 11, 345–356.

Mindel, C. H., & Habenstein, R. W. (Eds.). (1976). *Ethnic families in America*. New York: Elsevier.

Minuchin, S. (1974). *Families and family therapy*. Cambridge, MA: Harvard University Press.

Olson, D. H. (1986). Circumplex model VII: Validation studies and FACES III. *Family Process*, 25, 337–352.

Olson, D. H., & Killorin, E. (1984). Clinical rating scale for circumplex model. Minneapolis: Department of Family Social Science, University of Minnesota.

Olson, D. H., McCubbin, H. A., Barnes, H., Larsen, M., Maxen, M., & Wilson, M. (1983). *Families: What makes them work*. Newbury Park, CA: Sage.

Olson, D. H., Russell, C. S., & Sprenkle, D. H. (1983). Circumplex model of marital and family systems: VI. Theoretical update. *Family Process*, 22, 69–83.

Olson, D. H., Sprenkle, D. H., & Russell, C. S. (1979). Circumplex model of marital and family systems: I. Cohesion and adaptability dimensions, family types, and clinical applications. *Family Process*, 18, 3–29.

Openshaw, D. K., & Thomas, D. L. (1986). The adolescent self and the family. In G. K. Leigh & G. W. Peterson (Eds.), *Adolescents in families* (pp. 104–129). Cincinnati: South-Western Publishing.

Pardeck, J. A., & Pardeck, I. T. (1990). Family factors related to adolescent autonomy. *Adolescence*, 98, 311–319.

Perloff, R. (1987). Self-interest and personal responsibility redux. *American Psychologist*, 42(1), 3–11.

Peterson, G. W. (1986a). Family conceptual frameworks and adolescent development. In G. K. Leigh & G. W. Peter-son (Eds.), *Adolescents in families* (pp. 12–35). Cincinnati: South-Western Publishing.

Peterson, G. W. (1986b). Parent-youth power dimensions and the behavioral autonomy of adolescents. *Journal of Adolescent Research*, 1, 231–249.

Peterson, G. W., & Cromwell, R. E. (1983). A clarification of multisystem-multimethod assessment: Reductionism versus wholism. *Family Process*, 22, 173–177.

Peterson, G. W., & Leigh, G. K. (1990). The family and social competence in adolescence. In T. P. Gullotta, G. R. Adams, & R. Montemayor (Eds.), *Developing social competency in adolescence: Advances in adolescent development: Vol. 3* (pp. 97–138). Newbury Park, CA: Sage.

Peterson, G. W., & Rollins, B. C. (1987). Parent-child socialization. In M. B. Sussman & S. K. Steinmetz (Eds.), *Handbook of marriage and the family*. New York: Plenum.

Peterson, G. W., Rollins, B. C., & Thomas, D. L. (1985). Parental influence and adolescent conformity: Compliance and internalization. *Youth and Society*, 16, 397–420.

Peterson, G. W., & Stivers, M. E. (1986). Adolescent behavioral autonomy and family connectedness in rural Appalachia. *Family Perspective*, 20, 307–322.

Powers, S. I., Hauser, S. T., Schwartz, J. M., Noam, G. G., & Jacobson, A. M. (1983). Adolescent ego development and family interaction: A structural developmental perspective. In H. D. Grotevant & C. R. Cooper (Eds.), *Adolescent development in the family*. San Francisco: Jossey-Bass.

Pratt, D. M., & Hansen, J. C. (1987). A test of the curvilinear hypothesis with FACES II and III. *Journal of Marital and Family Therapy*, 13, 387–392.

Reiss, D. (1981). *The family's construction of reality*. Cambridge, MA: Harvard University Press.

Riesman, D., Glazer, N., & Denney, R. (1950). *The lonely crowd: A study of the changing American character*. New Haven, CT: Yale University Press.

Roderick, J., Henggler, S., & Hanson, C. L. (1986). An evaluation of the Family Adaptability and Cohesion Evaluation Scales (FACES) and the circumplex model. *Journal of Abnormal Child Psychology*, 14, 77–87.

Rohner, R. P. (1986). *The warmth dimension: Foundation of parental acceptance-rejection theory*. Newbury Park, CA: Sage.

Rollins, B. C., & Thomas, D. L. (1979). Parental support, power, and control techniques in the socialization of children. In W. R. Burr, R. Hill, F. I. Nye, & I. R. Reiss (Eds.), *Contemporary theories about the family: Vol. 1* (pp. 317–364). New York: Free Press.

Sampson, E. E. (1977). Psychology and the American ideal. *Journal of Personality and Social Psychology*, 35(11), 767–782.

Sampson, E. E. (1985). The decentralization of identity: Toward a revised concept of personal and social order. *American Psychologist, 40*(11), 1203–1211.

Sampson, E. E. (1988). The debate on individualism: Indigenous psychologies of the individual and their role in personal and societal functioning. *American Psychologist, 43*(1), 15–22.

Scharff, D., & Scharff, J. (1987). *Object relations family therapy.* New York: Aronson.

Segal, M. (1964). *Introduction to the work of Melanie Klein.* New York: Basic Books.

Shaver, P. R., & Hazan, C. (1988). A biased overview of the study of love. *Journal of Social and Personal Relationships, 5*, 473–501.

Skynner, A. C. R. (1976). *Systems of family and marital psychotherapy.* New York: Brunner/Mazel.

Skynner, A. C. R. (1981). An open-systems, group analytic approach to family therapy. In A. S. Gurman & D. P. Kniskern (Eds.), *Handbook of family therapy.* New York: Brunner/Mazel.

Slipp, S. (1984). *Object relations; A dynamic bridge between individualism and family treatment.* New York: Aronson.

Slipp, S. (1988). *Technique and practice of object relations family therapy.* New York: Aronson.

Smith, P. (1987). *Redeeming the time: A people's history of the 1920s and the New Deal: Vol. 8.* New York: McGraw-Hill.

Spence, J. T. (1985). Achievement American style: The rewards and costs of individualism. *American Psychologist, 40*(12), 1285–1295.

Sroufe, L. A., & Fleeson, J. (1986). Attachment and the construction of relationships. In W. W. Hartup & Z. Rubin (Eds.), *Relationships and development* (pp. 51–71). Hillsdale, NJ: Erlbaum.

Staub, E. (1979). *Positive social behavior and morality: Socialization and development: Vol. 2.* New York: Academic Press.

Steinglass, P. (1987). A systems view of family interaction and psychopathology. In T. Jacob (Ed.), *Family interaction and psychopathology* (pp. 25–65). New York: Plenum.

Stierlin, H. (1974). *Separating parents and adolescents: A perspective on running away, schizophrenia, and waywardness.* New York: Quadrangle.

Thomas, V. K., & Cierpka, M. (1989). *FACES III and FAM III: A comparison of family assessment instruments.* Presentation at the National Council on Family Relations Annual Conference, New Orleans.

Tocqueville, A. de. (1969). *Democracy in America* (G. Lawrence, Trans., J. P. Mayer, Ed.). New York: Doubleday (work originally published 1835).

Walker, L. S., McLaughlin, F. J., & Green, J. W. (1988). Functional illness and family functioning: A comparison of healthy and somaticizing adolescents. *Family Process, 27*, 317–325.

Walters, L. H. (1982). Are families different from other groups? *Journal of Marriage and the Family, 44*, 841–850.

Waters, E., & Sroufe, L. A. (1983). Social competence as a developmental construct. *Developmental Review, 3*, 79–97.

Weiss, R. S. (1986). Continuities and transformations in social relationships from childhood to adulthood. In W. W. Hartup & Z. Rubin (Eds.), *Relationships and Development* (pp. 51–71). Hillsdale, NJ: Erlbaum.

Whyte, W. H. Jr. (1956). *The organization man.* New York: Simon & Schuster.

Winnicott, D.W. (1965). *The maturational process and the facilitating environment: Studies in the theory of emotional development.* New York: International Universities Press.

Youniss, J., & Smollar, J. (1985). *Adolescent relations with mothers, fathers, and friends.* Chicago: University of Chicago Press.

Gender Interactions in Families

Peggy Quinn
University of Texas, Arlington

Men and women experience family differently. We are socialized into our masculine or feminine gender and the roles and behaviors that our society sees as gender-appropriate. Our interactions within families and our expectations regarding family and gender roles are affected by these disparate experiences.

Over the last four decades, stimulated in part by the work of Talcott Parsons, new knowledge has been developed with regard to gender and the roles that women and men play in families. The first section of this chapter describes the situation of families during each decade from the 1950s to the 1990s. In addition, some information about the perspective of family professionals during this period is included.

During the 1970s and 1980s, feminist scholars began intensive examination of the family and the role of gender. These studies were developed in part to begin to compensate for the fact that previous data about women and their roles had been based on the norm of white, heterosexual men. In the second section of this chapter, ideas from various researchers, feminist-based and others, are presented in order to assist you in forming your own ideas about gender and family. Some implications and applications are also suggested.

The goal of this chapter is not to provide all the answers to questions about gender and family. Instead, it is designed to assist you in asking appropriate questions and in maintaining an investigative stance. Families are undergoing rapid change, and researchers, therapists, educators, and other family scientists must be continually learning and changing as well.

Family and Gender: Forty Years of Change

Changes in social and economic circumstances have dramatically affected families and their functioning. Trends have changed in each recent decade. The 1950s were characterized by a sense of family and tradition. The 1960s featured youthful rebellion, and the 1970s had a sense of rootlessness. The 1980s saw families once again putting down roots and rediscovering traditional values (Russell & Exter, 1986).

The 1950s

During the post–World War II years, the United States experienced an increase in the number of births as well as a dramatic expansion in spending on consumer goods. The savings accumulated during the war were being spent, thus expanding the economy, providing jobs, and supporting the country. Family scientists saw the family as being in transition from the old patriarchal system to a new, more democratic, egalitarian order (Dyer & Urban, 1958).

Within the academic realm, attention was focused on the family as Parsons (1951) developed his views of the appropriate gendered division of labor and roles within families. Parsons viewed the transition from rural families who worked at home to urban settlers whose men worked in factories as having had dramatic effects on the family and its organization.

During the 1950s, it was not unusual for women to be employed outside the home for particular periods of their lives. Most young women were employed for several years after completing school. They were expected to marry by age 20 and withdraw from the labor force at the birth of their first child (Leopold, 1958). They would probably reenter the work force when their children entered school. For those women who worked outside the home when their children were small, child care was a major concern (Leopold, 1958).

Despite Parsons' (1951) proclamations about the gender roles of men and women, ambiguity and confusion reigned. In the traditional view, the ideal man was a good provider, was the ultimate source of knowledge and authority, and was strong enough in character to support his wife and family financially and emotionally (Hacker, 1957). Men were also expected to demonstrate some of the softer attributes typically relegated to women. They were to be patient, understanding, and gentle in their dealings with others (Hacker, 1957). In their role as fathers, men were expected to perform more than their typically authoritarian roles of judge and arbiter of society's rules. Their participation with the children was seen as important (Mogey, 1957). The transition from tough to tender caused considerable confusion among men within the home.

Men were also confronted more and more frequently with women in the workplace, generating fear that women would take the jobs that "rightly" belonged to men and that, even worse, women who could obtain jobs on their own might no longer depend on men as the link to the world outside the home (Hacker, 1957) or be subject to the paternal power of their husbands (Mogey, 1957).

Even if they were employed, women were expected to retain their traditional roles within the home. They were still the "scullions" who had full responsibility for housework and child care (Mogey, 1957).

African-American families. For African-American families, although school desegregation had become law, social and economic segregation was still a fact of life. Family scientists were focused on white families. Information about African Americans was generally limited to studies of individuals or groups, such as Whyte's (1943) *Street Corner Society*. A large number of African-American families lived in the large cities of the East and the North. High unemployment was a chronic problem for African-American men, while African-American women could generally find work as domestics.

Latino families. The decade of the 1950s saw large numbers of Mexican-American families moving to large cities. In the Southwest, the *bracero* employment program and illegal entry resulted in a huge immigration from Mexico.

Some family scientists studied Mexican-American families during the postwar years. Traditional parenting styles, patriarchy, and folk healing were characteristics applied to these families. The researchers basically concluded that the ethnic family and its values and traditions prevented Mexican Americans from fully assimilating into American life (Griswold del Castillo, 1984).

Summary. Looking back, the 1950s appear to have been a blissfully simple time in which the nuclear family thrived. In theory, gender roles were clear, and a successful life was available to anyone who wished to work hard. The actual experience of families who were not white and middle class was probably quite different. Unemployment and insufficient education as well as inadequate housing presented tremendous problems for large numbers of African-American and Latino families.

A blissful snapshot of the two-parent, 2.5-child family gleefully adhering to prescribed gender roles continues to influence the expectations of family professionals. The fact that this picture was probably never accurate for a majority of the population has not prevented our establishing programs, policies, and therapeutic goals designed to reach this ideal. Further research is needed on the experience of people of color as well as those who were not middle class. This could lead to a revision of the characteristics of the ideal family—perhaps reflecting the experience of a much wider section of the population.

The 1960s

The economic boom of the 1950s receded in the mid-1960s and led to even more women entering the workplace. The introduction of the contraceptive pill changed attitudes toward sexual activity within marriages as well as outside. Reliable contraception meant that women no longer needed to be bound to home by unintended pregnancy. The ensuing "baby bust" dropped the number of births in 1965 to below 4 million for the first time in 13 years (Cooper & Kosterlitz, 1986).

Nye's (1967) article on changing family values pointed out that girls were still traditionally counseled into such careers as teaching, nursing, and secretarial work, where they faced little competition from men and where their careers would cause little conflict with the requirements of homemaking and child care. If this gendered segregation of occupations was to change, several issues would need to be addressed. There might be a larger number of families in which the wife was the principal provider. The number of divorces might increase, and the need for child care provision would certainly rise. In terms of extramarital sexual activity, women's sexual lives might approximate those of men. The birthrate might drop, and the age at which women married might rise. These changes in the lives of women were frightening to many who would have the values of families remain unchanged from the carefully divided instrumental/expressive dichotomies of former times (Nye, 1967).

During the 1960s, despite changes begun during the previous decade, the transformation of family dynamics was slow. The decision-making processes in some families still left husbands in charge of jobs, cars, and life insurance while wives dominated in the areas of food shopping and choosing doctors (Hallenbeck, 1966).

In the decade of the 1960s, family-systems therapy was developed by Jay Haley and Salvador Minuchin (Goldner, 1988). They based their ideas on what had appeared to be the ideal family: the two-parent, father/breadwinner, mother/homemaker unit. The new possibilities of family types—single-parent, homosexual, or other—were not included in the construction of the "ideal" or "normal" family.

African-American families.   High rates of male unemployment continued to affect families. Women were still able to bring in some money from their jobs as domestic workers. In lower-class families, male and female roles continued to be separate and traditional. The man was the provider, with little responsibility at home. His wife was in charge of home, children, church, and kin (Rainwater, 1970).

Probably the most influential and controversial research on African-American families was that of Daniel Moynihan in *The Negro Family: The Case for National Action*. His conclusion was that the problems of African Americans in general resulted from that "tangle of pathology" (Moynihan, 1967, p. 74), the black family headed by a woman with no strong man available. He acknowledged that a patriarchal system was not necessarily superior, but since American life was predicated on men having more influence than women, he saw any subculture that functioned differently as inherently disadvantaged.

Latino families.   In the 1960s, the heaviest convergence of Mexican Americans was still in the Southwest—namely, Texas and California. They generally lived in concentrated neighborhoods known as barrios. Birthrates were high, leading to large families. Income levels were relatively low (Moore, 1976).

Summary.   During the 1960s, society was changing rapidly. The divorce rate was rising, psychological and social turmoil raged around the issues of the Vietnam War, and college students protested, defected, and dropped out. The women's movement and the civil rights movement were in place. No studies had yet begun to interpret the impact of these changes on families. As evidenced by Haley and the other initiators of family-systems thinking, family professionals continued to maintain a very limited view of what was appropriate for a properly functioning family.

The 1970s

The restlessness and rootlessness of the 1970s were based on the social and economic changes that were occurring. Many families of the middle and upper classes faced frequent moves to fit the needs of employers. Traditional social values, some based on fear of pregnancy, were being questioned. Young people who had challenged authority in their college years were now working for the very bureaucracies they had previously questioned. Within families, issues of communication and division of responsibility continued to ferment.

In attempting to address family problems concerning household roles, Rice and Rice (1977) proposed a nonsexist approach to marital therapy and suggested that equal sharing of household and child care duties should be arranged, because these traditionally female areas carried little social and economic value. The resolution of power disparity within the family would require the development of quality child care, giving either parent the option of working or remaining home.

Feldman's (1976) article on family therapy did not address gender at all. He followed the typical systems therapist's view that a healthy, flexible family would allow its members periodically to assume dominant or submissive roles. Like Haley and Minuchin before him, Feldman ignored the possibility that women might not have enough power within their families to assume dominant roles.

Therapists and family theorists continued to scrutinize the increasing numbers of married women in the workplace and the impact of this phenomenon on families. Humphrey (1975) stated that ancient values no longer kept women solely within the home. Women did continue, however, to take the man's name and to follow him wherever his job led. Burke and Weir (1976) determined that wives' employment led to greater satisfaction in their lives but more stress and health problems for their spouses. The husbands lost their support within the home as well as the dominance they had maintained as sole breadwinners. As men were forced into greater participation within the home, they were expected to attempt tasks that had never been demanded of them before. This was much more difficult for them than was women's task of moving from domestic chores to employment responsibilities (Burke & Weir, 1976).

Changes in the family life cycle as predicted by Paul Glick (1977) indicated that families would be smaller than in the 1950s. Women would not be required to devote so many years full time to child rearing, and couples would have a greater ability to provide adequately for their children. Although discussion of changing gender roles had been prominent in writings about the family for over 20 years, the fact that men were still dominant continued to be a concern. Women's place was still largely expected to be within the home, and the man's home was still his castle (Brashear & Willis, 1976).

Perhaps the most disturbing area of continued gender misalignment was the husband's right in several states to demand sexual intercourse from his wife or have a ground for divorce if she refused him. Still worse, the prosecution of rape within marriage was not even a possibility. One of the most punitive results of this continued male dominance was the increasing incidence of wife battering. For some women, gender-role expectations contributed to their motivation for remaining with a battering spouse: they had grown up with the expectation that men were supposed to beat their wives (Gelles, 1976).

One study on family roles examined changes in marital role divisions. A husband's sharing in child care was defined as his looking after the children without his wife present at least once a week (Ericksen, Yancey, & Ericksen, 1979). The explanation for this extremely narrow definition of sharing care was that if the definition required any more of the husband, none of the sample would qualify as sharing child care at all. This continued doubling of demands on employed wives' time was a major factor in the limited ability of many women to maintain continuity within the workforce and thus reap increased financial benefits (Hudis, 1976).

African-American families.   The economic recession continued to have a strong impact on lower-income African-American families. Manufacturing jobs and other manual labor slowed because of reduced demand for merchandise and construction. Some African Americans were able to enter college programs or professions through the assistance of student loans and affirmative-action programs.

School dropout rates continued to rise, further reducing the number of men who were regarded as good marriage material. The incidence of teenage pregnancy also increased, leading to even more single-parent households (Wilson, 1987).

Latino families.   During the 1970s, family scientists questioned the methods and assumptions of past studies that had perpetuated negative stereotypes about Latino families. Two prominent assumptions involved the subordination of women and their passivity and dependency. The new studies determined that few Hispanics lived in extended families and that, contrary to public assumptions, as many as 30% of homes consisted of a single parent and children. Within two-parent families, there was some patriarchal authority, but there was also some joint decision-making. For both boys and girls, there was a strong emphasis on a good education and on firm discipline (Griswold del Castillo, 1984).

Summary.   Economic struggles required increasing numbers of women to enter the paid work force. Concurrently, gender roles were expected to change to accommodate these alterations in family role performance. Either men were compelled to take on more household duties, or women effectively held two full-time jobs. Issues of domestic violence became more visible. Traditional roles were suitable in very few families, yet there were few models for the new ones.

The 1980s

The 1980s saw further change in the structure of families. The divorce rate continued to rise, as did the number of women in the workplace. Birthrates dropped, with women in their late 30s experiencing the greatest percentage of increase in births (National Center for Health Statistics, 1987). Life expectancy continued to increase, leading to larger and larger numbers of the old-old—those 85 years and older. Families began to experience the "baby boomerang," or returning-young adult syndrome. Young people graduated from college or left unhappy marital situations and returned home until they could gain control of their financial or social circumstances (Riche, 1987).

The increasing numbers of elderly who needed assistance and the numbers of young people returning home resulted in a squeeze, both social and financial, for middle-aged couples. The wives especially seemed to experience the stress of these new demands. They were concerned about having enough time to manage the family responsibilities along with the demands of the workplace. At the same time, they worried about the consequences on their financial situation when they

retired. The funds they had saved for the future were being spent on the current needs of all those in the expanding nest.

African-American families.   The reduction of social programs such as Women, Infants, and Children (WIC), the tightening of rules on Social Security, the cutback of funds for college grants, and other decreases in spending by the Reagan and Bush administrations were accompanied by continued increases in unemployment. The results of these economic problems were exacerbated by the extremely high rates of African-American male joblessness (Wilson, 1987). Gender issues within African-American families were intensified by these economic difficulties.

Latino families.   A major concern regarding Latino families in the 1980s was the rapidly increasing rate of poverty, especially in the inner cities. Concomitantly, Latinos fell behind the rest of the population in jobs, income, education, housing, and health care (Zinn, 1989).

The traditional, conservative values espoused by the Reagan and Bush administrations were appropriate for the family as it had supposedly existed in the 1950s. Lack of accessible, affordable health care, child care, and facilities for the elderly, however, continued to plague most families. An excessive amount of often-contradictory information about communication, parenting, and other family management issues poured forth from all the media almost daily. From all sides, families were confronted with their deficiencies and encouraged to learn more so they could function better. The strain on family members was exacerbated by the lack of clarity about gender roles. In general, the 1980s produced a large amount of information about and for families. Sadly, the result was merely more confusion and difficulty for families.

Conclusion

In the 1990s, as in the previous four decades, the issue of gender continues to provoke feelings of confusion in families. The roles of various family members are in flux, as are the expectations of society for these members. Contradictory information and messages are common. Research by family scientists and by others produces conflicting data. It is important that family professionals have some understanding of this material in order to be able to assist families in making informed, appropriate choices about their roles and interactions. To assist you in providing this assistance, the following section provides information on some theorists and family scientists about major issues confronting families.

Concepts and Controversies

Gender, self-identity, and family appear to be intricately related. The experience of women and men in families continues to be different even after decades of movement away from strict role distinctions such as those proposed by Parsons (1951). Several concepts are important in understanding the effects of gender on family interaction. These include roles and expectations about roles, communication, and power. The ideas and suggestions of a number of family scientists will be used to enlighten, and perhaps perplex, you regarding these concepts.

Roles

The roles that women and men play in families and in other settings have changed dramatically during the last four decades. Traditional gender roles, identified by Parsons (1951), divided the responsibilities for family maintenance into instrumental duties, such as providing resources and making rational decisions (for men), and expressive activities, such as nurturing and supporting family members (for women).

The economic realities of the 1980s and 1990s, however, have drastically altered gender roles in families from the ideal represented by the nuclear family of the 1950s. No longer is the husband solely responsible for financial support. Most women are employed outside the home, no matter what the age of their children. Since women and men are both playing the instrumental provider role, logic would say that both also perform the expressive, nurturant, caretaking activities formerly relegated to women. Arlie Hochschild (1989) investigated this area and determined that the alterations

women had made in order to engage in paid employment had not been matched by their husbands. Women were going to work for a full day and then returning home to carry out a full schedule of all of their traditional duties as well; they worked the second shift after they completed the first. As mentioned in the introductory section, the idea of men's participating in the nurturing responsibilities of family was not new in the 1980s. Family scientists have been investigating this issue for decades. It appears that within families, however, a satisfactory resolution has yet to be reached because feelings about these roles are deeply rooted.

The roles that women and men occupy within families are strongly related to the ideals established in the families of origin of both wife and husband. If the couple have grown up expecting that men will be strong, bring home the money, mow the lawn, and fix the car while women will be emotional, cook good meals, and successfully prepare the children for integration into the community, any variation can be problematic for family harmony.

Lifelong indoctrination into gender roles is a difficult thing to change. Women who expected to remain within the home to perform their tasks may feel very uncomfortable when they enter the world of commerce.

One of the roles that women play within the family is that of preliminary educator. Women provide the space and equipment, reduce intrusions and interruptions, and generally provide an appropriate environment in which children can do homework and prepare for school. The preparation for education appears to be critical for children (Smith, 1987). Other tasks assigned to women involve the nurturing and protecting responsibilities that Ruddick (1989) discusses. In addition, women are still expected to provide a restful haven in which men can recuperate and regain their energies in order to go back to the world of work and earn money for the family. There is a huge gender gap in these expectations, for women have no restful refuge in which a "wife" provides support, nurturance, and care.

Nancy Chodorow (1978) observes that traditional family structure, in which mothers only nurture and fathers only provide, is a major source of problematic gender identity for men. Girls are raised by someone similar to themselves whom they can emulate. Boys are raised by someone different from themselves and may see their father as marginal to the family and its interactions. As they develop, boys must differentiate from their mother, this incredibly powerful person who holds the key to nurturance and acceptance. For some men, this differentiation may be carried so far that it leads to such drastic actions as abuse, rape, and murder.

Although no particular arrangement of gender roles has been determined to produce ideally functioning families, it appears that some softening of extremes in behavior is helpful. In families, as in other societal settings, the ideal for gender roles seems to involve some presence of both masculine and feminine in each person (Rossi, 1985).

Family professionals can assist families in investigating their expectations about various gender roles. They can also determine whether these roles are appropriate given current circumstances. At that point, a therapist may suggest some new activities for the family. A family life educator could recommend some reading materials or utilize clips from movies or television shows to demonstrate both old and new gender role behaviors. The area of gender roles remains fertile ground for further investigation by family researchers. Both quantitative and qualitative methods are appropriate as researchers study the ever-changing dynamics within families.

Summary.   Family members are socialized into gender roles that are appropriate for that particular family. The inculcation of these ideas is subtle and pervasive. We tend to presume that our beliefs are the correct ones. Within families, the collision between disparate ideas about appropriate gender roles can be painful and disruptive. The lack of models for these new gender roles, in families and even in the media, means that family members are not clear either on how they should act or even on what the possibilities are for various gender-related behaviors.

Communications

Beginning in their families and continuing into other societal interactions, women and men communicate differently (see Chapter 11). The sources of this disparate approach to a very common tool have been identified by a number of researchers and theorists. The difficulty for family scientists is that all of these experts have varying views of how and why differences occur in the communications styles of women and men. Studies by Ruddick (1989) and Belenky, Clinchy, Goldberger, and Tarule (1986) examine thinking patterns and how these affect communication and other interactions. Gilligan (1982) has based her work on Chodorow (1978) and examined how moral development is different for the two genders. Recently, Tannen (1990) has explored communication patterns, basing her work on Chodorow as well.

Ruddick.   Sara Ruddick (1989) is a philosopher who has examined the practices and behaviors of "mothering" as they relate to how a person thinks. Although she acknowledges that most "mothers" are women, she asserts that being a woman is not a necessary component of maternal thinking. Those who nurture children must meet the three demands of maternal practice: preserving children's health and well-being, nurturing their emotional and intellectual growth, and guiding them so they become socially acceptable.

The intense and long-term demands made on nurturers as they assist growing children result in a different mode of thinking. Nurturers fight tenaciously for what they believe is vital for children. These caretakers are not capable of solving problems by instigating or pursuing violence such as wars. Instead, they seek to determine who was wronged and to help end the conflict. They personalize events and examine the effects on the lives and experience of individuals: there is no such thing as a just war, because people were hurt and killed. The nonviolent peacemaking that emerges from maternal thinking demands renunciation of violent strategies and weapons, resisting the violence of others, seeking reconciliation that is responsible, and attempting to avoid battles (Ruddick, 1989). If women in their roles as mothers do indeed think differently from men in their potential roles as warlords and generals, this truly leads to some wide variation in how they communicate.

Gilligan.   Carol Gilligan (1982) has examined the development of women and determined that whereas masculinity is defined through separation, femininity is defined through attachment. Men are socialized to need independence and to struggle to reach the top. Women spend their energies establishing connections and ensuring that they are embedded in a network of communications and relations. This can lead to very different ways of communicating.

If a woman is feeling insecure, she may want the man to let her know he feels close to her and will be available should she need him. When a man expresses the same insecurity, he may be overwhelmed and terrified if the woman, believing his need to be the same as hers, offers an enveloping support. Neither may understand the other's response.

The morality underlying their actions differs between the genders as well. Men proceed from an ethic of justice, which assumes that everyone should be treated the same. They are certain that it is possible to develop an abstract principle that can be applied generally. Women, on the other hand, develop an ethic of care, in which no one should be hurt. These very different moral voices put very different faces on any problems or issues. Attempts to solve the same problem may have drastically different outcomes depending on the philosophy and tactics one has chosen. Men and women approaching identical issues may assume that any reasonably intelligent person would emerge with the same outcome as they did. Huge gaps in communication can result from this assumption.

The basic assumptions, the ethics that undergird decisions, and the communication patterns that result led Gilligan (1982) to conclude that "men and women may speak different languages that they assume are the same, using similar words to encode disparate experiences of self and social relationships" (p. 173).

Tannen.   Deborah Tannen (1990) has provoked considerable discussion with her research on female/male communications. She concurs with Gilligan that women relate in terms of networks and intimacy, whereas men focus on independence and hierarchies. This results in a number of discrepancies when the two genders attempt to interpret what is said to them. In their search for connection, women seek symmetry in conversation, and men protect their position in the hierarchy with asymmetrical communication. As women show their connection in dialogue, men perceive them to be dependent, incompetent, and insecure.

When women and men discuss their problems with each other, they seek different outcomes. Women want understanding, and men strive for solutions. The content of talk is also dissimilar. "Rapport," talk as used by women, is directed toward building connections. "Report talk," for men, aspires to deliver information. These variations are evident at all ages when girls and women engage in intimate conversations with their friends for hours, discussing personal and secret ideas. Boys and men tend to give information and to discuss activities rather than confidential matters.

Even their handling of disagreement may cause tension when men and women talk. She may see the expression of any disagreement as a threat to their intimacy, while he feels that his disagreement indicates that he is comfortable with their relationship and is not threatened by the difference of opinion.

Summary.   It is not at all impossible for women and men to communicate, but they must learn to identify accurately what is taking place. They must be willing to understand the other's point of view and to adjust their communication styles as needed. It is vital for family therapists to understand the complexities of gender-differentiated communication and to be able to assist families in analyzing communication problems and developing solutions. Family life educators have ideal opportunities to convey information about potential gender gaps in communication in almost any kind of programming. Researchers may attempt to corroborate the findings of Tannen, Gilligan, Ruddick, and Chodorow.

Power

Power in families has been studied with much interest by family scientists for several decades. Scanzoni (1979) sees power as "the capability to achieve intended effects" (p. 302). He also says that power can refer to the ability to get others to change or to prevent others from changing—to maintain the status quo. Goodrich (1991) gives another definition of power: "the capacity to produce a change" (p. 38). She also provides a different perspective on power by dividing it into power-to and power-over. "Power-to refers to the ability to perform or produce and implies also the freedom and resources to do so. Power-over refers to domination and control" (p. 8). Both of these aspects of power have traditionally belonged to men. It is threatening to this traditional division of control when women begin to assert their power-to define themselves and their place, say no in business or personal relationships, or act on behalf of themselves. When women act on these powers, the ability of men to have power-over women, the only useful purpose of patriarchy, becomes shaky at best (Goodrich, 1991).

Within the family, the issue of power can become quite problematic. Many people regard power as an either/or matter. If the wife has it, the husband doesn't. Because of their lower level of participation in the instrumental sphere of commerce, wives often have less power in their marriages.

Okin (1989) describes the source of women's lack of power as being within the economic realm. Work for wages is valued, but women are valued for their work within the home—unpaid work. Women are assumed to be responsible for matters within the home. There is a concomitant assumption that the man will be engaged in paid employment. He needs to preserve his strength and energy for his role as provider. She is accountable for maintaining the household so that he has a place to recuperate from his work.

Goldner (1985) regards power as a key to understanding family interactions. She mentions that family systems therapy was developed by Minuchin and Haley based on the idea that within the home, people of the same generational level have interchangeable roles and therefore equal power. In reality, the power of women is considerably less than that of men. Women earn less than men, and this financial deficit carries over to their ability to control their own lives.

Given that work outside the home is valued and rewarded and that work within the home is devalued, women must move out of their appointed sphere of influence to gain the economic and political power to effect change in their lives. Goldner (1988) insists that power based on gender is not a mediating variable in families, but constructs family life.

The power distribution in African-American families appears to be similar to that which has been in place for several decades. In some lower-class African-American families, although women have some power based on their economic contribution to the family, the men may use beatings and knifings to gain control during quarrels. In middle-class families, the higher income of the man provides him with a power base. He can threaten to withdraw from the family, thus leaving them economically strapped, just as white men can (Staples, 1973). On the other hand, some African-American women have not been economically dependent on their husbands and may be less subservient than some white women. These women, however, have an added task of protecting their children from the hostile environment in which they live (Staples, 1973).

One extremely frightening and deleterious outcome of unquestioned patriarchal power is violence, especially within families. In this presumed haven in a heartless world (Lasch, 1977), men may strike out when they feel that their last vestiges of power are being threatened. Concurring with the ideas about gender roles and communications discussed earlier, Goldner, Penn, Sheinberg, and Walker (1990) posit that violence is a result of the man's desperate attempt to assert his difference from the feminine. He can be masculine only to the extent that he is not-feminine. As his wife gains power in the relationship by increasing her economic and social resources, he sees his position deteriorating. If a lack of verbal ability precludes his talking himself back into power, his socialization has left him with only one guaranteed means of asserting himself— he hits her.

An ultimate goal of power, properly utilized within families, is that of mutual empowerment, "participating in the development of another in a way that increases the other's strengths" (Miller, 1991, p. 45). The expansion of women's power need not mean the reduction of men's. The use of power to empower means that a family has an unlimited amount of this essential resource for all.

Summary.   For family therapists, the appropriate use of power is a critical issue. A therapist's training may not have provided information on power but only on hierarchy based on generational level. The therapist, therefore, must engage in self-retraining to ensure the inclusion of both power and generational levels when assessing and working with families. Family life educators can provide information on appropriate expressions of power and assist families in avoiding violence as they learn suitable mechanisms for evaluating the escalation of disagreements and for defusing these situations. Family researchers can well follow the lead of Gelles (1976) in investigating violence as an outcome of power differential. They can also assist by evaluating various programs developed by therapists and educators for establishing appropriate choices for expressing power within families.

Conclusion

An examination of the work of family scientists over the last four decades demonstrates that issues currently considered new and important have recurred in each decade, utilizing new terminology and sometimes adding current concepts. There have been enough alterations in families and in society, however, to virtually eliminate the viability of models that had been considered inviolate. Most women can no longer expect to replicate the behaviors of June Cleaver by staying at home, wearing pearls, and soothing their spouse's and childrens' problems. Most wives are employed. In the workplace as well as in other settings, they learn new methods of communication and interaction and new perspectives on power and its use. Therefore, these women may no longer be willing even to attempt to manage all household tasks and all child-rearing projects, plus the maintenance of internal and extended family relationships. The demand for new ways of assigning duties requires new ideas about power, gender roles, and communications.

It is probably not possible for most families to function in the idealized manner popularized by the 1950s television shows and the ideas of many family therapists. As family professionals, it is our obligation to understand the history of families and the current economic and social situation, and to constantly to update our knowledge and skills.

The system of each family is in some ways constructed and constrained by the historical, economic, and social conditions in which it exists. Within the family, each member's gender socialization, gender-role expectations, economic contributions, and attributions of power all contribute to decisions about roles as well as to their level of comfort in these roles and the perception of the family's success in its functioning.

Gendered interactions in families have been studied by family scientists for at least 40 years. Issues such as communications, changes due to women's employment, and sharing of household responsibilities recur in every decade. New information on communication and decision-making may provide tools for enhancing family interactions. Reminding family members that there are several possible approaches to any problem may give them the flexibility to develop new skills and to manage their lives more comfortably.

Chapter Summary

Discussion Questions

1. According to Quinn, the issues of men's and women's roles have changed dramatically over the last 50 years. Identify those changes, and comment on how such changes may have influenced the roles within families over the last half-century.

2. Give three examples of how changes in the cultural context have affected families. Specifically, how have changes in family size, women working outside the home, and our perception of women's roles influenced family functioning?

3. Quinn suggests that men and women think and communicate differently. Do you agree with this proposal? What evidence would either support or challenge this idea?

4. How do issues of the family life cycle interact with issues of gender? For example, do you think that women's roles change more or less than men's over time? Can you think of other issues, over the life cycle, that may have gender differences?

Additional Resources

Goldner, V. (1985). Feminism and family therapy. *Family Process, 24,* 31–47.

Gilligan, C. (1982). *In a different voice*. Cambridge, MA: Harvard University Press.

Ruddick, S. (1989). *Maternal thinking: Toward a politics of peace*. New York: Ballantine.

References

Belenky, M. F., Clinchy, B. M., Goldberger, N. R., & Tarule, J. M. (1986). *Women's ways of knowing*. New York: Basic Books.

Brashear, D. B., & Willis, K. (1976). Claiming our own: A model for women's growth. *Journal of Marriage and Family Counseling, 2,* 251–258.

Burke, R. J., & Weir, T. (1976). Relationship of wives' employment status to husband, wife and pair satisfaction and performance. *Journal of Marriage and the Family, 38,* 279–287.

Chodorow, N. (1978). *The reproduction of mothering*. Berkeley: University of California Press.

Cooper A., & Kosterlitz, J. (1986). Baby bust: Coming of age. *American Demographics, 8,* 546–557.

Dyer, W. G., & Urban, D. (1958). The institutionalization of equalitarian family norms. *Marriage and Family Living, 20,* 53–58.

Ericksen, J. A., Yancey, W. L., & Ericksen, E. P. (1979). The division of family roles. *Journal of Marriage and the Family, 41,* 301–313.

Feldman, L. B. (1976). Goals of family therapy. *Journal of Marriage and Family Counseling, 2,* 103–113.

Gelles, R. J. (1976). Abused wives: Why do they stay? *Journal of Marriage and the Family, 38,* 659–668.

Gilligan, C. (1982). In a different voice. Cambridge, MA: Harvard University Press.

Glick, P. C. (1977). Updating the life cycle of the family. *Journal of Marriage and the Family, 39,* 5–13.

Goldner, V. (1985). Feminism and family therapy. *Family Process, 24,* 31–47.

Goldner, V. (1988). Generation and gender: Normative and covert hierarchies. *Family Process, 27,* 17–31.

Goldner, V., Penn, P., Sheinberg, M., & Walker, G. (1990). Love and violence: Gender paradoxes in volatile attachments. *Family Process, 29,* 343–364.

Goodrich, T. J. (1991). *Women and power: Perspectives for family therapy*. New York: Norton.

Griswold del Castillo, R. (1984). *I a familia*. Notre Dame, IN: University of Notre Dame Press.

Hacker, H. M. (1957). The new burdens of masculinity. *Marriage and Family Living, 19,* 227–233.

Hallenbeck, P. N. (1966). An analysis of power dynamics in marriage. *Journal of Marriage and the Family, 28,* 200-203.

Hochschild, A. R. (1989). *The second shift*. New York: Viking.

Hudis, P. M. (1976). Commitment to work and to family: Marital-status differences in women's earnings. *Journal of Marriage and the Family, 38,* 267–278.

Humphrey, F. G. (1975). Changing roles for women: Implications for marriage counselors. *Journal of Marriage and Family Counseling, 1,* 219–227.

Lasch, C. (1977). *Haven in a heartless world*. New York: Basic Books.

Leopold, A. K. (1958). The family woman's expanding role. *Marriage and Family Living, 20,* 278–282.

Miller, J. B. (1991). Women and power: Reflections ten years later. In T. J. Goodrich (Ed.), *Women and power: Perspectives for family therapy.* (pp.36–47). New York: Norton.

Mogey, J. M. (1957). A century of declining paternal authority. *Marriage and Family Living, 19,* 234–282.

Moore, J. (1976). *Mexican Americans*. Englewood Cliffs, NJ: Prentice-Hall.

Moynihan, D. P. (1967). The Negro family: The case for national action. In L. Rainwater & W. L. Yancey (Eds.), *The Moynihan Report and the politics of controversy* (pp. 39–124). Cambridge, MA: MIT Press.

National Center for Health Statistics. (1987). *Annual summary of births, marriages, divorces, and deaths*. Hyattsville, MD: U. S. Public Health Service Statistics.

Nye, I. V. (1967). Values, family, and a changing society. *Journal of Marriage and the Family, 29,* 241–248.

Okin, S. M. (1989). *Justice, gender and the family*. New York: Basic Books.

Parsons, T. (1951). *The social system*. Glencoe, IL: Free Press.

Rainwater, L. (1970). *Behind ghetto walls*. Chicago: Aldine.

Rice, D. G., & Rice, J. K. (1977). Non-sexist "marital" therapy. *Journal of Marriage and Family Counseling, 3,* 3–9.

Riche, M. F. (1987). Mysterious young adults. *American Demographics, 9,* 38–43.

Rossi, A. (1985). *Gender and the life course*. New York: Aldine.

Ruddick, S. (1989). *Maternal thinking: Toward a politics of peace*. New York: Ballantine.

Russell, C., & Exter, T. G. (1986). American at mid-decade. *American Demographics, 9,* 23–29.

Scanzoni, J. (1979). Social processes and power in families. In W. Burr, R. Hill, F. I. Nye, & I. Reiss (Eds.), *Contemporary theories about the family* (pp. 295–316). New York: Free Press.

Smith, D. E. (1987) Women's inequality and the family. In N. Gerstel & H. E. Gross (Eds.), *Families and work* (pp. 23–54). Philadelphia: Temple University Press.

Staples, R. (1973). *The black woman in America*. Chicago: Nelson-Hall.

Tannen, D. (1990). *You just don't understand*. New York: Morrow.

Wilson, W. J. (1987). *The truly disadvantaged*. Chicago: University of Chicago Press.

Whyte, W. F. Jr. (1943). *Street corner society*. Chicago: University of Chicago Press.

Zinn, M. B. (1989). Family, race and poverty in the eighties. *Signs, 14*(4), 856–874.

Multicultural Family Science

Karen Schmid
St. Cloud State University

Ethnic heritage is an important influence on families. Ethnic background affects a family's access to resources and opportunities, and helps us understand familial exchanges, frequency of interaction, rules, rituals, communication patterns, emotional expression, and so on. In family-science classes I have students discuss their ethnic backgrounds; here are some examples of their experiences, in their own words:

Rob: When my father was ill, my mother was a typical Scandinavian who did not ever show emotions or discuss feelings, so that his serious illness and death were a total surprise to me.

Jennifer: My father is half Mexican, which makes me a quarter Mexican. I have been brought up with many Mexican traditions. We share the family tradition of making tortillas and tamales on Christmas Eve. My grandma and my mother prepare the tamale meat and masa, then everyone helps wrap the tamales in corn husks for steaming. It has been a tradition for as long as I can remember. My grandma is teaching me how to make them for my family one day. I plan on carrying on my family traditions like my grandma taught me. It is important that my children have something to identify themselves with, like their Mexican heritage.

Bridget: I was adopted when I was 10 months old. My family never discussed the fact that I am Korean. I grew up thinking I was blonde-haired and blue-eyed, like everyone else in town. Then I looked in the mirror. I now consider myself a Korean who happens to live in the United States.

Relevance of Ethnicity in Family Science

Awareness of ethnicity is essential in family science, for several reasons. Ethnicity is very closely related to family (Schneider, 1977). It is often conceptualized as being part of one's "blood," one's genetic heritage, related to the deeply felt emotions we have about procreating. Ethnic identity derives primarily from our family of origin and is passed on from generation to generation. It is usually learned through socialization in the family (Alba, 1990; McGoldrick, 1982). Two common methods parents use to teach children about their ethnic background are telling family histories and studying genealogy (Alba, 1990). Ethnicity involves one's basic roots and connections, familial heritage, identity, and lineage consciousness.

Many ethnic practices are interwoven throughout everyday practices such as eating, recreation, and esthetic habits (see Chapter 9). Ethnicity shapes many family rituals (Zeitlin, Kotkin, & Baker, 1982). For example, Americans of British ancestry often take a "no muss, no fuss," practical approach to death and funerals, while other ethnic groups, such as Irish and African Americans, more often take a "going out in style," "gathering of the clan" approach to death (McGoldrick, Pearce, & Giordano, 1992).

Definitions of Ethnicity

In this chapter ethnicity is defined broadly as "a shared sense of peoplehood that includes a body of shared cultural meanings" (Rosenthal, 1986, p. 20).

While this definition seems a bit stuffy and dry, the elements its discusses are very important. The defining factors alluded to in this definition are distinctiveness, originality of culture, and links with the culture of ancestors (Roosens, 1989). For some, ethnic identification is voluntary, but for others it does not stem from skin color or other physical characteristics. The concept of ethnicity can be analyzed further and conceptualized in a variety of ways. In simple terms, ethnicity affects social allocation—access to education, jobs, and housing. Ethnicity can represent a form of social solidarity, with ethnic groups advocating for rights, providing services through ethnic organizations, and so on (Alba, 1990). Ethnicity additionally can be conceptualized as a major factor in shaping identity, both self-concept and deep psychological structures such as values, attitudes, needs, modes of expression, and sense of security (Alba, 1990; Phinney, 1990). The concept of ethnicity also comprises the culture associated with ethnic groups; culture is defined as "a social group's design for surviving in and adapting to its environment" (Bullivant, 1989, p. 27).

Each family interprets this culture in a unique way, depending upon its family history and needs. It is important not to stereotype and expect that just because a family is from a certain ethnic group, it will reflect one or all aspects of the culture of this group.

Life Cycle

The importance of ethnicity often varies depending upon the stage in the family life cycle. For single young adults, ethnicity may not seem important. When a mixed marriage is contemplated or a child is born, however, ethnic background typically becomes central. Ethnic heritage and customs are often very important in later life (Luborsky & Rubinstein, 1990). For example, ethnic heritage and practices were essential in providing a sense of meaning for a community of elderly East European Jews in Los Angeles (Myerhoff, 1978). Their rituals and shared world views enabled them to survive despite the losses of their families, communities, and traditional way of life in the Holocaust; the trauma of immigration to the U. S.; and estrangement from Americanized children.

"Minority" Groups

Some ethnic groups also are commonly labeled *minority groups*, due to their unequal access to power and stigmatization because of assumed inferior characteristics (Mindel, Habenstein, & Wright, 1988). "Minority," in this sense, does not refer to numbers but to power and social allocation of desired resources.[1] "Race"[2] or ethnicity, age, gender, religion, and other characteristics may lead to minority status. However, because of the need for family science to more fully incorporate the perspectives of ethnic minority groups, this chapter emphasizes those most commonly labeled as "minority" in the United States: American Indians, Asians, African Americans, and Latinos.[3] These broad groupings can be misleading. Each group is very diverse. For example, Latinos can be of any race or social class, from many different countries, and of rural or urban background (Abbey, Brindis, & Casas, 1990).

By the middle of the next century, minorities will become the majority in the United States (O'Hare, 1992). Many American children already live in a world in which minorities are often the majority: in the nation's 15 largest school systems, minority enrollment ranges from 70% to 96% of the total (Kellogg, 1988). The "emergent majority" has been proposed as a more accurate term (Abbey et al., 1990; Staples, 1988). Ethnic diversity as an issue will be important simply due to population trends.

For some, the term *minority* has negative connotations (McAdoo, 1993; Sue, 1991). However, the term may be used deliberately to underscore exploitation and disadvantaged status. Some use "ethnic minorities" to distinguish groups that have received unequal treatment (Dilworth-Anderson, Burton, & Turner, 1993; Preli & Bernard, 1993). Other frequently used terms are "people of color" and "nondominant ethnic groups," which emphasizes the political nature of these classifi-

[1] Of course, globally, Europeans and their descendants are very much in the minority.

[2] "Race" is placed in quotation marks to make the point that race is a social construct, with little or no scientific basis.

[3] The term *Hispanic* is used in this chapter to correspond with the term used by the U.S. census. A variety of other terms have been proposed; for discussion, see Marin and Marin (1991).

cations.[4] When feasible, it is preferable to use a more specific term, such as "Puerto Rican" or "Oglala Lakota," reflecting the great diversity within these groups.

European Americans

Ethnicity also is important for European Americans—that is, those whose ancestors came primarily from Europe or who identify themselves as primarily of European heritage. European Americans vary enormously, ranging from Italian-Americans to East European Jews to WASPs (White Anglo-Saxon Protestants). It is misleading to place all European Americans together in a "white lump" (Webb-Watson, 1989). For purposes of broad comparison, however, European-Americans often are joined into one category. For information on a variety of European-American families, good starting places are McGoldrick, Pearce, and Giordano (1982) and Mindel and his colleagues (1988). For information about the wide range of ethnic groups that make up the United States, see the *Harvard Encyclopedia of American Ethnic Groups* (Thernstrom, 1980).

Bicultural or Multicultural Families

"Bicultural" can refer either to participating in both nondominant and dominant ethnic cultures or to being of mixed heritage as an individual or family. Increasing numbers of families are bicultural or multicultural in the second sense, through marriage, childbearing, or adoption. It is estimated that there are 1 million biracial children and adolescents in the United States (Gibbs & Hines, 1992). In some groups, mixed-race children are especially common; for example, in more than half of the births to a American Indian parent in 1989, the other parent was of a different race (O'Hare, 1992).

[4]Ethnic and "racial" classifications are human constructs, subject to change. For example, in 1890, the official U.S. census classifications were White, Black, Mulatto, Quadroon, Octoroon, Chinese, Japanese, and Indian (O'Hare, 1992, p. 7). In 1980 the official U.S. census classifications were White, Black, Hispanic, Japanese, Chinese, Filipino, Korean, Vietnamese, American Indian, Asian Indian, Hawaiian, Guamanian, Samoan, Eskimo, Aleut, and Other. In England in 1981, the official categories were White, West Indian, African, Arab, Turkish, Chinese, Indian, Pakistani, Bangladeshi, Sri Lankan, and Other (Spickard, 1992, p. 18). Many do not fit these classifications. If one does not fit, what does that signify? What about people of mixed heritage?

Bicultural or multicultural families have special issues. Concerns of parents in black/white families include racial/ethnic labels, openness of the neighborhood, and preparation of children for anticipated discrimination (Kerwin, Ponterotto, Jackson, & Harris, 1993). In order to facilitate healthy biracial/bicultural identity development, parents can take several steps: acknowledge that their children's racial/ethnic heritage is different from their own and recognize that as positive, encourage their children to discuss their racial heritage, provide opportunities for their children to develop relationships with those from varied backgrounds through multicultural schools and neighborhoods, facilitate the development of role models for their children through participation in activities held by support groups for biracial/multicultural families, and form a family identity as an interracial/multicultural unit (McRoy & Freeman, 1986).

For some children and adolescents, mixed heritage can be problematic, leading to conflicts about racial/ethnic identity, social marginality, autonomy, sexuality, and educational and occupational aspirations (Gibbs, 1989). For many, however, a bicultural or multicultural heritage is advantageous. In one study conducted in New York state, children and adolescents of black/white parentage did not perceive themselves as marginal but saw themselves as part of two groups (Kerwin et al., 1993). Children of cross-group marriages in Hawaii showed no signs of psychological disturbances, were not alienated, and performed better on tests of cognitive ability than children of within-group marriages (Johnson, 1992). Adults of black/Japanese heritage were positive about the experience. They made statements such as "I've got the best of both worlds," "It makes me more sensitive and understanding to other minorities," and "I feel like a richer, more diverse person" (Hall, 1992, p. 264).

Ethnic Identity

Not everyone has a strong sense of ethnic identity. Some, especially those of European heritage, may identify as "just American." However, ethnicity influenced their ancestors and probably still influences religious practices, rituals, expressions of affection, methods of conflict resolution, and so on. Lack of strong ethnic identity is possible only for some; many, such as immigrants, those for whom English is not the native language, and those labeled "minority," do not have the privilege of glossing over ethnicity. Lack of understanding of the importance of ethnicity and race has been termed "cultural insensitivity" (Preli & Bernard, 1993) or "white privilege" (McIntosh, 1988).[5]

Multiculturally Sensitive Practice

The focus of this chapter is multiculturally sensitive theory and practice in family science.[6] Multiculturalism is an approach in which we seek "a shared community that maintains the integrity of the different groups composing it" (Levine, 1991). Metaphors for this are the stew pot, tossed salad, mosaic, or rainbow, in which the different components remain unique and all contribute to and improve the whole.

Some fear that a multicultural approach may lead to lack of unity and dissension (see Schlesinger, 1992; Willie, 1992). Others believe that diversity can lead to cultural synergy, in which the differences in people lead to mutual growth and more creative problem solving (Hayes-Bautista, 1992; Kessler-Harris, 1992; Levine, 1991; Sleeter & Grant, 1988). In other words, the whole is greater than the sum of the parts.

Ethnicity often arouses passions, which may become destructive, as has been seen in Bosnia, South Africa, and many other countries. While celebrating diversity and using the dynamism it brings, the challenge is simultaneously to create and maintain community and national unity (Takaki, 1993; Taylor, 1992; Wong, 1991).

Obviously no one can be an expert on every ethnic group. A reasonable approach would be to (1) examine one's own ethnic background (see Table 4.1), (2) seek knowledge and appreciation of the more common eth-

nic groups in the area in which one lives and with whom one works, and (3) be open-minded and strive to understand families from within their culture and frame of reference. Resources for further reading and learning about multicultural practices are listed at the end of this chapter.

Value Frameworks

Historically, a variety of value frameworks has been used to think about ethnicity and to conceptualize nondominant ethnic families (Dilworth-Anderson, Johnson, & Burton, 1993). An early framework was that of Anglo-Saxon genetic supremacy, which assumed that non–Anglo-Saxons were genetically inferior. "Inferior" ethnic groups were to be eliminated (American Indians), enslaved, removed (blacks sent back to Africa), minimized (immigration quotas), or kept in their place (segregation, internment camps, limited employment opportunities for Irish, Jews, and others) (Marden, Meyer, & Engel, 1992).

Another early value framework was that of cultural pathology, in which it was assumed that non–Anglo-Saxons had inferior cultures and had to assimilate, or adopt the culture of the dominant culture. The metaphor was the melting pot, as all were to be homogenized into the dominant culture. Traditional cultural identities, customs, and language were to be discarded. Practices that reflected this way of thinking were Indian boarding schools, which did not allow any display of American Indian culture (Noley, 1990), and punishment of children for speaking Spanish or other non-English languages in school.

More recently, much research and many programs have been based on the idea of sociocultural pathology of nondominant ethnic groups, with the assumption that the lower economic well-being of ethnic minority groups is due to deviant, dysfunctional cultures. Perhaps the most famous research from this perspective is the Moynihan Report (Moynihan, 1965). Moynihan asserts that "matriarchal" families are the root problem for African Americans; he blames mothers and deviant families, rather than "economic, political, and educational deprivation," for African Americans' comparatively poor economic situation (Billingsley, 1992, p. 79).

[5]McIntosh (1988) provides numerous examples of "white privilege"—for example, "I can remain oblivious of the language and customs of persons of color who constitute the world's majority without feeling in my culture any penalty for such oblivion" and "I do not have to educate my children to be aware of systematic racism for their own daily physical protection."

[6]The related literatures in anthropology, comparative sociology, history of immigration and ethnic groups, and cross-cultural psychology and human development have been largely omitted due to space limitations.

TABLE 4.1   Understanding One's Ethnic Heritage

1. What is my cultural heritage? What was the culture of my parents and my grandparents? With what cultural group(s) do I identify?
2. What is the cultural relevance of my name?
3. What ethnic customs do my family and I practice? What values are represented in these customs?
4. What ethnic or cultural characteristics were disapproved of or purposefully suppressed or concealed in my family?
5. When have I felt my ethnic, racial, or national identity most strongly? What do these situations have in common?
6. What values, beliefs, opinions, and attitudes do I hold that are consistent with the dominant culture? What are inconsistent? How did I learn these?
7. What unique abilities, aspirations, expectations, and limitations do I have that might influence my relations with culturally diverse individuals?

Sources: Garbarino and Kostelny (1992, p. 199); Locke, (1992, pp. 2, 14); Preli and Bernard (1993, p. 13).

All of the above approaches are ethnocentric. They are based upon the assumed superiority of one culture.

In recent years the cultural relativity value framework has been applied to ethnic minority families (Dilworth-Anderson, Burton, & Turner, 1993). This framework is consistent with a multicultural approach. It is assumed that a variety of cultures and family systems can be viable. Research and practice using this framework focus on dynamics of families within specific nondominant ethnic groups and on meaning within those groups. However, the cultural-relativity value framework does not mean that "anything goes." Some have tried to use the "it's cultural" justification for behaviors such as oppression of women. However, there are agreed-upon standards. Obviously, individuals from all ethnic groups must obey the law. To illustrate, even if early marriage is a traditional cultural practice in the country of origin, such as among the Hmong (Thao, 1986), U. S. laws must be followed in order to have a legally recognized marriage. In addition, human rights as agreed to by the United Nations provide universal standards. For example, the International Convention on the Rights of the Child states that, among other things, the state is "to protect children from all forms of physical or mental injury or abuse, neglect, and exploitation by parents or others"; the best interests of the child shall prevail in all legal and administrative decisions; and the state is to ensure equal access to secondary and higher education (UN Convention, 1991, pp. 50–51). The 54 articles in this convention, along with other U. N. human-rights conventions, constitute widely agreed-upon principles that would set standards, regardless of cultural traditions.

Ethnicity and Change

We must keep in mind that cultures change and that people use ethnic cultures in various ways to meet the challenges they face (Hareven & Modell, 1980; Roosens, 1989; Rosenthal, 1983). For example, older Southeast Asian refugees use traditional cultural norms of filial piety and respect for the elderly, along with desire for continuity, to promote their own status and well-being. This strategy is used to counteract the values of individualism and freedom that the young learn in the United States (Detzner, 1992; Seabloom, 1991).

This cultural change can lead to or exacerbate conflict between generations within a family. Children typically acculturate, or adapt to a new culture, more quickly than parents and grandparents. Acculturation divergence interacts with generational differences. For instance, in Cuban-American families, adolescents combine the striving for independence that is typical of this generation with the dominant cultural value on individualism, while parents combine the striving to maintain family integrity that is typical of the parental generation with the cultural value on parental control. Bicultural effectiveness training, in which conflict between parents and adolescent is reframed as cultural conflict, is recommended to deal with this problem. Parents learn to understand and accept aspects of the dominant culture, and adolescents learn to understand

and accept aspects of ethnic culture (Szapocznik & Kurtines, 1993).

It was assumed that ethnicity would become increasingly less important and that assimilation was inevitable (Petersen, 1980). The growing emphasis on ethnicity in recent years has several sources, among them the appeal of roots and tradition as antidotes for the anonymity, homogenization, and constant change of modernity, bureaucracy, and mass society; the quest for community; the need for history and symbols in establishing one's identity; social movements, such as the civil rights movement; and the large number of recent immigrants. (Eight million immigrants arrived in the U. S. during the 1980s; the only decade with more immigration was 1900–1910, with 8.8 million immigrants [Gelf & Yee, 1991].)

The Ecology of Ethnicity

Building upon the work of Bronfenbrenner (1979), the individual can be conceptualized as embedded within the family microsystem, which is embedded within the macrosystem, in a series of concentric circles. The macrosystem consists of both the majority, or dominant, culture and ethnic subcultures, in an increasingly pluralistic mix. The relationships between various microsystems, such as the family, school, and social-service agencies, compose the mesosystem. Dissonance between the subcultures of the family and other microsystems can be problematic. Greater multicultural understanding is essential in decreasing this dissonance.

Benefits of Multiculturalism

Multiculturalism broadens and deepens our understanding of families. By examining families in cultures other than our own, we realize the range of survival strategies and creative approaches that families have used and therefore can better think about our own families, assumptions, and values. For example, European-American postdivorce families may be able learn a great deal from African-American families, who have long experience with complex extended families. African-American families traditionally have been centered on children and inclusive of all those who are involved in care for a child, regardless of household membership, and more flexible and tolerant of ambiguity than families in the dominant culture (Crosbie-Burnett & Lewis, 1993).

Attention to cultural diversity requires us to focus more on social inequality and economic issues affecting families (Smith & Ingoldsby, 1992). Ethnicity is a major factor in social allocation of education, jobs, housing, and other valued resources. Analysis of social allocation of desired resources may lead family scientists to focus on economic and other policies that affect family well-being and to connect private troubles to public issues (Mills, 1959).

As our population becomes more diverse, family-science professionals must be able to work with families from many ethnic groups. We all need some basic information on and sensitivity to ethnic differences, and we need ideas of where to go for further information and understanding of groups with whom we are interacting. In addition, greater attention to cultural diversity is necessary if we are to encourage the participation of all ethnic groups in studying and working professionally in family science (Hogan & Womack, 1990).

Learning about ethnic identity also encourages pride, a sense of belonging, and deeper connection between generations. Listen to the words of Clarence W. Blount, a Maryland state senator, after meeting distant relatives at a gathering at the plantation where his slave ancestors had lived: "I feel proud! I feel redeemed! I understand me and mine a little better. . . . For the first time in my life, I love my parents and grandparents and those before them in a way I never knew them, nor loved them before" (Redford, 1988, p. 263).

Factors Distinguishing Nondominant Ethnic Families

Ho (1987) proposes six major factors that particularly distinguish nondominant ethnic families from European-American families: (1) the reality of racism and poverty, (2) the impact of the conflict between value systems, (3) biculturalism, (4) the status of particular nondominant groups, (5) language, and (6) social class. These factors can help us organize our understanding of ethnic nondominant families.

Racism and Poverty

The reality is that racism persists and that median income is lower for ethnic nondominant families than for nonminorities. For example, 1991 U. S. median family income was $37,783 for whites, $23,895 for Latinos, and $21,548 for African Americans (U. S. Bureau of the Census, 1991). An example of racism is the preference of many employers to hire immigrant men or women from any background rather than African-American men (Raymond, 1991). (This example also illustrates the complexity of minority status, as some minorities are seen as preferable or higher status than others, and gender interacts with nondominant ethnic status.) Racism and poverty intermingle with cultural factors to affect family adaptations. For example, single-parent families have become much more prevalent among African Americans in the last 30 years, as employment opportunities for African-American men have declined (Billingsley, 1988; Levitan, Belous, & Gallo, 1988).

Conflict between value systems.   The value systems of European Americans and of nondominant ethnic groups may conflict (Spiegel, 1982). Typical European-American and American Indian values can be contrasted (see Table 4.2) (MacDermid, 1993).

As another example, a common value for American Indians is autonomy, including autonomy for children. Children are allowed choices and are expected to learn from the consequences. Adults are expected not to interfere, as children are not the property of parents but equal individuals. Punishment is not common, nor is praise for doing what is required or expected (Burgess, 1980; Carson, Dail, Greeley, & Kenote, 1992; LaFramboise & Low,

TABLE 4.2   Typical European-American and American Indian Value Statements

European Americans	American Indians
Look to the future.	Look to tradition.
Learn the language of where you live.	Cherish your language.
Religion is for the individual.	Religion is the universe.
I'll raise my children; you do the same.	Children are a gift of God to be shared with others.

1989). This philosophy of child rearing may be seen as permissive or negligent by non–American Indians, who may value a more directive or controlling approach.

Biculturalism.   Ethnic minority individuals must learn to go back and forth between the ethnic culture and the dominant culture. This can be enriching, but it also is complicated and can lead to family conflict. Detzner (1992) and Seabloom (1991) found conflict related to filial piety (respect, deference, and obedience to those who are older) and appropriate gender roles to be the norm in Southeast Asian refugee families. An elderly Laotian said:

> In my family, the children must be respectful to the elders and polite to the guests. They must bow their heads, greet the elders, and they must serve tea to the guests in the proper way. The children must speak Laotian at home. When they are at home, they are Laotian, and when they leave home, they are American. (Detzner, 1992, p. 100)

Status of Particular Nondominant Ethnic Groups

Historical and contemporary circumstances affect each nondominant ethnic group and subgroup differently. Some groups were forced to become a part of the U. S. through slavery or conquest. Some nondominant ethnic families have extensive contact with relatives and the culture of their homeland, and others do not. Determination of membership varies. There are legal rules for determination of official American Indian status. The same person may be considered white in Puerto Rico and black in the mainland U. S.

Language.   Language differences between nondominant ethnic families and the dominant culture or between family members obviously impede communication, one of the major components of intimate relationships (see Chapter 9). Rodriguez (1981) describes how his family changed after family members started speaking English in the family:

> There was a new quiet at home. The family's quiet was partly due to the fact that, as we children learned more and more English, we shared fewer and fewer words with our parents. Sentences needed to be spoken slowly when a child addressed his mother or father. [Often the parent wouldn't

understand.] The child would need to repeat himself. [Still the parent misunderstood.] The young voice, frustrated, would end up saying, "Never mind"—the subject was closed. (p. 23)

As ethnic minority children become fluent in English and comfortable with the public culture, they move away from the isolation and intimacy of their families of origin and mother tongue (Rodriguez, 1981).

Social class.   Class issues can be complicated. For example, a middle-class minority individual may be accused of "acting white" while at the same time not feeling fully accepted by European Americans. Often the family of origin is of lower socioeconomic status, and there may be difficulties of communication, values, and gender-role expectations related to social class. Families may experience intergenerational conflicts about "spoiling" children and children being overindulged materially rather than learning survival skills (Hines, Garcia-Preto, McGoldrick, Almeida, & Weltman, 1992). Upward mobility can be problematic, as described by this student (Wilson, 1991):

> I grew up in a low-income, single-parent family on the far south-side of Chicago. . . . Plain and simple, our goal was to survive. Survival to us was to get a job and hopefully wake up the next morning. I didn't think about college. . . . But, somehow, somewhere an idea was instilled in me. "To be 'somebody,' I must go to college; if I didn't go, I would be a nobody." Because I believed this, I became more distant from my family and friends. I felt ashamed of my family. (p. 4)

If others in the family are struggling for survival, those who are upwardly mobile may feel ambivalent or guilty (Hines et al., 1992).

Cultural Diversity in Family-Science Practice

Five Approaches to Multiculturalism

There are many ways to incorporate more on ethnicity and diversity into practice in family science. It is helpful to reflect and make deliberate choices about what we implement. Below are five approaches to multiculturalism adapted from Sleeter and Grant (1988).

Focusing on the exceptional and culturally different.   Family scientists help families and individuals adjust to the existing social structure and culture by building upon needs and strengths. Our task is to help families cope with the "real world" and to garner more resources for themselves. For example, a parent educator might work with Southeast Asian immigrant families on understanding American concepts of child development and appropriate discipline, while building upon their own approaches. The parent educator also would act as a resource, with information on healthcare providers, literacy and job-skills programs, nutrition programs, and the like.

Human relations.   The focus of the second approach is on promoting tolerance and positive feelings toward varied groups, attempting to reduce stereotyping. In this approach family scientists concentrate on increasing students' or clients' self-esteem and knowledge about the contributions of their own ethnic group. An example might be a counselor working in a shelter for battered women and their children. The counselor would set ground rules and an environment that would be positive for all ethnic groups. Speakers, films, and reading materials would feature positive role models, particularly of the ethnic groups of those served.

Single-group emphasis.   The third approach focuses on one group—its culture and victimization and current social issues—from the group's perspective. Family scientists and those served may work toward social action that would benefit that group. For example, the family scientist may work as a therapist on an American Indian reservation. The therapist would need to understand the political sovereignty of tribal nations[7] and how it affects families and the therapist's work. The specific circumstances of the tribe or pueblo would be stressed, such as the lasting legacy of Indian boarding schools on parenting, discipline, intergenerational relations, and so on. The family scientist would emphasize the impact of past practices upon the group's current situation and particular approaches and programs that

[7]Tribes are "domestic dependent nations" and "have retained, with some limitations, the authority to structure their own governments, to administer justice, to regulate domestic relations," and so on (O'Brien, 1991, p. 19).

are needed to overcome the legacy of discrimination, such as intergenerational programs in the schools and culturally appropriate child-welfare practices.

Multiculturalism.   The fourth approach promotes cultural pluralism, respect for differences, and social equality. The perspectives and contributions of different groups are valued, and the perspectives of a variety of ethnic and cultural groups are integral in university family-science curricula and research. Race, ethnicity, and oppression are not be afterthoughts, and teaching and research on diversity in families are rewarded (Smith & Ingoldsby, 1992). Cultural pluralism is seen as adding to the richness of human experience.

Social reconstructionism.   The fifth approach is similar to multiculturalism, but it also prepares citizens to work actively toward social equality. The goal is for those with whom we work to (1) develop decision-making and political skills, (2) learn how to analyze their own life experiences to learn about how society works, (3) develop social-action skills, and (4) learn to form coalitions of people of color, women, those with moderate and low incomes, and individuals with disabilities. For example, a family scientist working for a family service agency would work with various support groups to analyze how their "private troubles" are related to "public issues" (Mills, 1959). From this, the groups would decide to work together to support state and federal legislation guaranteeing health care to all who live in the United States, which includes support for family caregivers. Members of these groups would inform others, gain the attention of the media, and lobby legislators. These support groups would include those for single parents, adoptive families, Alzheimer's families, immigrant families, and families with a member with a chronic illness or disability.

Research on Nondominant Ethnic Families

Research on nondominant ethnic families can be based on any of the approaches given above. For example, should research focus on how families can adjust to the existing social structure and culture, or should it take a critical stance and promote social reconstructionism? What are the pros and cons of researching a single group versus several groups?

Several factors inhibit research on nondominant ethnic families. Some constraints have to do with data collection, such as costs associated with locating subjects from various nondominant ethnic groups, who are scattered throughout the population; language problems; the issue of whether an insider, or someone from the group being studied, is needed to conduct the study; and community resistance. Some issues are more related to data analysis—for example, separating ethnicity from confounding factors such as social class and recency of immigration; dealing with variation within ethnic groups; focusing on the extended-kin network prevalent in most nondominant ethnic groups, which leads to problems of unit of analysis, complexity, and cost; and defining an individual's or family's ethnicity. Does the researcher use the participants' self-identification, the origin of their ancestors, or his or her impressions? How are bicultural and multicultural individuals and families classified?

Lack of theory on family and ethnicity discourages research (Burton, Dilworth-Anderson, & Bengston, 1991; Dilworth-Anderson, Johnson, & Burton, 1993). Researchers may be uncertain whether their work will be published, for fear that editors may subscribe either to the "theoretical myth of sameness"—the assumption that a theory applies universally to all families, regardless of ethnic or other variability (Ben David & Erickson, 1990, p. 212)—or to "Eurocentrism," or focusing on European-American families and comparing nondominant ethnic families to the European-American norm (Boynton, 1987; Wilkinson, 1987). Many researchers may fear to take on a "touchy" subject, and be uncertain of how their work will be received, particularly if they are not of the group(s) being studied.

In order to increase the cultural relevance of research, Dilworth-Anderson, Burton, and Turner (1993) have suggested the use of insights from clinical practice and the humanities, and grounded theory. In the grounded-theory approach, concepts emerge inductively from the data and therefore are more likely to reflect concerns or meaning structures that are "emic," or from inside the culture being studied, rather than "etic," or imposed upon the culture from another cultural tradition.

Research on nondominant ethnic families may be complicated, but the benefits outweigh the costs. The following works provide strategies to deal with the above issues: Demos (1990), Dilworth-Anderson, Johnson, and Burton (1993), Dilworth-Anderson and McAdoo (1988), Jackson (1989), Marin and Marin (1991), Markides, Liang, and Jackson (1990), Root (1992a), Sue (1991), and Vega (1990).

Impact of Multiculturalism on Family Science

If we take multiculturalism seriously and acknowledge the cultural context of all family processes, we must rethink basic concepts in family science. Below are examples of a reexamination of several concepts common in family science: family stress, adaptation, family systems, and the definition of family.

Family Stress

Ethnicity affects the ways in which families perceive, define, and address stressful events (Boss, 1988; McAdoo, 1982a; McAdoo, 1982b; Peters & Massey, 1983). For example, Puerto Ricans tend to perceive and define stressful events as due to external factors and expressed through physical complaints. For assistance, they typically turn to family members, who recommend seeing a doctor or perhaps a spiritist (Garcia-Preto, 1982). Managing stress is complicated by the fewer material resources typically available to those from ethnic minority groups.

In addition to stressor events that may affect any family, African-American (and other nondominant ethnic) families experience additional stress factors including the mundane extreme environmental stress of ongoing oppression and chronic unpredictable acts of racial discrimination (Peters & Massey, 1983). As a result, African-American individuals and families must deal with their reactions to racism, on top of other sources of stress.

Adaptation

Due to limited access to societal resources, many nondominant ethnic families share the adaptive strategies of ancestral world views, family extendedness, and role flexibility (Harrison, Wilson, Pine, Chan, & Buriel, 1990). Salience and details of these strategies vary, of course.

Ancestral world views refer to an emphasis upon collectivism or loyalty to the group. The well-being of the individual is interwoven with collective well-being. Individualism is less common than in the dominant culture; nondominant ethnic cultures typically stress connection, attachment, and a common spiritual/philosophical heritage (Harrison et al., 1990).

Family extendedness and role flexibility have been common survival strategies. For example, familism, or close kinship ties, has often been considered a defining characteristic of Mexican-American families. Chicano familism comprises a triad of systems: the immediate family unit, or *la casa*; the extended family, or *la familia*; and the godparents, or *los compadres*. In times of stress, there is a consistent preference for relying on the extended family for support, rather than relying on other support systems (Baca Zinn & Eitzen, 1990; Rothman, Gant, & Hnat, 1985). Role flexibility has been a coping mechanism of nondominant ethnic families out of historic necessity. Common strategies include older siblings parenting younger siblings, sharing of the breadwinner role among adults, and alternative family arrangements (Harrison et al., 1990).

The very concept of adaptation as conceptualized in family-stress theory has been questioned. According to Dilworth-Anderson, Johnson, and Burton (1993), adaptation "connotes adjustment, conformity, assimilation, compliance, and at some level a passive acceptance of change." However, nondominant ethnic families may have a different goal: that of survival, "to maintain without loss of identity or integrity." Families may develop strategies to "keep from adapting" (Dilworth-Anderson, Johnson, & Burton, 1993, p. 641). For example, American Indian families, communities, and cultures managed to survive despite nearly 100 years of forcible removal of children to boarding schools, where native customs and languages were strictly forbidden. Despite the concerted effort of many in the dominant culture, indigenous cultures survived. As Webb-Watson (1989) says, "Not all people want to be absorbed into the dominant culture. . . . Many . . . want to be respected and have an opportunity to be successful (by their own standards) without having to give up so much of themselves" (p. 477)

Family Systems

Several concepts in family systems will be analyzed briefly: autonomy and connectedness, boundaries, enmeshment, and the family's construction of reality. By examining ethnic variation, we can come to better understanding of these concepts.

Autonomy and connectedness.   Connectedness (see Chapter 2) typically has a high value in nondominant ethnic groups. As pointed out in the section on adaptation, the subcultures of nondominant ethnic groups are often group-oriented and expect high family connectedness. Rather than focusing on individual rights, they typically stress family needs, cultural survival, and collective goals (Taylor, 1992). For example, according to Willie (1985, p. 275), black parents urge their children on to greater achievements than their own because they visualize their family not as an autonomous unit but as a part of a great racial movement for equality and justice. Through the achievements of the individuals in each generation, African Americans believe that the condition of minorities is improved. They believe that each generation builds on the other. In contrast, Willie asserts, middle-class whites often emphasize self-fulfillment and freedom and can learn about family connectedness from African Americans. The degree of autonomy that is considered desirable varies greatly depending upon the ethnic group. Autonomy is highly valued by most American Indians (see the section on conflict between value systems). By comparison, in traditional Japanese-American and Hmong families, dependence and conformity with family are stressed (Locke, 1992; McInnis, 1991).

Boundaries.   Boundaries and boundary ambiguity of nuclear families are less of an issue for many nondominant ethnic families because of the strong sense of extended family and group identity. For native

peoples, for example, the tribe or community may be the major kin organization, with fluid nuclear families (Carson et al., 1992; Curtis, 1992). All those of the appropriate age may be addressed as "grandfather" or "cousin." The establishment of a kin-type relationship may be more important than actual blood relation. Child rearing may be shared by a number of people, with grandparents particularly central. Grandparents are often preferred to parents as primary child rearers because of their superior ability to pass on traditional customs and because of the importance of the elderly (Weibel-Orlando, 1990). Discipline may be provided primarily by relatives, not parents (Burgess, 1980; Gonzales, 1992).

Emmeshment.   Some scholars have pointed out cultural complexities that we should consider when thinking about the family-systems concept of enmeshment (Bernal, 1982; Watson & Protinsky, 1988). For example, what appears to be enmeshment to nonminority individuals may be seen as strong family ties to African Americans or Cuban Americans. These strong family ties are related to "external societal factors," are positive, and are not dysfunctional. This is related to focus on the group rather than the individual.

Enmeshment in an extended family is different from enmeshment in a nuclear family. In the extended family, enmeshment may be the result of intentional commitment to traditions and customs and the sharing of instrumental and emotional support. An enmeshed extended family can be an effective problem-solving mechanism and support system due to its wide range of resources. For example, employment and business opportunities may be passed on through the extended family. Many frequently used tools such as the circumplex model have been used mainly to analyze nuclear families. Most families with strong ethnic backgrounds, however, must be conceptualized as nuclear families functioning inextricably within extended families (Woehrer, 1988).

Olson (Chapter 9) recognizes the impact of cultural and ethnic diversity on family cohesion and adaptability. He points out that some ethnic and religious groups have high expectations for family togetherness and low adaptability. Many of these families might be described as rigid-enmeshed, but as long as all family members go along with these expectations, the family will not necessarily have problems. In fact, what may appear to someone from the dominant ethnic group as an enmeshed family may reflect a "healthy balance of cohesion that best facilitates expression of family strengths" in a family from a nondominant ethnic group (Tiesel & Olson, 1992).

The family's construction of reality.   In family-systems theory, reality is seen as a social construction molded by culture, and families are the final authority in this reality construction (see Chapter 6). Family paradigms vary greatly, and "enabled," or functional, families can take many forms (see Chapter 2). Given different adaptive strategies and cultures, families will have paradigms and realities that vary according to ethnic background. Webb-Watson provides an illustration of one family paradigm (1989, pp. 463–465). Mrs. Washington happens to catch a rerun of *The Brady Bunch* on television. She perceives that the parents are wishy-washy, lacking the proper strictness to bring up children adequately. The children have too much say in the day-to-day operation of the family. She would never allow her household discipline to become so lax. Her children would be more respectful, and they would be more careful in their contacts with the outside world. Mrs. Washington also notices that the children are not really responsible for one another. She wonders how Mrs. Brady can tolerate her children being so immature. They barely seem able to do anything on their own. She concludes that white people have strange ways and that their children are overindulged and self-centered. It is essential for family-science practitioners to try to understand and work with the paradigms, realities, and strengths of families from varied ethnic groups. If not, we are not empowering families; we are committing "cultural imperialism," or imposition of another culture, and we will not be very effective.

Definition of Family

When we focus on cultural diversity, we are forced to reflect upon the definition of "family." The appropriate unit of analysis for many nondominant ethnic families is the multigenerational extended-family network (Dilworth-Anderson, Johnson, & Burton, 1993; Jarrett, 1992; Wilkinson, 1987). In the dominant culture in the United States, for example, adoption is generally conceptualized as a formal, legal process in which a child is permanently transferred from one family to another. In contrast, child keeping, or fosterage, is very common in several nondominant ethnic cultures, especially African-American, American Indian, Latino, and Pacific Island. Among Hawaiian-Americans, biological parents remain in contact with their children even if they are in another's care.[8] The mother who gives up her child is not stigmatized. Children are seen as a benefit, especially to older people, who may adopt even if they are of advanced age, are poor, or are in ill health (Werner, 1991).

Whether family membership is restricted to the living varies. For many Asian Americans, for example, continuity of family relationships after death is very important. Ancestor worship may be practiced, and family record books, which trace family members over many centuries, may be kept. The spirits of the dead may exert a strong presence, and communication with dead ancestors may be common (McGoldrick, Almeida, Hines, Rosen, Garcia-Preto, & Lee, 1991; Shon & Ja, 1982).

Conceptualizing families as multigenerational and extended will help us better understand all families, including European-American families. Many scholars have established the multigenerational, extended nature of most American families (Brubaker, 1990; Freeman, 1992; Hill, Foote, Aldous, Carlson, & MacDonald, 1970; Litwak, 1985; Rossi & Rossi, 1990; Sussman & Burchinal, 1962). The study of ethnic-minority families provides additional support for the need to conceptualize families as multigenerational kin networks, and to emphasize generational connections and familial heritage.

If we ignore ethnicity, we send the message that ethnic identity and heritage, and experiences as a member of an ethnic-minority group, are not important. It may be complicated and sometimes uncomfortable to study nondominant ethnic families; it also can be strengthening and inspiring. Our society is becoming increasingly diverse. Multicultural practice, research, and theory are essential if family science is to be useful in this diverse

---

[8]As open adoptions, in which there is ongoing contact between the birth mother and the adoptive family, become increasingly common, European-American families can learn from ethnic-minority families.

society. Indeed, multiculturalism has been called the "key issue of our epoch" (Kalantzis & Cope, 1992).

In addition to all of the reasons given above, another reason to study the impact of ethnicity on families is because it is interesting! Fictional works on nondominant ethnic families have become popular. Books such as *Roots, Beloved, Love Medicine, The Joy Luck Club, The Woman Warrior*, and *The House on Mango Street* are best-sellers. Learning about the human mosaic can only increase the depth of our understanding and our appreciation of the strength, endurance, and creativity of families.

Chapter Summary

Discussion Questions

1. How does ethnicity affect your family's construction of reality (see Chapter 5)? In what ways has our increasingly multicultural world affected your family?

2. Discuss bicultural or multicultural families using the following family-science concepts: second-order issues, morphogenesis, morphostasis.

3. Imagine the fifth edition of this text published in the year 2014. What content on ethnic-minority families would you imagine included? Why?

Additional Resources

Abbey, N., Brindis, C., & Casas, M. (1990). *Family life education in multicultural classrooms*. Santa Cruz, CA: Network Publications. (ERIC Document Reproduction Service No. ED 324 595).

Arms, K. G., Davidson, J. K., & Moore, N. B. (Eds.) (1992). *Cultural diversity and families*. Dubuque, IA: Brown & Benchmark.

Baca Zinn, M.B., & Eiken, D.S. (1990). *Diversity in families* (2nd ed.). New York: HarperCollins.

Banks, J., & Banks, C.M. (Eds.). (1989). *Multicultural education: Issues and perspectives*. Boston: Allyn & Bacon.

Dilworth-Anderson, P., Johnson, L.B., & Burton, L.M. (1993). Reframing theories for understanding race, ethnicity, and families. In P. Boss, W. Doherty, R. LaRossa, W. Schumm, & S. Steinmetz (Eds.), *Sourcebook of family theories and methods: A contextual approach*. New York: Plenum.

Family Relations. (July 1988). 37 (whole issue).

Ho, M. K. (1987). *Family therapy with ethnic minorities*. Newbury Park, CA: Sage.

Lewis, C. H. (1990). *Developing an inclusive curriculum: A curriculum guide for multicultural education*. (ERIC Document Reproduction Service No. ED 326 089.)

Locke, D. C. (1992). *Increasing multicultural understanding*. Newbury Park, CA: Sage.

McAdoo, H. P. (Ed.). (1993). *Family ethnicity*. Newbury Park, CA: Sage.

McGoldrick, M., Pearce, J. K., & Giordano, J. (Eds.). (1982). *Ethnicity and family therapy*. New York: The Guilford Press.

Mindel, C. H., Habenstein, R. W., & Wright, R. (Eds.). (1988). *Ethnic families in America* (3rd ed.). New York: Elsevier.

Vega, W. A. (1990). Hispanic families in the 1980s: A decade of research. *Journal of Marriage and the Family, 52*, 1015–1024.

References

Abbey, N., Brindis, C., & Casas, M. (1990). *Family life education in multicultural classrooms*. Santa Cruz, CA: Network Publications. (ERIC Document Reproduction Service No. ED 324 595).

Alba, R. D. (1990). *Ethnic identity*. New Haven, CT: Yale University Press.

Baca Zinn, M. B., & Eitzen, D. S. (1990). *Diversity in families* (2nd ed.). New York: HarperCollins.

Ben David, A., & Erickson, C. A. (1990). Ethnicity and the therapist's use of self. *Family Therapy, 17*, 211–216.

Bernal, G. (1982). Cuban families. In M. McGoldrick, J. K. Pearce, & J. Giordano (Eds.), *Ethnicity and family therapy* (pp. 187–207). New York: Guilford Press.

Billingsley, A. (1988). The impact of technology on Afro-American families. *Family Relations, 37*, 420–425.

Billingsley, A. (1992). *Climbing Jacob's ladder*. New York: Simon & Schuster.

Boss, P. (1988). *Family stress management*. Newbury Park, CA: Sage.

Boynton, G. (1987). Cross-cultural family therapy. *American Journal of Family Therapy, 15*, 123–130.

Bronfenbrenner, U. (1979). *The ecology of human development.* Cambridge, MA.: Harvard University Press.

Brubaker, T. (1990). An overview of family relationships in later life. In T. W. Brubaker (Ed.), *Family relationships in later life.* (pp. 13–28). Newbury Park, CA: Sage.

Bullivant, B. M. (1989). Culture: Its nature and meaning for educators. In J. S. Banks & C. A. M. Banks (Eds.), *Multicultural education* (pp. 27–45). Boston: Allyn & Bacon.

Burgess, B. J. (1980). Parenting in the Native-American community. In M. Fantini, & R. Cardenas (Eds.), *Parenting in a multicultural society* (pp. 63–73). New York: Longman.

Burton, L. M., Dilworth-Anderson, P., & Bengston, V. L. (1991). Creating culturally relevant ways of thinking about diversity and aging. *Generations, 15,* 67–72.

Carson, D. K., Dail, P. W., Greeley, S., & Kenote, T. (1992). Stresses and strengths of Native American reservation families in poverty. *Family Perspective, 24,* 383–400.

Crosbie-Burnett, M., & Lewis, E. A. (1993). Use of African-American family structures and functioning to address the challenges of European-American post-divorce families. *Family Relations, 42,* 300–310.

Curtis, T. (1992, November). *Understanding Native American family structure: Alternative genograms.* Paper presented at the meeting of the National Council on Family Relations, Orlando, FL.

Demos, V. (1990). Black family studies in the *Journal of Marriage and the Family* and the issue of distortion: A trend analysis. *Journal of Marriage and the Family, 52,* 603–612.

Detzner, D. F. (1992). Life histories: Conflict in Southeast Asian refugee families. In J. F. Gilgun, K. Daly, & G. Handel (Eds.), *Qualitative methods in family research* (pp. 85–102). Newbury Park, CA: Sage.

Dilworth-Anderson, P., Burton, L. M., & Turner, W. L. (1993). The importance of values in the study of culturally diverse families. *Family Relations, 42,* 238–242.

Dilworth-Anderson, P., Johnson, L. B., & Burton, L. M. (1993). Reframing theories for understanding race, ethnicity, and families. In P. Boss, W. Doherty, R. LaRossa, W. Schumm, & S. Steinmetz (Eds.), *Sourcebook of family theories and methods: A contextual approach* (pp. 627–645). New York: Plenum.

Dilworth-Anderson, P., & McAdoo, H. P. (1988). The study of ethnic minority families: Implications for practitioners and policymakers. *Family Relations, 37,* 265–267.

Freeman, D.S. (1992). *Multigenerational family therapy.* New York: Haworth Press.

Garbarino, J., & Kostelny, K. (1992). Cultural diversity and identity formation. In J. Garbarino (Ed.), *Children and families in the social environment* (2nd ed.) (pp. 179–200). New York: Aldine de Gruyter.

Garcia-Preto, N. (1982). Puerto Rican families. In M. McGoldrick, J. K. Pearce, & J. Giordano (Eds.), *Ethnicity and family therapy* (pp. 164–186). New York: Guilford Press.

Gelfand, D., & Yee, B. W. K. (1991). Trends and forces: Influence of immigration, migration, and acculturation on the fabric of aging in America. *Generations, 15,* 7–10.

Gibbs, J. T. (1989). Biracial adolescents. In J. T. Gibbs, L. N. Huang, & associates (Eds.), *Children of color* (pp. 322–350). San Francisco: Jossey-Bass.

Gibbs, J. T., & Hines, A. M. (1992). Negotiating ethnic identity: Issues for black and white biracial adolescents. In M. P. P. Root (Ed.), *Racially mixed people in America.* Newbury Park, CA: Sage.

Gonzales, J. L. (1992). *Racial and ethnic families in America.* Dubuque, IA: Kendall/Hunt.

Hall, C. C. I. (1992). Please choose one: Ethnic identity choices for biracial individuals. In M. P. P. Root (Ed.), *Racially mixed people in America* (pp. 250–264). Newbury Park, CA: Sage.

Hareven, T. K., & Modell, J. (1980). Family patterns. In S. Thernstrom (Ed.), *Harvard encyclopedia of American ethnic groups* (pp. 345–354). Cambridge: Harvard University Press.

Harrison, A. O., Wilson, M. N., Pine, C. J. Chan, S. Q., & Buriel, R. (1990). Family ecologies of ethnic minority children. *Child Development, 61,* 347–362.

Hayes-Bautista, D. E. (1992). Academe can take the lead in binding together the residents of a multicultural society. *Chronicle of Higher Education, 39,* B1, B2.

Hill, R., Foote, N., Aldous, J., Carlson, R., & MacDonald, R. (1970). *Family development in three generations.* Cambridge, MA: Schenkman.

Hines, P. M., Garcia-Preto, N., McGoldrick, M., Almeida, R., & Weltman, S. (1992). Intergenerational relationships across cultures. *Families in Society,* 323–338.

Ho, M. K. (1987). *Family therapy with ethnic minorities.* Newbury Park, CA: Sage.

Hogan, M. J., & Womack, W. J. (1990, September). *Project 2000: Building minority participation in family science and child development.* Paper presented at the conference Project 2000: Building Minority Participation in Home Economics—A Time for Action. American Home Economics Association and U.S. Department of Education, Office of Educational Research and Improvement, Washington, DC.

Jackson, J. S. (1989). Methodological issues in survey research on older minority adults. In M. P. Lawton & A. R. Herzog

(Eds.), *Special research methods for gerontology* (pp. 137–161). Amityville, NY: Baywood Publishing Co.

Jarrett, R. J. (1992). A family case study: An examination of the underclass debate. In J. F. Gilgun, K. Daly, & G. Handel (Eds.), *Qualitative methods in family research* (pp. 172–197). Newbury Park, CA: Sage.

Johnson, R. C. (1992). Offspring of cross-race and cross-ethnic marriages in Hawaii. In M. P. P. Root (Ed.), *Racially mixed people in America* (pp. 239–249). Newbury Park, CA: Sage.

Kalantzis, M., & Cope, W. (1992, November 4). Multiculturalism may prove to be the key issue of our epoch. *Chronicle of Higher Education*, pp. B3, B5.

Kellogg, J. B. (1988, November). Forces of change. *Phi Delta Kappan*, pp. 199–204.

Kerwin, C., Ponterotto, J. G., Jackson, B. L., & Harris, A. (1993). Racial identity in biracial children: A qualitative investigation. *Journal of Counseling Psychology, 40*, 221–231.

Kessler-Harris, A. (1992). Cultural locations. *American Quarterly, 44*, 299–312.

LaFromboise, T. D., & Low, K. G. (1989). American Indian children and adolescents. In J. T. Gibbs, L. N. Huang, & associates (Eds.), *Children of color* (pp. 114–147). San Francisco: Jossey-Bass.

Levine, A. (1991, September/October). The meaning of diversity. *Change*, pp. 45, 22.

Levitan, S. A., Belous, R. S., & Gallo, R. (1988). *What's happening to the American family* (rev. ed.). Baltimore: Johns Hopkins University Press.

Litwak, E. (1985). *Helping the elderly*. New York: The Guilford Press.

Locke, D. C. (1992). *Increasing multicultural understanding*. Newbury Park, CA: Sage.

Luborsky, M. R., & Rubinstein, R. L. (1990). Ethnic identity and bereavement in later life. In J. Sokolovsky (Ed.), *The cultural context of aging* (pp. 229–240). New York: Bergin & Garvey.

MacDermid, S. (1993). Native American families. In M. J. Sporakowski (Ed.), *Family life education teacher's kit*. Minneapolis: National Council on Family Relations.

Marden, C. F., Meyer, G., & Engel, M. H. (1992). *Minorities in American society* (6th ed.). New York: Harper Collins.

Marin, G., & Marin, B. V. (1991). *Research with Hispanic Populations*. Newbury Park, CA: Sage.

Markides, K. S., Liang, J., & Jackson, J. S. (1990). Race, ethnicity, and aging: Conceptual and methodological issues. In R. H. Binstock & L. K. George (Eds.), *Handbook of aging and the social sciences* (3rd ed.) (pp. 112–129). San Diego: Academic Press.

McAdoo, H. P. (1982a). Levels of stress and family support in black families. In H. I. McCubbin, A. E. Cauble, & J.

M. Patterson (Eds.), *Family stress, coping, and social support* (pp. 239–252). Springfield, IL: Charles C Thomas.

McAdoo, H. P. (1982b). Stress-absorbing systems in black families. *Family Relations, 31*, 479–488.

McAdoo, H. P. (1993). Ethnic families: Strengths that are found in diversity. In H. P. McAdoo (Ed.), *Family ethnicity: Strength in diversity* (pp. 3–14). Newbury Park, CA: Sage.

McGoldrick M. (1982). Ethnicity and family therapy: An overview. In M. McGoldrick, J. K. Pearce, & J. Giordano (Eds.), *Ethnicity and family therapy* (pp. 3–30). New York: The Guilford Press.

McGoldrick, M., Almeida, R., Hines, P.M., Rosen, E., Garcia-Preto, N., & Lee, E. (1991). Mourning in different cultures. In F. Walsh & M. McGoldrick (Eds.), *Living beyond loss: Death in the family* (pp. 176–206). New York: Norton.

McGoldrick, M., Pearce, J. K., & Giordano, J. (Eds.). (1982). *Ethnicity and family therapy*. New York: Guilford Press.

McInnis, K. (1991). Ethnic-sensitive work with Hmong refugee children. *Child Welfare, 70*, 571–580.

McIntosh, P. (1988). *White privilege and male privilege*. Unpublished manuscript, Wellesley College, Center for Research on Women.

McRoy, R., & Freeman, E. (1986). Racial identity issues among mixed-race children. *Social Work in Education, 8*, 164–175.

Mills, C. W. (1959). *The sociological imagination*. New York: Oxford University Press.

Mindel, C. H., Habenstein, R. W., & Wright, R. (Eds.). (1988). *Ethnic families in America* (3rd ed.). New York: Elsevier.

Moynihan, D. P. (1965). *The Negro family: The case for national action*. Washington, DC: U.S. Government Printing Office.

Myerhoff, B. (1978). *Number our days*. New York: Dutton.

Noley, G. (1990). The foster children of American education. In G. E. Thomas (Ed.), *U. S. race relations in the 1980s and 1990s*. New York: Hemisphere.

O'Brien, S. (1991). Tribal governments. *National forum: The Phi Kappa Phi journal, 71*, 18–20.

O'Hare, W. P. (1992). *America's minorities: The demographics of diversity*. Washington, DC: Population Reference Bureau.

Peters, M. F., & Massey, G. (1983). Mundane extreme environmental stress in family stress theories: The case of black families in white America. In H. McCubbin, M. Sussman, & J. Patterson (Eds.), *Social stress and the family* (pp. 193–218). New York: Haworth Press.

Petersen, W. (1980). Concepts of ethnicity. In W. Petersen, M. Novak, & P. Gleason (Eds.), *Dimensions of ethnicity* (pp. 1–26). Cambridge, MA: Harvard University Press.

Phinney, J. S. (1990). Ethnic identity in adolescents and adults: Review of research. *Psychological Bulletin, 108,* 499–514.

Preli, R., & Bernard, J. M. (1993). Making multiculturalism relevant for majority culture graduate students. *Journal of Marital and Family Therapy. 19,* 5–16.

Raymond, C. (1991, October 30). Results from Chicago project lead social scientists to rethinking of the urban underclass. *Chronicle of Higher Education, 38,* pp. A11–A13.

Redford, D. S. (1988). Somerset homecoming. New York: Anchor Books.

Rodriguez, R. (1981). *Hunger of memory.* Boston: David R. Godine.

Roosens, E. E. (1989). *Creating ethnicity: The process of ethnogenesis.* Newbury Park, CA: Sage.

Rosenthal, C. J. (1983). Aging, ethnicity and the family: Beyond the modernization thesis. *Canadian Ethnic Studies, 15,* 1–16.

Rosenthal, C. J. (1986). Family supports in later life: Does ethnicity make a difference? *The Gerontologist, 26,* 19–24.

Rossi, A. S., & Rossi, P. H. (1990). *Of human bonding.* New York: Aldine de Gruyter.

Rothman, J., Gant, L. J., & Hnat, S. A. (1985). Mexican-American family culture. *Social Service Review, 59,* 197–215.

Schlesinger, A. M. (1992). *The disuniting of America.* New York: Norton.

Schneider, D. (1977). Kinship, nationality, and religion in American culture: Toward a definition of kinship. In J. L. Dolgin, D. S. Kemnitzer, & D. M. Schneider (Eds.). *Symbolic anthropology* (pp. 63–71). New York: Columbia University Press.

Seabloom, M. (1991). *Filial beliefs in the life histories of Vietnamese elders.* Unpublished master's thesis, Family Social Science Department, University of Minnesota, St. Paul.

Shon, S. P., & Ja, D. Y. (1982). Asian families. In M. McGoldrick, J. K. Pearce, & J. Giordano (Eds.), *Ethnicity and family therapy* (pp. 208–228). New York: Guilford Press.

Sleeter, C. E., & Grant, C. A. (1988). *Making Choices for multicultural education.* Columbus, OH: Merrill.

Smith, S., & Ingoldsby, B. (1992). Multicultural family studies: Educating students for diversity. *Family Relations, 41,* 25–30.

Spickard, P. R. (1992). The illogic of American racial categories. In M. P. P. Root (Ed.), *Racially mixed people in America* (pp. 12–23). Newbury Park, CA: Sage.

Spiegel, J. (1982). An ecological model of ethnic families. In M. McGoldrick, J. K. Pearce, & J. Giordano (Eds.), *Ethnicity and family therapy* (pp. 208–228). New York: Guilford Press.

Staples, R. (1988). The emerging majority: Resources for nonwhite families in the United States. *Family Relations, 37,* 348–354.

Sue, S. (1991). Ethnicity and culture in psychological research and practice. In J. D. Goodchilds (Ed.), *Psychological perspectives on human diversity in America* (pp. 51–85). Washington, DC: American Psychological Association.

Sussman, M. B., & Burchinal, L. (1962). Kin family network: Unheralded structure in current conceptualization of family functioning. *Marriage and Family Living. 24,* 320–332.

Szapocznik, J., & Kurtines, W. M. (1993). Family psychology and cultural diversity. *American Psychologist. 48,* 400–407.

Takaki, R. (1993). *A different mirror: A history of multicultural America.* Boston: Little, Brown.

Taylor, C. (1992). *Multiculturalism and "the politics of recognition."* Princeton, NJ: Princeton University Press.

Thao, T. C. (1986). Hmong customs on marriage, divorce and the rights of married women. In B. Johns & D. Strecker (Eds.), *The Hmong world.* New Haven, CT.: Yale Center for International and Area Studies.

Thernstrom, S. (1980). *Harvard encyclopedia of American ethnic groups.* Cambridge, MA: Harvard University Press.

Tiesel, J. W., & Olson, D. H. (1992). Preventing family problems: Troubling trends and promising opportunities. *Family Relations, 41,* 398–403.

U.N. Convention on the Rights of the Child, unofficial summary of articles. (1991). *American Psychologist, 46,* 50–52.

U. S. Bureau of the Census (1991). *Money income of households, families, and persons in the United States: 1991* (U. S. Department of Commerce Publication Series P-60, No. 180). Washington, DC: U. S. Government Printing Office.

Vega, W. A. (1990). Hispanic families in the 1980s: A decade of research. *Journal of Marriage and the Family, 52,* 1015–1024.

Watson, M. F., & Protinsky, H. W. (1988). Black adolescent identity development: Effects of perceived family structure. *Family Relations, 37,* 288–292.

Webb-Watson, L. (1989). Ethnicity: An epistemology of child rearing. In L. Combrinck-Graham (Ed.), *Children in family contexts* (pp. 463–481). New York: Guilford Press.

Weibel-Orlando, J. (1990). Grandparenting styles: Native American perspectives. In J. Sokolovsky (Ed.), *The cultural context of aging* (pp. 109–126). New York: Bergin & Garvey.

Werner, E. (1991). Grandparent-grandchild relationships amongst U. S. ethnic groups. In P. K. Smith (Ed.), *The psychology of grandparenthood* (pp. 68–82). London: Routledge.

Wilkinson, D. (1987). Ethnicity. In M. B. Sussman & S. K. Steinmetz (Eds.), *Handbook of marriage and the family* (pp. 183–210). New York: Plenum.

Willie, C. V. (1985). *Black and white families*. Dix Hills, NY: General Hall.

Willie, C. V. (1992, January/February). Multiculturalism bashing. *Change*, pp. 70–75.

Wilson, B. (1991). Never leave your past behind. In J. Kilbom (Ed.), *Kaleidoscope: A collection of multicultural writings* (pp. 4–5). St. Cloud, MN: St. Cloud State University.

Woehrer, C. E. (1988). Ethnic families in the circumplex model: Integrating nuclear with extended family systems. *Journal of Psychotherapy and the Family, 4*, 199–237.

Wong, F. F. (1991, July/August). Diversity and community. *Change, 23*, 50–54.

Zeitlin, S. J., Kotkin, A. J., & Baker, H. J. (1982). *A celebration of American family folklore*. New York: Pantheon.

Theories and Research in Family Science

Once we begin to understand that the family lives in a context, the next step is to gain a clear understanding of how professionals in family science study those contexts and the attendant family processes. For example, how do they begin to understand how "close" a family "should" be, who makes family rules and enforces them, and how both desirable and undesirable family traits are transmitted from one generation to another? Of course, by understanding the contexts and process better, we can begin to design more effective interventions.

At the heart of understanding family-science intervention is understanding the theories that are used. In Part II, you will read about how family scientists construct and use theories. Two examples of more frequently used family theories are presented, family-systems theory and behaviorism. Keep in mind that the theories presented here are but examples; the two that are discussed are prominent in family research and intervention. As you begin the intellectual journey into the study of the family, however, it will quickly become apparent that a plethora of theoretical approaches is used by family-science teachers and interventionists. In Chapter 5, Wesley Burr leads us through an overview of why we use theories, where they come from, and how they are used. Burr is something of a master at developing, using, and analyzing family theory. For over 25 years he has been a leading exponent for the development and use of theories. One of his first books, *Theory Construction and the Family*, is one of the most cited works in family science.

Chapter 6 is an introduction to a theoretical perspective that is widely used in family-science research. Randal Day asks us to explore the idea that the cause-and-effect world of much of science does not work very well in explaining family processes. His chapter is not meant to be an exhaustive overview of the systems approach. You may have had similar introductions to these ideas in a beginning-level course on family science. However, Day reminds us how important this approach is and how some of the more visible terms in systems theory are being used in research. He shows how some family scientists are attempting to explain the world of the family as a unique example of a complex systemic process.

Chapter 7 presents a vastly different view of individual and family interaction. In this chapter, Eugene Mead suggests that family interaction can be best understood from a reinforcement/punishment perspective.

The challenge for the astute family-science student is to begin forming a *position*. As you develop in your academic career, you must take a position on how you will approach the problems families face as you assist them. The perspective that you choose will greatly influence the intervention you choose. Your primary task, therefore, is to "take a stand." You must decide which theories, which ideas, and which approaches fit your world view. You must also find out which approaches work best for each different situation. Of course, there is no one perfect theory. Instead theory-building and theory-using are somewhat private and personal exercises. The results of these exercises is a personal construction of how the world is put together and how it works.

In addition, part of the science of family science comes in the process of validating and (dis)confirming a theoretical idea. Chapter 8, by Karen Carver and Jay Teachman, is a short introduction to how family scientists use scientific methods to refine their thinking about a theoretical idea. Through the use of qualitative and quantitative methods, one begins to accept or reject the validity or usefulness of theoretical ideas.

Using Theories in Family Science

Wesley R. Burr

Brigham Young University

We humans are a curious and meddlesome bunch. We are always asking what is happening around us and what we can do to make things better. *What* happens to the children when their parents divorce? *What* can we do to make divorce as constructive as possible? *What* is happening that leads one child in a family to turn out well and another to turn into such a brat? *What* can we do to create intimacy, peace, love, and closeness? And we don't ask these questions just to be asking. We want answers!

As we try to answer these questions, we develop *theories*. Our theories give us *explanations* and help us know how to *intervene*. For example, the question about why some children in a family are more difficult than others led Vogel and Bell (1960) to develop a theory of scapegoating. They reason that some families tend to blame one child for the family difficulties and that when this occurs it often sets up a vicious circle. The child who is the scapegoat tends to misbehave more than before, and the family may then be even more sure that he or she is the source of the family's problems. Gradually, the scapegoated child acts more and more rebellious, and the family treats him or her more and more as a problem child. The scapegoating helps some families operate fairly normally in other ways as long as they can put the blame for their difficulties on the one child, and as long as the rest of the family, and sometimes the child, believes that he or she is the root of the family problems. This "solution" helps perpetuate the problem.

The theory about scapegoating is a minor theory, but it is an example of the way the term *theory* is used in the sciences. Thus, as mentioned above, scientific theories can be defined as groups of ideas that give us explanations that can be used as the basis for intervening.

All scientific fields have a number of theories. In geology, for example, there are theories of sedimentation and theories of glaciation. The theories of sedimentation help geologists understand how layers of rock and dirt are formed. The theories of glaciation help them understand how large segments of earth have been scooped up and removed. Family science is just like all the other fields in that it has many theories about family processes.

Six Important Aspects of General Theories

One way to understand the nature of theories is to recall the fable of the six blind men who approached an elephant. Remember that the men all had different "theories" about what they were encountering.

Theories Answer Questions about "What Is Going On"

Each of us constructs our private theory about "what is going on." The fable of the blind men helps us understand that the theory each man constructed gave him an explanation of what elephants were like. The man who felt the leg thought of how large, firm, and sturdy the leg was, and his insights satisfied his intellectual curiosity. The one who felt the side thought of how massive the "wall" was and how he couldn't move it when he pushed on it. His ideas accurately helped him understand one aspect of elephants. Each of the others had a different explanation because of his theory about elephants.

Theories about family processes help us understand what is going on in various aspects of the family realm. For example, some theories help us know what is happening when 2-year-old children are always saying "No!" Other theories help us understand what is going on when marriages succeed or fail, and others help us understand what is going on when some teenagers rebel and others cooperate.

Theories Are in the Minds of the Scientists

Another way the fable of the blind men helps us understand the nature of theories is that the theories were not part of the elephant. The blind men developed, or constructed, the theories. The theories were not "in" the elephant. They were "in" the *minds* of the six men.

It is the same in family science. Our theories about families are not "in" families; they are in the minds of the scientists who study families or the counselors or educators who try to help families. The theories are the sets of ideas that the scientists "think with" to help them understand and give them a basis for interventions.

Another way to describe theories is that they are intellectual "models," frameworks, or sets of ideas that exist in a scientific field. When students are learning any field, they learn a new language. They learn how to talk the "theory" language and think with the ideas that make up the field.

One way family scientists have described this aspect of theories is to observe that "the map is not the territory." If we have a map of a state or city, the map is not the state or the city; it is merely a description that people make to help them understand the state or city. Our theories about family processes are intellectual maps we use to describe families.

Theories Give Us Power

Good theories do more than just satisfy intellectual curiosity. They also help scientists and practitioners devise methods of changing things or solving problems so people can better attain their goals. Using the ele-

phant analogy, for example, the man who felt the trunk and thought the elephant was like a rope had some "new" ideas in his head. He could then use these ideas to help him attain goals such as moving large logs or carrying other objects. Thus, as Sir Francis Bacon said over three centuries ago, *knowledge is power*.

How do family scientists use this power? It helps therapists know how to help families solve their problems and cope with difficult situations. It helps extension specialists know what to write in pamphlets. It also helps them know what to do and say in television and other educational programs that are designed to help the families improve their lives. And it helps people in business know how to make work environments more supportive of workers and their families. Thus, the ultimate payoff of theories is that they give us ideas that we can use to better attain our goals.

The Search for One Integrating Theory Is Futile

Another aspect of the elephant fable is also helpful in understanding theories in family science. Theorists and practitioners in family science are somewhat like the blind men in that we are all blind to many things. None of us is able to understand all of the aspects of the "elephant" in family science. Families are so complex, they interact in such complicated ways with their many environments, and they have such long and complicated histories, that it is impossible to understand all of their arms, legs, trunks, and tails.

Families are so complex that it is impossible for any one theory to explain everything. The result is that family science has different theories about different aspects of the elephant. One theory is about the trunk of families, and another theory is about legs. Other theories deal with the elephant's skin and eyes, the food it eats, and the oxygen it needs to stay alive.

Thus, we should not try to get one grand or great theory that will explain everything about families (Holman & Burr, 1980). It would be too large to manage, understand, and use. We mortals need to be satisfied with having several different theories that focus on different parts of our elephants.

Another implication is that it is helpful for family scientists to learn several different theories. Then we can use each of them when it is helpful. If we only have a theory about an elephant's tail, and the problem we are trying to deal with is in the leg, we are seriously handicapped. It is impossible for any one family scientist to learn all of the theories that can be used to understand family processes, but it is possible to learn more than one and then shift among them when it is helpful.

Usefulness Rather Than Truth Is What Matters

Since theories are analytic tools that scientists use to explain and understand, and they are "true" to the group of scientists that views them as true, it is therefore not very helpful to argue, debate, or bother to do research about whether theories are true or false.

If a theory makes sense to a group of scientists, it exists and is true to the scientists who think with it. In fact, to push this point further, a theory could be fairly untrue in some objective or ultimate sense, but if it is helpful to a group of scientists and if there is no better theory, it could be quite valuable.

Scientific theories are developed because a group of scientists make observations about a part of their elephant, and each theory, even if it is inconsistent with another way of thinking, is truth—as seen by that group of scientists. Thus, the truth or falsity of theories is fairly irrelevant, and worrying about it can actually get in the way of developing new and helpful ideas.

If the ultimate or objective truth of theories should not demand our concern and attention, what does matter? The important thing is whether theories help theorists, researchers, and practitioners accomplish their goals. Therefore, it is helpful to evaluate theories in terms of their utility, their practical value, their usefulness, and their helpfulness.

Thus, the theories that help scientists understand important questions and help them solve important problems are valuable. Valuable theories become widely known in the field, and they are taught in universities, research centers, and clinics. A large number of people learn them and use them to satisfy their intellectual curiosity and accomplish their goals. The theories that are not helpful or useful—or that are so unrealistic, irrelevant, or inconsistent with empirical observations that they are not helpful—are gradually ignored, and eventually they are forgotten.

The conclusion to this point is that there is a natural selection process in the rise and demise of theories, and it has little to do with truth or falsity. It is a selection based on the pragmatic value of theories. When theories are helpful in satisfying intellectual curiosity, providing explanations, or solving human problems, they remain part of scholarly fields. When old theories are replaced by better ones, the old theories, like old soldiers, fade away.

The moral: Good theories are helpful. Bad theories fade away, and trying to prove a theory bad or untrue is usually not worth the effort.

Theories Give Us Perspectives

Another helpful aspect of the elephant fable is that it illustrates differences in *perspectives*. When we understand the theory about the legs of elephants, it gives us a certain "point of view." We think differently than if we are thinking about the theory of the chemistry in the digestive system of the elephant.

In terms of family science, when we think with behaviorism, we assume that humans are malleable. We also assume that the environment can change humans a great deal by changing the rewards and punishments. This is a very different point of view from that of psychoanalysis, which assumes that all people have innate, biological drives that influence what they do. These two theories, behaviorism and psychoanalysis, make such different assumptions about the nature of humans and the nature of families that family scientists don't usually think with both of them at the same time. One is a theory about legs, and the other is a theory about tails. Both are true, but they deal with very different parts of the elephant. It is helpful to know both of them, but they have very different perspectives, and they give us very different concepts, insights, generalizations, and ideas.

The Essential Parts of Theories

When we read something, how do we know if it is a theory? For example, does a set of ideas need to have mathematical formulas to be a theory? Does there need to be a large amount of research into some ideas before the ideas become a theory?

The answer to both of these questions is no. We don't need a mathematical formula, and we don't need a large amount of research.

What, then, are the minimal, essential components of a theory? The answer is that the ideas in a theory have six essential characteristics. One of these characteristics, that the ideas give us a *perspective*, has already been discussed. The other five are that the ideas have *concepts*, *assumptions*, *generality*, *explanations*, and a *history* of evolving in a scientific community.

Theories Have Concepts

The theories used by scientists have words, or terms, that are carefully defined. This helps all scientists think the same way when they learn the theory, and it minimizes misunderstandings and confusion. The terms in scientific theories are called *concepts*, and they are the basic building blocks of scientific thinking.

Theories Have Assumptions

The dictionary tells us that assumptions are facts or statements that are taken for granted, supposed to be true, or assumed to be true. Different theories make different assumptions. For example, behaviorism assumes that people are born with minds that are *tabulae rasae* (empty slates, blank chalkboards). This assumption is made in behaviorism. After the theorists made it, they were able to develop some new ideas about how people learn. They probably would not have developed their ideas or would not have been able to convince their colleagues that the ideas were valuable if they had not been able to assume a tabula rasa condition.

Family-systems theory does not assume that the mind is a *tabula rasa*. Why? The *tabula rasa* assumption is about the mind, and family-systems theory is not a theory about the mind. Using the elephant analogy, behaviorism is about one part of the elephant, and systems theory is about a different part.

When we want to think with family-systems theory, we assume that family systems can change and that the flow of information is an important part of the system. These assumptions then focus our attention on patterns of dealing with information rather than on how people learn.

What about the truth of assumptions? Do they need to be true? Do we need a lot of research into assumptions so we can have confidence that they are true? The answer is no. Assumptions merely identify the starting point for our reasoning. They identify what we want to begin with, what we want to take for granted while we think with or use a theory. They can be true, but they can also be hypothetical.

Theories Have Generality

Some theories are very narrow or specific. For example, Adams's (1979) theory of mate selection helps explain why people marry the people they do. Since it deals with a small part of the world, it is a fairly *specific* theory. Other theories deal with larger parts of the world. Behaviorism, for example, is an attempt to explain how humans learn, and it can be applied to any type of human learning. Since it can be used to explain more things than Adams's theory of mate selection can, it is a more *general* theory.

Systems theory is an example of a very general theory. It can explain why things happen in many different systems. It can be used to understand biological systems such as the circulatory or nervous system, and it can be applied to large and complex systems like armies and governments. Since it can be used to answer "why" questions in a wide variety of situations, it is a very general theory.

The highly general theories are the most valuable because we can use them in many situations. If we have a very narrow theory, for example, such as a theory about why a 2-year-old child broke a window, it is not helpful in very many situations. A more general theory, such as a theory about why children obey and disobey, can help us understand the child's breaking the window and many other situations. Therefore, scientists try to develop theories that are as general as possible.

Theories Have Explanations

The payoff of theories is that they give us explanations. The explanations are true statements that satisfy our intellectual curiosity. These true statements are sometimes called generalizations, postulates, propositions, or laws, and they are the main reason we have theories.

The concepts and assumptions help provide the explanations because they provide the foundation for the true statements, or generalizations. The concepts give us words with which to think and communicate. The assumptions help us know what to focus on, what to assume, and where to start reasoning. But the payoff part, the fruit of all the work, is in the true statements that give us the explanations.

Theories Have a History

Theories are not static sets of ideas or perspectives. They are always changing. Theories change and grow as new concepts are developed, as new discoveries are made, and as new problems are encountered.

There is also a pattern in the way that most theories change. They grow in uneven cycles. There are periods of rapid change when a brilliant scholar makes some unusual contributions. These periods are then usually followed by some minor refinements or reactions to the innovations and a period of little or no change.

Sometimes the periods of stability in theories last for decades or even centuries. At other times periods of major development are fairly close together. In most of the general theories used in family science, the periods when major developments were made are not numerous. It is usually a matter of learning about the work of a few creative people at certain periods.

Since it is almost impossible to understand general theories in family science without being aware of the historical patterns of change, it is helpful to know some strategies for remembering these changes. The following three ideas can help this process:

1. *Remember the names of major theorists.* Science is a social phenomenon. It is groups of individuals trying to find answers to their questions. Also, advances are usually made by one or two main individuals, so it is not necessary to learn long lists of names.

2. *Remember the approximate dates of the major publications.* Most of the advances in theories are made in reaction to advances in other theories or as reactions to unique historical events. They are also usually published in a small group of articles or books, and they have publication dates. It is therefore helpful to be aware of a few publications and dates.

3. *Pay attention to the roots and branches.* Most of the ideas in the general theories have long histories, and it is helpful, whenever possible, to be aware of these intellectual roots. Many new developments in general theories are reactions to or modifications of previous theories, and it is helpful to see how theories divide and branch into new perspectives.

General Theories Used in Family Science

The later chapters of this book use a number of general theories, and it is helpful to understand the main differences among these theories. To help you understand these theories, this chapter provides a brief description of six theoretical approaches that are widely used in family science: (1) hedonistic theories (which include economic theory, behaviorism, and exchange theory), (2) developmental theories, (3) humanistic theories, (4) symbolic interaction, (5) family-systems theory, and (6) feminist theory.

The six theories summarized in this chapter are not all of the theories that are used in the field. They were selected because they illustrate the three different paradigmatic approaches that we use, they are a manageable group, they are widely known and used, and they illustrate the variation in the many theories that are used. Some of the other theories that could have been included are Erik Erikson's developmental theory, the hermeneutic approach, Alfred Adler's theory of personality, phenomenology, and Jean Piaget's theory of development.

Before we examine the six theories, it is helpful to understand that our general theories are part of several different *scientific paradigms.* Scientific paradigms are philosophies about what knowledge is, what knowledge ought to be, and how we discover it. Before the scientific revolution in the 1500s and 1600s, most scholars had a "paradigmatic" orientation that can be called a *prescientific* paradigm or world view:

> Before 1500 the dominant world view in Europe, as well as in most other civilizations, was organic. People lived in small, cohesive communities and experienced nature in terms of organic relationships, characterized by the interdependence of spiritual and material phenomena and the subordi-

nation of individual needs to those of the community. The scientific framework of this organized world view rested on two authorities—Aristotle and the Church. Thomas Aquinas combined Aristotle's comprehensive system of nature with Christian theology and ethics and, in doing so, established the conceptual framework that remained unquestioned throughout the Middle Ages. The nature of medieval science was very different from that of contemporary science. It was based on both reason and faith and its main goal was to understand the meaning and significance of things, rather than prediction and control. (Capra, 1982, p. 53)

The scientific revolution occurred under the leadership of Nicolaus Copernicus, Galileo Galilei, René Descartes, and Isaac Newton in the 1500s and 1600s. This intellectual revolution created a new paradigm for scholars that is quite different from the organic view that preceded it.

The new paradigm has a number of different labels. Some call it *positivism*; some call it the *instrumental-technical* paradigm; since it is a marriage of rational and empirical approaches, some prefer to call it *logical positivism* (Mead, 1953, p. 249). The main assumptions in the positivistic way of getting knowledge are that (1) there are phenomena and processes that operate independently of human awareness of them, (2) there are laws that govern at least some of these phenomena and processes, (3) at least some of these laws can be discovered through the scientific method, (4) knowledge of these laws can be used by humans to predict and at least partially control some of the phenomena and processes, and (5) this type of prediction and control can help humans better meet their needs and desires (Capra, 1982; Doherty, 1986; Morgaine, 1992).

The positivistic approach has been enormously successful in creating knowledge in the physical and biological sciences, and it has become the dominant intellectual perspective in the modern scientific community. It has been less successful in creating knowledge about social phenomena, but it is the main approach in the social sciences in the 20th century.

Two other scientific paradigms are used in contemporary family science, but before we look at them, it seems useful to examine the main ideas in three of our general theories that are part of the positivistic mode of inquiry. The three that are discussed here are hedonistic theories, developmental theories, and humanistic theories.

Positivistic Theories in Family Science

Hedonistic Theories

The term *hedonism* refers to the idea that humans seek pleasure and avoid pain. The basic ideas in this school of thought are as old as scholarship itself. Aristippus, who lived in Cyrene on the African coast of the Mediterranean Sea in the fourth and fifth centuries B.C., is the first known advocate of hedonism, and his view was one of the most extreme. He argued that all good was determined by pleasure and that intensity and immediacy were the only criteria for evaluating pleasures. He thought that the most intense pleasure of the moment was the best and the most motivating.

This extreme view of hedonism was soon modified by other Greek scholars, such as Epicurus, who proposed that some forms of pleasure lasted much longer than others and that some were purchased at a higher cost. Epicurus also introduced the idea that the greatest pleasure was the absence of pain and the best life the one most free from want, suffering, and agitation of strong passion.

Three different versions of hedonism are used in contemporary family science. Scholars who approach the field with a psychological orientation tend to call this theory *behaviorism*. Chapter 7 in this volume is a more extensive discussion of this theoretical perspective. Scholars who approach the field from an economic orientation tend to call this perspective *economic theory*. Scholars who approach the field from a sociological orientation tend to call it *exchange theory*. Each of these groups uses slightly different terms for the basic concepts, and each uses them for slightly different purposes, but they are essentially all the same theory.

Where did hedonistic theories come from? John Locke was an English philosopher and physician who helped lay the foundation for behaviorism in his *Essay Concerning Human Understanding* (1690). He identified a number of laws that he called the "laws of association," and they became the cornerstone of this theory. These laws state that people tend to repeat behavior when it is associated with pleasurable results and that they discontinue behavior when it is associated with painful results.

Adam Smith was the first scholar to apply these ideas to economics in his volume *An Inquiry into the Nature and Causes of the Wealth of Nations* (1776). Contemporary economists who use this theory in studying family processes are Becker (1981), Fuchs (1983), and Boulding (1973).

Few additions were made to the basic "laws of association" until the early 1900s, when a Russian physiologist conducted a number of experiments on conditioning in dogs. Ivan Pavlov's experiments were widely publicized, and this school of thought became a major theory in psychology and sociology. The psychological branch of these ideas was expanded by scholars such as John Watson and B. F. Skinner.

As sociologists developed the study of how people are hedonistic in their interrelationships, they developed the exchange-theory branch of hedonistic theory. The two scholars who first articulated exchange theory were George Homans, *The Human Group* (1950) and *Social Behaviors: Its Elementary Forms* (1961), and Peter Blau, in *Exchange and Power in Social Life* (1964). Ivan Nye (1976, 1979) made helpful contributions in showing how exchange theory could be applied to the family.

What assumptions are made when we use hedonism?   All general theories make a number of basic assumptions. The assumptions are a group of ideas that are supposed to be true or are taken for granted. They are the "givens" that scholars start with in a theory. Those who use hedonistic theories usually assume that (1) people are influenced a great deal by what happens in their environment, (2) humans are rational, and (3) humans are profit-seeking. The psychological branch also assumes that the mind of an infant is a tabula rasa. The economic branch also assumes that resources are scarce, and the sociological branch assumes that the nature of profit is determined by social values (Nye, 1979, pp. 6–7).

What are the main concepts (terms) in hedonism?   The main concepts in this approach are the duo of reward (pleasure, reward, reinforcer, income, profit) and loss (pain, cost, negative reinforcer). Some of the other terms that are used are conditioning, extinction, discrimination, values, marginal, reciprocity, scarcity, exchange, grants, and comparison level.

What are the main ideas in hedonistic theories? Hedonistic theory provides explanations of how people learn and what motivates them to make the choices they do. Scholars who like to use this theory are aware that there are also genetic determinants of many things, such as physical growth, but they do not think that learning occurs or choices are made because of genetic maturation. They believe that learning occurs and choices are made because different things are "associated" together. Pavlov's (1927) famous experiments with dogs are a classic example. Dogs salivate when food is placed in front of them, and the salivation is apparently an innate reflex rather than something that is learned. Pavlov would ring a bell or turn on lights at the same time food was placed in front of his dogs, and after a period the dogs would salivate when the bells sounded or the lights appeared—even if there was no food. They had "learned" by somehow associating the bells and food.

These simple ideas have since been expanded into a more elaborate set of propositions about how positive and negative reinforcers increase and decrease behavior. When reinforcers such as food, praise, or the removal of pain occur, they increase and decrease rates of behavior.

Sociologists apply the basic idea of maximizing pleasure and minimizing pain to arrive as propositions such as the following. Each of these ideas assumes that, if other costs and rewards are equal (Nye, 1979, p. 6):

- Individuals choose the alternatives that supply or can be expected to supply the most social approval (or those that promise the least social disapproval).
- Individuals choose statuses and relationships that provide the most autonomy.
- Individuals choose alternatives characterized by the least ambiguity in terms of expected future events and outcomes.
- Individuals choose alternatives that promise the most security for them.

Foa (1971) has pointed out that this theory, like all the other theories, can deal effectively with only part of the "elephant." Hedonistic theory provides considerable understanding about the parts of the elephant where people make "rational" decisions, but it doesn't provide many answers about the less rational parts of the family, the parts that have to do with love, trust, compassion, and bonding.

What can family scientists do with hedonistic theories?   This theoretical perspective has been used extensively by family scientists. It is used in several schools of thought in marriage and family therapy. It is also used in educating parents and in marriage-enrichment programs. The ideas in behaviorism have become such a central part of our culture that they are used in everyday language.

A tradition in home economics that is known as "home management" has used this theory to help home-makers increase their efficiency, improve their con-sumer skills, make decisions more rationally, and manage homes more effectively. Scholars such as Becker (1981) and Fuchs (1983) have used economic theory to show how humans could be more rational in everything from birthrates to education.

An evaluation of hedonistic theories.   The he-donistic theories are some of the most useful and widely used theories in contemporary family science. Different family scientists, however, use different versions. Coun-selors and therapists tend to use the behavioral version. Home economists use the economic perspective, and family sociologists use exchange theory.

The hedonistic theories are the most useful in studying or helping very specific or limited phenomena. In other words, they are helpful in getting a child to have manners at the table or in getting a date to show up on time. They are less helpful with general or abstract parts of life, such as teaching generosity, charity, kindness, compassion, or consideration. They are the most effec-tive when the pleasures and pains are fairly easy to identify and control.

Another aspect of the hedonistic theories is that they have a clear perspective on human beings, human life, and goodness and badness. The perspective is true in that a substantial part of the human condition seems to be best described by hedonistic thinking. Unfortu-nately, in my opinion, this part is not the noble or lofty part. It is the more base, selfish, banal, infantile, irre-sponsible, and ignoble part of . . . the elephant. The learning that occurs for other than selfish motives is ignored in this perspective. The exchanges that occur in the grants economy (Boulding, 1970), as opposed to the market economy, are ignored in this perspective. The beliefs, definitions, and interpersonal interactions that involve love, compassion, charity, altruism, con-cern about others, service, sacrifice, giving, nobility, and beauty—*for their own sake*—are ignored. It is only the selfish, pleasure-seeking parts of the elephant that are described and studied. Metaphorically speaking, the conniving, self- seeking, and manipulative parts of the elephant's mind seem to be the parts that are studied, and the heart is not included.

A number of modern scholars probably do not agree with the above descriptions of the perspective provided by the hedonistic theories. One reason is that hedonism has become the hallmark of the 20th-century Western world. The trend toward individualism and the inclination to emphasize rights without responsibili-ties are such dominant themes in our culture that many modern scholars have come to believe that the hedon-istic perspective is the total view. They think it is the view of the whole elephant. Admittedly, it is a part of the elephant, and it is a part that a wise family scientist cannot ignore, but it is only a part.

Developmental Theories

Developmental theories began in the 18th century when a group of thinkers began to realize that children were fundamentally different from adults. Prior to that time the prevailing view was that children were mini-ature adults. Until the 14th century, for example, paint-ings invariably portrayed children with adult body proportions and facial characteristics (Aries, 1960).

The publication of Emile (1762/1948) by Jean-Jacques Rousseau is usually viewed as the beginning of the developmental theories. This volume is an essay on developmental processes and the education of children, and it became the cornerstone for a new way of thinking. No major innovations were made in the developmental perspective in the 19th century, but a number of relatively different theories appeared in the 20th century.

The developmental perspective has spawned many developmental theories in this century, and some of them are integral parts of family science. Most of them are theories about the development of individuals. For example, Freudian psychoanalysis, Erikson's theory of personality, Piaget's theories, and Adler's theories are all theories about the development of individuals. Gradually, however, a theory has emerged that deals with family development.

Where did family-development theory come from? Evelyn Duvall and Reuben Hill were the two scholars who developed this theoretical perspective. They began to develop their ideas in the 1940s in their volume *When You Marry* (1946). Duvall expanded their ideas in her book *Family Development* (1957), and Waller and Hill included this perspective in their revision of *The Family* (1951). Their initial work was later expanded by Roy Rodgers in his *Family Interaction and Transaction* (1973). It was refined and expanded further in the 1980s by Celia Jaes Falicov in her volume *Family Transitions* (1988) and by Betty Carter and Monica McGoldrick in *The Changing Family Life Cycle* (1989). James White's *Dynamics of Family Development* (1991) has continued to add ideas to this perspective.

What assumptions are made when we use family-development theory? The perspective that is provided by developmental theories has two characteristics that are fairly distinct from the other major intellectual traditions. The first of these is the assumption that there is some order in the developmental patterns of individuals and families. According to this assumption, genetic and environmental factors that are related to development have a combined effect in determining a substantial amount of what individuals and families are and do. The developmental theories, therefore, develop explanations (answers to the "why" questions) that are based in or inherent in changes in genetic and environmental factors.

The second characteristic of developmental theories is more of an attitude or expectation. It is pervasive, but it is not as not well articulated in most of the theories. It is the belief that people or families can be improved through healthy maturation and growth. This view is more a sense of optimism, a sense of hope, a frame of reference than a stated belief. Even though this perspective acknowledges that life cycles include old age and death in individuals and the empty nest and contracted family in the later stages of life, there is still an "onward and upward" aura to the developmental theories. This is a very different view from the self-oriented emphasis in the hedonistic theories or the sense of complexity, confusion, and lack of control in the systems perspective. It is an implicit expectation that "life can improve," "things can get better," and "people can grow and develop." The result is an orientation that we ought to "look for the best in the human condition" and "see what can be done to make things better." This is a subtle assumption, but it tends to be a part of the developmental perspective. Scholars who use this perspective, therefore, are frequently at odds with the hedonistic scholars, and there is usually little collaboration, overlap, or tolerance for the other point of view in the writings or research in these two intellectual traditions.

What are the main concepts in family-development theory? Some of the major concepts in this theory are developmental task, family life cycle, stages, transitions, norms, roles, positions, role sequence, structure, career, boundaries, epigenesis, and families being stuck, or arrested, in their development.

How do family scientists use this theory? Family development is useful in explaining a variety of phenomena. It explains why family systems move from an emphasis on rule creation in the formation stage of the life cycle to rules being implicit and assumed later. It helps us understand why families deal with some issues, such as inclusion, before they deal with managing emotional distance. It helps explain variations in consumption patterns in families, patterns of giving and receiving help across generations and among other kin, variations in marital satisfaction, and patterns of mobility.

Evaluation of family-development theory. This theory is one of the narrower and less general theories in family science. It is less general in that it deals with a fairly small part of the elephant. It is also not widely used in research or application in the field. Therefore, it is a useful but very limited perspective. Most of the efforts of the theorists in this perspective have been in developing the concepts rather than expanding the explanations, so it may have more potential than present usefulness.

Hill (1971) suggested over two decades ago that it was useful to broaden this perspective by integrating it with the systems theories. Since that time a number of scholars have integrated many developmental and systemic ideas (Falicov, 1988, chap. 1).

Humanistic Theories

Humanistic psychology emerged in the middle of the 20th century as one of the reactions to the emphasis on determinism and experimentation that had gained such popularity. Scholars such as Abraham Maslow made important contributions to this perspective.

Carl Rogers developed a theory that has been used in family science more than the other humanistic theories. His approach is sometimes called Rogerian theory, and at other times it is called self theory. The term *self theory* is used here.

Rogers published *Client-Centered Therapy* in 1951. It built upon the earlier work of a number of scholars, but the book was so well received that it was an important milestone in the development of this perspective. Rogers's view is more than just a theory of personality or human behavior. It is, like Freud's psychoanalysis, also a theory of how to "help" people, and this combination dramatically influenced family science. It stimulated, for example, innovative works on theory and practice, such as Thomas Gordon's *Parent Effectiveness Training* (1970).

What are the main assumptions in self theory? This theory makes a number of distinctive assumptions about that nature of humans. It assumes, for example, that humans are innately good and that they have an innate desire and drive to ennoble themselves. These assumptions are very different from those made in behaviorism and symbolic interaction—that people are asocial or empty slates when they are born. They are also very different from the assumptions of inner turmoil and conflict that are such a fundamental part of psychoanalysis. These traits can be disrupted by the social conditions in which people live, but in a "normal" life they are inherent.

What are the main concepts in self theory? Some of the main terms in this school of thought are self, real self, perceived self, ideal self, self-actualization, active listening (reflective listening), I-statements, and You- statements.

What are the main ideas in the theory? The central idea in this theory is that humans have an inherent drive to improve, grow, and develop. The term that is used to describe this motivation is self-actualization. As people mature, they develop a sense of who and what they are, and this is their self-concept. They also develop a complex set of beliefs about what they should be like, and this is their ideal self. When the perceptions of the self are less noble than the ideal self, the resulting guilt and anxiety can interfere with normal development and progress toward actualization.

Since this theory assumes that people want to grow and improve, the best way to help others is to "free" them from excessive pressures and constraints. The best way to do this is to treat others with unconditional positive regard, and allowing them to feel safe enough to pursue their noble desires.

How do family scientists use self theory? No theory is universally liked and used by family scientists. There are behaviorists and analysts, systems theorists and interactionists. Self theory is the same way. A sizable group of family scientists believes that this theory is a useful set of ideas, and a sizable group doesn't like it.

Those who use this theory behave in ways that are quite different from those who use the other theories. According to this theory, the best way to "help" individuals and families is to create a feeling, an atmosphere, of safety and love. This ambiance frees the basic human strivings, and people are unbelievably creative in solving their problems, finding ways to cooperate, and moving on to the task of self-actualizing themselves.

Some of the strategies that have been developed to help create the desired feelings of safety are to listen carefully to what people are saying, to try to understand their uniqueness, and to accept them. This led to the development of "active listening" as a method of relating to others. It consists of concentrated listening and stating back to the person the fundamentals of what is heard. This method of relating has a number of advantages. It shows interest in, and acceptance of, the other person. Also, since the object is to listen with empathy and warmth rather than to give advice or suggest solutions, it communicates that the listener has confidence that the person is the best one to find the solutions for his or her life. This tends to be enabling and strengthening to others.

This theory has had a major impact on educational, enrichment, and therapeutic programs in the family field. The most widely used educational programs in the last several decades use the concepts of active listening when someone else has a problem and using I-statements when you have a problem (Gordon, 1970; Guerney, 1977).

An evaluation of self theory.   This theory was developed as a reaction to the hedonistic and mechanical approach in behaviorism. It was also partly a reaction to the sense of turmoil and inner conflict that is such an inherent part of psychoanalysis. It is very different from the more neutral ideas in symbolic interaction, but there is no evidence that Rogers was reacting to George Herbert Mead and his co-workers. Self theory is an optimistic view of humans and societies, asserting that the human condition can be primarily peace, fulfillment, and harmonious growth.

This theory is more of a psychological theory than a family theory, since it is a theory of individuals. It therefore deals with a very limited part of the elephant. Many family scientists find it useful, but it is not as broad or inclusive as some of the other theories. Its stress on the positive, uplifting, and upward-reaching parts of the human process is not accepted by many theorists in the other perspectives, but in my view it too is part of the elephant.

Interpretive Theories in Family Science

The positivistic theories are useful, but some aspects of the human condition are not included in them. Also, a number of scholars have been uncomfortable with several elements of the positivistic approach. Positivism emphasizes the external and objective reality of phenomena. It also assumes that it is possible to predict and control, and this assumes that causal laws are operating. This ignores the parts of humans and families that deal with ethical choices, values, ideals, and morality. It also ignores the spontaneous and unpredictable parts of humans and families.

These concerns about the limitations of positivistic inquiry led several groups of scholars to try to develop alternative methods of inquiry. Many of the scholars who have been aware of the limitations of the positivistic approach have been in the artistic departments of universities, and the divisions between these two approaches is sometimes summarized by referring to the academic community as consisting of the arts and sciences. Thus, scholars in fields such as art, the humanities, theology, philosophy, literature, and drama have developed methods of understanding humans that are quite different from the scientific methods of positivism.

In addition to scholars outside the sciences trying to use nonpositivistic approaches, a number of scholars inside the physical and social sciences have tried to develop alternatives to the positivistic paradigm. One of these alternatives has become an important part of the family-science field. This alternative paradigm has been described with several labels. Some call it interpretive science (Brown & Paolucci, 1979); some call it an interpretive paradigm (Morgaine, 1992). Others call it hermeneutics (Osmond, 1981; Thomas & Wilcox, 1987). In this chapter, the term *interpretive paradigm* is used:

> Assumptions underlying this paradigm include: (a) Natural science methods are not always appropriate for gaining insight into human interaction; (b) many human actions cannot be predicted or controlled; (c) attempts to manipulate and control others are not ethical; (d) there is no single reality of life—knowledge is created by individuals living in an historical era; and (e) gaining understanding or reflecting on meaning will serve as a catalyst for action [Morgaine, 1992, p. 13].

Thus, this point of view does not believe in certainty, law-seeking, or objectivity. The objectives of scholarly inquiry are to develop a conceptual framework, create a "universe of discourse" that provides insights, understand processes, communicate about specific events that have meaning, or have conversations about the interpretations and meanings people have.

Two theoretical perspectives that are widely used in family science attempt to use this paradigmatic approach. They are *symbolic interaction* and *family-systems theory*. (Incidentally, a third approach has been identified recently that uses this paradigm. It is known as hermeneutics. There is a growing philosophical literature [Gadamer, 1975; Heidegger, 1962], but thus far so little has been published in the family field that there are not enough ideas to form a unique perspective.)

Symbolic Interaction

The ideas that led to symbolic-interaction theory began appearing in the late 1800s. Publications such as William James's *Principles of Psychology* (1890) and Charles H. Cooley's *Human Nature and the Social Order* (1902) laid the groundwork.

George Herbert Mead, a social philosopher at the University of Chicago, was the main developer of this perspective. His ideas were basically a reaction to behaviorism, and they were published after his death by his students in *Mind, Self and Society* (1934). Later developments were made by scholars such as Erving Goffman in *The Presentation of Self in Everyday Life* (1959).

What are the main assumptions in symbolic interaction?   Four of the main assumptions in this theory are (Rose, 1962, pp. 5–6):

1. Humans live in a symbolic environment as well as a physical environment, and they acquire complex sets of symbols in their minds.
2. Humans value.
3. Symbols are important in understanding human behavior.
4. Humans are reflexive (they think about themselves), and their introspection gradually creates a definition of self.

What are the main concepts in symbolic interaction?   Some of the main terms in this theory are self,

society, mind, the "I" and "me," values, roles, norms, meaning, perceptions, definitions, role expectations, role behavior, role making, and identity.

What are the main ideas in symbolic interaction?   Two illustrative propositions in this theory are that the clarity of people's expectations about a new role influences the ease with which they can move into the role and that the more strongly people value something, the more they will be influenced by it. Other ideas are that people who desire to interact in a relationship need at least a minimal consensus on the meaning of their perceptions and that the quality of the role enactment influences how satisfied people are in relationships such as marriage and parenthood.

How do family scientists use symbolic interaction?   This theory has stimulated a great deal of research on many topics. It is also widely used by educators and therapists as they attempt to educate and counsel. It is useful in explaining complicated behavior and also behavior that seems to be irrational until the individuals' perceptions are taken into account.

An evaluation of symbolic interaction.   Symbolic interaction has had an enormous impact on the family field. The theory is almost universally understood in the field, and people use it in a variety of settings. It tended, however, to have its greatest impact in the middle part of the 20th century, and it has not continued to grow, expand, or be modified. Therefore, the ideas in this theory are increasingly assumed to be true, but young scholars are unaware of their roots.

The ideas are also so fundamental in understanding human behavior that they are helpful in a variety of settings. They are also so self-evident that most of them are accepted as valid without empirical research or testing. They become more of a basic philosophy of life than a set of scientifically verified propositions.

Another interesting aspect of this theory is that many of its main ideas tended to be discovered and articulated by several different groups at about the same time. Piaget, for example, discovered many of the same ideas at about the time that the Chicago group was clarifying its ideas, and apparently these two groups had no contact. Two decades later a group of psychiatrically oriented scholars discovered many of the same ideas in what came to be known as the "family process" literature, and they too seem to have had no contact with the writings of Mead.

Family-Systems Theory

The systemic approach uses some ideas that are as old as the human intellectual tradition, but this theory did not emerge as a unique perspective until fairly recently. The systems approach became a general theory in biology in the 18th century when processes such as the circulatory system and nitrogen cycle were recognized. This theory became a central perspective in fields such as engineering when they began to focus on how the interrelationships of parts in a whole made a difference.

Systems theories were dramatically expanded in the era 1940–1960 when a great deal of research focused on telecommunication networks and computers became an integral part of our culture. During the 1960s a number of volumes clarified and expanded the concepts and ideas in this perspective. Chapter 6 in this volume is a more extensive discussion of systems theory.

Where did family-systems theory come from? The systemic approach became an important part of family science because of two fairly separate trends. First, a group of psychiatrists began developing "family therapy" as a reaction to the limitations in the individually oriented therapies in medicine and psychology. Volumes such as Gregory Bateson's *Steps to an Ecology of the Mind* (1972) and *Mind and Nature: A Necessary Unity* (1979) and Murray Bowen's *Family Therapy in Clinical Practice* (1978) were some of the influential volumes in the therapeutic branch of family systems theory. More recently, scholars such as Keeney and Sprenkle (1982) and Auserwald (1985) have added a number of refinements to this perspective.

The second trend involved a group of home economists and family scientists who developed an ecologically oriented systems perspective in the 1970s. Influential volumes in this movement were *Family Decision Making: An Ecosystem Approach* (Paolucci, Hall,

& Axinn, 1977), Ruth Deacon and Francille Firebaugh's *Home Management: Context and Concepts* (1981), and Urie Bronfenbrenner's *The Ecology of Human Development* (1979).

What are the assumptions in family-systems theory? The basic assumptions in all of the systems theories have not been stated as clearly as they are in the hedonistic approach, but systems theorists seem to assume that it is helpful to take a holistic perspective. They like to back up and look at the "total picture" as much as possible. All of the systems theories also seem to assume that there are enough regularities in the ways parts and wholes are composed and function that it is helpful to study them. They assume that life has great complexity and that focusing on complex interrelationships can provide valuable insights. This perspective also assumes that families cannot be effectively understood unless the *patterns* in the relationships within the family and between the family and external systems are taken into account.

The assumptions unique to ecosystem theory are that the environment around families is fragile and has limited resources and that, not only does it influence families in a number of ways, but families also influence it in important ways. Ecosystem theorists also assume that the systems perspective can provide insights about these relationships that will help families and society better attain their goals.

What are the main concepts (terms) in family-systems theory? Many of the concepts in family-systems theory are the same as in general systems theory—for example, terms like input, output, feedback, rules of transformation, and boundaries. In addition, however, a number of concepts are primarily limited to the family-systems theory: individuation, mystification, paradoxical bonding, double bind, complementary and parallel relationships, metacommunication, rules and metarules, boundaries, openness, pseudomutuality, coalition, and triangulation.

The ecological branch of systems theory also uses terms such as information and energy flows, resources, mesosystem, adaptation, goals, standards, consumption, and styles of decision-making. Bronfenbrenner's (1979) approach to human development is one of the ecosystemic branches of this theory, and he uses terms such as microsystem, mesosystem, and macrosystem.

What are the main ideas in therapeutic systems theory?   Two propositions emerged early in the development of this theory, and they illustrate the ideas that this approach creates. One of these is called by Jay Haley the homeostasis hypothesis, and it holds that when something tries to create a change in a family system there is usually a tendency to resist the change, a tendency to toward homeostasis. The second proposition is known as paradoxical communication. It holds that emotional disturbances tend to occur when there is a long-term pattern of powerful members of a family sending inconsistent messages and making inconsistent demands (Broderick & Pulliam-Krager, 1979, pp. 604–611).

The ecological parts of family-systems theory focus on the relationship between the family and its "near" environment. It has developed ideas about the ways the physical, technological, and social-regulatory systems influence and, in turn, are influenced by the family. It has demonstrated that a number of nonrational factors such as bonding, intense affect, and commitment in long-term relationships are essential for the well-being of children and adults. These theorists have also demonstrated that some environmental systems, such as neighborhoods and churches, can help provide, or at least assist in the provision of, these essentials.

What can family scientists do with systems theory?   This theory was designed by and for practitioners who wanted to make a difference in the quality of family life. Therefore, it tends to be a pragmatic theory, and it is extensively used in the field. Many of the ideas that were first identified in this theory have also been adapted for educational and enrichment programs.

The ecological branch is useful in a number of different contexts. It has been helpful in policy and impact analyses in government and industrial settings. It has helped families manage limited resources, and it provides useful ideas for decision-making and home management.

An evaluation of the systemic perspective.   The systemic perspective has provided many useful insights, but it also has a number of important limitations. The scholars who developed this perspective ignored gender issues and abusive processes in family systems. For many years the therapeutically oriented scholars also generally paid little attention to the "eco" aspect of family systems or the subsystems inside them. They focused their attention almost exclusively on the internal processes of conjugal families.

Several other aspects of the systemic perspective are limiting. This perspective is a very broad and general way of thinking. Also, it focuses on the complicated and complex patterns in life, so it is inherently a complex and abstract way of thinking.

Critical / Emancipatory Theories in Family Science

The third paradigmatic approach, in addition to the positivistic and interpretive paradigms, has been called critical theory (Brown & Paolucci, 1979) and the critical/emancipatory paradigm (Morgaine, 1992). It is one of the points of view that has been developed as an alternative to positivism. The primary goals in this mode of inquiry are to raise the consciousness of people about oppression and to help them become emancipated from their subjugation. This paradigm does not try to acquire scientific laws about cause-and-effect relationships or to focus on interpretive processes.

There is a long tradition of scholarship about the evils of domination and exploitation and the value of personal autonomy, justice, and freedom. Rousseau's (1750/1964, 1762/1948) writings on these issues helped spawn political revolutions in the United States and France in the 18th century, and they also helped equality and freedom become ideals that many believe are important. Several groups of scholars believe that these ideals are compromised in many ways, and they are dedicated to trying to develop ideas and strategies that are "critical" analyses of existing orders and "emancipatory" for those who are oppressed.

Some of these scholars have focused on political oppression. They tend to take an activist approach in trying to develop ideas that will help emancipate people from oppressive governments (Fromm, 1942; Habermas, 1971, 1981). This branch of scholarship has been widespread in Europe, but it has not become an important part of family science.

Feminist Theory

A different group of scholars has focused on sexual inequality and discrimination, and it has developed an approach that is called feminism, or feminist theory. The feminist perspective has become an important part of family science in the last several decades of the 20th century.

Where did feminist theory come from? The attempts to eliminate sexual discrimination have a long history. It was a difficult and gradual process that created the changes in our legal system which gave women legal identities separate from their husbands. As women acquired legal identities, they gradually acquired the rights to do such things as own property, vote, and sue and be sued.

During the 1950s and 1960s, feminist issues began to receive increased attention, but the literature during that period had little impact on the social sciences. However, considerable literature began appearing in the 1970s that helped feminism become a central part of family science, such as Adrienne Rich's *Of Woman Born* (1976), *Rethinking the Family: Some Feminist Questions* (Thorne & Yalon, 1982), and Carol Gilligan's *In a Different Voice* (1982). More recently, feminist scholars have found ways to include feminist thinking in a wide variety of theories and practical issues in the field (Gouldner, 1988; MacDermid, Jurich, Myers-Walls, & Pelo, 1992).

What are the assumptions in feminist theory? There is considerable diversity among feminist scholars, but a number of assumptions are widely shared. Some of these assumptions are the same as those in the interpretive paradigm—for example, the four listed earlier in the subsection on symbolic interaction. In addition, the critical/emancipatory approach assumes that women are oppressed, that personal and family experiences are also political experiences whether people recognize it or not, and that feminists need to have a double vision of reality: "The 'double vision' is the ability, and the need, to be successful in the current social (and educational) system while being attentive to, and working to change, oppressive practices and institutions" (MacDermid et al., 1992, p. 31). Most feminists also assume that it is ethical to work actively toward emancipation, that a wide range of ideas and methods that promote emancipation should be used, and that the positivistic approach is harmful when it is used to distance people from the emancipatory struggles and to promote the status quo.

What are the main concepts (terms) in feminist theory? Some of the central concepts in feminist theory are: gender, oppression, discrimination, emancipation, political, connectedness, personal experience, enlightenment, and power.

What are the main ideas in feminist theory? There is a clear thread in the ideas in feminist theory: gender inequality exists at many levels in contemporary societies. The inequality is oppressive and stifling for women, and it is morally imperative that emancipation occur. Thus, the driving force in this mode of inquiry is to promote gender equality, and scholarly ideas are one of the means that can help this end.

What can family scientists do with feminist theory? One of the goals of feminist thought goes beyond demonstrating that sexual bias is pervasive in our theories, our research, and the way practitioners such as educators and therapists intervene. The goal is to have the feminist perspectives enlighten theorists, researchers, therapists, educators, and students so they help eliminate gender bias in their own lives, in their professions, and in society generally. Feminist scholars differ considerably in the means they advocate to accomplish this goal. Some advocate radical and militant changes. Others are in favor of moderate and gradual changes, but an activist orientation is a central part of this perspective.

An evaluation of feminist theory. There are many reasons why this perspective has become widely used in recent years. Probably the main factor is its usefulness in social action. A secondary reason is because it is an idea-producing alternative to positivism.

Feminist theory has developed a large body of literature that is critical of the established order. The scholars who use this perspective have demonstrated serious and previously unrecognized gender biases in widely accepted theories, research, and practices in many fields of inquiry (Gilligan, 1982), and their arguments are so persuasive that they are literally (but unfortunately also slowly) revolutionizing academia and the professions.

Chapter Summary

Theories have immense value to scientists and practitioners. They help us understand the world around us. We can use them to predict events, and we can use them to help train children, send rockets to the moon, develop new technologies, and help criminals reform. In family science they help us understand why people get married and divorced, and they help us understand what we need to do to adjust effectively when we get married or divorced. They help us know why children respond the way they do to praise and punishment, and this type of knowledge is *power*. It is power because it helps family scientists help others attain their goals.

Discussion Questions

1. Why do we have theories?
2. If different theories make different assumptions, should we select only one theory we like? How is it possible to use different theories if they make different assumptions?
3. Which theories are more general and less general? What are the advantages of having theories of different levels of generality?
4. What is the practical value of theories?
5. Some scholars think we do not need theories. Why might they believe this?
6. What can we do with theories that we couldn't do without them?

7. How can theories interfere with scholarly or practical work?

Additional Resources

Bowen, M. (1978). *Family therapy in clinical practice.* New York: Aronson.

Constantine, L. L. (1986). *Family paradigms.* New York: Guilford Press.

Paolucci, B., Hall, O. A., & Axinn, N. W. (1977). *Family decision making: An ecosystem approach.* New York: Wiley.

Kantor, D., & Lehr, W. (1975). *Inside the family.* San Francisco: Jossey-Bass.

References

Adams, B. (1979). Mate selection in the United States: A theoretical summarization. In W. R. Burr, R. Hill, F. I. Nye, & I. L. Reiss (Eds.), *Contemporary theories about the family,* chap. 11. New York: Free Press.

Aries, P. (1960). *Centuries of childhood: A social history of family life.* New York: Knopf.

Auserwald, E. H. (1985). Thinking about thinking in family therapy. *Family Process, 24,* 1–12.

Bateson, G. (1972). *Steps to an ecology of the mind.* New York: Ballantine.

Bateson, G. (1979). *Mind and nature: A necessary unity.* New York: Dutton.

Bateson, G., Jackson, D. D., Haley, J., & Weakland, J. H. (1956). Toward a theory of schizophrenia. *Behavioral Science, 1,* 251–264.

Becker, G. S. (1981). *A treatise on the family.* Cambridge, MA: Harvard University Press.

Blau, P. M. (1964). *Exchange and power in social life.* New York: Wiley.

Boszormenyi-Nagy, I., & Sparks, G. M. (1973). *Invisible loyalties: Reciprocity in intergenerational therapy.* New York: Harper & Row.

Boulding, K. (1973). *The economy of love and fear.* Belmont, CA: Wadsworth.

Bowen, M. (1966). The use of theory in clinical practice. *Comprehensive Psychiatry, 7,* 345–374.

Bowen, M. (1976). Theory in the practice of psychotherapy. In P. Guerin (Ed.), *Family Therapy.* New York: Gardner.

Bowen, M. (1978). *Family Therapy in Clinical Practice*. New York: Aronson.

Broderick, C., & Pulliam-Krager, H. (1979). Family process and child outcomes. In W. R. Burr, R. Hill, F. I. Nye, & I. L. Reiss (Eds.), *Contemporary theories about the family*, chap. 23. New York: Free Press.

Bronfenbrenner, U. (1979). *The ecology of human development*. Cambridge, MA: Harvard University Press.

Bronfenbrenner, U. (1986, July 4). *Recent advances in research on the ecology of human development*. Paper presented at the Developmental Conference, Berlin.

Brown, M., & Paolucci, B. (1979). *Home economics: A definition*. Washington, DC: American Home Economics Association.

Buckley, W. (1967). *Sociology and modern systems theory*. Englewood Cliffs, NJ: Prentice-Hall.

Buckley, W. (Ed.). (1968). *Modern systems research for the behavioral scientist*. Chicago: Aldine.

Capra, F. (1982). *The turning point*. New York: Simon & Shuster.

Carter, B., & McGoldrick, M. (Eds.). (1989). *The changing family life cycle*. Boston: Allyn & Bacon.

Constantine, L. (1986). *Family paradigms*. New York: Guilford Press.

Cooley, C. H. (1902). *Human nature and the social order*. New York: Scribner's.

Deacon, R. E., & Firebaugh, F. (1981). *Family resource management*. Boston: Allyn & Bacon.

Doherty, W. (1986). Quanta, quarks, and families: Implications of quantum physics for family research. *Family Process*, 25, 249–263.

Duvall, E. (1957). *Family development*. New York: Lippincott.

Duvall, E., & Hill, R. (1945). *When you marry*. New York: Heath.

Duvall, E., & Miller, B. C. (1985). *Family development*. New York: Lippincott.

Erikson, E. (1950). *Childhood and society*. New York: Norton.

Erikson, E. (1959). *Identity and the life cycle*. New York: International Universities Press.

Erikson, E. (1964). *Insight and responsibility*. New York: Norton.

Falicov, C. J. (Ed.). (1988). *Family transitions: Continuity and change over the life cycle*. New York: Guilford Press.

Foa, U. (1971). Interpersonal and economic resources. *Science*, 171, 345–351.

Fromm, E. (1942). *Escape form freedom*.

Fuchs, V. R. (1983). *How we live*. Cambridge, MA: Harvard University Press.

Gadamer, H. G. (1975). *Truth and method*. New York: Crossroad.

Gilligan, C. (1982). *In a different voice*. Cambridge, MA: Harvard University Press.

Goffman, E. (1959). *The presentation of self in everyday life*. New York: Doubleday.

Gordon, T. (1970). *Parent effectiveness training*. New York: Wyden.

Gouldner, V. (1988). Generation and gender: Normative and covert hierarchies. *Family Process*, 27, 17–31.

Guerney, B. G. (1977). *Relationship enhancement*. San Francisco: Jossey-Bass.

Habermas, J. (1971). *Knowledge and human interests*. (J. Shapiro, trans.) Boston: Beacon Press.

Habernas, J. (1981). *The theory of communicative action*. (T. McCarthy, trans., 1987). Boston: Beacon Press.

Haley, J. (1976). *Problem solving therapy*. San Francisco: Jossey-Bass.

Hall, G. S. (1904). *Adolescence: Its psychology and its relations to physiology, anthropology, sociology, sex, crime, religion and education*. New York: Appleton-Century-Crofts.

Handel, G. (1985). *The psychosocial interior of the family* (3rd ed.). New York: Aldine.

Heidegger, M. (1952). *Being and time*. (Macquarrie & Robinson, trans.). New York: Harper and Row.

Hess, R. D., & Handel. G. (1959). *Family worlds*. Chicago: University of Chicago Press.

Hill, R. (1971). Modern systems theory and the family: A confrontation. *Social Science information*, 10, 7–26.

Hoffman, L. (1981). *Foundations of family therapy*. New York: Basic Books.

Holman, T. & Burr, W. R. (1980). Beyond the beyond: The development of family theories in the 1970s. *Journal of Marriage and the Family*, 42, 723–729.

Homans, G. (1950). *The human group*. New York: Harcourt Brace.

Homans, G. (1961). *Social behavior: Its elementary forms*. New York: Harcourt Brace Jovanovich.

James, W. (1890). *Principles of psychology*. New York: Holt.

Kantor, D., & Lehr, W. (1975). *Inside the family*. San Francisco: Jossey-Bass.

Keeney, B. P. & Sprenkle, D. H. (1982). Ecosystemetic epistemology: Critical implications for the aesthetics and pragmatics of family therapy. *Family Process*, 21, 1–20.

Kuhn, T. S. (1970). *The structure of scientific revolutions* (2nd ed.). Chicago: University of Chicago Press.

Locke, J. (1690). *Essay concerning human understanding*. London: J. M. Dent and Sons.

MacDermid, S. M., Jurich, J. A., Myers-Walls, J. A., & Pelo, A. (1992). *Feminist teaching effective education*. *Family Relations*, 41, 31–38.

Malinowski, B. (1929). *The sexual life of savages in northwestern Melanesia* (2 vols.). New York: Liveright.

Mead, G. H. (1934). *Mind, self and society.* Chicago: University of Chicago Press.

Morgaine, C. A. (1992). Alternative paradigms for helping families change themselves. *Family Relations, 41,* 12–17.

Mead, H. (1953). *Types and problems of philosophy.* New York: Henry Holt.

Nye, F. I. (1976). *Role structure and analysis of the family.* Beverly Hills, CA: Sage.

Nye, F. I. (1979). Choice, exchange, and the family. In W. R. Burr, R. Hill, F. I. Nye, & I. L. Reiss (Eds.), *Contemporary theories about the family.* New York: Free Press.

Osmond, M. W. (1981). *Rethinking family sociology from a critical perspective: Applications and implications.* Paper presented at the NCFR Theory and Methods Workshop.

Paolucci, B., Hall, O. A., & Axinn, N. W. (1977). *Family decision making: An ecosystem approach.* New York: Wiley.

Parsons, T. (1951). *The social system.* Glencoe, IL: Free Press.

Pavlov, I. P. (1960). *Conditioned reflexes.* New York: Dover. (Original work published 1927.)

Piaget, J. (1964). *Six psychological studies* (A. Tenzer & D. Elkind, trans.). New York: Vintage Books.

Rich, A. (1976). *Of woman born: Motherhood as experience and institution.* New York: Norton.

Rich, A. (1979). *On lies, secrets, and silence: Selected prose (1966–1978).* New York: Norton.

Rodgers, R. (1973). *Family interaction and transaction.* Englewood Cliffs, NJ: Prentice Hall.

Rogers, C. (1951). *Client-centered therapy.* Boston: Houghton Mifflin.

Rose, A. (1962). *Human behavior and social processes.* New York: Houghton Mifflin.

Rousseau, J. J. (1948). *Emile, or Education.* London: J. M. Dent and Sons. (Original work published 1762.)

Rousseau, J. J. (1964). Discourse on the sciences and arts. In R. D. Master (Ed.), *The first and second discourses.* New York: St. Martins Press. (Original work published 1750.)

Ruddick, S. (1982). Maternal thinking. In B. Thorne & M. Yalom (Eds.), *Rethinking the family: Some feminist questions.* New York: Longman. (Originally published in *Feminist Studies, 6,* 343–367.)

Ruddick, S. (1983). Preservative love and military destruction: Some reflections on mothering and peace. In J. Trebilcot (Ed.), *Mothering: Essays in feminist theory* (pp. 231–262). Totowa, NJ: Rowan & Allanheld.

Skinner, B. F. (1971). *Beyond freedom and dignity.* New York: Knopf.

Smith, D. E. (1979). Sociology. In J. A. Sherman & E. T. Beck (Eds.), *The Prism of Sex.* Madison: University of Wisconsin Press, pp. 135–187.

Thomas, D. L. & Wilcox, J. E. (1987). The rise of family theory: Critiques form philosophy of science and hermeneutics. In M. Sussman & S. Steinmez (Eds.), *Handbook on marriage and the family.* New York: Plenum.

Thomas, W. I., & Thomas, D. S. (1928). *The child in America.* New York: Knopf.

Thorne, B., & Yalom, M. (Eds.). (1982). *Rethinking the family: Some feminist questions.* New York: Longman.

Vogel, E. F., & Bell, N. W. (1960). The emotionally disturbed child as the family scapegoat. In N. W. Bell & E. F. Vogel (Eds.), *A modern introduction to the family.* Glencoe, IL: Free Press.

Waller, W., & Hill, R. (1951). *The family: A dynamic interpretation.* New York: Henry Holt.

White, J. M. (1991). *Dynamics of family development.* New York: Guilford Press.

CHAPTER 6

Family-Systems Theory

Randal D. Day
Washington State University

Scholars and practitioners have viewed the world of the family in many ways. This chapter presents the view that the family is a group of interacting individuals composing a whole, or unit. An important feature of this approach is the idea that family units have a *synergistic* quality; when a group combines with a relatively unified purpose, the energy produced by the group is greater than the energy produced by members individually. The description of this energy and how the unit solves problems, makes decisions, maintains balance, and achieves collective goals is called *family-systems theory*. Scholars have described this process in various ways. The following is one way to organize the primary concepts and ideas in that perspective.

One popular way of organizing what happens in families is by thinking of the various *levels* of interaction that occur. Authors have written about these levels in several ways and have used different labels to describe this process. I have decided to use the convention presented in the text *Family Science* (Burr, Day, & Bahr, 1993). In this text, we struggled with the various tiers, planes, or layers of association that occur within a family. At the simplest level *(Level I)* the association, or interaction, is rather open to view and is focused on the everyday event. (See Chapter 10 for an expansion of this idea.) For example, the functional interactions as described in Chapter 7 fall into this category. These are the daily routines, responses, and exchanges that characterize family interaction. Like a race car on a track, we move along with the pack, avoiding crashes, changing lanes, and "humming" right along.

Level II describes the *meta*processes occurring in family settings. These processes include the unspoken rules and redundancies, the scriptlike miniplays that each family knows when a given situation arises. Level II association describes the historical assumptions we make about our bonds: "What do I do when my husband is blue?" "What does Tommy do when he is scared of elevators?" Each of life's situations seems to demand a response. Like the framing behind the wallboard of a house, the studs of Level II interaction are unseen but hold it all together.

To continue the metaphor, *Level III* describes the general context in which a family operates. It is more abstract and, unseen, much like the foundation of the house. Foundations are usually composed of one simple material (concrete); they are plain, unpainted, and rarely visible. Such basic assumptions drive family interaction. As you will see in Chapter 9, families can be closed, open, or random. They can be very adaptable or very rigid. They can be highly enmeshed or very separate in contact. Like an overarching theme, the foundation of Level III pervades much of what happens in family life. And, as can well be imagined, changing the foundation of a house is one of the more difficult tasks in building.

The Level I world of the family is deterministic. This is the world of cause and effect, objectivism, and the epistemology of empiricism (Simon, 1992). Intervention is prescribed when such an independently existing "social system deviates from some norm, which also has a stable, independent existence" (p. 377). Intervention consists of identifying deviations from normative behavior and helping the system return to some level of behavior that reduces its deviation from the norm.

In this type of Level I thinking, an automatic hierarchy is established that implies that the therapist is the standard bearer and helps the system back to a comfortable and effective level of function. Positivism suggests that the foreground of understanding human behavior is to understand "cause and effect." We often hear discussions of "What *causes* divorce?" "Why did that child become a delinquent?" or "Why are African-American youths much more likely to have sexual intercourse at an earlier age?" The implication, of course, is that if we are good enough scientists, we can disassemble the presenting human problems (like divorce, delinquency, or teen pregnancy) and by dissecting the event can begin to understand "why" something happened. The assumptions of the positivistic approach, therefore, hinge on isolating cause and effect. Like the physical scientists of our age, many social scientists believe in the "medical" model of discovery and intervention. In the positivistic, medical model, there is some disease (divorce, teen pregnancy). Carefully and astutely, the social scientist tries, usually *post hoc*, to discover what led to that condition, or what caused it to emerge.

This approach mostly employs measuring (usually by survey questionnaire) several variables thought to be "associated" with the problem. In the field of divorce, for example, researchers for years have wondered what makes the divorce rate in the United States go up or down. Is it related to economic conditions, marital unhappiness, conflicts over children, sexual problems, or lack of communication? Many studies have attempted to unravel and "discover" which factors contribute to marital breakup. (For an excellent treatise on this approach to divorce see Kitson, 1992.)

The driving force behind this type of research is the hope that understanding and comprehension will lead to intervention and change. If one knows that a primary "cause" of divorce is communication problems and excessive conflict, for example, one can intervene and alter the chances of divorce occurring by developing courses, books, or counseling strategies that increase positive communication. Like a disease-control specialist, the social scientist should be able to identify the

problem, isolate the antecedents, or causes, of the problem, and finally prescribe the relevant "antidote." The foreground, therefore, is predicting which of several possible factors *cause* the identified problem. The game of science is afoot to identify, isolate, prescribe, and change.

In the past 150 years social science (economics, sociology, psychology, and anthropology) has emerged, and much discovery, understanding, and even social change have resulted. For example, one prominent area in family studies is the work done in family violence. Murray Straus and his colleagues have clearly shown us in the past 20 years the nature and depth of the problems of physical abuse in the family and our society. There are many such examples of significant work in the social sciences that has changed how we view the world and how we respond to it. As important as those findings have been, another approach to the study of family relations has recently emerged that asks different questions and suggests a different foreground; this is called the nonpositivistic approach.

The Nonpositivistic Assumption

While the most popular way of viewing human interaction (particularly in the United States) is through the eyes of first-order thinking (positivism), another view of the family and its functioning is that of the Level II and Level III world. In this world, the family scientist or therapist sees the family as interacting within a *shared reality* (Anderson, Goolishian, & Winderman, 1986; Simon, 1992). In this view, the behavior of the family revolves around the needs of the interaction; "as conversation goes, so goes the membership . . . of the system" (Simon, 1992, p. 378). Instead of the therapist acting as standard bearer of stable, normal behavior, it is the family group that discovers, constructs, and decides on which problems will be explored and even which ones exist. How the family arrives at agreement and negotiates interaction defines and describes the nature of the system. The family scientist (or the counselor) must join this conversation (not objectively) and facilitate a group process that leads to problem solving and eventual solution.

In one sense, Level I issues in families are like the bed of a river. They are the tasks and daily issues that draw so much of our attention. Level II and III issues are more like the river flowing and changing. The two ideologies are not irreconcilable but instead are a matter of focus. Indeed, these formulations can and should be complementary (Hoffman, 1985). As Hoffman explains, the pragmatic strategies of Level I schemes may take on rich importance in the context of Level II and Level III systemic processes. The focus of this chapter is on the nature of Level II and Level III thinking; it is about the processes and dynamics that flow over the riverbed of the more stabilized, normal aspects of daily living.

Systems Theory in Family Science

Over the past two decades, therapists and researchers have increasingly viewed the world in terms of constructions of reality, Level II and Level III thinking (Sprenkle & Piercy, 1992). As was mentioned in Chapter 1, the social constructions of reality do not pretend to deal with "truth." Instead of seeking for the ultimate answers to life's complexities, we look at how families construct reality and how those constructions direct family life. According to Sprenkle and Piercy (1992), the therapist is also responsible for molding a reality when working with a family. Importantly, social scientists and field workers are being taught the value of promoting empowerment (Dunst, Trivette, & Deal, 1988) in addition to instrumental intervention. For example, the family-service caseworker is being taught that it is less effective to prescribe instrumental interventions when trying to change Level II and Level III issues. In the pragmatic, medical approach, the family is seen as "having a problem" that the members did not create and cannot solve. When doing Level I thinking and intervention, the "trained" professional is assumed to know best for the "patient" and instrumentally prescribes an intervention. In Level II and Level III thinking, the emphasis is upon what is created rather than why it was formulated.

When the reality of the family is placed in the foreground, the effective family-service worker realizes that he or she must *collaborate* with the family members and empower them to solve their own problems. Rather than "giving them a fish," the help provider "teaches them to fish." The helper and help-seekers work together to assess and mobilize the resources available and promote new skills and resources that will assist the family to help itself.

Therefore, family-systems theory helps us know how to enable families to create change in Level II and Level III issues. The family helper spends very little time trying to identify why things have occurred. Instead, when the focus is upon the family system, attention is directed to *how* things work within the system and how to interrupt those patterns of behavior that are not effective.

Origin

Family-systems theory was originally developed from general systems theory. General systems theory was developed as a way to describe a variety of mechanical and biological systems. In the past 40 years or so, professional responses to the idea of systems theory have been mixed. In 1979, Broderick and Smith presented a major effort to demonstrate the difference between general systems theory and family-systems theory. Additionally, they showed how systems theory could be applied to specific family issues, such as relationship formation and communication patterns (Broderick & Smith, 1979, p. 124). Since that time, the attention given to the systems approach has primarily been in research projects that use system ideas. (Several of those will be mentioned in this chapter.)

Few, however, have written longer books or chapters that attempt to present an integrated overview of this theory and how it has been used in research and intervention. (Two exceptions are Becvar & Becvar, 1982, and Broderick, 1994.) While the individual concepts are used profusely in the therapy and family-science literature, only a few theorists and researchers, relatively speaking, have challenged or advanced the constructs introduced several decades ago. Among the exceptions are feminist writers, who suggest that an important element in a systems model is the element of power in relationships. Another example is the work of Imber-Black, Roberts, and Whitting (1988), who demonstrate how family rituals are an integral aspect of the family process. Also, the work of Carter and McGoldrick (1989) has broadened our understanding of how family processes mesh with important concepts of the family life cycle. The above examples represent the fairly small group of researchers and theorists who have been working on a variety of different components of the family system. The authors of *Family Science*, (Burr, Day, & Bahr, 1993) have attempted to present the diverse concepts in the family-process arena as an integrated picture. For the most part, theory construction and research about family processes remains fairly fragmented and relatively unsystematic. Those who seem to do the most significant work are the researchers oriented to therapy and family science.

The Family as Ecosystem

Many individuals live within small groups called families. Families live within the context of a community environment, and the community is within a culture. When one part of the system is moved or energized, that, in turn, has an effect on the other parts of the interconnected environments.

Family-systems theory evolved as clinicians and scholars recognized that it was increasingly efficacious to speak of the families within a community context and the individual within a family context. One could not really understand individual behavior until that behavior was observed in the setting of the special groups to which the individual belonged. One of the primary strengths of this approach is that it does not interpret events in isolation from other events (Becvar & Becvar, 1982). At the basis of this approach is the idea that within families there are rulelike patterns of repetitious behavior. As if following the script of a complex play, each family member knows his or her role in this daily drama. We only know about families and how they solve the problems of life as we observe the members in these daily interactions with one another. From these repetitive interactions we can make guesses about many family attributes, such as family goals and values, the nature of familial boundaries, communication rules, and allocation of resources.

The primary directive of this approach is that by studying such things as family redundancies, rules, rituals, and boundaries, we learn far more about the family than if we studied each member individually. The following are several main terms and assumptions that are commonly used to describe this theory.

Assumptions, Terms, and General Principles

System

A key concept in systems theory, obviously, is the term *system*. A system refers to the enduring, repetitious (redundant) patterns and the way the parts of the system interact. When we first try to understand how the term *system* is used, we are inclined to define a system as "a whole made up of interacting parts." This definition is widely used, yet it miscommunicates. When we use this definition, we usually think of a family system made up of individuals. When we think this way, we are probably thinking *individualistically* rather than *systemically*. The focus of the discussion of family systems is the group interaction and processes, not on the individual parts within the system.

Patterns and Process

In family-systems theory, we recognize that the key elements or interesting aspects of the family "system" are the *patterns* in the *processes* as the individuals interact. For example, a family may have an implicit rule that "the father can criticize others, but others can't criticize the father." This rule will create a pattern in the processes of the family. Rules like this are the fundamental components of the system, not the individuals. Individuals are necessary to a system, but they are not sufficient to explain what goes on in the group. There isn't a system until there is *pattern in the processes*, and it is the pattern in the processes that creates "systemness."

A metaphor may be useful here. Imagine a family in a rubber raft floating down the river of life. Of course, the members are individuals and have individual experiences during that adventure. However, family-systems theory is interested in what they do in the raft as they meet a rock in the river or turbulent water. How do they solve problems, and how do they choose who is in charge? We are not as interested in why they are there, how many people are in the raft, why they wore the clothes they wore, why the rocks are in the river, or why the sun is not shining on them. Instead, it is the processes of communication, position, and patterns of interaction that attract the attention of the family scientist.

Some of the other questions about rocks, forest, and color of clothing may be important to others (perhaps as analyses of the Level I world), but the rich information gained by observing the group in the raft is family-systems theory.

Wholeness

In family-systems theory, the primary focus is on the idea that the family is unique and something more than a summing of its individual members. The family is viewed as a coherent composite that behaves as an irreducible organismic unit (Nichols, 1984). This characteristic is sometimes described as "wholeness," or a "holistic" aspect of families. "The whole is more than the sum of its parts," is a phrase commonly used to describe a system.

The characteristic of wholeness is illustrated in Murray Bowen's idea of the family as an emotional unit (Bowen, 1978; Kerr & Bowen, 1988). His observations of relationships between mothers and schizophrenic patients, and later observations of entire families in "live-in" research, reveal a complex network of what he calls "fusion of selves" in an "undifferentiated family ego mass." The problems of a schizophrenic child, it turns out, are not "individual" problems, nor are they "mother-and-patient" problems as had commonly been assumed. Instead, certain families are fragmented. There is a larger family emotional system in which fathers are as intimately involved as the mothers. These emotional boundaries are fluid and shifting and can extend to involve the entire central family unit, and even nonrelatives. (Bowen, 1978, pp. 104–105). There is a systemic wholeness about this interaction. It cannot be described without understanding all the parts and processes that go with it. Every family seems tied together in ways that make it impossible to understand each member without understanding the whole.

Interdependence

The definition of most family roles depends upon the existence of another. One cannot be a mother without an offspring; a husband without a wife; a sibling without a brother or sister (Nichols, 1984; Searight &

Merkle, 1991). How people in those "system-defined" positions behave is an ongoing net consequence of actions and reactions, perceptions and interpretations, of family members. The behavior of any one family member is related to and dependent upon past and current behaviors of the others (Burr, Day, & Bahr, 1993).

The Symptomatic Family Member

That one behavior by a family member defines and influences the others is a critical aspect of this theory. This interdependence is a means of preserving the delicate balance among the system's parts, or members. As events affect the system, and as family members respond to situations, the members seek balance and move through evolutionary periods that affect all members (Galvin & Brommel, 1982).

Virginia Satir's (1972) comparison of the family to a mobile also illustrates the nature of interdependence. A touch to any part of the mobile creates change in other parts and temporarily alters the system as a whole. Similarly, "as events touch one member of the family, other family members reverberate in relationship to the change in the affected member" (Galvin & Brommel, 1982, p. 5). In effect, this means that when a person displays a symptom, he or she is broadcasting and reflecting the distress of the family unit. Conversely, the symptomatic family member's behavior is seen as the balancing behavior. That is, he or she acts in a way that keeps the family in balance, even at high personal cost. An excellent example of this notion is demonstrated in the docudrama book *The Family Crucible* (Napier & Whitaker, 1978). In this story, written by two leading family therapists, the daughter (who is originally the identified patient in the story) is projecting the unhappiness and distress of the marriage relationship of her parents.

To return to the metaphor of the family on a rafting adventure, the turbulent water and many of the problems encountered when rafting affect all who are on the journey. All participate in one way or another.

Boundaries

A primary element of the systemic process is the concept of boundary. Boundaries are defined in several ways in the family-systems literature. First, Minuchin

(1974) writes that boundaries are the defining elements of subsystems within a family. One type of subsystem in the family may be the executive subsystem. It usually consists of the parents or adults in the family, but it may have other configurations. The boundaries of these subsystems, therefore, are the rules defining who participates, and how (Minuchin, 1974, p. 53). There is a variety of rules within families (as discussed later in this chapter), and only some of those pertain to the notion of boundary. Such boundary-defining rules guide family members. Rules may dictate in which rooms of the house one is welcome and where access is limited. There may be boundary rules about which topics can be discussed and who is allowed to interrupt another's conversation.

Another way to define boundary is more concrete and visual. Some boundaries are physical. For example, there are often property lines between one's lot and the neighbor's. Inside homes there are physical boundaries between private rooms, private drawers, and toothbrushes. In addition, there are many subtle physical boundaries in family systems. There may be strict boundary lines at the dinner table or for favorite chairs in front of the television set. At the more individual level, scientists have long noted the well-defined boundaries of personal space shown in greetings, farewells, and expressions of intimacy or anger.

In addition to these rules and physical elements of boundaries, other researchers indicate that the primary distinguishing element of a family boundary is that it tells us who belongs in the family and who does not (cf. Becvar & Becvar, 1982). The boundary specifies what information can come in and what cannot. Usually, it is easy to tell who family members are—that is, where the family ends and the public world begins. Family members also, for the most part, know who can leave and when, how long they can stay away, and what needs to be done upon return.

Another aspect of boundary is the idea of *emotional boundaries*, which are used to control how "close" we want other people to be to us emotionally. The bulk of the people we know in our lives are not family members. With most of these individuals we have superficial relationships, with some, close relationships, and with a few, intimate relationships. We grade these relationships with a great deal of ease and know the differences between the close and distant so naturally that we manage them almost unconsciously.

Boundaries in families are dynamic and nonstatic. Some are very changeable, and others are fairly rigid. They change at different times, change at different rates, and sometimes vary drastically depending on contextual elements. For example, there may be strict boundary rules about entering the parents' (executive subsystem) bedroom. On the other hand, there can be great variability in how late a child can stay out, depending on the age and responsibility of the child. Boundaries also change as a result of changing states within the family. Imagine the family that has just lost a grandparent. In some families, at times of loss and grief, the general family boundaries may be more *impermeable*. This means that fewer people and less information would be allowed in or out.

The variable of openness refers to the permeability of family boundaries, or how "open" the system is to inputs and outputs from the environment. The family system is an open system, influencing and influenced by its environment.

Boundary density.   Recently, researchers have attempted to expand the idea of boundaries in families by suggesting that boundaries have identifiable characteristics that help us understand how families process information and interact with the surrounding environment. Boss (1988) suggests that marital relationships have boundary *density*. This term is used to define a network of family connections. In understanding crisis situations, one important aspect of the process is the idea of social support. Social support has to do with the connections we make with people in times of stress. These people provide friendship, assistance, caring, and relief. Often the informal (familial) social-support connections, rather than formal ones (such as community agencies) are critical in recovering from a traumatic event.

Within that context, imagine that husband, wife, and children are connected to an "outside" world with both informal and formal social-support connections. Boundary density is a measure of the membership overlap between two or more family members (Kazak & Marvin, 1984), suggesting that the level of boundary density within a family has an impact on how the family approaches the problems of severe crisis. Kazak and Marvin interviewed families who had a child with spina bifida, a birth defect in which the spinal cord is formed incorrectly during the prenatal period. The frequent result is lower-body paralysis in the child. Most spina bifida children use braces and/or crutches for mobility. Much of the time they also require special bladder and bowel care. Both of these problems result in major child-care responsibilities for the parents. Kazak and Marvin showed that the spina bifida families had significantly more stress than similar families without a handicapped child. Importantly, they also found that these families in times of high stress had very high levels of boundary density. The family obtained support from "many of the same members of a small, highly interconnected, family dominated network " (Kazak & Marvin, 1984, p. 75). It would appear that the stress of having the handicapped child pushed the family into more of a closed family system. The density was high, which precluded family members from seeking different connections outside the family. If they did seek connections outside family boundaries, both husband and wife were likely to have the same social-support associations. In summary, stress and crisis seem to have the effect of increasing boundary density because family members focus their social-support network down to fewer individuals. More work needs to be done in this area to examine other factors that may contribute to the creation of denser family systems with more closed boundaries.

Boundary definition. Researchers have been interested in the concept of how boundaries within families are established and maintained (Aldous, 1978). Simply stated, this idea involves the level of confusion in a family about who is in and who is out of the family system (Boss, 1988). Boss uses the term *ambiguity* to delineate this concept; it may be easier to see this idea by thinking about boundary definition as having a range of possibilities varying from clarity to ambiguity. In other words, the larger idea is how boundaries are established and maintained and, finally, how well defined the boundary is at any given point.

According to Boss (1988) several situations that families experience can create more boundary ambiguity. The most boundary clarity occurs when the target family member is obviously physically and psychologi-

cally present. In other words, the person is regularly to be found within the family and has an emotional investment. Similarly, there is also a high decree of clarity when a family member is clearly *out* of the family. For example, it is more adaptive to have the family member either there or not. Situations where others are not sure about the status of a family member create disequilibrium in the system. For example, imagine a family taking care of an aged parent who has Alzheimer's disease. In this case, one would expect more system disruption because the membership of one person is unclear. He or she may be physically present but is psychologically absent.

Equifinality

Simply put, equifinality means that "many beginnings can lead to the same outcome" (Bavelas & Segal, 1982, p. 103). This idea is clearly one that assists us in understanding how the family is different when viewed from an indeterministic perspective. When one considers any *final* event (any outcome or result), that event could have been the result of many *causes*, or determinants. In Level I theorizing and thinking about the family processes, attention is paid to identifying specific causal determinants of a final event (like bed-wetting, divorce, mental illness, or alcoholism). In second-order thinking and theorizing, one would realize the nature of the interchangeability of "causes." In fact, it may be that in family systems there are many "true" explanations of a given circumstance (Burr, Day, & Bahr, 1993). The opposite term for equifinality could be coined as "specific-finality." Specific-finality is the goal of deterministic, first-order thinking. Those who seek specific-finality causes for events assume that by knowing the causal ordering and sequences of behavior, one can induce general principles of counseling and intervention that will apply to the next case or incident that comes along. Family scientists who focus on equifinality do not pay as much attention to the specific causes of a final event. Instead, when Level II and Level III thinking is used, one assumes the final event as a given and explores ways of interrupting the patterns of behavior. For example, it may be less important to discover why people are getting a divorce and more important to focus on what that means to them and how they muster resources, make decisions, and define the results. Okun and Rappaport (1980) give an excellent example of how thinking in terms of equifinality can redirect intervention and research. In their book *Working with Families*, they give the example of a family that is scapegoating. *Scapegoating* means that the negative interaction in a family is directed toward one person, who is somehow chosen to be the "lightning rod" for the pain a family is feeling. The anger and hostility between parents, for example, is acted out as hostility toward a wayward child. When scapegoating is occurring, family members blame the wayward child for the pain of the family and even for the crisis through which the family is going. Therefore, in order to help a family that is scapegoating, it is not necessary to understand or even recount how that process began, whose fault it was, or why it started. Instead, the skillful therapist simply recognizes the family pattern from current interactions.

Likewise, one needs to consider the notion that a single event can "cause" a host of results. This aspect of the equifinality principle is illustrated by Friedman (1985). Friedman lists several examples of how one starting event can have different outcomes. For example, researchers have been puzzled for many years by the role of parental investment in adolescent achievement. The research in this area shows us a clear example of equifinality. In some cases, when parents become invested in their children's lives by giving them higher amounts of attention and resources, there are two clear results: overachievement and underachievement. In other words, there is no clear-cut result of the single strategy. The cause and the effect are seriously muddled. Likewise, an overly strict father can result in a son who is strict himself (when he is a father) or one who turns 180 degrees from his father and becomes very permissive, and there does not seem to be a sure way to tell which result will happen.

Another example comes to us from the alcohol-studies literature. In some cases, alcoholism is transmitted to one child in a family, yet another will become an adamant abstainer. There has also been a plethora of research about interpersonal relationships, which states that dependency can lead to two quite different outcomes: helplessness or overcontrolling attitudes.

The point of understanding the equifinality principle is, again, the difference between second and first levels of analysis. When one persists in understanding *why* a person is an alcoholic, Level I thinking is the focus. The researcher searches the labyrinth of possible causes and connections that lead to the target outcome. When considering Level II and Level III analysis, the focus is on the results and patterns that are known. We also make the assumption that even if one were to carefully track down the causal sequence of one or even several alcoholics, that information would not be particularly applicable to the next family we encounter that has an alcohol problem. Instead, the foreground must be the patterns of interaction that happen *once* a family is alcoholic and how to interrupt those patterns. When equifinality is our foreground, we tend to ask questions about *what* instead of *why*. The more appropriate questions may be "What is going on here?" and "What can be done to change it?" The background, or even unimportant, questions become "Why did that happen?"

Watzlawick, Weakland, and Fisch (1967) almost 30 years ago wrote that "the possible or hypothetical causes of behavior assume a secondary importance. . . . A rule of thumb can be stated in this connection: where the *why* of a piece of behavior remains obscure, the question of *what for* can still supply a valid answer" (p. 45).

Morphogenesis and Morphostasis

Morphogenesis and morphostasis describe how a system responds to processes of change (Becvar & Becvar, 1982; Burr, Day, & Bahr, 1993; Speer, 1970). As a system seeks stability (*homeostasis*), it must be able to change. Morphogenesis describes the family as changing (*morpho*) through growth, creativity, and innovation (*genesis*). The morpheme *genesis* simply means the creation of that which is new or different. Successful families, when faced with a new situation, must be innovative and creative and exhibit growth. Families learn new ways of solving problems, new strategies, and new approaches to that which they encounter. In fact, one of the things they are called regularly to examine is how they deal with the events of life with respect to family rules and patterns of behavior. Morphogenesis describes the idea that families can (and must) change their rules and rule sequences in response to such challenging situations.

For example, the same rules and rule sequences a young family uses with preschool children are usually not appropriate as that child enters elementary and eventually secondary school. The way daily problems are handled, the approaches to discipline, and the strategies used to direct household activities necessarily change as the family passes through the various stages of life. Some families try to remain rigid and unbending in their structure and approach to daily life, while others are chaotic and unpredictable. Morphostasis reflects the idea that there must be an element of stability in the family structure. In other words, too much change is also resisted. Somewhere in the balance, each family finds equilibrium. A plethora of research about this level of balance, or level of adaptability, has come forth in the last 15 years. At the forefront of this research is David Olson (see Chapter 9). Olson and his associates have been attempting to describe the blend of appropriate cohesion and adaptability for nearly two decades. In Chapter 9, the latest version of this important and exciting work can be found.

Critiques of Family-Systems Theory

As with any endeavor that attempts to explain the complex world in which we live, family-systems theory is not without its detractors and critics. Early in its formulation it was seen as a panacea and cure-all for the problems within families. Its nondeterministic foundation is appealing and attractive to many who work with families. However, as Searight and Merkle (1991) so aptly point out, it is unrealistic to think one explanation can explain the nature of the family interaction for all. Over the past decade, there has been a movement away from seeing the family-systems approach as the cure-all. There are some family problems for which behavioristic/positivistic approaches seem to work better. This is especially true when working with problems that do seem based in the individual. For example, when working with antisocial adolescents (Anderson, Goolishian, & Winderman, 1986), a strong and direct behavior cost-and-reward approach seems to be quite effective. Drug therapy for certain psychological disorders may be much more effective than family-systems analysis and intervention.

Another problem with systems theory, in general, is the difficulty of conducting convincing research. One clear problem is that most of what we think of as reliable and valid research on a social or familial problem requires that we use methods and scientific approaches that are essentially based in the deterministic/positivistic world. Most methods of science assume a causal model of some kind with attendant appropriate statistics and analysis, which suggest a linear, and time-sequenced, cause-and-effect world. When boundaries, patterns, and rules of behavior are central topics in the family-systems world, it is difficult, time consuming, and costly to measure or record what happens in families. Even at that, one is very limited in terms of generalizability. Only the most general of ideas and principles in this approach can be induced and abstracted out of case studies and other qualitative methods of research.

Family-systems theory and its attendant therapy interventions may also be seen more as philosophically and ethically divergent from the current emphasis on studying and understanding the individual (Searight & Merkle, 1991). It can be argued that the level of analysis in our society for most of what we do is the individual. Individuals make contracts, break laws, can be sued, and can sue. We have organized our society (in the United States) to reflect the idea that we ultimately hold the individual responsible for his or her actions and activities.

Family-systems theory informs us that reality is a social construction molded by culture. Family intervention, therefore, is also a construction of a reality by those who participate. It is less instrumental and more collaborative (Sprenkle & Piercy, 1992). And importantly, the family is seen as the final authority on this collaborative venture (Andersen, 1987). When we consider the feminist critique, however, another view, or perspective, emerges with regard to the family's goal-attainment possibilities. According to this view, it is the individual who must take the foreground and precedence over the collaborative construction of the family (Avis, 1986; Goldner, 1985; McGoldrick, Anderson, & Walsh, 1989). As Sprenkle and Piercy (1992) remind us, feminism has forced us to question whether the family with its inherent patriarchal/status quo orientation is the best solution for the individual. "Seen through the feminist lens, patriarchy and oppression are seen as morally wrong while feminism itself serves as a moral compass, pointing families in the direction of equality, freedom, and empowerment" (p. 405). Increasingly, family-systems theory is characterized as a construction that demotes the woman and institutionalizes oppressive familial power structures.

The challenge of the next ten years will be to find ways of describing that which goes on inside the "raft" as families float the river of life. It is clear that while the family is changing, it is remaining as the predominant way in which we live and bring children into the world. The specific invitation of the next decade will be to find ways of refining the indeterministic approach so that familial power inequity is addressed and corrected. Additionally, expansion and improvement of the qualitative methodologies will need to move at a more rapid and systematic pace. That also implies a responsibility of the professional social-science community to learn how to think in nonpositivistic ways.

Chapter Summary

Discussion Questions

1. Explain how understanding the concept of boundary helps us work with families more effectively.
2. Think of three ways a family interventionist could use the following ideas: equifinality, wholeness, and morphostasis.
3. What is meant by the idea that families live in an indeterministic world where cause-and-effect issues are less important considerations?
4. How would you characterize the difference between Level I thinking (and intervening) and Levels II and III?

Additional Resources

Broderick, C. B. (1994). *Understanding family process.* Newbury Park, CA: Sage.

Becvar, R. J. & Becvar, D. S. (1982). *Systems theory and family therapy.* Lanham, MD: University Press of America.

Minuchin, S. (1974). *Families and family therapy.* Cambridge, MA: Harvard University Press.

Imber-Black, E., Roberts, J., & Whitting, R. A. (1988). *Rituals in families and family therapy.* New York: Norton.

Napier, A., & Whitaker, C. (1978). *The family crucible.* New York: Harper & Row.

References

Aldous, J. (1978). *Family careers: Developmental change in families.* New York: Wiley.

Andersen, T. (1987). The reflecting team: Dialogue and meta-dialogue in clinical work. *Family Process, 28,* 415–429.

Anderson, H., Goolishian, H. A., & Winderman, L. (1986). Problem determined systems: Towards transformation in family therapy. *Journal of Strategic and Systemic Therapies, 5,* 1–13.

Avis, J. (1986). Feminist issues in family therapy. In F. P. Piercy & D. H. Sprenkle (Eds.). *Family therapy sourcebook.* New York: Guilford Press.

Bavelas, J. B., & Segal, L. (1982). Family system theory: Background and implications. *Journal of Communication, 32,* 99–107.

Becvar, R. J., & Becvar, D. S. (1982). *Systems theory and family therapy.* Lanham, MD: University Press of America.

Boss, P. (1988). *Family stress management.* Newbury Park, CA: Sage.

Bowen, M. (1978). *Family therapy in clinical practice.* New York: Aronson.

Broderick, C. B. (1994). *Understanding family process.* Newbury Park, CA: Sage.

Broderick, C., & Smith, J. (1979). The general systems approach to the family. In W. R. Burr, R. Hill, F. I. Nye, & L. Reiss. (1979). *Contemporary theories about the family.* New York: Free Press.

Burr, W. R., Day, R. D., & Bahr, K. S. (1993). *Family science.* Pacific Grove, CA: Brooks/Cole.

Carter, B., & McGoldrick, M. (Eds.). (1989). *The changing family life cycle.* Boston: Allyn & Bacon.

Dunst, C., Trivette, C., & Deal, A. (1988). *Enabling and empowering families.* Cambridge, MA: Brookline Books.

Friedman, E. H. (1985). *Generation to generation.* New York: Guilford Press.

Galvin, K., & Brommel, B. (1982). *Family communication: Cohesion and change.* Glenview, IL: Scott, Foresman.

Goldner, V. (1985). Feminism and family. *Family Process, 24,* 31–47.

Hoffman, L. (1985). Beyond power and control: Toward a Level II and Level III family systems therapy. *Family Systems Medicine, 3,* 381–396.

Imber-Black, E., Roberts, J., & Whitting, R. A. (1988). *Rituals in families and family therapy.* New York: Norton.

Kazak, A. E., & Marvin, R. S. (1984). Differences, difficulties and adaptation: Stress and social networks in families with a handicapped child. *Family Relations, 33,* 67–78.

Kerr, M. E., & Bowen, M. (1988). *Family evaluation.* New York: Norton.

Kitson, G. (1992). *Portrait of divorce.* New York: Guilford Press.

McGoldrick, M., Anderson, C., & Walsh, F. (Eds.). (1989). *Women in families: A framework for family therapy.* San Francisco, CA: Jossey-Bass.

Minuchin, S. 1974. *Families and family therapy.* Cambridge, MA: Harvard University Press.

Napier, A., & Whitaker, C. (1978). *The family crucible.* New York: Harper & Row.

Nichols, M. (1984). *Family therapy: Concepts and methods.* New York: Gardner.

Okun, B., & Rappaport, L. J. (1980). *Working with families.* Belmont, CA: Wadsworth.

Satir, V. (1972). *Peoplemaking.* Palo Alto, CA: Science and Behavior Books.

Searight, H. R., & Merkle, W. T. (1991). Systems theory and its discontents: Clinical and ethical issues. *American Journal of Family Therapy, 19*(1), 19–31.

Simon, G. M. (1992). Having a Level II and Level III mind while doing Level I therapy. *Journal of Marital and Family Therapy, 18*(4), 377–387.

Speer, D. C. (1970). Family systems: Morphostasis and morphogenesis, or is homeostasis enough? *Family Process, 9,* 249–256.

Sprenkle, D. H., & Piercy, F. P. (1992). A family therapy informed view of the current state of the family in the United States. *Family Relations, 41*(4), 404–408.

Watzlawick, P., Weakland, J., & Fisch, R. (1967). *Change.* New York: Norton.

A Functional Analysis of Family Behavior

D. Eugene Mead
Brigham Young University

The application of modern behavioral theory to the study of family behavior holds great promise for family scientists. It is the purpose of this chapter to show the relationship of some behavioral laws and principles to family behavior. In addition, we will examine some of the methods of behavioral analysis and see how they can be used to study the family.

A functional analysis of family behavior is centered on the acts of members within the context of an environment known as the family. Family behaviors are the acts of individual members. These acts are to be understood as a function of the family environment, as opposed to acts originating inside the members. The most important aspect of a family environment is other family members.

The behavior-theory point of view suggests that much of our behavior was shaped in us as a result of interaction with our family of origin and continues with us throughout our life. Family members' behavior is largely responsible for shaping our language, our manners, our values, and our morals. The shaping of children's cultural history may be as important an inheritance as their genetic inheritance. The processes by which they gain their initial world outlook is a function of their interaction in their family.

According to this theory, the goal of the family scientist is to understand and predict family behavior. Once the family scientist can reliably predict family behavior, the phenomena may be well enough understood that the independent variables can be altered to bring about changes. For example, a family scientist may observe that on specific occasions one family member

does things that favor other members, puts the needs of others ahead of his or her own needs, and generally benefits others. In addition, the family scientist notes that in response to these altruistic acts, other family members respond by performing special and positive consequences. Over time, with frequent observations of this pattern, the family scientist can predict when these acts will occur and what events will typically follow. Then, if it is important, the family scientist can recommend changes in the frequency with which other family members provide special and positive consequences. If the predictions were correct, changes in family members' responses will alter the amount of altruistic behavior exchanged between family members. When family science can reliably produce changes in important family behaviors, the science of family behavior can be translated into a technology of change for use by practitioners such as family life educators and family therapists.

Functional Analysis

One way to gain an understanding of family behavior is to undertake a functional analysis. A functional analysis is concerned with discovering the consistent relationships between acts and the environment. If we are concerned about the development of altruism in family members, for example, we start by carefully defining the acts that we classify as altruistic behavior. Once defined, the altruistic acts are put into a code book, and observers are trained to observe whether an altruistic act occurred or did not occur within a specified unit of time (Baer, 1986). However, altruistic acts cannot be studied in isolation. They have a characteristic impact on the environment, which in this case consists of other family members. If the family members respond to the altruistic acts in such a way that their occurrence increases, we say that there is a functional relationship between the altruistic acts of one family member and the responses of others. Therefore, in a functional analysis of family behavior we must also define and codify the responses that family members make to altruistic acts and observe their occurrence or absence following the altruistic acts. The bidirectionality of family members' effects upon one another is an important characteristic of family behavior (Gewirtz & Pelaez-Nogueras, 1992).

Another word frequently used to indicate the correlated relationship between the act and the changes in the environment is *contingent*. The functional relationship between acts and the environmental contingencies that follow those acts has been extensively studied by behavioral analysts. The behavioral laws and principles that behavior analysts have found through experimentation become behavioral theory by the processes of induction. Modern behavioral theory, as set out by Skinner and others, is based upon Baconian induction (Chiesa, 1992; Delprato & Midgley, 1992; Hineline, 1992; Moxley, 1992; Schlinger, 1992; Skinner, 1953, 1969, 1989). Following extensive research, generalizations about the nature of behavior have been added until recently the concept of selection by consequences was put forward (Skinner, 1981). The very general principle of selection by consequences ties behavioral theory with the natural sciences by showing the role of selection at the phylogenetic (development of the species), ontogenetic (individual development), and cultural levels.

Principles of Reinforcement

When an act, such as an act of altruism in our example above, is followed by contingent changes in the environment that lead to an increase in the frequency of the dependent variable, in this case an increase in altruistic acts, behavioral theorists describe this functional relationship as *reinforcement*. We say that the probability of the behavior occurring was strengthened, or reinforced.

On the other hand, if family members ignore the altruistic acts of other family members, the altruistic behavior fades and is eventually "put out" or *extinguished*. If the altruistic act of family member A is aversive to family member B, B may *punish* A when A performs the act. Punishment may temporarily suppress the behavior, but if it has a history of reinforcement, only extinction will eliminate it (Skinner, 1953).

Figure 7.1 shows the interaction between giving a positive (and/or negative) response and taking one away. It is common for the term *negative reinforcement* to be misused. Punishment, as defined above, is the presentation of an aversive (as perceived by the receiver) stimulus, so that the target behavior disappears. Thus, family member A makes the situation uncomfortable following a displeasing event (spanking is the oft-cited example), and the target behavior decreases over time. With negative reinforcement, an aversive stimulus is presented, and when the target behavior improves, the negative stimulus is removed. For example, the child stays in her room until she changes her attitude. The difference between the two is subtle but important. In the first example, the parent is the locus of change and is effecting a response through an act of power. In the latter, the situation promotes change that must occur within the child. (For further examples of parent/child interaction, see Chapter 13.)

An act of altruism can be performed in a myriad of ways. Therefore, any single given act of altruism is a member of the class of acts that we call altruistic. When we undertake a functional analysis of altruism in the family, we are interested in predicting that a member of the class of behaviors we call altruistic will occur in response to certain events in the family. When an altruistic act is performed and reinforced in the context of the needs of other family members, the behaviors of the others that indicate "need" in that context become contingent with the altruistic act. These antecedent events also form a class of events that, if frequently present when the altruistic act is reinforced, serve to

	Give	Take Away
+	Positive reinforcement	Negative reinforcement
−	Punishment	Extinction

FIGURE 7.1   The elements of reinforcement

increase the probability that an altruistic act will occur in that context. The technical term in behavioral theory for antecedent events that increase the probability of an act is a *discriminative stimulus* (Skinner, 1953).

A functional analysis includes a thorough description of three terms: (1) the discriminative stimulus, (2) the act, and (3) the changes in the environment that serve to reinforce the act. These three terms form the "three term contingencies" of reinforcement (Glenn, Ellis, & Greenspoon, 1992; Skinner, 1953). The three terms *discriminative stimulus*, *act*, and *reinforcing changes* are connected by two sets of contingencies: first, the contingency between the act and the reinforcing consequences that follow and second, the contingencies between the antecedent discriminative stimulus and the act.

The environmental changes that follow an act, and are therefore contingent upon it, can vary in a number of ways. Reinforcement can follow each act, and when it does, it is known as continuous reinforcement. Reinforcement can also come on some schedule such as every so many minutes, an interval schedule, or after every so many repetitions of the act, a ratio schedule. In families where reinforcement is mediated by other family members, reinforcement is most often delivered on a random intermittent schedule. For example, a child asks for a drink, the parent is not preoccupied with something else, so the drink is delivered immediately. At other times the parent is busy, and the child must ask for the drink several times. Then a little later the child asks for a drink, and the drink is delivered after only two askings, and so on. That is a random intermittent schedule for the act of "asking for a drink" and the reinforcement of receiving a drink.

Each set of contingencies can vary in several ways. The first set can vary according to the frequency of changes that follow an act; the frequency can be every time the act occurs (continuously) or periodically (scheduled). Continuous reinforcement occurs when environmental changes follow every act. Scheduled reinforcement may come on some schedule. For example, if the parent, in the example above gives the child a drink only in the kitchen and the dining area, the kitchen and dining area become discriminative stimuli

for asking for drinks because they are contingent upon "asking for a drink" and the reinforcement of receiving a drink. If these are the only two rooms where drinks are ever delivered, the act of asking for a drink is tightly controlled. On the other hand, if drinks are occasionally delivered in the living room and bedroom, the act of asking for a drink is generalized. The more an act is generalized, the greater the probability of it showing up in other environmental settings.

The second set of contingencies also can vary, by environmental settings. If family scientists can describe the environmental changes that, when they are made contingent on that act, increase or decrease the frequency, amplitude, or duration of the act, the family scientists can predict the occurrence of the act. Family scientists' ability to predict the act will be improved if they can also accurately describe the context—that is, the antecedent events or discriminative stimuli—that have been contingent upon the act when reinforced. Family scientists can help families change behavior patterns by helping them manipulate the two sets of independent variables, the discriminative stimuli and the reinforcing changes in the environment.

A functional analysis of behavior (for Level I types of behavior) can be useful because it enables us to analyze the relationship between the independent variables to be manipulated, to determine their relationship to the dependent variable. Family scientists who use this approach want to know the nature of the functional relationship between the family behaviors under study. They seek to determine if changing the independent variables leads to systematic changes in the rate, amplitude, latency, duration, or interresponse time of the dependent variable. The method has meet with remarkable success over the past 60 years. A representative sampling of studies that have demonstrated the control described above using behavioral analysis includes these areas of interest to family scientists: child development (Gewirtz & Pelaez-Nogueras, 1992; Schlinger, 1992), community (Greenwood et al., 1992), education (Bijou, 1970; Johnson, & Layng, 1992), and family therapy with young children (Patterson, Reid, Jones, & Conger, 1975), with adolescents (Alexander & Parsons, 1982), and with couples (Jacobson & Addis, 1993).

Selection and Behavior

Use of the methods of behavioral analysis brings the study of family behavior closer to the natural sciences. Just as natural selection has been shown to be responsible for the evolution of species, so too does selection play a role in the evolution of behavior. Another way to think about an act is in terms of evolutionary selection (Alessi, 1992; Glenn et al., 1992; Hayes & Hayes, 1992; Skinner, 1989). An act can be considered as a single representative of a population of acts, just as an individual can be considered as a single representative of a species. Therefore, an altruistic act is a single representative of the class of acts described as altruistic. The survival of an act is a function of its effect upon the environment. If it has no effect upon the environment, it will not survive. As a result, the environment selects some acts through the principle of reinforcement and causes others to vanish due to the principle of extinction. A young child's altruistic act that goes unnoticed by the environment will not survive in the child's repertoire.

As an example of how this type of functional interaction works, consider how people choose partners for dating and eventual mating. In most cases, individuals feel that they have positive attributes that others may find attractive. They may, for example, think they are fun-loving, sexy, funny, or charming. When we seek out others for relationships (so this theory would postulate), we avoid those people whom we see as unrewarding and enjoy being around those who find us rewarding. They enjoy our sense of humor, we enjoy their charming ways. In this way, a series of interactions becomes the basis of the future relationship. (Note that this type of behavior, referred to in Chapter 6 as Level I behavior, is an essential element of daily life).

Recently, behavioral analysts have undertaken the study of more and more complex forms of behavior such as the study of the production of untaught cognitive processes (Sidman, 1986), cooperative play (Hart, Reynolds, Baer, Browky, & Harris, 1968), racial integration (Hauserman, Walen, & Behling, 1973), and teaching children to share and praise (Rogers-Warren & Baer, 1976). Complex responses are a function of complex environments. As we have seen, altruistic acts require an environment that consists of other people.

Not only must the environment consist of other people, but the other people must be disposed to respond to the child's act in a way that increases the probability of similar acts in the future. If a child performs an altruistic act in the physical environment devoid of other people, the physical environment is not likely to be changed in a way that will strengthen or reinforce the act. The probability of the act occurring again in an environment without people is diminished. If this process is repeated, the act will not survive but will be extinguished.

The development of altruistic acts depends upon variability in the child's behavior. Just as variations in species are necessary for nature to select some members of the species for survival, so too is variation in behavior necessary for some behaviors to survive. The child's family environment, over time, selects acts that more and more come to resemble altruistic acts. The process by which a complex behavior is developed over time is known as *shaping*, or *successive approximation* (Skinner, 1953).

Shaping of a complex behavior pattern need not be a conscious process on the part of other family members; in fact, most of the time it is not. This is why complex patterns, such as altruism, show so much variation, even among members of a family. As a result of the family environment's differential patterns of reinforcement, any given complex pattern of acts may be observed to range from not occurring at all in some family members to occurring at very high rates in others.

The Individual Family Member as a Carrier of Histories

It is clear from the discussion above that each family member becomes a unique individual due in part to his or her unique history of reinforcement. In fact, we are all the carriers of three unique histories. First, we each carry our own unique history of the human species embedded in our genes. This is our phylogeny, or phylogenetic history. The second unique history we carry around is our history of reinforcement. Our reinforcement history is part of our ontogeny, our individual developmental history. The third history we carry is a function of the second but is unique to humans, and that is our cultural history. Each of us inherits these histories through our family. Our phylogenetic history is inherited as a code in our DNA structure, which is then decoded in our genes. Our ontogenetic, or personal, history is a function of our interaction with our environment, which for most infants and children is their family environment. We "decode" our ontogenetic behavior in response to the discriminative stimuli in our current environment on the basis of our past history with similar environments. Our early cultural history is also an inheritance from our families, from whom we receive our language and our general world view. Our cultural inheritance is largely a verbal inheritance and can be best understood by a careful functional analysis of verbal behavior and how it creates "virtual" realities, or verbal environments, for family members (Guerin, 1992).

Phylogenetic History

Our phylogenetic history has prepared us to respond to environments that are past. That is, only those of our ancestors who adapted to environmental conditions in their time survived long enough to pass on their genes to us. Therefore, part of our adaptive system prepares us to respond to some aspects of our environment in fixed ways. For example, we move away from things that are hot, and the pupil of the eye contracts when a stimulus such as a bright light is suddenly shown into it. These reflexive actions can be modified slightly by a process of conditioning. We begin by pairing the unconditioned response of pupillary contraction in response to the stimulus of a bright light with another stimulus that does not have the same effect. After several pairings the secondary stimulus will be accompanied by contraction of the pupil. This form of conditioning is known as *respondent* conditioning (Skinner, 1938, 1953). Because of the fixed nature of the reflexes, however, this form of learning is fairly limited.

Respondent conditioning plays one of its most important functions in the conditioning of the responses we label fear, panic, and anxiety. When an individual is placed in a traumatic situation, the unconditioned startle, or "fight-or-flight," responses occur. When startled, we have changes in smooth muscles and glands. These reflexive changes may be conditioned to

the stimuli that were contingent on the traumatic event. Presentation of stimuli of this same class may be followed by the conditioned changes in smooth muscles and glands, and we refer to these bodily states as fear, panic, or anxiety. Family therapists are familiar with this type of response in their work with children who have been abused and with adults who have developed debilitating phobias such as agoraphobia—that is, fear of a panic attack in public places. Behavioral family therapists generally treat clinical cases of these conditions by using some form of systematic desensitization.

Ontogenetic History

Our phylogenetic history has prepared us for far more rapid adaptation to our environment than can be accomplished with respondent conditioning. The contingency learning described earlier allows each family member to respond to the environmental changes that occur in his or her lifetime—that is, over the course of his or her ontogenetic development. Contingency learning is also know as *operant conditioning* (Skinner, 1953).

Skinner (1938) defines operant behavior as what an organism is doing to the environment: "that part of the functioning of an organism which is engaged in acting upon . . . the outside world" (p. 6). The emphasis is clearly on the act and not the organism (Lee, 1992). Operant conditioning has been shown to be consistent across species and has been thoroughly demonstrated with human infants and children (Gewirtz & Pelaez-Nogueras, 1992; Hayes & Hayes, 1992).

However, the process of operant conditioning has not always held with adult humans (Hayes & Hayes, 1992). There are several possible reasons for these results. First, prior learning often makes later conditioning difficult, sometimes requiring extensive unlearning before the desired learning can take place. The process of unlearning and relearning is the domain of family therapists (Alexander & Parsons, 1982; Jacobson & Addis, 1993; Patterson et al., 1975) and other applied-behavior analysts (Baer, 1986; Baer, Wolf, & Risley, 1968; Greenwood et al., 1992).

Another important reason that direct operant conditioning sometimes appears not to work with adults is to be found in the role of instructions, or verbal rules.

For example, in research where reinforcement is being made available on a fixed interval, say, every six seconds, adolescents and adults give themselves verbal rules to count. When they count or keep track of time, the usual results of operant conditioning appear to be disrupted. When their ability to count is taken away by other instructions, however, the expected results are found (Hayes & Hayes, 1992). Counting and other verbal behaviors are the result of our third history, human cultures.

Cultural History

Experiences with the environment that have survival value can be learned by individuals through the processes of respondent and operant conditioning. Unfortunately, these experiences die with the individual; they cannot be passed on, "Lamarckian style," by means of the chromosomes and genes to later generations (Alessi, 1992). However, the evolutionary development that led to vocalization and language allows human experience to be passed on to later generations. The collection of human experience peculiar to a certain group is that group's culture. Each individual's first cultural inheritance is a function of his or her interaction with family members. Whether a child learns to speak Chinese, French, or English depends upon the verbal community of his or her parents. Embedded in language is much of that community's cultural history. In addition to teaching their children language, parents and other family members teach them "how to live." How to live is generally passed on by verbal instructions and rules. The contingencies that control verbal behavior are not different from the contingencies that control other forms of behavior, but they are much more subtle because verbal behavior, like much of family behavior, relies upon the mediation of other people (Skinner, 1953, 1957).

The Family as a Verbal Community

The family is a verbal community with its own family culture. The family is a part of a larger verbal community and that group's culture. For the children in the family, however, the larger community is represented to them by the verbal behavior of family members. In the family much of each family member's behavior is under the verbal control of others.

Verbal Behavior

Verbal behavior is any behavior in which reinforcement is dependent upon the mediation of others (Skinner, 1957). This definition is much broader than the usual definition of verbal behavior, which is generally limited to oral or written language and separated from "nonverbal" behavior such as hand signals, facial expressions, and so on. Verbal behavior as used by behavioral analysts and as used here includes both language and the so-called nonverbals. Verbal behavior is any behavior that signals another person to act or respond to the sender in some way. Therefore, it is not surprising that the family therapist Virginia Satir (1964) can say that in the family one "can never not communicate."

As stated above, verbal behavior is controlled by the same contingencies that control other forms of behavior. However, the relationships between the contingencies are far less conspicuous and require careful and special treatment.

We are concerned here primarily with the operant control of verbal behavior. Because space does not permit a full explanation of verbal behavior, we will limit our examination to that part of verbal behavior that is most directly related to how family members create the family verbal community. This community is embedded in the larger verbal community, but the infant or young child generally experiences very little of that larger community. The same is true for the child's learning of the culture. The child first learns the family culture, and he or she learns about the larger culture only through the verbal descriptions of family members.

Children come to "know" their culture in two ways: first by their direct experience and second, by being told about their culture, the world that is out there, by family members. A child learns to interact with the physical world through direct experience that is shaped by the principles of respondent and operant learning. This is knowledge about *how to* respond to a variety of environmental contingencies (Guerin, 1992). As more and more of our world is made by humans, this means responding to more and more complex environments (Skinner, 1953).

The second way children come to "know" their culture is *knowing that* such and such is whatever (Guerin, 1992). For example, the child is told *that* "Washington is the capital of the United States." This type of knowing is almost entirely verbal, and it is this part of the child's cultural heritage that is passed on by the family as verbal instructions and rules. Two types of verbal behavior involving *knowing that* are important in understanding how the family represents the family culture and the larger culture to the child. These two types of verbal behaviors are "tacts" and "intraverbals."

Tacts.   A tact is a verbal behavior, act, or operant that is strengthened by an object or event in the environment (Skinner, 1957). Verbal behavior that is used to report on direct experience with the world, including the world inside of one's skin, is tacting behavior (Skinner, 1957). A tact is a report about the environment. Tacts are, or should be, under the stimulus control of the environment. For example, a parent points to a ball and says to the child, "ball." The child is reinforced for calling a ball a ball and punished for calling a block a ball. This form of tight stimulus control is important in many verbal communities, especially the scientific community. However, it is the verbal community that structures and maintains the verbal behavior of calling a ball a ball, not the physical environment.

In some verbal communities less tight stimulus control is maintained over tacts. A family may not punish the child for saying "bally" instead of ball, and the child may continue with this behavior until punished by the larger verbal community. Verbal behavior of this type, sometimes called "baby talk," may not be any trouble within the family verbal community that originated it, but it sometimes can become troublesome. I was told of a preschool child who announced to his teacher on the first day that he needed to "tinkle." The teacher, not having been exposed to the child's family verbal community, told him to go ahead and play with the other children. He could "tinkle" with them if he wanted. He returned later holding his crotch and dancing about saying again that he needed "to go tinkle." At this point the teacher realized that "tinkle" was a tact for urinate and responded appropriately with directions to the toilet.

Intraverbals.   The second type of verbal behavior that is important for our understanding of how family verbal behavior is involved in constructing the family culture is intraverbal behavior. Verbal behavior that is under the stimulus control of other verbal behavior is called intraverbal behavior (Skinner, 1957). If someone says, "Salt and . . ." many English-speaking listeners will add "pepper" even when no other related stimuli are present in the environment. A functional analysis of intraverbal behavior suggests that prior history has prepared the listener for the response "pepper" but that the current stimulus control comes from the verbal community in the form of the speaker. Other forms of intraverbals include questions, counting, reproducing "facts" of history and science, and any other "facts" we acquire as intraverbal responses and to which we make intraverbal replies. Clearly, much of the family culture and the culture of the larger group received by the child will be received as intraverbal behavior from the other family members.

In addition to tacts and intraverbals, other forms of verbal behavior are described by behavioral analysts (see Oah & Dickinson, 1989; Skinner, 1957). However, these two types plus a description of rule-governed behavior will suffice for a discussion of the family as a verbal community.

Rule-Governed Behavior

Rule-governed behavior differs from contingency-based behavior inasmuch as the individual being directed by the rules may never have been exposed to the actual contingencies. Rules describe the contingencies and point up the reinforcing consequences (Skinner, 1953). For example, the instructions "If you turn your tennis racquet a quarter-turn forward and swing level with the ball, you'll keep more of your backhand shots in the court" describes the contingencies "turning the racquet" and "swinging level with the ball" and the consequences "more shots in the court." The act of listening to the coach give advice is under the control of the three term contingencies of control that are part of that setting. The reinforcement for taking the coach's advice is delayed until one actually practices on the court with racquet and ball. Taking advice is not controlled by what will happen but by the consequences that followed taking advice in the past.

Contingency-shaped behavior is far more effective than acts based upon advice. One reason is motivation. Rule-governed behavior is based upon a history of taking advice and finding the results reinforcing. As pointed out above, direct reinforcement is delayed in rule-governed behavior. Contingency-based learning, on the other hand, is reinforced directly as one acts.

In summary, family members gain knowledge of part of their group's cultural history by direct experience with the contingencies of the cultural environment. Much of that cultural environment is a human environment. In addition, families pass on much of the cultural history to other family members by the use of verbal behavior. Some of the verbal behavior that is used to share the cultural history is a tact. Tacts are verbal behavior used by a verbal community in conjunction with specific stimuli in the environment. The other form of verbal behavior that family members use to pass on the cultural history is an intraverbal. Intraverbals are verbal behaviors under the control of other verbal behavior.

The Family Verbal Community as a Socially Constructed Reality

Infants and children are introduced to their verbal community and its characteristic ways of living by those who serve as parents. In this way children inherit their culture from their parents, not in the genes as they inherit their genetic characteristics but through direct interaction in the family environment (Alessi, 1992). Survival of the species makes procreation the primary function of the family. Survival of the culture makes socialization of the children the family's second great function. How the family goes about constructing the child's world is of critical importance to the child, the family, the culture, and the family scientist.

The child's tacting behavior is maintained by generalized reinforcing consequences that are mediated by other family members (Guerin, 1992: Skinner, 1957). Some generalized reinforcers are approval, praise, encouragement, attention, affection, and submissiveness (Guerin, 1992; Skinner, 1953). The child's reporting about events in the family environment is strengthened

by family members' use of the generalized reinforcers. If the child says "dog" when the family dog enters the room, the child gets attention, praise, and affection. When the child reports that the stove is hot, and it is, more praise, attention, and affection follow. These verbal tacts are reinforced intermittently and in different ways, which makes the probability of the child making a tacting response high in the presence of the physical stimulus and an appropriate environment—that is, a family member or another person. In this way the child is prepared to respond later without any obvious consequences from family members (Guerin, 1992).

Intraverbals are under the control of the verbal behavior of others. As a result, the response may be shaped by the particular biases of the verbal community. The control of reinforcing consequences by other people, as in the family, may lead to distortion of the tacting process. For example, if the child is punished for saying "Daddy's drunk" even when its true, the information reported may become a "distorted tact" (Guerin, 1992; Skinner, 1957). For example, if the family instructs the child to report *that* "Daddy's tired," the child's report is no longer a tact under the control of the stimulus event, an inebriated father. The child's report is now an intraverbal under the control of the family's reinforcement or punishment. In this way families may create a "social reality" that is not consistent with events in the environment.

Of course, intraverbals need not be distorted tacts. Much of our knowledge of the world is based upon verbal reports from others. I may not have been at yesterday's basketball game, but if you ask me I can report that the score was 98-83 because I read it in the newspaper. Presumably, you or I could verify this information. Perhaps we could ask someone who was there, or we might see the score on the television news. Because the information is easily verified, it is less likely that the tact will be distorted. We tend to think of information that can be verified as "objective" information. As we have seen above, however, when the verbal community has a bias and when the information is not easily verified by others, the report may be distorted.

Information may become distorted when it is detached from the controlling stimuli. If the family culture does not maintain the necessity of validating the implied tacts or if, in fact, the family members reinforce inaccurate reporting (Guerin, 1992), family problem-solving processes may become ineffective, and trouble may follow. In this way, family myths can be shaped and maintained because family members control the intraverbal behavior of one another. Two other situations may prevail, according to Guerin (1992). Intraverbals may be reinforced as if they were remembered tacts. For example, if one family member states that an event occurred in a given way, others may agree, if for no other reason than to avoid an unpleasant disagreement. The third way verbal behavior can become detached from environmental controlling stimuli is for generalized reinforcing consequences to become too generalized and maintain tacting in completely nondiscriminating ways. An example of this later form of detachment might be the parent who gives direct or tacit approval to almost everything the child says. For example, when a child says, "I can't go to school today, I'm sick" and the parent acquiesces without checking to see if the child's verbal behavior is a tact to an actual illness or if it is an intraverbal aimed at avoiding some unpleasant consequences that may follow going to school, the parent is nondiscriminatively reinforcing the child's detached tacting behavior.

One form of trouble that may follow when family verbal behavior becomes detached from environmental control is that the usual checks and balances against behavioral excesses may not be available as countercontrols. When behavior has become detached from stimulus control, the probability of abuse, incest, and other forms of chaotic behavior may increase. This is an area in need of further empirical study.

From the point of view of an outside observer, the detached report may appear irrational. From the point of view of the family members making the report, however, it is rational inasmuch as it is a function of the verbal variables controlling their verbal behavior. For the family member making the report there are two competing sets of contingencies. The competing contingencies for reporting are (1) the individual's past history of reinforcement for reporting all historical and current stimuli accurately ver-

sus (2) the currently stronger family contingencies for reporting inaccurately (Guerin, 1992).

The issue, for the family scientist, may not be to what extent is the information supplied by family members is rational or irrational, true or not true. The issue might better be whether family members are reporting on tacts or reporting intraverbals based on remembered tacts or imagined tacts. To answer such questions, the family scientist may need to undertake a functional analysis to determine the extent to which tacts or intraverbals are controlling family members verbal behavior related to any important issue.

The Benefits of Applying Functional Analysis to Family Behavior

The potential for a family science based upon a functional analysis of family behavior is great. A functional analysis of family behavior can start with confidence "from a foundation of well-established principles derived from a rigorous program of basic research. This is the advantage that behavior analysis brings to the task of understanding that part of human behavior that has not yet been directly subjected to an experimental analysis" (Schlinger, 1992, p. 1400).

What are the "well-established principles" of functional analysis? The functional analytic approach demands careful stimulus control. The family scientist using this approach must go to great lengths to see that the descriptions of the family behavior under investigation are carefully crafted tacts that are matched to the issues and complaints of the family members (Baer, 1986). Then these tacts are written into intraverbal instructions or rules in the form of codes that are to be followed by observers. The "objectivity" of the observers is checked by the use of multiple observers, whose reliability is frequently checked against the written codes. Then the predictions of the family scientist are checked by actual manipulation of the assumed independent variables while maintaining the tightly controlled observations. The results of such studies, focused on variables of interest to family scientists, should yield new insights into the functional contingencies of family behavior. As this information is verified, it can then be turned into a technology to help families better socialize their children to become effective contributing members of their larger community.

Chapter Summary

Discussion Questions

1. What is the nature of a *functional analysis* of family behavior?
2. In what way is an *operant* the basic unit of analysis in a functional analysis of family behavior?
3. How do the *three term contingencies of reinforcement* operate in family behavior?
4. What is the role of *shaping, or successive approximation,* in family behavior?
5. How does *extinction* affect family behavior?
6. Describe the application of functional analysis of family behavior in studying complex behaviors such as thinking and problem solving.
7. Contrast the theory presented in this chapter with the family-systems ideas presented in Chapter 6. What do you consider to be five of the most important differences?

Additional Resources

Jacobson, N. S., & Addis, M. E. (1993). Research on couples and couple therapy: What do we know? Where are we going? *Journal of Consulting and Clinical Psychology, 61,* 85–93.

Patterson, G. R., Reid, J. B., Jones, R. R., & Conger, R. E. (1975). *A social learning approach to family intervention: Vol. 1. Families with aggressive children.* Eugene, OR: Castalia.

Moxley, R. A. (1992). From mechanistic to functional behaviorism. *American Psychologist, 47,* 1300–1311.

References

Alessi, G. (1992). Models of proximate and ultimate causation in psychology. *American Psychologist, 47,* 1359–1370.

Alexander, J. A., & Parsons, B. V. (1982). *Functional family therapy.* Pacific Grove, CA: Brooks/Cole.

Baer, D. M. (1986). In application, frequency is not the only estimate of the probability of behavior units. In T. Thompson & M. D. Zeiler (Eds.), *Analysis and integration of behavioral units* (pp. 117–136). Hillsdale, NJ: Erlbaum.

Baer, D. M., Wolf, M. M., & Risley, T. R. (1968). Some current dimensions of applied behavior analysis. *Journal of Applied Behavior Analysis, 1,* 91–97.

Bijou, S. W. (1970). What psychology has to offer education—now. *Journal of Applied Behavior Analysis, 3,* 65–71.

Chiesa, M. (1992). Radical behaviorism and scientific frameworks: From mechanistic to relational accounts. *American Psychologist, 47,* 1287–1299.

Delprato, D. J., & Midgley, B. D. (1992). Some fundamentals of B. F. Skinner's behaviorism. *American Psychologist, 47,* 1507–1520.

Gewirtz, J. L., & Pelaez-Nogueras, M. (1992). B. F. Skinner's legacy to human infant behavior and development. *American Psychologist, 47,* 1411–1422.

Glenn, S. S., Ellis, J., & Greenspoon, J. (1992). On the revolutionary nature of the operant as a unit of behavioral selection. *American Psychologist, 47,* 1329–1336.

Greenwood, C. R., Carta, J. J., Hart, B., Kamps, D., Terry, B., Arreaga-Mayer, C., Atwater, J., Walker, D., Risley, T., & Delquadri, J. C. (1992). Out of the laboratory and into the community: 26 years of applied behavior analysis at the Juniper Gardens Children's Project. *American Psychologist, 47,* 1464–1474.

Guerin, B. (1992). Behavior analysis and the social construction of knowledge. *American Psychologist, 47,* 1423–1432.

Hart, B. M., Reynolds, N. J., Baer, D. M., Brawley, E. R., & Harris, F. R. (1968). Effect of contingent and non-contingent social reinforcement on the cooperative play of a preschool child. *Journal of Applied Behavior Analysis, 1,* 73–76.

Hauserman, N., Walen, S. R., & Behling, M. (1973). Reinforced racial integration in the first grade: A study in generalization. *Journal of Applied Behavior Analysis, 6,* 193–200.

Hayes, S. C., & Hayes, L. J. (1992). Verbal relations and the evolution of behavior. *American Psychologist, 47,* 1383–1395.

Hineline, P. N. (1992). A self-interpretive behavior analysis. *American Psychologist, 47,* 1274–1287.

Jacobson, N. S., & Addis, M. E. (1993). Research on couples and couple therapy: What do we know? Where are we going? *Journal of Consulting and Clinical Psychology, 61,* 85–93.

Johnson, K. R., & Layng, T. V. J. (1992). Breaking the structuralist barrier: Literacy and numeracy with fluency. *American Psychologist, 47,* 1475–1490.

Lee, V. L. (1992). Transdermal interpretation of the subject matter of behavior analysis. *American Psychologist, 47,* 1337–1343.

Moxley, R. A. (1992). From mechanistic to functional behaviorism. *American Psychologist, 47,* 1300–1311.

Oah, S., & Dickinson, A. M. (1989). A review of empirical studies of verbal behavior. *The Analysis of Verbal Behavior, 7,* 53–68.

Patterson, G. R., Reid, J. B., Jones, R. R., & Conger, R. E. (1975). *A social learning approach to family intervention: Vol. 1. Families with aggressive children.* Eugene, OR: Castalia.

Rogers-Warren, A., & Baer, D. M. (1976). Correspondence between saying and doing: Teaching children to share and praise. *Journal of Applied Behavior Analysis, 9,* 335–354.

Satir, V. (1964). *Conjoint family therapy.* Palo Alto, CA: Science and Behavior Books.

Schlinger, H. D., Jr. (1992). Theory in behavior analysis: An application to child development. *American Psychologist, 47,* 1396–1410.

Sidman, M. (1986). Functional analysis of emergent verbal classes. In T. Thompson & M. D. Zeiler (Eds.), *Analysis and integration of behavioral units* (pp. 213–245). Hillsdale, NJ: Erlbaum.

Skinner, B. F. (1938). *The behavior of organisms: An experimental analysis.* Englewood Cliffs, NJ: Prentice-Hall.

Skinner, B. F. (1953). *Science and human behavior.* New York: Free Press.

Skinner, B. F. (1957). *Verbal behavior.* New York: Appleton-Century-Crofts.

Skinner, B. F. (1969). *Contingencies of reinforcement: A theoretical analysis.* New York: Appleton-Century-Crofts.

Skinner, B. F. (1981). Selection by consequences. *Science, 213,* 501–504.

Skinner, B. F. (1989). *Recent issues in the analysis of behavior.* Columbus, OH: Merrill.

The Science of Family Science

Karen Price Carver / Jay D. Teachman
Washington State University

What precisely do we mean by *science*? Many of us have the perception that science has something to do with complicated equipment, white lab coats, and perhaps mice in mazes. While these things are often associated with the doing of science, they are not science per se. Sometimes we associate science with a body of knowledge, like medicine, physics, chemistry, or engineering. On other occasions we may identify it with the creation of material objects, like computers, instrumentation, or robotics. However, none of these associations specify exactly what science is. More correctly expressed, science is the *scientific method*, a process. The scientific method is a way of asking questions and then going about the task of answering them. It is a system, or method, of knowing, a means of creating knowledge.

Your parents may tell you to wait until you are older before you marry. We generally listen to our parents because they are older and wiser, and hence, we often internalize such advice. We eventually come to think about this admonition as common sense, but are we or our parents also using the scientific method? In a sense, yes. Your parents may have observed that younger individuals sometimes come to change their opinions. Because divorce can be costly in many ways, they may have deduced that waiting to marry is a wise choice given the costs of divorce. The point to is that while commonsense knowledge and knowledge derived more formally are often the same, knowledge gained through the use of the scientific method is more systematic. The scientific method is very specific in its assumptions, specification of concepts, statements of hypotheses, and precision of observations.

More explicitly, someone using the scientific method specifies a set of concepts, states a hypothesis, and then collects data or makes observations related to the hypothesis. One then uses the observational information to either reject the hypothesis or not. For example, in order to use the scientific method to discover if marrying younger is associated with a greater risk of divorce (notice we did not say that marrying young "causes" divorce), one would observe whether individuals who married early were more or less likely to divorce. Through some statistical magic (to be discussed later), one would then be able to come to some conclusion about whether it's likely that marrying at older ages is beneficial in terms of deterring divorce.

Induction and Deduction

In the previous example, your parents may have come to their hypothesis in one of two ways, either deductively or inductively. If they used the deductive method, they would have derived the hypothesis from some theory. For example, your parents may subscribe to the notion that "when you get old, you become set in your ways." If one is young, therefore, one is probably less likely to be set in one's ways and more likely to vacillate in convictions and opinions. Then if one marries early, one will probably be more likely to change one's opinion and perhaps change one's mind about one's partner and hence, divorce. We began with a theory (albeit a less formal one) and then deduced a hypothesis from that theory. Explicitly, our theory stated that when you get old, you become set in your ways. Our hypothesis stated that an increase in age at marriage should be associated with a decrease in the probability of divorce. The greater the measure of one concept (age at marriage), the less likely the probability of observing another concept (divorce).

On the other hand, your parents could have used the inductive method to come to the same hypothesis. Perhaps they have some friends with whom they associate at cocktail parties. They go to these parties and talk to people who have had their own children go on to marry. Perhaps they have noticed that the parents of the children who married at younger ages are now dealing with the unpleasant tasks involved with divorce. If they noticed that many more younger marriers divorced than did older marriers, they may have come to the conclusion that if one values 50th anniversaries, one should wait until older ages to marry. In this scenario, your parents reasoned from particular cases to a more general theory. The particular cases are those individuals your parents observed who divorced, and the more general theory would be the hypothesis they derived about an increase in age being associated with a decrease in the probability of divorce. Both methods produced the same hypothesis; however, the routes by which it was obtained were distinctly different.

Causation and Association

Up until this point, we have avoided using words that intimate causation. Our hypotheses were crafted so as to suggest that an increase in one concept is *associated* with a decrease in another concept. On the other hand, one could correctly argue that it is really causation in which we are most interested. However, in order to "prove" something, we take on a monumental task. It might be argued that social scientists are never really able to "prove" anything. They can point to evidence that supports a hypothesis or negates a hypothesis; however, they are never able to really go through a mathematical-like "proof." And in practice, it is quite rare that a social scientist would even use the "p" word.

Hoover (1992, p. 80) has suggested that in order to prove that X *causes* Y, three criteria must be met:

1. X must precede the occurrence of Y.
2. The occurrence of X must be connected with the occurrence of Y; and
3. A third variable Z must not eliminate the variance in y associated with X.

In our example, we would not argue that marrying when young "causes" divorce. Logically, it's something associated with being young that "causes" divorce. Let's suppose that it's really the higher propensity to change one's mind that is a direct cause of divorce for these individuals. Therefore, we must show that one changes one's mind about one's partner before the occurrence of divorce (criterion 1). Second, we must show that having second thoughts about one's partner must be related to the occurrence of divorce (criterion 2). For example, we must show that higher rates of "mind-changing" must be associated with higher rates of "divorce." And, finally, we must show that some other variable, not yet mentioned, does not eliminate the variance in divorce associated with mind-changing (criterion 3). It is this last criterion that is so difficult to show, and precisely why social scientists very seldom use the "p" word.

Originally, we had stated our hypothesis in terms of age at marriage: the higher one's age when marrying, the less likely one is to divorce. It would be relatively easy to show such an association through the use of some previously collected data. In terms of criterion 3, however, we then added that it was probably not age at marriage per se that caused divorce but, rather, some other factor *associated* with age at marriage, like the propensity to change one's mind. Someone could now ask why it is that older individuals also get divorced. Another might argue that perhaps it is not the propensity to change one's mind but, rather, that younger individuals are more likely to have financial difficulties. Arguing about money may create a decline in "marital satisfaction," which then causes divorce. The web is very tangled. It should now be clearer why it is so difficult to convince others that you have "proved" that a higher proclivity for "mind-changing" causes divorce.

Objectivity and Ideology

There has been an underlying assumption that by using data to "test" our theoretical concepts, we have approached some measure of objectivity. And while it is undoubtedly true that without data we would be reduced to arguing opinion, we suggest that it is never possible to eliminate subjective bias from our research. Each individual has unique experiences that tend to color his or her view of the social world. On the other hand, these experiences are helpful in many ways. These biases provide us with interesting questions and useful insights. However, they also blind us to other avenues of thought and explanation. Researchers often attempt to answer questions by observing social phenomena through the lenses of their discipline. For example, sociologists who study divorce may only cursorily consider the explanations that have been developed by psychologists or other family researchers. In fact, given the breadth of the literature in sociology alone, they may not even be aware of the existence of a literature in these other fields. Additionally, because the sociologist is concerned with more macrolevel, or structural, "causes" of divorce, an approach that utilizes qualitative data to measure intrafamily processes for a necessarily small number of families would be completely unfamiliar ground for the sociologist. Likewise, demographic explanations of changes in divorce rates that necessarily consider such macrolevel processes as the changing nature of the age structure of a population would be unfamiliar turf to the intervention specialist. These academic boundaries create barriers and, hence, may obstruct important avenues of thought and explanation.

These biases are also relevant to problems inherent in data-collection efforts. Data problems create problems for the conclusions we may draw. Because we always have some underlying notion of the important forces influencing the question we are studying, we tend to collect data to allow us to test these notions. For example, assume that we hail from a discipline that takes an interventionist approach to family studies, an approach that hopes to help troubled families work through problems. As researchers, we may collect our data by observing families in their daily interactions with an eye for strategies to facilitate positive communication and conflict resolution (an inductive approach). By doing so, however, we may implicitly assume that all conflict is equal and focus our attention singularly on techniques for reducing strife. A family researcher from a background not quite as concerned with intrafamily processes might point out that data were not collected with an eye for types of conflict. This researcher might argue that more macro/structural data should be collected in an effort to understand some of the outside forces (like neighborhoods and economic disruption) that affect family systems. Without the collection of data aimed at understanding these macro/structural issues, the intervention specialist may conclude incorrectly that some techniques to reduce conflict are more successful than others when, in fact, the researcher should have set up scope conditions to show *when* one type of technique is superior to another. For example, one technique may be superior for conflict originating from processes internal to the family but quite useless for externally generated conflict.

Conceptualization and Measurement

Measurement of Concepts

In the preceding section, we used the word *concept* a number of times. It didn't seem necessary to explain the term. We just assumed that most people probably know what one means by a concept. When we begin to discuss how one goes about measuring such a notion, however, the realization occurs that maybe it's not so straightforward as one would like to think. Thus, let's begin with a definition of both concept and measurement. A concept is a thought or notion, something conceived in the mind—an abstract image of reality. So how would one go about measuring something as amorphous as a thought, notion, or abstract image? Furthermore, what's a measure? A measure is a basis for comparison, a way to differentiate one thing from another. In a sense, we create concepts to measure concepts. To illustrate, let's first consider an example from the physical sciences, since we tend to have the notion that the "hard sciences" are able to measure concepts more concretely than the social sciences. Consider the concept of velocity. Before a physicist could come along and measure this newly created concept, humans had to invent the concepts of distance and time. Assume that these concepts are fully defined: we'll call our measure of length a mile and define it as 5280 feet; likewise, our time measure is called an hour and is defined as 60 minutes. Velocity is defined as a movement from one point in time and space to another point in time and space. We will measure it as a ratio expressed as *x* miles per *y* hours. The point to come away with is that these measurements, or indicators, are arbitrary creations, abstractions. They didn't exist before we defined them. They have no substance in and of themselves. You cannot see an hour or touch a mile. They are concepts used only as a basis for comparison.

Critical to this discussion is an awareness that a group of physicists came to agree on the definition and measurement of velocity. The social sciences are no less abstract and perhaps equally concrete. We define concepts and then use these concepts to measure other concepts, the same as do the so-called hard sciences. However, the difference between the "hard" and "soft" sciences is the potential for agreement. It's relatively easy for individuals to agree to call a foot the distance between two marks on a stick. Nonetheless, high degrees of agreement also occur in the social sciences. Consider, for a moment, the concept of marital status. Social scientists have, for the most part, agreed that legal marital status should be defined by the concepts of married, divorced, widowed, separated, or single. They are concepts; you can't see or touch a marital status; but an agreement has been reached to define it accordingly.

Conversely, there are measures and concepts over which social scientists (and no doubt physicists as well) continue to argue. For instance, consider the concepts of marital quality and marital satisfaction. What is a quality marriage? Can we define and subsequently measure these concepts? And just because we are able to define them, does their existence necessarily follow? If we can't agree on a measure, does it exist? And how do we know? Furthermore, how do these two concepts differ from each other? Can you have marital quality without marital satisfaction, and vice versa?

Consider strategies for measuring these concepts. One strategy for measuring marital satisfaction might be to ask your subject, "How satisfied are you with your marriage?" To measure marital quality, one might ask, "On a scale of 1 to 10, how would you rate the quality of your marriage?" Are we measuring the concepts? Assume that we ask both partners the same question. What do we do if we get completely different responses? How do we interpret them? How do we know that both

partners are even perceiving the question in the same way? What happens if you are a more qualitative researcher, are observing family interactions, and are not really asking questions of your respondents? How do you know that you've interpreted a complex series of interactions the same way that the participants did? Assume that there are two of you. What do you do if you interpret an interaction differently? How do you come to agree?

Eventually, at least one researcher will probably specify a set of relatively objective indicators to measure the concept in question. On the other hand, another person will probably develop a completely different set of indicators to measure what we are calling the same concept. So how do we go about reconciling these differences? In practice, we often don't. We go about our research with our own conceptualizations and measurements and then argue about them at our professional meetings and in the journals. Fortunately, we use criteria to determine measurement quality. In a sense, these are the techniques that we use to argue our case, ways to convince one another. We call these criteria reliability and validity.

Reliability and Validity

Reliability is defined as the degree to which a measurement technique produces similar outcomes when it is repeated. Consider how reliable our measure of marital satisfaction might be. If our respondents had been throwing dishes at each other just before you knocked on the door, would you get the same answers next week to the question "How satisfied are you with your marriage?" Probably not. However, think if we had created a scale of marital satisfaction, a scale that asked a number of questions aimed at measuring separate dimensions of satisfaction. The scale would give us a total score of marital satisfaction. There is a higher probability that we would approach an acceptable level of reliability with a scale measure than with a unidimensional measure. But does this higher level of reliability ensure that we are indeed measuring marital satisfaction? One person's measure of marital satisfaction may be another's measure of marital quality. Which brings us to the conviction that reliability does not guarantee accuracy.

The degree to which the measurement being used is in reality measuring what one thinks one is measuring is called validity. This criterion is much more problematic because it is more subjective. It is much easier to show that one can obtain similar responses to a particular question than whether the question is measuring reality. So what is reality? Reality depends upon whom you ask. So how valid would our measures be? If you are a researcher who believes that people don't always know how they feel about their marriage or that their feelings change over time, then a scale of marital satisfaction may still be unacceptable to you. In fact, you may go so far as to argue that the concept is not meaningful because there is no acceptable way to measure it. If you believe the question to be unanswerable, you may eschew the debate altogether and work on an entirely different question.

It should be clear that there is a tension here. By trying to obtain precise, reliable measures, we may sacrifice the richness of questions that are perhaps less reliable. This tension translates very closely to the debate between those researchers who prefer quantitative methods and those who prefer more qualitative approaches. Those using the more qualitative approaches, like ethnographies, are often more contentious when it comes time to convince their colleagues that they can measure (that is, compare) what they think they are each and every time (reliability). On the other hand, quantitative researchers are often accused of not even coming close to measuring the concept that they claim is being measured (validity). Regardless, you should not come away from this debate with the idea that one method is preferable over the other. They are complements in the truest sense of the word. In fact, some of the most innovative and bright methodological minds in social research today are working on this very issue; that is, how does one combine qualitative and quantitative data without losing the best that each has to offer?

Variables and Units of Analysis

By this point, you should have some intuitive sense of what a variable is. To discuss a variable, however, we must have some notion of attribute. Variables are logical groupings of attributes that describe something that varies. Using our previous example, our measurement of marital quality asked the respondents to rate their response in terms of a value on a scale of 1 to 10. One might choose to call such a variable "marital quality" and assign it an attribute between 1 and 10; that is, it varies by respondent on a range between 1 and 10.

In order to study a particular question, a researcher will usually have in mind the type of subjects necessary to answer the question at hand. In most cases, individual respondents (or participants) will be the subject of research, although a researcher will sometimes study a question by focusing on a couple or a group. At other times, organizations, communities, or even nations will be the focus of inquiry. The type of question usually dictates the unit of analysis (groups versus individuals versus nations). Also, units of analysis prescribe the types of conclusions that can be drawn from the research. Two potential pitfalls should be avoided that are relevant to units of analysis: the ecological fallacy and reductionism.

Both notions refer to the danger of making assertions about one unit of analysis based on the examination of another. For example, say you are interested in why children are retained in a lower grade. Therefore, you go to a number of schools and compare the percentage of children who fail grades with the percentage of the children in a school who come from families that have experienced a divorce. You notice that the higher the percentage of children from divorced families, the higher the percentage of children in a school who fail grades. You would be tempted to conclude that divorce leads to grade failure for children. But you could not be sure that the children who had failed to move on to a higher grade were the same children who had experienced divorce. It could be just the opposite. You can't know for certain, because you are comparing aggregate variables, not individual-level variables. This is the *ecological fallacy.*

Reductionism is the tendency to reduce complex social phenomena to a single cause, and in some cases it is the reverse of the ecological fallacy. Reductionism reduces a group-level occurrence to an explanation at the individual level. For example, assume that Americans in 1928 were more likely to bootleg whiskey. If we argue that the onset of the Depression was caused by whiskey bootleggers, we have reduced the explanation of a complex phenomena to a single individual attribute. Similarly, consider the faulty logic in trying to attribute the increase in aggregate U.S. divorce rates to changing patterns of spousal communication. Explaining all or most of human behavior in terms of structural or sociological factors would be called sociological reductionism; explaining all or most of human behavior in terms of psychological factors is called psychological reductionism. This discussion should resonate with the previous discussion of objectivity and ideology in that disciplinary boundaries may be the driving force behind the tendency of researchers to engage in reductionism.

Research Design and Data Collection

This section moves our discussion in the direction of research design and data collection. It highlights designs common to a broad range of disciplines. In the case of family science, the ethnography is a common research design. Complementary to the work accomplished by family-science researchers is the work accomplished by sociologists, demographers, and economists who study the family. These researchers often use large-scale, population-based surveys. In turn, the family psychologist may be partial to the experiment. Within each of these traditions are both mixtures and subclasses of research methods. For example, the family-science researcher may utilize a blend of research designs by quantifying some of the more qualitative ethnographic data. The psychologist may use a population-based survey to try to correct some of the bias inherent in clinical-based samples. That is, by knowing something about the distribution of a sample of a larger population, scientists can attempt to correct estimates to reflect that they have collected data exclusively on subject's who were included because they met some criteria (like young persons who have been through the juvenile court system or children who are now in foster care). By focusing only on children in foster care, they may not be able to compare them with those not in foster care or those who have returned to live with their biological parents. Another reason to be cognizant of methods outside one's discipline relates to the conclusions one is able to draw from data collected in a cross- section (one point in time). These conclusions may be very different from what one would draw if data were analyzed from

within a more longitudinal framework. Some research designs are inherently more amenable to longitudinal analyses than others. The point here is that all research designs have strengths and weaknesses. The challenge to all of the disciplines that study the family is to propose ways to combine the different methods.

Survey Design

A survey allows one to query individuals in order to collect data for the analysis of some aspect of a larger group. While most surveys collect data on individuals, it is also possible to collect information on larger units of analysis like organizations. In fact, a single survey will sometimes collect information not only on individuals but also on schools, neighborhoods, and the governments of those individuals.

There are several distinct types of surveys, however. Most tend to be cross-sectional, meaning that they collect data to describe a population at a single time. Others are longitudinal and are designed to collect observations over an extended period. Some are administered by the respondent through the mail, while others are administered in person or by an interviewer over the telephone. Obviously, there are strengths and weaknesses with all the types of surveys in terms of cost, sampling frame, response rate, and the kinds of questions that can be answered. With the decrease in both the cost and size of computers, many surveys are now being administered by computer-assisted interviewers, sometimes in person (CAPI) and sometimes by telephone (CATI). The costs saved by the new computer technology can be substantial.

It can be difficult to identify a cross-sectional survey from a longitudinal survey. The problem with the distinction is that a cross-sectional survey sometimes also obtains retrospective longitudinal information. At other times, we call a survey longitudinal because it surveys a cross-section a number of times. The following three types of surveys fall in the latter category. They differ in the type of respondent group. *Trend studies* are usually cross-sectional surveys that measure certain characteristics of a population at different times. The decennial census is an example of a survey that can be used for trend studies; it collects information about the entire population of the United States every ten years.

Cohort studies survey more specific subpopulations (cohorts) at various times. Often a cohort is an age group, like individuals who were born during a particular week in 1965. Sometimes other time groupings will be used, like individuals who served in the military during the Korean War. For example, individuals born during 1965 might be surveyed every ten years. So in 1975 the survey would interview a sample of 10-year-olds; in 1985 a sample of 20-year-olds would be interviewed; and so forth. *Panel studies* are similar to the previously discussed longitudinal surveys; however, they usually reinterview the exact set of individuals that was interviewed previously. Trend studies and cohort studies obtain a different sample of individuals for each survey.

Distinctions among surveys must be made because they can be used to answer different types of questions. Longitudinal studies are useful because they can more correctly answer questions involving processes over time. However, it should be obvious that longitudinal studies can be more expensive to conduct because one must interview more than once; and in the case of panel studies, one must keep track of the individuals over time. The response rates of panel studies often become problematic due to the nonrandom nature of withdrawals.

Some cross-sectional surveys will try to approximate observations collected over time. They ask respondents to recall previous histories, such as their employment history. The respondents are asked to remember every job and occupation in which they have engaged since perhaps age 18. Information is collected in order to chronologically date these jobs. Other information on occupation type, whether the job was full time or part time, and other characteristics are also usually asked. These "event histories" are retrospective in nature. However, sometimes a true longitudinal survey will also attempt to collect "event histories" in a prospective fashion. Events will be assessed at periodic intervals, and therefore they are less prone to measurement error. A respondent's recall can oftentimes be imperfect. On the other hand, prospective studies have enormous costs associated with them, so trade-offs are usually made.

Experimental Design

While many types of experimental designs are available to the social science researcher, we will discuss only two: the classical experiment and the natural experiment. A *classical experiment* is an operation carried out under controlled conditions in order to discover some unknown effect or to illustrate some known law. This method is particularly suited to formal testing of hypotheses. Classical experiments usually involve two processes: (1) some action is taken, and (2) observations are made of the effect of that action. For example, suppose that we are interested in testing the hypothesis that graduate students in family science will perform better in a methods course that requires them to analyze secondary data if they take a computer-application course designed specifically for social scientists as compared with a computer course that teaches the application in more general terms. We could test this hypothesis experimentally by dividing an incoming graduate-student cohort into two groups and randomly assigning them to two differently organized computer courses. To minimize confounding effects, we would have the same instructor teach both courses.

One course would be taught in a way that emphasized the main points of the specific application software but used very generic examples (control group). The other course would be taught in a way that emphasized the software's applicability to specific topics in which family-science students might be interested (experimental group). At the end of the semester we would observe to see whether the students in the family-science-relevant computer course did significantly better in the methods course than those students who were enrolled in the more general course. The underlying assumption here is that randomly assigning students to two different classes should "control" for other variables that might influence the outcome; for example, perhaps the student also worked as a teaching assistant (less hours available to devote to studies), or perhaps the student worked as a research assistant (gaining more experience in data analysis), among other possibilities.

The problem with this experiment is that randomly assigning individuals to the two computer classes involves very small numbers of students. There is a real possibility that, because of the small numbers, we might not have gained a completely random group on all potentially important variables. For example, by chance alone, all of the very high achievers could be assigned to one group over the other. While this is rather unlikely, with small numbers it is distinctly possible. If such a scenario occurred, the very high achievers would bias the results so that what we were attributing to the different course styles might really be attributable to the overrepresentation of the high achievers in one of the courses. One way around this problem would be either to increase the size of the classes or to repeat the experiment over a number of semesters. We then have the additional problem of whether we can expect student populations to be similar on academic characteristics from one semester to the next. For instance, if all the failing students get kicked out of the university at the end of the fall semester, the spring semester might again overrepresent the higher achievers.

The other type of experiment, the *natural experiment*, entails no manipulation on the part of the experimenter. Individuals are not randomly assigned to groups but, rather, are just observed. The experimenter observes the predictor variable and relates it to an outcome variable. For example, suppose that a corporation decides to completely automate an automobile factory, effectively reducing its labor force by half. The company lays off 3000 of its 6000 employees. Many levels of the company are affected, from vice presidents to middle managers to assembly-line workers. You can follow both sets of employees for a number of years to determine if the individuals who were laid off are more likely to divorce than the non-laid-off employees. If you find significant differences, you might conclude that stressful events are associated with higher risks of divorce. In the case of experiments, we as researchers must carefully consider the ethical issues involved. This particular type of experiment could not ethically be performed by a researcher because of the consequences for the subjects affected. On the other hand, in natural experiments, we often really can't be sure that it is the "treatment," in this case the layoff, that is causing the outcome. Because we were not able to randomize the subjects, there may be some other factor associated with an increased risk of divorce that is correlated with the population experiencing the layoff. For example, suppose that the population being laid off was disproportionately younger than the population who stayed with the company. Past research has suggested that younger ages at marriage are associated with higher risks of divorce. Statistically, we would have to try to control

for these differences before we could draw any sort of conclusion.

Ethnography

Ethnography is a method of inquiry that is perhaps most often associated with anthropology. Sometimes it is referred to as field research, participant observation, or case studies. This type of research tends to study small groups in an intensive fashion. Ethnography is a method that can give a more extensive and perhaps more complete understanding of some social phenomenon. It allows one to observe intricate interactions and other phenomena that may not have been predicted and, likewise, planned for. It also has the advantage of allowing one to observe behavior in a more natural habitat, the social world (unlike the classical experiment). Furthermore, many times a researcher does not have a clear theory or hypothesis to test but, rather, needs further information about some context that is not available through a secondary data source. Ethnography can often help point a researcher in the right direction. It can allow a researcher to more fully understand some social process; and likewise, the process can be more formally tested with secondary data if the researcher has a clearer idea what to look for. A disadvantage to this method is that conclusions may not be generalizable to a larger population because of the small numbers of cases necessarily involved. We can't be certain that what is observed is a more general process or an idiosyncrasy of the subject or group involved. Additionally, observers may experience selective perception, a real hazard in that they may observe only those things that support what they expect to find.

Ethnographic research can vary on a number of dimensions. The researcher can at his or her discretion assume a number of roles in this type of research design. These roles revolve around the distinction made between researchers who interact with the participants in their study and those who simply observe said interactions. There is obviously a continuum in that one is always able to participate to some degree; that is, some researchers participate more than others. Another distinction relates to whether an interaction is observed in a more natural setting or in a situation that is more contrived. Likewise, the research question itself should drive the setting in which research is executed. Again, the cutting edge of methodological research requires us to combine aspects of many of the above-mentioned designs to answer our questions more globally.

Statistical Techniques

Hypothesis Testing and Statistical Inference

To this point, we have considered methods of scientific inquiry and have discussed concept measurement and data collection. Once we have our research question appropriately defined and have argued convincingly that our data are measuring our concepts adequately, we now proceed to hypothesis testing and statistical inference. Before we discuss hypothesis testing, however, think briefly back to that beginning statistics course where you learned all about scientific sampling. Once every ten years, the U. S. Bureau of the Census attempts to count every person in the United States by questionnaire and, in fact, comes very close to identifying the entire population. During this process, the Census Bureau also identifies a random subset of the population to which it gives a longer version of the questionnaire. This subset of the population is called a *sample*. The bureau issues the long questionnaire to a sample of individuals because it generally costs more money to collect, code, and analyze data from the long form than it does from the short form. The bureau uses this technique because the sample of individuals will contain enough respondents to approximate responses for the entire U.S. population. It is upon this relatively simple principle that statistical inference is based.

By hypothesis testing we can come to a more certain conclusion regarding the validity of our now-well-defined hypothesis. Hypothesis testing formally determines whether the observed sample data could have been generated by chance from a population in which the null hypothesis is true. In the above example, we would be testing to see if our sample of individuals could have been generated by chance from the general population of the United States. The null hypothesis usually tends to be a hypothesis that states that no relationship exists (although this doesn't have to be the case). If you can reject the null hypothesis, then you know that a relationship of some type does indeed exist,

at some level of probability. Rather clever, yes? But then how does one go about determining the criterion one could use to reject a null hypothesis?

While we will not go into the specific mechanics involved in the testing of hypotheses, we will make some general statements about the process. In order to reject a hypothesis, one must set up a statistical test. We first decide on a sampling distribution—for example, a normal distribution for small samples (t distribution) or large samples (z distribution), a chi-square distribution, and so on. Next, we select a significance level and critical region, compute the test statistic, and use the information to make a decision about whether we should reject the null hypothesis. If our data show a high probability that the sample data could have been generated by chance, we would not reject the null hypothesis. Not rejecting the null hypothesis leads us to believe that there may, in fact, be no relationship. Therefore, we would not be able to "accept" the alternative hypothesis, that a relationship does exist.

Univariate, or Descriptive, Statistics

Univariate statistics are often referred to as descriptive statistics. Social scientists usually want to collect data to test relationships between two or more variables. Most often, however, the first step of any good research project is to get an idea of what one's data look like. To describe one's data, it is necessary to understand that variables differ by level of measurement. That is, variables are measured in different ways. We will discuss four levels of measurement: nominal measures, ordinal measures, interval measures, and ratio measures. One example of a *nominal measure* would be marital status. This measure involves no rank ordering; it makes no sense to say that being widowed is higher than being separated. Other examples of nominal measures would be sex, state of residence, and religious affiliation. *Ordinal measures*, on the other hand, do involve some sense of rank ordering; however, these measures do not give an indication of how far apart the intervals are from one another. We can only say that one attribute is higher than another, not how much higher. For example, an ordinal measure of religiosity could ascertain whether you were highly religious, somewhat religious, or not religious at all. Measures that do allow us to express the interval between two attributes are called *interval measures*. IQ is often cited as an example of an interval measure. There are standard intervals between measures. Interval measures and *ratio measures* are similar to each other with the exception that a ratio measure has a true zero point. A score of zero on an IQ test would not indicate a complete lack of intelligence; hence, a zero score is not meaningful. On the other hand, income does have a true zero. It is entirely possible that an individual made no money last year. It is necessary to distinguish between the levels of measurement in order to more fully understand the advantages and limitations of each.

Data can be described in many ways; however, one way employs categorical data, and another uses continuous data. Categorical data are grouped data. In general, it probably makes no sense to just list out the attributes of a variable. If we did this, we might have 5000 individuals with a different value for each variable. Grouping the data allows us to tell a more meaningful story. For example, if we are concerned with the income levels of individuals in a data set, we might group the data into categories—for example, less than $6000; $6,000 to $20,000, and more than $20,000. We would then count the number of individuals who fell into each of these three categories. This is called a frequency distribution; there is a frequency of individuals associated with each category. Furthermore, you should be aware that by categorizing the variable income, we constructed an ordinal measure from a ratio measure. The measure is now ordinal because there are not equal intervals between the categories.

The other way of describing data utilizes continuous data. Measures of continuous data can give us information about the central tendency and dispersion of a distribution. Measures of central tendency include means, medians, modes, and percentiles. Measures of dispersion include ranges, standard deviations, variance, and skewness. For a more complete discussion of univariate measures see Blalock (1979, pp. 31–104).

Bivariate and Trivariate Statistics

Frequency distributions, means, and standard deviations are useful to describe the distribution of the attributes of one variable. As previously stated, however, social scientists are most interested in identifying relationships between distributions; for example, rather than just identifying proportions of individuals who cohabited before marriage, we would probably be more interested in whether those individuals who cohabited before marriage were more likely to divorce than those who didn't. Other examples: Are adults whose parents divorced during their childhood more likely to divorce than other adults? Are children who live in families with stepparents more likely to leave home early than children from intact families? Variables can be constructed so as to measure individuals who cohabited before marriage and those who didn't. Likewise, we can construct a variable that captures whether an individual divorced or not. If we *cross-tabulate* these two variables, we can calculate a statistical test to determine whether a relationship, or an association, exists between the two variables. We will discuss two frequently used bivariate statistical tests: the chi-square test and Pearson's correlation coefficient (Pearson's r).

Chi-square test of significance.   The chi-square test of statistical significance allows us to determine the probability that two variables in the sample are also related in the population. The null hypothesis is the hypothesis of no relationship. Chi-square tests are used with cross-tabulated categorical variables. The major limitation of the chi-square statistic is that it says nothing about the strength of the relationship or the direction. It tells us only the probability that the relationship between two variables in the sample is also present in the population. However, there are measures based on chi-square (phi-squared, the contingency coefficient, Tschuprow's T, and Cramer's V) that attempt to correct for this deficiency. Unfortunately, these measures also have limitations and can be hard to interpret. In the case of chi-square and some of the other similar tests, many statistical computer packages will calculate these statistics for us. Hand calculations can be time consuming, especially given many categories for each variable.

The correlation coefficient, or Pearson's r. The correlation coefficient measures the association between two variables that are continuous. Consider the variables age and income. These variables can be both continuous and categorical. Earlier in the discussion we showed how we could categorize income into three categories. However, it should be clear that by categorizing a variable, we lose some information. We may know that a person is between 25 and 35 years old, but we won't know whether that person is closer to 25 or 35. Conversely, marital status is inherently a categorical measure. There are no levels of marriage. You are either single, married, divorced, separated or widowed. If we calculate a correlation coefficient for the continuous measures of income against age, we will be able to estimate the direction and strength of the relationship. The correlation coefficient is a number between -1 and +1. A negative number indicates that an increase in one variable is associated with a decrease in the other variable. Conversely, a positive value indicates that an increase in one variable is associated with an increase in the other variable. The closer the number is to 1 (either negative or positive), the stronger the relationship. In addition, this statistic also provides a test of significance, the t-test.

Multivariate Statistics

The history of the development of the social sciences, in general, and family studies, in particular, revolves around significant advances in both theoretical knowledge and methodological sophistication (Miller, Rollins, & Thomas, 1982; Schumm, 1982). The development of theory about families has proceeded slowly. Following an early period of grand theorizing, the field was dominated in the first half of this century by an empirical approach that was mainly descriptive and lacked cumulation (Burr, Hill, Nye, & Reiss, 1979). As a result, the statistical procedures most often used in family research were descriptive (for example, cross-tabulations and correlations). Since midcentury, with attempts to develop theoretical foundations for family research, changes in statistical methods have necessarily occurred. As researchers developed propositions about the causal effects of one or more independent variables on a dependent variable, for instance, regression procedures became more common. Today, multivariate regression procedures dominate the journals in all of social science, including the family subfield. We now turn to a discussion of linear and nonlinear regression procedures, followed by a more cursory discussion of the limitations of nonrandom samples and analysis of change over time.

Linear regression techniques. Regression analysis is a procedure used to relate the level of one or more independent variables to the level of a dependent variable. Linear regression is often referred to as ordinary least squares (OLS) regression. This relationship is usually depicted by the following linear equation:

$$Y = a + bX + e \qquad (1)$$

where Y is the dependent variable of interest, a is a constant term, X is the independent variable of interest, b is a coefficient indicating the amount of shift along the Y axis associated with a unit shift along the X axis, and e is an error term. In most examples in the family field, e is assumed to be normally distributed (which is equivalent to assuming that Y is normally distributed), homoskedastistic (which means that the variances of two or more population distributions are equal), and uncorrelated with X. If the model is properly specified and Y and X are measured without error, ordinary least squares (OLS) regression estimates of a and b are appropriate. When these assumptions are not met, OLS regression estimates of a and b are potentially biased.

Let us now consider an example where linear regression would be an appropriate technique of investigation. First we will consider the bivariate case. Ordinary least squares regression usually specifies that the dependent variable be continuous. Suppose we have a theory that presumes that level of education is related to income. Our outcome measure (dependent variable) would be level of income (in dollars per year), and our predictor variable (independent variable) would be level of education attained (in years of education). Just to make things equal for our respondents, let's consider only a subsample of individuals who are 35 years of age. (Younger people have had less time to achieve the income levels of older people.) Suppose our coefficient, b, is calculated by the computer to be 5000. We can interpret this to mean that for every one-year increase in education, we can expect, on average, an increase of $5000 per year in income.

Suppose that by taking a subsample of our data we were able to obtain only 20 individuals who were exactly age 35. Because tests of significance are dependent on sample size, let's assume that the *t*-test for our coefficient was not significant at a given probability level (.05 level). Therefore, the null hypothesis that the coefficient (or slope) is not significantly different from zero cannot be rejected. We would have to assume that education has nothing to do with level of income. These results would indicate that we might want either to consider increasing our sample size to make certain that the significance test is not related to sample-size problems or to reconsider our theory. Certainly, it makes sense to try first to investigate the sample-size issue.

One way to increase our sample size would be to use the entire sample of individuals (of every age) and use multivariate analysis. We can now address both problems at once. By including all sampled individuals and "controlling" for age, we can now discover what the effect of education, net of age, is on yearly income levels. Our new equation would look like this:

$$\text{Income} = a + b_1(\text{education}) + b_2(\text{age}) + e \qquad (2)$$

Suppose that our results indicate that the coefficient for education (b_1) is now 3500, and the coefficient for age (b_2) is 500. These results indicate that every one-year increase in educational attainment is associated with a $3500 increase in yearly income. In addition, every one-year increase in age is associated with a $500 increase in yearly income. Assume that the constant is calculated to be 200. This implies that if both the level of education and the age of an individual are zero, we can still expect that person to receive $200 per year in annual income. It should be obvious that this result does not make a great deal of sense. A note of caution is appropriate. One should be wary when interpreting the constant term when all independent variables are set to zero, because values of zero are generally outside the realm of typical experience. It's very unlikely that we will identify individuals who either have zero education or zero age. Accordingly, social scientists tend to disregard the constant term when interpreting the model.

Earlier in the discussion, we laid out some basic assumptions underlying OLS regression. However, for a number of reasons, it is not always possible to meet these assumptions. Unfortunately, the development of statistical procedures for variables or concepts not meeting the assumptions for OLS regression has lagged.

In addition, procedures that have been developed to deal with departures from the usual assumptions have been slow to diffuse into the family literature. The problem has been compounded by the lack of easily available software for computing parameter estimates (for example, coefficients). As a consequence, when the usual assumptions are not met, it is difficult to test theoretically derived propositions and hypotheses with confidence. In addition, researchers may hesitate to gather data pertaining to important concepts and variables if they are unsure how to analyze such data. This situation has probably retarded the development of knowledge bases and slowed the development and modification of theories related to the family.

Nonlinear regression techniques. When are the usual assumptions of OLS regression likely to be violated? Perhaps the most common situation results when the dependent variable is measured on the nominal level, resulting in an error term that is not normally distributed. Nominal dependent variables are likely to occur in most theoretical orientations. Some theories, however, such as those pertaining to the life course (Scanzoni, Polonko, Teachman, & Thompson, 1989), are particularly wedded to concepts measured as discrete variables. One consequence is that the discrete concepts are often used as independent variables but are seldom analyzed as dependent variables, even though this would often be logical.

If both Y and X are measured on a nominal level, log-linear procedures can be applied (Reynolds, 1977). This is restrictive, though, because it is likely that at least one or more of the independent variables are measured on a continuous scale. If there are continuous independent variables, there are at least two alternatives for estimating their effect on a nominal dependent variable: logistic regression or prohibit regression. The two are similar, the difference depending on the assumption made about the nature of the error term. If a cumulative normal distribution is chosen, then the probit model is appropriate. If an extreme value distribution is chosen, the logistic model is correct. In practice, the choice is of little consequence because the shape of the two distributions is similar, and it is highly unlikely that any theoretical orientation would favor one over the other.

The point to note is that both probit and logistic-regression procedures allow the researcher to obtain unbiased (an estimator of a population parameter whose expected value equals the population parameter) estimates of the effects of both nominal and continuous independent variables on a nominal dependent variable. In addition, extensions of the probit and logistic-regression models further increase their usefulness. First, the logistic model can be extended to include aggregate characteristics of the choice set (for example, corresponding to values of the dependent variable) as predictor variables (Maddala, 1983). Second, both the probit and logistic models can be extended to deal with ordered values of Y and X (Winship & Mare, 1983).

Limitations of nonrandom samples. Even if Y is measured on a continuous scale and can be assumed to be normally distributed, there are important instances when OLS regression will yield biased estimates of a and b. The two instances we will discuss pertain to censored and truncated samples (Maddala, 1983). A censored sample refers to the situation where the researcher has information for all sample members on the independent variables but has information on the dependent variable only for a nonrandom subsample. In a sample of women, for example, it is likely that not all respondents will be employed outside the home. Unless employment is a random event (which is not likely), it is probable that estimates of the effects of variables such as education on wages that are based on the subsample of employed women will be biased. The effects of education and other independent variables on wages may be confounded with their effect on labor-force participation.

A truncated sample refers to the situation where information on both the dependent and independent variables is available for only a subsample of cases. For instance, a sample selected on the basis of contact with a spouse-abuse shelter would be truncated if no information was available on subjects not having contact with the shelter. Analyses based on the sample contacting the shelter will yield biased estimates of the effects of the predictor variables to the extent that contacting the shelter is not a random event.

Both censored and truncated samples are likely to be found in research using a wide variety of theoretical orientations. In many cases, the presence of a censored or truncated sample will be the result of sampling decisions made for reasons of availability, time, or cost. In other instances, though, censored or truncated samples are the result of theoretical direction. Theories concerned with the consequences of experiencing a stressful event are one example. Unless the event precipitating the onset of stress occurs randomly in the population, an OLS regression of the predictors of the consequences of the event using the subsample experiencing the event may yield biased parameter estimates.

The techniques available to deal with censored samples are generally called sample selection procedures (in part because the bias is due to sample selectivity). These procedures are relatively new but can be estimated, with some additional programming, using major software packages (SAS, SPSSX). Procedures are also available to deal with truncated samples. Unfortunately, these procedures are less accessible to family researchers and require special software packages for estimation.

Analysis of change over time. Family researchers have moved away from models emphasizing order and stability, turning more often to models that recognize that families are not stationary entities in equilibrium. Developmental theories, conflict theory, systems theory, and life-course perspectives are all examples of dynamic theoretical orientations that focus on family processes and change over time. While structure is not unimportant in these theories, it is but one context affecting the process of change, as well as a result of change (see the discussion in Scanzoni et al., 1989).

The movement toward an emphasis on theories of change requires a fundamental shift in statistical methodology. While most cross-sectional analyses focus on structure and implicitly assume equilibrium, dynamic theories assume that families are in flux and therefore not likely to be in equilibrium. Methods appropriate for cross-sectional data are not directly appropriate for the analysis of change over time, although researchers have used cross-sectional data to (inappropriately) make inferences about change over time. Dynamic theories require statistical methods that explicitly take into account the process of change. While we will not go into these methods, you should note that a growing body of literature on these models has appeared. These procedures include Markov models; event-history models; proportional-hazards, or hazard-rate, models; and differential-equation models. Many of these techniques can be quite complicated to apply correctly; but some, particularly hazard-rate models, are becoming increasingly more common in the family literature.

Future Direction of Family-Research Methods

While we have not explicitly addressed the theoretical frameworks utilized by family researchers, we should make it clear that there is necessarily a close link between statistical methodology and theory. On the one hand, theoretical frameworks, as abstract images of reality, determine the research questions that will be asked and the nature of the data gathered, and they require particular statistical procedures for description and testing. On the other hand, statistical procedures, by dictating a specific mathematical relationship between variables or concepts, influence the nature and form of observed empirical regularities used to develop theoretical propositions, limit the types of data that can be analyzed, and restrict the sorts of theoretical propositions that can be tested.

To date, we feel that the relationship between statistical methodology and theory has been reciprocal. The future, however, is likely to be different. In recent years advances in statistical methodology have occurred at an increasing pace. This situation has been generated by (1) the cumulative nature of statistical knowledge and (2) substantial increases in computational power available to statistical methodologists (problems virtually inconceivable a decade ago are now routinely handled using personal computers).

Changes have also occurred in theory, but we feel that these changes are less cumulative. There has been a shift away from theories emphasizing structure and stability toward theories emphasizing process and change—and a concurrent emphasis on causal relationships. Such changes in theory have generally been matched by developments in statistical methodology, especially the boom in techniques for the analysis of change over time.

However, most theories are so rudimentary that it is difficult to move beyond simple predictions about the presence and direction of a relationship. There is little theoretical work that builds consistently and logically on earlier work so that systems of relationships between concepts can be clearly stated mathematically. As a result, most researchers use only the most basic statistical techniques. In the immediate future, therefore, it is more likely that advances in statistical methodology will spur development in theory (by suggesting new lines of investigation) rather than the reverse.

Chapter Summary

Discussion Questions

1. Describe the scientific method. How is it different from other means of creating knowledge? Use examples to convey what is meant by inductive and deductive reasoning.
2. Explain how subjective bias colors research. Discuss why this bias can be useful as well as problematic.
3. Discuss the strengths and weaknesses of both quantitative and qualitative research. Explain how these approaches complement each other.
4. Discuss the differences between the three types of survey designs: trend studies, cohort studies, and panel studies.
5. Carver and Teachman argue that statistical methods are undergoing a significant transition. Discuss the nature of this shift, and explain why a change in statistical methods is important for the development of useful family theory.

Additional Resources

Burr, W. R. (1973). *Theory construction and the sociology of the family*. New York: Wiley.
Elder, G. (1977). Family history and the life course. *Journal of Family History*, 2, 279–304.

Espenshade, T. J., & Braun, R. E. (1982). Life course analysis and multistate demography: An application to marriage, divorce and remarriage. *Journal of Marriage and the Family, 44,* 1025–1036.

Miller, B. C., Rollins, B. C., & Thomas, D. L. (1982). On methods of studying marriages and families. *Journal of Marriage and the Family, 44,* 851–873.

O'Leary, K. D., & Turkewitz, H. (1978). Methodological errors in marital and child treatment research. *Journal of Consulting and Clinical Psychology, 46,* 747–758.

Schumm, W. R. (1982). Integrating theory, measurement and data analysis in family studies survey research. *Journal of Marriage and the Family, 44,* 983–998.

Schumm, W. R., Milliken, G. A., Poresky, R. H., Bollman, S. R., & Jurich, A. P. (1983). Issues in measuring marital satisfaction in survey research. *International Journal of Sociology of the Family, 13,* 129–143.

Schumm, W. R., Southerly, W. T., & Figley, C. R. (1980). Stumbling block or stepping stone: Path analysis in family studies. *Journal of Marriage and the Family, 42,* 251–262.

Snyder, D. K. (1979). Multidimensional assessment of marital satisfaction. *Journal of Marriage and the Family, 41,* 813–823.

Snyder, D. K., Wills, R. M., & Keiser, T. W. (1981). Empirical validation of the marital satisfaction inventory: An actuarial approach. *Journal of Consulting and Clinical Psychology, 49,* 262–268.

Sprenkle, D. H. (1976). The need for integration among theory, research, and practice in the family field. *The Family Coordinator, 24,* 261–263.

Teachman, J. D. (1982). Methodological issues in the analysis of family formation and dissolution. *Journal of Marriage and the Family, 44,* 1037–1054.

Wampler, K. S., & Powell, G. S. (1982). The Barrett-Lennard Relationship Inventory as a measure of marital satisfaction. *Family Relations, 31,* 139–145.

References

Blalock, H. M. (1979). *Social statistics* (2nd ed.). New York: McGraw-Hill.

Burr, W., Hill, R., Nye, F. I., & Reiss, I. (1979). *Contemporary theories about the family: Vol. 1.* New York: Free Press.

Hoover, K. R. (1992). *The elements of social scientific thinking* (5th ed.). New York: St. Martin's Press.

Maddala, G. (1983). *Limited-dependent and qualitative variables in econometrics.* New York: Cambridge University Press.

Miller, B. C., Rollins, B. C., & Thomas, D. (1982). On methods of studying marriages and families. *Journal of Marriage and the Family, 44,* 851–874.

Reynolds, H. T. (1977). *The analysis of cross-classifications.* New York: Free Press.

Scanzoni, J., Polonko, K., Teachman, J. D., & Thompson, L. (1989). *The sexual bond: Rethinking families and close relationships.* Newbury Park, CA: Sage.

Schumm, W. (1982). Integrating theory, measurement and data analysis in family studies survey research. *Journal of Marriage and the Family, 44,* 983–989.

Winship, C., & Mare, R. (1983). Structural equations and path analysis for discrete data. *American Journal of Sociology, 89,* 54–110.

PART III

Understanding Family Processes

The daily processes of family life have been systematically studied (as a theoretical approach) for only a little more than 30 years. Hill and Hansen (1960)[1] did a meticulous survey of theories used in the study of the family. They did not include any theories that targeted microlevel family processes. Broderick (1993) has recently suggested in his book *Understanding Family Process* that the history and foundation of the study of family processes is new but certainly legitimate. In his first chapter, he shows how a variety of scholars from an assortment of disciplines has approached this topic. The roots of the study of family process reach back into the disciplines of sociology, psychology, social work, and anthropology. Those who have advanced this perspective with the greatest voracity, however, have been those in the field of family therapy. In the 1960s researcher/clinicians began discovering that much could be gained by looking at those activities done by the family group. Certainly, there was a social context in which the family lived, and the individual brought his or her personality to the mix. But the new and exciting aspect of this research is that families seem to possess special and unique processes that are greater than the scope of the individual personality of each member. The following chapters are designed to illuminate some of those processes.

In Chapter 9, David Olson presents an excellent overview and expansion of his life's work. For more than 20 years Olson has been developing the concepts of cohesion and adaptability. These key systemic elements are, perhaps, at the heart of understanding how families interact, solve problems, and respond to crises. He shows us how families must maintain balance and regulate the amount of closeness and chaos in their lives. Included in this chapter is a short version of the research instrument used to assess this important idea.

The daily life in families is filled with peaks and valleys of emotion mixed with routine and ritual. In Chapter 10, Barbara Settles discusses how this daily life influences the family's choices and decisions. These decisions define family life. Among the more important are decisions about work and the division of roles among family members. As you consider the important issues in this chapter, assess how the daily routines of life become the texture and context of life itself.

In Chapter 11, Kip Jenkins takes us through a thoughtful and informative overview of how family scientists have come to view the important factor we call communication. Probably no other process within a family has received more attention. To strengthen the quality of communication in one's family is a critical and important venture. Much of what family therapists and social-service workers do is to help family members understand what communication means and how to increase its effectiveness.

One of the most important and least understood aspects of private daily life is the world of sexuality. In Chapter 12, Colleen Murray and Geoffrey Leigh alert us to the ever-changing ideas that surround intimate relationships. Of particular interest in this chapter is

[1]See the References section of Chapter 9 for citations in this Part III overview.

their discussion of how power and men's and women's roles influence the close, intimate expression of love.

Finally, Denise Ann Bodman and Gary Peterson present us with a challenging and innovative chapter. Chapter 13 (probably more than any other in the text) breaks new ground. These researchers have (for what we think is the first time) taken the family-process literature and merged it with the research on parent/ child interaction. These two theoretical perspectives have remained exclusive from each other. As can be seen, many of the concepts so important in the parent/child literature fit snugly into the family-process framework. Parents spend much of their time dealing with boundaries, rule formation, intergenerational transmission, emotions, and cyclic rule sequences. This chapter, we hope, will spawn more attempts to develop research and theory projects that illuminate the process of parent/ child interaction.

Family Systems: Understanding Your Roots

David H. Olson
University of Minnesota

In this chapter we will explore various types of marriage and family relationships. We will then look at three major components of an intimate relationship: cohesion (togetherness), adaptability (the capacity to change), and communication (Olson, 1993). At the beginning of this text, both Orthner (Chapter 1) and Peterson (Chapter 2) discuss the historical changes in our perceptions of individuality and separateness. In this chapter, I will take a closer look at how cohesion, adaptability, and communication are significant and important family processes.

We will see how relationships change over time in terms of couple and family relationships. Some relationships are capable of surviving the most terrible storms life may bring, whereas other relationships fail. We will try to account for these differences.

Finally, we will examine the family of origin, where people's first relationships begin, and see how it can affect the type of relationship the members of a couple would like to have and are able to achieve. We all carry parts of our family of origin—both its strengths and its weaknesses—into our marriages.

Cohesion, Adaptability, and Communication

There are three central dimensions in the circumplex model. Cohesion (defined as "togetherness") and adaptability (defined as "the ability to change") are the two dimensions used graphically in the model. The third dimension, communication, is a facilitating factor, in that it facilitates movement of families on the cohesion and adaptability dimensions. In short, if a couple or family has good communication skills, they are more likely to be close and more likely to be able to work out problems (adapt to change) when they arise.

Other professionals in the field of family studies have developed theoretical models for understanding relationships, and there is a good degree of agreement on the importance of these three concepts. For example, Beavers and Hampson (1990) describe forces that bring family members in toward one another (centripetal forces) and counteracting forces that tend to hurl them away from one another (centrifugal forces). A force bringing family members together might be social activities in which all family members participate as a group, or tasks around the house in which everyone has to help. Forces that tend to distance family members might include the world of work. Dad and Mom go off for long hours each day, and the problems at work are often brought home in the minds of the parents. Dad and Mom may be cranky around the house because they're mad at the boss; or they may be absent-minded in regard to the children's concerns because they have so much to worry about on the job. The working world can thus easily become a "centrifugal" force that serves to hurl family members away from one another.

Likewise, Kantor and Lehr's (1975) concept of affect is closely related to cohesion, and their concept of power is quite like adaptability. Another prominent conceptual framework of family relationships, the McMaster model of family functioning, uses concepts that fit very well into the three dimensions of cohesion, adaptability, and communication (Epstein, Bishop,

Ryan, Miller, & Keitner, 1993). And Reiss (1981) conducted intensive experimental studies on families, relying heavily upon a model focusing on problem solving. His dimension called coordination is quite similar to cohesion, and his concept of closure is similar to the concept of adaptability (change).

Finally, Nick Stinnett, John DeFrain, and numerous colleagues at the University of Nebraska–Lincoln studied 3500 strong families and found that their members shared six major qualities: appreciation for one another; commitment; communication; spending time together; religious/ethical values; and the ability to cope with stress and crisis (Stinnett & DeFrain, 1985). When you think about it, appreciation, commitment, and spending time together clearly are cohesion-building qualities; religious/ethical values and the ability to cope with stress and crisis are obviously related to adaptability; again, the concept of communication is an important dimension.

In summary, many researchers and theoreticians have spent countless years studying family interaction and talking with families, and the conclusions they come to are quite similar. The circumplex model is very well developed and has strength-building activities related to it that we will use in this textbook. Table 9.1 illustrates how all these various theoretical models are parallel with the circumplex model.

The Circumplex Model: A Relationship Map

Circumplex is a complicated term, but it simply refers to a two-dimensional graph. It is easier to think of the circumplex model as a relationship map (see Figure 9.1.). This relationship map makes it possible to identify 16 types of couple and family relationships. The logic is quite simple: the dimensions of cohesion and adaptability are broken down into four levels each (and 4 x 4 = 16). A marriage or family relationship can be described as being in one of the 16 types on the basis of how the family functions. The relationship map provides a graphic representation of how families and relationships operate.

Dynamic Balance of Cohesion and Adaptability

Like a seesaw, both cohesion and adaptability require that people balance between the extremes. On cohesion, couples and families need to balance their relationship between the levels of separateness and togetherness. Adaptability involves balancing between the extremes of stability and change.

It has been found in both research and clinical work with couples and families that they more typically are stuck at the extremes on these dimensions. More specifically, problem families often experience too much separateness (disengaged) or too much togetherness (enmeshment). On the adaptability dimension, extreme families often experience too much stability (rigid) or too much change (chaotic) (see Figure 9.1).

On the other hand, couples and families that function best across the life cycle seem to be able to balance between their levels of separateness and togetherness in that they have some components of each. That is, they are able to be separate and autonomous as individuals but at other times can be close and intimate. They are,

TABLE 9.1   Theoretical Models and the Circumplex Model

	Cohesion	Adaptability	Communication
Beavers & Hampson (1990)	Centripetal/centrifugal	Adaptability	
Epstein, Bishop, Ryan, Miller, & Keitner (1993)	Affective	Behavior control	Communication
Kantor & Lehr (1975)	Affect	Power	
Reiss (1981)	Coordination	Closure	
Stinnett & DeFrain (1985)	Commitment; time together	Ability to cope with stress stress and crisis; religious/ethical values	Positive communication; appreciation of values

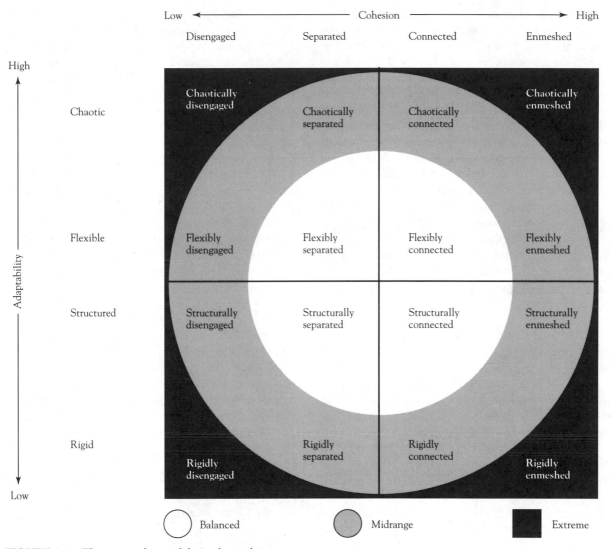

FIGURE 9.1 The circumplex model: A relationship map

in fact, not stuck at either extreme, but are able to balance between these two extremes.

Being balanced on these dimensions means that a couple and family can experience the extremes of the dimensions when appropriate but do not typically function at these two extremes for a long period. Balanced couples and families, therefore, are able to allow family members to be both independent from and connected to their family. Both extremes are tolerated and respected. But the family does not continually function at these extremes. Conversely, extreme families in the

circumplex model tend to function only at the extremes and seem to be stuck there.

It is also important to emphasize that there is a dynamic balance, in that it is assumed that change on both dimensions does occur in couple and family relationships. For example, when a balanced family (structurally connected) is under stress, it might change its family system to be more flexibly enmeshed. This style might, thereby, help members cope effectively with a stressor. As the stress subsides over time, however, the family system usually returns to the type it was previously.

This dynamic balance can also be illustrated by the fact that families will change the system they have as they develop across the family life cycle. The relationship that a young couple would have without children will change when the couple has three children, and then it will probably change again as these children become older and reach adolescence. Again, as these adolescents leave home, the family dynamics will probably change. This dynamic process occurs in a more fluid and functional way with the four balanced types of family systems than it does with families that fall within the four extremes of the circumplex model.

Because of the concept of balance, there is a curvilinear relationship between both cohesion and adaptability and family functioning. This means that families scoring either very low or very high in these dimensions tend to be more dysfunctional, or unhealthy. A linear relationship means that the higher the cohesion or the higher the adaptability, the better the family functioning (See Figure 9.2).

Balanced versus Extreme Families

The 16 types can be clustered into three more general types: balanced families, midrange families, and extreme families. (Look at the bottom of Figure 9.1 to see how these three general types fit into the relationship map.) Balanced families are those fitting into the four central categories of Figure 9.1. Balanced families are labeled flexibly separated, flexibly connected, structurally separated, and structurally connected. Midrange types of families have tested out to be extreme on one dimension (cohesion or adaptability) but balanced on another of the dimensions. For example, the family could be extreme on cohesion but balanced on adaptability, according to its test score. Extreme families are those that score at extreme levels on both dimensions.

Extreme types have the most difficulties functioning as a family. A number of scientific studies have validated this hypothesis. For example, Clarke (1984) focused on families with schizophrenics, families with neurotics, families who had participated in therapy at some time in the past, and a no-therapy control group. He found a high percentage of extreme families in the neurotic and schizophrenic groups compared with the no-therapy group; and he found a greater percentage of balanced families in the no-therapy group compared with the other groups (see Figure 9.3).

Studies of chemically dependent (alcoholic) families revealed that they had a significantly higher percentage of extreme families than did nondependent families (Killorin & Olson, 1984; Olson & Killorin, 1985).

A study of sex offenders found high levels of extreme family types in both their family of origin and their current family (Carnes, 1989). A study of families at risk for destructive parent/child relationships in the adolescent period found the majority of high-risk families to be extreme types (Garbarino, Sebes, & Schellenbach, 1984). And finally, a study of families with adolescent juvenile delinquents found only a small percentage to be balanced and a vast majority to be midrange or extreme types (Rodick, Henggler, & Hanson, 1986).

In summary, there is strong research support for the notion that balanced families as defined by the circumplex model are more functional than extreme families.

Balanced Families and Communication Skills

Another hypothesis is that balanced families will have more positive communication skills than extreme families. Communication can be measured at both the

FIGURE 9.2   Dynamic balance of cohesion and adaptability

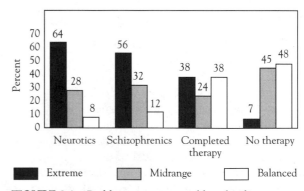

FIGURE 9.3   Problem versus nonproblem families

marital and family level. Using data from the national survey of 1000 families, researchers investigated parent/adolescent communication and family functioning in "nonproblem" families (Barnes & Olson, 1985; Olson et al., 1989). The hypothesis that balanced families would have better communication skills was supported when relying on data from the parents; this hypothesis was not supported for adolescents. Future research is needed to test hypotheses at both the marital and family level with both normal and problem families.

In addition to finding support for the hypothesis regarding balanced versus extreme families, Rodick and his colleagues (1985) also found clear support for the hypothesis that balanced families have more positive communication skills. Using observational measures of mother/adolescent interaction, the researchers found that mothers in the balanced group had significantly higher rates of supportive communication, explicit information, and positive affect than the extreme types, the majority of whose problem dyads were chaotically enmeshed.

Accounting for Cultural and Ethnic Diversity

In order to make the circumplex model relevant to a variety of families with different ethnic and cultural backgrounds, I developed a hypothesis to reflect this diversity. The hypothesis states that, if the normative expectations of families support behavior that is extreme on one or both of the dimensions, families will function well as long as all family members are satisfied with these expectations. In this way, the family serves as its own norm base. This approach, however, necessitates measuring the family satisfaction of each member.

Families in our culture still vary greatly in the extent to which they encourage and give support to individuals to develop in ways that differ from the family's values. While parents would prefer their children to develop values and ideas similar to theirs, most of them can enable their children to become somewhat autonomous and differentiated from the family system. A sizable minority of them, however, have normative expectations that strongly emphasize family togetherness, often at the expense of individual development. Their family norms emphasize emotional and physical

togetherness, and they strive for high levels of consensus and loyalty.

Some ethnic groups in this country, such as Slovak-American, Puerto Rican, and Italian families, and religious groups, such as the Amish and Mormons, have high expectations regarding family togetherness and have low adaptability. These expectations are also common, but less predominant, in many other American families regardless of their ethnic or religious orientation. Many of these families could be described as rigidly enmeshed, but they will not necessarily have problems in their families as long as the members are willing to go along with those expectations. These families have the potential to have more problems when their children reach adolescence and want more independence.

In general, the hypothesized curvilinear relationship between effective family functioning and the cohesion/adaptability dimensions primarily applies to families that accept the current cultural norms that support both family togetherness and individual development. The general hypothesis would not apply, however, for families that have different normative expectations.

Another important qualification of the hypothesis relates to our definition of "problem families." We tend to define problem families as those that are voluntarily or involuntarily involved in some treatment program. There is good clinical evidence that those couples or families in treatment programs are often extreme in one or both of these dimensions.

However, many families that are extreme in these dimensions do function well and never seek treatment. Other families extreme in these dimensions do have problems but never choose to seek treatment. Unfortunately, most studies have relied on problem families that enter treatment, and hence we know very little about those that do not. Hopefully, future studies will attempt to gather data from families not seeking or being placed in treatment and ones with extreme normative expectations, so that these hypotheses can be more adequately tested.

Marital and Family Togetherness (Cohesion)

Cohesion is defined as a feeling of emotional closeness with another person. We can experience four basic levels of cohesion with other people: disengaged, separated, connected, and enmeshed. The extreme low level, called disengaged, and the extreme high level, called enmeshed, are more characteristic of relationships that have problems in the long run. Although being disengaged or enmeshed is appropriate at times, it becomes more problematic when relationships are stuck at these extremes. The two levels of separated and connected seem to be the most functional across the life cycle. This is true, in part, because such relationships are able to balance separateness and togetherness, which is why they are called balanced.

The specific characteristics of the two unbalanced relationships, disengaged and enmeshed, are described in Table 9.2. Disengaged relationships emphasize the individual, and there is often very little closeness, a lack of loyalty, high independence, and high separateness. At the other extreme, enmeshed relationships emphasize togetherness, with very high closeness, high levels of loyalty, and high dependence on each other. Enmeshed relationships are typical of couples in love. They often become problematic when this level of intimacy occurs between a parent and child (for example, an enmeshed father/daughter relationship or an enmeshed mother/son relationship).

The two balanced types of family systems, as noted, are called separated and connected (see Table 9.2). At the separated level there is more emphasis on the individual and less on the relationship. Levels of closeness are often low to moderate, with moderate levels of loyalty. There is often more independence than dependence and more separateness than togetherness. At the connected level there is, again, a balance, but with more emphasis on togetherness and less on separateness. There is some loyalty to the relationship, and there is often more dependence than independence.

In the real world of loving relationships, few of us find this perfectly developed, almost spiritual balance with our partner. It is something to quest after, but it is rarely attained for long periods. It is useful to note that in our intimate relationships we experience and even enjoy, at least for a short time, both extremes on the togetherness/separateness continuum. We can remain in love with another person, even though we are away from him or her temporarily on a trip. Especially in the early stages of a relationship, we enjoy being totally together. When we are just "falling in love," it literally hurts to be away from each other for very long. We ache and pine and feel pent up with emotion and expectation of seeing each other again. Couples in this type of situation are enmeshed, and being so totally together can be very exciting—for a time. But too much togetherness leads to relationship fusion, or enmeshment. We get stuck to each other. While this feels good for a while, soon the enmeshment begins to prickle. We become like two porcupines living in a small cage. We get on each other's nerves and become bothered by our togetherness.

Two of the most common reasons why an enmeshed relationship becomes troublesome are jealousy and personification. If we are jealous, we need our partner so terribly that we do not feel we can afford to let the person out of our sight; we cannot risk losing the loved one to a competitor. Tied closely to this jealousy is the notion of personification: we make the foolish but

TABLE 9.2   Levels of Togetherness

Characteristic	Disengaged (Unbalanced)	Separated (Balanced)	Connected (Balanced)	Enmeshed (Unbalanced)
Separateness/ Togetherness	High separateness	More separateness than togetherness	More togetherness than separateness	Very high togetherness
I versus We	Emphasis on "I"	More emphasis on "I" than "we"	More emphasis on "we" than "I"	Emphasis on "we"
Closeness	Little closeness	Low to moderate closeness	Moderate to high closeness	Very high closeness
Loyalty	Lack of loyalty	Moderate loyalty	Some loyalty	High loyalty
Dependence/ Independence	High independence	More independence than dependence	More dependence than independence	High dependence

common mistake of taking everything that our partner does as a personal reflection on ourself.

To expect to be totally sheltered from the storms of life by our loved ones is a nice fantasy, but it is problematic for either individual or relationship development. It romanticizes a relationship and puts impossible expectations upon the partners. Simply put, it's unfair to expect another human being to meet all of our needs. And it's unrealistic to try to do this for a loved one. We should be good to each other, but those who try to smother each other with love only end up like the caged porcupines. One way to improve an enmeshed relationship is for each person to invest more time apart developing individual interests and abilities.

In the 1970s, the hippie generation represented an extreme that emphasized "doing your own thing." This overfocus on one's self was problematic for relationships, which require one to focus on another person. Successful couples—those who feel good about their relationships and who are functioning well in the judgment of trained professionals assessing the relationship—tend to be those couples in the center of the relationship map. They have found how to balance the "I" and "we" so they can have both their own individuality and their intimacy as a couple.

Relationship Adaptability

The second major dimension of the circumplex model, or relationship map, is adaptability. Adaptability is defined as the ability to change power structure, roles, and rules in the relationship. Cohesion, as you will recall, had various levels from low to high. Similarly, adaptability, as you can see in Table 9.3, also has various levels.

The four levels of ability to change range from very low, which is described as rigid, to extremely high, which is called chaotic. Both of these extremes are seen as problematic and as unbalanced, since families are often stuck there. In rigid relationships, there is very little change, and the leadership is often authoritarian. As a result, the discipline is strict, and the roles are very stable. At the other extreme, chaotic, there is too much change, often because of a lack of leadership. Discipline is erratic and inconsistent, partly because there are often dramatic shifts in the roles in the family.

The two balanced levels of adaptability are called structured and flexible. These two levels are characteristic of relationships that have a good balance between stability and change. Structured relationships have more moderate levels of change, with leadership that is sometimes shared. Discipline is often democratic, and the roles are stable. In flexible relationships, there is more change and often a more democratic relationship between the couple and family members. There is also more role sharing between the couple.

Jay Haley, a family therapist, suggests that families are by nature basically rigid in that they resist change. The normal family functions primarily to maintain the status quo: "When an organism indicates a change in relations to another, the other will act upon the first so as to diminish and modify the change" (Haley, 1959, p. 281).

In short, when a loved one moves to make changes in our relationship, our first reaction is often to defend against the process or at least slow it down until we can better understand what is happening. We fear the change will bring more harm than good. And the family that is solely maintenance-oriented or totally conservative in its approach is a dinosaur. As Lyman Wynne and his colleagues see it: "Families that rigidly try to main-

TABLE 9.3   Levels of Adaptability

Characteristic	Rigid (Unbalanced)	Structured (Balanced)	Flexible (Balanced)	Chaotic (Unbalanced)
Change	Very little	Moderate	Some	Great
Leadership	Authoritarian	Sometimes shared	Often shared	Lacking
Discipline	Strict	Somewhat democratic	Democratic	Erratic, inconsistent
Roles	Very stable	Stable	Shared	Dramatically shifting

tain homeostasis [the status quo] through successive developmental phases are highly disturbed and atypical. Enduring success in maintaining family homeostasis perhaps should be regarded as a distinctive feature of disorder in families" (Wynne, Ryckoff, Day, & Hirsch, 1958, p. 89).

In rigid families there is little room for change. The rules are always the same, even though the game of life outside the family continuously changes. This rigidity can be seen in such relatively trivial matters as styles of dress; the family members do not permit one another to make even the slightest changes even though styles in the community are changing. More important, the rigidity may be evidenced by resistance to changing roles in the family—maybe the mother wants to find work outside the home and the father refuses; or the daughter wants to become an engineer but her parents are not supportive.

At the other extreme are the chaotic families, almost completely without structure, without rules and roles. No one knows what to expect. For example, a young former prostitute whom I was interviewing in a court case described the family she had grown up in as very chaotic. Her mother divorced her father, and then another man moved in with her. The newcomer raped the daughter when she was 11 years old. The mother refused to believe her daughter when she told the story, or maybe the mother simply didn't want to believe it. At any rate, she decided to stay with the new man and also decided that the 11-year-old daughter was a divisive influence in the family. So the mother abandoned her daughter and left with the new lover and a younger son. The daughter was left to fend for herself on the street, and soon was involved in drugs and prostitution.

As the former prostitute described her chaotic family of origin: "It was like a sieve. Anybody could come into it, and anybody could leave, and anybody could fall through the gaps. The family wasn't safe or reliable for anybody at all." "Nothing is constant in life but change" is a reality of life. It doesn't make much sense to try to go through life without changes— changes in yourself and changes in your family. Change is inevitable, and individuals and relationships seem to do better if they are open to change.

Circumplex Types as Illustrated by the Movies

Movies often provide excellent examples of extreme couple and family relationships, because these types are more dynamically and dramatically interesting. Table 9.4 lists four movies that illustrate the four extreme types. A brief description of each movie and extreme type is given below.

The Great Santini: Rigidly Enmeshed

This is a military family, both inside and out. Dad (played by Robert Duvall) is a colonel in the Marines and wants to run his family the same way. His family is rigidly enmeshed, especially with his oldest son, whom he wants to follow in his footsteps into the Marines. On top of that, the son is supposed to excel in sports. For Dad, the son's achievement means his achievement.

But the father cannot just cheer his son from the sidelines. In a one-on-one home basketball game, the son beats the father, and the father cannot take the defeat, saying the boy must win by at least two points. He bullies the son, trying to get him to cry. He bounces the ball off the kid's forehead in a mocking, confrontive manner, trying to get his son to admit weakness after having just beaten him. None of the other kids has ever beaten the father at any sport, not at table tennis, checkers, cards, anything. Dad always has to win. So when the son beats him, Dad can't take it. He ridicules his son, trying to get him to cry so he will feel superior again. The mother acts in a codependent way. She makes excuses for him, defends him to the kids, and is careful not to cross him. This family has a very rigid system. Rules are set down and strictly enforced by Dad. There will be no defiance from them, no whimpering or complaining.

TABLE 9.4   Circumplex Types as Illustrated by Movies

Circumplex Type	Movies
Rigidly enmeshed	*Great Santini*
Rigidly disengaged	*Ordinary People*
Chaotically disengaged	*Shoot the Moon*
Chaotically enmeshed	*Who's Afraid of Virginia Woolf?*

This is a very enmeshed system. Loyalty is demanded. The son's achievements are a reflection on Dad and an extension of Dad's ego. There is no letting go of Dad. He is the center of the family and sets the tone. If he is up, the family is up; if he is down, the family had better watch out. This is an enmeshed system based on intimidation, not on affection or even feigned affection. But the intimidation works. Mom, who of course has lived with Dad the longest, has the typical way of putting herself last to keep Dad happy, and she does not question it.

Ordinary People: Rigidly Disengaged

The other extreme of the cohesion dimension is the disengaged family as seen in *Ordinary People.* There is also rigidity in this pleasant suburban family of wife (played by Mary Tyler Moore), husband (played by Donald Sutherland), and son. Unlike the angry, authoritarian rigidity of the Meechams in *The Great Santini,* this is a passive, controlling, but outwardly pleasant rigidity that maintains a good appearance to outsiders.

This rigidity was born in part out of a need to survive the family's loss of the elder son in a boating accident on Lake Michigan, just a few months before the beginning of the story. The son, Buck, was the star of the family—handsome, charming, an excellent student and fine star athlete—now tragically gone. His death has left an emptiness in his mother that she defends against through her rigidity and disengagement, which moves the rest of the family in this direction as well.

The family is characterized by emotional controlling, strictly defined roles, and unchanging rules, especially the rules about what feelings can be openly discussed. The surviving son, who has attempted suicide over his guilt surrounding the boating accident, cannot talk about his feelings in the family because of the implicit rules forbidding such intimate and painful self-disclosure. Likewise, the disengagement in this family is painfully apparent. Feelings are not discussed, and a distance is carefully maintained to prevent any further grief. There are attempts by the son and the husband to make contact with the mother, but they fail. Near the

end of the movie, she wakes up in the middle of the night and finds her husband not at her side. She goes downstairs and finds him sitting in the dining room in the dark, crying softly to himself. He says he doesn't think he knows her anymore. She is so cautious. When Buck died, a part of her died. He does not know the woman who is left behind. And he is not sure he loves her anymore. Without another word, she goes upstairs and begins packing her suitcase to leave. There is a brief moment when she gasps, and nearly cries. She regains control, resumes packing and leaves.

Both of these families are rigid, and the rigidity effects their degree of emotional closeness. In *The Great Santini,* the rigidity serves the purpose of controlling their level of enmeshment. The demands for family loyalty and the lack of individualization and emotional reactivity are thrust upon the system by the power they give to the father, who dictates the rules of the family: what people should do, how they should perform, and what their level of importance should be within his rigid view.

In *Ordinary People,* the rigidity serves the purpose of maintaining emotional disengagement in order to prevent the surfacing of grief and guilt over the loss of the elder son. It's as if Mom is keeping everyone at arm's length by emotionally stiff-arming her son and husband. And it's Mom's rigidity to which both husband and son respond by finally giving up in despair any real attempt at emotional contact.

Shoot the Moon: Chaotically Disengaged

This is a family falling apart. Dad (played by Albert Finney) has been having an affair. He has been trying to keep it from the family, but his oldest daughter is suspicious and listens in on a conversation he has with his lover from an extension at home. He has never called his lover from a phone at home before, but he is desperately in love and beginning to get careless. His wife (played by Diane Keaton) has been suspicious for some time but has not confronted him. However, his excuses for "working late" wear thin, and she finally does challenge him. A dish-breaking fight ensues. He suggests he should leave, and she says she packed his bag the night before.

The disengagement of the couple really shows in these early scenes of the movie. They have not been connected in a long time as their estrangement has become more extensive. When Dad finally does move out, the chaos in the family system takes its turn. The oldest daughter, Julie, takes over Mom's role. Mom sleeps late, buries her head under the pillow, moans, and turns over to try to escape her pain. This happens to a woman who has never before been tired and has always been patient and had time for her four daughters.

In a scene typical of the family chaos, the oldest daughter is trying to make breakfast, talk on the phone to a doctor's office to make an appointment for one of her sisters who has sprained her foot, and yell upstairs at her sisters to get downstairs for breakfast. The sisters yell back that they don't want her breakfast (that she so carefully has tried to prepare), so she yells back at them that she doesn't need this, throws the frying pan of scrambled eggs into the kitchen sink, and heads out to the school bus.

Dad is waiting at the end of the driveway to pick them up in his car to take them to school himself, trying to overcome his guilt and spend some time with his daughters at the same time. The oldest daughter just walks around his car and gets onto the bus without saying a word to him. The bus pulls out, and she can be seen looking through the bus window crying.

This couple has been disengaged for some time. And Dad is also disengaged from his daughters. Mom was close to her daughters before the separation, but even she gets disengaged from them through her depression. The rules and roles are all up for grabs in this family. The father has left, the mother is depressed and unable to function, and the oldest daughter has taken over some of the parenting roles while still wanting to have a mother and father care for her and be in charge.

Who's Afraid of Virginia Woolf?: Chaotically Enmeshed

This is a good example of a classically chaotically enmeshed alcoholic family. George (Richard Burton) and Martha (Elizabeth Taylor) have a dependent, love/hate relationship bound together by unseen but powerful forces of mutual dependence and kept toler-

able for each through the numbing and disorienting properties of alcohol.

George is an associate professor of English at a small college, and Martha is the president's daughter. Martha and her father were impressed with George at first but have become increasingly disenchanted with him over time. Martha thinks he's a "nothing," an enormous disappointment. And George thinks Martha is a monster, who, he says, used to howl and claw at the turf outside his window when he first came to the college. So he married her in order to get some work done.

They cannot let go of each other. They fight dirty: they know where to attack each other's vulnerability and don't hesitate to do so. To George, Martha is a promiscuous, liquor-ridden slut who never hesitates to make a fool of herself. And to Martha, George is a weak-willed, pretentious, academic flop. They even share a secret, mutual fantasy of a son. Since they were never able to have children, they created one. They even created a history for him and obviously invested a good deal of their hopes and dreams in this fantasy.

But one night, in an extended drunken battle in the presence of two guests, the secret is disclosed. For a while it looks as if their enmeshed relationship will come unraveled during the course of an endless nightmare of fighting. They break mutually agreed-upon rules but manage to stick together in the end, even though it looks as though they will destroy each other.

Dynamic Changes in Family Types

Change in a Marriage over Time

Let's look at one couple and their journey through married life. Steve and Sally were both raised in rather traditional homes. After three years of marriage they had their first baby, and Sally decided to resign from her teaching job. "How can I leave my own baby alone to go off to teach other people's kids?" she explained to an old friend.

Because their young son was totally dependent upon his parents and because they both felt unsure of themselves as young parents and wanted to be supportive of each other, Sally and Steve developed a connected level of family cohesion. Also, their traditional upbringing led them to the structured level on the adaptability scale of the circumplex model. Thus, they were comfortable at the time with the traditional husband-dominant power structure in their marriage. They preferred the relative security of these established patterns: Steve was the leader, and Sally usually agreed with his decisions. Rather than get into negotiations over innumerable issues, it seemed simpler to Sally to let Steve have his way. Using the circumplex model, this couple would be classified as structurally connected, and Steve and Sally liked it this way.

But life flows on. Their son was now a teenager, and Sally started pursuing a career outside the home. Both parents had been bombarded by media messages on sex-role issues for a number of years. Articles on "The New Fatherhood" and "Supermother" influenced Steve and Sally's thinking; and a television potboiler on a man in a midlife crisis really got Steve thinking. Sally attended a women's discussion group at their church. The group was ostensibly formed to give members a chance to share the joys and sorrows of childrearing; but it soon got off into personal issues, and Sally loved attending.

Steve was upset when he saw her enjoying such intimate conversations with other women, so he joined a men's group at the church, which met every Tuesday morning at 6:30. After a few weeks of nondescript talk about sports and the weather, the minister piped up and said quite sharply: "All right, let's be frank. This is all General Motors talk. It's safe, it's empty. Let's talk reality. Let's talk frankly." A few of the men had the courage to do so, and soon Steve was as happy about his discussion group as Sally. At the same time, their teenage son, Joe, was also experiencing his own need to try his wings a little. In fact, all three family members were enjoying the open space in their relationships. They began to operate at what we call a lower level of cohesiveness, moving from being connected to being more separated.

During this time the family power structure also began to change, from structured to flexible. Steve was deciding that he was sick and tired of making all the so-called big decisions in the family, and Sally began to realize that she was just as smart as he was and wanted a bigger say. Joe wasn't quite sure at the time that his parents knew anything at all, and he was always eager to offer his two cents' worth—and his parents were becoming more and more interested in his youthful ideas as they grew more open to change.

The transition period lasted about five years and was not without difficulty. The word *divorce* was mentioned a few times in a number of marital arguments, and Sally came close to having an affair with a friend at the office. But she decided against it when she saw Steve becoming more flexible in his approach to life, and happier because of it. Today Sally exercises much more control in the relationship than previously, and the couple struggles to decide how the rules, roles, and responsibilities are to be applied. Who's going to wash the dishes on Friday night, if it automatically isn't Mom's job? That issue and countless other issues take some discussing. Occasionally, Sally and Steve yearn for the good old days when things were simpler. But the excitement and challenge of their new life together are too great to give up. In the terminology of the circumplex model, they have become a flexibly separated type.

This brief case history illustrates the dynamic nature of marriage and family life, and the dynamic nature of the circumplex model. Couples and families are not locked into a particular mold forever. If family members agree to change and can agree on the direction and objectives of the change, they have a very good chance of doing so successfully. Agreeing is more than half the battle.

Of the four balanced types of families in the center of the circumplex model (see Figure 9.1), none is the so-called "ideal"—that is, none of the types is best suited for all couples at all times. Instead, the members of each couple will have to decide for themselves which of the four types they want to be their own individual "ideal." And they may change "ideals," as Steve and Sally have. Although a variety of the 16 circumplex types can work for some couples and families, therapists and researchers generally recognize that the unbalanced relationships are less functional—they simply don't work as well for people.

We can make a few generalizations about how relationships change successfully as time passes:

1. An intimate relationship is able to change (adapt) when appropriate.
2. An intimate relationship is able to balance between too much change (chaos) and too little change (rigidity).

3. Staying at either extreme too long can destroy an intimate relationship.
4. Too much change leads to unpredictability and chaos.
5. Too little change leads to high predictability and rigidity. It also leads to persons controlling each other, which is a barrier to intimacy.

Changes in Early Marriage

As we have seen in this chapter, relationships change as time passes. In the long run, the type of relationship may change in a developmental sense, as couples respond to the challenge of child rearing. You will remember how family cohesion and family adaptability tend to diminish in the middle years of the family life cycle. One of the essential goals of a family therapist is to help a family achieve a more balanced and functional relationship.

Even in the early years of marriage cohesion and adaptability can change relatively dramatically. Figure 9.4 charts the changes that one young couple, Susan and Henry, faced in only five years. As you can see, during the dating period the couple's test scores indicate a balanced relationship (within one of the four central squares of the relationship map); the couple is flexibly connected, in the terminology of the circumplex model. Henry and Susan feel close (connected) and have a flexible style of leadership and decision making.

One year later, the newlywed couple can best be described as structurally enmeshed. Susan and Henry are structured, because they are still getting organized in terms of their roles and leadership. Being in love and enjoying spending maximum time together, they are still enmeshed.

By the end of the first year of marriage, the so-called honeymoon effect has worn off, and the couple is now structurally connected. Henry and Susan's excitement with each other isn't as great as it was (this is perfectly normal, by the way), and their togetherness scores have dropped off into the more balanced range. Adaptability has increased somewhat. The couple is now in a balanced relationship—both cohesion and adaptability are in the center of the continuum.

A year passes. The second year of the marriage is ending, and Susan becomes pregnant. Pregnancy means change for any couple, and so this couple's adaptability scores go up slightly, but it is still in the balanced area on the relationship map in terms of adaptability. Henry and Susan's togetherness scores have also dropped off some; he is more involved in his work, and she is more involved in work and pregnancy. But they remain in the balanced area of the relationship map. They are now flexibly separated.

Another year passes, and the family can be described as chaotically connected. The baby has arrived, a momentous event in any couple's relationship. Change is almost inevitably high at this time. The couple is forced to adapt to the advent of this new member. A totally dependent, totally demanding person has come into the lives of the young mother and young father, and many pressures are made on their relationship. Their life is in relative turmoil, because they are up a couple times each night to feed the baby; because Susan has quit her job; because they can't go out with friends as they used to; because they're short on money; because there are 15 or 25 diapers to change each day, and so on. But they are so busy they don't have time to think about how chaotic it all is. The baby's presence has increased the sense of bonding between the husband and wife; they feel united in their goal of rearing a happy, healthy child. And they are young and energetic and seem to thrive on challenge. The chaotic connectedness seems to work for this particular couple, and Susan and Henry are happy.

Five years have passed since we first met this young couple in their dating period. The baby is 1 year old, life has stabilized, and Henry and Susan are now functioning as a rigidly separated family. They are experiencing very few changes now. She is home with a 1-year-old and enjoying the baby. He also spends a good deal of time with the infant. They have successfully scaled down their spending habits: they decided they could not afford to buy a house for a few years, and they traded the new Camaro in for an old Nova. The young couple is enjoying the stability, especially in comparison to the chaos they experienced when the baby was born. Susan and Henry's cohesion scores have also dropped off somewhat, but not dramatically. She is more involved with the baby than her husband; though he is aware of the demands his work places upon him, he cannot

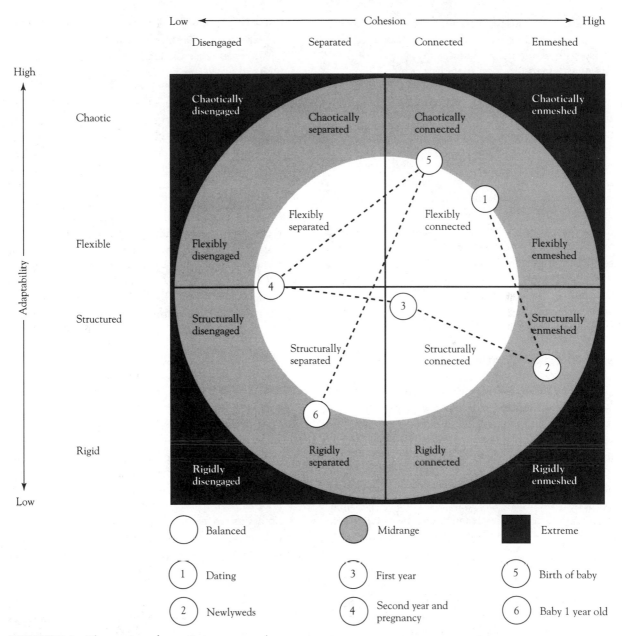

FIGURE 9.4   Changes in early marriage

control it to the extent he would like. The boss is still the boss.

In one short year Henry and Susan have bounced from one side of the relationship map to the other; but they remain a midrange family because they are balanced on cohesion, though unbalanced on adaptability.

As long as they agree that the type of relationship is working for them, the relationship will survive. But in the long run their chances for satisfaction increase if they manage to score in the balanced area of the relationship map. As this case clearly demonstrates, however, relationship dynamics do change as a way of coping with stress, and this is appropriate. In fact, Henry and Susan would have had more problems if they had resisted changing their relationship system to deal with the new demands put on them as a couple.

Cohesion across the Family Life Cycle

My colleagues and I recently surveyed 1000 couples and families nationwide (Olson et al., 1989). We studied many facets of family life, but we will look at only two in this section: how family cohesion and family adaptability change as time passes.

The levels of cohesion across the life cycle change in quite predictable ways. Figure 9.5 summarizes the results from the 1000 families, who were divided into four stages: young couples, families with children, families with teenagers, and older couples. Because these were normal families, most of the respondents' scores fell into the two balanced levels of cohesion, separated and connected. The table summarizes the percentage of families in these two levels.

As expected, a high percentage (71%) of young couples feel connected, with only 29% feeling more separated. This figure drops a few percentage points when young children arrive. By the time these children become teenagers, however, there is a reversal, with a majority (60%) of families feeling separated. This reversal is not only expected but also appropriate, because it enables the teenagers to develop more autonomy and independence, which is appropriate for that stage of the life cycle. After the children leave home, the older couples

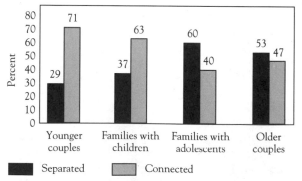

FIGURE 9.5   Family cohesion across four stages of the life cycle

shift back to an almost equal balance between those who feel separated and those who feel connected.

Adolescents see the family as significantly lower in cohesion than do the mothers and fathers. The teenagers report much lower levels of family cohesion. This is consistent with the interpretation that adolescents are seeking to differentiate themselves from the family. In order for them to accomplish this task, it is often necessary for them to become less cohesive with their parents. They say, in effect: "I don't need a lot of togetherness with Mom and Dad. So we really don't have a very close family."

Parents at this time have mixed emotions about how cohesive a relationship they wish to have with their youngsters. As one father explained: "Just two months ago I was feeling quietly perturbed that my daughter didn't go out with any other kids at all. She just hung around the house all the time and looked bored. I thought she should be running around a bit. But now—only two months later—she's turned 16. She's got her driver's license, and we never see her. She's always buzzing around. I miss her a lot. There's got to be some happy medium in between somewhere!"

Adaptability across the Family Life Cycle

Family adaptability is the "ability of a marital or family system to change its power structure, role relationships, and relationship rules in response to situational and developmental stress" (Olson et al., 1989, p. 24). Adaptability is a measure of the extent to which a family can adapt its structure, rules, and roles to meet the challenges presented by its changing needs and those of its individual members. Can the family change when it is appropriate or necessary?

For example, the grandfather in a family has died, leaving the blind grandmother alone. The family has decided it would be unfair to put her in a nursing home, because she simply needs a bit of help getting around the house and caring for herself—she really is not incapacitated to any great degree. The members of the family have decided to take Grandmother into their home; she will live in the spare bedroom. Will the family be able to make all the myriad adaptations necessary to accommodate a new household member? This is one example of the uncountable number of ways families find themselves adapting to changes in life.

In the study of 1000 families, my colleagues and I explored family adaptability across the four stages of the life cycle (Olson et al., 1989). In general, these nonclinical families fell into the balanced area of the circumplex model and were classified as either structured or flexible. Figure 9.6 summarizes these results.

Almost two-thirds of young couples without children, (62%) were flexible. When young children arrived, however, there was a reversal in this pattern, with about two-thirds (63%) being structured.

Another shift in adaptability occurred with families having teenagers. As is appropriate, these families shifted in the direction of being flexible. This is a style that would enable the family to loosen up its rules so the teenagers could have more freedom. After the teenagers have left home, almost two-thirds of the older couples (63%) developed a more flexible style of relating to each other.

When teenagers' descriptions of their family were compared with those of their parents on adaptability, teenagers tended to see their family as more structured and at times rigid. Their parents, however, tended to see their family as more flexible. These parent/adolescent differences are consistent with what was found regarding family cohesion. Because adolescents are seeking greater freedom, they tend to see the restrictions in their family as problematic and, therefore, tend to see more rigidity than their parents do. This difference in their perception can also create conflict in their relationships. However, it is an inevitable part of develop-

ment to have these differences emerge between generations as the adolescents seek more freedom and autonomy.

Although this is a cross-sectional study that provides snapshots of families at different stages, it does indicate significant differences in their style of cohesion and adaptability at the four stages of the family life cycle. One should exercise some caution, however, in these interpretations since the study is not longitudinal in nature and does not follow the same members across the various stages. However, there is a good probability that a longitudinal study would produce similar findings, since the results are predictable and have held up in other studies.

Common Problems in Marital and Family Systems

The relationship map is useful for family therapists who try to understand the various problems that families face. In this section I will present a few common relationship difficulties, as they relate to the circumplex model.

One problem that couples coming for counseling frequently describe is that the spouses feel that they are at opposite extremes on the same dimension of the relationship map. On the cohesion dimension, for example, one partner may want more togetherness than the other; the other partner may be perfectly happy with the situation as it stands. Similarly, on the adaptability dimension, one partner may wish for more flexibility in the family system, while the other partner is satisfied with the patterns of the family.

A second common problem for couples is that both partners are at the same extreme on one or both dimensions. Both may be disengaged from the relationship, so heavily involved in career or outside interests that they have no time for the marriage. Or both may be enmeshed in each other, so heavily invested in the other partner that they have no room to develop their own personal interests and skills.

This all may sound quite simple, but the difficulty comes because people see their relationship differently and have different expectations. For example, the wife and the husband often come up with different descriptions and goals for their family type. Add a teenage

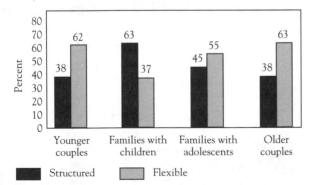

FIGURE 9.6   Family adaptability across four stages of the life cycle

child, and you may have three different definitions of the situation.

If we were to take 50 wives who were going through a divorce with 50 husbands and have each of the 100 people tell his or her story of why the marriage had broken down, it would be almost impossible for a trained professional to match up the partners with their spouse on the basis of the descriptions of the marriage and the spouses' personalities. A wife may describe her husband as a total monster who is drunk much of the time, has gone through numerous jobs in five years, and beats her and the young children on a regular basis. Her husband may describe himself as a "social drinker" with no real problem; he happens to change jobs occasionally because he has had a string of bad luck with a few lousy bosses. Although his wife is really a rotten, nagging woman who has made the young boys into a "bunch of sissies," he has never laid a hand on her or the kids.

The wife sees the marriage from her unique perspective, and so does the husband. The kids have their views. The family therapist also develops a picture of the marriage from observing interaction in the counseling setting.

There is no simple solution to this dilemma. If the counselor were to interview only one person in the family—say the husband or wife—it would be easy. The counselor would get one relatively coherent picture. But the picture wouldn't represent the complexity of the family. So the solution lies in getting everyone together, asking countless questions, and refereeing many arguments over what is true about the family and what is not true. After all this time-consuming effort, the therapist and the family members may develop a valid picture of the family dynamics.

A Premarital Couple and Their Families of Origin

Kathy and Jim, a premarital couple, have described how they perceive their families of origin. This analysis will compare their families and how this background influences the couple's relationship and the kind of relationship they want (see Figure 9.7).

Kathy's Family Is Structurally Enmeshed

Her family: There are six children, aged 18–27, Kathy being the third oldest. Her parents have been married for 28 years. All of the children, except Kathy, live and work in the same town.

Structured on adaptability: While growing up, the kids knew what was expected of them. The parents were firm yet fair with their discipline and enforcement of family rules. While the mother may be strong and a thorough organizer, the father has been equally strong, and even stubborn at times. He always acted as the head of the household but respected his wife's education, contributions, and ability. The mother has not minded playing a somewhat traditional role. She also works hard at keeping the family together. She is a superb organizer and is heavily involved in the lives of each of her six children.

Enmeshed on cohesion: This is a close-knit, Roman Catholic family from a small town. All of the children except John, 18, have left home and settled down in the local community. Only the third oldest, Kathy, has moved away, to a larger city about 120 miles away. The kids are in and out of their house two or three times during the week and at least once every weekend. On week nights they'll play cards or just sit around and talk. The whole family gets together at least every other weekend for Sunday dinner and to spend the afternoon. The mother feels excited when the children are excited, and guilty when they are down, and she is always trying to take care of them emotionally in some way. The father is also heavily involved in the lives of his kids. He has high expectations of them and doesn't mind letting them know whenever they have disappointed him.

Jim's Family Is Flexibly Disengaged

His family: There are two children, Jim and his brother, four years younger. His parents have been married for 27 years and are separated. After several years of frustration, his mother decided that she had had enough and asked for a separation. His father moved out several months ago. He has been asking for a reconciliation, saying he has changed. But she is suspicious of any "instant" changes in him, and she decided to wait and see if these changes (to be less controlling

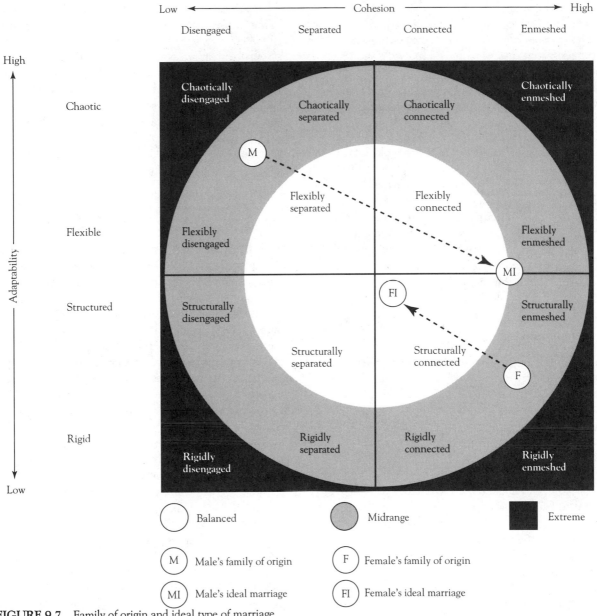

FIGURE 9.7 Family of origin and ideal type of marriage

and, reduce his drinking and verbally abusive behavior) are permanent.

Flexible on adaptability: This is a family that has undergone some changes over the past several years. It was closer to a structured family for many years. The mother and father had traditional male and female roles: he laid down the rules, and she backed him up. After 15 years as a housewife, however, she went back to school and got a two-year certificate in bookkeeping. Her self-esteem changed. She became more confident in herself and more assertive in her relationship with her husband. The family system became more flexible.

Jim's father would help out some with household chores and cooked some meals while his wife was in a night class or had to work late. He became more lenient with the boys as he saw that they were fairly responsible and willing to readily pitch in and help more around the house.

Disengaged on cohesion: The boys were heavily involved in school activities, and the parents had their own separate interests. Dad had his hunting and fishing, and Mom had her church activities. Dad would take the boys hunting and fishing when they got old enough, and he even went on several canoe trips with them. But these outings were the only time that they were close. Their ties to people on the outside are often closer than their ties to one another. Each person in the family has his or her friends, who are sometimes more important than other family members. Most of the time they go their own way and do their own thing. There are very few times when they are together.

Jim and Kathy: Two Types of Ideal Marriage

These two diverse family systems have presented some problems for this couple. Kathy would really like a connected marriage, in which she would have more emotional space and greater flexibility in the relationship's rules and expectations than is the case in her enmeshed family of origin (see Figure 9.7). Jim would like an enmeshed marriage in reaction to his disengaged family of origin. He has had a lot of pain and disappointment in the breakup of his parents' marriage, and he has pledged not to make the mistakes they did. He doesn't want to be in another disengaged system where people go their own way and do not connect emotionally.

One of the struggles Kathy and Jim are having as a premarital couple is negotiating just how much closeness they want from the relationship. Since it's hard for him to say what he is really feeling and to share his need for closeness in a more direct way with her, his desire to be closer to her is sometimes interpreted as an attempt to control her. She wants to avoid the overcontrolling atmosphere of enmeshment that existed in her family, so she sometimes backs away from him when he is needy and wanting closeness from her. He isn't always aware of how he tries to control her or even why he wants to do so. He is more aware of the outcome of his efforts: that she withdraws from him.

Both Jim and Kathy want a structured marriage. While Jim sympathizes with his mother, emotionally he still leans toward his father's value of a structured system, with more stable male and female roles and predictable family rules and patterns. This is the level of adaptability with which he is most comfortable. Kathy would also like a structured marriage, with fairly stable roles and a distribution of responsibilities. She likes the predictability of a structured system but also wants a career and wants to be respected for what she contributes economically.

Using the Circumplex Model in Treatment

The relationship map is often used by marital and family therapists to diagnose and treat various problems. The following is an example of how the circumplex model is used in the diagnosis and treatment of a chemically dependent family. Let's call it the Davis family. The family therapist diagnosed the family as rigidly enmeshed, extreme on both dimensions. The treatment plan was to move the family to being structurally connected, a family type that is balanced and one step toward the balanced level on both cohesion and adaptability (see Figure 9.1).

Family Diagnosis

The Davis family has five members: Mary and Don, the parents; 18-year-old Ann; 16-year-old Julie; and 9-year-old Peter. Mary is chemically dependent. She drinks to relieve feelings of inadequacy in the family, which is dominated by two high-achievers, Don and Ann. Mary is consoled by Julie, who also feels inadequate but does not drink and is responsible enough to be a surrogate mother to the youngest child, Peter. The family came in for therapy shortly after Mary began treatment for her alcoholism. Ann had left home, angry at Mary for all the problems she had caused. Julie felt lost because her mother was being "taken care of" by other people and Julie's role as chief consoler was gone.

In terms of cohesion, the Davises evidenced high emotional bonding as well as high mutual dependency. They were very enmeshed. The mother and two daughters were engaged in intense competition for approval from one another and from Don. Peter kept Julie connected to the rest of the family after she felt cast adrift when her mother went off to alcohol treatment.

The family's external boundaries were closed off. No one felt free to interact with other people outside the family, partly because they were afraid that Mary would be drunk and embarrass everyone. Friends and relatives were all kept at a distance by family members, who jealously feared losing one another. And when Julie tried to make friends with the family therapist, she was given a strong nonverbal message by the rest of the family that this was a mistake. The only time husband and wife really made contact with each other was to team up as parents when one of the children misbehaved. Then the two would support each other. Otherwise they did not interact much. The father/daughter coalitions were strong, especially the coalition between Don and Ann. In many ways they played the role of parents in the family, for Mary was often incapable because of her drinking.

Individual activities were permitted, but only within family-approved guidelines. Tennis was approved: Don and Ann spent a lot of time playing tennis together. But Julie's desire to spend the same amount of time away from the family "partying" with friends was not approved. Close friends, especially boys, were not allowed. Though no one ever said this in so many words, it was a fact of family life. The family tried desperately to have fun at their cabin on weekends. But the implicit message was "You will have fun!" because everyone was required to go to the cabin. The result was that nobody enjoyed these weekends. At home, Mary made life difficult for everyone else by insisting that each be just as compulsive about housekeeping standards as she was. When she felt upset about life, she tended to clean house or drink. Or both.

Much of the conflict in the family seemed due to the Davises' low level of adaptability. The family system and each of the members were too rigid to respond in new ways to a situation or problem. Also, no one in the family knew how to be appropriately assertive. Rather than making a point firmly but without malice or a loud voice, the family members were locked into aggressive behaviors: screaming, throwing things, and occasionally striking one another.

Family roles were stereotypic. Mary saw herself as in charge of the house and Don as boss of the children. Don was seen as the rule enforcer. When things got out of hand, he meted out punishment in a heavy-handed manner. Mary made many impossible threats but rarely carried them out. The children did not know how to negotiate their positions in the family. When their parents made demands, the most common response was an angry string of swear words, followed by an angry counter-response from the parents.

All in all, the family rules, roles, and leadership design were too rigid. But as new situations developed in the family, the members did not have the flexibility to negotiate and create solutions that were reasonable. Ann and Julie could not discuss possible changes in a rational fashion with their parents. The Davises were locked into a dysfunctional system; they were rigidly enmeshed.

Family Treatment

The family therapist sought to focus on those issues in the family where there was already some movement in a positive direction. On the dimension of cohesion, the goal was to increase the level of individual autonomy in the family—in short, to give each member more space.

A related goal was to strengthen the marriage. In terms of adaptability, the family therapist taught members how to negotiate and compromise, rather than alternating between times of quiet passivity and times of total war. They were taught to see family rules as general guidelines that would need to be discussed and interpreted as new situations arose in day-to-day living. Thus, the children had a chance to argue a particular point and even a chance to change their parents' minds occasionally. When the family as a whole had learned adequate negotiating skills, it was discharged.

Don and Mary continued as a couple in marital therapy. The therapist focused on ways they could learn to enjoy each other's company again. They were encouraged to go out on dates without the children and to do things together they hadn't felt they had time to do for many, many years.

As the marriage improved, the number of disagreements with the children began to diminish. How could this be? As the marital coalition strengthened, it was less necessary for Julie and Ann to struggle for a position in coalition with Don. Mary was taking back her rightful place in the parental team, and Ann didn't feel it was necessary anymore to try to fill the vacuum.

The family therapist got a good deal of help from the alcohol counselors and from Alcoholics Anonymous. The chemical-dependency specialists were adept at helping Mary maintain sobriety once she had attained it. Al-Anon, which focuses on the family of the alcoholic, gave Don and the children good support and ideas in their struggle to live with an alcoholic.

As Mary became more secure in her marriage with Don, she could be more supportive of Julie in her growth as an individual. The family members were becoming able to separate and connect freely with one another. This all may sound like a fairy tale, especially if you are in a troubled family. But families do change. Marital and family therapists specialize in the treatment of family behavior, and these professionals can guide families who want to deal with their problems. Also, many find the relationship map a useful tool in the treatment process.

Chapter Summary

Describing Your Family

It's now time for you to evaluate how you perceive your family. Answer the two sets of five questions about family cohesion and adaptability, and sum the total for each area. Then plot the location onto the family map, using your scores on cohesion and adaptability (see Figure 9.8).

Family Cohesion (Togetherness)

Circle the number that you feel best describes your family:

1. How close do you feel to other family members?

1	2	3	4
not very close	moderately close	very close	extremely close

2. How often does your family spend free time together?

1	2	3	4
seldom	sometimes	often	very often

3. How does your family balance separateness and togetherness?

1	2	3	4
mainly separateness	more separateness than togetherness	more togetherness than separateness	mainly togetherness

4. How independent or dependent are family members?

1	2	3	4
very independent	more independent than dependent	more dependent than independent	very dependent

5. Answer either part a or b:
   a. For married couples: how close are the husband and wife?

1	2	3	4
seldom close	moderately close	very close	extremely close

   b. For single-parent families: how close is the parent to another adult?

1	2	3	4
seldom close	moderately close	very close	extremely close

Add your responses to the five questions to get a total cohesion score.

Family Cohesion (Togetherness) Score ____

Family Adaptability (Flexibility)

Circle the number that you feel best describes your family:

1. What kind of leadership is there in your family?

1	2	3	4
One person usually leads.	Leadership is sometimes shared.	Leadership is shared.	No clear leadership.

2. How often do family members do the same things (roles) around the house?

1	2	3	4
almost always	often	sometimes	seldom

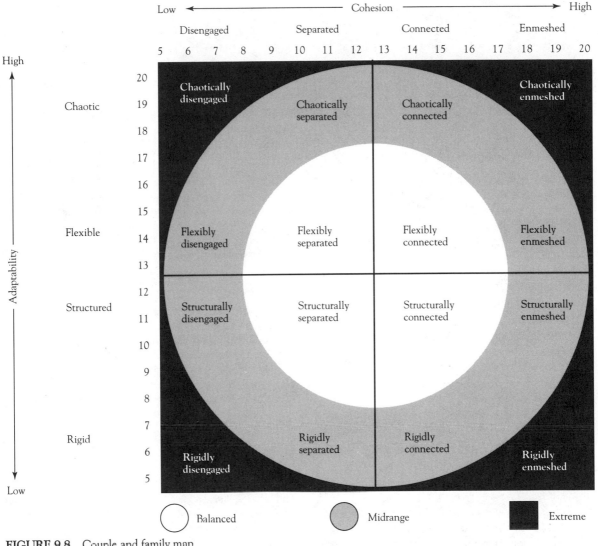

FIGURE 9.8 Couple and family map

3. What are the rules (written or unwritten) like in your family?

1	2	3	4
Rules are very clear and very stable.	Rules are clear and stable.	Rules are clear and flexible and change often.	Rules are seldom clear and change often.

4. How is discipline of children handled?

1	2	3	4
very strict	somewhat democratic	democratic	very lenient

5. How open is your family to making changes when they appear necessary?

1	2	3	4
seldom open	somewhat open	generally open	very open

Add your responses to the five questions to get a total adaptability score.

Family Adaptability (Flexibility) Score _____
Now consider the following questions:

1. What is it like to live in your type of family (for example, flexibly connected or rigidly enmeshed).
2. In what ways related to cohesion and adaptability was your family satisfying and frustrating?
3. How did your family change on cohesion and adaptability as you were growing up?
4. Did your family change on the circumplex model during times of high stress?

Discussion Questions

1. Change is inevitable in families. Your family of origin has gone through several relationship changes through the years. For this activity, sit down with your mother and/or father for at least 45 minutes. Explain the relationship map to them. Then asked them to plot out on a relationship map how the family has changed through the years. (Show them Figure 9.4 as an example to follow.) Discuss with your parent(s) these changes your family has gone through and the reasons for them. Then, with classmates in small groups, discuss the map you have done with your parents. Compare and contrast the differences in the maps.
2. Write a one-page description of your "ideal marriage" in terms of the circumplex model. Then compare it with your perception of reality in your family of origin. Compare your ideal and the reality of your family of origin with classmates in a small-group discussion.
3. If you are dating someone, are engaged, or are married, have your partner take the family cohesion and adaptability questionnaires, answering the questions in two ways: in terms of his or her family of origin and in terms of his or her ideal marriage. Compare your partner's scores with yours, and discuss similarities and differences.

Additional Resources

Constantine, L. L. (1986). *Family paradigms: The practice of theory in family therapy.* New York: Guilford Press.

Olson, D. H., McCubbin, H. I., Barnes, H. L., Larsen, A. S., Muxen, M. J., & Wilson, M. A. (1989). *Families: What makes them work.* Newbury Park, CA: Sage.

Reiss, D. (1981). *The family's construction of reality.* Cambridge, MA: Harvard University Press.

References

Barnes, H., & Olson, D. H. (1985). Parent-adolescent communication and the circumplex model. *Child Development, 56,* 438–447.

Beavers, W. B., & Hampson, R. B. (1990). *Successful families: Assessment and intervention.* New York: Norton.

Broderick, C. B. (1993). *Understanding family process: Basics of family systems theory.* Newbury Park, CA: Sage.

Carnes, P. (1989). *Contrary to love: Helping the sexual addict.* Minneapolis: Comp-Care Publications.

Clarke, J. (1984). *The family types of neurotics, schizophrenics and normals.* Unpublished doctoral dissertation, Family Social Science, University of Minnesota, St. Paul.

Epstein, N. B., Bishop, D. S., Ryan, C., Miller, I, & Keitner, D. (1993). The McMaster model of healthy family functioning. In F. Walsh (Ed.), *Normal family processes* (2nd ed.) (pp. 138–160). New York: Guilford Press.

Garbarino, J., Sebes, J., & Schellenbach, C. (1984). Families at risk for destructive parent-child relations in adolescents. *Child Development, 55,* 174–183.

Gilles, J. (1974). *My needs, your needs, our needs.* Bergenfield, NJ: New American Library.

Haley, J. (1959). The family of the schizophrenic: A model system. *Journal of Nervous and Mental Disorders, 129,* 357–374.

Hill, R., & Hansen, D. A. (1960). The identification of conceptual frameworks utilized in family study. *Marriage and Family Living, 22,* 299–311.

Kantor, D., & Lehr, W. (1975). *Inside the family.* San Francisco: Jossey-Bass.

Killorin, E., & Olson, D. H. (1984). The chaotic flippers in treatment. In E. Kaufman (Ed.), *Power to change: Alcoholism.* New York: Gardner.

Olson, D. H. (1993). Circumplex model of marital and family systems: Assessing family functioning. In F. Walsh (Ed.), *Normal family processes* (2nd ed.) (pp. 104–137). New York: Guilford Press.

Olson, D. H., & Killorin, E. (1985). *Clinical rating scale.* St Paul: University of Minnesota, Family Social Science.

Olson, D. H., Mc Cubbin, H. I., Barnes, H., Larsen, A., Muxen, M., & Wilson, M. (1989). *Families: What makes them work* (2nd ed.). Newbury Park, CA: Sage.

Reiss, D. (1981). *The family's construction of reality.* Cambridge, MA: Harvard University Press.

Rodick, J. D., Henggler, S. W., & Hanson, C. L. (1986). An evaluation of family adaptability, cohesion evaluation scales (FACES) and the circumplex model. *Journal of Abnormal Child Psychology, 14,* 77–87.

Stinnett, N, & De Frain, J. (1985). *Secrets of strong families.* Boston: Little, Brown.

Walsh, F., & Olson, D. H. (1989). Utility of the circumplex model with severely dysfunctional family systems. In D. H. Olson, C. S. Russell, & D. H. Sprenkle (Eds.), *Circumplex model: Systemic assessment and treatment of families* (2nd ed.). New York: Haworth Press.

Wynne, L., Ryckoff, I. M., Day, J., & Hirsch, S. I. (1958). Pseudo-mutuality in the family relations of schizophrenics. *Psychiatry, 21,* 205–222.

CHAPTER 10

Families in Everyday Life

Barbara H. Settles

University of Delaware

In Chapter 6 of this text (Family-Systems Theory), it was suggested that there are three levels, or layers, of family living. Level I is the visible daily interactions and associations of family life. This chapter is dedicated to that topic. Too often the daily, visible associations of life are ignored or thought of as mundane. I will propose in this chapter that the study of this topic can bring significant insight and attention to necessary and interesting processes within families.

Everyday life in families comprises the vast majority of the individual's and family's real experience and forms the fabric of our existence. The development of meaningful relationships, the choice of and investment in activities and resources that are essential to ordinary survival, the construction of meaning of the past, and the process of making decisions about the future occur as a rich and heterogeneous medley of events. Much of the action in daily life seems to go on without much conscious thought or awareness, and this background quality has meant that both families and family scientists have often taken it for granted. They have not paid attention to the processes of maintaining practices or the ordinary shifts in family and household maintenance of patterns of action. It is easy to think about families in crisis or transition as if those times were the most important events in defining family life. Under such challenging conditions, the family often brings the status quo to the level of awareness because its routines and practices of daily life are no longer adequate to handle the issues of the day. However, even when the family must face a major trauma or opportunity, there remains a need to get through the day. People must be

fed, sanitation attended to, bills paid, children and the elderly cared for, clothes cleaned, and some diversion found from the worries of the moment. The routines of daily life may provide a major coping mechanism under challenge, and research on both individuals and families frequently links successful strategies to a pattern of previously adequate coping with daily hassles and solving of problems (Hill & Hansen, 1964, Rettig, 1993; Tallman, 1993).

Background of the Study of Daily Life

Family crises and transitions are especially useful to scholars, because the disturbance to daily life makes members aware of their own family and household functioning and more easily available for study. In these times, providers of social and technical services, friends, and members of the extended kinship network may be drawn into the family members' lives and may participate in structuring the response and augmenting household resources. Much of our research in family studies is funded to address these problematic aspects of family life, and we know less about the time between such striking events. For example, disease and disability research groups are often willing to fund studies on family adaptation and coping with a specific syndrome. However, studies often compare situations and outcomes for "at-risk" families with those of "normal" families without a clear baseline or documentation of what constitutes normality either in the problematic family or its comparable counterpart. If enough data are gathered

154

for a full view of both groups, the variation and distribution on many variables may be found to overlap, and the so-called normal sample may be found to contain other problems that are simply unlabeled (Lucca & Settles, 1981; Settles, 1980). Since a good deal of the research on problems is funded by the interest groups for each problem, it has been difficult to rise above the labeled problem—that is, cystic fibrosis, unwed parenthood, mental illness, retirement, divorce, or adoption. Conceptually, there is little to tell us about the normal level of insult, injury, and disturbance in families and households and about the usual demands for flexibility and problem solving. There is a general belief that economic security and social status moderate the numbers and difficulties faced by families and provide the basis for household formation and maintenance (Adams, 1986). But the sophistication necessary to provide any standards for assessing stress and coping in the normal or expected range has continued to elude many family studies. Studies that describe how families respond to specific stresses and challenges may be helpful to those who would like to understand the general processes by helping scholars identify continuity as well as discontinuity with previous strategies. For example, Patterson's (1985) discussion of family response to home treatment for children with cystic fibrosis helps the practitioner understand the wide variety of responses that families can make to similar situations and see that these responses involve similar processes. Giele (1984) discusses the family's role in helping handicapped members in terms of the flexibility of its resources. As deinstitutionalization of people with special needs and earlier discharge from hospitals have increased, more families face the care of challenged members as part of everyday life (Settles, 1987).

While the limits to knowledge about everyday life in families and households are clear, there is also a large body of research and practice that speaks to important aspects of this concern and that can be used to generate larger theoretical questions and guide future work (McKenry & Price, 1984).

Home Economics and Rural Sociology

Two of the professional groups that have studied ordinary families going about their regular lives have been the home economists and the rural sociologists. Since these groups were frequently located in colleges of agriculture and these colleges had ongoing research programs funded through the agricultural experiment stations, they had an opportunity early on to look at the relationship between family and the work of farming as a normal situation without having to focus on families with problems. Rural sociologists have been interested in role relationships and the relationship of families to community development (Broderick, 1988). For example, many studies of mobility, part-time farming, and adoption of new technologies included both spouses as informants and looked at the effects on both husbands and wives. Studies of division of labor, time use, improving quality of home and work life, economic management, and the contributions of spouses and children to both work and family were studied quite early (Berger, 1984; Liston, 1993; Staab, 1993; Williams, 1993). These research studies and discussions provide us with a baseline for looking at today's families (Culley, Settles, & Van Name, 1976). For example, time-use studies that were begun in the 1920s and that have continued to be replicated typically find that the total time spent in homemaking is likely to be dominated by food preparation, clothes, and house care (Berger, 1984). Even though the wife's employment may slightly reduce the overall time spent in housework, the bulk of housework is not changed greatly by labor-saving devices or sharing of the work by husband or children (Nikols & Metzen, 1978; Vanek, 1974; Virginia Agricultural Experiment Station, 1981; Walker & Woods, 1976). Recent analyses of time-use data across the family life cycle show that the differential between the amount of time spent in work remains important even in retirement, with women retaining a longer work week (Rexroat & Sheehan, 1987, Szinovacz, 1992). Attempting to look at change and education for more equitable roles is in its infancy (Halkins & Roberts, 1992).

In addition, home economists have been interested in consumer and decision-making strategies and normal developmental growth and learning in children and youths. The education programs for secondary-school home economics teachers financed by federal legislation early in this century also supported research and curriculum work in the land-grant and traditionally black colleges and in the state departments of public instruction, which emphasized improving life for ordinary families and using technology for the betterment of all individuals and families (Wallace & Hall, 1984). The comprehensive research in nutrition and family food practices since the 1930s has included a broad range of family-living variables (Wyse, 1984) and an analysis of family structures and life-cycle and cultural differences as influences and constraints on family food choices and the social meaning of food (Lewin, 1943; Penfield & Axelson, 1984).

In the 1920s most departments or schools of home economics added two laboratory teaching and research situations to their curricula. First, early-childhood studies, or the nursery demonstration school, became a critical part of the program of preparation for high school teachers of home economics as an experiment in progressive child-development and parenting techniques (Frank, 1962). The schools demonstrated the possibility of educationally relevant programs for young children, showed that young children could be disciplined without physical punishment, and showed that with a professionally trained teacher, young children could work and learn in groups. While a complete history and an evaluation of these programs remain to be written, the legacy of interest in the positive study of ordinary children and in the centrality of families continues to be an important factor in most family-science programs (Dickerscheid, 1984). Early-childhood education has emerged as a major field of professional and research endeavor with its own professional organizations and journals.

The second laboratory that was widely adopted in training programs for high school teachers and nutritionists was the home-management house. This course, directed toward seniors, was usually taken before or after student teaching or fieldwork. It involved several students doing a living and learning experience together in a family-sized house, often with a foster child or baby-sitting component, modeling newer recommendations for managing the aspects of daily life and homemaking that were being suggested by research and theory in the field. Historically, for many students this experience was the first exposure to upper-middle-class options and materials and to an awareness that there are a vast number of alternatives in putting together

household and family routines. In contrast to the earlier tradition of college dormitory life, today's students have the choice of living in their own apartments and working while in school and being allowed to continue in or return to college when married. By now, the home-management house seems an awkward or artificial way to learn about managing daily life and decisions about lifestyle. Contemporary methods of instruction in home management include analysis of case studies, vignettes, game and computer simulations, fieldwork, and interviews (Rice & Tucker, 1986; Van Name, 1993). These current approaches attempt to provide a valuable check on reality. It would be helpful if professionals who are trying to help families had more opportunity to enter the reality of what adopting their own advice means in daily life. Some work in developing computer models of decision making and problem solving in life situations is under way in home-management and family-studies research, and interactive teaching techniques are also being used to help students get a stronger foundation in the reality of everyday life in families (Settles, 1993; Settles & Berke, 1989).

Psychology and Anthropology

Among other professional groups that have sought to look at the common threads in ordinary life are developmental psychologists and cultural anthropologists. From developmental psychology the field has gained an appreciation of the wide variation in how people normally change and the need to carefully measure phenomena used for analytic purposes and to estimate the measurement error inherent in this work. The invention and development of statistical analysis in the biological and developmental aspects of psychology have been critical to our use of a scientific paradigm in family studies. The use of physical measures as well as reports and observational techniques has been important to understanding daily life. Family therapy has not only used laboratory settings to conduct research on family processes (Doherty & Baptiste, 1993; Minuchin, Rosman, & Baker, 1978) but has also developed its entire program of professional training based on the use of observation and video documentation of the learning and interaction pattern with families in therapy (Nichols & Schwartz, 1991, pp. 129, 556). Both observation and physical measures have been especially useful in studies dealing with stress, coping with physical problems, and coping with situations where family members' verbal skills are limited or undependable. In family, child-development, nutrition, and time-use studies, self-report techniques have also been augmented by the use of physical tracking and input/output measures. For example, such technologies as beepers, voice-activated microphones, video monitors, and in-home observation have helped researchers get a better idea of family processes and practices. The use of physical tests such as blood sugar and heart rate have been made easier and less intrusive than previously and can be used to validate other social measures.

Cultural anthropology, which blossomed following the great findings in archaeology and field trips into undeveloped parts of the world in the 19th century, has, by documenting the great variety of culturally sanctioned living arrangements and daily routines, greatly expanded our perception of what qualifies as a normal and reasonable way to live (Lee, 1987; Lee & Haas, 1993). The strong interest by anthropologists in how family and tribal relationships can influence the organization of even fairly large cultural groups as a basic social-organizational tool has been useful in directing the ways sociologists and family scientists examine families' and individuals' participation in the larger bureaucratic organization of contemporary societies (Adams & Steinmetz, 1993). The development of comparative databases and cross-national studies has been an interesting advance in the study of daily life, although issues of measurement and comparability remain difficult to resolve (Lee & Haas, 1993). For example, the classic three-nation comparison of how parents and their adolescent children played a game helped us understand the difficulty of even doing the same experiment in differing cultural situations (Straus, 1968; Straus & Tallman, 1971).

In each culture the situations presented by the simulation game required parents and children to stretch their ordinary roles vis-à-vis each other but even that idea was differently received by subjects. It is often possible to find analogues cross-culturally and historically to practices in the society's current issues, but we can never be sure about all the elements to be compared. In the study of household work, for example, it

seems evident that tasks are circumscribed more by the total time and energy available than the time or effort level that is most efficient to do the task. Often, standards are increased as more time is liberated by changed technology (Cowas, 1983).

Newer Developments in the Study of Daily Life

The multidisciplinary concern about family life and its impact on other phenomena has become even more evident in recent developments in related fields. History has recognized as a specialty the work of specifying how daily life relates to broader events. Several scholars working between history and demography have found methods for looking at the life course of individuals and groups and relating critical cohort events to familial participation and the structure of daily life (Bengston & Allen, 1993; Hareven, 1987).

In nursing and medicine, family-centered care has emerged as an important movement for change in the way medical problems and treatment are addressed. At the two extremes of medical intervention, practitioners of critical and chronic care, at one end, and preventive education, at the other, have become aware that the family arrangements and lifestyle choices of individuals do make a major and critical difference in responsiveness and outcome of interventions (Doolittle & Wiggens, 1993). While most of this concern has centered on specific health or prevention practices that the professionals were involved in encouraging, the findings of these studies have created an interest in understanding the normal ways families behave and change, and many collaborative efforts in research and training have been undertaken recently involving medical, nursing, and other therapeutic specialties with family scholars.

Marriage and Family Therapy

In family studies itself the rapid development of the profession of marriage and family therapy within the past three decades has provided tremendous energy and demand for clearer understanding of how families work things out when they function without formal help and when different levels of intervention, education, and additional resources are available (Carter & McGoldrick, 1980). The essential problem of knowing when treatment can be viewed as successful has directed attention and resources to examining ordinary family functioning (Howe & Reiss, 1993). In Chapter 9, in Olson's work on examining two dimensions of family structure and process, cohesion and adaptability, it can be seen that the concepts came out of therapeutic hypotheses and have now been widely used in studies of many kinds of families and many levels of stressful situations. Frequently, studies using these variables and the instruments developed by the team note that extremes of these dimensions are more related to dysfunctional outcomes than the originally hypothesized direction of enmeshed and rigid family organization (Volk, Edwards, Lewis, & Sprenkle, 1989). Therapists are interested not only in knowing the big trends but also in estimating more proximate effects on specific people. Since their competency is judged by both clients and referral groups, they need and support qualitative study that emphasizes process and nondeterminent outcomes. Because many of their clients are not able to participate in long-term therapy, studies that identify continuing impact or lack of it are also highly desired. A similar situation existed for family-life and parent education for many years.

Further Research on Home and Family Life

In the 1930s a major funding effort from the Laura Spellman Rockefeller foundation provided a boost to activities in parent education and evaluation (Hendrickson, 1963). Many creative and interesting programs were developed and institutionalized, but with the end of this funding the field was not expanded. In the 1950s and 1960s interest was rekindled, but review of the small and discursive studies that had been done of the efficacy of parent education did not find any basis to indicate that it was particularly cost-effective or productive of change (Brim, 1959). Although parents involved seemed to follow the general precepts of the programs, it was not clear that it was the programs that made the difference, because control groups had similar views and practices. It was not until attention was drawn to people whose inability to function as a caring

parent had been identified by the discovery of child abuse and neglect that the efficacy of parent education was revisited (Noller & Taylor, 1989). To the surprise of many practitioners, classes in elementary child development and nonviolent disciplinary techniques proved to be far more effective than anticipated, and major psychiatric intervention appeared to be necessary less frequently than the development of some social support, social integration, and resocialization experiences. Apparently, one of the problems in understanding how fairly well-functioning families handle challenge is that they have multiple support and information resources. Only when we find a truly isolated and uninformed family can the impact of a single source of data be seen clearly. Currently the use of parental support and educational interventions to prevent problems for at-risk populations is being demonstrated and studied widely (Devlin, Brown, Beebe, & Porulis, 1992). For example, federal drug- and alcohol-prevention grants have funded several programs that reach out to various risk groups (Wood, 1992). Although the results are not complete, preliminary formative evaluation suggests that these approaches may have some impact. Certainly over the years evaluations of parent programs have suggested a role for family-life education in prevention (Sterne & Alvarez, 1992).

In social work and the legal professions the need to deal with estimating costs of everyday life in families for use in reimbursing foster care and administering divorce settlements and custody arrangements has led to the study of how information about usual expenditures and choices at different levels of living could or should be used in finding equitable solutions (Culley et al., 1976; Espenshade, 1973; Weitzman, 1985). The U. S. Department of Agriculture prepares and updates a cost estimate for family food expenditures at four different levels of living that can meet nutritional standards and serve the needs of those family members of different ages and sexes within the constraints of those budgets, although the lowest level is meant to be only temporary (Culley et al., 1976). This set of assumptions is not always really understood when it is used for many applications in service to families and for such programs as food stamps and nutrition aid for mothers and young children. Another indicator that is based on assumptions about family practices and needs is the Consumer

Price Index, which includes specific assumptions about a market basket of products needed by households, including food, shelter, clothing, medical care, and transportation. The surveys on which this market basket was based have attempted to chart the real expenditures of a sample of households that is thought to be representative of the country. This economic research is not any more value-free than other research, and there are specific ideas about what a household is, what the important indicators of level of living are, and when new items become a standard part of daily life. Consumer Price Index data are used in labor negotiations, salary administration, and other policy decisions that affect families directly. It is important to recognize that our perception and knowledge about the everyday life and expectations of families are used to shape programs and policies at every level of government and industry. Gubrium and Holstein (1990), in their analysis of how we view the family, discuss the ways social workers operate in triaging their caseloads for removing children from home environments. Often the frontline case worker uses housekeeping and home-management quality as indicators of family organization or disorganization.

The study of everyday life is now coming to the forefront of research and practice and holds great promise for the future of family science. Scholars and practitioners need to be aware of how interdisciplinary techniques and teams can be used to strengthen family science and increase our understanding of all families.

Diversity in Families and Daily Life

Many people use their own lives, families, and home situations as a point of departure when thinking about the ordinary family. Others use the mythological ideals of some past period when, they feel, families were indeed functioning better. The diversity of families and cultural backgrounds that is recognized as fundamental to the study of family life in general is particularly critical when daily life is described. Of course, everyone's activities of daily living include much the same elements, in order for people to meet their needs for food, sleep, socialization, entertainment, sexuality, communication, shelter, status, and support. But the style, the meaning, and the specific actions are embedded in cultural and economic institutions. Whether a household is even defined as a family may well depend on how the society tolerates the diversity found everywhere. Jessie Bernard (1987) in her book *The Female World from a Global Perspective* notes that within the household the use of the space and the division of labor and responsibilities vary greatly from culture to culture and among the classes within a society. She suggests that persons within the same home and family may live very different lives in parallel universes that intersect only rarely as life-course transitions and outside change challenge arrangements. Because there is limited documentation on everyday activities for ordinary people, focusing on special groups and examining differences and similarities are also difficult to accomplish. Case studies and qualitative data suggest that the structure of families and households does influence how families manage activities and develop patterns and rituals.

Class and ethnic differences often affect families when marriages or households are first established. While the preference in marriage is usually for homogeneity and most marriages bring together similar people, even minor differences in religiosity, national origin, or social class become magnified when routines and habits are being developed. The clashes of preference may be escalated into charges about the morality and propriety of the choices being made. There are so many small details to be resolved, and each is not only a practical matter but also a mode of establishing couple identity and a face toward the community. Arranging one's clothes in a closet or one's cooking pots in a kitchen can communicate character and religious commitment, fashion and social climbing, or something of both ideas. In a classic study of English working class life, for example, Bott (1957) details the continuing close interaction on a daily basis between mothers and their grown daughters, which included many activities and discussions together even though they usually lived in separate houses.

Structuring and Scheduling of Activities

In examining the Level I activities of everyday life, the family scientist is required to be alert to many different levels of structuring of activities and the pauses in between. Families live a daily life around multiple problems, tasks, and challenges. Attention is divided among many goals and different levels of demand. Most families have fewer resources than they would like and must develop a strategy of management to handle everyday logistics. Resources in this context include not only money and materials but also time, physical and emotional energy, and social support (Bulboltz & Sontag, 1993). Families also must make decisions within constraints of time and information and may not always be able to anticipate the consequences (Hanks, 1993). In addition to these obvious forces that affect when, how, and why families behave as they do, there is also a need to be aware of what is not happening. Lack of stimulation, the need for rest and recuperation, waiting for others to act, leisure, and unstructured time are part of daily life.

Impact of Resources

Even a wealthy family faces decisions about the use of time and energy and must develop methods for using its wealth to secure a lifestyle the members appreciate. In dealing with physical or mental health, the greater availability of professional services and medical interventions for the wealthiest households proves to be only a partial solution. Families still need to know how to use and monitor these services, and good health is not solely based on intervention, so that prevention and promotion of a healthy lifestyle may be more important than absolute material resources (Hanks & Settles, 1990). Those families at the lowest levels of financial and material resources often commit their time and energy to securing the minimum survival level of family needs. It has been estimated that of the women in Third World countries spend many hours a day searching for and preparing food or carrying water (Williams, 1992). Families who are pressed by continual and grinding poverty have little emotional energy to deal with abstract issues, and such concepts as quality time for child rearing may seem meaningless. In the new "home economics" theory of family expenditures, the family is seen to anticipate spending and saving in terms of its own understanding and sensing of future needs and spending rates (Getz & Becker, 1975).

Habits and Routines

Much of Level I activity in families is reduced to habits and routines in order to get the personal and emotional freedom necessary for more idiosyncratic and challenging issues. Habits and routines can be so well learned that individuals and their families are unaware of them unless they are disturbed or frustrated in carrying them out. That is not to say that habits and routines are simple. In fact, in families and households of any size the complexity and reciprocity of these activities may be quite extensive. The need to stage the family members to go to school or work on weekdays may require taking turns, establishing priorities, dovetailing, and the precision movements of a choreographed ballet. One slow, clumsy, or reluctant person can throw everyone off and create a momentary crisis and acrimonious exchange. Someone will miss breakfast or the bus altogether, and another will reluctantly try to fix things by rearranging transportation or taking a doughnut to eat in the car.

When a disturbance in the family habits continues into other activities, there may be many other consequences. Entry and exit routines are among the most difficult to develop and maintain. The literature on blended families and stepfamilies has many references to the difficulties in handling custodial visitation and the likelihood that both children and parents will be cross and irritable both on entry and exit. One of the likely reasons for these unresolved problems in transitions is the diversity in style of the households that have repeated contact. One can also see similar conflicts when grandparents care for their grandchildren and introduce their own child-care routines that differ from the parents' patterns and preferences. The amount of hostility and heat generated around the conflict of habits and routines suggests that they represented very strong attachments and higher-level values.

Variation in the style of routines and the intermeshing of family members and habits includes both normality across a wide range and dysfunctionality. Some families long ago adopted a management style popular in industry today, "just-in-time" services and products. In these households the families buy toilet tissue or milk only as the last bit is used up, often missing out on the timing so everyone notices the shortage.

Other families maintain houses that are more like civil defense shelters, with many backup supplies and alternatives tying up a lot of their spendable income in inventory that may never be used in its best condition. Most are somewhere in between these extremes. Subculture and peer groups and cohort events may influence the family's approach to resource allocation and staging. At least one contemporary religious group has a strong recommendation that a family should stock a year's supply of food and some other essentials. The elderly, whose security needs were shaped by the Depression of the 1930s, are often seen by their children and grandchildren as hoarders and savers whose households are overrun with plastic containers and paper bags. Young people who do not have such a history may appear to their elders as insufficiently aware of the importance of thinking ahead and having supplies in the house for projects you want to accomplish on the holidays when stores are closed. As a working parent, the worst moments come on Sunday afternoon or at 10:00 P.M. any evening when a child puts forth an unfinished class project requiring a piece of poster board, a birthday party invitation requiring an appropriate gift, a bake sale announcement requiring two dozen brownies, or a permission slip for a trip the next day requiring pickup after school but before work is over. Having a storehouse of supplies and a network of social support can help a lot, but households will have many unanticipated small crises to address.

Dysfunctional families may have developed habits and routines that perpetuate their difficulties without a conscious awareness of these relationships among activities. For example, family rituals may be related to how alcoholism is perpetuated or interpreted (Fiese, 1993). Berne (1964) describes in his book *Games People Play* two common cases of dysfunction within families that are repetitive and recur because they are habitualized. The "harried housewife" in his scenario is an already overworked person who, when faced with a major threatening overload such as unexpected company being thrust on her by her husband's emergency call, allows herself to further overload her capacity to cope by taking on more tasks from other family members and failing to seek any other help. She makes a total mess of the meal for the company, incurring both the wrath of her family and an inner sense of guilt and failure. Berne suggests that this scenario is repeated without improvement and feeds upon the anxiety of the former event to move the person toward a major breakdown if there is no intervention.

Another example is that of perpetual sexual dysfunction of the sort seen in frigidity and impotence in married couples. Berne notes that couples can use the symbolic language of the sexual invitation to keep sex activity at a distance. If the wife is frigid, she may occasionally tease about sexuality by nudity or provocative behavior, but when the husband initiates a sexual advance, she gets angry and says she wanted a little affection while all he wants is sex. She may bring up some other situation in which he has failed to do his duty, perhaps calling a plumber for a dripping faucet she can now hear or leaving the lights on in the garage. Both may get out of the sexual encounter implied in some romantic activity like going to a movie or opening a bottle of champagne by picking a ritual fight and slamming a door. The point of Berne's analysis in terms of everyday life is that a disappointing relationship can be maintained in the home by elaborate routines and standardized behaviors. Dysfunction can have a very long life expectancy in families.

The levels of tenacity and reverence a family has for routines also vary widely. In some families dinner time may be an important ritual occurrence, with the specifics of time, content, service, and menu being precisely observed. In the movie *Shirley Valentine* (Gilbert & Russell, 1989), one of the illustrations of how the British wife's boring life has become routine involves her challenging her husband's preference for steak on Thursday by feeding his steak to a dog she is watching for a neighbor and offering her husband eggs and french fries. He is most unhappy to have his routine changed. In a recent popular magazine, a young woman notes that in a deteriorating marriage she and her husband fell apart over when dinner should be, at 7 o'clock, as she preferred, or at his preference of 9 o'clock, which she considered near to being her bedtime. Satisfying hunger is only a part of the action, with moral, relational, communicative, and aesthetic content feeding more than bodily hunger.

Of course, when many families cannot secure regular meals or quell essential hunger, the inability to carry out even the simplest meal ritual will dominate every thought and moment. The pictures from the sub-Sahara of starving children and adults that have been with us repeatedly in recent years remind us that survival is still a major part of daily living.

Models and Methods for Managing Routines and Habits

Routines appear even though they are not consciously created. If we examine them in some detail, however, there is usually some connection to families of orientation, to outside institutional demands, and to power-assertion characteristics of the members of the household as well as the current needs of the family members.

It is clearly important what precedents are set from the start of relationships. The first time that a new couple celebrates holidays and initiates visits with relatives, these arrangements begin to form the history and perceptions of equity that govern later arrangements. The couple who have relatives nearby may feel lucky until they have spent a Thanksgiving day rushing from turkey dinner to turkey supper and on to dessert somewhere else. For families in transition and divorce and reconstituted families, working out holiday routines is a special challenge to avoid hurt feelings, anger, and exhaustion. Rigidity in habits and routines is particularly likely to be a problem for such families. The normal changes in the life course also pose challenges to cherished habits and rituals. It is necessary to address the functionality of the structure of daily life as these changes affect the costs and benefits of such investments.

The sense of rightness and comfort found in memories of one's earliest family experience, whether or not there actually was a high quality of life, may drive the couple in a new household to attempt to duplicate the ways each associates with essential family relationships. The day of the week to go shopping or wash clothes may be traditional in a community or a family heritage, and great efforts may be made to maintain this idea in the face of other demands (Bossard & Boll, 1950).

The power of the institutions with which the family must interface to affect the structure and substance of everyday choices is enormous. School bus schedules, work hours and shifts, holidays, and beliefs about proper procedure and appointments press upon the household. A common complaint in dual-work homes is the lack of flexibility of delivery and home-repair services. It is as if everyone assumes that every house is supposed to have a person waiting there just in case someone might bring something. The shift in the United States to more jobs in the service sector has meant that many families do not share mealtimes, leisure, or even planning and discussion time. To find a time when all family members are available to interact becomes more difficult when jobs and peer-group activities compete for time and attention. For those who are active in religious or other social-action groups, a contest for marginal time may mean that leisure and family experiences are built into these institutions' programs, and their schedules may become part of the family routine.

Personal preferences for immediate or long-term outcomes affect daily life by shaping the evaluation of the effectiveness of routines. If one member of a couple wants a set pattern and the other strives for spontaneity and quick response to new stimuli, there is likely to be some conflict and even certain routines for reciting the criticism. Families develop routines for complaining and praising, for testing and pushing on the rules and systems. Adolescents frequently question the family's values and press for change in the normal activities as part of their individuation and development of personal efficacy. The vast literature on family power has been focused on couple and parental relationships, and more recently interest in sibling and adult relationships with elders has been growing. In another part of this text more detail is given on the way power and preference are built into the family system (see Chapter 6). In this context it is important to note that much of the literature has assumed that final decisions are the most important turning point in the expression of power. The many research studies that used Blood and Wolfe's (1960) scale on spousal decisions made this assumption in the use of the measure. Among some of the interesting findings of these studies was the consistent pattern of more influence on final decisions by women when they had jobs outside the home and were somewhat better educated. Safilios-Rothschild (1970) led a critique of this approach by noting that in different cultures family process was also important and that there were other sources of marital power than work and education in some of these other settings. For example, normative expectations of fairness or domain could be important in examining the exercise of power. Recently, in a study examining middle school pupils' perception of family decision making and their own role, the importance of coaxing as a step in decision making was identified by these youths as common (Liprie, 1993). It is likely that, with the low level of awareness most families have of their routines, it would be difficult to unravel how power is exercised and how these activities reinforce the power arrangements in the household. When families notice transitions or seek outside assistance, an opportunity to observe the role of power may be available to the researcher.

In home-management research in the 20th century, models from industrial time-and-energy-management studies were adapted to examine home production and everyday routines. The famous Cornell kitchen projects examined how the arrangements of appliances and work centers affected the work demands on homemakers, and they suggested better floor plans and cupboard designs to improve the working conditions and reduce the time and energy involved (Cushman, 1936, Glenn & Boyer, 1952). These plans became standards in design, and further studies looked at how heart patients and other handicapped family members could be accommodated by design adaptations and understanding the energy demands of such tasks as vacuuming, bed making, and loading dishwashers. It was a surprise to many families that rather minor changes in procedure or order of tasks could make independent living possible. More recently, research has focused on the living arrangements of the elderly and accessibility for all to community institutions (Makela & Tripple, 1992; Moore & Ostrander, 1992). The Americans With Disabilities Act has given legal sanction to this movement for less restrictive options for all of our society and for support to families who attempt to manage more difficult living requirements on a daily basis. Internationally, interest is growing in terms of shaping housing policy. Although the specific focus of some of the studies on routines and housing seem unimportant to those younger adults who have a great deal of energy and time, it should be remembered that almost everyone has some periods in their lives in which a supportive environment would allow them to function

independently. The great change in medical treatment that encourages an early return home after surgery and treatment in hospitals and outpatient care whenever possible also requires us to take heed of the knowledge on housework and routines. For example, the information on the energy required to walk downstairs shows it to be nearly as demanding as going upstairs, although most people would think otherwise. Lifting a child may be the worst thing a person with a sprained back should do, but connecting that act to the general warning about being careful may not result in compliance. Without good patient and family education in the medical situation, families may not alter daily life appropriately.

Class norms and aspirations for social mobility have created a market for etiquette and how-to books that advise people on their choices of lifestyle and action. In these cookbooks for the newly arrived, specifics about the material goods and services are discussed, as well as how they fit into everyday life. The long-standing series from the U. S. government on infant care has given quite different advice in each publication about how to arrange a baby's life, but it has consistently given the current advice as though it were the best course of action and would with great certainty lead to good outcomes for the child (Malone & Orthner, 1988). One of the most commonly used books by Judith Martin (1989), *Miss Manners' Guide*, attempts to distill the principles of pleasant living so that one can venture to solve other problems from that basis. The fact that every gesture and action can communicate many messages about family relationships and the family members' presentation of one another to the community makes these choices critical to understanding the family's beliefs and values.

Novels and television illustrate the impact of outside influences on our own lives. The fact that housecleaning products are pitched to women and yard tools to men and teenagers both reflects the reality and reinforces it. The women's movement and the civil rights movement have made us aware of stereotyping and unexamined traditions and have provided the impetus for changes in expectations. In many households a stronger effort to shape habits and routines free of sex- and gender-role assumptions has been encouraged by media attention to these issues. New products also change our ways of doing things. The availability of backpacks makes it easy for men and women to take their babies anywhere. The disposable sanitary napkin and tampon and baby and adult diapers have given more freedom to women and made giving care a non-gender-based activity. The environmental impact of these technologies is now under discussion and review, but a solution is not likely to be a return to harder-to-manage approaches. It is also interesting that even the watching of television itself, which is one of the most prevalent activities of daily life in contemporary times, is again undergoing a major shift. In addition to overcoming scheduling problems by buying more television sets, viewers have radically changed their viewing habits by using video cassette records. The rating services continue to try to determine who in the family is watching what. Families, however, now use taping and video rental to manage their own lifestyle.

Models for managing routines and habits come from many theoretical and treatment stances. Intervention is thought to be possible, although awareness and knowledge by their very nature may be limited. Moments for change occur because of developmental and situational changes and because some family member or outsider identifies the possibility.

Planning and Implementing Action in Family Life

The active management of everyday life is a smaller aspect of family action than habit and routine but is highly influential. Because family members are overloaded with activities, interact with many separate institutions and other households, and have limited resources, successful living requires using a number of strategies for integrating and staging daily life and creating resources for future use. Some of these strategies are relatively simple. Having developed habitual and ritual scheduling of activities and allocating responsibilities to various members, families still have a great variety of demands and unanswered needs. Dovetailing and integrating action are useful approaches in busy lives. Driving home after work, we make some simple plans and, on entering the house, turn on all our equipment: we do a load of wash, microwave a frozen entree, and flip on the TV to the news. We open the mail, call Mother, change clothes, move the wash to the dryer,

and so on. At the same time, much family conversation and interaction is going on during a vast buzz of activity. In fact, hot or difficult topics may be brought up in situations where full attention is difficult or impossible. Dovetailing as a method of handling complexity is useful, but there are real limits to how much can be handled before the entire system becomes overloaded (Deacon & Firebaugh, 1988).

Energy, time, and money can be used to spare family members to some extent. Young adults often have more time than money and create interesting experiences if they are willing to "camp out" or "make do" without all the extras usual in leisure consumerism. In the early years of married life energy is often used to create "sweat" equity in household projects that have real economic value. In middle age the press of active careers, multiple familial demands, and lesser energy may make spending some cash for household repairs or vacation villas an attractive option. In contemporary society older Americans have had access to better medical care and have benefitted from the Social Security program and retirement benefits and savings. Consequently, they have had more discretionary income for travel than previous cohorts. The examination of how families deal with choices about balancing the use of different resources is an area that needs more research.

Technology and other innovations have brought creative solutions to the problems of restricted of energy and time. Computer and communication links can provide instant access. Many extended families are able to keep close ties because of regular telephone calls. Skills in using the telephone, fax machine, and computer greatly increase the range of choices for resolving these resource problems.

Households with really limited economic resources are especially challenged to provide a reasonable daily life. Questions of enough to eat, shelter, heat, and other necessities dominate every minute in such families. Children in poverty learn that their parents' best intent cannot solve daily problems of adequacy. Being hungry, isolated, and neglected is for many children their everyday existence. When families have more resources and manage them well, children may grow up without realizing that their parents have limits. For middle-class children their first experiences with the knowledge that they cannot have everything may occur as late as junior high school. Some upper-class youngsters may live into adult life with the perception that their parents can fix anything that happens.

In every culture there are norms about how money and resources should be addressed. In the United States, many areas of money management are viewed with great unease. It may be easier to talk about sex than money in the intimacy of the family. There are tremendous symbolic values in :

- Who earns what?
- What is saved or spent?
- Who makes what decisions?

For example, if you want to see real controversy develop in a parent-education class, just bring up the topic of children's allowances or pay for chores, and discuss what the long-term outcomes are thought to be of either strategy in child rearing. Some parents will be sure that an allowance will make a "welfare" dependent out the child; other parents will be equally concerned that pay for chores will wipe out all appropriate concern and teamwork in family life. As the debate heats up, many other concerns about the meaning of money expenditures will be put forward.

- Should the child have to save or contribute to a religious or charity collection box?
- What happens if children mismanage their money?
- What bailouts are appropriate for small "bankruptcies"?
- What if children earn money outside the home—is it all their money?
- When will the child be responsible to support part of the household expenses? At age 14, in high school, in college, or on the first real job?

Exchanges of money and other economic resources have a long history of importance in the sponsoring of new families. Dowries, bride prices, gifts, and personal jewelry are obvious transfers. The relationship of family interests to marriage choices was and often still is solidified by arranged marriages. In upper-class European and Indian societies these practices have continued well into the 20th century. The tradition of primogeniture (inheritance primarily by the oldest son) was also used to consolidate family holdings. In Amish communities there is still the custom of purchasing a farm for the young couple in order to provide a place for them to stay

within the community. Relationships between husband and wife have usually been defined with some specificity over money issues. For example, it was common in the 19th and early 20th centuries for American women not to know their husband's income or investments, and even today many widows are surprised to learn exactly what their assets are. Intergenerational transfers are now occurring earlier because of the underlying demographic trends. The extended lifetimes of the 20th century and long-term care problems of the elderly have changed the costs and benefits of the traditional testamentary rules. Although Sussman (1983) has found that people follow the general principles in the legal suggestions about the ways that money should be distributed in designing their own wills, the regulations for spending down resources in long-term care have made many families reconsider waiting until death to make such transfers, and trusts and early gifts are becoming more popular.

The impact of the near environment on family living is clearly visible to the observer, although the family may simply see it as natural and therefore normal. The house or apartment, design of furnishings, equipment, and organization influence how daily life is enacted. Rearranging the furniture may create havoc or smooth over a stressful situation. Adapting households for changing family needs is a useful strategy to improve everyday functioning. Making a home safe for children and the elderly is one of the easiest ways to shape family process in a positive direction. Such simple ideas as sturdy hand rails in bathrooms or safety gates on staircases can make daily life much more pleasant and friendly.

Activities such as eating meals together and promoting communication are supported by good design and appropriate artifacts. Many contemporary homes may have four or five different arrangements for eating a meal, from trays to formal dining room. Each situation can also be altered to create a different atmosphere and ambiance. The vast quantity of cookbooks, entertaining guides, and decorating magazines sold every year suggests how much people are searching for recipes for pleasant living and a little sense of status. In developing countries the appearance of a table and a chair or two may symbolize the same desire to have a family meal and respectability.

Often we buy a house or rent an apartment to solve our last problem and fail to anticipate how flexible our requirements will be in the future. Anticipating how all the elements of the physical structure, the outdoor areas, and the larger community contribute to quality of life for a family over the life course requires some skills and knowledge. For example, a small extra room on the ground floor might start out as a den, become a baby's room, then a playroom, and later an office or a guest room for an older relative. However, many families cannot put together the economic resources to secure housing that will be practical over time. Perhaps you know families who got their dream house just as the children left home, so it was not really the family's home of memory or shared future. Many families have been misled by real estate agents, friends, and relatives into viewing housing as primarily an investment. While it is true that if you want or need to sell it, you can realize your equity, ordinarily it simply ties up capital that is not earning income. Historically (except for a recent 20-year experience and in some isolated locations), housing has always just been a place to live and as an investment in real terms has yielded little or no return. However, home ownership has many symbolic and mythic values in our society and thus receives many subsidies. Questions that are worth considering in choosing housing include:

- How much of one's life and resources does it make sense to tie up in investing and maintaining housing?
- What activities is it most critical to provide space to carry out?
- What values do you want reflected in the decorative and functional choices in house and garden?
- What community resources do you need and want to support?

Stability of taste and choice of activities vary greatly among families. One family may see an investment in an Oriental or handmade modern rug as a lifetime purchase, and another wants to change indoor and outdoor carpeting colors every few years as a part of housecleaning. Life-span transitions may create the moment for shifting the way the family relates to housing and communities.

Homelessness has become a reality both in the developed nations and in the Third World. A plant closing, a divorce, a natural disaster, an illness, or a reorganization may threaten the family's financial underpinnings sufficiently to loosen the fragile grasp that many families have on housing. After the family's friends and relatives wear out while providing temporary shelter, the family members may disperse into community shelters or take up residence in cars and alleys. In the less-developed nations, homelessness is also associated with mobility in search of jobs or other urban opportunities. A great deal of research on the effects of homelessness on children is under way (Dail, in press), and as a nation the United States is faced with the real likelihood that homelessness is not just a momentary phenomenon.

Chapter Summary

Everyday life is defined as the visible and frequent associations we have with family members. It consists of a complex overlay of habitual, ritual, and spontaneous activities. Families do a wide variety of problem solving and planning to attempt to control the impact of the environment on their lives, and their realistic ability to anticipate and alter the course of events is limited. In today's fast-paced world those who have good skills at finding and evaluating information, seeking and mobilizing support, and revising decisions that are no longer appropriate have a greater opportunity to secure the quality of life they desire. Within families, different problem-solving styles and division of labor on tasks may create more alternatives as long as these preferences are not so rigid that families cannot take advantage of changing circumstances. Much of what we remember, romantize, or reject about our families comes from the accumulation of these daily events. When dysfunction, recurrent crisis, or simple lack of any reasonable fulfillment of individual needs characterizes everyday life, families may come into treatment or supportive programs. It is important to deal with these daily concerns as well as the larger problems. In developing one's own lifestyle, the long-term consequences of short-range choices should be examined and evaluated. It is quite possible that the values one has can be lost in the trivia of an unexamined daily routine.

Discussion Questions

1. Describe how some holiday or event like a birthday is always celebrated in your family. Find out how the specific practices originated and how they have changed with time. Analyze the values and meaning of this ritual.
2. What two or three most important housework practices would you want to initiate in your own home? Why do you think these practices would be helpful in daily life? If your spouse or housemate disagreed with you, what would you do?
3. Suppose an older relative of yours has recently become limited in mobility and you would like to help him or her remain independent. What are some of the issues on which you would seek information?
4. You are a caseworker interviewing at-risk families for possible enrollment in a parent-education class. What would you like to know about their daily life?
5. Describe your dream house in a paragraph or two. Then describe how you think this house would influence your daily routine if you were to have it.

Additional Resources

Berne, E. (1964). *Games people play: The psychology of human relationships.* New York: Grove Press.

Deacon, R. E., & Firebaugh, F. M. (1988). *Family resource management: Principles and applications* (2nd ed.). Boston: Allyn & Bacon.

Rettig, K. D. (1993). Problem solving and decision-making as central processes of family life: An ecological framework for family relations and resource management. In B. H. Settles, R. S. Hanks, & M. B. Sussman (Eds.), *American families and the future: Analysis of possible destinies* (pp. 187–222). New York: Haworth Press.

References

Adams, B. N. (1986). *The family: A sociological interpretation* (4th ed.). New York: Harcourt Brace Jovanovich.

Adams, B. N., & Steinmetz, S. K. (1993). Family theory and methods in the classics. In P. G. Boss, W. J. Doherty, R. LaRossa, W. R. Schumm, & S. K. Steinmetz (Eds.), *Sourcebook of family theories and methods: A contextual approach.* New York: Plenum.

Bengston, V. L., & Allen, K. R. (1993). The life course perspective applied to families over time. In P. G. Boss, W. J.Doherty, R. LaRossa, W. R. Schumm, & S. K. Steinmetz (Eds.), *Sourcebook of family theories and methods: A contextual approach.* New York: Plenum.

Berger, P. S. (1984). Home management research: State of the art 1909–1984. *Home Economics Research Journal, 12*(3), 252–264.

Bernard, J. (1987). *The female world from a global perspective.* Bloomington: University of Indiana Press.

Berne, E. (1964). *Games people play: The psychology of human relationships.* New York: Grove Press.

Blood, R. O. Jr., & Wolfe, D. M. (1960). *Husbands and wives.* New York: Free Press.

Bossard, J. H. S., & Boll, E. S. (1950). *Ritual in family living.* Philadelphia: University of Pennsylvania Press.

Bott, E. (1957). *Family and social network: Roles, norms, and external relationships in ordinary families.* London: Tavistock.

Brim, O. (1959). *Education for child rearing.* New York: Russell Sage Foundation.

Broderick, C. (1988). Family studies in the 1930's. *Journal of Marriage and the Family, 50*(3), 569–584.

Bulbolz, M. M., & Sontag, M. S. (1993). Human ecology theory. In P. G. Boss, W. J. Doherty, R. LaRossa, W. R.Schumm, & S. K. Steinmetz (Eds.), *Sourcebook of family theories and methods: A contextual approach* (pp. 419–447). New York: Plenum.

Carter, E. A., & McGoldrick, M. (1980). The family life cycle and family therapy: An overview. In E. A. Carter & M.McGoldrick (Eds.), *The family life cycle: A framework for family therapy.* New York: Gardner Press.

Cowas, R. S. (1983). *More work for mothers: The ironies of household technology from open hearth to microwave.* New York: Basic Books.

Culley, J. D., Settles, B. H., & Van Name, J. B. (1976). *Understanding and measuring the cost of foster care* (Reprinted, 1977). Newark: Bureau of Economic and Business Research, University of Delaware.

Cushman, E. M. (1936). *The development of a successful kitchen* (Bulletin for Homemakers #350). Ithaca, NY: Cornell Cooperative Extension Service.

Dail, P. W. (in press). Homelessness in America: Involuntary family migration. In B. H. Settles, D. Hanks III, & M. B. Sussman (Eds.), *Families on the move.* New York: Haworth Press.

Deacon, R. E., & Firebaugh, F. M. (1988). *Family resource management: Principles and applications* (2nd ed.). Boston: Allyn & Bacon.

Devlin, A. S., Brown, E. H., Beebe, J., & Porulis, E. (1992). Parent education for divorced fathers. *Family Relations, 41*(3), 290–296.

Dickerscheid, J. D. (1984). Child development research in home economics: State of the art. *Home Economics Research Journal, 12*(3), 363–380.

Doherty, W. J., & Baptiste, D. A. (1993). Theories emerging from family therapy. In P. G. Boss, W. J. Doherty, R. LaRossa, W. R. Schumm, & S. K. Steinmetz (Eds.), *Sourcebook of family theories and methods: A contextual approach* (pp. 505–524). New York: Plenum.

Doolittle, N. O., Wiggens, S. D. (1993). Present and future health care for an aging society: A proactive self-health approach. In B. H. Settles, R. S. Hanks, & M. B. Sussman (Eds.), *American families and the future: Analysis of possible destinies* (pp. 57–72). New York: Haworth Press.

Espenshade, T. J. (1973). *The cost of children in the United States* (Population Monograph Series #14). Berkeley: University of California.

Fiese, B. H. (1993). Family rituals in alcoholic and nonalcoholic households: Relations to adolescent health symptomatology and problem drinking. *Family Relations, 42*(2), 187–192.

Frank, L. K. (1962). The beginnings of child development and family life education in the twentieth century. *Merrill-Palmer Quarterly of Behavior and Development, 8*(4).

Getz. G. R., & Becker, G. S. (1975). *The allocation of time and goods over the life cycle.* New York: National Bureau of Economic Research and Columbia University Press.

Giele, J. Z. (1984). A delicate balance: The family's role in the care of the handicapped. *Family Relations, 33*(1), 91.

Gilbert, I., & Russell, W. (Producers). (1989). *Shirley Valentine* [Film]. Los Angeles: Paramont Pictures Corporation, Gulf & Western.

Glenn, N., & Boyer, H. (1952). *The Cornell kitchen: Product design through research.* Ithaca, NY: Cornell University Press.

Gubrium, J. F., & Holstein, J. A. (1990). *What is family?* Mountain View, CA: Mayfield.

Halkins, A. J., & Roberts, T. (1992). Designing a primary intervention to help dual-career couples share housework and child care. *Family Relations, 41*(2), 169–177.

Hanks, R. (1993). Rethinking family decision making: A family decision making model under constraints of time and information. In B. H. Settles, R. S. Hanks, & M. B. Sussman (Eds.), *American families and the future: Analysis of possible destinies* (pp. 223–240). New York: Haworth Press.

Hanks, R. S. & Settles, B. H. (1990). Theoretical questions and ethical issues in a family caregiving relationship. In D.E. Biegal & A. Blum (Eds.), *Aging and caregiving: Theory, research and policy* (pp. 98–120). Newbury Park, CA: Sage.

Hareven, T. K. (1987). Historical analysis of the family. In M. B. Sussman & S. K. Steinmetz (Eds.), *Handbook of marriage and the family* (pp. 37–58). New York: Plenum.

Hendrickson, N. J. (1963). *A brief history of parent education in the United States.* Columbus: The Ohio State University Center for Adult Education.

Hill, R., & Hansen, D. A. (1964). Families under stress. In H. Christensen (Ed.), *Handbook on marriage and the family.* Chicago: Rand McNally.

Howe, G. W., & Reiss, D. (1993). Simulation and experimentation in family research. In P. G. Boss, W. J. Doherty, R. LaRossa, W. R. Schumm, & S. K. Steinmetz (Eds.), *Sourcebook of family theories and methods: A contextual approach* (pp. 303–324). New York: Plenum.

Lee, G. R. (1987). Comparative perspectives. In M. B. Sussman & S. K. Steinmetz (Eds.), *Handbook of marriage and the family* (pp. 59–80). New York: Plenum.

Lee, G. R., & Haas, L. (1993). Comparative methods in family research. In P. G. Boss, W. J. Doherty, R. LaRossa, W. R. Schumm, & S. K. Steinmetz (Eds.), *Sourcebook of family theories and methods: A contextual approach* (pp.117–134). New York: Plenum.

Lewin, K. (1943). Forces behind food habits and methods of change. In *The problem of changing food habits.* (Report of the Committee on Food Habits, Bulletin 108). Washington, DC: National Academy of Sciences.

Liprie, M. L. (1993). Adolescents' contributions to family decision making. In B. H. Settles, R. S. Hanks, & M. B.Sussman (Eds.), *American families and the future: Analysis of possible destinies* (pp. 241–254). New York:Haworth Press.

Liston, M. I. (1993). *History of family economics research: 1862–1962.* Ames: Iowa State University.

Lucca, J., & Settles, B. H. (1981). Effects of children's disabilities on parental time use. *Physical Therapy, 61*(2).

Makela, C. J., & Tripple, P. A. (1992). Housing adaptations to ease the demands of everyday living. In N. B. Leidenfrost (Ed.), *Families in transition* (pp. 185–192). Vienna: International Federation for Home Economics and United Nations.

Malone, D. M., & Orthner, D. K. (1988). Infant care as a parent education resource: Recent trends in care issues. *Family Relations, 37*(4), 367–372.

Martin, J. (1989). *Miss Manners' Guide to the turn-of-the-millennium.* New York: Pharos Books.

McKenry, P., & Price, S. (1984). The present state of family relations research. *Home Economics Research Journal*, 12(3), 381–402.

Minuchin, S., Rosman, B. L., & Baker, L. (1978). *Psychosomatic families: Anorexia nervosa in context.* Cambridge, MA: Harvard University Press.

Moore, L. J., & Ostrander, E. R. (1992). *In support of mobility: Kitchen design for independent older adults* (Information Bulletin #225). Ithaca, NY: Cornell Cooperative Extension Service.

Nichols, M. P., & Schwartz, R. C. (1991). *Family therapy: Concepts and methods* (2nd ed.). Boston: Allyn & Bacon.

Nickols, S. Y., & Metzen, E. J. (1978). Housework time of husband and wife. *Home Economics Research Journal*, 7, 85–97.

Noller, P. A. & Taylor, R. (1989). Parent education and family relations. *Family Relations*, 38(2), 196–200.

Patterson, J. M. (1985). Critical factors affecting family compliance with home treatment for children with cystic fibrosis. *Family Relations*, 34(1), 81.

Penfield, M. P., & Axelson, M. L. (1984). State of the art: Food research. *Home Economics Research Journal*, 12(3), 311–324.

Rettig, K. D. (1993). Problem solving and decision-making as central processes of family life: An ecological framework for family relations and resource management. In B. H. Settles, R. S. Hanks, & M. B. Sussman (Eds.), *American families and the future: Analysis of possible destinies* (pp. 187–222). New York: Haworth Press.

Rexroat, C., & Sheehan, C. (1987). Family life cycle and spouses' time in housework. *Journal of Marriage and the Family*, 49(4), 737–750.

Rice, A. S., & Tucker, S. M. (1986). *Family life management* (6th ed.). New York: Macmillan.

Safilios-Rothschild, C. (1970). The study of family power structure: A review 1960–1969. *Journal of Marriage and the Family*, 32, 539–552.

Settles, B. H. (1980, October). *Conceptual framework for parenting inputs with special needs children.* Paper presented at the National Council on Family Relations, Portland, OR.

Settles, B. H. (1987). A perspective on tomorrow's families. In M. B. Sussman & S. K. Steinmetz (Eds.), *Handbook of marriage and the family* (pp. 157–180). New York: Plenum.

Settles, B. H. (1993). Expanding choices for long term planning for family futures. In B. H. Settles, R. S. Hanks, & M. B. Sussman (Eds.), *American families and the future: Analysis of possible destinies* (pp. 1–36). New York: Haworth Press.

Settles, B. H., & Berke, D. (1989). *Interactive planning for family futures—Demonstration of a computer simulation.*

Paper presented at the meeting of the Association for the Development of Computer-Based Instructional Systems, Crystal City, VA.

Staab, J. H. (1993). Historical development and trends in research in family economics. In M. I. Liston, (Ed.), *History of family economics research: 1862–1962.* Ames: Iowa State University. (Originally published 1935)

Sterne, M., & Alvarez, A. (1992). Knowledge of child development and caretaking attitudes: A comparison of pregnant parents, nonpregnant adolescents. *Family Relations*, 41(3), 297–302.

Straus, M. A. (1968). Communication, creativity, and problem solving ability in middle and working-class families in three societies. *American Sociological Review*, 73, 417–430.

Straus, M. A., & Tallman, I. (1971). SIMFAM: A technique for observational measurement and experimental design of families. In J. Aldous, T. Condon, R. Hill, M. Straus, & I. Tallman (Eds.), *Family problem solving: A symposium on theoretical, methodological, and substantive concerns* (pp. 379–438). Hinsdale, IL: Dryden Press.

Sussman, M. B. (1983). Law and legal system: The family connection. *Journal of Marriage and the Family*, 45(1), 333–340.

Szinovacz, M. (1992). Is housework good for retirees? *Family Relations*, 41(2), 230–238.

Tallman, I. (1993). Theoretical issues in researching problem solving in families. In B. H. Settles, R. S. Hanks, & M. B. Sussman (Eds.), *American families and the future: Analysis of possible destinies* (pp. 155–186). New York: Haworth Press.

Vanek, J. (1974). Time spent in housework. *Scientific American*, 231(5), 116–120.

Van Name, J. B. (1993, September). Personal communication.

Virginia Agricultural Experiment Station. (1981). *Family time use: An eleven state urban/rural comparison.* Backsburg, VA: Author.

Volk, R. J., Edwards, D. W., Lewis, R. A., & Sprenkle, D. H. (1989). Family systems of adolescent substance abusers. *Family Relations*, 38, 266–272.

Walker, K. E., & Woods, M. E. (1976). *Time use: A measure of goods and services.* Washington, DC: American Home Economics Association.

Wallace, S. A., & Hall, H. C. (1984). Research in home economics education: Past achievements, present accomplishments, future needs. *Home Economics Research Journal*, 12(3), 403–419.

Weitzman, L. J. (1985). *The divorce revolution: The unexpected social and legal consequences for women and children in America.* New York: Free Press.

Williams, D. K. (1992). Women in developing countries: Food technology and daily life. In N. B. Leidenfrost (Ed.), *Families in transition* (pp. 121–126). Vienna: International Federation for Home Economics and United Nations.

Williams, F. M. (1993). Studies of family living: The United States and Canada. In M. I. Liston (Ed.), *History of family economics research: 1862–1962*. Ames: Iowa State University. (Originally published 1935)

Wood, H. (1992). FACET, families and communities empowered together. Wilmington: Office of Prevention, Department of Children and Families, State of Delaware.

Wyse, B. W. (1984). Nutrition research: State of the art. *Home Economics Research Journal, 12*(3), 300–310.

Communication in Families

Kip W. Jenkins
University of Idaho

A marriage and family therapist is meeting a couple for the first time. After a few minutes of introductions and nondirected talking, the therapist asks Hank and Nancy why they have come:

Hank: I really don't know why we've come. She says we need counseling in order to "save" our marriage, but I really don't think our marriage is in that bad shape!

Nancy: Well that's just the problem! You sit around the house watching TV and think that everything is just fine between you and me. You never listen to me. We never talk. We just can't communicate!

Hank: That's not a problem! I talk with you. We talk about lots of stuff . . .

Nancy: Oh yeah, we talk about a lot of stuff—hunting, fishing, what's for dinner, or whatever you want to talk about. We never talk about the things I want to. We never talk about my feelings, things I'd like to do. Besides, it seems like whenever I do want to talk to you, you're too busy watching that damn TV! You pay more attention to the TV than you do to me!

Therapist: I think it might be wise to remember that communication is a very complex process. I'd like to talk about a number of other things before we talk about communication problems, but let me just say this before I change the subject. Each of us has a different perspective from which we view the world . . .

Kantor and Lehr propose that "we shall understand families when we understand how they manage the commonplace, that is, how they conduct themselves and interact in the familiar everyday surroundings of their own households" (1975, p. ix). According to Satir (1972):

> Once a human being has arrived on this earth, communication is the largest single factor determining what kinds of relationships he makes with others and what happens to him in the world about him. How he manages his survival, how he develops intimacy, how productive he is, how he makes sense . . . are largely dependent on his communication skills. (p. 1)

It becomes obvious that Hank and Nancy have a "communication" problem and that much of their problem may be in the way they perceive communication. It is the same with everyone. All of us have a perspective of what communication is and how it operates. Fortunately, many share a common perspective, but the complexity of the process precludes a universal acceptance of what it is and how it works.

Family scholars and researchers are quick to admit that communication undergirds family functioning and, given the complex problems and stress experienced by families throughout society, needs to be understood. But many remain ignorant of the different definitions and perspectives from which one can view this complex process. In addition, most of us tend to forget that our own perspective on what communication is and how it works is our primary source of "sensemaking." In other words, each of us has a view of what communication is and how it works—much of it right, some of it incomplete, and all of it never completely understood.

Definition of Communication

Communication scholars throughout the years have provided a wealth of insight regarding definitions of communication. Although scholars differ in their definitions, certain properties of communication have received greater emphasis than others. *Transmission properties* continue to be a popular way of defining communication. Berelson and Steiner (1964) define communication as a transmission of information, ideas, emotions, skills, and the like by the use of symbols, words, pictures, figures, graphs, and so on. Shannon and Weaver (1949) also accept the transmission property by contending that communication includes all the properties by which one mind can affect another. Fitzpatrick and Ritchie (1992), in their review of definitions of communication, write that "any instance of the creation of symbols in some medium in such a fashion that other people can notice the symbols and make sense of them" constitutes communication (p. 568).

Other scholars focus on *behavioristic properties* and see communication as the process of eliciting a response through verbal symbols (see Dance, 1967). Gray and Wise focus on these same properties by defining communication as the "presenting of stimuli as well as the response, real or imagined, as it comes into the awareness of the initiator of the process" (1959, p. 10). Other scholars have been concerned with *effectiveness and ineffectiveness properties* (see Fotheringham, 1966; Gode, 1969), or *social-integration properties* (see Cherry, 1964; Harnack & Fest, 1964; Newman, 1948).

An examination of the major components of each of these properties leads one to a summary definition that is in harmony with one proposed by Galvin and Brommel (1982) and that tends to have majority acceptance today: "the process of creating and sharing meanings" (p. 6).

One of the dangers all of us face is to assume that once we can agree on what communication is, we ought to be able to resolve communication problems easily. One might be tempted to say, "I've got this communication business figured out, so all I need to do now is to help family members understand things from a common perspective" (that is, *shared meaning*). In the dialogue between Nancy and Hank, seeing that they have a communication problem and lack a "shared meaning" of how they "communicate" is relatively easy, but adequately resolving the problem, helping them enjoy more effective family communication, can be very difficult.

Fisher (1978) maintains that "defining communication is incredibly simple [while] understanding communication is considerably more complex. It is infinitely more important to understand what the definition does or does not imply, what the definition considers to be or not to be the crucial properties" (p. 9). In other words, though defining communication sufficiently to satisfy our inquiry may be easy, it is also important to know the strengths and limits of the definition. It must always be remembered that understanding how communication takes place is a complex and difficult matter.

Perspectives on Family Communication

Fitzpatrick and Ritchie (1992) suggest that a "basic issue in communication theory has to do with the process by which ideas are given symbolic or representational form and the converse process by which symbols are recognized and interpreted" (p. 569). A consensual agreement on this process has never been achieved within the field of communication, and I doubt that it ever will. However, efforts at defining communication and finding central core operations lead one to an examination of a number of perspectives on the process of communication in the family. Fisher (1978) contends that communication processes, including those that take place in families, can be viewed through four basic perspectives: *mechanistic*, or *strong code* (see Fitzpatrick & Ritchie, 1992); *psychological*; *interactional*; and *pragmatic*, or *systemic*. The pragmatic perspective is the most popular way of viewing the communication process, and its broad framework for inquiry has prompted marvelous discoveries. For many its appeal is that it looks at family interaction as a whole and requires faithfulness to a systemic view of things. It would probably be of benefit to begin with the pragmatic orientation, but I believe you will be more appreciative of this perspective after reviewing the other perspectives first.

The Mechanistic Perspective

The mechanistic perspective proceeds from the conceptualization of an "ideal" state, a mechanical model in which, if all components are functioning properly, the communication process is adequate and accurate. The family communication process, viewed from this perspective, is a "communication machine." This perspective, developed from a classical physics model, makes several assumptions, including quasi causality, transitivity of functions, material existence of components, and reductionism.

Quasi causality refers to the mechanistic assumption that the present constrains the future. In other words, present events determine future events. In essence, to know the present is to predict, with confidence, the future. Applied to family communication, this assumption promotes the idea that the way the family has communicated in the past will probably be the way it communicates in the future. Let's go back to the dialogue at the beginning of this chapter. Nancy and Hank's friends, when asked to comment on their "communication patterns," may say, "Hank and Nancy have always had problems talking. Hank watches too much TV, and Nancy argues that Hank only talks about the things he wants to and never listens to her. That's just the way things work with them." A marriage and family therapist or social worker subscribing to this assumption may see that this disruptive pattern is highly predictable and will continue to occur and probably worsen unless things change.

Transitivity of functions relates to the manner in which functioning components or concepts are related to one another (A, B, and C are "transitively connected" in such a way that the functioning of A leads directly to the functioning of B, which leads to the functioning of C). Applied again to Hank and Nancy's situation, one might see that watching TV, in Nancy's mind, is directly related to Hank's "communication problems." Here are some other examples:

A father becomes verbally involved in communicating with his child's elementary school principal only after the mother has talked with the principal or after she has received a letter that addressed the principal's concerns.

A child asks her mother if a friend can stay overnight but only after getting approval from her father first.

Material existence of components assumes that a universe is composed of material entities possessing form and substance, whose structure can be ascertained. These entities are related to each other in terms of physical actions and reactions; everything operates in *time* and *space* (see Lazlo, 1972). Family-communication scholars will carefully examine the operation of a communicated message as it travels "through" the home, measuring the "time" taken from the initiation of the message to its reception and interpretation (or the "distance" the message travels).

Reductionism assumes that reality is capable of being analyzed into ever smaller units (see von Bertalanffy, 1968). An examination of the family-communication process is possible through the assumptive properties of reductionism, because scholars can "reduce" what they "see" into a model reflecting the communication process as it "really" happens.

The mechanistic model of the communication process. Typical components in a mechanistic model include: message/feedback, channel, source/receiver, encoding/decoding, transformation, and noise. A mechanistic model of communication is illustrated in Figure 11.1.

The *message* is defined as what is communicated and is usually referred to in terms of "information." The message has a *source*, is *encoded*, and travels through a *channel*, where noise and other sources of interference can influence message fidelity. Once received, the meaning and application of the message must be

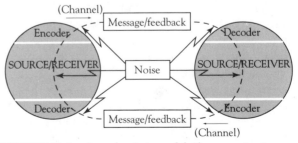

FIGURE 11.1   A mechanistic model of communication
Source: From *Perspectives on Human Communication* (p. 108), by B. A. Fisher. Copyright © 1978 by Macmillan Publishing Co. Reprinted by permission of the author.

assigned by a *receiver*, who does this by the process of *decoding*. Since communication typically involves a continuous exchange of messages, the source becomes the receiver, and vice versa. The concept of source/receiver contributes to another important model component, that being the simultaneous transmission process of encoding/decoding, which is the transformation of a message from one format to another at the point of transmission. Finally, *transformation* is the changing of thoughts into words and words into thoughts through a highly complex process involving linguistic codes, paralinguistic cues, learned behaviors, physiological interconnections, intentions, cognitions, informational biases, memories, and sociocultural norms. The notion of *fidelity* (the extent to which a message is similar at two points of the channel), *noise* (anything that interferes with the message), and *feedback* (any message that is a response to another message) are also related to this process.

Application of the mechanistic perspective to family communication.   Since each component in the mechanistic model of communication is located somewhere on the channel, adherents of this perspective tend to focus on the channel and accept it as the most appropriate place to examine the communication process. Family scientists accepting this perspective usually make inquiry into such things as message/feedback, barriers and breakdowns in the communication process, gatekeeping functions (especially of parents and older children), the functioning of mediated communication, and the study of family communication networks.

Let's return to Hank and Nancy's situation. A family practitioner viewing the communication process from this perspective might look at "channel noise"—the TV interfering with Nancy's messages to Hank—or "encoding/decoding problems"—Hank and Nancy's wrong assignment of meaning in their talk.

Though the mechanistic model was once the most popular way of looking at the communication process it has become weakened by the advent of new models. Many scholars still utilize the mechanistic perspective, if not as the best suited to study the family-communication process, at least as one of the easiest from which to formulate quick and effective therapy.

The Psychological Perspective

Fisher (1978) argues that the psychological perspective probably does not exist in any pure form and, in effect, many scholars see this perspective as augmenting the mechanistic model. However, the contribution of the psychological perspective is critical considering its strong focus on cognitive aspects of communication, which are essential to the understanding of communication processes.

Characteristic assumptions of this perspective include sensory reception of stimuli, internal mediation of stimuli, prediction of response, and reinforcement of response.

Sensory reception of stimuli focuses on the individual reception of stimuli and views an object as stimulus not simply because it exists in the environment but because it is received as a definable unit by one or more of the human senses; a stimulus is then the object converted to sensations.

Internal mediation of stimuli recognizes the "black-box" concept of organismic mediation. In other words, one can observe communicative inputs and outputs but cannot directly view the inner workings of the organism. The observation of these inputs and subsequent outputs can lead to an inference about the internal mechanism, but one cannot directly observe how a communicative input becomes an output.

Prediction of response makes the assumption that responses are predictable, at least in part, from past behavior. The concept of similar inputs is referred to as a "set," which, though predictably stable, is susceptible to change over time and experience.

Reinforcement of responses contends that S-R (stimulus-response) psychology is of necessity at least an S-O-R feedback psychology (Berger & Lambert, 1968, p. 97). Berger and Lambert explain that in understanding prediction of responses, it is necessary to add a feedback entity. Hence their model adds an additional R (reinforcement) to the model, becoming S-O-R-R. Probably the most significant effect of their concept is that it reverses the unidirectionality of time effects and suggests that the organism is not necessarily at the mercy of the environment but can influence its own internal state.

The psychological model of the communication process.   A representative model on the psychological perspective of communication is provided in Figure 11.2. The psychological perspective assumes that all humans exist in a *stimulus field* (shown by S's), which is usually defined by mechanical-communication scholars as the "informational environment." Surrounding each individual is a nearly infinite array of stimuli, which are capable of being processed through *receptor organs*. *Stimuli* compete for reception, but the organism can perceive and process only a certain amount. It must be remembered that stimuli are not only received but also produced, so the communicating organism is seen as both a *communicator* and an *interpreter*. It should also be remembered that the psychological model of communication differs from any general psychological model in the assumption that humans produce a significant amount of stimuli that are perceived by other organisms.

Any attempt to describe the communication process from a psychological perspective begins at an *arbitrary point of communication origin*. Under the black-box concept the internal states of a communicator/interpreter are referred to as *conceptual filters*, which have been described by proponents of this perspective as attitudes, beliefs, drives, images, cognitions, self-concepts, perceptions, orientations, and sets. Conceptual filters therefore are never directly observable but can be viewed indirectly through the modification of stimulus input into behavioral output. All *responses* (represented by the capital letter "R" in Figure 11.2) are not capable of being observed, and some of the response will always remain hidden.

The psychological perspective clearly focuses on the individual organism as the place where the communication process ought to be studied. As stated earlier, some proponents contend that this perspective, with its focus on the individual, is an addendum to the mechanistic model and that the communicator/interpreter of the psychological perspective is the same as the process of encoding/decoding from the mechanistic perspective. In other words, the process of receiving stimuli via conceptual filters is a process of interpretation, which is nothing more than a function of message encoding!

Application of the psychological perspective to family communication.   Again, let's use the little that we know of Hank and Nancy's problems to highlight the application of this perspective to family communication. The psychological perspective emphasizes individualism and the complexity of the communicator/interpreter. To begin, a family practitioner would focus on the internal process of communication within Nancy and Hank as individuals and how this process contributes to their "miscommunication." For example, Hank may be interpreting the amount of talk he and Nancy are doing as significantly stimulating and useful enough to qualify as effective communication. He feels that his needs are being met, his wife and he talk, she understands him, their marriage is not in trouble, and the communicative processing he participates in is very satisfactory. Nancy, on the other hand, does not feel the same. The stimuli she receives and processes lead her to believe that she and Hank may talk but don't talk about anything important. She sees the marriage as being in trouble because of the meaning she gives to the stimuli in her environment. A family practitioner would recognize the necessity of viewing the communication process first from the intrapersonal level and centrally organizing an analysis based on what the receiver perceives. The practitioner would investigate Hank and Nancy's attitude/behavior relationships and their selectivity of information.

It is easy to see that a family practitioner who subscribes to this perspective would tend to examine individual family members (rather than the family as a whole) and try to discover dysfunctional "black-box"

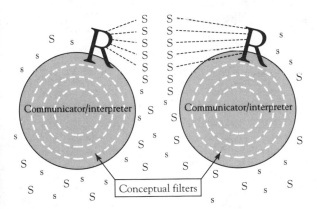

FIGURE 11.2   A psychological model of communication
Source: From *Perspectives on Human Communication* (p. 108), by B. A. Fisher. Copyright © 1978 by Macmillan Publishing Co. Reprinted by permission of the author.

functioning. Psychologists, social workers, family therapists, and others with background and training in psychoanalytic methods tend to form the greatest support for this perspective.

The Interactional Perspective

The interactional perspective developed out of symbolic-interaction theory. Characteristic assumptions involve the nature of self, the symbolic nature of the world, the nature of human action, and the nature of social action.

Nature of self. This perspective exalts the individual above all other influences. The human embodies the essence of culture, relationships, society, and the mind. Interactional-communication scholars refer to the process of experience and interpretation as *self-indicative* and see it as a social process that allows the individual to "transcend the immediate situation and go beyond the limitations of individual experiences, past and present" (Fisher, 1978, p. 167). Throughout the self-indication process is a continuous introspection: the self originates and functions as a social process. This concept of self thus differs from a mechanistic or psychological perspective in that there is no "filtering" process; rather, the individual acts upon experiences and organizes past, present, and future actions on the basis of an interpretation of these experiences. In other words, behavior is not so much a *response* as it is an *interpretative construction of self.*

Symbolic nature of the world. The interactional perspective recognizes *symbolic interaction* as well as *nonsymbolic interaction* functioning throughout human experiences. Nonsymbolic interaction is seen as a *reflex*, not requiring interpretation. Symbolic interaction, on the other hand, requires internal processes of self-indication and interpretation. The significance of a symbol is dependent on the ability of individuals to place themselves in the role of an *other* and ask themselves how the other would respond if in the same situation. This significance is related directly to the *sharedness* of the interpretative process (shared meaning). The interpretation of a significant symbol requires *role-taking.*

The nature of human action. In the process of self-indication, individuals are themselves an object of interpretation and may indeed see themselves as others see them. Within this interpretative, role-taking proc-

ess, individuals may take on the role of a *specific* or *generalized other.* It is through role-taking that people achieve individuality; they create their environment and self at the same time, rather than being merely the product of past experiences and past environmental stimuli.

The nature of social action. As the individuals participate in role-taking, they can allow others to direct actions, so that the actions of several people join in *group*, or *collective*, *action.* Individuals align their actions with those of another, even a generalized other. It should be remembered that collective action is not the result of some environmental force but is directly attributable to the individuals who coordinate their actions with those of others. Blumer (1969) has suggested three simple premises that underlie the nature of social symbolic interaction. First, "human beings act toward things on the basis of the meanings that the things have for them." Second, meanings are directly attributable to "the social interaction that one has with one's fellows." Third, these meanings are created, maintained, and modified through an "interpretative process used by the person in dealing with the things he encounters" (p. 2).

The interactional model of the communication process. Typical components in a model of interactional human communication (see Figure 11.3) include concerns for explaining the development of role and self by showing how humans develop through social interaction. The term that most accurately describes the communicator's individuality is *role.* The *self* develops exclusively through interaction with others, by taking

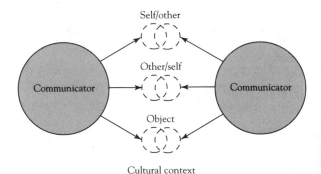

FIGURE 11.3   An interactional model of communication
Source: From *Perspectives on Human Communication* (p. 174), by B. A. Fisher. Copyright © 1978 by Macmillan Publishing Co. Reprinted by permission of the author.

the role of *other* and observing self as an object of orientation.

The *communicator* in an interactional model *performs*, or *acts*, a role. Part of this role behavior involves *role-taking*. The communicator views self from the perspective of other as well as the role of other from the perspective of self. The communicator can then adapt his or her behaviors to the other person by aligning actions.

Orientation occurs in the process of role-taking and behavioral alignment as communicators relate to an *object*, direct their attention to the object, and formulate an assessment. In Figure 11.3, orientation is modeled by the arrows toward the dotted circles. One communicator orients to both self and other while the same thing is happening with the other. Orientation, in other words, implies a *directiveness* in the process of role-taking.

Congruence occurs to the extent that the interpretative orientations of the communicators are similar (shown in Figure 11.3 by dashed overlapping circles). Nwankwo (1973) warns that congruence should not be confused with accuracy of interpretation. Two people may share congruent orientations yet may experience high levels of inaccurate interpretations; accuracy of communication may be an excellent measure of communicative effectiveness, but is not an integral element in the process of human communication.

Human communication always occurs within some identifiable *cultural context*. The term *culture* is usually defined in very broad terms (family, community, neighborhood), and every individual belongs to many overlapping cultural contexts and adapts to the ones that are the most relevant to the communicative event.

For the most part, the interactional perspective seems to be a humanistic reaction to the mechanistic and psychological perspective. It is seen as *dialogical communication* (see Matson & Montague, 1967). Johannessen (1971) argues that the essential movement in dialogue is turning toward and reaching for the other. A basic element of dialogue is "seeing the other or experiencing the other side" (p. 375). Neither the mechanistic nor the psychological perspective of the communication process takes into account this dialogical experience; hence, the communication process is best examined in the role-taking activities that make seeing yourself as others see you possible.

Application of the interactional model of family communication. How would a person taking this perspective view their communication problems? First, there would be a major concern to investigate the nature of their "self-development." It may be discovered that Hank has developed a view of self from experiences in his family of origin that is highly satisfied with the style of communication he employs. Perhaps he communicates in much the same way as his father reacted to his mother. Perhaps Hank interpreted that past interaction as not only significant but also effective and has modeled the role he pursues after the role he saw his father perform. On the other hand, she may have developed her ideas of interaction based on what she has read about "effective communication" in books or magazine articles, or perhaps she operates out of a "generalized other" role that has been developed from years of cultural orientation. In other words, she may have developed a generalized communication role that has come from interpreting the communication processes of significant others in society. In her interpretive construction of self, she is performing her role as it ought to be performed, but he is not, so it's his fault. If he could just perform an effective husband/communicator role, their problems would be resolved!

This perspective focuses on the search for self-understanding of members within the family setting. Interactional models tend to provide new meanings for perspectives of family sharing and place a greater emphasis on the social and joint actions.

The popularity of the interactional perspective as applied to family communication was beneficial in that it emphasized individual members and was helpful in explaining such things as child development, but its popularity was short-lived. The pragmatic (or systemic) perspective seemed to explain family process better, and it has become more popular.

The Pragmatic (Systemic) Perspective

The pragmatic perspective focuses on the behavior of the communicator as the fundamental component of human communication. In other words, behavior *is* communication and is not simply an outcome, or effect, of the communicative act. Most scholars trace the beginning of its application to family communication to

Watzlawick, Beavin, and Jackson's *Pragmatics of Human Communication* (1967).

This perspective's characteristic assumptions come from general systems theory and include concerns for a proper understanding of communication and behavior, a liberal application of systemic-framework ideologies, and information-theory applications.

Communication and behavior. This perspective concentrates on the behavior of the communicator within a whole system as the fundamental component of human communication. It assumes that behavior and communication are virtually synonymous.

Systemic framework. Pragmatics adheres to most of the major concepts of general systems theory, including the principle of nonsummativity (the whole is greater than the sum of its parts); systemic views of structure, function, and evolution, the identification of openness, closedness, and adaptability (see Chapter 9); and systemic hierarchical organizations.

The pragmatic perspective views communication socially, with the focus upon the processing of information at the level of the system and not at the level of an individual. Hence, the pragmatic perspective reduces the significance of the intrapersonal, focusing instead on interpersonal communication. In this perspective, the smallest system one could investigate would be a dyad.

The pragmatic perspective views individuals as possessing only one means to constrain the interaction of the system: behavior. In a social system, one person can affect others only by behavior, not by thoughts, feelings, or beliefs. One person may think, feel, or believe something, but the other person will remain unaware unless some behavior reflects it.

The nature of a relationship is contingent upon *punctuation* of the sequence of behaviors, or the grouping of them into recognizable patterns.

Information theory. Though information theory stems philosophically from Wiener's (1954) cybernetic thinking and statistically from Shannon and Weaver's (1949) mathematical theories of communication, the mechanistic philosophy of information theory is not particularly significant or even relevant to the pragmatic perspective. However, the functioning of information is.

The pragmatic model of the communication process. The fundamental unit of communication is the *act*, a behavior performed verbally or nonverbally by a participant in the communicative event). Acts are then categorized into the various *functions* performed by the communication.

Some act must precede every act, and some act follows every act; therefore, the most important analytical element is not the act itself but the relationship between the acts. In systemic language this relationship is referred to as the *interact*, or *double act*. Every interaction occurs at some level of probability, which is referred to as *transition probability*. Transition probabilities are determined for every interact possible in the period of interaction observed, and the most repeated interacts serve as *interaction patterns*. These patterns make up the structure and function of the communication system. In other words, if one is to understand communication from a pragmatic perspective, one must search for interactive patterns.

Interaction changes over time. The movement from one pattern to another constitutes a *phase*. Phases through which ongoing social systems evolve tend to repeat themselves. These repetitive phases are referred to as *cycles*. Patterns, phases, and cycles may change as a result of environmental or structural changes.

Adherents of the pragmatic perspective focus their examination clearly on the behaviors, or actions, performed by individuals who are members of the communicative system. However, one must be careful not to confuse individual behaviors in isolation. The primary place of communication, as constrained by the assumptions of the pragmatic perspective, is the *sequential* behavior of system players.

You may be thinking that a weakness of this perspective is the ignoring of certain intrapersonal communication processes that must certainly influence communication that can never be seen by simply looking at "interactive behavior." You're right. In some respects, the pragmatic perspective is blasphemous to principles of mechanism, psychology, and interaction, in that it views behavior as communication that is available only through the senses. The perspective does not deny such things as conceptual filters or role-taking; it simply considers them to be a different form of analysis and not to be that important to the systemic way of thinking. To a "purist," internalized processes enter the system as externalized behavior or do not enter at all.

Orienting to individuals rejects the systemic nature of social interaction.

Because of its orientation, the pragmatic perspective is the most distinctive of all the major perspectives on human communication. It is also the most recent in its development. Its examination of the ongoing sequences of interaction constraining and defining the social system is a departure from the interactional perspective's view of internalized role-taking, but the emphasis on interactive behaviors is a common link. The conceptualization of participating in or entering into communicative activities, rather than "doing" or "originating" communication, shows a dramatic departure from traditional communication philosophy.

Application of the pragmatic model to family communication. The pragmatic perspective is the approach most widely adopted by to scholars who study the family communication process. However, there has been significant straying from a number of the characteristics assumptions, and many of the principles from the mechanistic, psychological and interactional perspectives have been adopted. The popularity of the pragmatic perspective comes from its holistic view of family communicative activity. Scholars note how individual components of the system relate to one another and affect the whole, but they recognize that the whole is indeed greater than the sum of its parts. Thus, when one attempts to diagnose problems in a family's communication system, it is productive to focus not just on one or two elements but rather on as many parts of the system contributing to the dysfunctional communicative pattern as possible. In other words, system-theory proponents believe that it is inappropriate to try to identify a single, specific cause of an event; rather, it is more appropriate to view an event within a family system as an episode of continuing sequence.

The value of a systems perspective to family communication is that it can provide the investigator with a complex, open, adaptive, and information-processing framework for accurately understanding how family communication works (see Kantor & Lehr, 1975). It does not necessarily try to prescribe specific skills or behaviors to correct communication problems, but it does provide the tools to permit each family, each unique system, to better understand its own behaviors,

and it stresses the importance of being sensitive to available feedback to keep the family oriented toward its goals.

Can you accurately predict what comes next? If you can, you're probably thinking from a systems perspective and making a prediction based on transition probability, looking at the essence of a interaction pattern, phase, and cycle. Here come Hank and Nancy.

If you understand the basic philosophy of this perspective, you should realize that we now look at Nancy and Hank's interaction as the basic element of our investigation, not necessarily their feelings, attitudes, or social role models. We investigate their interactional behavior, looking for patterns and cycles. Hank began the conversation with the therapist by suggesting that he didn't know why they had come, because he thought the marriage wasn't in that bad shape. How did Nancy respond to that act? Basically, she said he didn't understand (especially his inability to understand things as she understands them). That is an example of an "interact." Nancy, as she responds to Hank, suggests that he assumes everything is fine but that for her it isn't: "You never listen to me. We never talk. We just can't communicate!" What is Hank's response? Again, he relates that he believes that's not a problem: "I talk with you. We talk a lot." Another interact. Nancy responds to this behavior with what we might be seeing as an interactional pattern: Hank "always" fails to understand her and see the problem (which she identifies for him in her response). If additional communicative acts were available, we would be able to identify additional patterns, phases, and cycles in Hank and Nancy's interactive behavior and eventually to identify their sequential behavior.

Blending the Perspectives: The Basic Elements of Family Communication

Very few scholars and researchers remain "faithful" to a particular perspective of family communication, making sure that their theories and explanations fall within the perimeters associated with each of the previously described perspectives. Indeed, there has been liberal borrowing of explanations, terms, and elements from all the different perspectives. This "borrowing" process has led scholars to accept a number of basic elements that adequately explain the functioning of communication in family life. The most popular of these major elements are shared family meanings, communication messages, communication patterns, and communication processes.

Shared Family Meanings

Some assume that communication is limited to the transmission of ideas, feelings, needs, and the like. Most family scholars also see communication as the process by which family form and structure and the interpersonal relationships of parents, children, siblings, and extended family members are established and maintained. Rogers-Millar writes that "how interactions proceed and are organized will at least primarily determine the psychological and sociological characteristics of the system and its members" (1979, p. 21). Altman and Taylor (1973) and Minuchin (1974) see communication as the process by which a young couple negotiates its "set of common meanings." Jenkins (1990) uses communication process to examine the establishment and maintenance of independent family culture. Scholars are quick to support the explanation that the family develops its own set of particular messages, behaviors, and expectations—in other words, its *shared family meaning*, through the process of communication.

Communication Messages

Burr, Day, and Bahr suggest that "the heart of understanding family communication is understanding messages" (1993, p. 234). All four perspectives address this issue. If there is any aspect of communication that becomes obviously important, it is the "message."

The mechanistic perspective of communication and informational theorists generally define a message as the conveyance of informational units, whether verbal or nonverbal. Mortensen defines message within the realm of a psychological perspective: "whatever unit of behavior serves to link the parties of communication" (1972, p. 57). Berlo (1960) sees communication messages mediated by a "treatment" that allows content elements to become coded structure.

Okun and Rappaport's (1980) suggestion that a communicated message has four parts, the subject, the predicate, the object, and the context, agrees mostly with the mechanistic perspective and is a favorite methodological assumption of numerous family researchers. Tubbs and Moss (1977) focus on the intentional/unintentional, verbal/nonverbal message, which tends to support assumptions made from the psychological perspective, and Watzlawick, Beavin, and Jackson's (1967) focus on the digital (report of information) and analogic (intent) context of communication messages has developed from the pragmatic perspective. The examination of communicated family messages generally leads all scholars to view "what" message is communicated, "how" it is done, and "why" it all happens.

Communication Patterns

Family communication patterns exist to provide order and precedent for family members. Patterns provide functional stability, reliability, and confidence. Most studies of family communication patterns focus on three areas: communication rules, communication networks, and communicator roles.

Cronen, Pearce, and Harris (1979) propose the existence of rules in social systems such as families for three reasons. First, behavior has regularities that are predictable even for an individual who seems to act in an unpredictable fashion. Second, individuals depend on accountability. Third, most individuals expect people to behave in a certain "right" way. Because of these expectations, the authors suggest, *communication rules* will naturally emerge as a result of multiple interactions among family members as they come to know what is expected of each family member. Often these expectations are passed on from the family of origin. Not only are individual rules developed, but over time each family system determines its own hierarchy of rules.

Knapp (1984) believes that rules exist to tell family members when communication is required, when it is preferred, and when it is prohibited. He also contends that there is an explicit and implicit nature to rules. Family members learn, subscribe to, and practice their communication rules. It is easy to see that once communication rules are established and practiced, they become difficult for most families to change, even if they become obsolete or dysfunctional, unless the family system is flexible and adaptive.

Besides developing and practicing communication rules, family systems also develop a number of metarules, or rules about the rules of communicating. Metarules serve as a type of "constitution" by which regular rules operate. A common example of a family metarule is that the rules cannot be changed, or if they are to be changed, it must be done in an orderly, predictable fashion.

The idea of family *communication networks* has its origins in the mechanistic perspective, but the pragmatic perspective has added greatly to the understanding of the operation of cycles and phases within networks. Basically, as a family develops its interactional rules and operations, networks are naturally established to assist it in accomplishing the tasks of daily family living. Galvin and Brommel (1982) say that the purpose of a family communication network is to "determine the flow of messages back and forth from one or more other members or significant others outside the family" (p. 53). Scholars agree that most families do not make a conscious decision regarding the types of family communication networks they will employ; rather, these networks evolve over time.

Adherents of the mechanistic perspective were the forerunners of communication network investigation, and their assumptions regarding the nature of networks remain popular. Allred (1976) promotes the idea that networks tend to be either vertical or horizontal. Vertical networks stress the idea of sequential and hierarchical message movement. Researchers discovered a number of existing family communication networks within this category, including the chain network, wheel network, and "Y" network (see Figure 11.4). Horizontal networks stress simultaneous and egalitarian message movement. The all-channel network (see Figure 11.5) is an example of a horizontal network. Network researchers tend to associate certain familial communication rules with the discovery of the type of channel utilized by the family. For example, Galvin and Brommel (1982) suggest that a family employing the "wheel" network is probably autocratic and authoritarian.

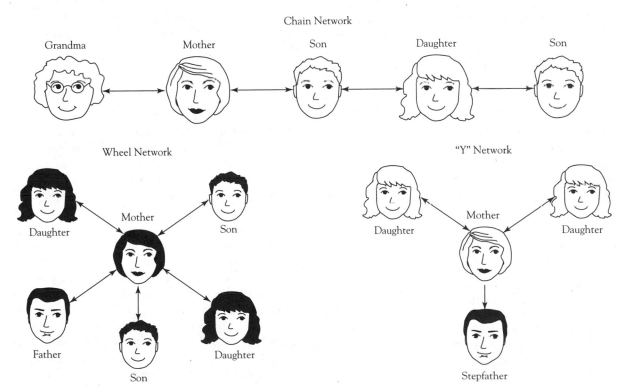

FIGURE 11.4 Models of chain, wheel, and "Y" communication networks

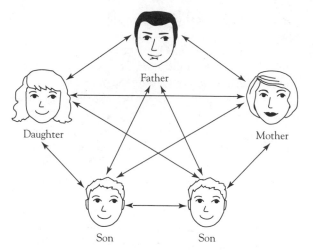

Daughter

Father

Mother

Son   Son

FIGURE 11.5   Model of an all-channel communication network

Associated with investigations into the patterns of family communication is the study of family *communicator roles*. In agreement with the assumptions promoted by the interactional perspective, family members, due to continual processing of communication rules and networks, adapt certain "expected" and "enacted" roles in day-to-day interaction. There is great discussion today regarding the interaction and communicated socialization of gender roles, with some researchers contending that what, how, why, when, and where we talk about and perform gender roles is probably the greatest determinant of the enactment of the gender role (see Beebe & Masterson, 1986; Galvin & Brommel, 1982).

Perhaps the best known and accepted findings regarding family communicator roles was proposed by Kantor and Lehr (1975). They contend that all family members, due to the nature of familial interaction, play four roles: mover, follower, opposer, and bystander. Accordingly, their premise is:

> Any social action initiated by one member of a family stimulates a reaction for the other members. The initiator of such an action is the *mover* of the action. The responders are co-movers. They may exercise one of three logical options: *following*—agreeing with the action taken by the mover; *opposing*—challenging the action of the mover; or *bystanding*—witnessing the mover's action but ac-

knowledging neither agreement nor disagreement with it. Any two or more people meeting for the first time have the same basic options at their disposal in the genesis of roles they evolve in relations to each other. Even when there are only two persons present there are four parts ready to be played, and if the relationship is to continue, all four parts most certainly will be played. This potential for parts remains the same whether the social system consists of two, three, four, seven, nineteen, or two thousand members. (p. 181)

Satir (1972) speaks of four communication styles (I define them as "roles" rather than "styles") and argues that they are used so often that they become "a personal interactional signature." The *blamer* identifies the problem and who caused it. The *placater* seeks to "please" at all costs. The *analyzer*, while denying his or her own feelings, seeks to explain how others feel and interact. The *distractor* offers lots of communicated messages but manages to keep conversation off the issue or resists solving the problem.

Scholars who study communicator roles assume that all families, to some degree or another, and at some particular time or another, will participate interactively in the roles previously described.

Communication Processes

Barnlund (1968) has promoted six useful assumptions about human communication that are applicable to understanding family communication regardless of the perspective employed. He contends that communication is dynamic, continuous, circular, unrepeatable, irreversible, and complex.

Communication is dynamic.   The communication process is always changing! The development of the pragmatic, or systemic, perspective of communication has helped show that communication does not occur in a simple linear fashion. Indeed, there may be a sequential passage of messages that can be traced in linear fashion from a sender to a receiver, but such an approach is recognized as only a snapshot of a small interactional episode. Scholars and researchers alike see a family and its communication processes as a living entity, constantly changing, growing, retarding, etc.

Communication is continuous. A general assumption supported by a vast majority of family communication scholars is that you cannot *not* communicate. Any study of human communication leads an inquirer to discover that the process does not have a definite beginning or an absolute ending. It is ongoing and continuous. It contains elements that are verbal and nonverbal. The psychological perspective on human communication assumes that even when a verbal message is not present between two or more communicators, "communication" still takes place. Even when one is alone, ever-present stimuli are perceived and interpreted. Human interaction and sociality provide a continuous assigning of meaning based on the reception of messages.

Communication is circular. The pragmatic perspective analyzes communication from the dyadic perspective and of necessity requires the assumption of circularity in a communicative "loop." Communication doesn't start with a sender of a message and end with a receiver of a message. Though sending and receiving messages are major parts of the communication process within any of the previously discussed perspectives, it must be remembered that preceding and following any reception, interpretation, or assigning of meaning is another message, and a message before that, and so on. The strength of the pragmatic perspective is its recognition of this aspect of human communication. It is unique in its focus on the nature of communication circularity.

Communication is unrepeatable. Even though you can say the same thing to the same person only a few seconds after you said it initially, you can never repeat the same feelings, emotion, and quality of the message. Time itself cannot be repeated, and so the assumption that communication is repeatable is quickly dismissed. It should be noted, however, that the repetition of communication process does contribute to communication rules, networks, and roles.

Communication is irreversible. The effect of communicating an idea, the interpretative feelings or assigning of meaning, is irreversible regardless of the intent of the sender of the message. Nothing can be "taken back." Indeed there is much alteration of mean-

ing, especially when it is perceived that there was miscommunication present in the interaction, but the memory of the "original message" (I use that term lightly) and the feelings associated with the perceiver are never completely reversed. In the words of Beebe and Masterson (1986), "Once we say something, no matter how badly we may wish we hadn't said it, we cannot take it back" (p. 16).

Communication is complex. It should be obvious from reading this chapter and reviewing Barnlund's previously discussed principles that communication is a very complex process. It is interwoven into every fiber of family functioning, throughout the life cycle. It is an essential characteristic, necessary to be investigated and understood if one desires to know of family-life experiences, but its complexity, like the other dimensions of communication, is continuous, dynamic, and irreversible.

In speaking of the complexity of communication, it should become obvious that each of the four perspectives cannot explain the whole process. However, scholars, researchers, students, therapists, and others must attempt to understand it, for only when we try to understand the complexity of communication will we understand families.

Future Directions in Family Communication

The pragmatic perspective is likely to remain the most popular view of communication for a long time. Its characteristic assumptions provide scholars, researchers, students, and others with a view of communication that is more applicable to "real" family process than the other perspectives. Borrowing from the mechanistic, psychological, or interactional perspectives will continue, but the field of family communication will turn its attention to refining theoretical assumptions and applications of the pragmatic perspective.

Message analysis will continue to be the heart of interest for family-communication scholars, but more attention will be paid to the idea of continual message transmission, reception, interpretation, and assigning of meaning. Attention will turn to dyadic and multiperson interactional patterns in association with message investigation. Researchers will no longer be satisfied with individual measures and coding techniques, and new research methods, measurement scales, and inquiry techniques will develop to measure more couples, triads, and family groups.

Steggell and Harper (1991) contend that in the future family-interaction research needs to turn its attention to more "two- way or more-way streams of action that are interrelated" (pp. 144–145). They call for investigation into a number of misunderstood areas, including going to more "naturalistic settings," inclusion of more qualitative data, more investigation of the "interplay between biological factors and social interaction in families," more coding schemes on the macrolevels of couple and family interaction, and more longitudinal studies. Their recommendations are in harmony with what should happen in the field of family communication.

Chapter Summary

The functioning of communication in the family is one of the most important if not *the* most important aspect of family functioning. In defining communication, scholars have cited its transmissional properties, behavioristic properties, effectiveness and ineffectiveness properties, and social-integration properties. The definition of "the process of creating shared meaning" is most in harmony with all these properties.

There are four major perspectives of human communication: mechanistic, psychological, interactional, and pragmatic (systemic), the latter being the most popular. The basic elements of family communication as accepted by the majority of scholars and researchers are shared family meanings, communication messages, communication patterns, and communication processes.

The pragmatic perspective of how communication operates in the family will no doubt undergo refining and extension. It provides a number of future directions for research.

Discussion Questions

1. What are the strengths of each of the four basic perspectives on the study of family communication? What are their weaknesses?
2. Which perspective best fits your view of family communication? Why?
3. Is there a danger in trying to view communication in the family from an artificially constructed perspective that borrows liberally from all? Explain your answer.
4. Why is it that shared family meanings, messages, patterns, and processes tend to be the major concerns of family scholars and practitioners? Are they that important?
5. How can Barnlund's list of "useful assumptions" help students of the family in their analysis and understanding of communication?
6. How do you think family communication will be studied 50 years from now? Why?

Additional Resources

Beebe, S., & Masterson, J. (1986). *Family talk: Interpersonal communication in the family.* New York: Random House.

Noller, P., & Fitzpatrick, M. A. (1991). *Marriage communication in the eighties: Looking forward, looking back.* Minneapolis: National Council on Family Relations.

Gottman, J. (1979). *Marital interaction: Experimental investigations.* New York: Academic Press.

References

Allred, H. (1976). *How to strengthen your marriage and family.* Provo, UT: Brigham Young University Press.

Altman, I., & Taylor, D. (1973). *Social penetration.* New York: Holt, Rinehart & Winston.

Barnlund, D. (1968). *Interpersonal communication: Survey and studies.* Boston: Houghton Mifflin.

Beebe, S., & Masterson, J. (1986). *Family talk: Interpersonal communication in the family.* New York: Random House.

Berelson, B., & Steiner, G. (1964). *Human behavior.* New York: Harcourt Brace Jovanovich.

Berger, S., & Lambert, W. (1968). Stimulus-response theory in contemporary social psychology. In G. Lindzey, & E. Aronson, (Eds.), *The handbook of social psychology: Vol. 1* (2nd ed.). Reading, MA: Addison-Wesley.

Berlo, D. (1960). *The process of communication.* New York: Holt, Rinehart & Winston.

Blumer, H. (1969). *Symbolic interaction: Perspective and method.* Englewood Cliffs, NJ: Prentice-Hall.

Burr, W., Day, R., & Bahr, K. (1993). *Family Science.* Pacific Grove, CA: Brooks/Cole.

Cherry, C. (1964). *On human communication.* Cambridge, MA: MIT Press.

Cronen, V., Pearce, W., & Harris, L. (1979). The logic of the coordinated management of meaning: A rules-based approach to the first course in interpersonal communication. *Communication Education, 23,* 22–38.

Dance, F. E. X. (1967). Toward a theory of human communication. In F. E. X., Dance (Ed.), *Human communication theory.* New York: Holt, Rinehart, & Winston.

Fisher, B. A. (1978). *Perspectives on human communication.* New York: Macmillan.

Fitzpatrick, M., & Ritchie, L. (1992). Communication theory and the family. In P. G. Boss, W. J. Doherty, R. LaRossa, W. R. Schumm, & S. K. Steinmetz (Eds.), *Sourcebook of family theories and methods: A contextual approach.* New York: Plenum.

Fotheringham, W. C. (1966). *Perspectives on persuasion.* Boston: Allyn & Bacon.

Galvin, K., & Brommel, B. (1982). *Family communication: Cohesion and change.* Glenview, IL: Scott, Foresman.

Gode, A. (1969). What is communication? *Journal of Communication. 9*(5).

Gray, G. W., & Wise, M. W. (1959). *The bases of speech.* New York: Harper & Row.

Harnack, R. V., & Fest, T. (1964). *Group discussion.* New York: Appleton, Century, Crofts.

Jenkins, K. (1990). *Inside the family's culture: A communicative-oriented analysis of culture within the family unit.* Ph.D. dissertation, Brigham Young University.

Johannessen, R. (1971). The functions of silence: A plea for communication research. *Western Journal of Speech Communication, 38,* 25–35.

Kantor, D., & Lehr, W. (1975). *Inside the family.* San Francisco: Jossey-Bass.

Knapp, M. (1984). *Interpersonal communication and human relationships.* Boston: Allyn & Bacon.

Lazlo, E. (1972). *Introduction to systems philosophy: Toward a new paradigm of contemporary thought.* New York: Gordon & Breach.

Matson, F. W., & Montague, A. (Eds.). (1967). *The human dialogue: Perspective on communication.* New York: Free Press.

Minuchin, S. (1974). *Families and family therapy.* Cambridge, MA: Harvard University Press.

Mortensen, C. D. (1972). *Communication: The study of human interaction.* New York: McGraw-Hill.

Newman, E. B. (1948). Hearing. In E. B. Boring et al. (Eds.), *Foundations of psychology.* New York: Wiley.

Nwankwo, R. A. (1973). Communication as symbolic interaction: A synthesis. *Journal of Communication. 23,* 105–216.

Okun, B., & Rappaport, L. J. (1980). *Working with families.* Belmont, CA: Wadsworth.

Rogers-Millar, L. (1979). Domineeringness and dominance: A transitional view. *Human Communication Review, 5,* 238–246.

Satir, V. (1972). *Peoplemaking.* Palo Alto, CA: Science and Behavior Books.

Shannon, C., & Weaver, W. (1949). *The mathematical theory of communication.* Urbana: University of Illinois Press.

Steggell, G., & Harper, J. (1991). Family interaction patterns and communication process. In S. Bahr (Ed.), *Family research: A sixty-year review, 1930–1990.* New York: Lexington Books.

Tubbs, S., & Moss, S. (1977). *Human communication.* New York: Random House.

von Bertalanffy, L. (1968). *General systems theory: Foundations, development, applications.* New York: Braziller.

Watzlawick, P., Beavin, J., & Jackson, D. (1967). *Pragmatics of human communication.* New York: Norton.

Wiener, N. (1954). *The human use of human beings: Cybernetics and society.* Boston: Houghton Mifflin.

C H A P T E R   1 2

Families and Sexuality

Colleen I. Murray / Geoffrey K. Leigh
University of Nevada, Reno

It may appear at first glance that the title of this chapter includes terms that are both synonymous and contradictory. The terms *family* and *sexuality* go together easily because the marital relationship typically involves a sexual relationship, and children are conceived from a sexual union. At the same time, however, notions and values about sexuality, sexual intercourse, sex education, and other related concepts are sometimes seen as foreign to the "family values" rhetoric that has become commonplace in our society and our politics today. Thus, to talk about family sexuality is to discuss the undiscussable, something that is not frequently mentioned in family conversation. In many cases, for example, people say that sex should not be talked about in schools because it is only appropriate for parents to discuss with their children. Yet most adolescents report that they learn about sexuality outside the family rather than from parents (Thornburg, 1982). Does this mean that families have little to do with learning about sexuality or sexual behavior? Despite these reports from adolescents, families seem to have an important influence on children and adolescents learning about sexuality. In addition, this current conflict, or tension, between families and sexuality illustrates the need to discuss sexuality in contexts such as the culture, society, and family.

In this chapter we will summarize some of the ways families "teach" about sexuality and what children and adolescents seem to learn about sex. In addition, we will raise some questions about current views of sexuality, both in terms of what we teach or do not teach within families as well as how professionals approach the study

of sexuality and families. Finally, we will make some suggestions about modifying some of our current perspectives and pose further questions that need to be addressed on this topic.

Generally, research on sexuality and research on families have been conducted independently. Research on sexuality has typically had an individual focus, often taking a physiological or clinical perspective focusing on sexual response, sexual problems, or deviance (McKinney & Sprecher, 1991). Such topics have lent themselves to examining the individual's sexuality, with the sexual relationship viewed as implicit. Sexuality, however, is primarily a social process, involving "real, imagined, or implied" interaction with others (Orbuch & Harvey, 1981, p. 10). Thus, the sexual relationship is probably best described as one form of social relationship (Weeks, 1986). Yet major reviews of literature typically treat sexuality as an individual characteristic. For example, recent reviews of adolescent sexual behavior in a family journal have summarized information about the timing of transition to sexual intercourse from "necking" to "intercourse" and have included discussion about the number of partners (Miller & Moore, 1990), as if adolescents were involved in sexual behavior without any emotion or any relationship, despite the importance of dating on transition timing (Leigh, Weddle, & Loewen, 1988). In addition, the concept of sexuality seems suddenly to appear in adolescence without much concern for any real developmental processes prior to "necking." In most cases, the main reason to discuss sexuality during adolescence has little to do with sexuality during adulthood and adult relationships; the primary focus is on dealing with problems of pregnancy, early childbearing, number of abortions that occur, and the like. There are a few exceptions, such as Laws's (1980) chapter on female sexuality or Sarrel & Sarrel's (1979) concept of sexual unfolding. For the most part, however, there is little developmental or contextual integration.

Because of the social nature of sexuality, one might expect family scholars to have closely examined its place within family processes. A review of major summaries of family research indicates that the role of sexuality in family interaction has not been thoroughly explored. In the first volume of *Contemporary Theories about the Family* (Burr, Hill, Nye, & Reiss, 1979), a major work in the field, the only chapters on sexuality are related to heterosexual permissiveness and to fertility. Sexual compatibility and sexual satisfaction are mentioned briefly in the chapter on quality and stability of marriage but are peripheral to the crux of the chapter. The majority of studies cited in this volume examine sexuality from the point of view of the individual, with little examination of process, and yet conclusions are implied about the relationship.

Sussman and Steinmetz's (1987) *Handbook of Marriage and the Family*, another landmark work, does include a chapter devoted to human sexuality by Francoeur. The foci of this chapter, however, are generally the development of the individual and the societal and cultural factors that contribute to similarities and differences among us.

Carter and McGoldrick's (1989) edited volume, *The Changing Family Life Cycle: A Framework for Family Therapy*, a basic work for family therapists, follows the problem, or deviance, focus. The discussion of sexuality for therapists is related to sexual abuse in the alcoholic home, adolescent sexual activity, privacy problems in families with children, and problems related to viewing sex as a wifely duty.

These works support Orbuch and Harvey's (1991) observation that reports from both members of a couple are rarely obtained. Much of what we call family-sexuality research does not contain a family, or even dyadic, perspective. Earlier works, such as those of Kinsey, Pomeroy, and Martin (1948, 1953) and Hunt (1974), which have frequently been considered major contributions to our understanding of sexual behavior for adults,

were not conducted from a dyadic perspective. Dyadic studies conducted on sexuality have often involved couples in a premarital (Christopher & Cate, 1985) or dating (Peplau, Rubin, & Hill, 1977) relationship, but most of the research in this field has been from an individual perspective.

Theoretical Perspectives on the Study of Family Sexuality

Traditionally, the study of family sexuality has been focused on general theoretical perspectives derived from the social sciences. For example, social-exchange theory, with its emphasis on costs, rewards, and comparison levels, has been used to explain why women remain in abusive relationships (Gelles & Cornell, 1990), with at least one-third of battered women also having been sexually assaulted by their partners (Finkelhor & Yllo, 1985); mate selection and relationship development (Scanzoni, 1979); and the bases for sexual behavior (Nye, 1979). This perspective also has been used to explain the patterns of racial disparity in premarital sex. With institutional racism blocking black achievement aspirations at every class level, and with a shortage of available black men, black women may perceive sexual favors as their only bargaining element in their relationships with men (Cortese, 1989).

Role theory has also been applied to sexual behavior "in terms of role prescriptions or proscriptions, and whether sanctions are provided for nonenactment" (Carlson, 1976, pp. 101–102). The sexual role is one of eight marital roles identified by Nye (1976). Role theory examines issues such as who initiates sexual activity, the importance and enjoyment of sexual activity, frequency of sexual desire, and role strain in coitus (Carlson, 1976). In addition to how people perceive their sexual roles, whom we choose to study may also influence our results. Spanier and Margols (1983) report that if the subjects themselves experienced extramarital coitus, they perceived it to be an effect of, rather than the cause of, marital problems. If their spouses experienced extramarital coitus, it was seen as a cause of marital problems. These perspectives, however, have not been central to the study of families and sexuality, nor do they seem to have had significant impact in modifying the way we think about family sexuality.

Life-Span Perspective

Another way in which perspectives about sexuality become segmented has to do with distinctions made between childhood sexuality, which is often viewed as innocent; adolescent sexuality; which usually is viewed as problematic; adulthood sexuality, which may be viewed as appropriate under limited circumstances; and sexuality among the elderly, which is often ignored completely. A life-span perspective tends to connect patterns of behavior or continuity in development over a period of time. Such a perspective is seldom used to connect sexual development, as if little that occurred in childhood had much to do with sexuality during adolescence or adulthood, unless the behavior is related to a traumatic experience, such as sexual abuse, or the development of a dysfunction, such as pedophilia. Yet children begin to learn about bodily response and physical pleasure, including sexual pleasure, as infants and young children (Langfeldt, 1981), possibly even prior to birth (Masters, Johnson, & Kolodny, 1988). Socio-sexual play also occurs during early childhood, even at the age of 2 (Spiro, 1956). While interest in sexual development and knowledge becomes less obvious as children move into and through middle childhood, Goldman and Goldman (1982) found from their cross-cultural research that children continued to be interested in and to learn about sexual development, gender differences, and sexual response as they got older. Rather than a perspective of discontinuity between childhood and adolescence, Goldman and Goldman suggest an increasing level of sophistication, comprehension, interest, and accuracy in children's understanding of sexuality as they mature to adolescents. This perspective has also been applied by Laws (1980) to female development on through middle adulthood and old age to demonstrate the continuity in sexual development.

Families also play a role in children's understanding of sexuality during early childhood. Parental response to autosexual arousal or sociosexual play begins to demonstrate and clarify attitudes and values about sexuality. Aspects of sexual relationships and social

restraints also begin to emerge during early childhood and continue to affect children through adolescence (Goldman & Goldman, 1982). Even aspects of appropriate sexual interaction in parental relationships and parental values are learned whether or not they are expressed by parents (Kahn & Kline, 1980). Parental values regarding communication about sexuality also become clear during adolescence, either because parents talk about sex with their children or because it is never all right to discuss such topics. These influences can continue through adolescence and adulthood.

Sexual Scripts

Social scripting is "the process whereby persons are subconsciously and consciously conditioned and gradually programmed to follow those rules, values, and behavioral patterns by a society, subculture, ethnic, or socioeconomic group" (Francoeur, 1990, p. 692). Sexual scripts are the mental plans we develop and use to organize our behavior along socially appropriate lines (Simon & Gagnon, 1987). Parents, in particular, influence the way children think and feel about sexuality. They provide models (scripts) for gender roles, expression and control of emotions and affection, family roles, and moral behaviors. Once internalized, these messages become our sexual scripts, influencing with whom we will be sexually intimate, our sexual values, and our sexual behaviors (Gagnon & Simon, 1973; Simon & Gagnon, 1987). Sexual development is viewed as episodic rather than continuous. This theory emphasizes individual experiences or development (ontogenic factors) and social influences (sociogenic factors) (Gagnon & Simon, 1973); it ignores biological factors. What is "sexual" or "nonsexual" is not mandated by the nature of our biological or social systems but takes on meaning with the individual in light of experiences in a given setting.

John Money (1988) has suggested that each of us has a unique and personalized sexual script, called a lovemap, of our idealized lover and the kind of erotic and sexual activities in which we would like to engage with that lover. During childhood and adolescence, we unconsciously elaborate on the physical characteristics of that ideal lover, and later we clarify the types of behaviors and objects involved. If, as the child's lovemap is developing, it becomes distorted, that person may experience long-term difficulties in developing intimate relationships. This scripting often occurs in intimate relationships and observations of those close to children, such as immediate and extended family members, peers, neighbors, family friends, and others.

Social-scripting concepts are often applied to the study of sexuality by sociologists. For example, Reiss (1989) uses them in constructing his definition of sexuality as "the erotic arousal and genital responses resulting from following the shared sexual scripts of that society" (p. 6). The culture of the family again becomes an important influence in learning about sexuality.

Family Systems

Family-systems concepts are useful in explaining family processes that involve sexuality. For example, family members influence the reactions of others in a bidirectional exchange, with patterns becoming circular and mutually reinforcing (Bateson, 1979; Hoffman, 1983; Patterson, 1982). Thus, the ways adolescents ask questions about sexuality, and the ways parents respond, influence the communication that takes place and may influence other aspects of sexual development in adolescents (Leigh & Loewen, 1987).

Family-systems theory has been utilized to address the changes that take place in parent/adolescent interaction during the period when an adolescent girl is experiencing puberty (Leigh & Loewen, 1987). Such changes have been explained in terms of both first-order and second-order developments. With first-order development, changes take place in the family patterns, but no change occurs in the family's prevailing consensual reality (Turkelson, 1980). In this example, the girl may begin to interact differently with her parents by asking general questions about physical development or appropriate social interactions between girls and boys. They, in turn, respond to her in different ways but without modifying their basic views of her as a child or of the characteristics of the parent/adolescent relationship.

Second-order developments involve changes in status and meaning that result in new interaction patterns and a new shared reality (Turkelson, 1980). For example, a daughter may ask: "What is a 'blow job?' My friend Tammy says they're awful, but Nancy says they're fun." Such questions may dramatically change the way a parent views a daughter. In this case, the family recognizes the changes in the pubertal adolescent girl and the changes in interaction patterns; they then treat her differently because they view her more as an adult (Leigh & Loewen, 1987).

Family systems could also be used to examine patterns of communication in sexual relationships. Traditionally, retrospective data have suggested that men appear to initiate sexual activity far more often than their female partners (Blumstein & Schwartz, 1983; Byers & Heinlein, 1989). O'Brien (1981) used multiple periodic interviews, however, to reveal that sexual initiation by wives is more common than originally thought. "The woman seemed to 'pace' the frequency of intercourse by subtly (or openly) signaling her readiness; then the husband 'initiated' the precoital behavior" (p. 117). Family systems could help place this example of interaction in context by investigating not only behaviors but also patterns that connect the behaviors, relationships, and people together in a different understanding of the process.

Family Processes

As mentioned earlier, little has been written about family sexuality specifically from a "family process" perspective. Yet, there are studies and applications that help us understand in a different way some of the issues related to sexuality in families. In this section we will review some of the relevant research and ideas related to family dynamics, structure, interactions, and processes.

Family Functioning

Families that tend to be fairly close and open seem to have an impact on children's later timing of transition to sexual intercourse. Students who have close ties with parents tend to be more sexually conservative than those who are not close (Teevan, 1972) and also are more likely to adopt parental values whether the families are conservative or liberal (Weinstein & Thornton, 1989). In addition, adolescents tend to disclose more to their parents when they perceive greater openness and adaptiveness in the family environment (Papini, Farmer, Clark, & Snell, 1988). Parental supervision also appears to be an important part of family functioning, with adolescents from very strict homes having higher levels of sexual activity than those from moderately strict families and those from the least strict families having the highest activity levels (Miller, McCoy, Olson, & Wallace, 1986). Such supervision also seems to be related to the probability of an adolescent girl becoming pregnant (Hogan & Kitagawa, 1985).

Many of these family variables are often closely interrelated, and it is not clear which are most important or whether a combination of factors is most influential. Closeness, adaptability, and supervision appear to be important, but little investigation has been done regarding how these interact or may build on one another. In some cases, supervision may have less to do with keeping adolescents from engaging in specific activities and more to do with affectional ties between parents and adolescents. Supervision can be a way of showing caring while also demonstrating respect for the adolescent's growing responsibility when families are not overly strict. In addition, closeness and openness may be important elements in an atmosphere that allows children to develop sexually while also learning appropriate social behaviors for the cultural context.

Cohesion and adaptability may also play an important role in adult relationships, especially in terms of developing sexual relationships, feeling open about communicating desires and feelings, and being clear and committed about whether or not outside sexual relationships are an option. Yet little of the research has focused on these aspects as they relate to sexual interaction. Hyde (1986), however, did find that a strong emotional connection to one's partner, an attitude of caring, and a willingness to learn about the partner's interests and desires were related to sexual satisfaction in a relationship.

Communication

One of the most studied topics concerning family processes has been communication about sexuality, something that is important at all ages of the life span. This process begins with very young children, whether parents are explicit or implicit in their messages (Cal-

derone & Ramey, 1983). We are always sharing symbols or demonstrating actions, and they often have meaning to others whether or not we intend to send such a message. Not only do parents communicate symbols, values, and messages to children, but they also communicate rules, many of which are negative directives focusing on "don'ts" rather than positive behaviors (Galvin & Brommel, 1991). "Often, communication about sexual issues remains indirect, resulting in confusion, misinformation, or heightened curiosity" (p. 97). Families that seem to be healthy sexually can communicate effectively about sex "using language that can accurately cover sexual information, reflect feelings and attitudes of members, and facilitate decision making and problem solving regarding sexual issues" (Maddock, 1989, p. 135). Yet communication is important for children to understand their own development, for long-term physical health and safety, and for learning about responsibility as adolescents and adults. Still, it is very difficult for many parents and frequently does not occur until children are much older, if at all (Thornburg, 1982).

Research on communication between parents and adolescents has yielded inconsistent results. Some researchers have found that adolescents are less likely to engage in early sexual intercourse when higher communication with parents has occurred (Fox & Inazu, 1980; Furstenberg, 1969; Furstenberg, Moore, & Peterson, 1985), while others have found that this holds only for girls and that boys are *more* likely to engage in sex (Kahn, Smith, & Roberts, 1984, as cited in Miller & Moore, 1990). Some have found no impact of communication (Newcomer & Udry, 1985), except when the communication occurs in conservative homes (Fisher, 1989; Moore, Simms, & Betsey, 1986). In addition, communication may be important because it "can make the daughter's sexual behavior explicit and can encourage the daughter's awareness and acceptance of her own sexuality, often a prelude to taking contraceptive responsibility for oneself" (Fox, 1980, p. 25).

Communication also plays a key role in adult sexual relationships. "Sexual expression needs to consist of clear messages that effectively communicate the feelings of both partners. Sexual pleasure that is freely given, in an honest and mutually intimate way, can draw two people together into a loving and passionate bond that is continually strengthened, enhancing the [relationship]" (Scoresby, 1977, pp. 45–46). Even among adults, however, sexual communication is often very difficult, but it is important to the quality of the sexual interaction and the quality of the relationship (Bell, 1987; Galvin & Brommel, 1991). Yet because people have not learned to communicate directly, feel awkward, or even feel that it is inappropriate to talk about sex, many may rely on nonverbal communication, which can lead to frustration and inaccurate interpretation of messages (Galvin & Brommel, 1991). Given the current threat of AIDS and other sexually transmitted diseases, clear communication about one's past is also important (Adelman, 1988). Lack of communication in this case can be a life-threatening response.

Family Scripts

Beginning in childhood, people begin to learn sexual scripts, which are repertoires of "acts and statuses that are recognized by a social group, together with the rules, expectations, and sanctions governing these acts and statuses" (Laws & Schwartz, 1977, p. 2). These collections of behaviors begin with personal scripts that individuals develop as standards for present behavior and plans for the future. These scripts typically include cultural norms, values, and meanings that have been incorporated into one's personal script, often beginning with one's family. They provide clear expectations regarding sexual behavior and define appropriate behavior. Such scripts become important in interpersonal relationships because they may, on the one hand, shared expectations of sexual interaction or may, on the other hand, be conflicting (Katchadourian, 1989). In the latter case, misunderstandings or distinct differences may occur between the individuals, which require some change or negotiation (Galvin & Brommel, 1991).

In some cases, individuals in families may develop a script early that later conflicts dramatically with larger social definitions. For example, a child may learn that any type of autoerotic play is "sinful and bad," leading to severe guilt and shame whenever there is any type of sexual arousal. Later, a partner who grew up feeling comfortable with sexual stimulation may not under-

stand the other person's difficulty feeling comfortable when they are sexually stimulating each other. In this case, not only does the interaction contradict one person's script, but sanctions easily come into play whenever sexual interaction occurs, even when the person says he or she is interested in the interaction or would like to participate with the partner (Laws & Schwartz, 1977).

Power and Hierarchy

In families, there is not typically equality between members, especially across generations. Families usually organize themselves with invisible sets of demands that influence the ways members interact (Minuchin, 1974). These organizations include differences in power and status, so that people form hierarchies within the system. Men often develop or maintain power over women, and parents often have greater power than children (Hoffman, 1981). This organization separates individuals in both positive and negative ways. For example, men with more power may abuse women and threaten them in such a way that they feel powerless not only to change the interaction but also to leave the relationship. Fathers can also use the power to eliminate the generational separation and sexually abuse a child in the family. More frequently and appropriately, the distance across generations is maintained by avoiding any sexual relationship between parents and children, providing an atmosphere where children can feel close and loved without any violation of their independent status and autonomy or without a coerced unpleasant sexual experience. Dramatic blurring of these boundaries with sexual abuse often creates confusion in families (Galvin & Brommel, 1991).

Distinct hierarchies in a couple relationship may be less beneficial and in fact may create some difficulties. In an atmosphere where there is less openness and comfort in self-disclosure, something more likely to occur when there are great discrepancies in power, partners may be less willing to share their desires and pleasures, creating a greater risk that sexual satisfaction will not develop within the relationship (Galvin & Brommel, 1991). When women feel inhibited and unable to be sexually assertive, they are less likely to meet their needs, and it is less likely that the satisfaction will be mutual (Feldman, 1982). While men may still be able to satisfy their needs, the relationship will be less mutual in interaction or responsiveness.

Subsystems

When a family has more than two members, subsystems often develop. Sometimes parents form one subunit within the system, for example, while children form another. The interactions within a subsystem are usually quite different from those between subsystems (Hoffman, 1981). Again, this may be quite appropriate, as parents have a close sexual relationship with each other but no sexual relationship with the children. In addition, children often have some affectionate expression or physical contact that is nonsexual, or they may have some sexual exploration, usually very different from a coerced experience with adults. For example, Finkelhor (1980) reports on a study of college students that 15% of the women and 10% of the men indicated having had some type of sexual experience with a sibling, although the true figures may have been higher given the likelihood of forgetting or concealing such behavior. Most of these experiences were between brothers and sisters, while a quarter were with a same-sex sibling. In most cases, the experience was predominantly sexual exploration, which is frequent among children and has little of the sexual meaning applied to interaction between adults or between adults and children. In some cases, however, especially when one sibling is much older, the experience may be very abusive, and traumatic and may occur over a long period, most often victimizing girls (again relating to a power hierarchy that can occur within the subsystem and be abused).

Sibling subsystems can also play an important function in the sharing of information and socialization of scripts. Older girls can be an important source of information about physical development, menarche, masturbation, or sexual response for younger sisters. Older brothers also share information about physical changes, sexual response, and masturbation with younger brothers. While older siblings may not be a primary source of information (Thornburg, 1982), they can often calm fears, normalize certain behaviors, and reassure siblings who are concerned about changes and who want some-

one to answer questions when it is difficult to ask anyone else, especially parents who have difficulty talking about sex to their children. Siblings may also be helpful in understanding the opposite sex and ways to respond that can improve sexual relationships as adults. On the other hand, siblings can also intensify fears, provide inaccurate information, or even coerce negative experiences, especially with younger siblings. The influence is not always positive.

Patterns and Rituals

As people develop sexual scripts, they are in part developing patterns of interactions that they carry with them into relationships. Individuals and couples also develop certain ways of interacting or certain stimuli that may become important "rituals" to sexual arousal. In some cases, people can become aroused only under these circumstances, and this may create limitations or problems in their relationships. For example, one man could only become aroused and have sex with his wife when his naked body was against leather. Others have rituals that are helpful but not limiting to their sexual arousal. For example, a man or a woman may come into the bedroom naked as a way of saying he or she is interested in sexual intercourse that evening. Or couples may put on certain music and light candles in order to create a romantic mood and stimulate arousal, but they can become aroused under other circumstances as well.

Some couples develop clear and consistent patterns of sexual interaction, and they continue in this pattern over a long period. Others feel uncomfortable or bored when they continue in the same pattern, often feeling refreshed when they create variations for themselves by going away to different places, making sure they approach each other in different ways, or varying the way they interact sexually (Cuber & Harroff, 1965).

Parents may also create patterns of noncommunication or rituals to avoid talking about sex with their children (Galvin & Brommel, 1991). Such patterns not only may be maintained in that family but also may occur in following generations. Children may learn these scripts and patterns so well that they practice them with precision when they have children, who also learn and maintain these patterns.

Challenges to the Traditional Views

Recently, traditional views of the study of sexuality and family have been challenged, particularly by feminists and with the advent of new physiological studies. In this section we outline some of the most essential challenges that help us think about family sexuality in a different and useful manner.

Sexuality from a Purely Problem-Oriented Approach

A great deal of information on family sexuality has been obtained from focusing on problems. Groups to which this approach is frequently applied are children, adolescents, women at midlife, the elderly, homosexuals, and subcultural groups (racial, ethnic, and social class). This seems to include almost everyone except white, middle-class, young-adults or midlife, heterosexual men! Examples pertaining to these groups will be presented throughout the remainder of this chapter.

In families with young children, we see this problem focus in an increased concern over sexual abuse. A child's first officially sanctioned exposure to sexual concepts may be in the negative context of child sexual assault programs (Comfort, 1985; Krivacska, 1990). In our well-intentioned efforts to protect children from abuse, we have developed child-sexual-assault prevention (CSAP) programs founded on principles derived from rape prevention and the women's rights movement (Krivacska, 1990). Although these principles may be appropriate for working with women, they may not be suitable for dealing with children. For example, the concept of empowerment proposes that individuals have a role to play in preventing themselves from becoming victims of sexual abuse. It presumes that they have the competence to care for themselves, can take responsibility for themselves, and have the freedom to make choices. Given the laws and structures of the United States, as well as the developmental levels of children, these may be inaccurate assumptions that result in children being more likely to feel guilty for not controlling the behaviors of the adults in their lives.

The CSAP programs also employ the concept of the touch continuum (Anderson, 1986). This concept was designed as an investigatory technique to assist in interviews of children suspected of having been sexually abused, and it includes "good touch," "bad touch," and "confusing touch." It assumes that children have an innate sense of appropriate touching. Depending on how a child is socialized, however, and under some circumstances, children fondled in a sexual manner may experience pleasure. Children are sexual beings and frequently have sexual experiences (such as masturbation or playing doctor). Vague references by adults to private parts or "the parts covered by a bathing suit" model adult discomfort with sexuality and "may compound the children's sense of shame and disgust with negative presentations of sexuality, such as those which describe contact with the genitals as bad touch" (Krivacska, 1991, p. 2).

Related to this concern over sexual abuse is the fear of sexual feelings between parents and children. Some mothers have experienced sexual arousal when breast-feeding their infants. Parents may feel turned on when children reach puberty or later. Fathers may experience erections during wrestling play with their children or when teenage daughters sit on their laps. Children also may have sexual feelings toward parents. These "feelings are common and, if managed reasonably, are nothing to be ashamed of" (Calderone & Johnson, 1990, p. 127). Such feelings arise out of uncontrolled thoughts (conscious, subconscious, or unconscious), but we can control our actions. Unfortunately, however, negative feelings about such sexual arousal can often interfere with gestures of affection between parents and children.

Viewing sexuality as a problem is particularly common in the literature on adolescents. Most work on adolescent sexuality focuses on intercourse as a precursor to teenage unwed pregnancy. Voydanoff and Donnelly's *Adolescent Sexuality and Pregnancy* (1990) focuses almost exclusively on coitus when it uses the term *adolescent sexuality*. Furstenberg, Brooks-Gunn, and Morgan (1987) and Stewart (1981) question whether it is appropriate to view all teenage pregnancy from a negative perspective. They also remind us that the teenage pregnancy rate in the United States peaked in the mid-1960s and then declined, as did rates for all women. Yet, teenage pregnancy was not identified as a national problem until the mid-1970s, when it was evident in families with white, middle-class, adolescent girls. While there are problems with early adolescent pregnancy, there is little focus on sexual development from infancy through old age, identifying the positive aspects as well as reaffirming responsibility. Interestingly enough, in societies where sexual communication is more open and consistent through childhood and adolescence, rates of both pregnancy and sexual abuse appear to be lower than in the United States (Goldman & Goldman, 1982).

Information on sexuality and the midlife woman also shows a problem focus. One indication is the nature of language used in menopause research (Cole & Rothblum, 1990). The term *symptoms* is used to describe women's experiences during climacteric and menopause. "Senile skin changes" and "vaginal atrophy" are terms commonly used in the medical literature (cf. Leiblum, 1990). But "it is untrue that a woman's skin decays as she ages, or that her vagina wastes away. We must stop . . . equating age with 'rotting'" (Cole & Rothblum, 1990, p. 510).

This negative image of the middle-aged woman is in part related to equating intercourse with sexuality and to equating reproduction with womanliness. Most studies of midlife women are based on clinical samples and define sexual interest and behavior in terms of intercourse. Assuming that vaginal intercourse is central to sexuality and continuing to use terms such as "foreplay" (something done before the real "game") limit our understanding of sexuality as a social process. Intercourse and orgasm have been the traditional goals of sexual activity. Progress toward those goals has often been described in terms used to describe winning in sports. Baseball terms such as "scoring," "getting to first base," "going all the way," and "striking out" (Roffman, 1991) reinforce men's views of sex as a goal-oriented game. Francoeur (1990) suggests that a preferable way to view sexual intimacy is as a non-goal-oriented game. This retains an element of playfulness but opens up potentially greater channels for communication, intimacy, and sexual pleasure. The focus is on enjoyment of the moment rather than on the game plan and its set objective.

The limited goal-oriented vision of sexuality becomes clearer when examined in light of findings about midlife experiences of lesbians. In a volunteer sample of nonpatient, midlife lesbians, the majority of whom were in a committed relationship, the picture presented is one of considerable and deepened sexual pleasure (Cole & Rothblum, 1991). Sex had a "celebratory quality" and was "discussed in the context of a relationship" (Cole & Rothblum, 1990, p. 512). In contrast, studies of heterosexual women indicate their concern with sexual functioning, arousal time, vaginal dryness, loss of clitoral sensation, and fear of disappointing one's partner (Bachmann, Leiblum, & Grill, 1989; Leiblum, 1990). It would appear that sexual difficulties might well be avoided by altering the sexual script commonly presented to heterosexual women, both in families and especially in the larger society.

An examination of literature on homosexuals shows that much is still written from a problem focus. This is even more true today in light of the HIV/AIDS epidemic. Much that is written about gays by healthcare and mental-health professionals deals with issues related to AIDS (for oneself or one's partner) or with still trying to find out what "makes" someone homosexual. Savin-Williams (1990) questions this problem focus and indicates that many gay adolescents have, for the most part, positive self-images and are coping remarkably well in American society. Many of our views about homosexuality as a "clinical problem" come primarily from biased clinical research on the small segment of the gay population that has had adjustment difficulties, especially in a society that is highly homophobic. Yet we do not characterize heterosexuals based on the clinical segment that also has difficulty adjusting in our society, which is more supportive of their sexual orientation.

Studies of the sexuality of the elderly, like studies of other age groups, cannot ignore the interaction of the biological and sociological aspects. With their changing physiological factors, however, the elderly are also one of the age groups most likely to be described from a problem focus. A problem that exists for sexuality research for all ages, but that people are willing to identify most readily for the elderly, is that sexual behavior has been measured in terms of intercourse. When coitus is evaluated, the elderly are usually dichotomized into the all or none groups (Ludeman, 1981).

Kinsey's work (Kinsey et al., 1948) found fewer men to be sexually active as they aged and found men to have increasing levels of erectile difficulty. A woman's decreased sexual activity was attributed to decreases in her mate's desires and his capacity rather than her own lack of interest (Kinsey et al., 1953). More recent studies indicate that the rate of decline is not as great as had been believed (Brecher, 1984; George & Weiler, 1981; Starr & Weiner, 1981). Recent studies have had larger sample sizes, but they still rely on convenience groups. Differences in findings also may be due to cohort effects, including improved health, longer life spans, and more leisure time, as well as "changing societal attitudes toward sex in general" (Riportella-Muller, 1989, p. 214).

Sexuality outside of Family and Relationship Contexts

Because so much work on sexuality has been conducted from an individual focus (looking at sexual response, sexual problems, and deviance), there has been a dearth of information on sexuality within the contexts in which it exists. Information on sexuality outside of its current context can lead to a misinterpretation of findings. For example, although studies often explain current behaviors in light of past trauma, Edwards and Booth (1976) indicate that the sexual behaviors of men and women are largely determined by present circumstances rather than past behaviors.

Context is also important in examining childhood experiences. Sex play functions as a learning experience, especially when parents fail to give children explicit information on basic topics such as sexual anatomy. Therefore, children "caught" in the act of sexual exploration and play are more likely to form negative or guilty feelings about sexuality in response to the adults' reactions than in response to the activity itself (Goldman & Goldman, 1988; Leitenberg, Greenwald, & Tarran, 1989). Context is also important in trying to assess "normal sexual behaviors" of children, since "there are individual differences due to developmental level of the child *and* due to the amount of exposure the child has had to adult sexuality, nudity, explicit television, and videos" (Johnson, 1991, p. 8).

Lack of a contextual perspective has also hindered our understanding of issues of sexuality for various subcultures and ethnic and socioeconomic groups. A typical example involves research on the sexuality of black adolescents. A study using a national sample of

adolescents aged 15 and 16 reported that blacks were approximately 4 times as likely as whites to have engaged in intercourse (Furstenberg, Morgan, Moore, & Peterson, 1987). Of those studied, blacks in isolated classrooms were over 3.7 times as likely as blacks in integrated classrooms to have had intercourse. Blacks in isolated classrooms were 18.6 times as likely as whites to expect parenthood before or at the same time as marriage. Blacks in integrated classrooms were 2.1 times as likely as whites to expect early parenthood. Hogan and Kitagawa (1985) also reported strong neighborhood effects on teenage pregnancy and childbearing rates. Social context is a necessary variable for the study of adolescent sexual behavior (Cortese, 1989).

Our knowledge about family sexuality of people who are disabled not only is scant but also suffers from the lack of a contextual perspective. For example, one cannot just examine divorce rates of people with spinal cord injuries. We must also account for the timing of the marriage in relation to the injury. Divorce rates for people who marry after a spinal cord injury are lower than the national average; for those who were married before the time of injury, the divorce rate is higher than average (Kettle, Zarefoss, & Jacoby, 1991). Our knowledge of sexual experiences of various groups is also hindered by what Mary Calderone has called "a tendency for society to castrate its dependent members: to deny the sexuality of the disabled, of prisoners, . . . the elderly" and children (Cross, 1993, p. 7). Cross suggests that this attitude may reflect a "subconscious desire to dehumanize those whom we believe to be less fortunate than ourselves in order to assuage our guilt feelings" (p. 7).

Information about homosexual family sexuality is often misinterpreted because of the lack of a contextual perspective. For example, it is impossible to discuss the sexuality of people who are gay without including the larger context of the effects of the HIV/AIDS epidemic on sexual behavior. The effects of losing the majority of one's network of friends, of dealing with one's own health issues and those of a partner cannot be isolated. In addition, when gay men and lesbians are studied, there has been little emphasis on variance within the group in social, economic, and familial characteristics. This is particularly problematic in the study of gay and lesbian adolescents (Savin-Williams, 1990).

Feminist Contributions

One of the greatest contributions of feminism to the study of family sexuality has been the push to reframe, reinterpret, and reconceptualize issues related to sexuality. In the Kuhnian sense (Kuhn, 1970), feminist scholarship is a paradigm shift that enables researchers to see things they did not see before and to see the familiar in a different way (Nielsen, 1990). Although there are diverse epistemologies within the feminist community, each of these perspectives (1) assumes that the everyday life and experiences of each person is valuable and deserves to be understood (DuBois, 1983); (2) considers women's experiences to be suitable problems for study, as well as potential sources for answers (Coyner, 1988–1989); (3) designs research *for* women, rather than *on* or *about* women; and (4) strives to empower women.

Feminists have challenged us to view sexuality within the broader issue of gender inequality, seeing it as a construct of male power (MacKinnon, 1987). They criticize existing theories of sexuality as sexist:

> Men author scripts to their own advantage, women and men act them out; men set conditions, women and men have their behavior conditioned; men develop developmental categories through which men develop, and women develop or not; . . . men have object relations, women are the objects of those relations. (p. 68)

Feminists can help family scientists reframe and reexamine sexuality by asking questions such as those presented by MacKinnon (1987): (1) Sex is described "as a central form of expression, one that defines identity and is seen as a primary source of energy and pleasure" (Snitow, Stansell, & Thompson, 1983, p. 9). Is it as much a woman's form of expression as it is a man's? Aren't violence and abuse equally central to sexuality as women experience it? (2) Why ask how women negotiate sexual pleasure? Women in a patriarchy do not have power or freedom to negotiate. Is the real sexual issue for women pleasure and how to get it, or dominance and how to end it?

Feminists can help us reexamine the terms we use in our research. Terms such as the male role and the female role imply complementary (separate or different but equal) roles during sexual interaction. These terms are depoliticizing and neglect questions of conflict, power, aggression, and dominance related to sexual relationships (cf. Stacey & Thorne, 1985).

Feminists have continually encouraged the reexamination of rape and sexual abuse. They first encouraged us to stop viewing rape as sex and to see it as violence, with its elements of power and dominance. But feminism is not stagnant, and it continues to critically examine even its own views. MacKinnon (1987) contends that the earlier feminist view led people to mistakenly dichotomize "sex that is good" from forced sex (that which is "not sex"). She asks, "If it's violence not sex, why didn't he just hit her?" and adds that "violence is sex when it is practiced *as* sex" (p. 73).

Although Masters and Johnson (1966) have indicated similar patterns of sexual arousal for men and women, feminists have questioned whether "objective" indexes of arousal, such as vaginal secretions, are preferable to self-reported arousal. When women exposed to pornography produce vaginal secretions but report no arousal, for example, the discrepancy has been typically reported as the result of repression (Mosher, 1971; Schmidt, 1975). Feminists ask: Is something sexual truth just because it is physically measurable? Could it also be that women disidentify with their bodies' conditioned responses (MacKinnon, 1987)?

Sexuality is viewed as rooted in a reality imposed by the sociohistorical context but as having varied little across time because most societies have been controlled by men (MacKinnon, 1987, p. 89). Feminists believe that we must analyze the current environment within which sexuality and relationships occur before it can be changed and that to seek an equal sexuality without political transformation is to seek "equality under conditions of inequality" (MacKinnon, 1987, p. 90).

Feminist postmodernism acknowledges the existence of varied social realities, rejects the notion of one privileged standpoint, and raises concerns about the existence of any universal reality or truth (Harding, 1986, 1987). Sexual experiences are viewed within a contextual format rather than as being based on gender alone. Therefore, postmodernism challenges the belief that there is one entity termed family or one universal definition for terms such as sexual satisfaction.

Equally as important as examining what theories and topics are studied is observing what topics have been omitted from the study of family sexuality. Among topics in family science that warrant greater attention are the experiences of victims of date and marital rape and abuse, the sexual experiences of women with AIDS, sexual experience in midlife, and the interrelationship of work, family, self, and sexual experiences.

An omitted topic that is particularly evident in the study of adolescent girls is the discourse of sexual desire (Fine, 1988; Tolman, 1991). Adolescent female sexuality is frequently discussed using a discourse of victimization (that boys take advantage of girls), a discourse of disease (that girls need to avoid infection from sexually transmitted diseases, including HIV), and a discourse of morality (that good girls are not sexually active) (Fine, 1988). Even in feminist research and theory, the role of sexual desire in female development is clouded (Tolman, 1991), and the focus of female sexuality is viewed in a relational context (Jordan, 1987).

These questions and issues raised by feminists play a critical role in modifying our view of family sexuality, sexual development, and sexual relationships. These become important modifications of the way we change our perception of sexual issues and influences within a family context.

Power of Biology and Abdication of Responsibility

According to Reiss (1989), sociologists do not deny the power of biology and psychology to explain aspects of sexuality. He posits that each discipline poses a different set of theoretical questions: one set related to the study of hormones, another to the study of therapeutic interventions, and a third the study of shared social scripts. He believes that an integrative approach to understanding human sexuality is too ambitious at this time.

Such might be the case if each discipline were truly asking different questions, but family science, as an integrative discipline, needs to venture into this ambitious territory. Questions are being posed for family scientists that cannot be adequately answered without an understanding of bio-psycho-social data and techniques. Miller (1993) concludes that a focus on envi-

ronmental issues alone is not sufficient for family scientists and that biological influences on experiences such as adolescent pregnancy are quite important.

One of the most pressing examples today relates to our understanding of how family stress, parent/child relationships, and the onset of puberty are related. Genetic factors (Plomin & Fulker, 1987) and nutritional factors (Marshall, 1978) strongly influence the timing of puberty. Therefore, developmental psychologists and family scholars have paid little attention to the effects of social ecology and behavioral development on pubertal maturation (Belsky, Steinberg, & Draper, 1991). Typically, the timing of puberty has been treated as an independent variable (Hill, Holmbeck, Marlow, Green, & Lynch, 1985, 1986; Steinberg, 1981, 1987). Conflict and distance between adolescents and their parents (especially mothers) have been assumed to increase in response to pubertal growth. Based on these studies, researchers concluded that it was the pubertal onset, independent of chronological age, that led to distancing between parents and adolescents. Interpretations have used psychoanalytic, social-learning, or ethological frameworks to explain the transformations in family interaction at puberty (Steinberg, 1981, 1987).

Recent work in socioendocrinology (Worthman, in press; cited in Belsky et al., 1991) indicates that a reciprocal relationship exists between social experience and the regulation of hormonal activity. It may be that the rate of pubertal maturation is also influenced by the quality of family relationships. Based on two longitudinal studies, researchers suggest that distance in the parent/child relationship may precede the onset of puberty for girls and that girls living in homes with stressful family relations mature earlier than their peers in homes with closer family relations. Steinberg (1987) found that girls who reported greater strain in their relations with their parents physically matured faster during a 12-month period than did their peers, although both groups began the period at an equivalent stage of puberty. Moffit, Caspi, and Belsky (1990) found that family conflict when a girl was age 7 was predictive of earlier menarche, even after the effects of parental divorce and the girl's weight were considered.

Belsky et al. (1991, p. 651) have proposed a model to account for the different developmental pathways of divergent reproductive strategies. The model suggests that interaction exists between family context (level of discord, stress, and resources), patterns of early child rearing, the child's psychological/behavioral development, somatic development (timing of puberty), and reproductive strategy (for example, early versus later sexual activity, stability of pair bonds). Such research and theoretical discussion have resulted in extensive dialogue. In responding to the Belsky et al. article, Maccoby (1991) suggests that "nonevolutionary factors are more than adequate to account for precocious sexuality in individuals" (p. 676). However, Hinde (1991) has responded to Belsky et al. by indicating that "an evolutionary approach is useful if it integrates diverse facts, if it aids clinical practice, and if it helps us toward a full understanding of human nature" (p. 671).

Further challenges that family scholars will face arise from books such as Moir and Jessel's *Brain Sex* (1991). The authors synthesize a plethora of research on male and female differences based on differences in brain organization (in which functions are housed in different brain locations for men and women), brain structure (differences in the thickness of the corpus callosum message-exchange center of the brain), and hormonal types, levels, and fluctuations. From this information, Moir and Jessel address differences in such factors as emotions and displays of affection, approaches to problem solving, sexual drive and arousal, breaking up of relationships, orgasm, and homosexuality. Some of their points may be uncomfortable to social scientists: "The desire for sexual novelty is innate in the male brain" (p. 133). "The happily married woman who has an affair is a rare creature. The happily married male adulterer is not" (p. 134). "The reluctance men have with feeling and with communicating emotion has a biological root" (p. 136). "The sexual revolution is largely built upon the misapprehension that each sex has an equal appetite and is equally receptive. It will be seen as a mere blip of social fashion in the history of our evolutionary selves" (p. 108). The debate regarding genetics and environment will continue to rage (cf. Christen, 1991), but unless family scientists are versed in fields such as physiology and endocrinology, they will be inadequately prepared to dissect and respond to these sorts of comments.

A concern that arises from such explanations for behaviors is that one can blame biology instead of society for problems such as rape or teenage pregnancy. This abdication of responsibility can exist at the individual level ("Teens are at the mercy of their hormones" and "Men just can't control themselves") and at the societal level ("Sex education should focus on abstinence only" and "The woman is responsible for provoking her own rape"). Implications for family policy are disconcerting unless such research is used in a scientific rationale for why society has the responsibility to try to solve such social ills (Sapolsky, 1992).

Where Do We Go from Here?

Family science has the potential to address several of the challenges to traditional sexuality research, and in doing so, contribute to our understanding of sexuality.

General Challenges

1. Family science can broaden the use of the term *sexuality* to mean more than coitus. Family science already has experience at encouraging the reconstruction of terms, such as the more inclusive definition now used in discussing families. We can respond in a similar way to what is included in the definition of sexuality. We need not only to teach this broader interpretation but also to conduct our research to measure sexuality in more holistic terms. Riportella-Muller (1989) calls this studying the "phenomenology of the sexual experience" (p. 213).

2. Family science can lessen the sex-negative, problem-focus orientation of traditional sexuality literature. Family scientists would not tolerate the lack of pluralism (the belief that there is more than one morally acceptable way for people to behave) in religion, political preference, or race. So too we should demand "sexual pluralism" (Reiss, 1990, 1991). This does not mean that we must try all kinds of sexual behaviors or that all behaviors are equally acceptable. Rather, we assert that honesty, equality, and responsibility are essential to all sexual relationships and that these three factors serve as the measure of what is sexually legitimate. To do so we must first analyze our own value systems. We can also discourage the problem focus of sexuality literature

by reconstructing our views of adolescent sexuality. Is promoting "compulsory abstinence" a safe goal when it results in less responsibility or planning and increases the likelihood of disease and pregnancy? What effect does the abstinence-based, sex-negative message presented in childhood and adolescence have on the later development of intimate relationships in adulthood? Are aspects of sexual activity (not coitus) desirable during adolescence? Should we be advocating the channeling of adolescent sexual energies through self-exploration? What sex-positive issues can we study? Family scientists have been able to reconceptualize the study of families to focus on family strengths rather than weaknesses (Stinnett, Chesser, & DeFrain, 1979; Stinnett & DeFrain, 1985); we should be able to use a similar approach to reconceptualizing family sexuality. Before we can study family sexuality, the family needs to be deconstructed and reconstructed in a variety of ways related to gender, age, and adult/child relationships (cf. Thorne, 1982). In addition, we need to begin viewing sexuality as a natural, positive developmental process with some changes occurring at different points of the life span. Children and adolescents develop sexually whether or not we address the issue directly. While the *timing* of the transition to sexual intercourse may still be a concern, it does not have to outweigh all aspects of sexual development or negatively orient our entire focus. Rather, we can examine the development of sexual acceptance, readiness, and responsibility in terms of effective timing.

3. Family science can improve the study of subcultural differences in family sexuality. There is a shortage of valid and reliable data on sexuality for black and Latino families (Cortese, 1989). What data there are have generally been studied through the normative system of white America, with dysfunction or deviation being anything that veers from white norms and scripts. From the family systems or ecosystems perspectives, family scientists can study the interaction of environment and social context to identify neighborhood effects (Furstenberg et al., 1987; Hogan & Kitagawa, 1985), subcultural effects, social class, and structural factors (Francoeur, 1987). In light of immigration and population trends, we need to learn more about the social and sexual scripting of various Latino and Asian-American groups, particularly as we try to understand the linkage between assimilation and sexual values (Cortese, 1989).

4. Finally, we need to begin examining directly how family dynamics, interactions, and relationships influence and are influenced by sexual development and sexual interactions. We need to address not only problem behaviors but also positive aspects of sexual development and interaction.

Challenges in Education

1. It would be important to require course work on family sexuality. Sexuality courses frequently are not required of our undergraduate or graduate majors. They generally exist but are taken as an elective, if students have the time and money. Students need to see the relevance of such courses, and instructors in other family-science courses need to show this relevance by drawing in examples from the study of sexuality.

2. We need to incorporate family-sexuality concepts, information, and issues in other courses in family departments, including courses on individual development in infancy, early and middle childhood, adolescence, adulthood, and old age. Such courses could take a life-span and normative perspective of sexuality within a family and cultural context so that they are integrated throughout the curriculum.

3. We also need to include course work in anatomy and physiology, biology/sociobiology, or endocrinology/socioendocrinology at the undergraduate and graduate levels. In interdisciplinary fields such as sexuality, students need to be able to speak the language and understand the principles of other disciplines. Only then can they critically evaluate some of the challenges to social science and contribute to the understanding of the interaction of biology and social conditioning.

4. A positive view of sexuality and sexual development needs to be included in our educational programs. This does not eliminate issues of appropriate timing for new behaviors, such as sexual intercourse, nor of sexual responsibility, including timing, avoiding pressure for others to participate, and using appropriate contraceptives.

Challenges in Research

Family science is particularly well suited for the study of interdisciplinary topics such as sexuality. Our background draws from an array of behavioral sciences, including sociology, psychology, communication, and anthropology. The study of family sexuality (particularly from a dyadic perspective) is a recent endeavor, and many questions are still to be explored.

1. We need to know more about the phenomenology of sexual experience, information that can be obtained only from cross-sequential studies over a long period; only then can we truly isolate cohort differences. With an understanding of the phenomenology of sexual experience we can improve our research instruments to get useful measures related to family sexuality—that is, measures of sexual aspects that people feel are important across the life span.

2. We need information comparing insiders' and outsiders' views of relationships (Olson, 1977; Orbuch & Harvey, 1991). Interviewing previous mates/spouses, close friends, adolescents, or adult children as "outsiders" may provide some interesting insights.

3. We need more representative samples, with greater numbers of subjects and more than one person responding from a family. In addition, we need to sample adequately by subcultural, ethnic, and class groups. Studies of adults need representative sampling of the elderly. Research on "family" sexuality needs to be conducted at least at the dyadic level, or we will continue to have studies based on one person's perspective of a sexual relationship.

4. We need to include more of a normative and life-span perspective in our research on sexuality and families. Such a perspective would help connect both the resilient and the dysfunctional aspects of individual development and would allow the more positive aspects of sexuality to be understood without focusing solely on problems.

Chapter Summary

Discussion Questions

1. How would a normative and life-span perspective change our current views about sexuality in families, cultures, and societies?

2. Discuss some of the ways a family-systems perspective would change the way sexuality is typically viewed in families, cultures, and societies.

3. Feminist scholarship encourages a reframing, reinterpretation, and reconceptualization of sexual issues in a broader context of gender inequality. (a) Describe ways in which a feminist perspective on sexuality can benefit the lives of men. (b) Identify some terms or issues related to sexuality that, if reexamined, could benefit family scientists in their teaching, research, and clinical work.

4. What is your reaction to the idea that biology (genetics and hormones) may be a stronger determinant than environment (social learning) of one's family interactions, sexual choices, and behaviors? What are some ways in which family scientists can integrate both nature and nurture into their research and clinical work?

5. In what ways would a sexuality course taught from a family-science perspective be different from one taught in psychology, sociology, or biology?

Additional Resources

Calderone, M. S., & Ramey, J. W. (1983). *Talking with your child about sex: Questions and answers for children*. New York: Random House.

Fisher, T. D. (1989). Family sexual communication and adolescent sexual behavior. *Journal of Marriage and the Family, 51,* 637–639.

MacKinnon, C. A. (1987). A feminist/political approach: "Pleasure under patriarchy." In J. H. Geer & W. T. O'Donohue (Eds.), *Theories of human sexuality*. New York: Plenum.

References

Adelman, M. (1988, November). *Sustaining passion: Eroticism and safe sex talk*. Paper presented at the convention of the Speech Communication Association, New Orleans.

Anderson, C. (1986). A history of the touch continuum. In M. Nelson & R. Clark (Eds.), *The educator's guide to preventing child sexual abuse* (pp. 87–114). Santa Cruz, CA: Network Publications.

Bachmann, G., Leiblum, S., & Grill, J. (1989). Brief sexual inquiry in gynecologic practice. *Obstetrics and Gynecology, 73,* 425–427.

Bateson, G. (1979). *Mind and nature.* New York: Dutton.

Bell, R. (1987). Did you bring the yarmulke for the cabbage patch kid? The idiomatic communication of young lovers. *Human Communication Research, 14,* 47–67.

Belsky, J., Steinberg, L., & Draper, P. (1991). Childhood experience, interpersonal development, and reproductive strategy: An evolutionary theory of socialization. *Child Development, 62,* 647–670.

Blumstein, P., & Schwartz, P. (1983). *American couples.* New York: Pocket Books.

Brecher, E. (1984). *Love, sex, and aging.* Boston: Little, Brown.

Burr, W. R., Hill, R., Nye, F. I., & Reiss, I. L. (Eds.). (1979). *Contemporary theories about the family: Vol. 1.* New York: Free Press.

Byers, E. S., & Heinlein, L. (1989). Predicting initiations and refusals of sexual activities in married and cohabiting heterosexual couples. *Journal of Sex Research, 26,* 210–231.

Calderone, M. S., & Johnson, E. W. (1990). *Family book about sexuality* (rev. ed). New York: Perennial Library/Harper & Row.

Calderone, M. S., & Ramey, J. W. (1983). *Talking with your child about sex: Questions and answers for children.* New York: Random House.

Carlson, J. (1976). The sexual role. In F. I. Nye (Ed.), *Role structure and analysis of the family.* Newbury Park, CA: Sage.

Carter, B., & McGoldrick, M. (Eds.). (1989). *The changing family life cycle: A framework for family therapy* (2nd ed.). Boston: Allyn & Bacon.

Christen, Y. (1991). *Sex differences: Modern biology and the unisex fallacy* (N. Davidson, Trans.). New Brunswick, NJ: Transaction.

Christopher, F. S., & Cate, R. M. (1985). Premarital sexual pathways and relationship development. *Journal of Social and Personal Relationships, 2,* 271–288.

Cole, E., & Rothblum, E. (1990). Commentary on "Sexuality and the midlife woman." *Psychology of Women Quarterly, 14,* 509–512.

Cole, E., & Rothblum, E. (1991). Lesbian sex at menopause: As good or better than ever. In B. Sang, A. Smith, & J. Warshow (Eds.), *Lesbians at midlife: The creative transition.* San Francisco: Spinsters/Aunt Lute.

Comfort, R. L. (1985). Sex, strangers, and safety. *Child Welfare, 64,* 541–545.

Cortese, A. J. (1989). Subcultural differences in human sexuality: Race, ethnicity, and social class. In K. McKinney & S. Sprecher (Eds.), *Human sexuality: The societal and interpersonal context.* Norwood, NJ: Ablex.

Coyner, S. (1988–1989). Feminist theory in research and teaching. *National Women's Studies Association Journal, 1,* 290–296.

Cross, R. J. (1993, June/July). What doctors and others need to know: Sex facts on human sexuality and aging. *SIECUS Report, 21,* 7–9.

Cuber, J. F., & Harroff, P. B. (1965). *Sex and the significant Americans: A study of sexual behavior among the affluent.* Baltimore: Penguin.

DuBois, B. (1983). Passionate scholarship: Notes on values, knowing and method in feminist social science. In G. Bowles & R. D. Klein (Eds.), *Theories of women's studies* (pp. 105–116). London: Routledge & Kegan Paul.

Edwards, J. N., & Booth, A. (1976). Sexual behavior in and out of marriage: An assessment of correlates. *Journal of Marriage and the Family, 38,* 73–81.

Feldman, L. B. (1982). Sex roles and family dynamics. In F. Walsh (Ed.), *Normal family process* (pp. 345–382). New York: Guilford Press.

Fine, M. (1988). Sexuality, schooling and adolescent females: The messy discourse of desire. *Harvard Educational Review, 58*(1), 29–53.

Finkelhor, D. (1980). Sex among siblings: A survey on prevalence, variety, and effects. *Archives of Sexual Behavior, 9*(3), 171–194.

Finkelhor, D., & Yllo, K. (1985). *License to rape: The sexual abuse of wives.* New York: Holt, Rinehart & Winston.

Fisher, T. D. (1989). Family sexual communication and adolescent sexual behavior. *Journal of Marriage and the Family, 51,* 637–639.

Fox, G. L. (1980). The mother–adolescent daughter relationship as a sexual socialization structure: A research review. *Family Relations, 29,* 21–28.

Fox, G. L., & Inazu, J. K. (1980). Patterns and outcomes of mother-daughter communication about sexuality. *Journal of Social Issues, 36,* 7–29.

Francoeur, R. T. (1987). Human sexuality. In M. B. Sussman & S. K. Steinmetz (Eds.), *Handbook of marriage and the family.* New York: Plenum Press.

Francoeur, R. T. (1990). *Becoming a sexual person* (2nd ed.) New York: Macmillan.

Furstenberg, F. F., Jr. (1969). Birth control knowledge and attitudes among unmarried adolescents: A preliminary report. *Journal of Marriage and the Family, 31,* 34–42.

Furstenberg, F. F., Jr., Brooks-Gunn, J., & Morgan, S. (1987). *Adolescent mothers and their children in later life.* Cambridge: Cambridge University Press.

Furstenberg, F. F., Jr., Moore, K. A., & Peterson, J. L. (1985). Sex education and sexual experience among adolescents. *American Journal of Public Health, 75,* 1331–1332.

Furstenberg, F., Morgan, S. P., Moore, K. A., & Peterson, J. L. (1987). Race differences in the timing of adolescent intercourse. *American Sociological Review, 52,* 511–518.

Gagnon, J. H., & Simon, W. (1973). *Sexual conduct: The social sources of human sexuality.* Chicago, IL: Aldine-Atherton.

Galvin, K. M., & Brommel, B. J. (1991). *Family communication: Cohesion and change* (3rd ed.). New York: Harper-Collins.

Gelles, R. J., & Cornell, C. P. (1990). *Intimate violence in families* (2nd ed.). Newbury Park, CA: Sage.

George, L. K., & Weiler, S. J. (1981). Sexuality in middle and late life. *Archives of General Psychiatry, 38,* 919–923.

Goldman, R. J., & Goldman, J. D. (1982). *Children's sexual thinking.* Boston: Routledge & Kegan Paul.

Goldman, R. J., & Goldman, J. D. (1988). *Show me yours: Understanding children's sexuality.* Ringwood, Austria: Penguin Books.

Hammond, B. E., & Ladner, J. A. (1969). *The individual, sex, and society.* Baltimore: Johns Hopkins University Press.

Harding, S. (1986). *The science question in feminism.* Ithaca, NY: Cornell University Press.

Harding, S. (1987). Introduction: Is there a feminist method? In S. Harding (Ed.), *Feminism and methodology* (pp. 1–14). Bloomington: Indiana University Press.

Hill, J., Holmbeck, G., Marlow, L., Green, T., & Lynch, M. (1985). Pubertal status and parent-child relations in families of seventh-grade boys. *Journal of Early Adolescence, 5,* 31–44.

Hill, J., Holmbeck, G., Marlow, L., Green, T., & Lynch, M. (1986). Menarcheal status and parent-child relations in families of seventh-grade girls. *Journal of Youth and Adolescence, 14,* 310–316.

Hinde, R. A. (1991). When is an evolutionary approach useful? *Child Development, 62,* 671–675.

Hoffman, L. (1981). *Foundations of family therapy: A conceptual framework for systems change.* New York: Basic Books.

Hoffman, L. (1983). A co-evolutionary framework for systemic family therapy. In J. C. Hansen & B. P. Kenney (Eds.), *Diagnosis and assessment in family therapy.* Rockville, MD: Aspen.

Hogan, D., & Kitagawa, E. (1985). The impact of social status, family structure, and neighborhood on the fertility of black adolescents. *American Journal of Sociology, 90,* 825–855.

Hunt, M. (1974). Sexual behavior in the 1970s. Chicago: Playboy.

Hyde, J. S. (1986). *Understanding human sexuality* (3rd Ed.). New York: McGraw-Hill.

Johnson, T. C. (1991). Understanding the sexual behaviors of young children. *SIECUS Report, 19*(6), 8–15.

Jordan, J. (1987). Clarity in connection: Empathic knowing, desire and sexuality. *Work in Progress, No. 29.* Wellesley, MA: Stone Center Working Papers Series.

Kahn, J., & Kline, D. (1980). Toward an understanding of sexual learning and communication: An examination of social learning theory and nonschool learning environments. In E. Roberts (Ed.), *Childhood sexual learning: The unwritten curriculum.* Cambridge, MA: Ballinger.

Katchadourian, H. (1989). *Fundamentals of human sexuality.* Chicago: Holt, Rinehart & Winston.

Kettle, P., Zarefoss, S., & Jacoby, K. (1991). Female sexuality after spinal cord injury. *Sexuality and Disability, 9*(4), 287–295.

Kinsey, A. C., Pomeroy, W. B., & Martin, C. E. (1948). *Sexual behavior in the human male.* Philadelphia: Saunders.

Kinsey, A., Pomeroy, W., Martin, C., & Gebhard, P. (1953). *Sexual behavior in the human female.* Philadelphia: Saunders.

Krivacska, J. J. (1990). *Designing child sexual abuse prevention programs: Current approaches and a proposal for the prevention, reduction and identification of sexual misuse.* Springfield, IL: Charles C Thomas.

Krivacska, J. J. (1991). Child sexual abuse prevention programs: The need for childhood sexuality education. *SIECUS Report, 19*(6), 1–7.

Kuhn, T. S. (1970). *The structure of scientific revolutions* (2nd ed.). Chicago: University of Chicago Press.

Langfeldt, T. (1981). Sexual development in children. In M. Cook & K. Howells (Eds.), *Adult sexual interest in children* (pp. 129–157). London: Academic Press.

Laws, J. L. (1980). Female sexuality through the life span. In P. B. Baltes & O. G. Brim, Jr. (Eds.), *Life-span development and behavior: Vol. 3* (pp. 207–252). New York: Academic Press.

Laws, J. L., & Schwartz, P. (1977). *Sexual scripts.* Hinsdale, IL: Dryden.

Leiblum, S. R. (1990). Sexuality and the midlife woman. *Psychology of Women Quarterly, 14,* 495–508.

Leigh, G. K., & Loewen, I. R. (1987). Utilizing developmental perspectives in the study of adolescence. *Journal of Adolescent Research, 2,* 303–320.

Leigh, G. K., Weddle, K. D., & Loewen, I. R. (1988). Analysis of the timing of transition to sexual intercourse for black adolescent females. *Journal of Adolescent Research, 3,* 333–344.

Leitenberg, H., Greenwald, E., & Tarran, M. J. (1989). The relation between sexual activity among young children during preadolescence and/or early adolescence and sexual behavior and sexual adjustment in young adulthood. *Archives of Sexual Behavior, 18,* 299–213.

Ludeman, K. (1981). The sexuality of the older person: Review of the literature. *The Gerontologist, 21,* 203–208.

Maccoby, E. E. (1991). Different reproductive strategies in males and females. *Child Development, 62,* 676–681.

MacKinnon, C. A. (1987). A feminist/political approach: "Pleasure under patriarchy." In J. H. Geer & W. T. O'Donohue (Eds.), *Theories of human sexuality.* New York: Plenum.

Maddock, J. (1989). Healthy family sexuality: Positive principles for educators and clinicians. *Family Relations, 38,* 130–136.

Marshall, W. (1978). Puberty. In F. Falkner & J. Tanner (Eds.), *Human growth: Vol. 2* (pp. 212–244). New York: Plenum.

Masters, W., & Johnson, V. (1966). *Human sexual response.* Boston: Little, Brown.

Masters, W., Johnson, V., & Kolodny, R. C. (1988). *Human sexuality* (3rd ed.). Boston: Little, Brown.

McKinney, K., & Sprecher, S. (Eds.). (1991). *Sexuality in close relationships.* Hillsdale, NJ: Erlbaum.

Miller, B. C. (1993). Families, science, and values: Alternative views of parenting effects and adolescent pregnancy. *Journal of Marriage and the Family, 55,* 7–21.

Miller, B. C., McCoy, J. K., Olson, T. D., & Wallace, C. M. (1986). Parental discipline and control attempts in relation to adolescent sexual attitudes and behavior. *Journal of Marriage and the Family, 48,* 503–512.

Miller, B. C., & Moore, K. A. (1990). Adolescent sexual behavior, pregnancy, and parenting: Research through the 1980s. *Journal of Marriage and the Family, 52,* 1025–1044.

Minuchin, S. (1974). *Families and family therapy.* Cambridge, MA: Harvard University Press.

Moffit, T., Caspi, A., & Belsky, J. (1990, March). *Family context, girls' behavior, and the onset of puberty: A test of a sociobiological model.* Paper presented at the biennial meeting of the Society for Research in Adolescence, Atlanta.

Moir, A., & Jessel, D. (1991). *Brain sex.* New York: Carol Publishing Group.

Money, J. (1988). *Gay, straight, and in-between: The sexology of erotic orientation.* New York: Oxford University Press.

Moore, K. A., Simms, M. C., & Betsey, C. L. (1986). *Choice and circumstance.* New Brunswick, NJ: Transaction Books.

Mosher, D. (1970). Psychological reactions to pornographic films. In *Technical Reports of the Commission on Obscenity and Pornography: Vol. 8* (pp. 286–312). Washington, DC: U. S. Government Printing Office.

Newcomer, S. F., & Udry, J. R. (1985). Parent-child communication and adolescent sexual behavior. *Family Planning Perspectives, 17,* 169–174.

Nielsen, J. M. (1990). Introduction. In J. M. Nielsen (Ed.), *Feminist research methods: Exemplar readings in the social sciences* (pp. 1–37). Boulder, CO: Westview.

Nye, F. I. (Ed.). (1976). *Role structure and analysis of the family.* Newbury Park, CA: Sage.

Nye, F. I. (1979). Choice, exchange, and the family. In W. R. Burr, R. Hill, F. I. Nye, & Reiss, I. L. (Eds.) *Contemporary theories about the family: Vol. 2.* New York: Free Press.

O'Brien, C. P. (1981). Commentary. *Medical Aspects of Human Sexuality, 15,* 117.

Olson, D. H. (1977). Insiders' and outsiders' views of relationships. In G. Levinger & H. L. Raush (Eds.), *Close relationships* (pp. 112–135). Amherst: University of Massachusetts Press.

Orbuch, T. L., & Harvey, J. H. (1991). Methodological and conceptual issues in the study of sexuality in close relationships. In K. McKinney & S. Sprecher (Eds.) *Sexuality in close relationships.* Hillsdale, NJ: Erlbaum.

Papini, D. F., Farmer, F. L., Clark, S. M., & Snell, W. E. (1988). An evaluation of adolescent patterns of sexual self-disclosure by adolescent pubertal status, gender, and family member. *Journal of Adolescent Research, 3,* 387–401.

Patterson. G. (1982). *Coercive family process.* Eugene, OR: Castalia.

Peplau, L. A., Rubin, Z., & Hill, C. T. (1977). Sexual intimacy in dating relationships. *Journal of Social Issues, 33,* 86–109.

Plomin, R., & Fulker, D. (1987). Behavioral genetics and development in early adolescence. In R. Lerner & T. Foch (Eds.), *Biosocial-psychosocial interactions in early adolescence* (pp. 63–94). Hillsdale, NJ: Erlbaum.

Reiss, I. L. (1989). Society and sexuality: A sociological theory. In K. McKinney & S. Sprecher (Eds.) *Human sexuality: The societal and interpersonal context.* Norwood, NJ: Ablex.

Reiss, I. L. (1990). *An end to shame: Shaping our next sexual revolution.* Buffalo, NY: Prometheus Books.

Reiss, I. L. (1991). Sexual pluralism: Ending America's sexual crisis. *SIECUS Report, 19*(3), 5–9.

Riportella-Muller, R. (1989). Sexuality in the elderly: A review. In K. McKinney & S. Sprecher (Eds.), *Human sexuality: The societal and interpersonal context.* Norwood, NJ: Ablex.

Roffman, D. M. (1991). The power of language: Baseball as a sexual metaphor in American culture. *SIECUS Report, 19,* 1–6.

Sapolsky, R. (1992). Growing up in a hurry. *Discover: The world of science, 13*(6), 40–45.

Sarrel, L. J., & Sarrel, P. M. (1979). *Sexual unfolding: Sexual development and sex therapies in late adolescence.* Boston: Little, Brown.

Savin-Williams, R. (1990). Gay and lesbian adolescents. In F. W. Bozett & M. B. Sussman (Eds.), *Homosexuality and family relations.* New York: Harrington Park Press.

Scanzoni, J. (1979). Social exchange and behavioral independence. In R. Burgess & T. Huston (Eds.), *Social exchange in developing relationships.* New York: Academic Press.

Schmidt, G. (1975). Male-female differences in sexual arousal and behavior during and after exposure to sexually explicit stimuli. *Archives of Sexual Behavior, 4,* 353–365.

Scoresby, A. L. (1977). *The marriage dialogue.* Reading, MA: Addison-Wesley.

Simon, W., & Gagnon, J. H. (1987). A sexual scripts approach. In J. H. Geer & W. T. O'Donohue (Eds.), *Theories of human sexuality.* New York: Plenum.

Snitow, A., Stansell, C., & Thompson, S. (1983). *Powers of desire: The politics of sexuality.* New York: Monthly Review Press.

Spanier, G. B., & Margols, R. L. (1983). Marital separation and extramarital sexual behavior. *Journal of Sex Research, 19,* 23–48.

Spiro, R. (1956). *Children of the kibbutz.* New York: Shocken.

Stacey, J., & Thorne, B. (1985). The missing feminist revolution in sociology. *Social Problems, 32,* 301–316.

Starr, B. D., & Weiner, M. B., (1981). *The Starr-Weiner report on sex and sexuality in the mature years.* Briarcliff Manor, NY: Stein & Day.

Steinberg, L. (1981). Transformations in family relations at puberty. *Developmental Psychology, 17,* 833–840.

Steinberg, L. (1987). The impact of puberty on family relations: Effects of pubertal status and pubertal timing. *Developmental Psychology, 23,* 451–460.

Stewart, M. W. (1981). Adolescent pregnancy: Status convergence for the well-socialized adolescent female. *Youth and Society, 12,* 443–464.

Stinnett, N., Chesser, B., & DeFrain, J. (Eds.). (1979). *Building family strengths.* Lincoln: University of Nebraska Press.

Stinnett, N., & DeFrain, J. (1985). *Secrets of strong families.* Boston: Little, Brown.

Sussman, M. B., & Steinmetz, S. K. (Eds.). (1987). *Handbook of marriage and the family.* New York: Plenum.

Teevan, J. J. (1972). Reference groups and premarital sexual behavior. *Journal of Marriage and the Family, 34,* 283–291.

Thornburg, H. D. (1982). *Development in adolescence* (2nd ed). Pacific Grove, CA: Brooks/Cole.

Thorne, B. (Ed.). (1982). *Rethinking the family: Some feminist questions.* New York: Longman.

Tolman, D. (1991). Adolescent girls, women and sexuality: Discerning dilemmas of desire. In C. Gilligan, A. G. Rogers, & D. L. Tolman (Eds.), *Women, girls and psychotherapy: Reframing resistance* (pp. 55–69). New York: Harrington Park Press.

Turkelson, K. G. (1980). Toward a theory of the family life cycle. In E. A. Carter & M. McGoldrick (Eds.), *The family life cycle: A framework for family therapy.* New York: Gardner Press.

Voydanoff, P., & Donnelly, B. W. (1990). *Adolescent sexuality and pregnancy.* Newbury Park, CA: Sage.

Weeks, J. (1986). *Sexuality.* Chichester, England: Ellis Horwood.

Weinstein, M., & Thornton, A. L. (1989). Mother-child relations and adolescent sexual attitudes and behavior. *Demography, 26,* 563–577.

Parenting Processes

Denise Ann Bodman / Gary W. Peterson
Arizona State University

Parents and their children, whether young, old, or middle-aged, are compelling subjects of inquiry for family scientists. Historically, concern about the parent/ child relationship goes back about as far as written records exist. One of the earliest inscriptions unearthed from ancient Mesopotamia, the cradle of civilization, deplores the fact that "children no longer obey their parents. . . . The end of the world is evidently approaching" (Sommerville, 1982).

It was not until the beginning of the 20th century, however, that social scientists began to systematically study the child (and often, by default, the parents). Because of our current "child-oriented" models of parenting, however, even some of the early 20th-century scientific writings may seem disconcerting to contemporary observers. For example, the behavioral psychologist James B. Watson, in his popular book *Psychological Care of Infant and Child* (1928), advised:

> There is a sensible way of treating children. Treat them as though they were young adults. Dress them, bathe them with care and circumspection. Let your behavior always be objective and kindly firm. Never hug or kiss them, never let them sit on your lap. If you must, kiss them on the forehead when they say good-night. Shake hands with them in the morning. Give them a pat on the head if they make an extraordinary good job of a difficult task. (pp. 81–82)

Such recommendations for emotional distance raise concerns today about the quality of parent/child relationships that would result. Nonetheless, remnants of

Watson's "hands-off" policies toward children continue to the present through some experts' advice to parents to ignore infants when they cry, thus avoiding reinforcing the need for excessive parental attention (Bigner, 1989).

Despite these residues of a more distant or firmer parenting in the past, experts on parent/child socialization have described how the typical child-rearing practices of 20th-century North America have moved toward more democratic strategies characterized by a combination of rational control, mutual communication, and high levels of affection (Baumrind, 1978, 1991; Bronfenbrenner, 1958; Peterson & Rollins, 1987). Furthermore, some of the frequently used disciplinary practices of the past, involving severe punitiveness, have been redefined in recent times as child abuse (Gelles, 1990).

With these changing views of child rearing as a backdrop, the purpose of this chapter is to examine several key ideas from the scholarship on parent/child relationships in terms of systems concepts that are frequently used by family scientists. Although focusing on the special qualities of the parent/child relationship within the context of families, we also look at other social contexts that impinge on these systems or subsystems. We focus special attention on reinterpreting traditional parent/child research (for example, parental styles and power), utilizing such systems constructs as the family paradigm, the executive subsystem, boundaries, and communication processes. Central aspects of well-functioning parent/child relationships, consisting of parental love, parental guidance, parental authority, and communication are reexamined in terms of systems concepts from a family-science perspective. We also give consideration to the role of children as providers of love and as socializers of parents.

A Systems View of Parent/Child Relations

The scientific study of parent/child relationships has undergone a gradual but quite extensive transition. Today's family scientists have increasingly shifted from examining this relationship only in terms of how parents "shape" their children to a more complex representation of what transpires between parents and children (Peterson & Rollins, 1987). Of special importance for family scientists is the relatively recent recognition that the parent/child relationship is not an island unto itself. Instead, what initially appears simply to be a dyadic relationship between parents and children is in reality at least a three-person relationship among mother, father, and child(ren). Furthermore, although families have unique qualities that provide each parent/child relationship with its own texture and substance, the processes occurring among mothers, fathers, and children are impinged upon and constrained by a great variety of social relationships beyond family boundaries.

A Systems View of the Larger Social Context

Such a conception implies that a "systemic perspective" should be used to understand how social phenomena beyond the dyad redefine both the processes and outcomes that emerge within the parent/child relationship. Stripped of much of its complexities, a systems perspective provides the view that all aspects of families are interrelated through dynamic, mutual, and circular mechanisms. Furthermore, the family system and its subcomponents have substantial interconnections with other social environments such as the workplace, neighborhood, community, school, socioeconomic milieu, and ethnic subculture (Bateson, 1979; Bertalanffy, 1969; Broderick, 1990; Bronfenbrenner, 1979; Buckley, 1967; Skynner, 1976, 1981; Steinglass, 1987).

Suppose, for example, that a single parent, Alice, lives in an area of a community characterized by pov-

erty, crime, extensive drug traffic, and gang activities. Compared to Barbara, who lives in a "safer," more affluent, middle-class neighborhood, Alice may place greater value on obedience and use more direct forms of discipline (strict rules, physical punishment) to "protect" her children from the wide variety of threats (as she perceives them) in the immediate social environment. Barbara, on the other hand, may be more inclined to allow autonomy and practice democratic (indirect) forms of control (reasoning or persuasion) that have the long-term aim of teaching her children to become responsible in managing their own behavior.

Likewise, parent/child relationships in a Chinese-American family may be quite different from those that exist in the dominant middle-class culture. A Chinese family that recently immigrated from Hong Kong, for example, may face many new expectations for changes in the parent/child relationship as the pressures for acculturation (learning and adjusting to the dominant culture) increase (Harrison, 1990). Specifically, generational conflict may be fostered as children assimilate the new (or dominant) culture, whereas adults may relinquish their traditional culture more reluctantly. Compared to "mainstream" American parents who emphasize individualism, autonomy, and democratic controls, Chinese parents may be more inclined to foster collectivism, cooperation, and firmer rules in their child rearing.

Corresponding with such examples, therefore, social scientists have presented evidence indicating that the values and behavior of parents are influenced by their membership in work, socioeconomic, ethnic, or neighborhood environments (Gecas, 1979; Harrison, 1990; Kohn, 1977; Peterson & Rollins, 1987). A comprehensive view of the parent/child relationship, therefore, must consider social phenomena far beyond the face-to-face exchanges among mothers, fathers, and children.

An example of such complex systemic relationships is provided in the model of "dynamic person/context interactions" by Richard Lerner (1984). Specifically, this model considers the characteristics of children along with the characteristics of parents and then examines how the individuals in such relationships interact with and affect each other. In other words, family scientists who assume this perspective view the parent/child relationship as a dynamic bidirectional process (from parent to child as well as from child to parent). However, instead of stopping at the face-to-face level of parent/child relations, a systemic perspective gives ample recognition to the likelihood that they may be directly and indirectly influenced by a multitude of sources. Consequently, such a model makes it apparent that the parent/child relationship is further influenced by the parent's or child's work, marriage relationship, social network, and the larger social environment. Consider the following examples:

Work network. Father is a police officer who deals daily with situations where criminal acts have been committed against children. How might this influence the way that he interacts with his child? How might the child respond to the father if he is authoritarian and/or treats the child as he treats the people he sees at work? How might having a child and being a father influence his work?

Marital network. Mother has a stormy relationship with her teenage daughter. How might this relationship affect her relationship with the father? How might the mother/father relationship affect the father's relationship with the daughter?

Social network. A young father has many single male friends who enjoy spending a lot of time together doing "things with the guys." How might this affect his relationship with his son or daughter? How might having a child affect his relationship with his friends?

A systemic perspective also recognizes that reciprocal influences occur among the various subsystems. For example, the workplace interrelates with the parents' marriage, and both of these social contexts, in turn, may have mutual connections with the parent/child subsystem. Furthermore, each level of the social system such as the parent/child relationship, entire family, neighborhood, and community are mutually influential in reference to one another (Brofenbrenner, 1979).

Finally, as the model by Lerner recognizes, all of these interrelationships take place within the context of time. Family scientists must take special note that the development of individuals, dyadic relationships, entire family systems, and social contexts beyond family boundaries occurs longitudinally. Consistent with this idea, Lerner's systemic model is just as relevant to adult children and their parents as it is to earlier periods of development. Although children's relationships with their parents change with aging, each of the listed subsystems continues to exert influence in different ways across time. It is certainly the case, for example, that children will be influenced as parents experience divorce, remarriage, promotions at work, unemployment, religious conversions, or moves to new neighborhoods. Besides the influence of changing contexts themselves, we must also consider how the developmental status of children will interact with the alterations in contexts outside the parent/child subsystem. For example, research indicates that adolescents may be affected differently than younger children by marital transitions (such as divorce and remarriage (Hetherington, Hagan, & Anderson, 1989) and parents' employment status (Elder, 1978; Hoffman, 1989). In short, we are only beginning to understand how the parent/child subsystem is interconnected with social environments beyond its boundaries.

The Family as a System Encompassing Parent/Child Relations

The family is a distinctive social environment that encompasses the parent/child relationship and is organized hierarchically in successively decreasing levels of generality (Brofenbrenner, 1979; Cromwell & Peterson, 1983; Kantor & Lehr, 1975; Skynner, 1976, 1981; Steinglass, 1987). According to this viewpoint, each system is composed of smaller component subsystems. Although all subsystems of families are complex and different from other components, each level maintains boundaries that are variably permeable to input from other subsystems and the surrounding social environment. Consequently, the individual, dyadic, and systemic levels of families occur in a hierarchical arrangement and are simultaneously interdependent and distinct.

The *individual,* from this perspective, is a biological and psychological system conceptualized as the basic component, or level, of the larger family system. Although partially explainable with biological and psychological models, individuals cannot be adequately understood without reference to their social context (for example, the family) or without examining how their behavior has consequences for their interpersonal environment (part of which is the family). Next, the more encompassing *dyadic* level consists of the parent/child relationship, marital, and sibling subsystems, in which mutual social processes are of primary concern among family members. Finally, the *family unit level* is the more general social context that circumscribes the marital, parent/child, and sibling subsystems (Cromwell & Peterson, 1983; Peterson & Cromwell, 1983).

Each of these levels of the family system has some elements that are unique and some that are held in common with other levels of the system. The family unit, which immediately encompasses the parent/child relationship, must be conceived of in terms of multiple levels of analysis. Specifically, the larger family system consists of several subsystems, which are reciprocally interrelated so that a larger entity is produced that is not reducible to the sum of its parts. Thus, the family system is best understood by attending to relationships as the core subsystems created by interacting individuals. More specifically, such a perspective demands that attention be paid to parents as well as children, to marital as well as parent/child relationships, and to triadic relationships as well as parent/infant and spousal dyads (Broderick, 1990; Minuchin, 1985; Steinglass, 1987). As a result, families are both holistic entities having common themes throughout the system and a collection of components having differences that define the constituent subsystems.

Family Paradigms and Parent/Child Relations

Because family systems are holistic entities, family members are thought to develop shared views, or paradigms, of the social world that have important implications for parent/child relations. Specifically, the concept of family paradigm refers to a jointly held perspective by family members composed of basic assumptions about (1) how the world within and outside family boundaries is viewed, (2) how members are expected to relate to one another, and (3) how the surrounding environment is to be dealt with (Constantine, 1986; Reiss, 1981). That is, family paradigms offer a sense of meaning and order, which in turn provide a rationale for selecting goals, making decisions, governing behavior, and managing resources (Reiss, 1981).

Although family paradigms may have some things in common with other families' perspectives, it is important to recognize that each family constructs its own view of "reality" that is partially unique.

The important advantages of such paradigms include the tendency to define family roles, organize the environment, and clarify family goals, while disadvantages are illustrated by their inclination to foster resistance to change and new ideas. Part of the reason for such rigidity in the face of change is that family paradigms are automatic components of everyday thinking that are largely unconscious. In fact, such conceptions are so much a part of routine assumptions that particular families may incorrectly believe that all other families view the world and function in the same way. Although families vary greatly in their extent of agreement about paradigms, a reasonable speculation would be that family paradigms follow a five-stage pattern similar to those of scientific paradigms conceptualized by Thomas Kuhn (1970).

Pre-paradigm stage. The first stage corresponds to the formative period of paradigm development described by Burr, Day, and Bahr (1993). This phase would occur when a man and woman begin thinking about marriage and family. Specifically, all people enter such a relationship with their own ideas about marriage and family life based on their personal experiences as well as their observations of others' experiences, media portrayals, and a diverse array of other information sources. Lacking actual experience, their ideas are often diffuse, and some ideas may even be competing (for example, the complexities of being the perfect wife/mother/career woman). A tremendous amount of sharing occurs during the early stages of the relationship, with these ideas being formulated and integrated, leading to the next stage:

She: I believe that men and women should be equal shareholders in relationships. They should participate equally in rearing children. My mother did most of the parenting, and I always believed that having all that responsibility was unfair.

He: I believe that men should work outside and women inside the home. Fathers should have the final say on all decisions about children and be the ultimate disciplinarians. That's how it worked in my home when I was growing up.

Paradigm emergence.   At the second stage, husbands and wives are beginning to establish an accepted view of the family. Ideas that disagree with the emerging paradigm begin to be ignored and dropped.

She: If the woman doesn't work outside the home, she should be in charge of parenting to a large extent. If she does work outside the home, both partners should take equal responsibility for the care of the children.

He: I think I might come to accept that with time.

Friend: Men work so hard they shouldn't have to "baby-sit" too.

He and She: We disagree with our friend.

Paradigm established.   At the next stage, the family paradigm is strongly established and becomes an integral part of the family's unconscious way of thinking. The total family lifestyle reflects the paradigm. Other paradigms outside the family may be judged as inappropriate and incorrect. As long as the family runs smoothly, the paradigm remains intact.

She: I'll be late coming home from work this afternoon. Can you pick up Johnny at the day-care center?

He: Yes, I'll take care of it. Can you believe the Johnsons? He wouldn't pick up their daughter at the day care if she were on her death bed.

She: Yeah, she'll get tired of it eventually and probably leave the bum! He's such a chauvinist pig.

Paradigm shift.   A paradigm shift could occur for many reasons, including education, experience, or crisis. When a family's basic beliefs, values, and constructs do not adequately address a situation or when a severe crisis occurs, the family may be forced to reevaluate and reformulate its paradigm.

She: I'm glad I got promoted and got such a big raise. I'm sorry you got laid off, but I'm making as much as we used to earn together.

He: Yeah, maybe I should consider being a househusband and stay home to take care of Johnny.

She: Maybe we could try it and see how it works.

Paradigm dissolves.   Finally, the old family paradigm dissolves and is replaced by a modified or completely different one. There may be a tremendous reaction against the former paradigm. Sometimes, dissolution of the family paradigm can also result in dissolution of the family, especially if one family member is unable to embrace and share a new paradigm.

She: I'll be home at five.

He: I just love staying home and rearing Johnny.

She: I can't understand how two people can work when they have children.

He: You can sure say that again!

Although family paradigms are often much more complex and deal with many more issues than these illustrations, it should now be evident that these frameworks influence the relationship between parents and children in a variety of important ways. Suppose, for example, that a family paradigm has a component emphasizing that family members should focus on individual goals and be self-oriented. Such an egocentric paradigm implies that parents will give greater priority to their own desires, needs, and schedules than to other family interests. Parents who accept such a paradigm are more likely to choose child-rearing strategies that are insensitive to the needs of the children (Dix, in press). Consequently, parents who view the social world through this perspective would be more likely to devote less time to lengthy processes of reasoning with and providing nurturance to children. Instead, they are more likely to deal with problems quickly through such convenient strategies as coercion or punishment that serve their own interests and are less sensitive to children's needs.

In contrast, other family paradigms tend to emphasize being more group- or child-oriented and encourage parents to organize their daily behavior around the needs and wants of children. This group-focused, or other-oriented, paradigm may encourage parents to spend more time with children and engage in more playful interactions with them (Dix, in press). The experience gained in interaction with children, in turn, may foster increased sensitivity to their needs, feelings, and viewpoints, and children may become reciprocally aware of the parents' needs and feelings.

Finally, it is important to recognize that the relationships between parents and children can influence family paradigms. If a self-oriented family paradigm leads parents to be neglectful or punitive, for example, the young may eventually rebel, become delinquent, and reject parental values (Barber, 1992; Rollins & Thomas, 1979). As a result, a paradigm shift may occur, and efforts may be made in the future to more effectively balance a self-orientation with a child orientation. As children grow and develop, in fact, such paradigm shifts may be necessary within parent/child relationships for adaptive development to occur. For example, a family paradigm that emphasizes control and conformity during the early years of childhood must undergo substantial changes over time so that adolescents can achieve greater autonomy and make more of their own decisions as they approach the transition to adulthood.

Love in the Parent/Child Relationship

One of the essential ingredients of a competent parent/child relationship is love, a complex emotion with perhaps endless subtleties and forms of expression. Different definitions of love were reflected in a question by the 7-year-old daughter of one of the authors, who asked, "Do you love ice cream?" "Yes," the author replied innocently, unaware of the trap that had been set. "Then why don't you marry it!" her daughter exclaimed, bursting into laughter.

Because of such difficulties in clearly defining love, many scientists have avoided studying it; although its fundamental importance is unmistakable, as evidenced by the numerous love songs, poems, and stories written today and throughout the ages. Despite such reluctance, the scientific arena has not ignored the concept of love completely. For example, in his book *Learning to Love*, Harry Harlow (1974) notes that little has been written on the theory and facts of love, "though love is at least as concrete as it is abstract." Based on his work with monkeys, Harlow conceived of love as "a process, and a developmental process, of enormous importance in both the creation and causation of human social behavior. It is often said that love makes the world go round, and even if the world is not perfectly round, love is all round" (p.vii).

Work such as Harlow's is scarce, and in the social science literature, love is often transformed into concepts such as attachment, acceptance, warmth, support, nurturance, or bonding (Barber & Thomas, 1986; Bowlby, 1988). It is probably true that social scientists feel more comfortable using terms that are less emotionally laden and somewhat sterile. In reality, love may encompass these concepts, but they certainly do not encompass love in its entirety. They are only small portions of the whole.

Because love is viewed as such a "basic, enabling family process, a core dimension of healthy families," family scientists focus on this process more than do other disciplines (Burr et al., 1993, p. 97). And why not? Ask most parents what they feel for their children, and they will say "love." Ask children what they feel for their parents, and they will say "love." Many family members have frequent dialogues that express their love for one another. Although some families are less verbal about their affections, the love they feel is expressed through their caring, protective behaviors and their attitudes. We suspect, for example, that many so-called distant or inexpressive fathers convey their love in countless ways, such as by keeping things repaired, making a good living, and being someone whom one can count on during times of adversity. Love is an undeniable and multifaceted part of well-functioning family systems.

Burr et al. (1993) present a model of family love based on other conceptions of affect in families (reciprocal altruism and the rule of amity, grants and exchanges, altruistic commitment and individualism, and maternal love). According to their conception, the kind of family love necessary for healthy individual and family life is other-oriented, action-oriented, unconditional, and enduring. It is probably true, in turn, that family or parental love of such complexity has no equal as a basis for the healthy development of children and the larger family system.

Despite the crucial role that love plays in healthy parent/child relationships, a balanced view that accounts for a somewhat "darker side" must also be acknowledged. Even the best aspects of the human condition can take strange twists or develop problematic qualities when prevalent in extremely high levels. Some authorities, for example, have argued forcefully that irrational or intrusive forms of emotional closeness may be harmful to the developmental progress of both adolescents and young adults toward autonomy and individuality (Bowen, 1978). Others have identified intrusive or suffocating forms of love as part of overprotective parenting that leads to excessive dependency and diminished maturity in children (Becker, 1964). Some observers also worry that high levels of parental affection may encourage too much conformity and dependency in girls (Baumrind, 1980; Bronfenbrenner, 1958).

Problematic forms of love also appear within families as actions "done for your own good, because I love you," even though such actions may be potentially harmful. For example, parents who severely spank their children may justify this action by saying that "I discipline my son because I *love* him and want him to turn out right." Recently, we read detailed accounts of a mother who committed suicide but first shot her 5-year-old daughter in the head "out of love." Such an incident illustrates one of the greatest ironies of the human experience: that the one who provides children with love, the greatest gift of all, can also render some of the most destructive behaviors in its name. Unquestionably, love is the most splendid, complicated, and even contradictory phenomenon within both family systems and parent/child subsystems.

The Development of Love between Parents and Children

Although no other factor may be as important for the healthy development of children and the larger family, the love between parents and their young is not an automatic consequence of a child being born and the transition into parenthood. In a study by MacFarlane, Smith, and Garrow (1978), for example, 97 new mothers were asked, "When did you first feel love for your baby?" About two-thirds felt love during pregnancy or at birth, but the remaining one-third indicated that they did not feel love until the first week or thereafter. Consequently, even maternal love for an infant cannot be taken for granted.

Instead, in its most basic form, parental love may result from a combination of biological and experiential factors that emerge initially through interaction with the child. One way that love manifests itself is in the "synchrony" that occurs between parents and children (Beebe, Jaffe, Feldstein, Mays, & Olson, 1985; Brazelton, Koslowski, & Main, 1974; Field, 1985; Field, Healy, Goldstein, & Guthertz, 1990; Peterson & Rollins, 1987; Schaffer, 1977). Similar to partners in a dance, parents and children touch, vocalize, gaze, and interact in a way that is complementary and mutually responsive. Baby coos, mother smiles, baby reaches toward mother, mother kisses baby's fingers. Such early interactions, characterized by high levels of maternal sensitivity, responsiveness, and warmth, are also associated with infants who display a secure form of attachment (Ainsworth, Blehar, Waters, & Wall, 1978; Bretherton, Biringen, & Ridgeway, 1991; Grossman & Grossman, 1984). Perhaps this synchrony and the emerging bond extend beyond the parent/infant relationship into childhood, adolescence, and adulthood, becoming a finely tuned but increasingly complex system of interactions that compose the "waltz" of interpersonal relationships (Bowlby, 1988).

As children grow, the love that their parents communicate to them through warmth and trust fosters the development of self-esteem (Bachman, O'Malley, & Johnson, 1978; Barber & Thomas, 1986; Becker, 1964; Openshaw, Thomas & Rollins, 1981, 1983; Peterson & Rollins, 1987; Rohner, 1986; Rollins & Thomas, 1979). Love, which is often referred to as parental support, warmth, nurturance, or acceptance, with its attendant hugging, encouragement, kissing, praising, and so forth, tells the child that he or she is a person of worth. In response, the child may be more likely to identify with the parents, conform to their expectations, incorporate their attitudes and values, and accept their guidance and authority (Coopersmith, 1967; Peterson & Rollins, 1987; Rohner, 1986).

Besides being the primary source of togetherness, the expression of parental love also provides the paradoxical function of fostering the opposite development: the progress of children toward autonomy. Parent/child relationships characterized by considerable love provide a secure base from which children can explore and meet challenges that exist beyond family boundaries (Bowlby, 1988; Peterson & Leigh, 1990; Peterson & Stivers, 1986). From the solid basis of loving family relationships, children acquire the confidence to tackle the world outside the family and face both the risks and benefits of independent activity. Children who receive sufficient parental love are more likely to be socially competent through the careful balancing of continued ties with parents and gradual progress toward autonomy (Peterson & Leigh, 1990). Failure to have such a secure base of love, on the other hand, may mean that children are more likely to suffer from feelings of separation, hostility, aggression, diminished self-confidence, emotional unresponsiveness, and disturbed peer relationships (Becker, 1964; Rohner, 1986; Rollins & Thomas, 1979).

Parental love remains a powerful force even when adolescents mature and young adults leave home. Phone calls, mutual assistance, visits, and sharing continue across both short and long distances. Some observers have also indicated that the quality of parent/child relationships improves as children make the transition from adolescence to adulthood. Across time, for example, middle-aged parents report that relationships both with their younger adult children and their own elderly parents either remain stable or continue to improve (Richards, Bengtson, & Miller, 1989).

Contrary to a systems perspective, however, much of the work on love among mothers, fathers, and children is limited to the perspective that parents provide affection to the young. A systemic orientation, on the other hand, is equally interested in other relationship directions of socialization, such as the love expressed from child to parent, to provide a more comprehensive picture. We know, for example, that love expressed by children plays a key role in why parents value and are satisfied with child rearing (Chilman, 1980; Goetting, 1986; Umberson, 1989). Even at a very young age, children reciprocate parental expressions of affection with their own forms of loving, dependent, and proximity-seeking behavior (Bowlby, 1988). It is likely, for example, that children's love may affect both the behavior and responses of parents, including the degree that parental love is expressed and the child-rearing strategies that are used (Ambert, 1992).

Unfortunately, our understanding of the development and expression of children's love and what it means to parents remains quite limited. What are the ways in which children express love to parents? How does the love of children for mothers and fathers affect the parent/child relationship? How do children's ex-pressions of love for parents change over time? What do these changes mean to parents, and how does parental responsiveness change as these transitions take place? These are only some of the issues that remain for future investigators. Consequently, further examination of the child-to-parent love relationship would be a fruitful area of research and intervention for family scientists.

Parental Guidance and Authority

An effective parent/child relationship is also characterized by certain kinds of guidance and authority that parents provide to the young. Many of today's parents may recall, for example, their own father saying, "Do it or else . . ." If we dared ask why, the reply was a curt, "Because I told you so." It was understood that he was the boss and we were the children. His word was law. With time, however, such autocratic guidance has increasingly been replaced by the more democratic approaches recommended by contemporary parenting experts.

To understand the nature of parental "guidance," one needs to examine child-rearing styles as partial reflections of the family paradigm. It is also important to understand that competent parents are most capable of exercising influence when the young recognize and accept their authority. Consequently, the following sections focus on the parental executive subsystem and how parental guidance and authority contribute to the socialization of children. Consideration is also given to the authority of children and the extent to which parents are provided guidance by the young.

The Parental, or Executive, Subsystem

A common arrangement in the structure of families consists of an *executive subsystem* and a *child subsystem*. The executive subsystem, usually made up of parents (but sometimes including stepparents or parent substitutes), is responsible for much of the family decision-making and the approaches to child rearing. The executive subsystem determines the rules, limits, traditions, and disciplinary practices that are used in the family. These decisions and actions, of course, are strongly affected by the family paradigm, part of which exists before children are born.

When children enter the family system, a *boundary* is often established between the executive subsystem and the newly established child subsystem. This boundary consists of several components. First, the boundary assumes a concrete, or physical, manifestation through such actions as the preparation of a separate nursery or the initial "No" command given to a toddler who is approaching a hot stove. In a psychological sense, however, a boundary is established, in part, when parents come to think of themselves as "parents"—that is, as being responsible for making the rules and for taking care of and socializing children. Another component of the boundary is established through *guidance*, or the style of child rearing that parents use to influence the young. Finally, the boundary is reinforced when the children themselves recognize and accept the idea that parents have the *authority*, or competence, to exercise influence.

At the beginning of the parent/child relationship, these boundaries often become quite clearly defined, with parents making most of the decisions. As children develop, however, adjustments must be made in the permeability of the boundary that differentiates the executive responsibilities of parents from those of the young. The concept of permeability, in this case, refers to the extent to which the executive subsystem boundary becomes selectively open to information and influence from the child subsystem. If children are to progress developmentally, they must be increasingly allowed to participate in more of the decision-making, which earlier was a near monopoly of the parents.

Parental Guidance

The concept of degree of permeability in the executive subsystem can also be viewed in terms of an older research tradition on styles of child rearing, referred to here as parental guidance. The most prominent conceptions of child rearing are the authoritarian, authoritative, permissive, negligent, and overprotective parental styles, as developed by Diana Baumrind and other investigators who view parent/child relations in a similar manner (see Baumrind, 1978, 1991; Becker, 1964; Maccoby & Martin, 1983; Peterson & Rollins,

1987; Rollins & Thomas, 1979). From a family-science perspective, parental styles can be viewed as behavioral expressions of the degree to which permeability is prevalent in the executive subsystem. In addition, each child-rearing approach is a behavioral manifestation of those aspects of the family paradigm that are concerned with the guidance and socialization of children.

The *authoritarian* style, for example, which combines high (often punitive or arbitrary) control and low affection, is reflective of an executive-subsystem boundary that tolerates little permeability to information and influence from the child subsystem. The family paradigm that supports this approach often defines the role of parent as that of rule maker, disciplinarian, planner, and head of household. A fairly rigid system of values and uncompromising principles is an important aspect of the family paradigms of authoritarian parents. Children are expected to have very limited impact on family decisions, to keep in their place, and to be seen and not heard. Very little dialogue and negotiation occur within such relationships, while verbal and physical punitiveness are common techniques of control used by parents. Although these autocratic mothers and fathers may feel and profess love for their children, affectionate behavior is not a frequent expression. Some authoritarian parents, in fact, may view themselves as communicating a kind of love expressed as "interest in our child's welfare" through the use of strict discipline and punishment: "I'm doing this for your own good. It hurts me more than it hurts you." If these parents are fortunate, however, the most problematic outcomes of authoritarian child rearing can be lessened when children actually do come to perceive such "forceful interest" as expressions of concern by their elders.

Given some troubling features, therefore, the most common consequences of authoritarian parenting (Baumrind, 1978, 1991; Peterson & Leigh, 1990; Peterson & Rollins, 1987; Rollins & Thomas, 1979) are the growth of hostility and the hindrance of social competence in children and adolescents (Baumrind, 1978; Peterson & Leigh, 1990). Although the children of authoritarian parents may conform, they often comply in a manner that results from fear of retribution, not as a product of reasoned moral decisions. Furthermore, the self-esteem of children is inhibited by authoritarianism, probably because such strategies communicate that children are of little value to parents (Coopersmith, 1967).

Contrasting with authoritarian child rearing is *permissive* parenting, which combines low amounts of control with high amounts of support. From a systems perspective, a permissive style is characterized by very permeable boundaries between the executive and child subsystems. Parents use this approach to implement a family paradigm that defines their roles as that of a resource person and facilitator rather than as a source of control. Most goals in these families are quite idiosyncratic to each member, and minimal effort is devoted to reinforcing an agreed-upon system of family beliefs. Children are allowed (and possibly encouraged) prematurely to take over many responsibilities of the executive subsystem and to set their own goals and objectives. Although permissive child rearing provides high levels of love and encouragement, the lack of parental guidance (or control efforts) fosters diminished sensitivity to the cooperative abilities needed in group situations. Children who are exposed to an executive subsystem that is permissive often exhibit the socially competent attributes of high self-esteem, autonomy and creativity but lack the ability to easily subordinate their own interests when necessary to that of the group (Baumrind, 1978; Peterson & Leigh, 1990).

An even more problematic form of child rearing, referred to as *negligent* parenting, is characterized by diminished use of both control and love. If one can even refer to this as an intentional parenting approach, its best description would probably be an effort by adults to virtually resign from child-rearing responsibilities. Such a style also implies that parenting is not a very important aspect of the family paradigm and that the parental subsystem is virtually abolished, except perhaps to serve the parents' self-interest. Correspondingly, the boundary of the executive subsystem is quite permeable but does exist, primarily to protect the parents from much involvement with the children. Because the parental subsystem is weak in socialization goals, children are unclear about the expectations and rules of the family. They are left alone both psychologically and physically to flounder in a family world that appears to be uncaring. The common results of such parenting are children whose psychosocial attributes include lower self-esteem, low conformity, and substantial amounts of emotional distance from parents.

The most adaptive form of parenting, *authoritative* child rearing, combines both high levels of control and affection. Like authoritarian parenting, authoritative child rearing involves the use of control techniques to set rules, limits, traditions, and expectations. Instead of using arbitrary force, however, authoritative child rearing achieves control through rational justifications and efforts to seek voluntary compliance from children. The family paradigm that defines this style places parents in charge but encourages mothers and fathers to listen and negotiate with the young. The executive-subsystem boundary is semipermeable to allow for a balance between the need for parental influence and growing autonomy for the young.

Authoritative parenting involves discussing why rules and limits exist as well as opening the possibility that such parameters will be modified in the future. These parents also practice effective listening so that children can have growing input into the family decision-making process. Furthermore, love expressed as encouragement, praise, and companionship is an important component of authoritative parenting. The common psychosocial outcomes of this form of child rearing are children who are socially competent in the sense of having high self-esteem plus the ability to balance the requirements for interpersonal cooperation and for progress toward autonomy (Peterson & Leigh, 1990).

Finally, another form of child rearing, *overprotective* parenting, combines high levels of control and love in a different manner and with different outcomes than the authoritative style. Specifically, overprotective parents use both controlling and loving behaviors in psychologically intrusive ways to manipulate children's emotional experiences (Becker, 1964). From a systems perspective, although these parents structure a very influential executive subsystem, they also seek on many occasions to manipulate or obscure the boundary between themselves and children as a means of fostering dependency in their young. Consequently, the executive-subsystem boundary is variable and semipermeable so that parents can gain access to information from children that helps maintain their dependency. The subsystem boundary is closed, however, to any expectations from children for change or individuality. A primary objective of the family paradigm, therefore, is to foster intrusive control and emotional closeness between parents and children. In efforts to foster a pervasive sense of "we-ness" in the family system, parents often use high levels of anxious control and suffocating love to keep children responsive to parental perspectives, inhibit movements toward autonomy, and discourage individuality. The excessive use of overly protective behaviors often functions to foster the internalizing of problems, which manifest themselves in self-destructive patterns including depression, suicide, and eating disorders, and in failure to achieve autonomy in adulthood (Barber, 1992; Becker, 1964; Schaefer, 1959; Symonds, 1939). Probably the most frequent negative consequence of overprotective parenting is the persistence of excessive dependency in the young that prevents them from eventually assuming the responsibilities of a mature adult on schedule (Bowen, 1978).

Difference versus Similarity in Parental Guidance

Because child rearing can vary so widely across many styles, a frequent result is that the two parents differ over their choice of approaches (Deal, Halverson, & Wampler, 1989). For example, a father may be inclined to be authoritarian, whereas a mother may prefer a more permissive approach. Such a combination may mean that while he works to establish rules and set standards, she inadvertently undermines these standards by failing to enforce them. He may order a child to "Go to your room without dinner!" while she may secretly provide a tray of goodies delivered to the child's bedroom later that night. Likewise, he may say, "No TV before homework," but she may often allow "Mommy's boy" to watch his favorite show before all of his math homework is completed.

Some disagreement over parenting approaches is probably inevitable and, in moderate amounts, may contribute to healthy development in child-rearing styles as mothers and fathers respond to various situations, rethink their preferences, and renegotiate their strategies. Continuous and extensive differences in parental styles, however, can lead to serious violations of the necessary boundary between parents and the young so that effective guidance and socialization cannot re-

sult. Widely divergent child-rearing styles can be viewed as behavioral symptoms of the likelihood that each parent has established a very different kind of relationship with his or her children. What this implies is that a unified hierarchy is necessary that gives recognition to the idea that parents, not children, are the primary sources of socialization in the family. The work of Salvadore Minuchin and several others, for example, indicates that familial disturbances are likely to occur when the marital relationship is not the primary bond, loyalty, commitment, alliance, or source of common objectives within the family (Minuchin, 1974; Minuchin, Rossman, & Baker, 1978; Teyber, 1983a, 1983b). Instead of the marriage being the primary relationship, leading to a unified parental strategy, a possible development is the emergence of "cross-generational alliances" (for example, a coalition between mother and daughter) within these families. A troubling feature of such coalitions is that children and adolescents are believed to develop problematic symptoms as a result of one parent being cut off from the children, generational boundaries and role definitions being blurred, or children being triangulated into parental conflicts (Bowen, 1978; Hayley, 1976, 1980). Such cross-generational alliances may appear in unhappy marriages or divorce situations, with the children being treated as peers, confidants, or surrogate adults rather than as the youngsters they really are (Burr et al., 1993). The young who are exposed to such family circumstances may be difficult to discipline and may have problems disengaging from parents as adolescence proceeds.

Contrasting with such incongruent parenting, however, is the increased recognition that parents need to establish a common front or "parental alliance" in reference to children. As Burr et al. (1993) say:

> In ideal situations the parents are a cohesive, integrated, and coordinated team. They are supportive of each other and unified in the way they relate to their children, and the boundaries between parents are few and permeable. At the same time, there are a number of more rigid or impermeable boundaries between the parental alliance and the children. (p. 67)

When parental alliances do not exist, children are quick to play one parent against the other for their own benefit. Even when a parental alliance is established, children may test its strength. Younger children's attempts are sometimes transparent and humorous.

Child: Mom, can I go over to Johnny's house to play?
Mother: No, it's almost time for dinner.

The child then finds his father in another room.

Child: Dad, can I go over to Johnny's house to play?
Father: Go ask your mother.

As the child gets older, of course, his attempts are more subtle and persuasive:

Teenager: Mom, can my curfew be moved to 1:30 A.M.? All my friends have a late curfew.
Mother: No, your curfew is midnight. Not one minute later.

The teenager then goes to his father.

Teenager: Dad, I've always admired how you've trusted me in the past and could see when I was ready to do new things. Your wisdom, sensitivity, awareness of my growing needs, and trust have made me who I am. Do you think we could move back my curfew to, say, 1:30?
Dad: Yeah, I suppose so.

Parental Authority as Perceived Competence

Besides guidance, or the behavioral aspect of parental influence, maintenance of the executive subsystem boundary is also based on *perceptions* by the young that their elders have authority, or *competence*. Although previous family scholars have often used the word *power* to represent this idea (McDonald, 1980; Rollins & Thomas, 1979; Smith, 1986), we prefer the terms *perceived authority* or *competence* because power has been used in so many different and confusing ways in the family literature (Szinovacz, 1987).

The authority of parents in relation to a child is a product of the young person's perception of their interpersonal resources, or competence. That is, the authority resides in the eyes of the beholder, or the child's subjective assessment of the parents' abilities to exercise influence within their relationship. Because authority is based on subjective interpretations of the parents' competence, a very different assessment may be made by a third party (for example, another child or sibling) outside a specific parent/child relationship. Consequently, the perceived authority of parents may differ from one relationship to another.

Parental authority differs from guidance by referring to the perceived *potential* ability of parents to influence the young or establish a subsystem boundary, rather than the *actual use* of overt behavior (child-rearing styles) to establish and maintain a parental subsystem. Thus, parental authority consists of subjective assessments by children and adolescents that parents have the ability to exercise influence, but it may not actually translate into action (or behavior). The important difference between authority as potential influence, and guidance as actual (or behavioral) influence is that parental authority does not have to be used for the executive-subsystem boundary to be reinforced. Instead, the boundary is maintained, in part, because the young acknowledge and accept their parents' authority.

Beyond its subjective nature, authority also takes several different forms, as follows (Cromwell & Olson, 1975; French & Raven, 1959; McDonald, 1980; Peterson, Rollins, & Thomas, 1985; Smith, 1986): (1) *reward authority*, or the perceived ability to supply gratifications; (2) *coercive authority*, or the perceived ability to administer punishments or adverse consequences; (3) *legitimate authority*, or the perceived right to exercise influence based on social norms; (4) *expert authority*, or the perceived potential to provide useful information; and (5) *referent authority*, or the potential to function as an identification object or significant other. These dimensions of parental authority, in turn, have been reported to predict such dimensions of social competence as conformity to parents, identification with parents and autonomy in reference to parents (Henry, Wilson, & Peterson, 1989; McDonald, 1980; Peterson et al., 1985; Smith, 1983, 1986).

Expert authority.   Children of any age may turn to a parent for help if they perceive a mother or father as having expertise that they value. Young children usually attribute great expertise to their parents and believe that they can turn to them at any time for information, advice, and assistance. They are often willing to ask parents questions about a variety of subjects from "Why is there rain?" to "Where did I come from?" As children grow and develop, they become increasingly attuned to the limits of their parents' knowledge and distinguish what mother knows from what father knows. A youngster may want her father to fix her bicycle but her mother to fix her breakfast. Although her father may be an accomplished chef, if the child continues to perceive her mother as the "expert," she will turn to her when needed. So the parent may sometimes have expertise in an area, but the child fails to recognize it. A parent may be well-versed in styles of dress, sexuality, or dating, but many teenagers would rather die than listen to Mom and Dad about such things or acknowledge their expertise.

Legitimate authority.   Family scientists have become increasingly aware of the influence that society and culture have on the parent/child relationship. By virtue of society and its "norms," parents are given certain authority, or social legitimacy, over their children (for example, "Honor thy father and mother"). Consequently, they have a "legitimate right" to control and influence the young. This perceived social legitimacy is instilled from birth in children as they are socialized and enculturated by parents and other social agents. Most youngsters will admit that it is the parents' "right" to do such things as setting curfew times, monitoring their comings and goings, and overseeing school activities.

Rewards and coercive authority.   The potential of parents to administer both rewards and punishments is also recognized as an aspect of parental authority. According to this conception, the child perceives that parents have certain abilities that they can use to make the youngster feel either better or worse. In fact, the perceived potential of parents to be either rewarding or punitive (rather than the actual use of rewards and punishments) may be all that is needed to influence the behavior of children. Consequently, it is probably wise for parents to retain the perception that they have some control over their youngster's access to such things as affection, money, or the car keys for a weekend date. The potential to provide or deny access to such valued aspects of their relationship gives parents the ability to control, in part, the positive or negative experiences of the young.

Referent authority.   Finally, potential as a "referent," or object of identification, is considered part of parental authority. When a parent has reference potential, the child knows that he or she can turn to that parent for guidance that is based on the perception of long-term security in their relationship. This potential has grown out of love and affection for the parent and is based on a history of trust and admiration of the parent' qualities. Referent authority often derives from the desire of the young to incorporate or identify with their parents' attributes.

Children's Guidance and Authority: The Other Side of the Coin

Another important idea is the awareness that children and adolescents play a substantial role in socializing (guiding) their parents and acquire increased authority as development proceeds (Ambert, 1992; Bell & Harper, 1977; Peterson & Rollins, 1987). Most boundaries between the parent subsystem and the child subsystem, therefore, must be semipermeable to some extent and must move toward greater permeability as development proceeds.

What this means in terms of guidance and authority is that relationships between parents and children are a two-sided coin, with influence flowing in both directions. The differential temperaments, states, and attributes of children, for example, all evoke varied child-rearing strategies from parents (Peterson & Rollins, 1987; Thomas, Chess, & Birch, 1968). Furthermore, children become increasingly adept at devising their own behaviors designed either to influence their parents or to counteract many of the parents' disciplinary behaviors. If serious obstacles to adaptive development are to be avoided, the changing competencies of children and adolescents require that parents become less authoritarian or overprotective as the young progress toward maturity (Peterson & Leigh, 1990). The best advice of child-rearing experts, in turn, is for parents increasingly to emphasize the democratic aspects of the authoritative style, which balances the need for continuing parental influence with the growing recognition that autonomy must be expanded (Baumrind, 1980; Peterson & Leigh, 1990).

Besides being aware of mutual socialization behavior, competent parents are capable of readjusting their perceptions of children's and adolescents' capabilities as development unfolds. Consequently, based on the changing attributes of the young, parents must recognize that children and adolescents will acquire greater authority in their relationship (Peterson, 1986; Peterson & Rollins, 1987; Smith, 1983, 1986). Specifically, a recent study has indicated that parents view their teenage sons and daughters as having reward, coercive, expert, legitimate, and referent authority. Such results support the idea that authority in the parent/child relationship is a two-way street, with both the young *and* their parents viewing each other as having interpersonal competencies (Peterson, 1986). Changing resources and competencies means that "authority" between parents and children is constantly renegotiated to allow for the eventual emergence of an egalitarian relationship between an "adult" parent and an "adult" child.

An overall view of influence in the parent/child relationship, therefore, is that *guidance* and *authority* play different but very important roles in defining the boundary between the parental executive and child subsystems. Furthermore, both of these mechanisms of influence are constantly being renegotiated and redistributed between parents and their children as part of a reciprocal relationship that changes. Finally, although we have dealt with guidance and authority as separate concepts, it is quite likely that one cannot be fully effective without the other (Peterson & Hann, in press). It is probably true that parents have to be viewed as "competent" in their children's eyes before their socialization behavior can have its maximum effect.

Communication

Communication is another facet of family life that is central to parent/child relationships and fosters effective development. The communication process may well be the keystone of family development, with the success or failure of the entire system being dependent on the adequacy of communication among family members. In reality, communication both includes and goes far beyond the behavioral expressions of love, guidance, and authority discussed in previous sections. At its most basic level, however, communication is an exchange of information between a sender and a receiver, with the message sent being either verbal or nonverbal. Verbal communication is primarily concerned with linguistic symbols that have cultural meaning and are referred to as language. Nonverbal communication includes gestures, facial expressions, body language, intonation, and other behavior that may define the nature of relationships between communicators (Galvin & Brommel, 1991; Watzlawick, Beavin, & Jackson, 1967).

Verbal and nonverbal communication may be direct or indirect. For example, a parent may directly tell a child who is inappropriately dressed for school: "Those clothes are not what you should wear to school. Go change!" Indirectly, on the other hand, the parent may try to send the same message in a less confrontational manner by asking: "Are you sure that's what you want to wear to school?" or "Why don't you wear that new outfit today? It looks so nice on you!" Such indirect messages run a greater risk of not being received as intended, a result that often leads to misunderstandings. In contrast, indirect messages may be useful in a variety of situations, such as when trying to save face or to avoid insult or conflict.

The message itself has at least two levels: (1) the *content* level, and (2) the *relationship* level. The content level consists of the actual words, while the relationship level provides nonverbal information about the relationship between the sender and receiver, as well as additional information that helps to explain the message. For example, the statement "You bought some condoms" at its content level is simply a statement of fact. The relationship level, however, will supply more of its true meaning when one considers that it may be communicated in greatly different ways by an adolescent boy's mother, father, sex-education teacher, peer, or girlfriend! A parent may make this statement and convey a critical meaning by glowering angrily, pointing a finger, and using an indignant tone of voice. The same adolescent boy, however, may receive a very different meaning when the identical statement is made in a parked car by his girlfriend who has a flirtatious look on her face.

The various aspects of communication (verbal/nonverbal, direct/indirect, content/relationship) may disagree, or be incongruent, with one another. For example, a father may say to his young son, "You did a great job combing your hair" while picking up the comb and recombing the son's hair; or a mother may say to her adolescent daughter, "Whatever you decide is all right with me," using an icy tone and avoiding eye contact. Incongruent communication of this kind is believed by some family scientists to be a source of problems varying from minor misunderstandings to serious individual and relationship pathologies.

For family scientists, such a cursory description of communication only begins to help in understanding how communication in families may differ from the exchange of information in other social environments. Fitzpatrick and Ritchie (1992) outline various models of communication and suggest that an "inferential model" may assist in developing theories of family communication. Specifically, in the inferential model, communicators do more than simply produce a verbal or nonverbal message and respond to that signal. Instead:

> Communication occurs when one person produces an utterance (a set of symbolic patterns) as a public representation of his/her thoughts and another person constructs a mental representation based on this utterance . . . Discourse (i.e., speech, writing, gestures) comprehension depends on one's knowledge of the plans and goals of the participants in the interaction. We supply missing information from our knowledge, including general word knowledge, knowledge of the context, the speaker, and what has already occurred in the present sequence of utterances. (p. 570)

For example, suppose the parent is getting ready for work while the young child is getting ready for school. As the parent busily packs school lunches, the child asks, "Can you tie my shoes?" In an exasperated tone, the parent replies, "I can't afford to be late for work today!" Taken by itself, the statement simply provides information about promptness at work and does not directly answer the question. However, given the context (the parent's history of investment in work), and the child's past experience and knowledge of the parent (previous history when exasperated), the child constructs the meaning of the parent's response: "No!" The child may respond either by tying his own shoes or by quickly finding a pair of slip-ons. What this illustrates is that constructing the meaning of a message requires knowledge of the family paradigm, hierarchy, past experiences, and conceptions of family roles.

Functions of Communication in the Parent/Child Relationship

Communication serves a systems function. One function of communication is to define parent/child roles, relationships, boundaries, power structures, control, and disciplinary strategies. Such definitions about expected behavior and authority are not lost on even the youngest members of the family. One father, for example, who was playing with his 5-year-old daughter told her, "I'm the boss of the house." Quickly and emphatically the daughter replied: "No you aren't, Daddy. You're just the play boss. Mama's the real boss!" Parent/child communication patterns and styles develop and can affect the child's behavior, the parent/child relationship, and the entire family system (Leigh, 1986).

Discipline and control techniques also depend on adequate communication and may be verbal or nonverbal. Parents may say, "No, no, don't touch!" or simply shake their heads while moving an object away from curious hands. At times, different levels of a messages may be in conflict. For example, one of the authors remembers finding her 2-year-old son throwing asparagus from an open can at the kitchen cabinets, delighting in the new, green splotches that decorated the kitchen. Laughing heartily, she said, "No, no, honey, we don't throw asparagus at the cabinets." Rather than looking chastened, her son seemed quite pleased that he had made Mommy laugh.

Communication serves a support function. "I love you" can be expressed verbally or expressed nonverbally through looks, hugs, and touching between parents and child. Such positive communication can strengthen family bonds and foster the development of self-esteem. As indicated in the previous section on parental love, positive communication from parent to child tells the child that he or she is a worthwhile human being (Openshaw et al., 1981, 1983). Words and actions by either parent or child can communicate respect, trust, and confidence.

Another way of saying this is that parent/child communication sets an emotional tone through verbal and nonverbal behavior. Positive communication in the form of praise, encouragement, and expressions of empathy results in a positive, loving climate that fosters unity, connectedness, cooperation, and common family goals. Negative communication expressed as verbal abuse, name-calling, defensiveness, ignoring, and disagreement between verbal and nonverbal messages contributes to resentment, resistance, rebellion, animosity, tension, and separateness (Alexander & Barton, 1976).

It is important for parents to send the same positive message with different channels of communication. Mothers and fathers should strive to support the verbal messages they send with nonverbal behavior that is *congruent*. For example, parents who praise their children for school achievement should make eye contact with them and smile, rather than continuing to read the newspaper or thinking about a work issue that makes them stressed, angry, or unconcerned. Fathers and mothers must increasingly become aware of different communication channels and send congruent messages.

Communication serves a teaching function. Some people believe that the ability of humans to teach their young effectively about both concrete and abstract ideas differentiates human beings from animals. Effective communication is necessary for teaching of this kind to occur. As children develop, parents alter their communication patterns to allow for the effective teaching of increasingly more complex behavior patterns and ideas. The term *motherese* has been used to describe the simpler language structures, slower speech rate, special intonation pattern, and higher pitch utilized by parents when talking with their infants, perhaps providing the first language lessons (Schaffer, 1977; Zigler & Stevenson, 1993). Current research indicates that mothers adjust their interactions with their children according to the child's developmental level. In one study, for example, mothers were asked to work with their children in coordinating a number-matching system; that is, the children were asked to pick up the same number of pennies as there were cookie-monster faces displayed in the research stimuli. Mothers of low achievers were found to provide the basic guidance

necessary, even to the point of defying researcher instructions. Lower-order structures, or those matched to their children's abilities, were used most frequently by these mothers. In contrast, greater flexibility in teaching styles was used by mothers of high-achieving children. Specifically, higher-order structures, or those designed to challenge children's abilities, were used initially in the teaching process. If the child was not successful, however, these mothers were often quite willing to move to a lower level of instruction (Saxe, Gearhart, & Guberman, 1984).

The importance of teaching for the communication process lies in its link with parenting strategies. The authoritative parenting style, for example, involves considerable teaching as parents use induction or rational control to instruct children in the reasons for behavior and the principles upon which moral development is based (Hoffman, 1970, 1980). In seeking to teach or instill such principles, however, parents must also remember that "all behavior is communication" and guard against the possibility that one mode of communication will be incongruent with another. Although some of the content that parents seek to teach may be intentional, other things are taught to children unintentionally by example during everyday situations. In other words, parents may say one thing but do another. Such inconsistent communication is illustrated when parents intentionally tell children that bad language is wrong but use expletives to describe other drivers on the road or nasty bosses at work. Or parents may tell their children not to steal but later hedge a bit on their taxes and bring home "little extras" from work. Such contradictions are not without their impact on children. Parents unintentionally teach much by example or by modeling (Bandura, 1976).

Consistent with a systems perspective, teaching as a form of communication occurs in directions other than from parent to child. "Generational transmission" can also occur in reverse, with children teaching things to parents and grandparents. To illustrate, many adults have become computer literate (or addicted to computer games) because of communication with (or instruction from) their children. More fundamental are various "keynote" issues upon which youths have focused their efforts and taught their parents. The young teach parents about issues that vary from the most fundamental to the most trivial, ranging from politics to sports to personal appearance and grooming (Ambert, 1992; Bengtson & Troll, 1978; Peters, 1985).

Communication serves an informational function.   Communication allows parents and children to share thoughts, feelings, facts, and events of the day. Parents use good communication to monitor the development of their children even in settings where they cannot be present to observe their behavior. "What did you do in school today?" a parent will ask, hoping that the reply will be more than "Nothing."

Communication serves a historical function. Communication allows parents and children to discuss ancestors, family stories, legends, and traditions. Such verbal exchanges reinforced by nonverbal cues (the amount of time devoted and the positive or negative affect used to describe the "revered" topic) serve to communicate the importance of events, accomplishments, and aspirations that are part of the family history. Sharing information about such topics helps to build the family paradigm, communicate expectations, shape the "family character," and foster a sense of continuity and togetherness.

One of the authors, for example, can vividly remember many long family conversations about a particular legendary uncle—Grover Cleveland Alexander, a Hall of Fame baseball pitcher who "won the most games in National League history, almost singlehandedly beat the New York Yankees with Babe Ruth in a World Series, and had a Hollywood movie made about his life, starring a prominent actor who later became a recent U. S. president." Although some of the "legend" was a little tarnished in real life, his rough edges were often ignored, and the real mastery of his pitching skills was often used to send the more general message that "we expect members of our family to give their best in the face of adversity—even if the bases are loaded with Babe Ruth at the plate!" This became a special feature of the family tradition that is powerfully etched in many of the author's childhood memories.

Communication also serves an entertainment function.   "Tell me a story" is a common refrain from childhood. Whether the story is read, remembered, fact, or fiction, parents and children often enjoy this special activity together. Children love to communicate in this fashion, and parents must endure age-old jokes: "No, I don't know. What's black and white and red all over? A newspaper? Oh you're so funny; I never could've guessed!"

Communication in the form of entertainment may begin during infancy, with an exchange of "raspberries" blown by mother and child, and continue through adulthood in conversations about TV soap operas, sharing an off-color joke, or talking about someone's faux pas from the past: "Remember the time you stepped out in the cold garage on a frigid Nebraska evening when no one else was home, in your undershorts and bare feet, and had to tippy toe through the snow next door to the neighbors for help?" Such conversations are important processes that help to forge strong bonds in parent/child relationship based on common experience, intimacy, and connectedness.

Communication serves a developmental function.   Communication allows families to change and make transitions to new stages in the parent/child and larger family relationships. Development in the parent/child relationship requires that rules, expectations for behavior, and new freedoms be continually renegotiated and clarified. Such a complex process also requires that problems be solved and conflicts be resolved or managed. All of these social skills (negotiation, clarifying rules and expectations, problem solving, and conflict management), in turn, require effective communication skills. Learning to accept parental authority, succeed in school, adjust to peers, cope with puberty, seek greater autonomy, and make the transition to adulthood all require a constant, clearly communicated dialogue between parents and their young. Such a process is most likely to clarify expectations in families, make relationships predictable, and define how change will proceed. Both parties in this relationship must change substantially to accommodate these necessary developmental transitions. Adolescents, for example, do not progress toward autonomy in healthy ways without corresponding changes in the control strategies used by parents and modifications in how family rules are enforced.

What this means is that communication is the engine that drives the family system and encompasses the meaningful exchanges of behavior that occur between parents and children. No matter what changes occur in parent/child communication while the young progress from infancy to adulthood, it is almost inevitable that corresponding changes will result in the larger family system and its paradigm.

Chapter Summary

The poet Kahlil Gibran writes that parents "are the bows from which . . . children as living arrows are sent forth." Just as the archer knows that the bow and arrow function together within a system, the family scientist knows that parents and children function together within a family system. Failure to account for the effects of the entire system may lead to erroneous conclusions, as in the old story of the scientist who decided to look at the effects of removing a frog's legs. After the removal of one leg, the scientist demanded, "Jump, frog." And the frog jumped as commanded. The scientist continued this process until he had reached the fourth leg. At last, he removed the leg and commanded, "Jump, frog." The frog did not jump. The scientist then made the following notation in his journal: "When the four legs of a frog have been removed, the frog becomes deaf." Studying the parent/child relationship through an isolationist perspective, therefore, is a bit like studying a Mozart symphony by examining the individual notes or a Monet painting by examining the primary colors. While one may gain limited insight into the symphony or painting, one misses the impact of listening to the symphony or gazing at the painting as a whole.

This chapter has focused on parent/child relationships using family-systems theory, the theory most commonly used by family scientists. Consistent with systems theory, the parent/child relationship is bidirectional, or even multidirectional, with parents affecting children, children affecting parents, and their relationship existing as part of systemic relationships with many other aspects of the social environment. Time is also part of this system,

with development occurring within all levels of the family system and its surrounding social context.

Traditional research on such central aspects of the parent/child relationship as love, parental guidance, parental authority, and communication has been recast into ideas from a systems perspective, including family paradigms, boundaries, and parental subsystems. Family scientists have added new dimensions to the study and understanding of the complex structures and processes that form the parent/child subsystem.

Discussion Questions

1. Consider an 8-year-old child in a "typical" two-parent family. What are some of the specific subsystems one might observe, and how might these subsystems interact? How might these subsystems differ for an adult child whose parents are living nearby?
2. What are some positive and negative outcomes of love in parent/child relationships?
3. Contrast authoritarian, authoritative, permissive, neglectful, and overprotective styles of parenting using a family-science perspective; utilize such concepts as executive and child subsystems, permeability of boundaries, support, and control.
4. How does parental guidance differ from parental authority? How do these concepts interact?
5. Give examples of expert, referent, reward, coercive, and legitimate authority in parents. Give examples of the same in children.
6. What are some functions of communication in the parent/child relationship? How might the family paradigm affect such communication?

Additional Resources

Ambert, A. M. (1992). *The effects of children on parents.* New York: Haworth Press.

Broderick, C. B. (1990). Family process theory. In J. Sprey (Ed.), *Fashioning family theory: New approaches.* Newbury Park, CA: Sage.

Constantine, L. L. (1986). *Family paradigms.* New York: Guilford Press.

References

Ainsworth, M. D. S., Blehar, M. C., Waters, E., & Wall, S. (1978). *Patterns of attachment: A psychological study of the strange situation.* Hillsdale, NJ: Erlbaum.

Alexander, J. F., & Barton, C. (1976). Behavioral systems therapy for families. In D. H. Olson (Ed.), *Treating relationships.* Lake Mills, IA: Graphic.

Ambert, A. M. (1992). *The effects of children on parents.* New York: Haworth Press.

Bachman, J., O'Malley, P., & Johnson, J. (1978). *Adolescence to adulthood: Change and stability in the lives of young men.* Ann Arbor, MI: Institute for Social Research.

Bandura, A. (1976). *Social learning theory.* Englewood Cliffs, NJ: Prentice-Hall.

Barber, B. K. (1992). Family, personality, and adolescent problem behavior. *Journal of Marriage and the Family, 54,* 69–79.

Barber, B. K., & Thomas, D. L. (1986). Dimensions of fathers' and mothers' supportive behavior: The case for physical affection. *Journal of Marriage and the Family, 48,* 783–794.

Bateson, G. (1979). *Steps to an ecology of mind.* New York: Ballantine.

Baumrind, D. (1978). Parental disciplinary patterns and social competence in children. *Youth and Society, 9*(3), 239–276.

Baumrind, D. (1980). New directions in socialization research. *American Psychologist, 35,* 639–652.

Baumrind, D. (1991). Effective parenting during the early adolescent transition. In P. A. Cowan & M. Hetherington (Eds.), *Family transitions.* Hillsdale, NJ: Erlbaum.

Becker, W. C. (1964). Consequences of different kinds of parental discipline. In M. L. Hoffman & L. Hoffman (Eds.), *Review of child development research: Vol 1* (pp. 169–208). Chicago: University of Chicago Press.

Beebe, B., Jaffe, J., Feldstein, S., Mays, K., & Olson, D. (1985). Interpersonal timing: The application of an adult dialogue model to mother-infant vocal kinesic interactions. In T. Field & N. Fox (Eds.), *Social perception in infants* (pp. 217–248). Norwood, NJ: Ablex.

Bell, R. Q., & Harper, L. V. (1977). *Child effects on adults.* Hillsdale, NJ: Erlbaum.

Bengtson, V. L., & Troll, L. (1978). Youth and their parents: Feedback and intergenerational influence in socialization. In R. M. Lerner & G. B. Spanier (Eds.), *Child influences on marital and family interaction: A lifespan perspective.* New York: Academic Press.

Bertalanffy, L. von (1969). *General systems theory: Essays in its foundation and development* (rev. ed.). New York: Braziller.

Bigner, J. J. (1989). *Parent-child relations: An introduction to parenting* (3rd ed.). New York: Macmillan.

Bowen, M. (1978). *Family therapy in clinical practice.* New York: Aronson.

Bowlby, J. A. (1988). *A secure base: Parent-child attachment and healthy human development.* New York: Basic Books.

Brazelton, T. B., Koslowski, B., & Main, M. (1974). The origins of reciprocity: The early mother-infant interaction. In M. Lewis & L. A. Rosenblum (Eds.), *The effect of the infant on its caregiver.* New York: Wiley.

Bretherton, I., Biringen, Z., & Ridgeway, D. (1991). The parental side of attachment. In K. Pillemer & K. McCartney (Eds.), *Parent-child relations throughout life.* Hillsdale, NJ: Erlbaum.

Broderick, C. B. (1990). Family process theory. In J. Sprey (Ed.), *Fashioning family theory: New approaches.* Newbury Park, CA: Sage.

Bronfenbrenner, U. (1958). Socialization and social class through time and space. In E. E. Maccoby, T. M. Newcomb, & E. L. Hartley (Eds.), *Readings in social psychology.* New York: Holt, Rinehart & Winston.

Bronfenbrenner, U. (1979). *The ecology of human development.* Cambridge, MA: Harvard University Press.

Buckley, W. (1967). *Sociology and modern systems theory.* Englewood Cliffs, NJ: Prentice-Hall.

Burr, W. R., Day, R. D., & Bahr, K. S. (1993). *Family science.* Pacific Grove, CA: Brooks/Cole.

Chilman, C. S. (1980). Parent satisfactions, concerns, and goals for their children. *Family Relations, 29,* 339–345.

Constantine, L. L. (1986). *Family paradigms.* New York: Guilford Press.

Coopersmith, S. (1967). *The antecedents of self-esteem.* San Francisco: Freeman.

Cromwell, R. E., & Olson, D. H. (1975). *Multidisciplinary perspectives of power. Power in families.* New York: Wiley.

Cromwell, R. E., & Peterson, G. W. (1983). Multisystem-multimethod family assessment in clinical contexts. *Family Process, 22,* 147–163.

Deal, J. E., Halverson, C. F., & Wampler, K. S. (1989). Parental agreement on child-rearing orientation: Relations to parental, marital family and child characteristics. *Child Development, 60,* 1025–1034.

Dix, T. (in press). Parenting on behalf of the child: Empathic goals in the regulation of responsive parenting. In I. E. Sigel, A. V. McGillicuddy-De Lisi, & J. J. Goodnow (Eds.), *Parental belief systems: The psychological consequences for children: Vol. 2.* Hillsdale, NJ: Erlbaum.

Elder, G. H. (1978). Family history and the life course. In T. Haraven (Ed.), *Transitions* (pp. 17–64). New York: Academic Press.

Field, T. (1985). Attachment as psychobiological attunement: Being on the same wavelength. In M. Reite & T. Field (Eds.), *Psychobiology of attachment and separation* (pp. 415–454). New York: Academic Press.

Field, T., Healy, B., Goldstein, S., & Guthertz, M. (1990). Behavior-state matching and synchrony in mother-infant interactions of nondepressed versus depressed dyads. *Developmental Psychology, 26*(1), 7–14.

Fitzpatrick, M. A., & Ritchie, L. D. (1992). Communication theory and the family. In P. G. Boss, W. J. Doherty, R. LaRossa, W. R. Schumm, & S. K. Steinmetz (Eds.), *Sourcebook of family theories and methods: A contextual approach*. New York: Plenum.

French, J. R. P., & Raven, B. H. (1959). The bases of social power. In D. Cartwright (Ed.), *Studies in social power* (pp. 118–249). Ann Arbor: University of Michigan Press.

Galvin, K., & Brommel, B. (1991). *Family communication: Cohesion and change*. Glenview, IL: Scott, Foresman.

Gecas, V. (1979). The influence of social class on socialization. In W. R. Burr, F. I. Nye, & I. L. Reiss (Eds.), *Contemporary theories about the family: Vol. 1*. New York: Free Press.

Gelles, R. J. (1990). Methodological issues in the study of family violence. In G. R. Patterson (Ed.), *Family social interaction: Content and methodology issues in the study of aggression and depression* (pp. 49–74). Hillsdale, NJ: Erlbaum.

Goetting, A. (1986). Parental satisfaction: A review of research. *Journal of Family Issues, 7*, 83–109.

Grossman, K. E., & Grossman K. (1984). *The development of conversational styles in the first year of life and its relationship to maternal sensitivity and attachment quality between mother and child*. Paper presented at the congress of the German Society for Psychology, Vienna.

Harlow, H. F. (1974). *Learning to love*. New York: Aronson.

Harrison, A. (1990). Family ecologies of ethnic minority children. *Child Development, 61*, 347–362.

Hayley, J. (1976). *Problem-solving therapy: New strategies for effective family therapy*. San Francisco: Jossey-Bass.

Hayley, J. (1980). *Leaving home: The therapy of disturbed young people*. New York: McGraw-Hill.

Henry, C. L., Wilson, L. M., & Peterson, G. W. (1989). Parental power bases and processes as predictors of adolescent conformity. *Journal of Adolescent Research, 4*, 15–32.

Hetherington, E. M., Hagan, M. S., & Anderson, E. R. (1989). Marital transitions: A child's perspective. *American Psychologist, 44*, 303–312.

Hoffman, M. L. (1970). Moral development. In P. H. Mussen (Ed.), *Charmichael's manual of child psychology: Vol. 2* (pp. 261–359). New York: Wiley.

Hoffman, M. L. (1980). Moral development in adolescence. In J. Adelson (Ed.), *Handbook of adolescent psychology*. New York: Wiley.

Hoffman, M. L. (1989). Effects of maternal employment in the two-parent family. *American Psychologist, 44*, 283–292.

Kantor, D., & Lehr, W. (1975). *Inside the family*. San Francisco: Jossey-Bass.

Kohn, M. L. (1977). *Class and conformity: A study in values* (2nd ed.). Chicago: University of Chicago Press.

Kuhn, T. S. (1970). *The structure of scientific revolutions* (2nd ed.). Chicago: University of Chicago Press.

Leigh, G. (1986). Adolescent involvement in family systems. In G. K. Leigh and G. W. Peterson (Eds.), *Adolescence in families* (pp. 38–72). Dallas: South-Western Publishing Co.

Lerner, R. M. (1984). *On the nature of human plasticity*. New York: Cambridge University Press.

Maccoby, E. E., & Martin, J. A. (1983). Socialization in the context of the family: Parent-child interaction. In E. M. Hetherington (Ed.), *Handbook of child psychology: Socialization, personality, and social development: Vol. 4*. New York: Wiley.

MacFarlane, J. A., Smith, D. M., & Garrow, D. H. (1978). The relationship between mother and neonate. In S. Kitzinger & J. A. Davis (Eds.), *The place of birth*. New York: Oxford University Press.

McDonald, G. W. (1980). Parental power and adolescents' parental identifications: A reexamination. *Journal of Marriage and the Family, 42*, 289–296.

Minuchin, S. (1974). *Families and family therapy*. Cambridge, MA: Harvard University Press.

Minuchin, P. (1985). Families and individual development: Provocations from the field of family therapy. *Child Development, 56*, 289–302.

Minuchin, S. Rossman, B. L., & Baker, L. (1978). *Psychosomatic families: Anorexia nervosa in context*. Cambridge, MA: Harvard University Press.

Openshaw, D. K., Thomas, D. L., & Rollins, B. C. (1981). Adolescent self-esteem: A multidimensional perspective. *Journal of Early Adolescence, 1*, 273–282.

Openshaw, D. K., Thomas, D. L., & Rollins, B. C. (1983). Socialization and adolescent self-esteem: Symbolic interaction and social learning explanations. *Adolescence, 18*, 317–329.

Peters, J. F. (1985). Adolescents as socialization agents to parents. *Adolescence, 20*, 921–933.

Peterson, G. W. (1986). Parent-youth power dimensions and the behavioral autonomy of adolescents. *Journal of Adolescent Research, 1*, 231–249.

Peterson, G. W., & Cromwell, R. E. (1983). A clarification of multisystem-multimethod assessment: Reductionism versus wholism. *Family Process, 22*, 173–177.

Peterson, G. W., & Hann, D. (in press). Socializing children and parents in families. In M. B. Sussman & S. K. Steinmetz (Eds.), *Handbook of marriage and the family.* New York: Plenum.

Peterson, G. W. & Leigh, G. K. (1990). The family and social competence in adolescence. In T. P. Gullotta, G. R. Adams, & R. Montemayor (Eds.), *Developing social competency in adolescence: Advances in adolescent development.* Vol. 3 (pp. 97–138). Newbury Park, CA: Sage.

Peterson, G. W., & Rollins, B. C. (1987). Parent-child socialization. In M. B. Sussman & S. K. Steinmetz (Eds.), *Handbook of marriage and the family.* New York: Plenum.

Peterson, G. W., Rollins, B. C., & Thomas, D. L. (1985). Parental influence and adolescent conformity: Compliance and internalization. *Youth and Society, 16,* 397–420.

Peterson, G. W., & Stivers, M. E. (1986). Adolescent behavioral autonomy and family connectedness in rural Appalachia. *Family Perspective, 20,* 307–322.

Reiss, D. (1981). *The family's construction of reality.* Cambridge, MA: Harvard University Press.

Richards, L. N., Bengtson, V. L., & Miller, R. B. (1989). The generation in the middle: Perceptions of changes in adults' intergenerational relationships. In K. Kreppner & R. M. Lerner (Eds.), *Family systems and life-span development.* Hillsdale, NJ: Erlbaum.

Rohner, R. P. (1986). *The warmth dimension: Foundation of parental acceptance-rejection theory.* Newbury Park, CA: Sage.

Rollins, B. C., & Thomas, D. L. (1979). Parental support, power, and control techniques in the socialization of children. In W. R. Burr, R. Hill, F. I. Nye, & I. R. Reiss (Eds.), *Contemporary theories about the family: Vol. 1* (pp. 337–357). New York: Free Press.

Saxe, G. B., Gearhart, M., & Guberman, S. R. (1984). The social organization of early number development. In B. Rogoff & V. Wertsch (Eds.), *Children's learning: The zone of proximal development* (pp. 19–30). San Francisco: Jossey-Bass.

Schaefer, E. S. (1959). Children's reports of parental behavior. *Child Development, 36,* 413–424.

Schaffer, H. R. (1977). *Mothering.* Cambridge, MA: Harvard University Press.

Skynner, A. C. R. (1976). *Systems of family and marital psychotherapy.* New York: Brunner/Mazel.

Skynner, A. C. R. (1981). An open-systems, group analytic approach to family therapy. In A. S. Gurman & D. P. Kniskern (Eds.), *Handbook of family therapy.* New York: Brunner/Mazel.

Smith, T. E. (1983). Parental influence: A review of the evidence of influence and a theoretical model of the parental-influence process. In A. Kerckhoff (Ed.), *Research in the sociology of education and socialization, an annual compilation: Vol. 4.* Greenwich, CT: JAI Press.

Smith, T. E. (1986). Influence in parent-adolescent relationships. In G. K. Leigh & G. W. Peterson (Eds.), *Adolescents in families* (pp. 130–154). Dallas: South-Western Publishing Co.

Sommerville, J. (1982). *The rise and fall of childhood.* Newbury, CA: Sage.

Steinglass, P. (1987). A systems view of family interaction and psychopathology. In T. Jacob (Ed.), *Family interaction and psychopathology* (pp. 25–65). New York: Plenum.

Symonds, P. (1939). *The psychology of parent-child relationships.* New York: Appleton-Century-Crofts.

Szinovacz, M. E. (1987). Family power. In M. B. Sussman & S. K. Steinmetz (Eds.), *Handbook of marriage and the family* (pp. 651–693). New York: Plenum.

Teyber, E. (1983a). Effects of the parental coalition on adolescent emancipation from the family. *Journal of Marital and Family Therapy, 9,* 305–310.

Teyber, E. (1983b). Structural family relations: Primary dyadic alliances and adolescent adjustment. *Journal of Marital and Family Therapy, 9,* 89–99.

Thomas, A., Chess, S., & Birch, H. (1968). *Temperament and behavior disorders in children.* New York: New York University Press.

Umberson, D. (1989). Relationships with children: Explaining parents' psychological well-being. *Journal of Marriage and the Family, 51,* 999–1012.

Watson, J. B. (1928). *Psychological care of infant and child.* New York: Norton.

Watzlawick, P., Beavin, J., & Jackson, D. D. (1967). *Pragmatics of human communication.* New York: Norton.

Zigler, E. F., & Stevenson, M. F. (1993). *Children in a changing world.* Pacific Grove, CA: Books/Cole.

PART IV

Challenges and Choices for Families

For the most part, families engage in the activities of everyday life as described in Chapter 10. Sometimes, events will challenge those patterns of life. These events may cause them to question the ways in which they view their family, how they act in the family, and perhaps even the choices they see themselves able to make.

One way to think of these challenges and the choices that result from them is to recall the metaphor that was introduced in Chapter 6, on "Family Systems Theory." In this metaphor, Level III issues are considered to be the foundation of the family. Some events shake that foundation, rattle the walls, and cause plaster to fall. The challenges explored in Part IV involve events that are more than just inconveniences or daily problems. They involve the reorganization of the meaning of family itself.

Chapter 14 addresses a topic that few people would have even considered only a few years ago. As technology and social attitudes advance, couples have increased reproduction options. Kerry Daly explores those options and the impact they have on couples who eagerly seek alternatives when they cannot have a child in the usual way. This is an example of a stressor event that can force the members of a couple to reexamine who they are and what the purpose of their relationship is.

Chapter 15, by Linda Matocha, describes the effects of illness on the family and the stresses and strains inherent in what, to some families, becomes a "normative" crisis. Like so many of the various stressors that

affect a family, health crises can have a multitude of effects: economic, morale, losses, and dramatic changes in role definition.

Chapter 16, on family violence, is written by Suzanne Steinmetz. She and her colleagues (most notably Murray Straus and Richard Gelles) have been at the forefront of describing a family crisis that need not happen. Family violence is a severe and ubiquitous problem in our society. It is found at every income and social level. Steinmetz asks us to consider the larger question of why it continues to plague families.

Chapter 17, written by Linda Wark, Suzanne Bartle, and Patrick McKenry, takes a family-process approach in their discussion of divorce. Various theories focusing on individual and family-systems factors help us to understand the family's struggle to regain a sense of balance as they move through the changes in their family.

Remarriage and stepfamilies are the focus of Chapter 18, by Larry Ganong, Marilyn Coleman, and Mark Fine. Often struggling under the weight of myths, stepfamilies share certain characteristics and have unique challenges related to their characteristics. Yet, as this chapter shows, stepfamilies can be healthy places to rear children and to grow up.

Finally, Kathleen Gilbert introduces us to emerging concepts about family loss and the resulting grief. In Chapter 19, she challenges our current understanding about the grief process and provides an excellent critique of the "stages of grief" approach, which has received much attention over the last 20 years. While family losses are inevitable and unalterable, they are still some of the most traumatic and devastating events we experience. Gilbert provides practical suggestions about how family-science workers can be more effective in dealing with those who are passing through these crises.

CHAPTER 14

Reproduction in Families

Kerry Daly
University of Guelph

Reproduction is a central organizing force in family experience. Four major themes are explored in this chapter. First, reproduction serves as a key referent for defining who the family is. Second, the meaning of reproduction in families is comprehensible only when considered within the broader social and political context. Third, reproduction shapes how men and women in families differentially gear into the social world. Fourth, it reflects a technological ethos that has profound implications for control, autonomy, and power both within the family and between families and the technical experts to whom they turn for help.

Reproduction, in its narrowest definition, encompasses a range of physiological processes from conception to birth. What is critical in this analysis of reproduction in families, however, is the idea that these physiological processes give rise to a set of social relationships. Most fundamental among these is the ensuing relationship between parent and child. In this regard, the definition of reproduction must include the "reproductive labor" of nurturing and socializing children to the point of personal independence (Clark & Lange, 1979). This reproductive labor is clearly differentiated by gender. Men and women have a different consciousness of reproduction that is at the root of a set of historical disparities in their involvement with, valuing of, and control over reproduction (O'Brien, 1981). This different consciousness has been shaped by material and ideological structures that continue to idealize motherhood and assign to women the primary responsibility for the domestic sphere. Technology has been paramount in changing the historical meaning of repro-

duction, because it has introduced choice and has fragmented the traditional definition of parenthood into biological and social components. Reproduction, then, in its broadest definition, involves a set of social relationships, rooted in the physiological process of procreation, that is shaped by the broader sociohistorical context.

When one takes the analysis of reproduction beyond mere physiology, it becomes an important forum for understanding cultural notions of what constitutes a family, the differential experience of men and women, and the role of technology in changing the meaning of reproduction. This chapter focuses on the social construction of reproduction: What social meanings are attached to the biological processes of reproduction? How does reproduction shape meanings within family systems? How do social policies, organizational procedures, and the prevailing political climate affect the way that reproduction is defined? What is the difference in the meaning of reproduction for men and women? What are the implications of technology in helping family systems achieve greater control over the reproductive function?

Reproduction and Family Definition

The reproduction of oneself represents one thread in a larger family genealogy. Reproductive tradition in families is characterized by lineage, genetic transmission, family loyalties, and inheritance, each of which gives shape to an evolving set of meanings for the family system. From this perspective, reproduction plays a central role in defining who the family is. Beutler, Burr, Bahr, and Herrin (1989) argue that reproduction is the basis for defining the family realm: "The irreducible parameter of this realm is the biological, emotional, social and developmental processes that are inherent in the procreation and the nurturing of dependent children" (p. 806). Reproduction, then, defines families in terms of generational links. Kinship, which is based on consanguineous bonds, reflects the horizontal links that one has with contemporary relatives and the vertical links that one has with ancestors. The bearing and rearing of children are seen to create ties that are both unique and permanent to the family realm (Beutler et al., 1989). Nevertheless, these links are always in flux. Since family relationships are continually created through time, reproduction has a "dynamism" that involves not only birth and maturation but also aging and mortality (Robertson, 1991).

Deeply embedded within these assumptions about the role of reproduction in the definition of families is the cultural importance of blood ties. Terms like consanguinity, procreation, generational links, and lineage have a biological element that is taken for granted. The family is deemed a biological unit until some problem arises to cast doubt on this assumption. Reproduction, biological continuity, and family are natural bedfellows. The permanence of social relationships in the family realm, in comparison with the relatively transitory relationships with friends or associates, is typically seen as a product of the genetic links that lie at their root.

Infertile Families

The importance of blood ties for the creation of family meanings becomes most obvious when one studies examples in which reproduction is problematic or atypical. In the infertility literature, for example, the pursuit of genetic parenthood by infertile couples is often characterized as desperate and obsessive. The obsession, of course, is to have a child *of one's own*. Couples go to great lengths to get pregnant, including years of painful tests and treatments, often followed by efforts with reproductive technologies that can be frustrating, time-consuming, painful, and seldom successful. In my own research with infertile couples, I

interviewed one woman who had persisted with this process for 22 years (Daly, 1988, 1989a, 1989b, 1990). The biological link is an important impetus to keep going. When she and others were asked how they felt about adoption as an alternative to their own reproductive success, they clearly identified it as *second best*. Blood ties continue to have ideological primacy for defining the family realm in our culture.

The importance of having children of one's own reflects the need not only to have a blood tie with one's own child but also to maintain and preserve the family lineage. For example, one of the difficult aspects of a couple's inability to have children of its own is the sense that it is creating "grandchildlessness." Not only do couples suffer the loss of the parenting experience through the loss of their own reproductive capacity, but they feel that they are depriving their own parents of the grandparenting experience. Here the generational links are profound: their inability to reproduce both thwarts biological continuity and disrupts the expected life-cycle transitions not just of themselves as parents but also of their own parents.

Adoptive Families

Adoptive families are another example of a contrast to the "natural" pattern of biological continuity. Although adoptive families provide social continuity with respect to family patterns, customs, and values, the absence of the biological tie can have a significant impact on family meanings. Modern adoptees are still treated in many ways like orphans: excluded from their biological clan, forced out of the natural flow of generational continuity, and often deprived of essential parts of their biographical heritage (Lifton, 1988).

In his classic theoretical work on adoption, David Kirk (1964) identifies the central tension in an adoptive family's development as the "acknowledgment" versus the "rejection of difference." The challenge for an adoptive family is to manage the tension between creating a system of family meaning *as if* it were a biological family and creating a system that openly accommodates the differences of adoption. Whereas biological reproduction is the typical method of family formation, adoption calls into question, in the eyes of others, the way in which the family is defined. Routine questions for biological families about the circumstances of pregnancy, labor, and birth become problematic for adoptive families. Defining the adoptive-family realm for others involves decisions about whether and to what extent to include the biological parents as members of the system. Unknown elements in the biological history, fear of ridicule or stigma, and uncertainty about what or when to disclose information present different, and often stressful, challenges to adoptive families. It is the fracturing of biological reproduction and social parenting that calls for a different construction of family identity.

Perhaps the most obvious indication of the importance of blood ties can be found in the way that adoption is treated in the news media. Two stories dominate the public presentation of adoption in the media, both of which emphasize the importance of genes for successful family relationships. Story 1 is the glorified celebration of reunion between the child long ago placed for adoption and the biological parent. Here the adoptees find their "real" parents. The message is clear: adoption may temporarily disrupt the social relationship between birth parents and their children placed for adoption, but it can never sever the blood tie between a child and his or her "real" mother. Story 2 is less glamorous. Here the adoptee is portrayed as the sociopath who burns down the family home with the adoptive parents inside. The importance of the genetic link for successful family functioning is equally obvious: adoption, or the absence of a blood tie, is the focus for explaining the family horror. Not only are blood ties seen as a natural part of family relationships, but as these examples would suggest, they are publicly presented as a necessary part of successful family functioning. Of course, what the media fail to present are the stories that attest to the strength and positive adjustment that are typical of adoptive families or the stories of anxiety, uncertainty, or disappointment associated with birth-parent reunions. Nevertheless, biases such as these preserve the ideological primacy of blood ties.

Reproductive Technologies

The new reproductive technologies also challenge the way in which family reality is traditionally defined by separating social and biological aspects of parent-

hood. By using a combination of these technologies, it is possible for a child to be born with five parents instead of the traditional two: a genetic (sperm donor) father, a social father, a genetic (egg donor) mother, a uterine mother (surrogate), and a social mother. In these families, as in adoptive families, there is potential for "genealogical bewilderment" as the offspring attempt to sort out biological origins and construct an identity from their fragmented biological heritage (Edwards, 1991; Lifton, 1988). These technologies challenge the traditional meaning of both family and kinship and result in the construction of a very different family realm. When there is a shift from natural to artificial reproduction (for example, artificial insemination by donor or egg or embryo donation), genetic parenthood no longer guarantees familial relationship. By introducing a number of different players into the conception equation, the new reproductive technologies "make the consanguineal bond highly diverse, often indirect, and in some cases altogether fictive" (Edwards, 1991, p. 357).

Nevertheless, the "as if" principle of defining the family realm is still operative in families that have used reproductive technologies. Like adoption, reproductive technologies maintain a filtered "awareness context" by keeping secret or playing down the contribution of other biological parents (Glaser & Strauss, 1965). In its place, the family chooses to present itself to the world around it *as if* it were a traditional nuclear family. This is nowhere more obvious than in families formed through the use of artificial insemination where the anonymity of the donor parent is assured by medical practitioners and the families accordingly keep secret the identity of the biological parent.

Hence, although reproduction plays an important role in shaping family genealogy, it now occurs within a wider spectrum of alternatives. The various permutations of parental contribution disturb and challenge the accepted meanings of family, parenthood, lineage, genealogy, and kinship. In their place, they call out for a more idiosyncratic method of defining the family realm. Although the deconstruction of the mythical monolithic nuclear family is well advanced because of increases in divorce, voluntary childlessness, and gay unions, the new reproductive alternatives give rise to new questions about the meaning of parent and family (Eichler, 1988). While reproduction is central to the way that we define families, it is impossible to separate it from the cultural meanings that have been brought to bear on it throughout history.

Reproduction in a Sociohistorical Context

Although we typically think of reproduction within the private-family realm, its social meaning is only fully comprehensible when placed within the context of the broader historical and social milieu. For example, individual actors privately make sense of their reproductive experience when they talk about the good or bad timing of a pregnancy or when they grieve over the inability to produce a child when one is desired. Yet these private definitions are shaped by the society within which they live. For the 25-year-old married woman, a pregnancy may be defined as badly timed because it disrupts a socially expected career trajectory. Thirty years ago, when a minority of women were in the paid labor force, social expectations were different, and a private definition of bad timing was therefore less likely. Similarly, the private grief over infertility is understandable against the public backdrop of pronatalist standards that continue to emphasize the importance and necessity of parenthood to marriage. While infertile couples may privately wish to have a child, there are tremendous social pressures that come to bear when they do not make the expected transition from young married couple getting established to proud parents. Private definitions of reproduction are shaped by the public meanings of reproduction. Of course, the influence of these systems of meaning on one another are not unidirectional, for as Mills (1959) astutely reminds us, the frequent occurrence of private troubles is also the basis for the emergence of public issues.

Marxist analysis further underscores the relationship between private and structural meanings of reproduction. From this perspective, the family household appears as the private locus of generational reproduction. In this separate sphere outside of production, Marx sees family members engaged in reproductive activities arising from their instinct for self-preservation and procreation (Dickinson & Russell, 1986). Here family members experience some self-determination

with respect to their need for generational continuity. Nevertheless, these private activities of reproduction in the family play a vital role in the reproduction of labor power on both a daily and generational basis. The private consciousness of reproductive activities is a necessary condition for the success of the capitalist social structure.

Given how it is embedded in systems of public meaning, reproduction is profoundly political. As Handwerker (1990) suggests, the birth of a child is a political event insofar as it may be part of a strategy to acquire or extend power or create or break ties of dependence. Teenage pregnancy provides an excellent example of how reproduction is a political event at both the private and the public level. In early research with adolescents, the term *teenage pregnancy* was used interchangeably with *unplanned pregnancy*. Of course, as more was learned about the motivations for these pregnancies, it became very clear that not all of them were unplanned. In fact, many of them could be seen as teenagers' deliberate attempts to violate the rules of the family system in order to break the ties of dependency with their own parents. These are political dynamics within the private-family realm. At the public level, teenage pregnancy is also intensely political. Debates about abortion, parent-support programs, and adoption continue to be hotly contested. However, as Vinovskis (1988) has pointed out, the notion of an "epidemic" of teenage pregnancies is simply unfounded when one looks at the demographic trends. In the early 1970s, when funding bodies and policymakers were focusing intensively on teenage pregnancy programming, adolescent fertility rates were actually declining. In the United States, for example, the fertility rate for 15- to 19-year-olds declined from a peak of 97.3 in 1957 to 51.7 in 1983. Although the fertility rate was falling, the number of out-of-wedlock births in this age group rose from 30% to 72% between 1950 and 1981 (Vinovskis, 1988). This increase in the number of births outside of marriage may account for heightened political concern about early childbearing (Vinovskis, 1988). When pregnancy occurs outside of marriage, a greater burden is placed on federal and state welfare programs. It is precisely this increased dependency on the state that makes teenage pregnancy an important political issue in the public forum.

As a political phenomenon, reproduction is characterized by issues of power, competition, rights, privilege, and control. Consider the following ways in which the political nature of reproduction is manifested:

• Reproduction is a political event when one looks at history. Reproduction changed meaning as the meaning and value of children changed. For example, whereas children were seen as objects of affection and discipline in the 17th century and as a valuable source of labor in the 18th and 19th centuries, they are now seen as a source of developmental satisfaction that is accompanied by a set of monetary costs.

• Reproduction is a political event when one looks across cultures. In many cultures, women have been exploited because of their reproductive biology (Handwerker, 1990). Clitoridectomies, menstrual taboos, and manipulation by contemporary Western doctors reflect the control and domination of women's reproductive capacity by men.

• Reproduction is at the root of a different experience for men and women. Women's unique capacity for reproduction has been credited with shaping the social division of labor. Although there is no necessary link between bearing children and rearing children, women have historically been responsible for the reproductive labor of nurturing them. Of course, this social division of labor typically favors men in terms of power. The dependency of a helpless infant contributes to a pattern of dependency of wives on husbands. It has also resulted in the exclusion of women from the economic and political spheres.

• Reproduction is susceptible to public control. When birth control information or abortion services are inaccessible due to geographical location, social class, or government policies, reproduction is political. Likewise, policies and legislation for parental leave can significantly affect reproductive labor done by men and women in the private sphere.

• Reproduction is political in light of the separation between sex and reproduction. Assisted conception and artificial reproduction are now possible with the use of reproductive technologies. The use of these technologies removes reproduction from the private sphere and puts it squarely into the public domain, where technicians, ethics committees, doctors, and lawyers play a part in the decisions. These relationships have power dynamics and are inherently political. As Brodribb (1989) asserts, there is an emerging distinction between the "private ordering of reproduction" and the "state regulation" of reproduction (p. 145).

• Reproduction is also political because of the many differing opinions among medical practitioners, lawyers and judges, ethicists, religious groups, feminists, and the infertile about the merits and detriments of reproductive technologies. Each of these groups presents a different set of interests with the desire to uphold a different set of principles. Although some would argue that the new reproductive technologies are inherently harmful, others would argue that they are highly beneficial in meeting a variety of needs. Arising from these different orientations is conflict over the use of available resources, legislation, and entitlement. These technologies thereby politicize reproduction, parenthood, and the family itself.

• Reproduction is becoming more political because of the increasing fragmentation of parenthood into its biological and social components, creating an escalating potential for competing interests. Where once we could think of whole mothers and fathers, reproductive technologies push us to think about genetic, uterine, or social mothers, on the one hand, and genetic or social fathers, on the other. Where once reproduction could be thought of as natural or as an instance of biological destiny, it may now involve several parental parties who have a different stake in the child. The highly publicized Baby M case, involving the competing interests of a surrogate mother and the commissioning parents, is an example of these power dynamics.

Although a study of reproduction leads one into many domains, from physiology to family definitions to political control, gender remains at the center of the debate. Accordingly, gender is a central axis for the social analysis of reproduction. Specifically, it raises issues of the role of biology in gendered experience, the links between private and public domains, and the historical changes in the relationship between production and reproduction.

Reproduction and Gendered Experience

When one seeks to explain the differences between men and women in their relation to reproduction, at least two perspectives are possible. One is to think about their contribution to the reproductive process as different but complementary. From this traditional perspective, men and women participate in the physical aspects of reproduction with the guidance of nature and subsequently negotiate a set of roles for managing the reproductive labor that is necessary for rearing a healthy child.

A second and more critical perspective also examines the reproductive differences between men and women but emphasizes the unequal and oppressive nature of these differences. Specifically, the process of human reproduction is viewed as the historical root of women's oppression. In light of our increasing awareness of the deep-rooted nature of sexism and patriarchy in our culture, it is with this latter perspective in mind that the discussion proceeds.

There are two arguments explaining the genders' unequal experience of parenthood. One suggests that biology plays a major role in determining the experience of parenthood, and the other argues that differences in reproductive capacity are not as important as social and historical conventions for explaining these gender differences in parenting.

The Biological Argument

Alice Rossi's (1977) work on the biosocial aspects of parenting emphasizes the importance of biology in explaining gender differences in parental behavior. Focusing on studies of mother/infant bonding, Rossi argues for the importance of maternal instincts to explain why mothers parent differently from fathers. To this end she identifies a set of inherently female qualities among mothers: how infant crying stimulates the secretion of oxytocin, which in turn triggers breast and uterine responses; how women, regardless of handedness, cradle their infants in their left arm so that the child can hear the heartbeat; and how women have a common sequence of tactile approach when their infants are placed next to them. Rossi's work has been criticized for focusing only on maternal responsiveness (as opposed

to the responsiveness of others, including fathers) and for failing to account for the role that social expectations play in shaping mother/infant interactions (Rothman, 1987).

Consistent with this work, but from a very different perspective, Firestone (1970) argues that biological differences in reproductive capacity are the base from which to explain unequal social relations in society. Specifically, by virtue of bearing a child who is helpless and dependent at birth and having lactation capacity, women have historically assumed responsibility for rearing children. This, in turn, has resulted in their dependence on men for material support. Women's reproductive capacity is a key basis for biological differentiation from men, which in turn is critical for culturally differentiating men and women in terms of identity, role, and social status. For Firestone, this biological difference is at the root of women's oppression. Although she has been criticized for the biological determinism of her theory (O'Brien, 1981; Rose, 1987), the theory does, nevertheless, focus attention on the fundamental biological difference between men and women in their relation to reproduction. The solution for Firestone is to revolutionize the means of reproduction through the use of reproductive technologies so that men and women will share equally in the burden of reproductive labor.

The Sociohistorical Argument

Although biology plays an important role in how men and women experience physiological reproduction, it ignores the fact that the roles of mother and father are social constructs. Rothman (1987), for example, suggests that although biological roles in reproduction are different, the social roles of parents *can be* interchangeable, with both having the ability to hold, comfort, teach, discipline, love, and guide. From this perspective, the different relations of the sexes to reproduction is not explained by nature but by convention (Clark & Lange, 1979). These conventions are rooted in a long tradition of gender socialization. Chodorow (1978) talks about the social reproduction of mothering as a result of men's failure to become full partners in the parenting experience. As she points out, "Women's mothering is one of the few universal and enduring elements of the sexual division of labor" (Chodorow, 1978, p. 3). In the absence of strong father/child relations, the relationship between mothers and children is "supercharged" (Goldner, 1985, p. 39). The result is that mothering has come to be taken for granted as a natural and necessary function for women. Hidden from view are powerful ideological beliefs that reinforce the importance of motherhood while at the same time keeping women in a position of economic disadvantage.

The historical-materialist analysis offers insight into the fact that women do the primary parenting while men do not. As this perspective would suggest, industrial capitalism created a separation of family life and work life (Zaretsky, 1976). As Engels (1967) pointed out in the 19th century, changes in the organization of production in society, which allowed for the accumulation of private property, had profound implications for the changes in the organization of reproduction. With the emergence of industrialized society, men were called to work in the factories, while women remained in the home in order to bear and rear children and provide the emotional rejuvenation that was required by husbands working in an alienating place. This resulted in a separation of gender, with women charged with maintaining the private, domestic domain while men presided over the public domain of the exchange economy.

Motherhood and domesticity were seen to be "women's natural destiny and responsibility" because of their reproductive capacity (Goldner, 1985, p. 35). As production moved out of the private sphere of the home, reproduction became paramount within that sphere. These spheres, as Goldner reminds us, are not only separate and different but also unequal. As a result, power at home for women stands in a dialectical relationship to power in the outside world for men.

In the same way that new forms of production in industrial capitalism reshaped reproduction, so too one would expect that current changes in the organization of production would have an impact on reproduction. Most significant in this regard has been the dramatic increase in the number of women in the paid labor force. This change has led some to argue for the "rise *and fall* of dual spheres" (Bose, 1987, p. 267; my emphasis). However, contrary to the expectation that full participation in the public sphere of paid work would result in a lessening of responsibility in the private sphere of family life, this change has not occurred in a significant way. Empirical evidence suggests that when women enter the paid labor force, men do not significantly increase their share of work in the private family sphere (Eichler, 1988; Geerken & Gove, 1983). Rather, there has been an increased demand for professional child care, which is consistent with Chodorow's idea that when biological mothers do not parent, other women, rather than men, virtually always take their place (1978, p. 3). Furthermore, heightened standards of child care as a result of the proliferation of literature in sociology, psychology, social work, and therapy have served to reinforce the importance of women's role as mother.

Men and women participate differently in the social world by virtue of their gendered experience of reproduction. Based on the Hegelian concept of dialectics, O'Brien (1979) argues that the process of human biological reproduction is a dialectically structured process involving the coming together of two opposites: the male and female seeds. This fundamental biological dialectic is at the root of a social structural dialectic between the private world of women and the public world of men. Reproduction separates men and women into the different spheres of work and home, public and private, or the economy and the family (Zaretsky, 1976).

When the reproduction of private and public spheres is historicized in this way, the implications for systemic understanding of family reproduction are profound. No longer can reproduction be seen simply as a set of insular physical and affective behaviors within the system that results in the introduction of a new member to the system. Rather, seen within its broader social, historical, and political context, reproduction sets into play power dynamics that profoundly shape the way men and women differentially experience life course events.

Family-systems theory has been criticized for its failure to account adequately for issues of gender and social-structural influence (Goldner, 1985). For example, "the feminist assertion that power in family life is socially constructed by gender simply offends the systemic aesthetic," insofar as systemic principles focus on circularity, balance, and interchangeability (Goldner, 1985, p. 33). So might it offend the systemic aesthetic to suggest that reproduction plays a major role in the way power is established along gender lines.

What is not well accounted for in the systemic view, because of the conceptual boundary that is placed around the family, is the role of sociohistorical influences. By focusing on the family as a separate, intimate, and isolated sphere, systems approaches may "tacitly endorse the nineteenth century fiction that the family is a domestic retreat from the market place economy" (Goldner, 1985, p. 43). This has important implications for how families are viewed in therapy. Most significant in this regard is the propensity to blame mothers. When the focus is on the private, intimate sphere, women are more likely to be blamed for the family dysfunction.

In keeping with the distinction between public and private spheres, the history of reproduction is essentially a history about women. Men, as essential partners for successful reproduction, are curiously absent in the literature. This absence would almost seem to reflect a set of historical beliefs that men played no part in procreation. As Corea (1985) points out, in Neolithic society a man knew nothing of his part in creation and made no connection between intercourse and the birth of the baby nine months later!

The underanalysis of men in the reproduction literature may be partially accounted for by their limited involvement in the reproductive process. Working within a Marxist framework, O'Brien (1979) talks about the "alienation of male seed in copulation," suggesting that men are separated materially from both nature and biological continuity (p. 107). Whereas a woman's experience of reproduction is a continuous process from intercourse, conception, pregnancy, and labor to postpartum nurturance, a man's experience is discontinuous. Once he ejaculates his sperm into the woman, he is marginalized from the process of reproduction. When the child is born, the attribution of paternity requires the intellectual act of conceptualizing a cause-and-effect relationship between intercourse and birth (Corea, 1985). In the same way that men are alienated from the products of their labor in the economic sphere, they are alienated from the product of their reproductive activity. Women, by contrast, establish a relationship to the child through childbirth that is similar to that which autonomous workers have to a product of their own making. Through this sense of reproductive unity, women experience themselves as a critical link between generations, while men's discontinuous experience of reproduction results in a lack of generational continuity (Corea, 1985).

Reproductive choice for men has historically focused on maintaining control over power, wealth, and inheritance. As Engels (1967) clearly identified, the emergence of surplus and wealth in agrarian and industrialized societies was the root of monogamous marriage whereby men insisted on fidelity from their wives in order to protect their accumulated wealth. This reflects men's response to "the alienation of their seed": to insist on fidelity through the act of appropriating children in order to preserve biological continuity, lineage, and inheritance. In this regard, men's control over reproduction has been defined in economic terms.

Men have typically been less involved in reproductive decision-making. For example, until the awareness of AIDS increased condom use for health protection, contraception was almost exclusively a female responsibility. Similarly, in instances of unplanned pregnancy, fathers are unlikely to play a major role in parenting the child or placing the child for adoption. For men, sexual behavior appears to be of much greater importance than reproductive behavior. This should come as no surprise, for as O'Brien (1981) reminds us, sexual intercourse represents "the male moment of inclusion in genetic continuity" (p. 75). Hence, for men who receive a diagnosis of azoospermia, the impact is often defined more in terms of a wounded sexual identity than in terms of blocked reproductive capacity. Likewise, female partners in infertile couples are more likely to cover the stigma of the man's infertility by telling others that they themselves have the medical problem, thereby keeping his sexual identity intact (Miall, 1986). The continued secrecy concerning the use of artificial insemination by donor might be interpreted as yet another mechanism for protecting men's identity from the public shame of infertility.

The idea that sexuality is more important than reproduction for men is also reflected in the continued prominence of impotence. A recent review of the psychological literature suggests that while the pejorative term *frigidity* has declined dramatically since 1970, the term *impotence* has increased significantly since that time (Elliott, 1985). As Tiefer (1987) has suggested, the persistence and increased use of this label provide significant insight into the social construction of male sexuality. This continued emphasis reflects the deep importance that is placed on strength, power, and vigor in male sexuality.

In the feminist literature, men's voice in reproductive decision-making has been silenced. McCormack (1989), for example, identifies reproduction as a feminist issue: "Reproductive freedom means the right of all women to manage their own fertility" (p. 89). As the feminist slogan "Control our bodies, control our lives" suggests, control over reproductive capacity is seen as central to the liberation of women. Here the paradox of political change becomes apparent: In order for women to make choice meaningful and authentic against the backdrop of a long tradition of patriarchal governance over reproduction, men must be excluded as partners in the decision-making. Yet attempts to overturn the control that male experts have had over reproduction may inadvertently reinforce the primacy of parenthood within the female role constellation.

Reproduction in a Technological Age

Within modern, industrialized, technological society, there is an assumption that reproduction can be controlled, either through the use of birth control to prevent unwanted conception or through the use of reproductive technologies to facilitate a wanted conception. The locus of this control varies considerably. It can range from the use of a relatively simple contraceptive device like the diaphragm that is controlled by the user to the complex medical procedures involved in in vitro fertilization that are controlled by the physician (Achilles, 1990).

This modern control of reproduction affects family experience in many ways. Most significantly, fertility is more likely to be taken for granted, because of the emphasis placed on control. Corresponding to the widespread use of contraceptives to avoid an unwanted pregnancy is the expectation that one will be able to achieve a pregnancy when desired. In contrast with the pretechnological era, when reproduction was allowed to follow its natural course, there is now a presumption that fertility can be turned on and off at will. Hence, loss of reproductive capacity results in a loss of control over one's life plans.

Similarly, people expect and are expected to have more control over the timing and number of children. As a result, being too early (teenage parenthood) or too late (delayed childbearing) or choosing to have none at all (voluntary childlessness) can violate social norms about appropriate reproductive behavior. In addition, family rules and traditions about the appropriate number of children are easily violated when control is assumed as part of the reproductive process. The choice of a couple to have only one child, for example, can be interpreted by the grandparents as a rejection of their values of the importance of a little brother or sister to play with.

Reproductive technologies also affect families by increasing the risk of "commodifying" children. The commercialization of reproduction not only makes the child a commodity, but the social parents become the consumers, and the donors become suppliers. As technologies increase the level of control over reproduction, the expectations for the final "product" are heightened accordingly. As expectations for the perfect baby are heightened, the tolerance for disabilities and other imperfections is lowered. Through the selection of embryos, donor sperm, or a surrogate mother, reproduction becomes yet another act of consumerism with implications for the definition of the parent/child subsystem. When the child misbehaves, for example, what parent could resist the temptation to blame it on the genes, especially when the genetic parent was a donor? The implications for the marital subsystem are also significant: How does the family formed through artificial insemination by donor manage the imbalance when one of the partners is a genetic parent and the other is not?

Although reproductive technologies have direct consequences for family experience, their impact is perhaps most salient for mothers. In the feminist literature, a central concern is the way in which reproductive technologies have further removed the process of reproduction from women themselves and put it into the hands of medical scientists (Spallone & Steinberg, 1987). The control of reproductive technologies by men has resulted in the further oppression of women (Morgan, 1989). Specifically, reproductive technologies are identified as "further examples of medical abuse, class-gender exploitation and the victimization of women" (McCormack, 1989, p. 83). Corea (1987) argues that women have throughout history been viewed as sexual and reproductive chattel and that the new reproductive technologies are simply another step in this long patriarchal tradition. Paralleling prostitution, technologies such as surrogate motherhood give rise to the same issues of men controlling women. Dworkin (1983) argues that the brothel model fits equally to the new reproductive technologies: "Women can sell reproductive capacities the same way old-time prostitutes sold sexual ones" (p. 182).

Individuality and integrity are compromised in the face of the objectification and commodification of the female body for either sexual pleasure or reproductive efficiency. With technologies, the traditional experience of whole, integrated, and natural fertility becomes fragmented into a set of body parts and procedures. When conception is mechanized as it is through reproductive technologies, the woman's body is controlled, monitored, and stimulated by machines and technicians. When women become the site for *harvesting* eggs or providing a uterine *environment*, the result is that women's reproductive processes become disembodied (Raymond, 1987). With these procedures, a woman becomes the "mother machine" who is exploited and objectified by the male "technodocs" (Corea, 1985).

There is a paradox of choice and control with regard to these technologies. On the one hand, reproductive technologies offer a promise of choice: sperm is chosen according to the characteristics of the donor, procedures can be followed that increase the chances of sex selection, or in vitro fertilization (IVF) can be chosen as a way of bypassing blocked fallopian tubes. On the other hand, this choice is available only through the assistance of the medical experts who control the technology that creates a dependency on these medical intermediaries. It is the experts who coordinate and monitor the procreative experience. Physicians, lab technicians, and hospital screening committees become the gatekeepers who make the experience accessible and possible. As Stanworth (1987) argues, reproductive choice is a double-edged sword:

> On the one hand, they have offered women a greater technical possibility to decide if, when and under what conditions to have children; on the other, the domination of so much reproductive technology by the medical profession and by the state has enabled others to have an even greater capacity to exert control over women's lives. (p. 16)

This dependency is consistent with a long tradition of medical interference in women's control of their own reproductive lives. In North America, medical practitioners have institutionalized contraception, conception, and childbirth as medical events and in so doing have subjugated these processes to medical authority (Sherwin, 1989). Increasingly sophisticated reproductive technologies result in further oppression of women as the "patriarchal control of women's reproduction takes on more radical and complete forms" (Morgan, 1989, p. 72).

Furthermore, in light of the high demand for reproductive technologies, a variety of screening procedures is in place designed to determine who is appropriate for or deserving of treatment. As Poff (1989) has pointed out, screening patients is essentially an "interventionist, discriminatory procedure which limits access on the grounds of marital status, sexual orientation and ability to pay" (p. 221). These are decisions about who is fit to be a mother. The fact that single, homosexual, disabled, or older women are typically excluded from the definition of "fit mother" is a strong indication of the power dimension that is operating within reproductive technologies (Corea, Hanmer, Klein, Raymond, & Rowland, 1987). In this regard, the choice afforded by the new reproductive technologies may be more illusory than real.

Not only does the dependence on the medical profession temper the degree of choice that is available to infertile couples, but the mere availability of reproductive technologies may foreclose the option of *not* using them (Achilles, 1990). Against the backdrop of cultural pronatalist pressures, an infertile couple will probably feel the pressure to pursue every possible avenue, including the appropriate reproductive technology, to achieve a pregnancy. Even if women control the decisions they make regarding reproductive technologies, McCormack (1989) questions whether this is freedom for women or whether it simply reinforces some of the oppressive dimensions of motherhood that are manifested in traditional families where there is a clear division of labor and an idealization of motherhood. Presumed fertility control exists within a cultural milieu that emphasizes the belief that motherhood is natural, desired, and instinctual and that for a woman to deny her maternal instincts through voluntary childlessness is selfish, peculiar, or disturbed (Stanworth, 1987). In fact, to bypass motherhood in our culture is to jeopardize self-realization, for motherhood is seen to represent the greatest achievement of a woman's life (Oakley, 1974).

The Changing Family

These ideas about reproduction in families can provide family scientists with a window on social change. They bring into focus several key developments that give insight into the ways families are changing. Specifically, changes in reproduction have implications for understanding change in family structure and ideology, they provide insight into the different relationships of men and women to reproduction, and finally, they raise new questions about what it means to control reproduction.

Considerable attention in the family-science literature has been focused on the increasing variability in family structure. Divorce, stepparenting, and voluntary childlessness are frequently identified as key manifestations of these changes in family structure. As this analysis would suggest, however, the changing landscape of reproduction also has implications for family structure. Most significantly, reproductive technologies have challenged the traditional conceptualization of parenthood as natural and holistic and have fragmented it into its genetic, uterine, and social parts. Although reproductive technologies directly affect only a relatively small portion of families, their implications for all families are enigmatic. In the same way that the presence of divorce affects all marriages, the reproductive technologies affect all families by redefining the very meaning of parenthood.

In spite of the fact that the kinds of families that can be created in a technological age are very different, there continues to be a strong gravitation to definitions based on traditional nuclear-family models. For example, in families that have used artificial insemination by donor (AID), there are three parents: the donor father, the social father, and the mother (both biological and social). The typical experience for the AID family is to act *as if* there were only two parents. The identity of the donor father is not only protected through medical confidentiality, but the social parents are usually quite adamant about preserving the secrecy of the child's biological heritage. The emphasis on secrecy and the presentation of themselves as if they were a normal family is a testimony to the continued power of traditional family models. Although the structure of the nuclear family is no longer the norm, its ideology continues to be a central organizing force for family experience.

The social organization of reproduction also points to the continued presence of a strong patriarchal tradition in family experience. As this analysis suggests, reproduction shapes gendered experience in an unequal fashion. Whether one focuses on differences in biological capacity or the increasing medicalization of reproduction, women continue to be more vulnerable in the reproductive experience. Where once reproductive technologies were championed as the solution to women's oppression (Firestone, 1970), they are now seen as another example of women being exploited and commodified at the hands of men.

Technology has afforded families a measure of control in many domains of family experience. For example, modern appliances allow one to accomplish household tasks more quickly than ever before, modern travel allows some families to maintain commuter marriages, and video equipment allows one to preserve family history more effectively than ever before. For some, reproduction holds the same promise: effective contraceptives allow one to have greater control over the number and timing of births, fetuses can be screened for genetic disorders in order to provide more choice in medical decision-making, and reproductive technologies like in vitro fertilization provide an alternate choice for having children in the face of infertility. Although these are real choices for families, they are also choices with a catch. The catch is that as the technologies become increasingly sophisticated, there is deepening dependence on experts for guidance in making these choices. In this regard, reproductive choice within families may be misconceived choice.

These reproductive themes have implications for family scientists on several levels. For family-science researchers, there must be an ongoing vigilance of two major biases associated with the analysis of reproduction: one that overlooks the differences in the gendered experience of reproduction, the other that assumes that the traditional, monolithic family form is normative and thereby fails to account for wide variations in family structure. Educators and policymakers need to be attentive to the implications of increasing genealogical bewilderment as the biological aspects of reproduction become more complex and technologically governed. Policies are required that are sensitive to issues of gender and power in reproductive decision-making as well as to the preservation of the rights of the children who result from the use of reproductive technologies. Family therapists are in a position either to reinforce or to challenge traditional family patterns. Changes in the nature of generational links and distinctions between public and private spheres are rooted in reproductive experience and warrant attention in the therapeutic process.

Chapter Summary

Discussion Questions

1. Pretense and secrecy continue to be central elements in the use of artificial insemination by donor. What are the advantages and disadvantages of moving toward a procedure that would require full disclosure of donor identity?
2. One of the most common social-psychological responses to infertility is an experience of loss of control. On the one hand, the body cannot be controlled in order to make a pregnancy happen; and on the other hand, there is a loss of control over one's own developmental process, insofar as parenthood is being thwarted in spite of one's best efforts. Identify the roots of the expectation that reproduction can be controlled, and discuss the consequences for coming to terms with the loss of reproductive capacity.
3. O'Brien has argued that men, by virtue of their biological characteristics, are naturally "alienated" from the experience of reproduction. Do

you agree with this statement? What are the implications of this premise for the way that men and women negotiate and renegotiate parenthood roles?

Additional Resources

Lifton, B. J. (1988). Brave new baby in the brave new world. In E. H. Baruch, A. F. Adamo, Jr., & J. Seager (Eds.), *Embryos, ethics, and women's rights: Exploring the new reproductive technologies* (pp. 149–154). New York: Harrington Park Press.

Brodribb, S. (1989). Delivering babies: Contracts and contradictions. In C. Overall (Ed.), *The future of human reproduction* (pp. 139–158). Toronto: Women's Press.

Corea, G. (1985). *The mother machine: Reproductive technologies from artificial insemination to artificial wombs.* New York: Harper & Row.

References

Achilles, R. (1990). Desperately seeking babies: New technologies of hope and despair. In K. Arnup, A. Levesque, and R. R. Pierson (Eds.), *Delivering motherhood: Maternal ideologies and practices in the 19th and 20th centuries* (pp. 284–312). London: Routledge & Kegan Paul.

Beutler, I. F., Burr, W. R., Bahr, K. S., & Herrin, D. A. (1989). The family realm: Theoretical contributions for understanding its uniqueness. *Journal of Marriage and the Family, 51*, 805–816.

Bose, C. E. (1987). Dual spheres. In M. M. Feree & B. B. Hess (Eds.), *Analyzing gender: A Handbook of social science research* (pp. 267–285). Newbury Park, CA: Sage.

Brodribb, S. (1989). Delivering babies: Contracts and contradictions. In C. Overall (Ed.), *The future of human reproduction* (pp. 139–158). Toronto: Women's Press.

Chodorow, N. (1978). *The reproduction of mothering: Psychoanalysis and the sociology of gender.* Berkeley: University of California Press.

Clark, L. M. G., & Lange, L. (1979). Introduction. In L. M. G. Clark & L. Lange (Eds.), *The sexism of social and political theory: Women and reproduction from Plato to Nietzsche* (pp. vii–xvii). Toronto: University of Toronto Press.

Corea, G. (1985). *The mother machine: Reproductive technologies from artificial insemination to artificial wombs*. New York: Harper & Row.

Corea, G. (1987). The reproductive brothel. In G. Corea et al. (Eds.), *Man-made women* (pp. 38–51). Bloomington: Indiana University Press.

Corea, G., Hanmer, J., Klein, R. D., Raymond, J. G., & Rowland, R. (1987). Prologue. In P. Spallone & D. L. Steinberg (Eds.), *Made to order: The myth of reproductive and genetic progress* (pp. 1–12). Oxford, England: Pergamon Press.

Daly, K. J. (1988). Reshaped parenthood identity: The transition to adoptive parenthood. *Journal of Contemporary Ethnography, 17*, 40–66.

Daly, K. J. (1989a). Anger among prospective adoptive parents: Structural determinants and management strategies. *Clinical Sociology Review, 7*, 80–96.

Daly, K. J. (1989b). Preparation needs of infertile couples who seek to adopt. *Canadian Journal of Community Mental Health, 8*, 111–123.

Daly, K. J. (1990). Infertility resolution and adoption readiness. *Families in Society: The Journal of Contemporary Human Services, 71*, 483–492.

Dickinson, J., & Russell, B. (1986). Introduction: The structure of reproduction in capitalist society. In J. Dickinson & B. Russell (Eds.), *Family, economy and state: The social reproduction process under capitalism* (pp. 1–22). Toronto: Garamond Press.

Dworkin, A. (1983). *Right-wing women*. New York: Perigee Books.

Edwards, J. N. (1991). New conceptions: Biosocial innovations and the family. *Journal of Marriage and the Family, 53*, 349–360.

Eichler, M. (1988). *Families in Canada today: Recent changes and their policy consequences* (2nd ed.). Toronto: Gage.

Elliott, M. L. (1985). The use of "impotence" and "frigidity": Why has "impotence" survived? *Journal of Sex and Marital Therapy, 11*, 51–56.

Engels, F. (1967). *The origin of the family, private property and the state*. New York: International Publishers.

Firestone, S. (1970). *The dialectic of sex: The case for feminist revolution*. New York: Morrow.

Geerken, M., & Gove, W. R. (1983). *At home and at work: The family's allocation of labor*. Newbury Park, CA: Sage.

Glaser, B., & Strauss, A. (1965). *Awareness of dying*. Chicago: Aldine-Atherton.

Goldner, V. (1985). Feminism and family therapy. *Family Process, 24*, 31–47.

Handwerker, W. P. (1990) *Births and power: Social change and the politics of reproduction*. Boulder, CO: Westview Press.

Hansen, D. A., & Hill, R. (1964). Families under stress. In H. T. Christensen (Ed.), *Handbook of marriage and the family*. Chicago: Rand McNally.

Kirk, D. (1964). *Shared fate*. New York: Free Press.

Lifton, B. J. (1988). Brave new baby in the brave new world. In E. H. Baruch, A. F. Adamo, Jr., & J. Seager (Eds.), *Embryos, ethics, and women's rights: Exploring the new reproductive technologies* (pp. 149–154). New York: Harrington Park Press.

McCormack, T. (1989). When is biology destiny? In C. Overall (Ed.), *The future of human reproduction* (pp. 80–94). Toronto: Women's Press.

Miall, C. (1986). The stigma of involuntary childlessness. *Social Problems, 33*, 268–282.

Mills, C. W. (1959). *The sociological imagination*. London: Oxford University Press.

Morgan, K. P. (1989). Of woman born? How old fashioned!: New reproductive technologies and women's oppression. In C. Overall (Ed.), *The future of human reproduction* (pp. 60–79). Toronto: Women's Press.

Oakley, A. (1974). *Housewife*. London: Penguin.

O'Brien, M. (1979). Reproducing Marxist man. In L. M. G. Clark & L. Lange (Eds.) *The sexism of social and political theory: Women and reproduction from Plato to Nietzsche* (pp. 99–116). Toronto: University of Toronto Press.

O'Brien, M. (1981). *The politics of reproduction*. Boston: Routledge & Kegan Paul.

Poff, D. C. (1989). Reproductive technology and social policy in Canada. In C. Overall (Ed.), *The future of human reproduction* (pp. 216–225). Toronto: Women's Press.

Raymond, J. G. (1987). Fetalists and feminists: They are not the same. In P. Spallone and D. L. Steinberg (Eds.), *Made to order: The myth of reproductive and genetic progress* (pp. 58–66). Oxford, England: Pergamon Press.

Robertson, A. F. (1991). *Beyond the family: The social organization of human reproduction*. Oxford, England: Polity Press.

Rose, H. (1987). Victorian values in the test-tube: The politics of reproductive science and technology. In M. Stanworth (Ed.), *Reproductive technologies: Gender, motherhood and medicine* (pp. 151–173). Cambridge, England: Polity Press.

Rossi, A. (1977). Biosocial aspects of parenting. *Daedelus, 106*, 1–32.

Rothman, B. K. (1987). Reproduction. In M. M. Feree & B. B. Hess (Eds.), *Analyzing gender: A handbook of social science research* (pp. 154–170). Newbury Park, CA: Sage.

Sherwin, S. (1989). Feminist ethics and new reproductive technologies. In C. Overall (Ed.), *The future of human reproduction* (pp. 259–272). Toronto: Women's Press.

Spallone, P., & Steinberg, D. L. (1987). Introduction. In P. Spallone and D. L. Steinberg (Eds.), *Made to order: The myth of reproductive and genetic progress* (pp. 13–17). Oxford, England: Pergamon Press.

Stanworth, M. (1987). Reproductive technologies and the deconstruction of motherhood. In M. Stanworth (Ed.), *Reproductive technologies: Gender, motherhood and medicine* (pp. 10–35). Cambridge, England: Polity Press.

Tiefer, L. (1987). In pursuit of the perfect penis: The medicalization of male sexuality. In M. S. Kimmel (Ed.), *Changing men: New directions in research on men and masculinity* (pp. 165–184). Newbury Park, CA: Sage.

Vinovskis, M. A. (1988). *An "epidemic" of adolescent pregnancy?* New York: Oxford University Press.

Zaretsky, E. (1976). *Capitalism, the family and personal life.* New York: Harper & Row.

Families and Health Crises

Linda Matocha
University of Delaware

Families are responsible for the health of their members from birth to death. Parents take their children to a health-care provider when they become ill or to maintain their health. They ensure that their children's immunizations are kept up to date, they take them to dentists, and they take them for checkups to make sure that they stay healthy and are growing at an acceptable rate. They teach their children about healthy habits and about what things can harm them. When children become teenagers, parents usually allow them to assume some responsibility for their own health. Adolescents begin to go to their health-care providers alone. They may go to school clinics without their parents' knowledge. They begin to feel that they can make a difference in their future as a healthy person. Many teenagers may feel that they are invincible and may try to test their health boundaries by smoking, drinking, experimenting with sex, and putting themselves at risk by driving fast and participating in other risky pastimes.

Young adults usually begin to realize that they are not invincible, and they try to prepare for a healthy future by eating nutritious foods and exercising regularly. Many young adults quit smoking and limit their drinking and put limits on taking unnecessary risks. They begin to see the illnesses of their parents as part of their future, and they want to make their future different. Middle-aged adults realize that their bodies are changing as health problems increase. Their lives are very busy, and they tend to deny that those problems exist. They frequently put off health care until the illness incapacitates them. As these illnesses and health problems increase, adults at midlife search for alternatives that can promote their health. They try new diets, they begin to exercise again, and they begin to follow recommended health guidelines such as yearly checkups.

Older adults continue to visit their health-care providers, and they alter their lifestyles to further reduce their risk of injury. As their health deteriorates, their children begin to assist them in monitoring their pursuit of health and long life. The roles change from the parents being the guardians of the family's health to the children assuming that important role.

Impact of Illness on the Family

Accidents and acute illnesses occur in most families. Family members usually unite and help one another when this occurs. For a short time most families can adapt to the necessary changes. Roles are altered, and relationships temporarily change. The expense of the illness may mandate that resources be reallocated. Coping strategies are utilized and improved, and family goals change to include the need for giving care. Eventually, most families will be able to identify a time when the disorganization in their lives will be over. Caregivers learn to recognize their competence and proficiency in providing care. New coping strategies are learned, and families recognize who can be regarded as successful caregivers in a crisis.

The impact of illness on families and their members is characterized by four variables: (1) the diagnosis and its meaning to family members, (2) the relationship of the person who is ill with each other family member, (3) the symptoms exhibited by the patient, and (4) the passage of time. Change in each of these variables results in change in the impact of the illness on each family member.

Many families rally around the ill person and bring food and emotional comfort. Roles within the family may be altered as a specific member of the family either takes on or is assigned the task of providing direct care for the ill member. For example, if the mother takes on the task of caring for a sick or injured child, the father frequently takes on many of her family duties, such as cooking for the other children, transporting them to day care, and doing laundry and other housework.

Since it is not possible for some family members to provide care over time, one person usually assumes the role of primary caregiver. This special person is recognized as being able to meet the needs of the ill person. The family caregiver is usually the person who puts others' needs first, has cared for an ill person in the past, and seems to have the most time and energy.

Diagnosis and Its Meaning to Family Members

The diagnosis of disease or disability affects families in several ways. If the diagnosis is socially stigmatizing, families and their caregivers may choose to keep it from friends and relatives. For example, when the diagnosis involves a sexually transmitted disease, mental illness, or a drug-borne disease, the patient, caregivers, and other family members often want to keep it secret. Fearing that, if the true diagnosis is made known, relatives and friends will turn away from them, families may substitute a false diagnosis that is more "socially acceptable," like leukemia, cancer, or respiratory infection. When families believe that the diagnosis needs to be hidden, problems arise. Caregivers need to constantly be on guard that they do not give "clues" to others that would give away the true diagnosis. The secret must be kept at all times. Even after the death the secret must be kept. Family members cannot grieve openly with others who would give them support.

Another effect of diagnosis is the support accessible to families and their caregivers due to available funding. At different times, certain diseases are indicators of resources that can be drawn upon to facilitate healing.

Those supports may be research, agencies that can supply treatments, support groups, and even financial assistance. Cancer, heart problems, respiratory problems, Alzheimer's disease, and HIV infection seem to have those supports available at this time. Families can use these support groups to obtain knowledge about funding, they can use them to learn about the disease and treatments, and they can learn about the local health-care system and how to interact with the health-care professionals so that care their needs can be met.

The Patient/Caregiver Relationship

It is the bond of affection and long-term relationship that usually determines who in the family will be primary caregiver during an illness or recovery from an accident. Most often, spouses care for spouses, and daughters care for mothers and fathers. Traditionally, women have generally been caregivers (Brody, 1974; Shanus, 1979; Steinmetz, 1988). Parsons and Bales (1955), Block (1973), and Shields (1987) document that it is women who exhibit a caring, compassionate, and empathetic attitude; therefore, they are more capable of providing care. Gilligan (1977, 1982) asserts that it is not their gender that promotes caregiving in women but, rather, that they are socialized into the role of caregiver as children and adolescents. Eisenberg, Fabes, and Shea (1989) researched this attribute and concluded that, indeed, it is not until boys and girls are 12 years old that there are differences between them in caregiving abilities.

The benefits of a close relationship between the caregiver and the ill family member are many. Each knows what the other likes and dislikes. They tend to know how and when to communicate with each other. The caregiver knows how much power and control to leave in the hands of the person who is ill and when it may be necessary to assume some of that power. However, a negative effect of a close relationship is that the caregiving is generally more stressful. Marjorie Cantor's (1983) study of support utilized by 111 older Americans in New York City asserts that stress in the caregiving role increases the closer the bond is between the caregiver and the ill person. That same closeness, which facilitates the choosing of the caregiver, results in an increased desire to do the best possible job of caregiving.

Often, the caregiver believes that no one else can provide the quality care needed by the loved one. This places the perceived burden for all care on the family caregiver: professionals just "cannot give the love and attention to my family member that I can." This is heard over and over.

The Patient's Symptoms

The characteristics and number of symptoms of the patient affect the family and the caregiver. It is obvious that those symptoms that require a great deal of time and physical energy deplete the physical energy of the caregiver. There is a significant relationship between the level of disability of the family member and the physical strain on caregivers (Cantor, 1983). The more disabled the adult, the more the physical health of the caregiver declines. Providing activities of daily living such as bathing, turning, lifting, transfer in and out of wheelchairs and beds, feeding, and providing elimination facilities all require enormous expenditures of physical energy, energy that must be used day in and day out, every day of the week. Stress levels eventually increase, and reservoirs of energy become depleted.

Symptoms that produce additional stress and depletion of energy are those that result from mental impairment and emotional impairment of the ill family member (Deimling & Bass, 1986; Pearson, Verma, & Nellett, 1988; Yaffe, 1988; Zarit, Todd, & Zarit, 1986). The emotional swings and varying elements of mental impairments of a loved one needing care contribute to caregiver distress and physical damage. After time, that distress and damage become a burden to the caregiver and, ultimately, to the family.

The Passage of Time

Caregiving for a family member suffering from a chronic illness or a lifetime disability is very different from caring for a family member with an acute, time-limited illness. Chronic illnesses account for 75% of the deaths in the United States and for a large portion of related disabilities (Centers for Disease Control, 1989). Heart disease, cancer, stroke, diabetes, liver disease, and diseases of the lung are the six major areas of chronic diseases. Families who have members with chronic illnesses have to assume responsibilities for caring over time.

The issue of extended time affects family members in many ways. If one spouse becomes ill, the shared support and companionship are lost, and the healthy spouse shoulders the responsibility of maintaining the physical and emotional support of the family. Relationships within the family are strained. Family functioning is a struggle. Any small change in daily living further strains family life, even when those changes are usually considered positive. Heartache, misery, and torment seem to become components of the family's existence. Families learn to exist day to day. Some days are good, some days are bad. Life becomes a roller coaster of ups and downs. The dreamed-about future becomes an uncertainty.

Who Are the Family Caregivers?

Family caregivers provide not only physical support but also reassurance and unlimited devotion to loved ones who are ill. Perhaps it is the love offered freely and without hesitation that really makes the difference in the care given by family members and that provided by professional caregivers. The love and dedication offered by family members allow the interventions of the treatment team to succeed and heal.

Few studies have profiled the characteristics of family caregivers; however, caregivers seem to share certain attributes. They generally have lower education levels than noncaregivers (Haley, Levine, Brown, Berry, & Hughes, 1987). Similarly, their income levels are significantly lower than those of noncaregivers (Haley et al., 1987).

Families also select caregivers on the basis of their physical and psychological health. They do not expect potential caregivers who are in poor physical health to provide primary care (Haley et al., 1987). And they select caregivers who have the necessary psychological strength (Haley et al., 1987).

The few available studies about characteristics of caregivers have examined people caring for elderly family members and those with Alzheimer's disease, cancer, and mental illness. The first characteristic of a caregiver is the ability to put the needs of others over one's personal needs (Miller & Eisdorfer, 1989). One caregiver described this orientation by the analogy of the stranger:

> It's like walking down the sidewalk, and there is someone lying on the sidewalk. There are three kinds of people in this world. The first stranger would walk on by. They wouldn't even notice that there was someone lying there. They are so wrapped up in their own lives that they are not even tuned in to the fact that there are others out there who need our help. There is a second stranger who comes along, and that person sees the person lying there. He may even stop and think for a minute about maybe helping the person, but after weighing the option, he will decide that he can't take the chance on helping the person. Maybe it would take too much time; maybe it might be dangerous in some way. That person would end up walking by as well. Then there is that third stranger who would not only see the person, but who would stop and help the person without even thinking of the possible harm it might do to him. Those are the caregivers in this world. They stop because it is the right thing to do; they just love people in general and want to help others who are in trouble. (Matocha, 1989, p. 27)

It is this "other" orientation that overwhelmingly signifies who is, and who is not, successful at providing care for family members.

Researchers cite the relationship to the ill person as the next characteristic. Most often spouses and daughters assume caregiving responsibility, followed by daughters-in-law, sons, other female relatives, and finally nonrelatives (Cantor, 1983; Kiecolt-Glaser et al., 1987; Soldo & Myllyluoma, 1983). Do nonrelatives give care in a familial way? Definitely, yes. With the advent of HIV infections there have been many instances of individuals providing care to loved ones who are not related legally or by blood. In many cases the person infected by the virus loses the support that many families provide in times of illness. Can those who do not have the support of family members still receive familial love and nurturance from someone who is not a blood or legal relation? Research confirms that this is possible (Matocha, 1989). For example, homosexual couples consider themselves a family, and they define

themselves as married in a spiritual and familial sense. In most states in the United States this relationship is not recognized as legally binding, and it is abhorred by many heterosexuals. In fact, however, the support received within the homosexual relationship is powerful and effective.

Are there other instances when nonrelatives assume a caregiving role? Again, yes. Health professionals need to be aware of this fact and allow that person or persons the opportunity to give care. It may be a lover or a friend. It may be a person who is a member of a volunteer organization and who, throughout the disease process, becomes very close to the ill person. Those people, because of the caring offered to the ill or injured, are considered family. The following example will illustrate such a situation:

> A young man of 23 becomes infected with HIV and is diagnosed with AIDS. He attempts to return to his mother's home in order to obtain physical, economic, and emotional support. He lives with her for two months. During that time she tries to provide what he needs but is unsuccessful. She treats him like a child, her child from years ago. He refuses to be that child again, but she does not understand this. She forces him to give up his job and stay in bed as much as possible. He rebels and tries to tell her to listen to him and to let him control his life. She cannot. He decides she is unable to love him as he is or provide him with the caring that is necessary for him to stay as well as possible for as long as possible. He moves out. He no longer has his job and is unable to support himself. He contacts the local AIDS support group and is assigned a support volunteer. That volunteer welcomes him into his home and begins to provide the emotional and physical support that he needs. Time passes, and his physical health improves. He moves out and becomes independent again. That healing promoted his emotional stability and allowed him to eventually return to work and support himself. The support volunteer continues to be with him when he needs someone and yet still allows the young man to control his life. The young man eventually becomes ill and is hospitalized. The support volunteer is there for him. He provides daily care and acts as an advocate when necessary. The young man begins to love the support volunteer as he would a brother, and the support volunteer loves the young

man. The two acknowledge the relationship, and many of the young man's friends also come to realize that this is a special relationship. The young man recovers once again, but the relationship continues to flourish. The young man gives legal responsibility to the support volunteer. Ultimately, the young man's immune system fails, and he is hospitalized for the final days of his life. The two remain close and caring. Death occurs, but the brotherly love does not diminish. The support volunteer grieves the death and loss of a future together just as a family member would. The caring results in a relationship that can only be described as familial.

This case illustrates not only that caregiving is a familial task but also that persons who participate are often considered family.

Effects of Providing Care on Family Caregivers

Caring has multiple effects on the caregiver, and these effects change over time. There are a variety of types of effects that impact the health process in families. The primary types are physical, psychological, social, economic, and spiritual. These effects are woven together and form a systemic response to the target presenting problem. But in reality, one cannot be viewed without considering all. When a child becomes ill, for example, and a mother assumes the primary caregiving role, the father recognizes a change in their relationship. She is tired and involved with the ill child; she has no time to prepare meals or to demonstrate her love to him. If a spouse becomes ill and the other spouse assumes the caregiving role, time spent on caregiving may be time that would normally have been spent with the children. The children will frequently be asked to assume roles and responsibilities that are usually not theirs. Families have the ability to adjust to the initial changes, but as the illness changes and responsibilities change, families must respond by continually readjusting and modifying roles and relationships.

Physical Effects

The physical effects of caring for an ill family member change over time (Matocha, 1992). These effects

may include changes in weight, sleep patterns, exercise patterns, and the home environment. For example, parents of chronically ill mentally retarded adults reported chronic fatigue (Lefley, 1987; Thobaben, 1988). Haley et al. (1987), using questionnaires and matched groups of 44 caregivers and 44 noncaregivers, report a significant decrease in the overall health of the caregivers of relatives with senile dementia. Snyder and Keefe (1985) report that 70% of their 117 responding caregivers of disabled adults experienced a negative effect on their physical health; in particular, they reported losses of exercise and sexual activities. Silliman, Fletcher, Earp, and Wagner's (1986) study of caregivers of elderly stroke patients found a 24% deterioration in general health of the caregivers; 40% scored in the "ill" range on a self-report questionnaire. Caregivers for cancer patients (Stetz, 1987) and the frail elderly (Horowitz, 1985; Snyder & Keefe, 1985) reported lost personal time from providing direct care and from the frequent need for their physical presence in doing other caregiving tasks. Direct care includes giving medications, assisting with activities of daily living (bathing, brushing teeth, turning, feeding, and dressing), and providing treatments ordered by the physician (such as range-of-motion exercises). Errands, transportation, health-care visits, daily telephone calls, and assisting in housekeeping chores keep caregivers physically involved, decreasing their time to attend to their own physical needs.

Family caregivers may also experience sleep deprivation, weight changes, and nausea and vomiting (Fischl et al., 1987; Searle, 1987). During the first six weeks, just after diagnosis, the physical demands frequently result in the deterioration of health for each caregiver, as direct caregiving is initiated and stress increases. If the ill family member has a period of time when health is improved and maintained, this second phase is usually signaled by a return to a pre-illness state for caregivers as direct caregiving demands decrease. During the third phase, the time when the health of the ill family member again deteriorates and the direct caregiving activities increase, the caregiver's health again declines. A gradual return of the caregiver's physical health occurs after the illness subsides or the ill person dies. It is interesting that some caregivers report a subsequent *increase* in the level of their health resulting from an increased awareness of the positive effects of good nutrition, sleep patterns, and exercise habits on family members during illness. Others report that when there have been extensive caregiving activities, there can be a decrease in the immune response of caregivers that lasts for many years beyond the actual caregiving. A study of 34 family caregivers of Alzheimer's patients and 34 comparison subjects, using self-report data, immunologic assays, and nutritional assays, reported a decrease in cellular immunity against common infections (Kiecolt-Glaser et al., 1987). The long-term effects of caring for an ill family member require further study.

Psychological Effects

The psychological effects of caregiving change over time as well. Initially, caregivers experience increased stress from attempting to cope with the diagnosis. Studies of caregiving for elderly demented adults, adults dying with cancer, and the frail elderly indicate that the psychological responses are more pervasive than physical or economic responses (Cantor, 1983; George & Gwyther, 1986; Holing, 1986; Horowitz, 1985). Family caregivers constantly live with the fear of a decline in health, and possible death, of a loved one. Horowitz (1985) says that caregivers of the frail elderly experience fear for the ill family member's safety and health even if death is not an expectation. She notes in her commentary that providing care can also produce a *positive* psychological effect: caregivers gain self-respect from the knowledge that they are successfully providing care for a loved one in need. There are additional positive aspects of giving care. Silliman et al. (1986) studied 89 caregivers of elderly stroke patients and report that 84% had increased self-esteem. Emily Holing (1986) studied 14 caregivers' perception of the death of a loved one. The results of the descriptive statistics and content analysis indicate that emotional stress is related to watching the family member die, but joy results from an increased feeling of drawing closer to that family member.

During long-term illnesses, changes in roles within the family may result in feelings of anger and depression from emotional exhaustion or stress. In her commentary recommending interventions for de-

pressed caregivers, Thobaben (1988) acknowledges that caregivers experience resentment and anger when caring for stroke patients. Kriesel (1987) notes a similar response of anger in caregivers of persons with malignancies. Anger occurs as caregivers recognize that their lifestyle will have to change. Changes in lifestyle continue as patients go through periods of remission and exacerbation. Thobaben's (1988) commentary also notes that caregivers experience guilt when they feel anger toward the ill family member.

Caregivers need knowledge to assist them in providing quality care. In their commentary, Hirst and Metcalf (1986) maintain that caregivers of institutionalized demented patients need knowledge about the disease, how it affects patients, the expected prognosis, the expected treatments and their effects, and the availability of resources.

The results of studies on the effects of planning seem to be contradictory. Horowitz (1985) indicates that planning is not considered valuable in reducing the stress of caregivers of the frail elderly. However, Rakowski and Clark's (1985) study of 90 pairs of geriatric caregivers found that those with a perspective of planning tended to experience a decrease in personal life stress.

Depression is another effect, especially among caregivers of Alzheimer's patients. Two research studies found that depression occurred when caregivers felt overwhelmed by the disease and relatives' responses to the disease (Kiecolt-Glaser et al., 1987; Light & Lebowitz, 1988). Thobaben (1988) reports that the incidence of depression in care providers 65 years of age and older ranged from 20% to 50%.

Frierson, Lippmann, and Johnson (1987) provide illustrative vignettes selected from case studies of 50 relatives of 15 AIDS patients. The authors provided psychiatric counseling for those caregivers over four and a half years. AIDS caregivers experienced helplessness, loss of control, and powerlessness as they watched their family members slowly dying. They reported psychological stress when they had to acknowledge the lifestyle of the person with AIDS. The authors recommend the use of specific intervention strategies in counseling caregivers: (1) Counselors should provide information concerning the epidemiology of AIDS, precautions needed during care, and expected treatment protocols.

(2) They should use a nonjudgmental approach when advising clients who practice alternative lifestyles. (3) Finally, counselors should facilitate grief work.

Caregivers also experience grief and mourning as they deal with terminal illnesses. Stress increases as caregivers grieve for the lost promise of the future of the ill family member (Lefley, 1987; Macklin, 1988). Macklin (1988) explains that stress ensues when caregivers notice dying persons with AIDS begin to distance themselves from caregivers in order to ease their own sense of impending loss. She also notes that anticipatory grief is possible in terminal cases when caregivers begin the grief process before the person with AIDS dies. In another commentary, Ross-Alaolmoiki (1985) writes that anticipatory grief when a child is dying may either interfere with or sharpen a caregiver's decision-making skills. The change over time in the caregiver's psychological response reflects the change in the patient's state of health. Caregivers in the first phase experience a decline in psychological well-being. They feel they are alone in attempting to cope with the illness. They often do not know any other caregiver who is in a similar situation. During the second phase, of reduced severity of illness, their psychological well-being deteriorates even more as they have more time to think about the future demands of caring for the family member, the patient's potential death, and life without the person whom they love. Psychological well-being continues to deteriorate during the third phase as the family member becomes sicker and the psychological stress from direct caregiving, making decisions, dealing with health-care professionals, and anticipatory grieving increases. Many caregivers' psychological well-being improves during the fourth phase and return to a pre-illness level, and they have learned effective coping mechanisms that can be used in similar situations. Some caregivers may experience a lower level of psychological well-being, often attributed to an inability to grieve over the losses associated with the illness or death of the loved one.

Sociological Effects

There are sociological effects on family members caring for those with acute and chronic illnesses. Miller (1983) indicates that caring for those with chronic illnesses often prevents caregivers from participating in family leisure activities and other special activities. Direct care dramatically decreases the time available for socializing with others. This is compounded by the increased use of technology in the home, which results in more direct caregiving by the family. Peterson's (1985) study of 19 female caregivers of home hemodialysis patients reveals that 61.1% of the respondents reported the increase in time needed for direct care reduced the time available for socializing.

Caregivers also report that they are often unable to relate socially to family members in their traditional manner because of mood changes and fatigue. Haley et al.'s (1987) study examined matched groups of caregivers of senile dementia patients with controls. The decrease in the social activities with family and friends was statistically significant. The authors further report little change in the *number* of social contacts with family and friends; rather the decrease was in the *frequency* of contact. Observations made by Lefley (1987) are similar; she notes that the constant need for the physical presence of the caregiver and the time needed to do things for the ill person encroach on the time available for social contact and social relationships. For instance, caregivers of stroke patients describe a 40% to 45% decrease in social contacts such as going to church. Family members who care for dying children report reduced time to interact with family and friends (Ross-Alaolmoiki, 1985).

Family and friends usually provide social support when they are told of the diagnosis. Those parents who continue social contact with family and friends after learning that their child is dying receive support and increase their ability to cope with the diagnosis (Ross-Alaolmoiki, 1985). Zarit, Reever, and Bach-Peterson (1980) find that the caregiving burden decreases when family and friends visit regularly with caregivers.

Social distancing of family members from the ill member may occur. The degeneration of the relationship between caregiver and patient is cited by Bader (1985) in her discussion on caring for chronically ill patients. Kriesel (1987) reports that secrets are kept by both caregivers and cancer patients. Caregivers attempt to protect the ill person from painful knowledge, while the ill person attempts to protect the caregiver from similar information. This protection seems to hinder communication, and the caregiver and the ill family member are distanced from each another.

Sociological effects on caregivers change over time, but during the newly diagnosed phase they are generally unfavorable. Social isolation occurs from friends and family members distancing themselves from the illness and from the caregiver spending increased time at the bedside of the patient. Relationships improve during the second phase as the ill person gets better and more time is available for affiliation with others. New friendships are made with others experiencing the same problems; old friendships are strengthened when continued support is demonstrated, and some shallow friendships are lost when friends remove themselves from the circle of support. During the third phase, the social contacts and relationships again diminish as the demands of direct caregiving control lives and no time is available. Caregivers during the fourth phase generally acknowledge a return to the pre-illness level of socializing. An improvement in social effects occurs whenever the caregiver acknowledges the diagnosis and shares that diagnosis with family and friends. Honesty in relationships ensues as caregivers develop genuine caring relationships with others.

The social discrimination experienced by AIDS patients frequently touches family caregivers (Macklin, 1989; Tibler, Walker, & Rolland, 1989). Social isolation occurs as caregivers become aware of this discrimination. Cleveland, Walters, Skeen, and Robinson (1988) studied 763 parents of homosexuals. Through open-ended questions and questionnaires they found that 3% of the parents would not maintain contact with a child who contracted AIDS. Forty-seven percent reported that they would not tell anyone outside the family of the diagnosis, and 16% said they would not inform other family members. Family caregivers who try to keep the diagnosis of AIDS a secret, from fear of becoming social outcasts, find it more and more difficult to keep the secret as time passes (Tibler et al., 1989). Furstenberg and Olson (1984) say AIDS patients do not tell family members of their diagnosis for fear that they will cause the family pain and for fear that they will be socially ostracized by the family. When families and AIDS patients keep the secret of the diagnosis, the result may be social isolation.

Economic Effects

Economic effects on families can be minimal or catastrophic. Those who care for a family member with access to adequate medical insurance or who do not experience significant spending are not disadvantaged during the first phase. However, those families that do not have adequate insurance or finances can be devastated by the expenses. During the second phase, the spending for illness-related items decreases, and caregivers report an increase in responsible spending as they realize the need to plan for adequate resources for the future. The first bout with stress related to the depletion of finances teaches families how to economize. The family may also become aware of various agencies that can assist them with future medical expenses. Economic planning and protection occur as caregivers and other family members make wills and decide on future disposal of belongings.

The third phase reflects a further decrease in income as the ill family member is no longer able to work or the caregiver must spend time away from an income-producing job because of the need to spend more time giving care (Horowitz, 1985; Soldo & Myllyluoma, 1983). Many women, recognized as caregivers for the elderly, remain out of the employment market just when their families need them to become employed (Bader, 1985). Muurinen (1986) discusses results of 1445 primary caregivers in a national hospice study. Sixty percent of the caregivers reported income losses due to time lost from work providing care. To maintain solvency, some spouses had to divorce just so the well spouse would have financial support if the ill person died. The effects of economic losses may continue long after the illness abates or the ill person dies. If funeral plans were made and prepaid during earlier phases, families experienced less of an impact on financial resources. Some families receive money from the estate, but that improvement in economy is generally minimal and unusual.

Spiritual Effects

The individuals potential for spirituality (Veninga, 1985) is not necessarily grounded in a religion, but it is frequently expressed as religious beliefs (Soeken & Carson, 1987). Studies characterize spirituality as grace, heroism, love, strength, dignity, energy, creativity, faith, and a hope that cannot be denied (Brommel, 1986; Gallagher, 1987; Norwood, 1987; Peabody, 1986). Modern medicine has begun to recognize the importance of studying the effects of spirituality on healing (Hiatt, 1986). Caregivers of family members with AIDS may experience a loss of hope when their grief becomes too much to bear (Tibler et al., 1989). Still others maintain hope and instill hope in others. Alcoholics Anonymous uses spirituality in its 12-step recovery process (Buxton, Smith, & Seymour, 1987). Individuals learn to draw from their inner strength to overcome alcoholism and other drug dependencies (Prezioso, 1987). Some caregivers experience a loss of life's inner quality. They have difficulty maintaining hope when they exist in a borderline state between life and death of a loved one.

A research study of 240 Alzheimer's patients supports the premise that a significant number of caregivers remain strong in their belief in a God and consider the illness and their needed care as a rejuvenation of faith (Pratt, Schmall, Wright, & Cleland, 1985). The literature also suggests that family caregivers need to seek spiritual help to maintain their strength and hope. Tibler et al. (1989) say that an important resource for family caregivers is the recognition that their strengths and the support they provide make a difference in life and death. This recognition of strength assists caregivers in renewing their own inner strength.

Spiritual effects are difficult for caregivers to identify and describe. The English language does not contain sufficient recognized terms to describe those effects. There is a decrease in spiritual strength during the first phase as caregivers begin to accept the diagnosis and recognize the potential bleakness of the future. During the second phase, as the health of the family member improves, the spiritual strength and hope increase. The third phase again reflects a decrease in spirituality. Death becomes a probable reality, and caregivers realize that the future may not include the loved one. Caregivers who talked with the family member about the possible death reported a positive spiritual uplifting (Matocha, 1992). Caregivers and the ill person functioned as a team to prepare for death. Plans were made and wishes revealed. Those caregivers who were able to participate in the planning of the death and the decision about when to withdraw life support described an enrichment in inner strength and ability to meet the demands of the impending death. During the fourth phase, spirits initially fluctuate day by day. Gradually, as time passes, spiritual strength increases, life gets better, and memories of the loved one remain.

Dealing with the Health-Care System

Health-Care Professionals

Caregivers need to learn how to interact with professionals in health care and social services. When this is accomplished, family goals are maintained. Families can be assisted in helping the caregiver conserve physical, emotional, and spiritual energy. Family functioning is optimized because everyone is aware of the goals and is working to achieve them. Professionals who include the family in the treatment and recovery plans for a patient find they have generated a comprehensive health-care team with not only the best knowledge of the technical information but also in-depth insight into each patient. This assists in an effective and efficient plan of care. Stress reduction within the health-care team is a result. Professional caregivers need to maintain contacts with family caregivers. Pratt et al.'s (1985) investigation of 240 caregivers of Alzheimer's patients found that caregivers who had the support of family members experienced lower stress even when there was no direct assistance.

Professional caregivers need to assess the emotional and physical stress of family caregivers and encourage respite care when needed. Respite allows the caregivers time to reorganize coping mechanisms and to have periods away from the stress of giving care. Without respite, caregivers will find their health deteriorating and the care they give to be a burden rather than a gift for someone they love.

Similarly, family caregivers need help to recognize how much they are doing to help the patient. Many times they feel out of control and ineffective. Family caregivers may feel as though it is the health-care system that has control over their lives and the lives of those for whom they care. There is a need for professionals to assist family caregivers to recognize successes they have had when dealing with systems providing care.

Caregivers will need a health-care advocate to assist them in "assertiveness training" so they can negotiate satisfying care for their loved one.

Family caregivers emphasize the need for information about medical and nursing procedures. Many times they experience anger, frustration, and fear when they do not understand the reason for procedures. As soon as caregivers are provided information, those feelings disappear. Health-care professionals who do not attempt to explain procedures, treatments, and alternatives lose the caregivers' trust. Caregivers feel that they cannot safely leave the sick family member and must remain at the bedside around the clock. They are afraid the professional will change the treatment plan without their input or knowledge.

Health-Care Institutions

Families use health care from institutions most often when an acute illness or accident occurs. Many times families depend on institutions to provide most of the care. Snyder and Keefe's (1985) study found that only 43% of the caregivers of the frail and disabled elderly received any assistance from family and friends. Eighty percent received formal social-service support at one time or another, but those who functioned as caregivers the longest reported the least contact with social-service agencies. With the increase in health-care costs, however, the ability to use institutions is decreasing. More and more families are caring for their ill and injured in the home. Institutions are often used only during the acute phase of illness and injury. Patients are being sent home sicker, needing advanced technology and procedures in the home. Families and caregivers now need to know how to manage the technology and recognize possible problems that might arise in the home. Institutions need to offer training and support for these families. Open communication between families and institutions is very important so that when families need information themselves or provide information about the health status of the ill person, there is a method whereby this can be accomplished. Rigid hours and lines of communication hinder the contact that is needed between family and institution. No longer can the health-care system afford to apply a biomedical model and consider only the patient. In-

stead, families must be included in the care; this necessitates use of a self-care/holistic model. Support resources must be explored and be made available not only for the patient but also for each family. The family will then be considered part of the health-care system rather than alien to it.

Chapter Summary

Discussion Questions

1. How can family scientists best study the roles that family members play in health care?
2. What roles do family members play in health promotion and disease prevention?
3. How can families be better consumers of health care to reduce the cost of caring for a member who is ill?
4. Name three specific ways family members can promote family wellness.

Additional Resources

Haley, W. E., Levine, E. G., Brown, S. L., Berry, J. W., & Hughes, G. H. (1987). Psychological, social, and health consequences of caring for a relative with senile dementia. *Journal of the American Geriatric Society, 35*, 405–411.

Horowitz, A. (1985). Family caregiving to the frail elderly. *Annual Review of Gerontological Geriatrics, 5*, 194–245.

Veninga, R. L. (1985). *A gift of hope: How we survive our tragedies.* Boston: Little, Brown.

References

Bader, J. E. (1985). Respite care: Temporary relief for caregivers. *Women's Health, 10*(3), 39–52.

Block, J. H. (1973). Conceptions of sex role: Some cross-cultural and longitudinal perspectives. *American Psychologist, 28*, 435–443.

Brody, E. M. (1974). Aging and family personality: A developmental view. *Family Process, 13*, 23–37.

Brommel, H. van. (1986). *Choices: For people who have a terminal illness, their families, and their caregivers.* Toronto: NC Press.

Buxton, M. E., Smith, D. E., & Seymour, R. B. (1987). Spirituality and other points of resistance to the 12-step recovery process. *Journal of Psychoactive Drugs, 19*(3), 275–286.

Cantor, M. H. (1983). Strain among caregivers: A study of experience in the United States. *The Gerontologist, 23,* 597–604.

Centers for Disease Control. (1989). Chronic disease prevention and control activities—United States 1989. *Morbidity and Mortality Weekly Report, 40*(41), 697–700.

Cleveland, P. H., Walters, L. H., Skeen, P., & Robinson, B. E. (1988). If your child had AIDS. . . : Responses of parents with homosexual children. *Family Relations, 37*(2), 150–153.

Deimling, G. T., & Bass, D. M. (1986). Symptoms of mental impairment among elderly adults and their effects on family caregivers. *Journal of Gerontology, 41,* 778–784.

Eisenberg, N., Fabes, R., & Shea, C. (1989). Gender differences in empathy and prosocial moral reasoning: Empirical investigations. In M. M. Brabeck (Ed.), *Who cares? Theory, research, and educational implications of the ethic of care* (pp. 127–143). New York: Praeger.

Fischl, M. A., Dickinson, G. M., Scott, G. B., Klimas, N., Fletcher, M. A., & Parks, W. (1987). Evaluation of heterosexual partners, children, and household contacts of adults with AIDS. *Journal of the American Medical Association, 257,* 640–644.

Frierson, R. L., Lippmann, S. B., & Johnson, J. (1987). AIDS: Psychosocial stresses on the family. *Psychosomatics, 28*(2), 65–68.

Furstenberg, A. L., & Olson, M. M. (1984). Social work and AIDS. *Social Work in Health Care, 4,* 45–61.

Gallagher, J. (1987). *Voices of strength and hope for a friend with AIDS.* Kansas City, MO: Sheed & Ward.

George, L. K., & Gwyther, L. P. (1986). Caregiver well-being: A multidimensional examination of family caregivers of demented adults. *The Gerontologist, 26,* 253–259.

Gilligan, C. (1977). In a different voice: Women's conceptions of self and of morality. *Harvard Educational Review, 47,* 481–517.

Gilligan, C. (1982). *In a different voice: Psychological theory and women's development.* Cambridge, MA: Harvard University Press.

Haley, W. E., Levine, E. G., Brown, S. L., Berry, J. W., & Hughes, G. H. (1987). Psychological, social, and health consequences of caring for a relative with senile dementia. *Journal of the American Geriatric Society, 35,* 405–411.

Hiatt, J. F. (1986). Spirituality, medicine, and healing. *Southern Medical Journal, 79,* 736–743.

Hirst, S. P., & Metcalf, B. J. (1986). Learning needs of caregivers. *Journal of Gerontological Nursing, 12*(4), 24–28.

Holing, E. V. (1986). The primary caregiver's perception of the dying trajectory. *Cancer Nursing, 9*(1), 29–37.

Horowitz, A. (1985). Family caregiving to the frail elderly. *Annual Review of Gerontological Geriatrics, 5,* 194–245.

Kiecolt-Glaser, J. K., Glaser, R., Shuttleworth, E. C., Dyer, B. A., Ogrocki, B. S., & Speicher, C. E. (1987). Chronic stress and immunity in family caregivers of Alzheimer's disease victims. *Psychosomatic Medicine, 49,* 523–535.

Kriesel, H. T. (1987). The psychosocial aspects of malignancy. *Primary Care, 14*(2), 271–280.

Lefley, H. P. (1987). Aging parents as caregivers of mentally ill adult children: An emerging social problem. *Hospital and Community Psychiatry, 38,* 1063–1070.

Light, E., & Lebowitz, B. (Eds.). (1988). *Alzheimer's disease treatment and family stress: Directions for research.* Washington, DC: National Institute of Mental Health (U. S. Government Printing Office).

Macklin, E. D. (1988). AIDS: Implications for families. *Family Relations, 37*(2), 141–149.

Macklin, E. D. (1989). Introduction. *Marriage and Family Review, 13,* 1–11.

Matocha, L. K. (1989). The effects of AIDS on family member(s) responsible for care: A qualitative study. *Dissertation Abstracts International, 51,* 648A. (University Microfilms No. 90–19, 300).

Matocha, L. K. (1992). Case study reviews: Caring for a person with AIDS. In J. F. Gilgun, K. Daly, & G. Handel (Eds.), *Qualitative methods in family research* (pp. 66–84). Newbury Park, CA: Sage.

Miller, J. F. (1983). *Coping with chronic illness, overcoming powerlessness.* Philadelphia: Davis.

Miller, M., & Eisdorfer, C. (1989). A model of caregiver's willingness to provide care. *Caring, 8*(12), 10–13.

Muurinen, J. M. (1986). The economics of informal care. *Medical Care, 24,* 1007–1017.

Norwood, C. (1987). *Advice for life: A woman's guide to AIDS risks and prevention.* New York: Pantheon.

Parsons, T., & Bales, R. F. (1955). *Family, socialization, and interaction processes.* New York: Academic Press.

Peabody, B. (1986). *The screaming room.* New York: Avon Books.

Pearson, J., Verma, S., & Nellett, C. (1988). Elderly psychiatric patient status and caregiver perceptions as predictors of caregiver burden. *The Gerontologist, 28,* 79–83.

Peterson, K. J. (1985). Psychosocial adjustment of the family caregiver: Home hemodialysis as an example. *Social Work in Health Care, 10*(3), 15–32.

Pratt, C. C., Schmall, V. L., Wright, S., & Cleland, M. (1985). Burden and coping strategies of caregivers to Alzheimer's patients. *Family Relations, 34*(1), 27–33.

Prezioso, F. A. (1987). Spirituality in the recovery process. *Journal of Substance Abuse Treatment, 4*, 233–238.

Rakowski, W., & Clark, N. M. (1985). Future outlook, caregiving, and care-receiving in the family context. *The Gerontologist, 25*, 618–623.

Ross-Alaolmoiki, K. (1985). Supportive care for families of dying children. *Nursing Clinics of North America, 20*, 457–466.

Searle, E. S. (1987, January 3). Knowledge, attitudes, and behavior of health professionals in relation to AIDS. *The Lancet*, pp. 26–30.

Shanus, E. (1979). The family as a social support system in old age. *The Gerontologist, 19*, 169–174.

Shields, S. A. (1987). Women, men, and the dilemma of emotions. In P. Shaver and C. Hendreck (Eds.), *Sex and gender* (pp. 229–250). Newbury Park, CA: Sage.

Silliman, R. A., Fletcher, R. H., Earp, J. L., & Wagner, E. H. (1986). Families of elderly stroke patients. *Journal of the American Geriatrics Society, 34*, 643–648.

Snyder, B., & Keefe, K. (1985). The unmet needs of family caregivers for frail and disabled adults. *Social Work in Health Care, 10*(3), 1–14.

Soeken, K. L., & Carson, V. J. (1987). Responding to the spiritual needs of the chronically ill. *Nursing Clinics of North America, 22*, 603–611.

Soldo, B. J., & Myllyluoma, J. (1983). Caregivers who live with dependent elderly. *The Gerontologist, 23*, 605–611.

Steinmetz, S. K. (1988). Parental and filial relationships: Obligation, support, and abuse. In S. K. Steinmetz (Ed.), *Family and support systems across the life span* (pp. 165–182). New York: Plenum.

Stetz, K. M. (1987). Caregiving demands during advanced cancer. *Cancer Nursing, 10*(5), 260–268.

Thobaben, M. (1988). What you can do for the depressed caregiver. *RN, 51*(1), 73–75.

Tibler, K. B., Walker, G., & Rolland, J. S. (1989). Therapeutic issues when working with families of persons with AIDS. *Marriage and Family Review, 13*, 81–128.

Veninga, R. L. (1985). *A gift of hope: How we survive our tragedies.* Boston: Little, Brown.

Yaffe, M. J. (1988). Implications of caring for an aging parent. *Canadian Medical Association Journal, 138*, 231–235.

Zarit, S. H., Reever, K. E., & Bach-Peterson, J. (1980). Relatives of the impaired elderly: Correlates of feeling of burden. *The Gerontologist, 20*, 649–655.

Zarit, S. H., Todd, P. A., & Zarit, J. M. (1986). Subjective burden of husbands and wives as caregivers: A longitudinal study. *The Gerontologist, 26*, 260–266.

CHAPTER 16

Violence in Families

Suzanne K. Steinmetz
Indiana University—Indianapolis

Domestic violence is not a new problem. Accounts of acts of violence between family members and intimates abound in court records, newspaper articles, and preambles to laws. In ancient societies, laws decreed that a woman who was verbally abusive to her husband was to have her name engraved on a brick that would then be used to knock out her teeth (Steinmetz, 1987). Euripides, the Greek playwright, argued that women should be silent, should not argue with men, and should not speak first. Roman law even justified the husband's killing of his wife for reasons such as adultery, drinking wine, or other "inappropriate" behavior.

The concept of children as the property of their parents is illustrated in the Hammurabi code of 2100 B.C. and the Hebrew code of 800 B.C., which considered infanticide to be an acceptable practice (Bates, 1977). In Roman times the Patriac Potestae permitted fathers to sell, sacrifice, mutilate, or kill offspring (Radbill, 1968). The Book of Proverbs provides parents with specific guidelines on discipline: "He who spares the rod hates his son, but he who loves him disciplines him diligently (13:24). British colonial law increased the value placed on women, who were vital to the survival of the American colonies, by recognizing that marital violence was not tolerable. For example, a Massachusetts law during the colonial period required that cohabitation be peaceful. This mandate did not mean that domestic violence was abolished, but it did mean that those who perpetrated violence would be punished. For example, the First Church of Boston excommunicated Mary Whorten "for reviling of her husband and sticking of him and other vile and wicked courses" (Morgan,

1966, p.141). One man in the Plymouth colony was punished for abusing his wife by "kicking her off from a stoole into the fire," and another for "drawing his wife in an uncivil manner on the snow." Joan Miller was charged with "beating and reviling her husband and egging her children to help her, bidding them to knock him in the head and wishing his victual might choke him" (Demos, 1970, p. 93).

Colonial America recognized the importance of protecting women from abuse; however, it considered the need for children to be properly reared to be so important that parents were given the power of life and death over their children. In 1646, a law was enacted to help parents control their rebellious children. This law noted that unless the parents had been "very unchristianly negligent in the education of such children or have so provoked them by extreme and cruel correction" any child over 16 years of age and of sufficient understanding who cursed, smiled and would not obey his natural mother or father, then "would be put to death" (Bremner, 1970, p. 37).

There is no indication that parents resorted to using this law. With industrialization and rapid population growth, our social sanctions of nonviolent marital interactions changed. A husband's right to chastise his wife with a whip or rattan no bigger than his thumb, a remnant of old English law, was upheld by a Mississippi court in 1824. This "rule of thumb" law, which prevailed for nearly half a century, limited a husband's use of corporal punishment to "great cases of emergency" and required "salutary restraints" (*Bradley* v. *State*, Walker, 158 [Miss. 1824]. The treatment of children at the onset of the Industrial Revolution was equally harsh. Children endured long hours, extreme physical hardship, and numerous beatings to ensure that they would exhibit no laziness.

Acknowledging the existence of violence between family members and labeling it unacceptable behavior is, however, a relatively new phenomenon. Only two decades ago, Maccoby and Jacklin (1974) noted that wife beating was probably rare in most marriages and that this behavior would be considered pathological and an endangerment to the species. What is the consensus on how frequently a behavior must occur to be considered rare? For example, Scanzoni (1978), in discussing women's use of violence to resolve conflicts, noted the frequency of reported active violence to be relatively modest, and 86% of his respondents reported that they had never hit their husband. Apparently, the remaining 14% of the women who had hit their husbands was considered inconsequential.

Despite the mistreatment of children in the United States and the need to rely on the Society for the Prevention of Cruelty to Animals to assist these children in 1874, nearly a century passed before all states had laws mandating the reporting of child abuse, requiring investigation of the reported cases, and providing services to these children and their families. It would be refreshing to consider this change in attitude to be a reflection of a kinder, more sophisticated society, a society that values all human beings. Unfortunately, the attention being given to this issue is more likely to reflect the economic costs to society for providing services to these family members combined with the loss of human capital (current and potential) in the marketplace.

For purposes of this chapter, family violence will be defined as an act carried out with the intention of, or perceived as having the intention of, physically, sexually, or psychologically hurting a family member; could be one's partner (either married, dating, or cohabitating), a child, or parent or other kin. Because family violence is also called "intimate violence," acts such as rape are sometimes included. Although nonconsenting sexual activity is molestation or rape (depending on the nature of the act) regardless of the relationship between the individuals involved, this chapter will not examine stranger rape. Physically violent acts can range from a slap to murder. Psychological violence, which is also called "emotional violence," can include denigration, such as telling a child that he or she is worthless, as well as verbal threats and insults. Sexual abuse includes molestation and rape. Under the general rubric of domestic violence we also include neglect (the deprivation of resources such as failure to provide food, clothing, or medical attention for a child or dependent elder) or misuse or theft of a person's property (resource abuse, a category of abuse of the elderly).

Although this is a basic definition of violence, it is usually necessary to consider a number of other characteristics of these violent acts: Was the act *instrumental* to some other purpose, such as disciplining a child for a specific wrongdoing? Or was it *expressive*—that is, an end in itself, (for example, a parent who lashes out at a child because the parent is frustrated and out of control)? Is it a culturally permitted or required act, such as spanking a disobedient child (which is unfortunately mandated in some school systems)? This would be considered a *legitimate* act in our society, as opposed to one that runs counter to cultural norms, such as beating a child to death, which is *illegitimate* violence. Thus, the basis for the "intent to hurt" may range from concern for a child's safety (as when a child is spanked for going into the street) to hostility so intense that the death of the other is desired. The former would be an example of "legitimate instrumental violence" and the latter of "illegitimate expressive violence."

The Dynamics of Family Violence

By examining the theoretical perspective used to explain a phenomenon, one can gain insights into the different interpretations of the dynamics of family violence. Theoretical perspectives are often categorized by the focus utilized by a particular perspective into three levels: intraindividual, social-psychological, and sociocultural (Steinmetz, 1987). Intraindividual theories locate explanations for family violence within the individual. Explanations focus on the causes or factors such as mental illness, physical or mental abnormalities, or the use of alcohol and drugs that can act as disinhibitors to violence. Also in this group are theories based on innate, or organic, factors—for example, genetic, hormonal, or medically linked violence.

Genetic and hormonal influences on violence are included in intraindividual theories. A study conducted in Denmark found that low intelligence rather than aggressive personality appeared to be related to the XYY chromosome configuration in males (Jarvik, Klodin, & Matsuyama, 1973). The relationship between XYY and violence that has been articulated in earlier studies is the result of the tendency for the XYY chromosome to produce low intelligence; this, in turn, is correlated with low education, limited occupational opportunities, and increased frustration, which can lead to antisocial behavior and violence. Organic brain syndrome has been linked to episodic, violent outbursts, and clinical observation has found this violence to include domestic violence (Elliott, 1978, 1982; Monroe, 1970) and temporal lobe and psychomotor epilepsy. EEG abnormalities have also been linked to violent and aggressive behavior (Benson & Blumer, 1976; Dossett, Burch, & Keller, 1982; Lewis, Pincus, Shanok, & Glaser, 1982; Williams, 1969).

The hormonal influence of testosterone in men and the women's hormonal imbalance resulting in the premenstrual syndrome have been linked to violence. The latter has been used successfully as a defense in France and England (Dalton, 1980), raising the specter of a return to the tactic of prohibiting women from working in certain jobs because of mental and emotional instability linked to their monthly cycle. However, this approach should not be overlooked as a contributing factor in understanding the behavior of a mother who is abusing her child. Tardiff (1982), in a comprehensive review of the hormonal influence on violence, notes that among samples of "violent" individuals, hormonal levels may act as the straw that breaks the camel's back for individuals with other problems, stresses, and frustrations. The intraindividual perspective also looks at that.

Personality Characteristics

A comparison of a matched sample of 65 abusing parents and 65 nonabusing parents found that the abusing parents were significantly more likely to score high on rigidity, unhappiness, and distress factor (easily upset, often frustrated, angry, mixed up, and rejected) than the nonabusing parents (Milner & Wimberley, 1980). Rosen (1979) compared the interpersonal values of 30 abusing and 30 nonabusing mothers and found that the abusing women valued conformity, benevolence, or nurturing less and authority and power needs more than did the nonabusing subjects. Six personality characteristics were found to be common to a group of 60 abusers: reliance on the child to satisfy dependency needs, poor impulse control, poor self-concept, disturbances in identity formation, feelings of worthlessness, and misperception of the child (see Sweet & Resnick, 1979, for a comprehensive discussion of this material). Individual differences in personality are also evident in partner abuse. Hiberman and Munson (1977–1978), in a study of 60 battered women, found that almost the entire sample had sought medical help for stress-related complaints and that many evidenced symptoms commonly associated with the rape-trauma syndrome. More than half had evidence of prior psychological dysfunction, including classic depressive illness, schizophrenia, manic-depression, alcoholism, and severe character disorders; and 22% had been hospitalized because of violent psychotic behavior. Post-traumatic stress disorder (PTSD) is of growing interest because it can manifest itself in both receivers (battered woman syndrome [Sonkin, Martin, & Walker, 1985] and physical child abuse [Green, 1978]) as well as in perpetrators of violence, especially combat veterans who experience sudden outbursts of anger (Sonkin et al., 1985).

Research describing the personality characteristics of a battered wife often leaves an impression that these victims, by their own weaknesses, have enabled the battering to occur. A woman is likely to become a victim of spouse abuse when she displays the characteristics of a weak, vulnerable woman: she is isolated (Gelles, 1979; Prescott & Letko, 1977: Roy, 1977; Straus, 1977–1978); she is overcome by anxiety (Gelles, 1975; Prescott & Letko, 1977; Ridington, 1977–1978); and she is full of guilt and shame (Hilberman & Munson, 1977–1978; Resnick, 1976). Some researchers suggest that violence can be reduced by changing the women's social and economic resources, increasing their education and job skills, teaching them to be less submissive, helping them to have a better self-concept, or teaching them to interpret their husband's moods. Infante and colleagues conceptualize verbal aggressiveness as a communication "trait" (Infante & Wigley, 1986; Infante, Chandler, & Rudd, 1989; Infante, Sabourin, Rudd, & Shannon, 1990). However, Whitchurch and Pace (1993) suggest that verbal aggression is relational (not intraindividual) and that skills training that attempts to change an individual's communication patterns runs the risk of further increasing the verbal violence, with the potential of escalation into physical aggression. They note that conceptualizing verbal aggression (a communication *behavior*) as verbal aggressiveness (a psychological *construct*) instead of in a transactional perspective disregards contradictory prior literature. Gondolf (1988), Saunders and Hanusa (1987), and Shields and Hanneke (1983) all found that a comparatively small proportion of physically violent husbands in their samples were violent in all of their relationships. The majority were physically violent only with their wives and children.

Although possessing these skills and resources may be a valid mechanism for helping a victim escape from the battering environment at its onset or for decreasing the likelihood of violence, those who suggest these remedies tend to assume that the battered woman has the ability to control her environment and that not to do so implies a satisfaction with the status quo. This display of learned helplessness allows such women to be further victimized (Walker, 1977–1978).

It is suggested that contrary to the notion that battered women have personality characteristics or psychiatric conditions that "cause" them to be at risk of being beaten, (for example, they are poor, uneducated, anxious, lacking in self-confidence, or weak), rather, it is the dynamics of the beating itself that produce these manifestations (Steinmetz, 1979). This phenomenon is closely related to the processes involved in brainwashing: isolation from family, friends, and social-support systems. Each reinforces the victim's dependency on the abuser for confirmation of her worth. Unfortunately, the confirmation supports the woman's negative self-image, filling her with shame and guilt. In this "trapped" learned-helplessness state, even well-educated women with resources are unlikely to leave without intervention because they don't see these resources as valid mechanisms for allowing them to leave.

Such abuse may result in personality traits that increase the likelihood of further abuse. Kinard (1980) compared 30 children who had been physically abused at least one year earlier with a control group matched in age, sex, race, birth order, number of children in family, parental structure, socioeconomic status, and type of residence and neighborhood. Although a battery of psychological tests revealed small differences in self-concept, the abused children were more unhappy, nonconforming, extrapunitive, and aggressive in child/child relationships (but not in parent/child relationships) than the nonabused children. While an intraindividual perspective suggests that individual characteristics produce aggressiveness, social and cultural characteristics clearly shape how the response is displayed. These factors are discussed in the following section.

A Sociocultural Perspective

Unlike intraindividual theories, which locate the sources of violence within the individual, sociocultural theories of violence focus on the macrolevel conditions that lead to family violence, such as sexism, racism, ageism, poverty, inadequate housing, unemployment or underemployment, and unequal opportunity.

One cannot help but wonder whether the methods that family members use to resolve family conflict somehow reflect the general attitudes of society toward the use of physical aggression to resolve other social problems. This becomes a chicken-and-egg problem. Does society influence individual behavior, or is the individual the constructor of society? Although the starting point might be an intraindividual psychological perspective that sees people's natural aggression as a determinant of their ability to survive (Tiger, 1969), we must also address the sociocultural influences on learning aggressive behavior as an acceptable response.

While caution must be used in linking societal levels of aggression to interpersonal and familial levels of aggression, there is both theoretical and empirical support for this position. Langman (1973) found that the child-rearing methods that parents used and the amount of interpersonal aggression considered tolerable were related to the level of aggression considered appropriate in the culture, an observation that has been supported in anthropological literature (Mead, 1935; Whiting, 1965). In a study of playground behavior,

Bellak and Antell (1974) found that the aggressive treatment of a child by his or her parents was correlated with the aggressiveness displayed by the child. The authors found that the levels of both parental and child aggression were considerably higher in Frankfurt than in Florence or Copenhagen. The rates for suicide and homicide, considered by Bellak and Antell to be additional indications of personal aggression, were also much higher in Germany. DeMause (1974, p. 42) reports that 80% of German parents admitted having beaten their children and that 35% had done so with canes. A German poll showed that up to 60% of the parents interviewed believed in beating (not slapping or spanking) their children (Torgerson, 1973, as cited by Bellak & Antell, 1974). Studies based on the data in the Human Relations Area Files reveals that the incidence of wife beating in 71 primitive societies was positively correlated with invidious displays of wealth, pursuit of military glory, bellicosity, institutionalized boasting, exhibitionistic dancing, and sensitivity to insults (Slater & Slater, 1965). These descriptions sound curiously similar to the macho attempts to dominate that are often linked to wife abuse in the United States.

Lester (1980), also studying primitive cultures, found that wife beating was more common in societies characterized by high divorce rates and societies in which women were rated as inferior. Societies that experienced not only high rates of drunkenness but also high rates of alcohol-related aggression also had higher rates of wife beating.

In an examination of 86 primitive societies, Masumura (1979) found that wife abuse was correlated with overall societal violence—for example, homicide, suicide, feuding, warfare, personal crime, and aggression. Whereas matrilocal societies were found to be characterized by intrasocietal "peacefulness" (Divale, 1974; Van Valzen & Van Wetering, 1960) and exhibited less feuding (Otterbein & Otterbein, 1965), Masumura reports weak, but positive, correlations between wife abuse and patrilocal residence and patrilineal inheritance, thus providing limited support for male dominance leading to higher rates of wife beating. Prescott (1975), using the Textor cross-cultural categorization of contemporary societies, found that in 36 of 49 societies, physical violence decreased when physical affection increased, and physical violence increased when physical affection decreased.

Whiting (1965) reports less wife beating in societies that lived in extended-family forms. I compared the societal-violence profiles from a number of studies with marital-violence scores from Finland, Puerto Rico, Canada, Israel, Belize, and the United States (Steinmetz, 1981, 1982, 1987). In general, political and civil profiles of violence and marital-violence scores were similar within each society. One exception was the high levels of violence among kibbutz families, where norms of sexual equality and the availability of numerous kin would have predicted lower levels of spousal violence, as compared with similar nuclear Jewish families living in America.

One explanation for these findings among kibbutz families might be that offered by Demos (1970), who notes that to survive cramped living quarters, early American colonists went to great lengths to avoid family conflict. They apparently vented their hostilities on their neighbors, because the rate of conflicts between neighbors was extremely high. Is it possible that preserving the community tranquillity is of extreme importance and that, therefore, the kibbutz family keeps the conflicts within the family?

I also examined sibling violence cross-culturally (Steinmetz, 1982). Finland and Puerto Rico, societies shown to be consistently low on all societal measures of violence, had relatively low scores on sibling violence. However, Canada and the United States, societies that scored fairly high on all measures of societal violence, had somewhat higher sibling scores.

In a study of validated cases of child abuse and neglect in Texas from 1975 to 1977, Lauderdale, Valiunas, and Anderson (1980) found that the rates for all types of abuse were highest among African Americans, followed by Mexican Americans, with Anglos having the lowest rates. However, analysis within each group indicated that the Anglos had the highest percentage of abuse followed by African Americans, with Mexican American families having the lowest percentage of abuse.

A study of abuse and neglect in Hawaii revealed that Japanese Americans had significantly lower rates of abuse than Samoan Americans (3.5% versus 6.5%) (Dubanski & Snyder, 1980). However, Japanese Americans represented 27% of the population, and Samoan Americans constituted less than 1% of the population.

One of the few studies to systematically assess the ethnic effects on family violence in the United States was undertaken by Blanchard and Blanchard (1983). They administered a modification of the Conflict Tactics Scale (CTS) used by Straus et al. (1980) to 475 college students in Hawaii. They divided the sample into European, Japanese, Chinese, Filipino, and Hawaiian/part Hawaiian. They asked about violence toward *any* family member rather than specifying a particular family member (parent, sibling, or spouse). They found that the Hawaiian students had the highest scores, with a mean score of 7.8; the Europeans were the next highest with 4.2, followed by the Filipinos, 3.75, and the Chinese, 3.20. The lowest scores were obtained by the Japanese, who had a mean score of 3.05. These scores, however, did not include slapping, pushing, grabbing, or shoving, as these acts were not violent enough to qualify "as a violent crime charge" or to "inspire a reputation as a bully" (Straus et.al., 1980, p. 182).

A Social-Psychological Perspective

I have discussed intraindividual characteristics such as inherited factors, personality, and attitudes and sociocultural factors that are related to cultural or ethnic differences in viewing violence as a way to resolve family problems. The third level to be discussed is the social-psychological perspective. This perspective examines the interface between the individual and society. Several aspects of this interface need to be mentioned—issues of power, control, social class, employment, and transfer of property. The resolution of each of these issues has a significant impact on how violence is muted or amplified within the family realm.

Power

First is power differentials. Power can be defined as the ability of one individual (or group) to exercise his or her wishes over another. The resources that one individual can muster, such as social class, education, income, physical appearance, personality, family, and business or social network, are components of power. The ability to influence others can also be based on age, gender, or race.

Power is a critical aspect of violence for several reasons. First it characterizes and legitimizes intrafamilial interactions such as those between wife and husband, parent and child, or siblings. Second, it provides an indication of the intrinsic value that society places on a particular family member—for example, the value of women during colonial times. Third, the power available to a particular family is based on the value accorded this family; for example, the abuse or murder of a member of a prominent family is defined as being more tragic. Media coverage, law enforcement, judicial opinion, and public feelings are all shaped by the social position that the individuals involved in family violence occupy in the society. Perhaps this is because we assume that families with greater resources have alternative ways to resolve conflicts or that individuals with greater resources are able to afford greater protection from abuse.

Nonetheless, countless women in poverty or with few resources are battered daily with little or no attention, while Charlotte Fedders, the wife of a prominent politician, became a talk show regular. This is not to suggest that Fedders's abuse was any less real or less painful or that marriage to a wealthy man offers better protection from abuse than that afforded a welfare mother. However, it does provide evidence that when these events occur to members of the privileged class, more media attention is given to their story. Somehow we consider such treatment of poor women or women with few resources or power to be somewhat commonplace and not worthy of attention.

The impact of societally specific marital power was studied by Kumagai and O'Donoghue (1978). They examined relative power between husband and wife and the effect it might have on conjugal violence in Japan and the United States. They found that whereas U.S. couples were egalitarian in power and violence, Japanese wives were more powerful than their husbands but were considerably more likely to be the victims than the offenders in spouse abuse. Thus, when a wife had more power than her husband in the traditional, male-dominated society of Japan, she was considerably more likely to be the victim of violence than a similar situation in the United States.

Control

Control can be conceptualized as both direct control—the ability to successfully exert one's power to control another person—and indirect control—the ability of one individual to exert manipulation over another through indirect control of resources such as money, transportation, food, or freedom of movement. The control of resources is typically measured by social class. This variable is probably one of the most commonly used in family-violence research. Based on the definition used and the indexes or measures that make up "social class," different relationships will be found. When a working-class/middle-class, or blue-collar/white-collar classification based on type of occupation is used, slightly higher levels of violence are found among blue-collar workers. However, if the components of socioeconomic status (type of job, educational levels, and income) are examined separately, the data are inconsistent.

Social class.   One of the earliest myths to be examined was that of the class myth of family violence (Steinmetz & Straus, 1973). Current studies have verified the existence of family violence in all social classes, and they suggest that the almost exclusive representation of working- and lower-class child abusers noted in earlier studies may have resulted because poor people use public clinics and become part of the public record. Middle-class women have access to private social-support systems, such as family counselors, private doctors, ministers, and lawyers, who maintain the privacy of the professional relationship; lower-class families must rely on social-control agencies such as the police, social-service or family-court workers, clinics, and public agencies that keep "public" records.

Newberger, Reed, Daniel, Hyde, and Kotelchuck (1977) found that lower-class and minority children with injuries were more likely to be labeled as abused than middle- and upper-class children. Even when injury level was held constant in mock cases presented to physicians in which the race and the class of the family were varied, the physicians were more likely to label minority or lower-class children as abused (Turbett & O'Toole, 1980).

Clearly, violence is related to the resources that are available. When our society is facing a constricting economic situation with high unemployment and inflation, violence appears to increase. When families must use all their available energies to keep food on the table, a roof over their heads, and clothes on the children's backs, the stress becomes intolerable, and both street and family violence increase. This phenomenon was seen most recently after Hurricane Andrew devastated Miami and other towns in south Florida, leaving thousands without homes and jobs. The link between income levels and violence may be primarily an indirect one that provides families with resources useful for mediating many stress-producing and potentially violent situations. Greater financial resources enable parents to procure stress-reducing mechanisms, such as baby-sitters, vacations, nursery schools, and camps, which provide them with "timeout" from child-rearing and homemaking responsibilities, thus possibly preventing or reducing violence.

Employment status.   The employment status of the husband and satisfaction with occupational or homemaking roles are also predictors of family violence. Unemployment is often perceived by men as incompetence in fulfilling their provider roles, and it has been linked to child abuse and wife beating. Gill (1970) reports that nearly half (48%) of the fathers in his sample of abusers experienced unemployment during the year preceding the abuse. McKinley (1964) found that the lower the job satisfaction, the higher the percentage of fathers who used severe corporal punishment, a relationship that was not affected by social class. A study of battered women who replied to a request for information in Ms. magazine reported that husbands who were unemployed or who were employed part time were extremely violent compared with husbands who were employed full time (Prescott & Letko, 1977). Although this sample was nonrepresentative, a national survey (Straus et al., 1980) found similar results: a consistently lower level of child and spouse abuse among families where the husband was employed full-time. Furthermore, part-time employment was more likely to predict family violence than was unemployment.

Transfer of property.   The transfer of property, both through inheritance and deeds of gifts, provides insights into parents' attempts to use economic control as a hedge against maltreatment in their old age. In an attempt to provide for the surviving wife in colonial Massachusetts, many husbands included elaborate provisions in their will for her care, which required the children to furnish food, clothing, and shelter or forfeit their inheritance. Other parents deeded the land to their offspring before their death, but the provision of a lifetime of care was a requirement of keeping the land. For example, Henry Holt, by a deed of gift, gave the original homestead to his 30-year-old unmarried son. The deed required him to "take ye sole care of his father Henry Holt and of his natural mother Sarah Holt" for the rest of their days and to provide for all their needs, which were carefully detailed. Failure to supply any of the required articles resulted in forfeiture of the property (Greven, 1970, pp. 143–144).

The desire of the father to use economic means to control his adult children produced conflict when these children tried to establish independence. In one family, 32-year-old Robert Carter was forced to spend an additional ten years under his father's authority because he lacked the financial means to secure complete independence. Bitter arguments, mostly resulting from the middle-aged son's continued dependence on his father, nearly resulted in physical blows. Landon Carter, the father, feared for his life and went around with a pistol. He noted that "surely it is happy our laws prevent patricide or the devil that moves to this treatment would move to put his father out of the way. Good God, that such a monster is descended from my loin" (Greene, as cited by Fischer, 1977, p. 62).

Cotton Mather, in *Dignity and Duty*, complained that "there were children who were apt to despise an Aged Mother." Landon Carter, in 1771, wrote that "it is a pity that old age which everybody covets and everybody who lives must come to should be so contemptible in the eyes of the world" (Smith, 1980, p. 275). The elderly poor fared most miserably. Throughout the court records of Connecticut and Massachusetts are instances of attempts to bar these people from entering a given town, because they would increase the population of the almshouses. A 1772 New Jersey law required the justices of the peace to search arriving ships for old people as well as other undesirables and to send them away in order to prevent the growth of pauperism (Smith, 1980, p. 61). Neighbors often "warned out"

poor widows and forced them to wander from one town to another.

Sexual Inequality and Social Status

Because sexual inequality has been considered a major force behind the abuse of wives, reducing it is considered necessary to reduce wife abuse. However, some researchers suggest that violence may actually increase as women strive to obtain greater income, power, and status, and men attempt to maintain their dominant position in these areas (Marsden, 1978, Steinmetz & Straus, 1974; Whitehurst, 1974). Steinmetz and Straus (1974) contend:

> It will not be until a generation of men and women reared under egalitarian conditions and subscribing to equalitarian rather than male-superiority norms takes over that we can expect to see a reduction in violent encounters between spouses. In the meantime, the conflict between the emerging equalitarian social structure and the continuing male superiority norms will tend to increase rather than decrease conflict and violence between husbands and wives. (p. 76)

Straus (1976) suggests that the long-run consequences may be to lessen the frequency of wife abuse but the short-run impact may be to increase violence because many men may not easily give up their traditional role of dominance.

Using American states as a unit of analysis, Yllo (1983) obtained measures for the economic status of women, their educational accomplishments, their role in politics, and the laws protecting women's rights. The relationship between the overall status of women and the levels of violence, as measured by the CTS (Straus et al., 1980), was curvilinear. Violence was highest in those states where the status of women was lowest; violence decreased as status improved, but it increased in states in which the status of women was the highest. This relationship was not affected by measures of urbanization, statewide levels of education, or the state level of violent crime and was only slightly affected by state levels of income.

Intergenerational Transmission of Violence

In a comparison of wives who had been battered with wives who had experienced marital discord and were in therapy but had not experienced physical violence, Rosenbaum and O'Leary (1981) found that the children of the abused wives were more likely to exhibit behavior problems. The differences were not significant, and the abused wives were no more likely to have witnessed parental abuse than were the nonabused wives. However, the authors found a strong and significant relationship between the husband's witnessing of parental spouse abuse and his using physical violence on his wife. Furthermore, nearly 82% of the husbands who had witnessed marital violence as children had also been victims of child abuse by their parents. The researchers note that the male children of couples in which there is wife abuse are clearly at high risk for developing into abusive husbands in the next generation.

Walker (1984) demonstrated the cyclical nature of domestic violence in her study of over 400 battered women. She reports that 67% of the women were battered as children (41% by their mothers, 44% by their fathers); about 20% had brothers and sisters who were also battered; 44% of their fathers battered their mothers; and 29% of the mothers battered their fathers. Furthermore, 28% of these battered women reported that they had battered their own children, with 5% attributing this behavior to being angry at their husband; 15% used violence against their spouse (either in retaliation or self-defense) when in a battering relationship; and 5% continued this violent behavior after they left the first relationship and had entered a nonbattering relationship.

Studies of college students revealed a similar relationship. I found that 36% of the students reported courtship violence, 65% of the students had experienced the violence more than once (yet nearly all continued the relationship), and the same percentage had experienced the violence with more than one partner (Steinmetz, 1987). In over half (54%) of these couples, the physical violence had been used by both partners, and 23% reported female-to-male violence only. Of the students who reported that their mother had used physical means of disciplining them, 41% also reported courtship violence, as compared with only 16% of those whose mothers had been nonviolent. A similar but less dramatic trend was observed for father/student interactions.

The most striking link was found between the students' reports of their parents using violence and their own courtship violence experiences. Only 18% of the students who reported that their parents had used neither verbal nor physical aggression to resolve marital conflicts had experienced courtship violence. However, 42% of the students who reported mother/father physical violence and 33% of the students whose parents had used verbal aggression to resolve marital conflicts had experienced courtship violence. Similar findings were reported by Bernard and Bernard (1983) in their study of college students in which 15% had abused a partner; 77% of the abusers had also been abused, and 8% had been abused but had not abused their partner. The authors noted that 74% of male students and 77% of female students were using the same forms of violence (such as punching or throwing things) as had been used in the home.

Patterns of Communication

Spousal communication patterns have also been examined as a contributing factor to spousal abuse. Weitzman and Dreen (1982) argue that individual spouses' "traits" come together in a couple system that becomes violent for two reasons. First, they have learned through their previous interactions that violence is a rewarded behavior. Second, their relationship rules are marked by rigid sex-role polarization, a high degree of enmeshment, and fear of open conflict. Weitzman and Dreen suggest that violent couples are greatly inclined toward complementary roles.

Gage (1988) studied the interactional behavior of violent spousal relationships, focusing on the assertion of control (a "one-up" message), and the acceptance of the assertion of control (a "one-down" message). Gage also measured domineering (the assertion of control by one partner), and found that one spouse's domineering behaviors were strongly associated with similar behaviors by the other. This suggests that rather than one partner being domineering and the other accepting the controlling behavior, as Weitzman and Dreen (1982) maintain, complementary roles occur, and partners tend to mirror each other's communication patterns.

Whitchurch (1989) suggests that there are four types of violent interspousal relationships, which differ in the relationship characteristics of the couples. Using a sample of 247 couples that had reported interspousal violence within the previous year in the 1975 National Survey of Family Violence, she identified four distinct types of violent interspousal relationships: "agreeable-intimate" couples, who were very low in conflict, valued their relationships highly, and had high intimacy and satisfaction in their relationships; "conflictive-intimate" couples, who had the most conflict, the most intoxication, and a high level of intimacy but had thought about separation; "detached" couples, who had considered separation, had low levels of intimacy, and were unsatisfied with their relationships; and "volcanic" couples, who avoided conflict and had low levels of verbal conflict but exploded when conflict reached a certain point and tended to be among the most physically violent couples.

Agreeable-intimate couples had a moderate level of verbal violence, a high level of physical violence, and the lowest level of severe violence among the four couple types. Conflictive-intimate couples had a high level of verbal violence a moderate level of less-severe physical violence, but the highest level of severe violence. Thus, couple type may be able to predict the respondents' verbal and physical violence, as well as their deescalating of conflict behaviors.

A Case Study of Family Violence

Describing family violence in cold, objective terms does not convey the pain experienced by families in which violence occurs. The material below is taken from process notes of a support group for substance-abusing women who are pregnant or have delivered within the past year. The names have been changed. Although participation in the group is voluntary, the discharge plans for mothers whose newborns test positive for drugs frequently mandate that the women participate in the weekly sessions as part of the agreement with Child Protective Services. Because it is an open group, the membership changes each week, although there is a core of regulars. The interaction is quite different based on the balance of older to newer members and the racial composition of the group. All of the women in the group the day this recording was done were mandated to attend. The group was composed almost entirely of newer members, and a majority were black.

One young woman—I'll call her Barbara—began by telling how she had left an abusive home with her 3-week-old baby to enter a shelter because it was the only way she could get away from the drug culture. She sobbed and sobbed while telling how hard it was to be homeless without your own things. She said this had been the best decision, however, because she felt safe for the first time in a long time and was well fed and cared for. The shelter staff was helping her find an apartment in a safe neighborhood, and she was brushing up on math to occupy her leisure time. She sat crumpled on the floor, head lowered, in complete dejection. She described this as a low point in her life but one that was necessary to protect her baby. The sadness enveloped the room. Her story had elements that were shared by most of the women. Abused and molested as children, these women married or cohabited with the first man who could rescue them from their abusive home. Life on the run, characterized by unemployment, drug and alcohol abuse, evictions, legal problems, and men who ultimately left after stripping them of their possessions and self-esteem, was typical.

Another young woman, Sherry, told about marrying her husband right after high school in order to get out of an abusive home. She noted that she had had two children by this man and two children by her current partner, who was abusing her. She told the group that she had also lost two children. Members of the group asked about them. Sherry replied that "one was lost by miscarriage, and one died from SIDS." Another member, Vicky, noted that she had also lost a child from sudden infant death syndrome and had had that baby on a monitor. She asked if Sherry's baby had been on a monitor. The detachment with which these women announced the loss of babies and experiences of rape, sexual molestation, and battering is still jarring to me. The group at this point believed that the baby had died from SIDS, an experience that disproportionately affects blacks. Sherry replied that her baby had not been on a monitor and went on to explain, in tears, that she had some concerns about the death of the baby who had died from SIDS. She wondered if it had been SIDS. Now sobbing, Sherry told of putting the baby to bed, going in later to feed it, and finding the baby's face covered with blood, apparently coming from the nose. The baby was not moving and felt cold. As I listened to this account, I feel a sickening feeling in the pit of my stomach. Blood from the nose is not typically associated with SIDS. There were looks of concern and distress on the faces of the other women.

Barbara, who was lying on her stomach, covered her head. Sherry continued. She related that she had called her husband in terror and he had told her "Don't worry. I'll check the baby. You fix the bottle." Sherry did so, assuming that she was just a nervous new mother and that the baby was really all right. In her absence, her husband cleaned the baby, and when she returned with the bottle, he told her that the baby was dead. From the horror on the faces of the other women, it was obvious that they recognized that cleaning the baby was an attempt to get rid of the evidence. I could only wonder what kind of unfeeling brute would kill his baby, send the mother off to fix the bottle while giving her false hope that the baby was not dead, and then announce to the mother when she returned to feed her baby that the baby was dead?

Sherry told the group that her husband had resented the baby and had felt that the baby tied them down. "I always wondered about the death," she sobbed. Vicky, who could easily relate to the loss of a child to SIDS, was clearly suspicious. She was shaking her head and said emphatically: "I lost a baby to SIDS, and this doesn't sound right. What did the autopsy show?"

You could have cut the silence in the room with a knife. Through the sobs, Sherry relayed that her husband had had the baby cremated the next day. By now there was no doubt in anyone's mind that her husband had killed the baby. There was no way for Sherry to continue the denial that had enabled her to live with this man for several more years and have another child by him. I wondered whether the baby had been cremated or simply buried in a field somewhere.

At this point, Sherry shared events that had occurred earlier in the evening that the baby was murdered. Her husband had taken the newborn outside in the rain with nothing on but a diaper. It was very cold as well as raining. Sherry ran out and pulled the baby away from him and attempted to run back to the house. He continued to beat her and pushed her the entire way. Several motorists screamed at him in an attempt to get

him to stop beating her and lashing out at the baby. She eventually made it home, where she fed and clothed the baby and put it to bed. Her husband had gone out, so she went to bed. When she did not hear the baby cry and it was past time for the feeding, she became concerned and went to the baby.

The picture of this distraught young mother grabbing her infant away and attempting to get the infant to safety while enduring continued physical assaults on her baby and herself is overwhelming. How vulnerable and desperate she must have felt in her attempts to protect her baby. I doubt that anyone ever told her that the baby had died of SIDS. I assume that she created this explanation because it was believable and enabled her to be able to deal with the loss.

At this point, however, Sherry could no longer deny what had happened. She cried: "I know he killed the baby. He tried to do it when he took the baby outside. He told me he didn't want the baby. That's why he had it cremated and would never discuss it." Clearly, having spoken out loud the words that had been in her head and her heart for nearly ten years, she was no longer able to deny what had actually happened.

As a researcher in the field of family violence for nearly a quarter of a century, I know the language. I know that men often threaten to kill their baby because of jealousy, immaturity, and a desire to return to the childless state. I am also familiar with the statistics on wife and child abuse and child fatalities. However, none of this prepared me for witnessing the pain that Sherry experienced when she could no longer deny what had actually happened. In addition to experiencing beatings she had to recognize that not only had her husband killed their baby, he had had the baby cremated, thus denying her any symbolic remembrance of the baby or even an opportunity to grieve the loss. Because she was dependent on her husband and saw no other alternative, she was forced to live this lie in order to survive.

This was perhaps the most wrenching experience I have ever witnessed. Her sobbing and shaking were as intense as if the murder had just occurred. And in fact, given her denial and suppression of event, it was the realization of the murder intensified by ten years of repression. Statistics such as "child abuse based on self-report has decreased 47% between 1975 and 1985" will never seem quite so reassuring.

Chapter Summary

Clearly it is not possible to isolate totally the impact of external factors such as discrimination, sexism, racism, ageism, poverty, unemployment, and inadequate housing from an individual's characteristics that may contribute to family violence. Likewise, as science unravels genetic coding and medicine reveals the inner working of the body and mind, our understanding of intraindividual factors that lead to violence will expand. It is likely, in most instances, however, that family violence results from a combination of intraindividual and sociocultural factors. Individual characteristics provide the predisposition to engage in aggressive behavior, but it is the culture and the social context that enable, discourage, or prohibit the use of violence to resolve conflict or gain control.

The devastating, lifelong effects of being reared in a family where violence occurs can been seen in the media coverage of violent crimes and in the histories of prisoners. Fortunately, this is an area where intervention in terms of legislation, education, crisis lines and shelters, and programs to improve individuals' parenting and partnering skills have had an impact. A comparison of the levels of family violence in two national surveys found a nearly 50% decrease in child abuse and over a 25% decrease in wife abuse in a decade. The authors of these studies suggest that these reductions were directly the result of policy and legislative changes as well as prevention and intervention programs (Straus, Gelles, & Steinmetz, 1980; Steinmetz & Straus, 1974).

The link between street violence and family violence has been clearly documented. As street violence continues to rise and youths at increasingly younger ages become violent, it is important that our efforts to reduce all violence be approached in a comprehensive manner. Our youths must be taught not only responsibility and control of aggressiveness and violence but also empathy—the ability to put yourself in another's shoes so as to understand the pain of violence.

Discussion Questions

1. Explain how violence has changed (or not changed) over the centuries in America.
2. What is meant by power in relationships, and how does the use or abuse of power possibly lead to violence in families?
3. What is meant by a cycle of violence?
4. Write a short essay that describes the main points of the author's case study. What is she trying to demonstrate with this segment? Would you have a difficult time being a worker in the Child Protective Services area? Why? Why not?

Additional Resources

Gelles, R. J. (1979). Etiology of violence: Overcoming fallacious reasoning in understanding family violence and child abuse. In R. J. Gelles (Ed.), *Family violence*. Newbury Park, CA: Sage.

Rosenbaum, A., & O'Leary, K. D. (1981). Marital violence: Characteristics of abusive couples. *Journal of Consulting and Clinical Psychology, 49*, 63–71.

Straus, M. A., Gelles, R. J., & Steinmetz, S. K. (1980). *Behind closed doors: Violence in American families*. New York: Doubleday.

References

Bates, R. P. (1977, June). *Child abuse—the problem*. Paper presented at the second world conference of the International Society on Family Law, Montreal.

Bellak, L., & Antell, M. (1974). An intellectual study of aggressive behavior on children's playgrounds. American *Journal of Orthopsychiatry, 44*, 503–511.

Benson, D. F., & Blummer, D. (Eds.) (1975). *Psychiatric aspects of neurological disease*. New York: Grune & Stratton.

Bernard, M. L., & Bernard, J. L. (1983). Violent intimacy: The family as a model for love relationships. *Family Relations, 32*, 283–286.

Blanchard, D. C., & Blanchard, R. H. (1983). Hawaii violence: A preliminary analysis. In A. P. Goldstein & M. H. Segall (Eds.), *Aggression in global perspective.* New York: Pergamon Press.

Bremner, R. H. (1970). *Children and youth in America: A documentary history: Vol. 1.* Boston: Harvard University Press.

Dalton, K. (1980). Cyclical criminal acts in premenstrual syndrome. *Lancet, 2,* 1070–1071.

DeMause, L. (1974). *A history of childhood.* New York: Psycho-History Press.

Demos, J. (1970). *A little commonwealth.* New York: Oxford University Press.

Divale, W. T. (1974). Migration extended warfare and matrilocal residence. *Behavior Science Research, 9,* 75–133.

Dossett, R. G., Burch, N. R., & Keller, W. J. (1982, October). *An electrophysiological profile of violence: The EEG of juvenile offenders.* Paper presented at the Southwest Science Forum Symposium on Violence and Aggression, Houston.

Dubanski, R. A., & Snyder, K. (1980). Patterns of child abuse and neglect in Japanese- and Samoan-Americans. *Child Abuse and Neglect, 4*(4), 217–225.

Elliott, F. (1978). Neurological aspects of psychopathic behavior. In W. H. Reid (Ed.), *The psychopath: A comprehensive study of antisocial disorders and behavior.* New York: Brunner/Mazel.

Elliott, F. (1982). Neurological findings in adult minimal brain dysfunction and dyscontrol syndrome. *The Journal of Nerves and Mental Diseases, 170,* 680–687.

Fischer, D. H. (1977). *Growing old in America.* New York: Oxford University Press.

Gage, R. B. (1988). *An analysis of relational control patterns in abusive couples.* Unpublished doctoral dissertation, Seton Hall University, South Orange, NJ.

Gelles, R. J. (1975). Violence and pregnancy: A note on the extent of the problem and needed services. *The Family Coordinator, 24*(1), 81–86.

Gelles, R. J. (1979). Etiology of violence: Overcoming fallacious reasoning in understanding family violence and child abuse. In R. J. Gelles (Ed.), *Family violence.* Newbury Park, CA: Sage.

Gill, D. (1970). *Violence against children: Physical child abuse in the United States.* Cambridge, MA: Harvard University Press.

Gondolf, E. W. (1988). Who are those guys? Toward a behavioral typology of batterers. *Violence and Victims, 3,* 187–203.

Green, A. H. (1978). Self-destructive behavior in battered children. *American Journal of Psychiatry, 135,* 579–582.

Greven, P. (1970). *Four generations: Population, land and family in colonial Andover, Massachusetts.* Ithaca, NY: Cornell University Press.

Hiberman, E., & Munson, I. (1977–1978). Sixty battered women. *Victimology, 2,* 460–470.

Infante, D. A., Chandler, T. A., & Rudd, J. E. (1989). Test of an argumentative skill deficiency model of interspousal violence. *Communication Monographs, 56*(2).

Infante, D. A., Sabourin, T. C., Rudd, J. E., & Shannon, P. A. (1990). Verbal aggression in violent and non-violent marital disputes. *Communication Quarterly, 4,* 361–371.

Infante, D. A., & Wigley, C. J. (1986). Verbal aggressiveness: An interpersonal model and measure. *Communication Monographs, 53*(1), 61–69.

Jarvik, L. F., Klodin, V., & Matsuyama, S. S. (1973). Human aggression and the extra chromosome: Fact or fantasy? *American Psychologist, 28,* 674.

Kinard, E. M. (1980). Emotional development in physically abused children. *American Journal of Orthopsychiatry, 50,* 686–696.

Kumagai, F., & O'Donoghue, G. (1978). Conjugal power and conjugal violence in Japan and the U.S.A. *Journal of Comparative Family Studies, 9,* 211–221.

Langman, L. (1973). *Economic practices and socialization in three societies.* Paper presented at the annual meeting of the American Sociological Association.

Lauderdale, M., Valiunas, A., & Anderson, M. (1980). Race, ethnicity, and child maltreatment: An empirical analysis. *Child Abuse and Neglect, 4*(3), 163–169.

Lester, D. (1980). A cross-cultural study of wife abuse. *Aggressive Behavior, 6,* 361–364.

Lewis, D. O., Pincus, J., Shanok, S., & Glaser, G. (1982). Psychomotor epilepsy and violence in a group of incarcerated adolescent boys. *American Journal of Psychiatry, 139,* 882–887.

Maccoby, E. E., & Jacklin, C. N. (1974). *The psychology of sex differences.* Stanford, CA.: Stanford University Press.

Marsden, D. (1978). Sociological perspectives on family violence. In J. M. Martin (Ed.), *Violence and the family.* New York: Wiley.

Masumura, W. T. (1979). Wife abuse and other forms of aggression. *Victimology: An International Journal, 4,* 46–59.

McKinley, D. G. (1964). *Social class and family life.* New York: Free Press.

Mead, M. (1935). *Sex and temperament in three primitive societies.* New York: Morrow.

Milner, J. S., & Wimberly, R. C. (1980). Prediction and explanation of child abuse. *Journal of Clinical Psychology, 36,* 875–884.

Monroe, R. R. (1970). *Episodic behavioral disorders: A psychodynamic and neurophysiologic analysis.* Cambridge, MA: Harvard University Press.

Morgan, E. S. (1966). *The Puritan family.* New York: Harper & Row.

Newberger, E. H., Reed, R. B., Daniel, J. H., Hyde, J. N., & Kotelchuck, M. (1977). Pediatric social illness: Toward an etiologic classification. *Pediatrics, 60,* 178–185.

Otterbein, K. F., & Otterbein, C. S. (1965). An eye for an eye, a tooth for a tooth: A cross-cultural study of feuding. *American Anthropologist, 67,* 1470–1482.

Prescott, J. W. (1975). Body pleasure and the origins of violence. *Bulletin of the Atomic Scientists, 31,* 10–20.

Prescott, S., & Letko, C. (1977). Battered: A social psychological perspective. In M. M. Ray (Ed.), *Battered women: A psychosociological study of domestic violence.* New York: Van Nostrand Reinhold.

Radbill, S. X. (1968). A history of child abuse and infanticide. In R. E. Helper & C. H. Kempe (Eds.), *The battered child.* Chicago: University of Chicago Press.

Resnick, M. (1976). *Wife beating: Counselor training manual #1.* Ann Arbor, MI: NOW-WIFE Assault Task Force.

Ridington, J. (1977–1978). The transition process: A feminist environment as reconstitutive milieu. *Victimology, 2,* 563–575.

Rosen, B. (1979). Interpersonal values among child-abusive women. *Psychological Reports, 45,* 819–822.

Rosenbaum, A., & O'Leary, K. D. (1981). Marital violence: Characteristics of abusive couples. *Journal of Consulting and Clinical Psychology, 49,* 63–71.

Roy, M. (1977). A current survey of 150 cases. In M. Roy (Ed.), *Battered women: A psychosociological study of domestic violence.* New York: Van Nostrand Reinhold.

Saunders, D. G., & Hanusa, D. (1987, July). *Are there different types of men who batter? An empirical study with possible treatment implications.* Paper presented at the Third National Family Violence Research Conference, Durham, NH.

Scanzoni, J. (1978). Sex roles, women's work and marital conflict: A study of family change. Lexington, MA: Lexington Books.

Shields, N. M., & Hanneke, C. R. (1983). *Violent husbands: Patterns of individual violence.* Unpublished report presented to National Institute of Mental Health. Cited in Gondolf (1988).

Slater, P., & Slater, D. (1965). Maternal ambivalence and narcissism. *Merrill Palmer Quarterly, 11,* 241–259.

Smith, D. B. (1980). *Inside the great house: Planter family life in the eighteenth-century Chesapeake society.* Ithaca, NY: Cornell University Press.

Sonkin, D. J., Martin, D., & Walker, L. E. (1985). *The male batterer: A treatment approach.* New York: Springer.

Steinmetz, S. K. (1979). Wife beating: A critique and reformulation of existing theory. *Bulletin of the American Academy of Psychiatry and the Law, 6,* 322–334.

Steinmetz, S. K. (1980). Women and violence: Victims and perpetrators. *American Journal of Psychotherapy, 34,* 334–350.

Steinmetz, S. K. (1981). Marital abuse: A cross-cultural comparison. *Sociology and Social Welfare, 8,* 404–414.

Steinmetz, S. K. (1982). Marital abuse: A cross-cultural comparison of sibling violence. *International Journal of Family Psychiatry, 2,* 337–351.

Steinmetz, S. K. (1987). Family violence. In M. B. Sussman & S. K. Steinmetz (Eds.), *Handbook of marriage and the family.* New York: Plenum.

Steinmetz, S. K., & Straus, M. A. (1973). The family as cradle of violence. *Society, 10*(6), 50–56.

Steinmetz, S. K., & Straus, M. A. (Eds.). (1974). *Violence in the family.* New York: Harper & Row.

Straus, M. A. (1976). Sexual inequality, cultural norms and wife-beating. *Victimology, 1,* 54–76.

Straus, M. A. (1977–1978). Wifebeating: How common and why? *Victimology, 2,* 443–457.

Straus, M. A., Gelles, R. J., & Steinmetz, S. K. (1980). *Behind closed doors: Violence in American families.* New York: Doubleday.

Sweet, J. J., & Resnick, P. (1979). The maltreatment of children: A review of theories and research. *Journal of Social Issues, 35,* 40–59.

Tardiff, K. (1982, October). *Endocrine effects in aggression and violence.* Paper presented at the Southwest Forum Symposium on Violence and Aggression, Houston.

Tiger, L. (1969). *Men in groups.* New York: Random House.

Togerson, D. (1973, February 20). Violence in families. *Daily Times,* Mamaroneck, NY, p. 4.

Turbett, J. P., & O'Toole, R. (1980). *Physician's recognition of child abuse.* Paper presented at the annual meeting of the American Sociological Association, New York.

Van Velzen, H. U. E., & Van Wetering, W. (1960). Residence, power groups, and intra-societal aggression. *International Archives of Ethnography, 49,* 169–200.

Walker, L. E. (1977–1978). Battered women and learned helplessness. *Victimology, 2,* 525–534.

Whitchurch, G. G. (1989). *A typology of relationship process in interspousal violence.* Unpublished doctoral dissertation, University of Delaware, Newark, DE.

Whitchurch, G. G., & Pace, J. L. (1993). Communication skills training and interspousal violence. *Journal of Applied Communication Research, 21,* 96–110.

Whitehurst, R. (1974). Violence in husband-wife interaction. In S. K. Steinmetz, & M. A. Straus (Eds.), *Violence in the family.* New York: Harper & Row.

Whiting, B. (1965). Sex identity conflict and physical violence: A comparative study. *American Anthropologist, 67,* 123–140.

Williams, D. (1969). Neural factors related to habitual aggressives and others who have committed crimes of violence. *Brain, 92,* 503–520.

Yllo, K. (1983). Sexual equality and violence against wives in American states. *Journal of Comparative Family Studies, 14,* 67–86.

The Process of Divorce

Linda J. Wark / Suzanne Bartle / Patrick C. McKenry

Ohio State University

Although the divorce rate in the United States has stabilized in recent years, it is predicted that two-thirds of all marriages today will result in divorce (Martin & Bumpass, 1989). For all family members, divorce represents a sense of loss, personal disorganization, and failure in interpersonal relationships, as well as the beginning of a difficult transition to new life patterns (Price & McKenry, 1988). Divorced people are overrepresented in all psychiatric populations and have higher morbidity rates than married cohorts (Coombs, 1991).

In Chapter 6 ("Family-Systems Theory") the concept of levels of analysis was introduced. One aspect of that concept is the idea that during a crisis the various levels of interaction can be interrupted. Some would suggest that divorce is a Level II or even a Level III disruption for most people. For some it shakes the very foundation of their life. For others, it may not be so devastating, but certainly most divorces have a powerful impact.

Divorce is receiving increased attention as a stress-inducing life event, and there is a corresponding interest in ways of controlling or minimizing its disruptive experiences. Yet little is known about the coping mechanisms and circumstances that facilitate or hinder the process of divorce (Berman & Turk, 1981; Kaffman, 1993). Although there is substantial research to document the relationship between demographic variables and divorce, the interpersonal literature is limited primarily to a theoretical and speculative format (Price-Bonham & Balswick, 1980; White, 1990). We know very little about the relationship of divorce to relation-

ship quality, social-psychological factors, or family structure (White, 1990).

Recent research has indicated that divorce has both short- and long-term effects, suggesting that for some individuals recovery is perhaps never fully realized (Hetherington, 1989; Kitson, 1992; Wallerstein & Blakeslee, 1989). Also, there is increasing recognition that divorce is not a single life event but involves numerous changes as the marriage deteriorates and a new lifestyle is established (Kitson & Morgan, 1990; Price & McKenry, 1989).

A family-process approach to the study of divorce implies an analysis of the actions, intentions, beliefs, and feelings involved in the decision to divorce and the transition to a new lifestyle (Scanzoni, 1978; Sprey, 1990). A family-process analysis also involves a developmental perspective on the dynamics of divorce, assuming that the etiology of divorce and divorce adjustment are components of the same developmental progression. This perspective includes a number of prevailing conceptual approaches in family studies, especially symbolic interaction, social exchange, conflict, and systems (Holman & Burr, 1980; Scanzoni, Polonko, Teachman, & Thompson, 1989). The family-process approach is in contrast to more traditional, static approaches, which focus on the end products of decision-making, adjustment, and conflict as opposed to the dynamics of interactions in the separation period, including negotiations, utilization of resources, and coping mechanisms actually involved in divorce (Scanzoni, 1978).

This chapter will draw on various theoretical perspectives in an attempt to describe the process of divorce. We begin by discussing more individually oriented approaches and then move to more systemic approaches, which include all family members in describing the process of divorce. Specifically, attachment, grief/loss, stress, structural, and two intergenerational theories—Bowen's family systems theory and contextual family-therapy theory—will be used to depict patterns of marital dissolution and adjustment and to suggest appropriate intervention modalities.

Attachment Theory

Theoretical Background

Men and women frequently experience a wide range of conflicting and confusing emotions in response to marital separation. These ambivalent feelings are often the result of an attachment response that spouses draw upon as they cope with the stress associated with divorce. This attachment to the former spouse is composed of emotional bonds of ease, comfort, and security that develop between marital partners (Kitson, 1992).

Application to Divorce

Application of this concept to divorce is based on Bowlby's work on attachment in infancy (Bowlby, 1969, 1973, 1977). He has indicated that attachment figures provide children with a sense of security, comfort, and well-being, both psychological and physical. He maintains that attachment behavior is persistent, learned behavior. Once developed, attachment may continue to a significant degree even when a relationship is no longer rewarding, because the predictably familiar is preferred over the strange (Kitson, 1992).

It is thought that adult attachment may be a residuel of infant attachment, providing a psychological sense of security and safety more than physical safety (Berman, 1988). In adults, attachment behavior is most likely to occur when they are distressed, ill, or afraid. The changes produced by the decision to divorce may induce the need for the familiar and previously comforting attachment figure of the former spouse. Weiss (1975) compares spouses in conflict to battered children in their feelings: they may be angry, even furious with each other, but they become almost paralyzed with fear when they actually consider leaving their marriage.

When the bonds of attachment are severed, individuals react with separation anxiety (Bowlby, 1969, 1973), separation distress (Parkes, 1972; Weiss, 1975), or attachment distress (Berman, 1988). Weiss suggests that separation distress in adults is analogous to the child's response to threat of abandonment. These reactions may be overtly manifested by feelings of anxiety, panic, apprehensiveness, denial and disbelief, guilt, anger, depression, and tearfulness and behaviors that seek to maintain contact with the former spouse. Separation responses may also operate in a purely cognitive domain—for example, evoking a mental representation of the attachment figure or feelings of longing and emptiness (Berman, 1988). Many want to hear about their former spouses, to learn how they are doing. They may seek reassurance that the spouse remains accessible without recognizing that they are seeking it (Weiss, 1975). Sometimes the loss of attachment gives rise to a fragile period of euphoria or intervals of euphoria and distress; however, this euphoria is thought to be a component of separation distress and not to be an integrated or lasting aspect of the separated individual's personality. These separation reactions are thought to be the most confusing and difficult aspect of the divorce process for the divorcing couples as well as those who work with them (Berman, 1988; Weiss, 1976).

Various studies have indicated that attachment is highly related to emotional distress and postdivorce adjustment (Berman, 1988; P. Brown, Felton, Whiteman, & Manela, 1980; Kitson, 1992; Tschann, Johnston, & Wallerstein, 1989). Also, attachment anxiety or distress appears to be quite common in divorce. Kitson (1992) and Weiss (1976) suggest that attachment is nearly universal; however, some studies have indicated that a significant minority does not experience any separation anxiety or distress (Goode, 1956; Spanier & Casto, 1979). The differences in study findings may be related to how long after the divorce the interview was conducted, as Kitson (1992) found that strong feelings of attachment rapidly decreased one year after the divorce. Nevertheless, 60% of Kitson's sample was still experiencing lingering signs of attachment four years after the separation.

A variety of factors has been found to predict attachment after divorce. While Kitson (1992) found no gender differences in the extent of separation anxiety experienced, Brown and colleagues (1980) found that men reported more attachment than women, perhaps because they were less likely to initiate the divorce and to obtain custody of their children. Kitson has found racial differences in the extent of attachment distress experienced; nonwhites (largely black) experienced significantly less attachment than did whites; this was perhaps related to the fact that divorce is more normative in the African-American community. Social support has been found to mediate separation distress by providing meaningful attachments to other individuals (Tschann et al., 1989). Tschann and colleagues found that general social support was related to decreased attachment for both men and women; for men, however, an intimate relationship further reduced feelings of attachment to the former spouse. In addition, the intensity of the stressors (such as economic) and strains (such as conflict with the former spouse) accompanying the marital separation has been found to accentuate attachment distress (Hetherington, Cox, & Cox, 1976; Tschann et al., 1989). Thus, a particularly bitter, traumatic, and conflictual separation is likely to increase the extent of separation distress and length of time required to recover. Brown and colleagues (1980) found that high separation distress was related to more contact with the former spouse, not wanting the divorce, and not initiating the separation.

Berman (1985) specifically examined a variety of predictors of attachment behaviors in a sample of women. He found several variables related to prolonged attachment to the former spouse: presence of minor children, especially boys; having low-status jobs and little education; the quality of the relationship prior to and during the separation; not wanting the divorce at the time of separation; more positive feelings toward the former spouse prior to separation; and more tension and conflict in contacts with the former spouse—not the amount of contact per se. According to attachment theory, the presence of minor children, especially boys, and economic hardships creates more tension and anxiety, thus stimulating the attachment drive. Theory would also suggest that the loss of a loved one, as in the case of those who did not desire a divorce or who

experienced affection and love prior to separation, will also increase separation distress. The separation itself may create a kind of anxious attachment, leading the person with prolonged attachment to engage in hostile and conflictual contacts, even though he or she longs for and misses the former spouse.

Although most research suggests that attachment responses to a former spouse are negative, if not pathological, phenomena, Kelly (1988) contends that some forms of attachment after divorce contain elements of healthy adjustment to the termination of a marital relationship. For example, individuals who choose to mediate a divorce may do so because they have retained a friendly relationship with the spouse and wish to minimize hostility. Likewise, Ahrons (1983) has proposed that a positive relationship between divorcing spouses is crucial to their postdivorce adjustment. Finally, Wright and Price (1986) found that attachment to a former spouse was significantly related to a father's compliance with court-ordered child-support requirements.

Although attachment theorists view divorce as the severing of relationship bonds, with resulting anxiety and distress, other theorists view this transition as a time of crisis. The grief/loss perspective focuses on stages of loss and recovery during this crisis. Family-stress theory proposes that divorce may or may not result in a crisis for the family.

Grief/Loss Perspective

The grief/loss perspective views divorce as a critical life event that involves a specified developmental emotional reaction as one severs bonds of attachment and mourns the losses represented by divorce. This theoretical approach dates back to Waller's (1938) seven alienation crises and four-stage readjustment to the loss of the mate, but it was more fully developed in the 1970s by clinically oriented researchers and theorists to deal specifically with the consequences of separation and divorce. This theory is based on overlapping stages that describe some of the psychological consequences of separation and divorce (Raschke, 1987). Various models have been put forth to account for the developmental progression of both adults and children as they grieve the losses associated with divorce. These models are in basic agreement that successful coping with divorce involves a predictable series of stages of grief reaction: denial, anger, bargaining, depression, and acceptance; these models primarily vary in having different starting and ending points in the separation and divorce process. The models stipulate that each person experiences divorce differently; some individuals skip phases or change the sequence of their occurrence, and others are in more than one phase simultaneously. Also, the intensity of each stage may vary with the individual. Some of the models focus on feelings, and others delineate states of being that incorporate these feelings (Salts, 1979). Although their explanatory power appears high, these theoretical models are relatively recent, and considerably more research is needed for further development and refinement (Raschke, 1987).

Most consistent with a process approach, Kessler's (1975) seven-stage model of emotional divorce proposes that the process of divorce begins early in the marriage when *disillusionment* with the marriage or the spouse occurs for one partner. She suggests that when differences are not openly acknowledged and resolved, the partners move into the *erosion* stage, which is defined as the wearing away of marital satisfaction and is characterized by sexual problems, vindictive behaviors, and increased fulfilling of needs outside marriage. A couple may remain in the erosion stage for several years. If the erosion stage is not reversed, the couples move into a *detachment* stage, which is characterized by indifference and boredom. The reality of the unhappy marriage becomes very apparent, the individual moves from a past to a future orientation, and thoughts of separation or divorce become common. The *physical separation* stage is a distinct stage in the Kessler and other models; it is characterized by anxiety, loneliness, guilt, disorganization, and confusion. After separation, the individual moves into a *mourning* stage characterized by feelings of anger, depression, helplessness, and hurt; the focus is on the self and movement through the grief process toward the reconstruction of a new identity and lifestyle. When the individual begins to function as an autonomous individual, there is a reorientation of priorities and reevaluation of values, a stage that Kessler terms *second adolescence* because it is characterized by overreaction and new learning, through trial and error.

As the reestablishment of a coherent and stable identity and life pattern continues, the individual enters the last stage of the divorce process, which Kessler labels *hard work*. The anxious floundering is replaced by renewed vitality to pursue manageable, reachable goals.

For children, a similar pattern has been noted, although little is known about the interaction between child and parental stress responses (Kurdek, 1981). The research literature clearly indicates that divorce represents a major crisis for children as it does for adults. However, for children the period of adjustment may be longer and more intense, reaching into adulthood in some cases, because children lose the family structure and support that is fundamental to their development (Wallerstein & Blakeslee, 1989). In addition, children lose not just the noncustodial parent but several familiar supports, such as daily routine; the symbols, traditions, and continuity of the intact family; economic well-being; and the home, school, and neighborhood (Hetherington, Stanley-Hagan, & Anderson, 1989; Wallerstein & Blakeslee, 1989). For most children, the news of the divorce is received as both distressing and *shocking*. Wallerstein and Kelly (1980) found that few children ever expected their parents to divorce regardless of the extent of conflict, and children can be quite content even when their parents' marriage is profoundly unhappy for one or both partners (Wallerstein & Kelly, 1980). The child then enters a stage of *denial*; he or she may withdraw from others into a fantasy world of images of a happy family life prior to divorce. As the reality of the divorce is recognized, children characteristically respond with intense feelings of *anger* (internalized or externalized) as they feel personally rejected. Anger frequently is expressed to engage both parents in the hope of bringing about a reconciliation. When anger and denial prove nonproductive, children will enter the *bargaining* stage. They may imagine that some change in their behavior will result in a reconciliation. When children find that their efforts to reunite their parents have failed, they move into a stage of *depression*, feeling responsible and thus guilty about their parents' marital problems. *Acceptance* comes when children learn that an objective reality exists, whether or not they like it, but that a satisfactory relationship with the parents can still exist (Hozman & Froiland, 1977; Wallerstein & Kelly, 1980). Like the adult progression, these stages may not occur in a clear, progressive fashion; regression to a prior stage or an overlapping of stages is common. Also, for children these stages may be manifest in a wide range of somatic disturbances—for example, hyperactivity, anorexia, nausea, vomiting, diarrhea, urinary frequency, and sleep disturbances (Anthony, 1974).

While stages of mourning and loss during the crisis of divorce are the foundation of the grief/loss perspective, family-stress theory asserts that factors influence whether divorce will result in a crisis for a particular family.

The ABCX Family-Stress Model

Theoretical Background

Several theories of family stress and crisis have influenced the field of family science (Boss, 1987; Raschke, 1987). One of the most prominent and recently developed is the *ABCX model* (Hill, 1958), where A is a stressful event (stressor), B is the family's resources available to meet the event, C is the perception of the event—that is, whether it is viewed as a crisis—and X is the outcome, or degree of stress.

Originally, most of the stress research examined the impact of a single stressor event on the outcome (Lavee, McCubbin, & Olson, 1987). More recently, the concept of stressor pileup has been incorporated into family-stress theory to explain the accumulation of stressors that families can experience (McCubbin et al., 1980). Most recently, a refined model, the *Double ABCX*, focuses on family postcrisis behavior (McCubbin & Patterson, 1983a, 1983b). The four additional factors in this model are aA, the pile-up of stressors (including normative family life demands), bB, family adaptive resources, cC, family definition and meaning of the stressor events, and xX, the adaptation outcome (good or bad).

Boss (1987) expanded on the C factor of the ABCX model (perceptions of stressor events) with the construct *boundary ambiguity*. Boundary ambiguity is defined as "a state when family members are uncertain in their perception of who is in or out of the family or who is performing what roles and tasks within the family system" (Boss, 1987, p. 709). There are two components to an ambiguous situation: *physical presence or*

absence and *psychological presence or absence*. If these two components are incongruent—for example, a family member is physically absent but psychologically present—ambiguous perceptions regarding the boundaries of the family will result. This is illustrated by a family whose father is missing in action (physical absence) but that sets a place at the dinner table every evening for this parent (psychological presence).

Application to Divorce

With regard to divorce, the ABCX model can explain why some families experience a divorce as a crisis while others do not (Price-Bonham & Balswick, 1980). In addition, it demonstrates how stressors and perceptions of stressors can play a role in family functioning and well-being and, thus, postdivorce adjustment (Lavee et al., 1987). The large number of stresses and strains associated with separation decreases adult functioning after divorce (Tschann et al., 1989). Child social functioning after divorce has also been explained by the ABCX model (Peterson, Leigh, & Day, 1984). In this application of the model, the disengagement of a spouse/parent from the family is viewed as a potential stressor influencing children's social competence in two ways. First, it has a direct influence on the meaning of the divorce for the child. A second influence is the indirect consequences of the partner's disengagement on the residential parent's capacity to maintain a good relationship with the child.

The Double ABCX model explains how and how well a family manages the transition of divorce. Divorce will vary in its impact depending on the resources available to the family members and the family's perception of the divorce. It is important to note that a stressor event does not always result in stressor crisis but that the buildup of stressors or an unexpected stressor can *possibly* lead to a crisis. This can be understood by considering the B and C factors. In fact, the transition of divorce is considered by some to be a normative stressor (Ahrons, 1983; Price & McKenry, 1988) where losses and gains of family membership are events with potential for stress until the transition is complete (Boss, 1980).

Although divorce can be thought of as a normative event, the uncertainties of change that accompany a marital breakup are considered highly stressful. Boss

(1983) asserts that several stress factors have an impact on divorcing families: (1) There is a loss of one or more family members, which represents a change in the family system boundaries. (2) The loss is unclear; is the family member still a part of the family? (3) There are no societal rituals to reorganize the family. (4) Roles must be reassigned. (5) The loss includes one of the executives in the parental subsystem.

While coping resources may be important in recovering from the divorce transition, the ambiguity that makes the boundaries of the family's identity diffuse are thought to have a greater influence on adjustment of the members (Boss & Greenberg, 1984). It is this uncertainty that inhibits the family system from reorganizing after its membership has shifted. Remarriage and stepchildren also challenge the security of the original family boundaries (Pasley, 1987), but even before these possibilities arise, uncertainty regarding who is in or out of the family is a problem. Boss refers to this as ambiguous loss.

The shifting of membership and roles can be subtle. As the family members begin to reorganize, some of them may be denied a physical presence in the family system. For example, the first birthday party after a separation may not include one of the parents, yet this parent will be very present in the minds of the family members. One of the most prominent losses for children during divorce is the loss of a sense of the nuclear family (Isaacs, Leon, & Kline, 1987). For example, children may be accustomed to the routine of their father waking them up in the morning. When he has moved away from home, the morning ritual must change. The children and mother experience a loss of father who is still psychologically present but physically absent, and whose role in the family has now become blurred. Inconsistent visitation may also result in boundary ambiguity, which may explain why inconsistent visitation patterns are more stressful for children than consistent visitation or total absence of contact (Ahrons, 1983; Isaacs, Montalvo, & Abelsohn, 1986). Adults also experience this ambiguity of not knowing where they fit in. Where formerly a husband could walk casually into the couple's home, he may now be required to wait on the porch, and his ex-wife may display extreme anger if he does otherwise.

Family-stress theory bridges the gap between more individually oriented theories and more systemic theories. Systemic theories allow for an expansion of "cause/effect" relationships (refer to Chapter 7 for a discussion of how the deterministic model is different from a systems approach) to incorporate a wider view of the divorce process. In other words, from a systemic perspective one can look at the impact of divorce on the entire family system. One can find answers to several questions, such as how does conflict between former spouses affect children and how do children's responses affect the conflict? How does the type of relationship between spouses before the divorce decision make a difference to children's postdivorce adjustment?

Structural Family Theory

Theoretical Background

Minuchin (1974) proposes that meaningful information about families is gained by examining their *structure*—that is, how members are arranged in relation to one another. As in systems theory, the structure of families is determined by subsystems and hierarchical arrangements. *Subsystems*, meaning either two or more people or an individual member (Minuchin, 1974), must have both autonomy and interdependence with other subsystems. *Hierarchy* refers to the appropriate separation of generational subsystems in the family. Because of this separation, members within each generation take certain roles; adults earn money to support the family, and children have more leisure time than adults. Finally, the concept of *boundaries* is essential to this theory, because it is believed that various types of boundaries separate the subsystems of the family in different ways.

Boundaries are the rules of interaction defining who participates and how (Minuchin, 1974). Thus, boundaries determine the kind of shared space, or territory, in which the family members engage (Wood & Talmon, 1983). Boundaries, or invisible lines of demarcation, can facilitate good family relationships (*clear*, or balanced, boundaries), separate members too much (*rigid*, or closed, boundaries), or permit too much closeness (*diffuse*, or blurred, boundaries). These three types of boundaries lie on a continuum representing balanced combinations of closeness and distance or extreme types of closeness (enmeshment) and distance (disengagement).

Clear, well-demarcated, but flexible boundaries have been proposed as being optimal for healthy family functioning (Serovich, Green, & Parrott, 1992). When family members have rigid or diffuse boundaries, we can say that the family is having boundary problems. Boundaries can be "violated," and this mainly refers to diffuse boundaries, although boundary violations can occur when one family member should encourage closeness but instead shuts the other family member out (for example, a parent and small child).

Rigid boundaries among family members are demonstrated by refusing to listen, always finding reasons to spend time outside the family, and concealing emotions. Diffuse boundaries may be evident when family members are overresponsible for one another, when autonomy is squelched, or in cases of exploitation. Clear boundaries, on the other hand, are recognizable when family members are able to reveal their concerns without fear of being invalidated, when there is flexibility, within limits, in the household rules, and when individuality is preserved.

Application to Divorce

In transitional situations such as divorce, families have to modify a previously existing family structure (Wood & Talmon, 1983). Residential parents, typically mothers, and the children are more likely to have a continuing commitment to the previous system, making fathers peripheral to the old system (Minuchin, 1974). In this transition process, boundaries can fluctuate or change rapidly. Adaptation to this transition is usually stressful, but it does not have to be disastrous or dysfunctional (Abelsohn, 1992). If family boundaries are clear, rather than rigid or diffuse, the transition should be less distressing. Early in the transition to family reorganization, confusion results because of the fluctuation in boundaries. Later in the transition, the process of realigning clear boundaries by defining the coparenting relationship and deciding child custody issues can result in much distress (Ahrons, 1983). Finally, however, by the third year after the divorce, if the new boundaries have been established, many ex-spouses can discuss virtually any topic without creating a tense atmosphere (Isaacs et al., 1986).

Changes in family boundaries after divorce place all members in the task of restructuring these boundaries to make distinctions between the old family and the new families (Walker & Messinger, 1979). Children can experience contradictory situations, causing confusion because of changing boundaries. For example, children may have experienced a clear boundary in their two-parent home (for example, young children have some decision-making power, but not as much as adults) but may experience a more diffuse one in the new home of the nonresidential parent (for example, the young child gets to select a roomful of bedroom furniture).

Parents and their relationships with each other may influence how boundaries are reconstructed. Divorced parents often continue to be hostile toward each other, and the conflict is likely to alienate the child from the nonresident parent (Isaacs et al., 1987). In addition, one parent may deliberately try to construct a more rigid boundary between a child and the other parent to prevent the other parent from having a close relationship (Abelsohn, 1992). Unfortunately, parental hostilities may alienate the child from both parents (Isaacs et al., 1987). Rigid boundaries can also be unwittingly constructed when the residential parent must deal with grief and loss and becomes emotionally unavailable to a child. Divorce is thought to open up boundaries between mothers and their children. This boundary problem is exacerbated when the residential parent experiences the divorce as the loss of a spouse; overcloseness in the parent/child relationship tends to evolve to fill the void (Carter & McGoldrick, 1980). This diffuse type of boundary can also be created because of the fear of "losing" a child (Abelsohn, 1983).

From a systems perspective, one can move beyond the nuclear-family system and incorporate several generations of a family when exploring the process of divorce. These are known as intergenerational approaches. Two family-therapy theories focus on family patterns across the generations: Bowen's family-system theory (Bowen 1976, 1978; Friedman, 1991; Kerr, 1981, 1984), and contextual family therapy (Boszormenyi-Nagy & Krasner, 1987; Boszormenyi-Nagy & Spark, 1973; Van Heusden & Van Den Eerenbeemt, 1987). Both of these theories focus on how individuals function in relation to others in the family and how those others also influence the individual. Both have roots in the psychoanalytic perspective. The psychoanalytic perspective is focused to a large extent on the formation of self and on how early relationships with parental figures promote or inhibit the development of self. In the case of divorce, the focus moves to the children of divorce and how the interruption in relationships with noncustodial parents affects the formation of self, such as identification with the opposite-sex or same-sex parent.

Bowen Family-Systems Theory

Theoretical Background

Bowen's theory (1976, 1978) is based on a notion of *differentiation of self*. Bowen maintains that all individuals have the capacity to function using their emotions and using their intellect. Well-differentiated people can impose their intellect over their emotions. In essence, this allows individuals to observe themselves in relationships and make decisions about their next move, rather than simply reacting. When people are not well differentiated, they are *emotionally reactive*. Bowen contends that emotionally reactive people respond to emotion-evoking situations automatically, perceiving no choice in their response. People who are not well differentiated have three reactive tendencies: withdraw, counterattack, and defend self.

Individuals who are not as well differentiated tend to fuse in relationships. *Fusion* is a state in which the people in the relationship have highly permeable boundaries, as in Minuchin's enmeshment. According to Bowen, we all have tendencies toward fusion, and when we are under stress and experience *anxiety*, this tendency is even stronger. As fusion increases, emotional reactivity increases as well. Bowen suggests that people in fused relationships that are under stress use different distance regulators, or compensatory mechanisms, to break away from the fusion (Beal, 1985). Distance regulators include physical or emotional distance; emotional conflict; emotional, social, or physical dysfunction; and child focus.

Some couples use physical withdrawal or the silent treatment when the anxiety in their relationship is high.

Other couples use open conflict to create some distance between them. In other couples, one person will take the role of the "sick one" and the other the "caretaker." The "sick one" may be depressed, be addicted to some substance, or have any number of other symptoms that leave them dependent on their spouse. The roles of "sick one" and "caretaker" set up a hierarchical structure so that one spouse is almost functioning in a child role, while the other is in a parent role. This structure provides distance for the fused couple.

Finally, some couples focus their anxiety on one or more children. Bowen labels this the *family-projection process*. When this happens, the child may become dysfunctional in some way, perhaps acting out at school, getting involved with drugs, or having some other psychological or physical symptom. The child's symptom allows the parents to focus their attention on the child, away from their own fused relationship, breaking up the fusion in the process.

The level of fusion in the couple relationship and the intensity of the family-projection process determine the offspring's level of differentiation of self. Bowen suggests that the child who bears the brunt of the projection process will be less differentiated than his or her parents. Some children may be relatively unscathed by the process and stay at the same level of differentiation as their parents or attain a higher level of differentiation of self. These offspring then leave home and more than likely marry. Bowen asserts that people tend to marry others at similar levels of differentiation of self, and then the process begins again. This is known as the *transgenerational transmission process*.

Application to Divorce

Two authors have applied Bowen's theory to the divorce process: Haber (1990) and Beal (1979, 1985). Haber (1990) focuses on the adults' experience in the divorce process, using the concept of differentiation of self. She suggests that the higher the level of fusion in the relationship, the more the individuals use the relationship to define their self-identity. In relationships where the individuals are more differentiated, they are able to balance a sense of themselves as separate and a sense of themselves as connected (Anderson &

Sabatelli, 1990; see also Chapter 2 in this volume). In fused relationships, when the relationship ends there is a significant loss of self (Weiss, 1975). Haber (1990) does not suggest, within the theory, why people choose to divorce.

Beal (1979), on the other hand, writes that the reasons people choose to divorce are directly related to the kinds of compensatory, or distance-regulating, mechanisms that the couple uses to break away from the fusion. If it uses the "caretaker" and "sick one" roles, the "caretaker" is often the one who chooses the divorce, feeling "used up" by the spouse and believing that he or she can no longer maintain a sense of self in the relationship. Weiss (1975) has demonstrated that this may be the case when one spouse is depressed. If the spouses use overt conflict, it could be that the level of conflict no longer works as a distance regulator or that it has become so intense that the partners can no longer bear it. Finally, if the couple focuses its anxiety on a child, the divorce decision may involve one of the spouse's inability to care for the child, or the "odd man out's" decision to find a new relationship.

Once the separation has occurred, the distance-regulating functions of the couple must also be replaced. Haber (1990) writes that the individuals involved must be careful to adjust the pace of the move away from the marriage and into a new relationship. She and Beal (1985) suggest that one way to cover for the loss of self in the relationships is to immediately seek another relationship in which the same level of fusion can be experienced. The goal for the individual is to develop a higher level of differentiation of self than was experienced in the failed marriage before moving to a new relationship.

Beal (1979, 1985) focuses more on the impact on the children in the divorce process. If the couple uses a child focus to break away from the fusion, that child may then bear the brunt of the increased anxiety experienced by the parents through the divorce process. As Bowen suggests, as anxiety increases, so does the tendency toward fusion. With an increased tendency toward fusion, there is an increase in reliance on distance-regulating mechanisms. In the case of divorce, these mechanisms are no longer available in the forms they were before the separation, creating more anxiety. According to Beal (1985):

> as families develop greater anxiety or make greater use of compensatory mechanisms, cooperation disappears, cohesiveness dissolves, and altruistic behavior vanishes. Cooperation is replaced by selfish behavior, and actions taken are often at cross-purposes. As cohesiveness dissolves, the family is divided into subgroups that play one dyad against another. (p. 21)

It is often the children who suffer in this vicious circle of increasing anxiety and fusion. Beal (1979) suggests that parents who use a child focus automatically involve their children in their conflicts and directly or indirectly ask their children to take sides. In this situation, children tend to become dysfunctional in any number of ways (physical, psychological, or behavioral) (Shaw, 1991; Wallerstein & Kelly, 1980; Weiss, 1975). Beal (1979) also suggests, from clinical examples, that in families with a severe child focus, overt conflict that existed between the parents is shifted to overt conflict between the child and the custodial parent. He asserts that the most severe conflict is often between mothers and sons. Wallerstein and Kelly (1980) and others (Weiss, 1979) have demonstrated this as well.

Contextual Family-Therapy Theory

Theoretical Background

Boszormenyi-Nagy's contextual family therapy is also concerned with intergenerational processes in families. He takes a somewhat different approach than Bowen, focusing more on the *ethics of relationships*. Several key concepts within his theory pertain directly to the divorce process. Boszormenyi-Nagy suggest that relationships need to be built on *justice* (Boszormenyi-Nagy & Krasner, 1986; Boszormenyi-Nagy & Spark, 1973). That is, it is important that all members of the family get what they deserve. He maintains that when a child is born, he or she is *entitled* to due care from the parents. As the parents provide this care, they are also *entitled to loyalty*. Individuals in marriages go through a similar process. As they learn that they can *trust* the other through the process of caring for the other and being cared for by the other, they build a sense of loyalty.

If one takes a three-generational perspective, the ethics of relationships start from birth. For example, let us say that a child is born and does not receive proper care from a parent. Perhaps that parent did not receive proper care from his or her own parent and expects that child to provide the love and trust that he or she did not receive early on. In this process the child becomes what Boszormenyi-Nagy refers to as *parentified*, because the child is expected to fulfill a parenting type of role for his or her own parent. This child, however, from the mere fact of birth, is earning entitlement. This may become *destructive entitlement* later on, because the child was not given due care and will expect that from others. Individuals with destructive entitlement may become overly controlling or selfish in relationships, in order to acquire what they believe they deserve. This process may continue throughout generations, with each new generation having to make up for what the other lacked. This is referred to as the *revolving slate*. Boszormenyi-Nagy's goal in all therapeutic work is to repair relationships in order to give future generations a chance.

Application to Divorce

Boszormenyi-Nagy and Spark (1973) have written about the impact of divorce on the family system from a contextual perspective. They suggest that "divorce can only be considered in its three-generational ethical perspective. The burden of each spouse's invisible past loyalties and their obligations to the future of subsequent generations are a crucially important area" (p. 385). Divorce may be a direct result of destructive entitlement, which results in chronic mistrust. Each spouse may feel that he or she has not gotten a fair share within the relationship and that the situation has become intolerable. As the divorce process continues, the children of the couple may become parentified in order to meet the needs of the parent who feels that he or she has not been treated fairly. Weiss (1979) and Wallerstein and Kelly (1980) have found clinical evidence to support this. Boszormenyi-Nagy and Krasner (1986) suggest that children become captive referees of their parents' controversies.

Boszormenyi-Nagy and Krasner (1986) assert that "at worst, youngsters in all their helplessness function as insular sources of trustworthiness in a blatantly un-trustworthy and manipulative adult world. Hurt, puzzled and resentful, parents almost always feel compelled to use their children as a forum in which to vent their contempt, hatred and mistrust" (p. 346). Contextual family-therapy theory also asserts that divorce heightens the parents' inability to cooperate in raising their children, even though that is indeed what they owe their children. Through this process children's loyalties may become divided. There is research evidence to support this phenomenon (Shaw, 1991; Wallerstein, 1987; Wallerstein & Kelly, 1980; Weiss, 1979). The custodial parent may directly or indirectly make it clear that his or her former spouse is a terrible person in some way or another, leaving the child in a dilemma. Is it possible to remain loyal to the custodial parent and still have a relationship with the noncustodial parent? If the child wants a relationship with the noncustodial parent, he or she is often placed in the untenable situation of choosing between parents. In fact, according to Boszormenyi-Nagy, by the mere fact of birth to these parents, the child must be loyal to both, regardless of the parents' failed relationship with each other.

There is some support for taking a multigenerational view of the divorce process. Kaffman (1993) has demonstrated that parental support (the third generation) is important in postdivorce adjustment. Individuals whose parents were not supportive of their decision to divorce or sided with the son-in-law or daughter-in-law tended to have poorer adjustment in the postdivorce phase, even at two years after the separation (Kaffman, 1993). Most of the other research evidence that could be used in support of Bowen's theory or contextual family-therapy theory is about children of divorce. Several studies on college students have demonstrated difficulties in the separation/individuation process or differentiation of self (Allen, Stoltenberg, & Rosko, 1990; Lopez, 1991; Lopez, Campbell, & Watkins, 1988; Wallerstein, 1987). Lopez (1991) and others (Wallerstein, 1987; Wallerstein & Kelly, 1980) suggest that persistent conflict between former spouses, which is one way they react to their experience of fusion, increases the likelihood that the student will be asked to take sides in the argument, as Beal (1985) and Boszormenyi-Nagy have suggested. During this process, the college student is being asked to "get closer" to the family, so to speak, which may go against the developmental tendency to be more separate. Clearly, the student is having difficulty balancing separateness and connectedness in the family and may be dealing with loyalty conflicts as well.

Boszormenyi-Nagy also proposes that to gain a sense of autonomy, one must have been given due care resulting in a sense of trust (Boszormenyi-Nagy & Krasner, 1986). Thus, children of divorce may have difficulties with separation/individuation because they did not receive due care from both parents and thus have difficulty attaining a sense of autonomy. Boszormenyi-Nagy and Krasner (1986) suggest that "a child of divorced parents may lose a great source of self delineation and self validation in addition to losing the actual relationships with their non-custodial parent" (p 74). This loss of sources of self-identification may lead to difficulties in attaining a sense of autonomy and identity.

Kalter (1987), in reviewing the literature on the impact of divorce on children, suggests that children suffer from difficulties in modulating anger and aggression, difficulties with separation, and some difficulty with gender identity. All these may be a product of the increased anxiety in the family system over the divorce and the resultant fusion. With this increase in fusion, parents may project their anxiety onto the children, resulting in the children's dysfunctional behavior. This evidence may also be used in support of Boszormenyi-Nagy's notions that children of divorce may not be getting due care while earning entitlement. They may then engage in destructive entitlement through displays of anger and aggression to get what they deserve in relationships.

The foregoing theories provide some insight into the divorce process and the individuals and families involved. What is most important to understand is that the decision to divorce begins an often lengthy process of adjustment for families. All members experience a significant loss and may experience separation distress. As family members are experiencing the grief and mourning losses, the family system is transforming, changing its boundaries and the nature of the relationships within it. These changes can be both positive and negative and mean different things to different members of the family.

Therapeutic Applications

Theories guide the clinician in therapeutic intervention. Previously described theories will be discussed again as they may be used in practice. Certainly, divorce has the potential to place family members in distressing or confusing situations. Individuals who seek help from professionals for stress associated with divorce are more distressed than those who do not seek help (Kitson, 1992). Besides offering help for individual problems after a divorce, therapists can work effectively with willing couples in conjoint therapy, typically conducted by marriage and family therapists (Goldman & Coane, 1978). However, divorcing spouses who are seen together in therapy report less distress regarding the divorce than spouses seen separately (Kitson, 1992).

The primary goal of divorce therapy is to facilitate as constructive a divorce as possible, protecting children in the process. Other subgoals named by Ahrons (1983) are to (1) aid the parents in maintaining good coparental relationships, (2) assist the family in redefining itself as a binuclear family, and (3) facilitate the development of new rules of interaction. For example, a therapist might stimulate a discussion of how and when parents will notify each other when they would like to request changes in the children's visitation schedule, might encourage parental support for a child who needs to assert his or her right to refuse to be a "go- between" for the parents, or might help a nonresidential father in another part of town establish new routines with his children to create connectedness.

As mentioned earlier, some individuals seek therapy after divorce without other family members. Many of these persons have experienced an unexpected "sudden divorce" and suffer from feelings of extreme abandonment (Sprenkle & Cyrus, 1983). Proposed guidelines for therapy include unconditional *support* of the clients, *teaching* the clients about the recovery process, *confronting* them with their responsibility for their part in a failed marriage, maximizing their *personal coping resources*, and assisting them in *developing a constructive view of the event* (Sprenkle & Cyrus, 1983).

Attachment Theory

Similarly, attachment theory and supporting research indicate that attachment distress is a normal, developmental response to divorce, requiring varying amounts of time to resolve. Therapists and others working with separated individuals should expect an attachment response in most individuals. Also, helping professionals should be aware that attachment distress is distinct from postdivorce distress, thus requiring specific attention. As in the case of knowledge of the grief/loss process, knowledge that attachment responses are common and normal can be very encouraging to divorcing clients.

Helping professionals should be aware that some individuals are at greater risk for attachment distress than are others—for example, those not initiating divorce, not having considered divorce very long, or having a poor relationship with the former spouse. The presence of other stressors also appears to activate the attachment response. Helping professionals should thus take a holistic approach in considering economic issues and other major stressors related to divorce that could exacerbate attachment distress. Loneliness, too, appears to be highly related to attachment anxiety. Thus, interventions that facilitate social interaction may be very helpful—for example, group therapy or social support.

Attachment distress appears to be a systems phenomenon in that feelings toward the former spouse and the presence of children are highly related to the distress. Thus, interventions must move beyond individual treatment if at all possible. For example, mediation and conciliation counseling might obviate some of the conflict and negative feelings that lead to attachment distress.

Thus far, research on postdivorce attachment has focused on the disabling effects that compromise the adjustment process. However, there is some evidence that postdivorce attachment has both positive and negative components. Future research should consider positive forms of attachment that are healthy and adaptive.

Grief/Loss Perspective

The grief/loss perspective suggests that adjustment to divorce is a developmental process wherein individuals mourn their losses. The various models that have developed under this paradigm imply that the intervention modality should vary by stage of the grief process (Salts, 1979; Thweatt, 1980). For example, knowledge of the stage of the divorce dictates whether the therapist is more nondirective, facilitating the client's grief reaction, or more directive, in encouraging the client to establish new goals. These models also suggest the utility of a family-systems perspective, because adults and children undergo a similar reaction to divorce, and their responses are interrelated. In addition, all practitioners should be aware that the mere knowledge of a predictable course of postdivorce events can be very reassuring to the divorcing individual.

Family-Stress Theory

There is evidence that divorce can increase the likelihood of adverse effects on the psychological well-being of family members (J. H. Brown, Portes, & Christensen, 1989). The ABCX model would suggest that these effects differ depending on how the family members view the event of divorce. Therapists and other helping professionals who apply the principles of this theory should remember that vulnerability and risk of dysfunction may be mediated by the resources available to the family and how families (Burr, 1973) and individuals define the stressor of divorce (Weiss, 1975; Wiseman, 1975). Some research would imply that there is a crisis period of divorce from which children have greater difficulty recovering than adults (Wallerstein & Kelly, 1980). Family researchers may want to investigate the resources that children use to cope with divorce and the perceptions that children have regarding the breakup of the family.

With adjustment as a final outcome of the ABCX model, Isaacs et al. (1986) suggest criteria that the family should meet to demonstrate adequate adjustment: (1) whether the children and the adults have settled down into healthy patterns of behavior and whether the adults' resources for parenting are emerging now that stress is reduced; (2) how the parents are managing to communicate with each other about inescapable issues of logistics concerning the children; and (3) whether the parents have structured visitation so that the children have comfortable access to the visiting parent.

Structural Family Theory

Attention should be paid to the changing structure of the family during the transition to divorce. Divorce weakens the protective boundaries around the family because all the relationships in the family shift simultaneously (Simons & Sprenkle, 1985). Divorce also involves the gradual setting of new boundaries in both the spousal role and the parenting role (Hetherington, Cox, & Cox, 1978). Although undesirable for children, it seems to be typical for the nonresidential parent to disengage from his or her children (Hetherington et al., 1978), creating a rigid boundary that children find difficult to penetrate. This further substantiates the loss that children experience. The reduced parenting that takes place during the initial upset of divorce can set a pattern that becomes a part of the reorganized structure (Simons & Sprenkle, 1985). In addition, if roles and family patterns have not been adapted to the transition, family pathology can develop (Abelsohn, 1983; Isaacs, 1981). If possible, service providers may want to encourage joint custody to retain substantial involvement of both parents with their children. Service providers should urge divorcing spouses to meet as early as possible to define the coparenting roles, although this is sometimes difficult (Brown et al., 1989).

Family reorganization is influenced by clinging to the old family structure or rushing into a new one (Montalvo, 1982). If parents are still focusing on their marital problems rather than negotiating child-rearing practices, the past family structure predominates. Children also need assistance in letting go of old images of their parents. They tend to view their relationship with their parents as a unit. A goal for helpers, then, is to help them develop a separate relationship with each parent with enduring qualities.

Bowen Family-Systems Therapy

The overarching goal of all Bowen family-systems therapy is to increase the individual's level of differentiation of self, thus increasing the family system's ability to function effectively. In the case of a divorcing indi-

vidual, Haber (1990) suggests, the therapy process may take up to two years. The individual goes through several stages: engagement, increasing self-focus, exploring the family of origin, and defining the self. As the parents are able to increase their level of differentiation of self, the children in the system are also freed up from the family-projection process and may also be able to increase their levels of differentiation of self in line with their parents. These changes will also affect the parents' relationship after divorce.

Contextual Family Therapy

The central technique of Boszormenyi-Nagy's contextual family therapy is *multidirected partiality*. The therapist must be able to empathize and see the merit in all sides of a situation. This becomes crucial for divorce therapy. The therapist must be able realize the merit of both spouses' side of the story, in order to help the children realize that their loyalty to both parents is merited. The contextual therapist also focuses on what both parents have to offer the children and encourages the parents to set aside their differences in order to make decisions about the children. Boszormenyi-Nagy and Krasner (1986) suggest that "no parent is forever obliged to stay in an untenable marriage to make it right for their children. What they do owe their children is an honest attempt to consider and safeguard their interests" (p. 342).

Chapter Summary

Discussion Questions

1. What should you, as a therapist or other mental-health professional, use to guide your interventions with families experiencing divorce? Choose one of the theories discussed, and explain what you would try to do if a couple experiencing divorce came to you with a troubled child.
2. What makes intergenerational theories of family therapy different from other theories of family therapy? How can this difference help when applying these theories to divorce?

3. List the theories discussed in this chapter and one of the major concepts defined with each of them.
4. What is significant about viewing divorce as a process?
5. How does attachment theory explain how members of a couple relate with each other after divorce?
6. According to the grief/loss model, how do adults and children most successfully adjust to divorce?

Additional Resources

Beal, E. W. (1985). A systems view of divorce intervention strategies. In J. C. Hansen & S. C. Grebe (Eds.), *Divorce and family mediation, (family therapy collections, Vol. 12)*. Rockville, MD: Aspen.

Hetherington, E. M., Stanley-Hagan, M., & Anderson, E. R. (1989). Marital transitions: A child's perspective. *American Psychologist, 44,* 303–312.

Price, S. J., & McKenry, P. C. (1989). Current trends and issues in divorce: An agenda for family scientists in the 1990s. *Family Science Review, 2,* 219–236.

Price, S. J., & McKenry, P. C. (1988). *Divorce.* Newbury Park, CA: Sage.

References

Abelsohn, D. (1983). Dealing with the abdication dynamic in the post divorce family: A context for adolescent crisis. *Family Process, 22,* 359–389.

Abelsohn, D. (1991). Adolescent adjustment to parental divorce: An investigation from the perspective of basic dimensions of structural family therapy theory. *Family Process, 30,* 177–191.

Abelsohn, D. (1992). A "good enough" separation: Some characteristic operations and tasks. *Family Process, 31,* 61–84.

Ahrons, C. (1983). Divorce: Before, during, and after. In H. I. McCubbin and C. R. Figley (Eds.), *Stress and the family: Vol. 1. Coping with normative transitions.* New York: Brunner/Mazel.

Ahrons, E. R. (1980). Divorce: A crisis of family transition and change. *Family Relations, 29,* 533–540.

Allen, S. F., Stoltenberg, C. D., & Rosko, C. K. (1990). Perceived psychological separation of older adolescents and young adults from their parents: A comparison of divorced versus intact families. *Journal of Counseling and Development, 69,* 57–61.

Anderson, S. A., & Sabatelli, R. M. (1990). Differentiating differentiation and individuation: Conceptual and operational challenges. *American Journal of Family Therapy, 18,* 32–50.

Anthony, E. J. (1974). Children at risk from divorce: A review. In E. T. Anthony & C. Koupernils (Eds.), *The child in his family.* New York: Wiley.

Beal, E. W. (1979). Children of divorce: A family systems perspective. *Journal of Social Issues, 35,* 140–154.

Beal, E. W. (1985). A systems view of divorce intervention strategies. In J. C. Hansen & S. C. Grebe (Eds.), *Divorce and family mediation (Family therapy collections, Vol. 12).* Rockville, MD: Aspen.

Berman, W. H. (1985). Continued attachment after legal divorce. *Journal of Family Issues, 6,* 375–392.

Berman, W. H. (1988). The relationship of ex-spouse attachment to adjustment following divorce. *Journal of Family Psychology, 1,* 312–328.

Berman, W. H., & Turk, D. C. (1981). Adaptation to divorce: Problems and coping strategies. *Journal of Marriage and the Family, 43,* 179–189.

Boss, P. G. (1977). A clarification of the concept of psychological father presence in families experiencing ambiguity of boundary. *Journal of Marriage and the Family, 39,* 141–151.

Boss, P. G. (1980). Normative family stress: Family boundary changes across the lifespan. *Family Relations, 29,* 445–450.

Boss, P. G. (1983). Family separation and boundary ambiguity. In O. Hultaker & J. Trost (Eds.), Family and disaster [special issue]. *International Journal of Mass Emergencies and Disasters, 1,* 63–72.

Boss, P. G. (1987). Family stress. In M. B. Sussman, and S. K. Steinmetz (Eds.), *Handbook of marriage and the family.* New York: Plenum.

Boss, P. G., & Greenberg, J. (1984). Family boundary ambiguity: A new variable in family stress theory. *Family Process, 23,* 535–546.

Boszormenyi-Nagy, I., & Krasner, B. R. (1986). *Between give and take: A clinical guide to contextual therapy.* New York: Brunner/Mazel.

Boszormenyi-Nagy, I., & Spark, G. M. (1973). *Invisible loyalties: Reciprocity in intergenerational family therapy.* New York: Harper & Row.

Bowen, M. (1976). Theory and practice in psychotherapy. In P. J. Guerin (Ed.), *Family therapy: Theory and practice* (pp. 42–90). New York: Gardner Press.

Bowen, M. (1978). *Family therapy in clinical practice.* New York: Aronson.

Bowlby, J. (1969). *Attachment and loss: Vol. 1. Attachment.* New York: Basic Books.

Bowlby, J. (1973). *Attachment and loss: Vol. 2. Separation: Anxiety and anger.* New York: Basic Books.

Bowlby, J. (1977). The making and breaking of affectional bonds. I. Aetiology and psychopathology in the light of attachment theory. *British Journal of Psychiatry, 130,* 201–210.

Brown, J. H., Portes, P. R., & Christensen, D. N. (1989). Understanding divorce stress on children: Implications for research and practice. *American Journal of Family Therapy, 17,* 315–325.

Brown, P., Felton, B. J., Whiteman, V., & Manela, R. (1980). Attachment and distress following marital separation. *Journal of Divorce, 3,* 303–317.

Burr, W. (1973). *Theory construction and the sociology of the family.* New York: Wiley.

Carter, B., & McGoldrick, M. (1980). *The family life cycle.* New York: Gardner Press.

Coombs, R. H. (1991). Marital status and personal well-being: A literature review. *Family Relations, 40,* 97–102.

Freud, S. (1917). Mourning and melancholia. In J. Strachy (Ed.), *Standard Edition: Vol. 14* (pp. 237–260). London: Hogarth Press.

Friedman, E. H. (1991). Bowen theory and therapy. In A. S. Gurman & D. P. Kniskern (Eds.), *Handbook of family therapy: Volume 2.* New York: Brunner/Mazel.

Goldman, J., & Coane, J. (1978). Family therapy after the divorce: Developing a strategy. *Family Process, 16,* 357–362.

Goode, W. J. (1956). *After divorce.* New York: Free Press.

Haber, J. (1990). A family systems model of divorce and loss of self. *Archives of Psychiatric Nursing, 4,* 228–234.

Hetherington, E. M. (1989). Coping with family transitions: Winners, losers, and survivors. *Child Development, 60,* 1–14.

Hetherington, E. M., Cox, M., & Cox, R. (1976). Divorced fathers. *The Family Coordinator, 25,* 417–428.

Hetherington, E. M., Cox, M., & Cox, R. (1978). The aftermath of divorce. In J. H. Stevens & D. Matthews (Eds.), *Mother/child and father/child relationships.* Washington DC: National Association for the Education of Children.

Hetherington, E. M., Stanley-Hagan, M., & Anderson, E. R. (1989). Marital transitions: A child's perspective. *American Psychologist, 44,* 303–312.

Hill, R. (1958). Generic features of families under stress. *Social Casework, 49,* 139–150.

Holman, T. B., & Burr, W. R. (1980). Beyond the beyond: The growth of family theories in the 1970s. *Journal of Marriage and the Family, 42,* 729–742.

Hozman, T. L., & Froiland, D. J. (1977). Children: Forgotten in divorce. *Personnel and Guidance Journal, 5,* 530–533.

Isaacs, M. B. (1981). Treatment for families of divorce: A systems model of prevention. In I. R. Stuart & L. E. Abt (Eds.), *Children of separation and divorce: Management and treatment.* New York: Van Nostrand Reinhold.

Isaacs, M. B., Leon, G. H., and Kline, M. (1987). When is a parent out of the picture? Different custody, different perceptions. *Family Process, 26,* 101–109.

Isaacs, M. B., Montalvo, B., & Abelsohn, D. (1986). *The difficult divorce: Therapy for children and families.* New York: Basic Books.

Kaffman, M. (1993). Divorce in the kibbutz: Lessons to be drawn. *Family Process, 32,* 119–133.

Kalter, N. (1987). Long-term effects of divorce on children: A developmental vulnerability model. *American Journal of Orthopsychiatry, 57,* 587–600.

Kelly, J. B. (1988). Refining the concept of attachment in divorce. *Journal of Family Psychology, 1,* 329–332

Kerr, M. E. (1981). Family systems theory and therapy. In A. S. Gurman & D. P. Kniskern (Eds.), *Handbook of family therapy.* New York: Brunner/Mazel.

Kerr, M. E. (1984). Theoretical base for differentiation of self in one's family of origin. *Clinical Supervisor, 2,* 3–36.

Kessler, S. (1975). *The American way of divorce: Prescriptions for change.* Chicago: Nelson-Hall.

Kitson, G. C., with Holmes, W. M. (1992). *Portrait of divorce: Adjustment to marital breakdown.* New York: Guilford Press.

Kitson, G. C., & Morgan, L. A. (1990). The multiple consequences of divorce: A decade review. *Journal of Marriage and the Family, 52,* 913–924.

Kurdek, L. A. (1981). An integrative perspective on children's divorce adjustment. *American Psychologist, 36,* 856–866.

Lavee, Y., McCubbin, H. I., & Olson, D. H. (1987). The effect of stressful life events and transitions on family functioning and well-being. *Journal of Marriage and the Family, 49,* 857–873.

Lopez, F. G. (1991). The impact of divorce on college students. In R. I. Witchel (Ed.), *Dealing with students from dysfunctional families* (pp. 19–34) (New directions for student services, series 0164–7970, no. 54). San Francisco: Jossey-Bass.

Lopez, F. G., Campbell, V. L., & Watkins, C. E. (1988). The relation of parental divorce to college student development. *Journal of Divorce, 12,* 83–98.

Martin, T. C., & Bumpass, L. L. (1989). Recent trends in marital disruption. *Demography, 26,* 37–51.

McCubbin, H. I., Joy, C., Cauble, B., Comeau, J., Patterson, J. M., & Needle, R. (1980). Family stress and coping: A decade review. *Journal of Marriage and the Family, 42,* 855–871.

McCubbin, H. I., & Patterson, J. M. (1983a). The family stress process: The Double ABCX model of adjustment and adaptation. *Marriage and Family Review, 6,* 7–37.

McCubbin, H. I., and Patterson, J. M. (1983b). Family transitions: Adaptation to stress. In H. I. McCubbin, & C. R. Figley (Eds.), *Stress and the family I: Coping with normative transitions.* New York: Brunner/Mazel.

Minuchin, S. (1974). *Families and family therapy.* Cambridge, MA: Harvard University Press.

Minuchin, S., & Fishman, H. C. (1981). *Family therapy techniques.* Cambridge, MA: Harvard University Press.

Montalvo, B. (1982). Interpersonal arrangements in disrupted families. In F. Walsh (Ed.), *Normal family processes.* New York: Guilford Press.

Nichols, M. P., & Schwartz, R. C. (1991). *Family therapy: Concepts and methods.* Boston: Allyn & Bacon.

Parkes, C. M. (1972). *Bereavement.* New York: International Universities Press.

Pasley, K. (1987). Family boundary ambiguity: Perceptions of adult family members. In K. Pasley & M. Ihinger-Tallman (Eds.), *Remarriage and stepparenting: Current research and theory.* New York: Guilford Press.

Peterson, G. W., Leigh, G. K., and Day, R. D. (1984). Family stress theory and the impact of divorce on children. *Journal of Divorce, 7,* 1–20.

Price, S. J., & McKenry, P. C. (1988). *Divorce.* Newbury Park, CA: Sage.

Price, S. J., & McKenry, P. C. (1989). Current trends and issues in divorce: An agenda for family scientists in the 1990s. *Family Science Review, 2,* 219–236.

Price-Bonham, S., & Balswick, J. O. (1980). The noninstitutions: Divorce, desertion, and remarriage. *Journal of Marriage and the Family, 42,* 959–972.

Raschke, H. (1987). Divorce. In M. B. Sussman & S. K. Steinmetz (Eds.), *Handbook of marriage and the family.* New York: Plenum.

Rosbrow-Reich, S. (1988). Identity and growth: A psychoanalytic study of divorce. *Psychoanalytic Review, 75,* 419–441.

Salts, C. J. (1979). Divorce process: Integration of theory. *Journal of Divorce, 2,* 233–240.

Scanzoni, J. (1978). *Sex roles, women's work, and marital conflict.* Lexington, MA: Lexington Books.

Scanzoni, J., Polonko, K., Teachman, J., & Thompson, L. (1989). *The sexual bond: Rethinking families and close relationships.* Newbury Park, CA: Sage.

Serovich, J. M., Green, I., & Parrott, R. (1992). Boundaries and AIDS testing: Privacy and the family system. *Family Process, 41,* 104–109.

Shaw, D. S. (1991). The effects of divorce on children's adjustment. *Behavior Modification, 15,* 456–485.

Simons, V. A., and Sprenkle, D. H. (1985). Stages of family therapy with divorcing families. In D. C. Breunlin (Ed.), *Stages: Patterns of change over time.* Rockville, MD: Aspen.

Spanier, G., & Casto, R. (1979). Adjustment of separation and divorce: A qualitative analysis. In G. Levinger & O. C. Moles (Eds.), *Separation and divorce: Context, causes, and consequences.* New York: Basic Books.

Sprenkle, D. H., and Cyrus, C. L. (1983). Abandonment: The stress of sudden divorce. In C. R. Figley & H. I. McCubbin (Eds.), *Stress and the family II: Coping with catastrophe.* New York: Brunner/Mazel.

Sprey, J. (1990). *Fashioning family theory: New approaches.* Newbury Park, CA: Sage.

Thweatt, R. W. (1980). Divorce: Crisis intervention guided by attachment theory. *American Journal of Psychotherapy, 34,* 240–245.

Tschann, J. M., Johnston, J. R., & Wallerstein, J. S. (1989). Resources, stressors, and attachment as predictors of adult adjustment after divorce: A longitudinal study. *Journal of Marriage and the Family, 51,* 1033–1046.

Van Heusden, A., & Van Den Eerenbeemt, E. (1987). *Balance in motion: Ivan Boszormenyi-Nagy and his vision of individual and family therapy.* New York: Brunner/Mazel.

Walker, K. N., & Messinger, L. (1979). Remarriage after divorce: Dissolution and reconstruction of family boundaries. *Family Process, 18,* 185–192.

Waller, W. (1938). *The family: A dynamic interpretation.* New York: Holt, Rinehart & Winston.

Wallerstein, J. S. (1987). Children of divorce: Report of a ten-year follow-up of early latency-age children. *American Journal of Orthopsychiatry, 57,* 199–211.

Wallerstein, J. S., & Blakeslee, S. (1989). *Second chances: Men, women, and children a decade after divorce.* New York: Ticknor & Fields.

Wallerstein, J. S., & Kelly, J. B. (1980). *Surviving the breakup: How children and parents cope with divorce.* New York: Basic Books.

Weiss, R. (1975). *Marital separation.* New York: Basic Books.

Weiss, R. (1976). The emotional impact of marital separation. *Journal of Social Issues, 32,* 135–146.

Weiss, R. S. (1979). *Going it alone: Family life and social situation of the single parent.* New York: Basic Books.

White, L. K. (1990). Determinants of divorce: A review of research in the 1980s. *Journal of Marriage and the Family, 52,* 904–912.

Wiseman, R. S. (1975). Crisis theory and the process of divorce. *Social Casework, 56,* 205–212.

Wood, B., & Talmon, M. (1983). Family boundaries in transition: A search for alternatives. *Family Process, 22,* 347–357.

Wright, D. W., & Price, S. J. (1986). Court-ordered child support payment: The effect of the former-spouse relationship on compliance. *Journal of Marriage and the Family, 48,* 869–874.

Remarriage and Stepfamilies

Larry Ganong / Marilyn Coleman / Mark Fine

University of Missouri—Columbia

What does George Washington have in common with Dr. Seuss and Dr. Spock? What similarity links Nancy Reagan, Whistler's mother, and Yoko Ono? What do Abraham Lincoln and Gerald Ford share with Erik Erikson? What do all these people have in common? Answer: all belonged to a stepfamily at some point in their lives, either as a stepparent (Washington, Ono, Whistler's mother, and Dr. Spock) or as a stepchild (Lincoln, Ford, Erikson, and Dr. Seuss). Some, like Nancy Reagan, grew up in a stepfamily and then found themselves a stepparent as an adult. These famous people of the past and present share their "step" status with a growing number of others, due primarily to relatively high rates of divorce and remarriage in recent years. In this chapter we present an overview of important topics related to remarried spouses and their children, including the prevalence of remarriage and stepfamilies, characteristic differences between stepfamilies and nuclear families, beliefs about stepfamilies and how they may affect adjustment, dimensions of stepfamily systems, stepfamily development, family processes that facilitate adjustment, and some characteristics of healthy stepfamilies.

Prevalence of Remarriage and Stepfamilies

The United States has the highest rate of remarriage in the world. Approximately one-half to two-thirds of first marriages end in divorce (Glick, 1984; Martin & Bumpass, 1989). Of these divorced individuals, nearly 80% remarry within three to five years (Glick, 1984). Many of these remarrying adults have children, thus creating stepfamilies.

A stepfamily, often known as a blended, reconstituted, or remarried family, is one in which at least one of the adults has a child (or children) from a previous relationship. A stepparent is an adult who marries a person who has had a child from a previous relationship. A stepchild is someone whose parent (or parents) is married to someone who is not the child's biological parent. Notice that these definitions do not limit stepfamily status to those who reside in the same household. A stepparent and stepchild do not have to live together all of the time or even part of the time to have a relationship and to share stepfamily membership.

In fact, with joint legal and physical custody of children becoming more prevalent, children's membership in two households is increasingly common. Thus, a remarried household may be "linked" to another remarried household or to a single-parent household by children (Jacobson, 1987) and these "binuclear" households may contain several combinations of full-time and part-time steprelationships (Ahrons & Perlmutter, 1982). Based on whether or not each spouse has children living in and outside of the household and the gender of the stepparent (stepmother, stepfather, or both), Wald (1981) identifies 32 stepfamily configurations. In the cases of split custody (one biological parent has custody of one or more children, and the other biological parent has custody of a child or children as well) the number of possible configurations approaches infinity.

How many stepfamilies are there? The U. S. Bureau of the Census does not compile data, and estimates vary widely, but even the most conservative estimates indicate that stepfamilies make up a sizable minority of the population. Cherlin and McCarthy (1985) calculated that nearly 2.5 million households were postdivorce stepfamilies with residential children. To this number must be added an unknown number of postbereavement stepfamilies and single-parent households that are linked to stepfamily households. At any one time, about 10% of American children live with a stepfather and mother (Bumpass, 1984; Glick, 1984), and about 2% with a stepmother and father (Bachrach, 1983). If current divorce and remarriage rates continue, as many as 35% of U.S. children will be part of a stepfamily before they are 18 years old (Glick, 1989).

These figures are underestimates, because they do not include either heterosexual or homosexual cohabiting stepfamilies. Not all stepfamilies are legally sanctioned, as cohabiting adults may bring children from a previous relationship into their household. Although most stepfamily researchers, clinicians, and educators have focused their efforts on stepfamilies formed following marriage, we speculate that many of the dynamics in stepfamilies that have legal status also operate in cohabiting ones. Crosbie-Burnett and Helmbrecht (1993), in a study of adolescents and fathers in gay-stepfather families, supported this proposition by showing that the factors that were related to adjustment in these families were quite similar to those in heterosexual-stepfather families.

Stepfamily Characteristics

Stepfamilies are quite different from first-marriage, or nuclear, families. Even when stepfamilies appear structurally to be the same as nuclear families (the household contains a mother, a father, and children), they are different in three important ways:

1. Stepfamilies are more complex.
2. Members have different family histories.
3. Parent/child bonds are older than spousal bonds.

Complexity.   As a group, stepfamilies are complex units with characteristics that deserve special consideration. To begin with, stepfamilies often have more adults and children than nuclear families. Remarriages following divorce may result in four adults in parental

positions: a mother, a stepfather, a father, and a stepmother. Between the two households there may be several sets os "his" and "her" children, as well as the possibility of an "our" child if the remarried spouses reproduce. The addition of stepgrandparents, stepaunts, stepuncles, and stepcousins can expand the family instantly and substantially. It is probably an understatement that this greater number of people adds complexity to stepfamilies. More people means more relationships, and more relationships put a stress on communications between members.

The roles and responsibilities of stepmothers and stepfathers are poorly defined in our culture, which adds to stepfamily complexity (Cherlin, 1978; Crosbie-Burnett, 1989). Much has been written about the struggle stepparents and their spouses have in deciding how much a stepparent's role functioning will mimic that of a parent in a nuclear family (Visher & Visher, 1979). Various alternatives, such as "parent," "other parent," and "nonparent," have been discussed, but stepparents have few guidelines to follow in developing a place for themselves in the stepfamily (Cherlin, 1978).

Other roles and role-definition problems add to the complexity of stepfamilies as well. Few guidelines exist to aid stepsons, stepdaughters, stepsiblings, stepgrandparents, and half-siblings. How are former spouses to relate to each other? The roles of nonresidential parents, stepparents, and stepsiblings are even less well defined than roles for people who share a residence. Developing comfortable and workable roles and relationships is difficult and adds to stepfamily complexity.

Another complicating factor is that stepchildren may hold membership in two households. Of course, many stepchildren have virtually no contact with a nonresidential parent; Furstenberg and Nord (1985) report that about 50% of children in a national sample had no contact with their divorced, noncustodial parent in the previous year. For those who do hold membership in two households, however, the arrangements can range from almost full-time residence in one household with rare visits to the other household to half-time residence in both. Most stepchildren who "belong" to two households probably fall in between these two extremes, residing mostly with one parent but spending some time periodically with the other parent. The increased prevalence of joint legal and physical custody in recent years may result in more stepchildren being part-time members of two households.

Pragmatically, when children have membership in two households, stepfamily households find themselves gaining and losing children from time to time. For example, remarried spouses may find themselves with one or two children to raise during the week, and their weekends may vary from a houseful of residential and visiting nonresidential children to no children at all. This "accordion effect" creates logistical and emotional complications for adults and children. Children who go back and forth may have difficulty adjusting to different sets of rules and expectations. Adults must adjust to frequently changing numbers of people in the household; for some, it is stressful to be so flexible, whereas others thrive on the excitement of frequent changes.

The high degree of complexity of stepfamilies, it should be noted, does not imply that stepfamilies are inherently problematic and distressful. Although the tendency has been for our culture to assume that deviations from the nuclear family are undesirable (Coleman & Ganong, 1990), the difference in complexity may be an asset to some families and individuals and a deficit to others.

Different histories.   Another unique characteristic of stepfamilies is that the members have differing family histories. Adults in nuclear families enter marriage with individual family-of-origin histories, but they go on to develop a mutual family culture with its own rituals and history. Children raised in nuclear families share that history as part of a common family culture.

In stepfamilies, a parent and child(ren) have mutual experiences and shared recollections of a family life that does not include the stepparent (and any children he or she may have). This is important not only because some stepfamily members are excluded from "remember when . . ." stories but also because different histories can result in patterns of living or lifestyles that seem odd to those who were not involved in developing those patterns. This joining of cultures may cause confusion in the period of transition following remarriage and, if not resolved, may result in a chronic sense that things don't feel right and "natural" in the stepfamily (Goldner, 1982). Unless a premium is placed on communicating expectations clearly and being flexible in

adapting these different ways of "being a family," misunderstandings and mistaken assumptions will occur.

Bonds of different ages.   Another major characteristic that distinguishes stepfamilies from nuclear families is that the parent/child bond is formed prior to the marital bond. Spouses in stepfamilies lack the luxury of months and years alone to adjust to each other as is typical in first marriages. This may mean that in addition to the differences in shared history mentioned above, the primary emotional loyalty for newly remarried parents is to their child(ren) rather than to their new spouse. Unlike spouses in first marriages, those in stepfamilies must develop a cohesive marital unit at the same time they are maintaining parent/child relationships and beginning stepparent/stepchild ties. As a result, bonds may be somewhat tenuous and fragile.

Beliefs about Stepfamilies and Their Influence on Adjustment

A number of unrealistic beliefs about stepfamilies ("stepfamily myths") have been identified that may cause some adjustment problems. Some of these unrealistic beliefs are based upon a lack of understanding of how stepfamilies are different from nuclear families, as discussed above. Most of the evidence for the existence of these beliefs has come from authors who actually work with stepfamily members (for example, clinicians, educators) to help them improve their functioning. Primarily because few researchers have studied stepfamily myths, there are limited dates to support that these myths exist and that they have negative effects on stepfamily members.

Several common stepfamily myths have been identified by Visher and Visher (1988) and Burt (1989). Three of these are considered particularly important, because they may have the most negative effects on stepfamily members:

1. Stepfamilies are functionally equivalent to nuclear families.
2. Stepfamily adjustment will occur quickly.
3. Loving and caring will develop instantly in stepfamilies.

These myths may have negative effects on the adjustment of stepfamily members because they lead to unrealistic expectations about what individuals can expect from their own family lives. As mentioned earlier in this chapter, stepfamilies are not functionally equivalent to nuclear families, and there are important differences between these two family forms. Further, stepfamily adjustment does not occur quickly for most members, and loving and caring do not develop immediately between stepparents and stepchildren. Stepfamily adjustment is a gradual process, taking four to seven years for those families that successfully resolve the challenges facing them (Papernow, 1993).

Because adjustment and the development of positive feelings take time in most stepfamilies, family members who believe in these myths are likely to feel frustrated and disappointed because their day-to-day experience will not meet these unrealistic expectations. Further, individuals with high expectations sometimes make overly vigorous attempts to meet these lofty goals, and this may, paradoxically, make matters worse. For example, a stepfather who believes that he should immediately love his stepdaughter and yet finds himself frequently becoming angry with her may vigorously try to find a way to improve the relationship. This effort may appear "forced," and she may not be emotionally prepared to have positive interactions with him. Thus, the child may withdraw and the relationship may be even less positive than before he initiated his unsuccessful efforts.

In addition to the first three myths, others have been identified and deserve mention:

4. Withdrawing a child from a biological parent enhances the relationship with the stepparent of the same sex.
5. Anything negative that happens is a result of being in a stepfamily.
6. Forming a stepfamily after a death is much easier than doing so after a divorce.
7. Being a nonresidential stepparent is easier than being a residential stepparent.

These are considered myths because they are often incongruent with the actual experiences of stepfamily members. There is some research evidence, for example, that nonresidential stepmothers may experience more parenting stress than residential stepmothers (myth 7), possibly because nonresidential stepmothers

do not have sufficient exposure to their stepchildren to develop a satisfactory relationship and establish consistent household routines (Ambert, 1986). In addition, particularly in stepfather families, empirical evidence suggests that regular contact with nonresidential fathers does not negatively affect the quality of stepfather/stepchild relationships (myth 4) (Clingempeel & Segal, 1986; Furstenberg & Seltzer, 1983). Consistent with myth 4, however, these studies did find that in stepmother families, regular contact with the nonresidential mother was related to more negatively perceived stepmother/child relationships.

As with the first three beliefs, these are myths to the extent that they are inconsistent with the realities of daily living in stepfamilies. If perceived reality is different from the expectations generated by such beliefs, frustration and disappointment may develop. However, it should be noted that some of these myths may actually accurately reflect the experiences of some stepfamily members. They are considered myths because they do not accurately reflect the experiences of *most* stepfamilies. As noted earlier, empirical support for the presence of these myths and their negative effects on adjustment is limited. Kurdek and Fine (1991) developed a scale that assesses the extent to which stepfathers and mothers endorse stepfamily myths. They found that the strength of belief in myths was negatively related to both stepfathers' and mothers' reported adjustment, supporting the claim made in the clinical literature that believing in stepfamily myths *causes* problems for stepfamily members. However, it is not possible to draw the conclusion from studies that use correlational designs that believing in myths causes poor adjustment. It is possible that poor adjustment causes individuals to adopt certain beliefs about stepfamilies or that some other variables are responsible for the observed relation.

Dimensions of Stepfamily Systems

As stepfamilies develop, they must address important issues related to each of several dimensions common to all family systems. These dimensions—rules, roles, hierarchy, boundaries, subsystems, and emotional distance—are reviewed below as they relate to stepfamilies. In this section we also offer examples of unresolved research questions, thorny issues facing clinicians, and issues of concern for stepfamily members. What is known about factors contributing to adjustment over time is also presented.

Rules

One of the primary tasks in newly formed remarriages and stepfamilies is to develop rules for the new system. Clinicians observe that people often assume that the stepfamily will function just as nuclear families do (Fishman & Hamel, 1981; Visher & Visher, 1988) and that relationships will undergo few, if any, changes following parental remarriage (Ganong & Coleman, 1989b). In other words, it is often assumed that household rules will undergo little change. Consequently, many remarried couples do not plan adequately for remarriage, and they are surprised if their family does not function smoothly (Ganong & Coleman, 1989b).

Rules in nuclear-family systems are developed over time. Newlyweds in first marriages have only each other to negotiate with as they try to adapt household and family rules brought from their families of origin. Rules related to being a married couple, to parenting, to child behavior, and to other aspects of family life are gradually, and implicitly, developed (Schwebel & Fine, 1993). By the time a baby becomes an adolescent, for example, parents in first-marriage families have had several years to evolve family rules related to raising an adolescent, even though this is seldom done with purposeful, conscious planning. Stepfamilies do not have this "luxury" of time in which to implicitly negotiate household rules; newlyweds are determining how to be marital partners at the same time they may be learning to relate with stepchildren. In the absence of discussed, explicitly negotiated rules, stepfamilies often rely on nuclear-family models of functioning, a pattern that works for some but not all (Fishman & Hamel, 1981; Visher & Visher, 1988).

Because members of the new unit lack shared family rituals (Goldner, 1982; Papernow, 1993; Visher & Visher, 1982) and rules (Whiteside, 1983), conflict is likely during the early period following remarriage, as stepfamily members become used to one another's different styles (McGoldrick & Carter, 1989; Wald, 1981).

For example, minor matters like where food should be stored in the refrigerator and how children should ask to be excused from the dinner table can be fuel for blazing arguments. Even more "flammable" are rules about role performance.

Roles

Newly formed stepfamilies have to determine what roles will be performed in their families and who will perform them. Although roles must be defined and all family members must achieve some comfort in how these roles will be filled, the greatest difficulty seems to center on defining appropriate roles for stepparents and stepchildren (Giles-Sims, 1984; Mills, 1984). Should a stepparent function as a parent, as a friend, as a "second parent," or as a stepparent (however that might be defined)? What *is* the function of the stepparent? Who decides what the step roles will be? Once these questions are decided, how easy is it for families to alter role expectations? These and other challenging questions face newly formed stepfamilies.

The clearest example of the importance of role definition in stepfamilies involves discipline issues. Discipline is a frequent problem in stepfamilies, particularly in the early stages when household rules are evolving (Messinger, 1984; Mills, 1984; Visher & Visher, 1988). Discipline problems can arise over value differences between the parent and stepparent, perceived inequities in punishments, and differing expectations regarding the behavior of children. Children's rejections of the stepparent's efforts to discipline may also create havoc in the home.

Some problems related to roles stem from the lack of societal institutionalization of remarried families (Cherlin, 1978). In other words, stepfamilies do not have the advantage of "automatically" knowing how to fulfill their roles; there are few societal norms to guide them. This contributes to confusion about roles (role ambiguity) (Fast & Cain, 1966), family identity (Ahrons & Perlmutter, 1982), and how much affection to show stepkin (Fast & Cain, 1966; Mowatt, 1972). The absence of legal ties between stepchildren and stepparents (Fine & Fine, 1992), the dearth of kinship terms for steprelationships (Jones, 1978), and the lack of societal rituals to support stepfamilies (Goldner,

1982; Jacobson, 1987) can contribute to role-definition problems for stepfamilies.

In addition to learning new step roles, stepfamily members must deal with changes in the roles they performed prior to remarriage. Compared with the courtship period before remarriage, for example, a newly remarried woman may find herself confiding more in her new spouse, spending more time with him (leaving less time to spend with her children, in all likelihood), and letting him do more of the disciplining of the children. A college-aged woman revealed that when her mother remarried, she promised her that "nothing between us will change." In actuality, almost every aspect of living in the household changed with the addition of the stepfather (including what they ate, when they ate, and where they ate it)! Parents often have difficulty viewing family change through the eyes of the children and may be unaware of the difficulty the children are experiencing.

Remarriage changes roles of nonhousehold kin as well as those in the home. Nonresidential parents must develop modified roles related both to their parenting tasks and to their relationship with their former spouse. Similarly, parents of divorced and remarried adults, and parents whose adult children have died, will probably be expected to assume roles in the extended family system.

We lack names for some of the new roles created by remarriage. For example, the relationship between a remarried person's former spouse and current spouse has no "official" name ("wife-in-law"? "husband-in-law"?). Similarly, we have known people who take care of their ex-spouses' stepchildren (the stepsiblings of their biological children) on weekends. No label exists for this relationship. Relationships without labels are surprisingly difficult to explain to other people.

Role ambiguity in stepfamilies is illustrated in the names that stepkin use to refer to one another. Children are sometimes confused about what to call a stepparent (Wald, 1981). Parents may push children to use terms like Mom and Dad when addressing stepparents, without considering the children's feelings. We have talked to young adult stepchildren who were still bitter about being forced to call a stepparent Mom or Dad when they were younger. If the use of such terms is important to adults, children learn to use the labels as a way to manipulate. For example, one stepson told us that when he wanted something from his stepmother, he always called her Mom because he knew it pleased her and she was more likely to give him what he wanted.

New roles may be created for children as well as adults in stepfamilies. For example, changes in birth order may force a child who was the oldest to consider what the role of a "middle" child might be (McGoldrick & Carter, 1989). Gender-constellation changes may result in an only son being confronted with relating to other boys in the family. Stepsiblings and half-siblings introduce new roles for children also.

Hierarchy

Children in single-parent households may be assigned more rights and responsibilities than is the case in nuclear families (Papernow, 1993; Weiss, 1979). In systems terms, children in these households move up the status hierarchy to become nearly equal to their parent. The parent may rely on the children for support and companionship, and the children function as if they were peers or friends. Older children may be given responsibilities for caring for younger siblings to a far greater extent than in nuclear families.

Remarriage puts pressure on the system to alter the hierarchy that may have been established in the single-parent household. Often, single parents become quite accustomed to making decisions on their own following marital dissolution, and they may logically prefer this to the conflict that may have accompanied decision-making in their marriage. However, the new spouse usually expects to have more say in decisions than children do, and if the adults are assuming the nuclear-family model, the new spouse expects control over stepchildren, financial decisions, and other concerns of running a household. Conflict may occur if stepchildren feel a loss of status and control. Spouses may also dislike sharing decisions with a new partner.

There is little research on the process of hierarchy establishment in stepfamilies. It appears that women take a greater role in financial decision-making in their remarriage than they did in their prior marriages (Ganong & Coleman, 1989a) and that mothers have more decision-making power than stepfathers and adolescents (Giles-Sims & Crosbie-Burnett, 1989), indications that women retain some of the hierarchical status they had as single parents. We do not know how stepfamilies can best resolve hierarchy issues. Family-life educators and family therapists advise stepparents to "go slow" in assuming a disciplinary role with stepchildren, particularly with older children and adolescents (Mills, 1984; Visher & Visher, 1988). In systems terms, the best advice to the stepparent may be to gradually find a place in the status hierarchy, rather than to immediately assume a family position that displaces children too rapidly for their comfort level.

Boundaries

Newly formed remarried families must establish internal and external boundaries (McGoldrick & Carter, 1989). The roles and hierarchy issues discussed earlier can also be seen as tasks associated with the definition of internal boundaries. For example, adults must establish boundaries around the marital subsystem, and stepfamilies (adults *and* children) need to figure out how the stepparent "fits" into the parental subsystem. Sometimes, boundary coalitions form along biological lines, with one parent and his or her offspring forming a coalition against the other adult and his or her children (if any). This way of defining internal family boundaries is probably to be expected in the early years of stepfamily life, before members have had the opportunity to develop a shared history and a degree of emotional bonding (Papernow, 1993).

Many families following divorce become "binuclear," consisting of divorced former spouses who reside in separate households and their children, who share part-time residence in both houses (Ahrons & Rodgers, 1987). This binuclear living pattern can create boundary difficulties for stepfamily members in several ways described below.

Coparental conflicts (those between the ex-spouses) may begin or increase following the remarriage of either or both parents (Whiteside, 1983). Custody issues that had apparently been resolved may flair again (Crohn, Sager, Brown, Rodstein, & Walker, 1982). Children may experience loyalty conflicts between parent and stepparent, and biological parent/child ties may become strained (Sager et al., 1983; Visher & Visher, 1988). Children may also feel tension trying to bridge

membership in two households (Greif, 1982); this tension can be heightened when parents and children disagree over family boundaries (who is in and is not in the family) or when family boundaries are too vague for most members' comfort (Crohn et al., 1982).

External boundaries (those defining who is a member of the stepfamily and who is not) are likely to be somewhat ambiguous (Pasley, 1987). There are several reasons why this may be so. First, family members within the same household are likely to disagree about who is in their family. For example, children are likely to include their nonresidential parent as a family member, but former spouses seldom continue to consider each other as family members. Stepparents may be excluded by children as family members early in the life of the remarriage, stepparents may not consider residential stepchildren to be members of their family (Furstenberg, 1987), and stepsiblings who live far away may not be counted as kin (Gross, 1986). This lack of consensus creates unclear boundaries.

Second, for some stepfamilies the number of household residents changes frequently due to visits by nonresidential children and to shared physical custody of children. This movement of children in and out of the house can be confusing and probably contributes to what has been labeled boundary ambiguity (Pasley, 1987).

A third reason for boundary ambiguity is societal. In North America, households and families are usually considered to be the same. However, in postdivorce families in which both parents maintain contact with the children and may have joint legal and physical custody of those children, households are *not* the same as families (Ahrons & Rodgers, 1987). The nuclear-family model (household = family) may cause confusion about external boundaries for stepfamilies. It almost certainly confuses the larger social systems in which stepfamilies reside (for example, schools, religious groups). It should be noted, however, that there has been considerably more speculation about the effects of boundary-definition problems in stepfamilies than there has been research (Pasley, 1987).

Subsystems

Part of the greater complexity of stepfamilies is due to the greater number of subsystems they have (see Fine

& Kurdek, in press). In addition to the "standard" subsystems found in families (for example, marital, parent/child), there may be new ones such as stepsibling. Existing subsystems (for example, the former spousal subsystem) may undergo changes in how they function following remarriage. For example, the parental system may gradually expand to include the new stepparent.

Emotional Distance

Stepfamilies are not as cohesive as nuclear families (Kennedy, 1985; Peek, Bell, Waldren, & Sorell, 1988; Pink & Wampler, 1985), and stepparent/stepchild dyads are not as emotionally close as parent/child dyads (Ganong & Coleman, 1986). These are fairly robust findings; that is, consistent results have been found by researchers who have used several different methods with varying samples to assess emotional closeness.

It is not clear what meaning to assign to the lower reported cohesiveness in stepfamilies. For example, how much of an issue should closeness be in stepfamilies? *Should* stepfamilies and step relationships be as close as nuclear families and blood-kin relationships? Is it possible for well-functioning stepfamilies to have optimal levels of closeness that differ from those of nuclear families? Research on a nonclinical sample of stepfamilies using standardized instruments found that although stepfamilies were not as emotionally close as nuclear families, they were well within the "functional" range on these instruments. This suggests that patterns of effective stepfamily functioning may differ from those of nuclear families (Anderson & White, 1986; Coleman & Ganong, 1987; Orleans, Palisi, & Caddell, 1989). Obviously, this is an area that needs to be much more fully researched.

If differences in optimal levels of closeness exist between well-functioning stepfamilies and nuclear families, can questionnaires developed for nuclear families be appropriately used with remarried families? If instruments standardized on nuclear families are used with stepfamilies, should the data collected be interpreted differently? These questions have not been adequately addressed by family scholars but are likely to be the focus of research in the future.

Do stepfamilies become closer over time? One implicit assumption held by many family clinicians and researchers alike is that functional stepfamilies grow closer until they are nearly indistinguishable from nuclear families in emotional closeness and patterns of functioning. Because few longitudinal studies have been conducted on stepfamilies, little empirical evidence exists to support this speculation.

We noted earlier in this chapter that stepfamilies are sometimes called blended or reconstituted families. An implicit expectation of both these labels is that stepfamilies will be as close as first-marriage families and that the basic dynamics will be similar to those of nuclear families. Remarried adults frequently expect more cohesion and closeness than children find comfortable (McGoldrick & Carter, 1989). This push for cohesion is stressful for children (Kompara, 1980) and can result in "pseudomutuality," an unwillingness to honestly express disagreements (McGoldrick & Carter, 1989), or rebellion and withdrawal by children (Sager et. al., 1983). An unintended result of this adult push for cohesion is that stepfamilies become less rather than more cohesive because children pull away (McGoldrick & Carter, 1989; Visher & Visher, 1979).

Stepfamily Development

In the context of stepfamily development, it should be noted that at least some members in stepfamily households have experienced multiple family transitions prior to the remarriage. For example, remarried parents probably have had these transitions:

1. from their family of origin to being a married adult
2. from being married to being married with children
3. from being married to being single due to separation and divorce or bereavement
4. from being single with children to being remarried

Their children have experienced the structural transitions from nuclear family to single-parent/binuclear family to stepfamily.

A small but growing number of remarried adults are "serial marriers," people who have married three or more times (Brody, Newbaum, & Forehand, 1988). In families where adults have experienced a series of marriages, the number of transitions is obviously much greater. This is also true, of course, for families in which the adults have cohabited several times without marrying.

An Ecological Approach to Stepfamily Development

An ecological model developed by Bronfenbrenner (1979) to explain child development may also be applicable to stepfamily development. This model suggests that development is jointly determined by the competencies and skills of the developing individual and the environmental settings in which the individual functions. According to Bronfenbrenner, development is affected by multiple levels of environmental systems, which proceed from being focused, specific, and direct in their effects to diffuse, broad, and indirect in how they affect individuals: (1) the *microsystem* consists of the characteristics of the individual's immediate setting, including the behaviors, roles, and relations in which influence the person's daily life, (2) the *exosystem* consists of settings with which the individual, does not come in contact directly but in which events occur that affect the developing individual, such as parents' places of employment; and (3) the *macrosystem* consists of characteristics of the culture or subculture, such as beliefs, values, and attitudes, that have an impact upon the individual.

Although Bronfenbrenner's model was not designed to explain how newly formed stepfamilies adjust to the changes they will experience, adjustment in stepfamilies may also be affected by multiple layers of nested environmental systems (see also Clingempeel, Brand, & Segal, 1987). Certainly, the development of an individual stepfamily member is affected by the behaviors, roles, and relations in which the individual is involved (the microsystem), the settings in which the individual is not directly involved but in which events occur that affect the individual, such as a stepchild who is affected by his or her parent's relationship to the ex-spouse or a stepparent who is affected by what a stepchild experiences at school (the exosystem), and cultural beliefs and values regarding stepfamilies (the macrosystem).

There has been some research on each of these systems. With respect to the microsystem, for example, researchers have found that the quality of stepparent/stepchild relationships is associated with children's psychological adjustment and parents' marital satisfaction (Brand & Clingempeel, 1987). Although there has been relatively little work on the exosystem, as noted earlier, investigators have shown that the quality of stepmothers' relations with their stepchildren may be related to the extent to which the children have contact with their nonresidential mothers (Clingempeel & Segal, 1986; Furstenberg & Seltzer, 1983). Finally, with respect to the macrosystem, studies have shown that members of stepfamilies are negatively culturally stereotyped, as they are perceived more negatively than members of first-marriage families (Ganong, Coleman, & Mapes, 1990). Further, stepparents and stepchildren have few legal rights (Fine & Fine, 1992), which may reflect the cultural belief that stepfamilies are not as "legitimate" as first-marriage families.

Although some studies have examined how the microsystem, exosystem, and macrosystem levels affect individuals, little work has been directed at how these levels affect the well-being of the entire stepfamily system. Despite this lack of empirical evidence, however, several authors have attempted to explain how the stepfamily system develops over time, identifying tasks and stages (Mills, 1984; Papernow, 1993; Ransom, Schlesinger, & Derdeyn, 1979; Rodgers & Conrad, 1986). Most have focused primarily on the microsystem—the dynamics of the stepfamily *household*—rather than the exosystem—dynamics related to the *binuclear system* and *extended-family networks* (including stepkin not living in the household)—or the macrosystem.

Models of Stepfamily Development

The processes of development in a stepfamily system are different from those in a nuclear family. To capture these differences, a number of models of stepfamily development have been proposed. We will briefly examine three of these models, all of which are based at least in part on family-systems concepts.

McGoldrick and Carter's developmental phase model. The McGoldrick and Carter (1989) model emphasizes resolving issues related to the prior marriage and divorce before confronting remarriage and stepfamily issues. This model was based partly on an earlier clinically inspired model (Ransom et al., 1979) and consists of three phases, or steps, each of which is accompanied by "prerequisite attitudes" and developmental issues that must be addressed. The prerequisite attitudes are emotional tasks that must be resolved before individuals and families can work on the accompanying "developmental issues." The phases are labeled: (1) entering the new relationship, (2) conceptualizing and planning the new marriage and family, and (3) remarriage and reconstitution of the family.

According to this model, the goal for stepfamilies is to have an "open system with workable boundaries." Tasks are outlined for individuals, family subsystems, the binuclear family unit, and the extended-family system.

McGoldrick and Carter, based on their clinical experience as social workers, have identified several factors that predict difficulty in making the transition to remarriage:

1. a wide discrepancy in the life-cycle stages of "his" family and "her" family
2. denial of earlier losses and a short time period between divorce and remarriage
3. unresolved, intense feelings for the former spouse
4. a general lack of understanding of children's emotional reactions to remarriage
5. inability to give up the ideal of the nuclear family
6. efforts to draw firm boundaries around the stepfamily household and pushing for cohesiveness too fast
7. attempts to exclude the nonresidential biological parents and grandparents
8. denial of difficulties
9. a shift in physical custody near the time of remarriage

These clinical speculations are interesting, but they have not yet stimulated empirical work. It is difficult to determine how potent these predictors actually are without further study by researchers investigating nonclinical samples of remarried families.

The stepfamily cycle.   A model drawn from Gestalt psychology and family-systems theories identifies seven stages of stepfamily development: (1) fantasy, (2) immersion, (3) awareness, (4) mobilization, (5) action,

(6) contact, and (7) resolution (Papernow, 1993). In the first three stages, the family remains primarily divided along biological lines, with most support and agreement on rules occurring between parents and children. In the fourth and fifth stages, the stepfamily begins the tasks of loosening old boundaries and restructuring itself to strengthen its subunits. In the final two stages, contact finally becomes consistent within the step subsystems, and the stepparent role becomes clear for the first time. Not all families satisfactorily complete the stepfamily cycle, as some remarried couples experience another divorce. As noted earlier, however, those who complete the cycle take between four and seven years to do so.

This model clearly blends individual and family dynamics to describe stepfamily processes. It has received quite a bit of attention from clinicians. The model was originally developed via a qualitative study of stepfamilies and has since received some validation in further qualitative work by Papernow.

Mills's model of stepfamily development.   Before setting forth his clinically based model, Mills (1984) outlined what he saw as requirements for any useful developmental model of stepfamilies:

1. It should not be identified as the only way that a stepfamily can develop but as one of several paths that a stepfamily might follow.
2. It must allow for the simultaneous achievement of a number of different, and sometimes competing, developmental tasks of individual family members and the stepfamily as a whole.
3. It must take into account the fact that parent/child bonds are older and more enduring than stepparent/child bonds.
4. It must be aware of the binuclear nature of many stepfamilies, even in situations when the nonresidential parent is not physically available.
5. It should be useful not only during the formative period but also in later periods of stepfamily life.

Unlike Carter and McGoldrick's and Papernow's models, Mills's model is prescriptive (it details how remarried parents *should* behave to achieve positive stepfamily outcomes over time) rather than normative (it does not describe how stepfamilies *typically* develop).

Components of the model serve as a set of recommendations to remarried couples for how to facilitate positive stepfamily development.

Mills emphasizes the necessity for the marital pair to assume executive control of the family. To be successful, the members of the new couple must decide on appropriate goals for their stepfamily. For example, appropriate goals might be to reach a point where stepfamily members can effectively solve problems together as a unit and the stepparent and stepchild enjoy spending time together. Based on these goals, the couple must plan the roles the stepparent(s) will play as well as the type of structure to establish within the family that will enable family members to meet their personal and collective goals. A basic underlying theme is to place most of the responsibility for decision-making on the subsystem that presumably has the greatest motivation to make the family a success: the adults who decided to marry. The focus of the majority of decisions is on the stepparent/stepchild relationship, the subsystem that may be the most important in determining stepfamily satisfaction (Crosbie-Burnett, 1984).

Stepfamilies are encouraged not simply to assume the nuclear-family model but also to be creative in choosing roles and rules that work for the specific needs of the family members. For example, families can consider drawing upon ideas related to a variety of roles (coach, sister or brother, friend, aunt or uncle, adviser, parent) when deciding on the stepparents' roles. Some families could even decide that the stepparent should assume different roles for different stepchildren, based on the children's expressed needs, ages, and genders.

Biological parents are put in control of setting limits for children, reducing the opportunity for conflicts among stepchildren and stepparents, and eliminating "triangulation" dynamics among parent, stepparent, and child. Stepparents are given the task of bonding emotionally with stepchildren by engaging in enjoyable and nurturing interactions. Household rules are established with an eye toward building a set of rituals and traditions for the stepfamily.

This brief summary does not do justice to the rationale or to the flexibility of Mills's model. Although it would be difficult to research some of the propositions of this model, it is not impossible to examine them empirically.

It should be obvious that we think more research needs to be done on stepfamily development over time. Longitudinal research on families is expensive and time-consuming, but certain questions can be answered only with such research design. Rodgers and Conrad (1986) have helped future family researchers who are interested in the transition to remarriage by identifying 25 propositions based on systems theory and on prior empirical work. It is up to the family scholars of the future to take up their challenge and test those propositions.

Family Processes That Facilitate Children's and Adolescents' Adjustment in Stepfamilies

One important aspect of the microsystem in stepfamilies is the nature of family interaction. Although family interactions, or processes, affect all stepfamily members, most of the research and clinical attention have been directed to how these family processes affect children and adolescents.

The impetus for examining family processes in stepfamilies came from early research that compared children and adolescents in stepfamilies with those in other family structures on a variety of measures of adjustment (Coleman & Ganong, 1990). These studies sometimes found significant differences between children and adolescents in stepfamilies and those in first-marriage families, but the sizes of the differences were typically quite small, and some studies did not find these differences. Because of the inconsistent findings and the small effect sizes, stepfamily scholars have called for a decreased emphasis on comparing family structure and an increased focus on processes that occur in families, such as how much conflict, support, and supervision there are in the home and how parents behave toward their children (Coleman & Ganong, 1990).

In fact, recent research has suggested that family processes may be more important for children's and adolescents' well-being than is the type of family in which they live (for example, single parent, first-marriage, or stepparent families) (Demo & Acock, 1988; Grych & Fincham, 1990). Unfortunately, relatively few studies have examined the relations between family processes and children's adjustment in stepfamilies.

As an example of work that has been done in this area, we review a study by Fine and Kurdek (1992), who assessed which family-process variables were linked to the well-being of adolescents in stepfather and stepmother families. Particularly for girls in stepmother families, high levels of perceived warmth ("There's a feeling of togetherness in my family"), supervision ("Someone in my family makes sure that my homework is done"), order ("There are set ways of doing things in my home"), and interest ("Someone in my family takes an interest in the things I do") and low levels of conflict ("There's a lot of yelling and fighting in my family") were related to the young adolescents' adjustment (good grades, high self-esteem, few health problems, little drug usage).

In addition, adolescents' perceptions of their biological parent's and stepparent's behavior were related to their adjustment. Authoritarian parenting by both the biological parent and the stepparent (parents exert rigid controls on the children without much warmth and nurturance: "If I don't agree with my father, he usually forces me to do what he thinks is right") was negatively related to the young adolescents' well-being. When adolescents reported that their biological parents behaved in an authoritative way (parents provide high levels of both warmth and supervision to their children: "My mother usually gives me a reason why family rules are made"), their well-being was high.

The results from this study need to be viewed cautiously, because on most measures only the adolescents' perceptions were measured. Further caution is indicated because, in a correlational design, we cannot infer that healthy family processes cause adolescents to adjust positively. It is possible that other causal mechanisms explain the observed relations. Despite these important limitations, however, these findings are noteworthy in several respects. First, they support the view that family processes and parenting styles are strongly related to the well-being of adolescents in stepfamilies. Second, they also suggest that the same family processes that are related to the well-being of adolescents in first-marriage families are also associated with adolescent well-being in stepfamilies (see Hetherington & Clingempeel, 1992). Finally, by examining how processes are related to

adjustment, we may begin to acquire a picture of how successful stepfamilies are able to function effectively in their difficult circumstances.

Characteristics of Healthy Stepfamilies

Developmental models have been useful in identifying factors that help stepfamilies adjust positively to their circumstances. Unfortunately, however, much of the stepfamily literature has focused on problems experienced by stepfamily members. There are stepfamilies that function quite well, and we believe that family practitioners and family scholars can learn a great deal about how all families can function better by studying healthy stepfamilies that have learned to adapt to their changed circumstances.

Because few studies have identified characteristics of healthy stepfamilies, there is a great need for future research in this area (Coleman & Ganong, 1990). However, authors who work with stepfamily members have identified several of these family characteristics. Visher and Visher (1990) list six characteristics of adults in successful stepfamilies, and these are described below. It should be noted that successful stepfamilies need not have all of these characteristics; rather, they have made substantial progress on a number of them. Typically, this progress occurs gradually over the life span of the stepfamily.

Losses Have Been Mourned

Stepfamily members have typically experienced a number of losses, including those associated with the previous family arrangement (for example, loss of spouse, reduced financial security, less social support). Some of these losses may not be obvious to outside observers. For example, a stepmother who has not previously married may experience the loss of her goal of marrying someone who also was marrying for the first time and having children be a part of her family only after several years of marriage. These losses must eventually be acknowledged and accepted before individuals are emotionally ready to devote their attention to adjusting to their new family arrangement.

Expectations Are Realistic

As discussed earlier, adults in successful stepfamilies are unlikely to have the unrealistic expectations reflected in "stepfamily myths." When stepfamily members hold realistic expectations about what their family life will be like, they are unlikely to experience substantial disappointment and frustration. Family members in well-functioning stepfamilies develop progressively more realistic expectations over time, although there is little empirical evidence to support this claim.

There Is a Strong, Unified Couple

Particularly because the parent/child relationship preceded the marital relationship, couples in successful stepfamilies make special efforts to nurture and build their relationship. The primary core of the stepfamily is a strong marriage (Mills, 1984) that must withstand any efforts by children to "divide and conquer." While children still need alliances with their parents, they also need the security that comes from a strong marriage and the assurance that the stepfamily will continue. This characteristic is also important in first-marriage families, but because the marital relationship preceded the addition of children into the family, a strong marriage is easier to achieve than it is in stepfamilies.

Constructive Rituals Are Established

Successful stepfamilies have established rituals and traditions that allow a sense of shared history to develop. While many of these traditions may be new, some may be flexible adaptations of those that existed in the previous family arrangement. For example, if the mother and child have become accustomed to Thanksgiving dinner around noon and the new spouse/stepfather has typically had the meal in the evening, the stepfamily may compromise by having the meal in the early afternoon or alternating mealtimes from year to year. Flexibility and creativity are characteristics often mentioned by adults in stepfamilies when referring to what helps them succeed.

Satisfactory Steprelationships Have Formed

It takes time for satisfactory steprelationships to develop, whether between stepparents and stepchildren or between stepsiblings. Typically, except when children are very young, stepparents are advised not to take on primary responsibility for discipline, because the children do not wish to comply with demands from a stranger they may resent. In addition, stepparents who initially take on an active role in discipline may have problems with their new spouse. As Hetherington, Cox, and Cox (1985) and Bray (1988) have found, stepparents in well-functioning stepfamilies initially take on a secondary, or "monitoring," function by supporting (but not themselves initiating) the disciplinary activities of the biological parent. These authors advise stepparents to enter the family system slowly and to form a friendly relationship with stepchildren before becoming active disciplinarians.

Relatively little attention has been devoted to the formation of stepsibling bonds (Ihinger-Tallman, 1987). Sibling bonds are often a great source of strength for children, particularly when parenting is inadequate (Bank & Kahn, 1982). However, conditions in stepfamilies make this process potentially problematic. With the addition of new and strange stepsiblings, children may feel that they will lose attention and affection from their biological parent, that they will have to share friends and possessions, or that they will have to make a major change if they move to another residence. As suggested by Ihinger-Tallman (1987), there are also benefits to children when stepsiblings are added to their lives. For example, stepsiblings provide companionship that may not have been present before and bring an expanded set of friends and community contacts. As postulated by Ihinger-Tallman, stepsibling cohesion will develop to the extent that stepsiblings are similar, they perceive that there is mutual benefit to relate to one another, there are few perceived personal costs, and there is an approximate equality in the extent to which stepsiblings have had to relinquish aspects of their former lives (for example, giving up possessions or changing routines).

The Separate Households Cooperate

Visher and Visher (1988) have referred to the importance of a "parenting coalition," which means that the adults from both of the child's households are cooperating. Unfortunately, it is very difficult for some formerly married spouses to cooperate in child rearing, and instead they maintain a competitive relationship. A particularly difficult challenge that successful stepfamilies have been able to meet is that ex-spouses are able to cooperate in this one important area, even though they may have negative and hostile feelings in many others.

Roles Are Clear

In addition to Visher and Visher's (1990) listing of attributes of successful stepfamilies, one additional characteristic warrants mention. Family members in well-functioning stepfamilies have clear perceptions of the roles they are expected to fulfill and the roles they expect others to perform. In addition, there is general consensus among individuals on perceptions of the various family roles (Fine & Schwebel, 1991). When these role perceptions are not clear, role ambiguity is experienced. Role ambiguity is not typically a problem in intact families because parent and child roles are usually quite clear.

In stepfamilies, stepparent roles, in particular, are likely to be ambiguous because there are few societally accepted standards that help stepparents decide how they should function (Cherlin, 1978; Leslie & Epstein, 1988; Visher & Visher, 1988). In addition, other family members may also lack clarity about how the stepparent should behave. In fact, ambiguity surrounding the stepparent role has been identified as the core difficulty encountered by members of stepfamilies (Crosbie-Burnett, 1989).

Some empirical support for the importance of role clarity in stepfather families was generated by Kurdek and Fine (1991), who found that the extent of role ambiguity was negatively related to mothers' perceptions of the overall quality of their lives and stepfathers' satisfactions with parenting. Consequently, although empirical support is limited, role clarity is posited to be an attribute of well-functioning stepfamilies.

Conclusions

Stepfamily members are the pioneers of family living in the final quarter of the 20th century. The rapid increase in the number of stepfamilies has caught helping pro-

fessionals, family social science researchers, and legal experts poorly prepared to deal with the complex demands of this family form. Although in recent years society has struggled to "catch up" with stepfamilies, members of such families still lack clear cultural role guidelines, still encounter clergy, counselors, and educators who are ignorant of their unique dynamics, and still find themselves on the frontier of constructing strategies for successful stepfamily living. We hope that the progress made in these areas in the last decade will continue into the next century.

Chapter Summary

Discussion Questions

1. In what ways are stepfamilies qualitatively different from first-marriage families? How might it be frustrating for members of stepfamilies if they believed that stepfamilies were functionally equivalent to first-marriage families?
2. What evidence have you seen in our society of negative cultural stereotypes of stepfamilies? How might these negative stereotypes affect stepfamily members?
3. What do you believe is the appropriate role for a stepparent to take in the stepfamily? How might this role change over the life course of the stepfamily?
4. After a divorce, how might processes within the family change? How might they change yet again when the residential parent remarries and a stepparent enters the family?

Additional Resources

Ihinger-Tallman, M., & Pasley, K. (1987). *Remarriage*. Newbury Park, CA: Sage.

Visher, E. B., & Visher, J. S. (1988). *Old loyalties, new ties: Therapeutic interventions with stepfamilies*. New York: Brunner/Mazel.

Visher, E. B., & Visher, J. S. (1979). *Stepfamilies: A guide to working with stepchildren.* New York: Brunner/Mazel.

References

Ahrons, C. R., & Perlmutter, M. S. (1982). The relationship between former spouses: A fundamental subsystem in the remarriage family. In L. Messinger (Ed.), *Therapy with remarried families* (pp. 31–46). Rockville, MD: Aspen.

Ahrons, C. R., & Rodgers, R. H. (1987). *Divorced families: A multidisciplinary developmental view.* New York: Norton.

Ambert, A. (1986). Being a stepparent: Live-in and visiting stepchildren. *Journal of Marriage and the Family, 48,* 795–804.

Anderson, J., & White, G. (1986). An empirical investigation of interactive and relationship patterns in functional and dysfunctional nuclear families and stepfamilies. *Family Process, 25,* 407–422.

Bachrach, C. A. (1983). Children in families: Characteristics of biological, step-, and adopted children. *Journal of Marriage and the Family, 45,* 171–179.

Bank, S., & Kahn, M. D. (1982). *The sibling bond.* New York: Basic Books.

Brand, E., & Clingempeel, W. G. (1987). Interdependencies of marital and stepparent-stepchild relationships and children's psychological adjustment: Research findings and clinical implications. *Family Relations, 36,* 140–145.

Bray, J. H. (1988). Children's development during early remarriage. In E. M. Hetherington & J. Aresteh (Eds.), *The impact of divorce, single-parenting, and step-parenting on children* (pp. 279–298). Hillsdale, NJ: Erlbaum.

Brody, G., Neubaum, E., & Forehand, R. (1988). Serial marriage: A heuristic analysis of an emerging family form. *Psychological Bulletin, 103,* 211–222.

Bronfenbrenner, U. (1979). *The ecology of human development: Experiments by nature and design.* Cambridge, MA: Harvard University Press.

Bumpass, L. (1984). Some characteristics of children's second families. *American Journal of Sociology, 90,* 608–623.

Burt, M. (Ed.). (1989). *Stepfamilies stepping ahead: An eight-step program for successful family living.* Lincoln, NE: Stepfamilies Press.

Cherlin, A. (1978). Remarriage as an incomplete institution. *American Journal of Sociology, 84,* 634–650.

Cherlin, A., & McCarthy, J. (1985). Remarried couple households: Data from the June 1980 current population survey. *Journal of Marriage and the Family, 47,* 23–30.

Clingempeel, W. G., Brand, E., & Segal, S. (1987). A multi-level-multivariable-developmental perspective for future research on stepfamilies. In K. Pasley & M. Ihinger-Tallman (Eds.), *Remarriage and stepparenting: Current research and theory* (pp. 65–93). New York: Guilford Press.

Clingempeel, W. G., & Segal, S. (1986). Stepparent-stepchild relationships and the psychological adjustment of children in stepmother and stepfather families. *Child Development, 57,* 474–484.

Coleman, M., & Ganong, L. H. (1987). Marital conflict in stepfamilies: Effects on children. *Youth and Society, 19,* 151–172.

Coleman, M., & Ganong, L. H. (1990). Remarriage and stepfamily research in the 1980s: Increased interest in an old family form. *Journal of Marriage and the Family, 52,* 925–940.

Crohn, H., Sager, C., Brown, H., Rodstein, E., & Walker, L. (1982). A basis for understanding and treating the remarried family. *Family Therapy Collection, 2,* 159–186.

Crosbie-Burnett, M. (1984). The centrality of the step relationship: A challenge to family theory and practice. *Family Relations, 33,* 459–464.

Crosbie-Burnett, M. (1989). Application of family stress theory to remarriage: A model for assessing and helping stepfamilies. *Family Relations, 38,* 323–331.

Crosbie-Burnett, M., & Helmbrecht, L. (1993). A descriptive study of gay male stepfamilies. *Family Relations, 42,* 256–262.

Demo, D. H., & Acock, A. C. (1988). The impact of divorce on children. *Journal of Marriage and the Family, 50,* 619–648.

Fast, I., & Cain, A. C. (1966). The stepparent role: Potential for disturbances in family functioning. *American Journal of Orthopsychiatry, 36,* 485–491.

Fine, M. A., & Fine, D. R. (1992). Recent changes in laws affecting stepfamilies: Suggestions for legal reform. *Family Relations, 41,* 334–340.

Fine, M. A., & Kurdek, L. A. (1992). The adjustment of adolescents in stepfather and stepmother families. *Journal of Marriage and the Family, 54,* 725–736.

Fine, M. A., & Kurdek, L. A. (in press). A multidimensional cognitive-developmental model of stepfamily adjustment. In K. Pasley & M. Ihinger-Tallman (Eds.), *Stepfamilies: Issues in research, theory, and practice.* Westport, CT: Greenwood Press.

Fine, M. A., & Schwebel, A. I. (1991). Stepparent stress: A cognitive perspective. *Journal of Divorce and Remarriage, 17,* 1–15.

Fishman, B., & Hamel, B. (1981). From nuclear to stepfamily ideology: A stressful change. *Alternative Lifestyles, 4,* 181–204.

Furstenberg, F. F., Jr. (1987). The new extended family: The experience of parents and children after remarriage. In

K. Pasley & M. Ihinger-Tallman (Eds.), *Remarriage and stepparenting: Current research and theory* (pp. 42–61). New York: Guilford Press.

Furstenberg, F., & Nord, C. (1985). Parenting apart: Patterns of childrearing after marital disruption. *Journal of Marriage and the Family, 47*, 893–904.

Furstenberg, F. F., & Seltzer, J. A. (1983, April). *Divorce and child development*. Paper presented at the annual meeting of the American Orthopsychiatric Association, Boston.

Ganong, L., & Coleman, M. (1986). A comparison of clinical and empirical literature on children in stepfamilies. *Journal of Marriage and the Family, 48*, 309–318.

Ganong, L., & Coleman, M. (1989a). Financial management in stepfamilies. *Lifestyles: Family and Economic Issues, 10*, 217–232.

Ganong, L., & Coleman, M. (1989b). Preparing for remarriage: Anticipating the issues, seeking solutions. *Family Relations, 38*, 28–33.

Ganong, L., Coleman, M., & Mapes, D. (1990). A meta-analytic review of family structure stereotypes. *Journal of Marriage and the Family, 52*, 287–297.

Giles-Sims, J. (1984). The stepparent role: Expectations, behavior, and sanctions. *Journal of Family Issues, 5*, 116–130.

Giles-Sims, J., & Crosbie-Burnett, M. (1989). Adolescent power in stepfather families: A test of the normative-resource theory. *Journal of Marriage and the Family, 51*, 1065–1078.

Glick, P. C. (1984). Marriage, divorce and living arrangements: Prospective changes. *Journal of Family Issues, 5*, 7–26.

Glick, P. C. (1989). Remarried families, stepfamilies, and stepchildren: A brief demographic analysis. *Family Relations, 38*, 24–27.

Goldner, V. (1982). Remarriage family: Structure, system, future. In J. C. Hansen & L. Messinger (Eds.), *Therapy with remarried families* (pp. 187–206). Rockville, MD: Aspen.

Greif, J. B. (1982). The father-child relationship subsequent to divorce. In J. C. Hansen & L. Messinger (Eds.), *Therapy with married families* (pp. 47–57). Rockville, MD: Aspen.

Gross, P. E. (1986). Defining post-divorce remarriage families: A typology based on the subjective perceptions of children. *Journal of Divorce, 10*, 205–217.

Grych, J. H., & Fincham, F. D. (1990). Marital conflict and children's adjustment: A cognitive-contextual framework. *Psychological Bulletin, 108*, 267–290.

Hetherington, E. M., & Clingempeel, W. G. (1992). Coping with marital transitions: A family systems perspective. *Monographs of the Society for Research in Child Development, 57* (2–3, Serial No. 27).

Hetherington, E. M., Cox, M., & Cox, R. (1985). Long-term effects of divorce and remarriage on the adjustment of children. *Journal of the American Academy of Child Psychiatry, 24*, 518–530.

Ihinger-Tallman, M. (1987). Sibling and stepsibling bonding in stepfamilies. In K. Pasley & M. Ihinger-Tallman (Eds.), *Remarriage and stepparenting: Current research and theory* (pp. 164–182). New York: Guilford Press.

Jacobson, D. S. (1987). Family type, visiting, and children's behavior in the stepfamily: A linked family system. In K. Pasley & M. Ihinger-Tallman (Eds.), *Remarriage and stepparenting: Current research and theory* (pp. 257–272). New York: Guilford Press.

Jones, S. M. (1978). Divorce and remarriage: A new beginning, a new set of problems. *Journal of Divorce, 2*, 217–227.

Kennedy, G. (1985). Family relationships as perceived by college students from single-parent, blended, and intact families. *Family Perspective, 19*, 117–126.

Kompara, D. R. (1980). Difficulties in the socialization of stepparenting. *Family Relations, 29*, 69–73.

Kurdek, L. A., & Fine, M. A. (1991). Cognitive correlates of satisfaction for mothers and stepfathers in stepfather families. *Journal of Marriage and the Family, 53*, 565–572.

Leslie, L. A., & Epstein, N. (1988). Cognitive-behavioral treatment of remarried families. In N. Epstein, S. E. Schlesinger, & W. Dryden (Eds.), *Cognitive-behavioral therapy with families* (pp. 151–182). New York: Brunner/Mazel.

Martin, T., & Bumpass, L. (1989). Recent trends in marital disruption. *Demography, 26*, 37–52.

McGoldrick, M., & Carter, B. (1989). Forming a remarried family. In B. Carter & M. McGoldrick (Eds.), *The changing family life cycle: A framework for family therapy* (2nd ed.) (pp. 399–429). Boston: Allyn & Bacon.

Messinger, L. (1984). *Remarriage: A family affair*. New York: Plenum.

Mills, D. (1984). A model for stepfamily development. *Family Relations, 33*, 365–372.

Mowatt, M. (1972). Group psychotherapy for stepfathers and their wives. *Psychotherapy: Theory, Research and Practice, 9*, 328–331.

Orleans, M., Palisi, B., & Caddell, D. (1989). Marriage adjustment and satisfaction of stepfathers: Their feelings and perceptions of decision making and stepchildren relations. *Family Relations, 38*, 371–377.

Papernow, P. L. (1993). *Becoming a stepfamily: Patterns of development in remarried families*. San Francisco: Jossey-Bass.

Pasley, K. (1987). Family boundary ambiguity: Perceptions of adult remarried family members. In K. Pasley & M.

Ihinger-Tallman (Eds.), *Remarriage and stepparenting: Current research and theory* (pp. 206–224). New York: Guilford Press.

Peek, C., Beel, N., Waldren, T., & Sorell, G. (1988). Patterns of functioning in families of remarried and first-married couples. *Journal of Marriage and the Family, 50,* 699–708.

Pink, J. E., & Wampler, K. S. (1985). Problem areas in stepfamilies: Cohesion, adaptability, and the stepfather-adolescent relationship. *Family Relations, 34,* 327–335.

Ransom, J. W., Schlesinger, S., & Derdeyn, A. P. (1979). A stepfamily in formation. *American Journal of Orthopsychiatry, 49,* 36–43.

Rodgers, R., & Conrad, L. (1986). Courtship for remarriage: Influences of family reorganization after divorce. *Journal of Marriage and the Family, 48,* 767–775.

Sager, C. J., Brown, H. S., Crohn, H., Engel, T., Rodstein, E., & Walker, E. (1983). *Treating the remarried family.* New York: Brunner/Mazel.

Schwebel, A. I., & Fine, M. A. (1993). *Understanding and helping families: A cognitive-behavioral perspective.* Hillsdale, NJ: Erlbaum.

Visher, E. B., & Visher, J. S. (1979). *Stepfamilies: A guide to working with stepparents and stepchildren.* New York: Brunner/Mazel.

Visher, E. B., & Visher, J. S. (1982). Stepfamilies in the 1980's. In J. C. Hansen & L. Messinger (Eds.), *Therapy with remarried families* (pp. 105–119). Rockville, MD: Aspen.

Visher, E. B., & Visher, J. S. (1988). *Old loyalties, new ties: Therapeutic interventions with stepfamilies.* New York: Brunner/Mazel.

Visher, E. B., & Visher, J. S. (1990). Dynamics of successful stepfamilies. *Journal of Divorce and Remarriage, 14,* 3–12.

Wald, E. (1981). *The remarried family: Challenge and promise.* New York: Family Service Association of America.

Weiss, R. S. (1979). Growing up a little faster: The experience of growing up in a single-parent household. *Journal of Social Issues, 35,* 97–111.

Whiteside, M. F. (1983). Families of remarriage: The weaving of many life cycle threads. *Family Therapy Collections, 7,* 100–119.

Family Loss and Grief

Kathleen R. Gilbert
Indiana University

Family feelings were very mixed. . . . These differences created bad feelings and breaks within the family that will probably never heal. . . . Mother has not adapted well to the loss of her life's companion of almost 55 years. She never will. . . . I am still carrying very bitter feelings that I thought I had dealt with and put behind me.

—Adult daughter of an 82-year-old man killed by a drunken driver

It's so hard to deal with. No one helps. No one recognizes that I lost a daughter. If it's not a loss, why, after a year, do I still cry? Why does it still hurt?

—Mother, one year after terminating her pregnancy because her fetal daughter was anencephalic

People were so busy judging each other that they didn't seem to have any time for anything else. One relative came up to me at the funeral, poked her finger in my face, and said, "What I want to know is, with all your education, why he didn't talk to you?" Well, maybe he didn't want to. . . . Haven't spoken to her since then, either.

—Adult sister of a man who committed suicide at age 40

Loss and the grief that results from it are normative elements of family life. Yet loss is often treated as an unusual occurrence, something that happens to others but not to oneself or someone in one's own family.

Not all losses are the result of a death; we grieve over such things as the loss of a relationship through divorce or the end of a friendship, the loss of hopes when we realize we will not attain childhood dreams, or the loss of memories resulting from Alzheimer's or other organic brain diseases. Our experience of loss and grief begins in infancy and extends through life to our own, anticipated death. This chapter will explore the grief response of the family and its members to loss through death, but you should be aware that similar processes occur with other losses as well.

Grief consists of the emotional, physiological, and behavioral reactions resulting from the loss of a significant other, and *grieving* is made up of active efforts to cope with and come to terms with loss (Attig, 1991). Loss in a family context occurs as a private and as a public experience. Because of this, when we consider family loss, we must take into account both public and private expressions of grief. *Mourning*, the public expression of grief, is also important. Seen in this context, the extent to which one may and may not publicly express grief is restricted by cultural prescriptions and sanctions and, more directly, by the censure or approval of one's family members. Thus, *all* of these take place in the context of family.

Until recently, grief was depicted (in research, clinical treatment, and in the personal experiences of the lay populace) as a clear, uncomplicated, linear process through which individuals moved in order to recover from a loss. The deceased was someone to be mourned and then left behind. The family was generally seen as one element in the social environment of the bereaved individual, placing the research focus on the response of the family to the griever. This view provided a limited sense of how loss affects the family system and why family members must struggle, sometimes for the rest of their lives, to come to terms with their loss.

The first section of this chapter addresses the complexity of grief and the flaws inherent in considering grief only in the context of simple, linear stages. The second section examines grieving in the context of the family; that is, ways in which the family system adapts to the loss of a member as well as the place of the family in individual members' grief resolution are also discussed. Finally, implications of this chapter for family scientists are presented.

I encourage you to consider the difficulties of coping with loss and the pressures on the family system that result. For example, it may be that a family focus on reducing the strain of grief on relationships in the family may facilitate grief resolution among family members. However, it may also be that efforts to reduce the level of stress on a grieving family member may result in a strain on relationships in the family and added stress on other members. In either case, it is wise to remember that family members experience grief simultaneously at the individual and at the family-systems level.

The Complexity of Grief

Grief is commonly held to be a simple, linear process of "letting go" of one's connection to a loved one. This view presents grief as occurring in a series of identifiable stages directed toward recovery of one's old level of functioning. In working through these stages, old attachments must be replaced with new ones, and painful, strong emotions that are tied to the deceased must be expressed and worked through. Variations from this process are commonly seen as evidence of abnormal grief (Wortman & Silver, 1989).

In truth, the process of grieving a loss is much more complicated than this picture indicates. Although it is comforting to think that by working through a set of preordained stages, one can recover from a loss, a growing body of evidence suggests that the process of grief is far more complicated than this stage model would suggest.

Here, two of the most commonly used approaches, Elizabeth Kübler-Ross's five-stage model of grief and John Bowlby's four-stage model, will be presented as examples. A critique of stage models will then be discussed. Finally, a number of factors that contribute to the complexity of grieving will be addressed.

Grief as a Series of Stages

Perhaps the most popular stage model of grief is Kübler-Ross's (1969) five-stage model. It was originally intended to depict the process through which the dying individual needed to move in order to have a "good" death. However, she indicated that by moving through each of the stages, a bereaved person, such as a family member, could also successfully resolve his or her loss.

Kübler-Ross suggests that both the dying and the bereaved experience *five stages* as they adjust to the reality of death. As presented by her, the first stage of grief involves *denial* of the reality of the loss, which is often accompanied by self-isolation. The next stage, in which the reality of their situation can no longer be avoided, the bereaved express great *anger* at the loss. In this stage, they may focus their anger in any number of directions: medical personnel, their god, perhaps themselves. They may direct their anger at the person who is dying or has died for some perceived negligence on his or her part. The next stage is *bargaining*, in which they attempt to find some way to negotiate the recovery of the dying (or dead) person, possibly through prayer or by seeking unusual, sometimes unorthodox, medical treatment. When this bargaining is unsuccessful, the griever experiences *depression* over the reality of his or her loss. Finally, the griever comes to an *acceptance* of the loss and moves on with his or her life. According to Kübler-Ross, the bereaved must move through these stages in order to come to a successful resolution of their loss. Failure to do so would result in psychological impairment.

Another model that has served as the basis for much of the grief research during in the past 30 years was first proposed by Bowlby (1961), expanded upon by Parkes (1972), and later refined by Bowlby (1980). In this model, based on attachment theory, they suggest that the normal grief process follows a pattern of *four distinctly discernible phases* through which the bereaved must pass for successful resolution. The phases are similar to those of Kübler-Ross's. They involve emotional *numbing*, followed by *yearning and searching* for the lost loved one, then *disorganization and despair* over the loss, and finally, *reorganization and recovery.*

According to Bowlby (1980), individuals may oscillate between any two phases throughout this grief-resolution process. Over time, however, an overall pattern of movement through these phases should be discerned. A lack of movement would be a source of concern, as it might indicate avoidance of the emotions of grief or of the reality of the loss.

Such stage, or phase, models of grief resolution have been used widely in investigations of grief (see Edelstein, 1984; Frantz, 1984; Miles, 1984; Peppers & Knapp, 1980), and although they contain some minor variations, their overall structure is in agreement with the examples presented above. That is, they assume the following: a period of disorganization, emotional numbness, and denial of the reality; a middle period (which is often broken into at least two different phases) of highly variable duration, of emotional extremes accompanying the struggle to accommodate the changed reality; and a final stage, resolution, in which the changed reality is accepted.

Criticisms of Stage Models of Grief

Stage models are intuitively appealing, as they have a clean sense of beginning, middle, and end. Unfortunately, they do not appear to fit the reality of grief and may do more harm than good. Frantz (1984) identifies a more complicated pattern of parental grieving in which parents experience an increase in intensity between six and twelve months after their child's death. Parents in this study assumed that the grief would lessen with time; instead, they suffered from recurring, intrusive thoughts about their child. Many expressed their fear that they were "going crazy," because they were unable to move through anticipated stages of grief in the expected sequence. Thus, the expectation of stages appears to have compounded the negative effects of the loss.

Others have found it equally difficult to fit grief to a stage model. In an extensive review of the literature, Silver and Wortman (1980) were unable to find any evidence of movement through a series of stages following a traumatic event.

Rando (1983) looked at parents of children who had died of cancer and was unable to find evidence that they moved through stages of recovery. The same pattern of worsening grief over time was true for parents of homicide victims (Rinear, 1985).

Additionally, grief does not simply go away; it can recur many years after the loss (Rosenblatt, 1983; Rosenblatt & Burns, 1986). An examination of 19th-century diaries showed that the diary writers experienced episodes of thinking of the lost loved one alternating with periods when they did not mention that person (Rosenblatt, 1983). Others have found evidence of long-term grief that appeared to be triggered by events (Gilbert & Smart, 1992; Rando, 1989; Rinear, 1985). Clearly, grief does not follow a single, easy path.

Another criticism of stage models involves the assumption that most victims of loss will come to a resolution of their grief. An increasing body of evidence suggests that this may not be true (Silver & Wortman, 1980; Wortman & Silver, 1989). Studies of parental grief have found that not all respondents achieved the same degree of resolution (Frantz, 1984; Gilbert & Smart, 1992; Rando, 1983). In each study, there was tremendous range in the degree to which the individual parent had come to terms with and accepted the loss.

Factors That Contribute to the Complexity of Grief

The grief process appears to be much more complicated than the stage models would indicate. An alternative view, suggested by Davidson (1979), holds that emotions and behaviors described as aspects of grief phases by Bowlby (1961, 1980) and Kübler-Ross (1969) may be present simultaneously, with each becoming more or less apparent during the course of recovery. Issues surrounding the loss may *never* be resolved completely (Wortman & Silver, 1989), and recurrent episodes of grief may recur many years after the loss (Rosenblatt & Burns, 1986).

Many factors contribute to this complicated nature of the grief response. Several of these factors are discussed below.

The relationship with the deceased.   As shown above, grief does not appear to be tied to a fixed order of emotional states. Rather, it appears to be related to such factors as the closeness of the relationship with the deceased and the perception of preventability of the death (Bugan, 1983; Wortman & Silver, 1989). This relationship need *not* be a warm, loving one. Indeed, Rando (1984) has suggested that a conflictual relationship may result in a more complicated pattern of grief. For example, it may be that following the death of her mother from a heart attack, the daughter with whom she had a close, conflictual relationship may feel the most intense grief because she may feel that the stress of their embattled relationship in some way resulted in her mother's death.

Anticipating loss.   First identified by Lindemann (1944), anticipatory grief occurs in preparation for loss. Anticipatory loss incorporates "a range of intensified emotional responses that may include separation anxiety, existential aloneness, denial, sadness, disappointment, anger, resentment, guilt, exhaustion, and desperation" (Roland, 1991, p. 145).

The unique character of anticipatory grief is that it involves a period of preparation for grief that allows the bereaved person opportunities to rehearse the loss of a wished-for future with the dying individual (Rando, 1986). In this case, the family members experience a series of small losses that precedes the final death of the loved one. As they relinquish hopes for a future with this person and cope with the daily challenges of caring for him or her, they also cope with daily pressures related to social expectations and evaluations of their behavior.

Traumatic nature of loss.   At the other extreme from anticipatory losses are traumatic losses. These result from the sudden and unanticipated death of a loved one when family members have had little or no time to prepare. Losses are more likely to be traumatic if the survivors have had little or no previous experience with loss.

The impact of traumatic loss is intense. Survivors are left feeling out of control, helpless, and confused. These emotions are accompanied by a sense of the untimeliness of the death as well as a perception of injustice that such a thing should have happened (Figley, in press-a; Gilbert, in press-a). Examples that immediately come to mind include the loss of a family member to suicide or homicide. However, any sudden, unanticipated loss, such as the death of a child or the death of a spouse at a young age, can also be traumatic. In addition, children may find even anticipated losses

to be traumatic because of such factors as magical thinking or efforts of adults to "protect" them from the reality of the impending death (Koocher, 1985).

Ambiguous loss.   As the name indicates, ambiguous losses lack clarity. They receive little or no public recognition because there is uncertainty over who or what has been lost. Others may not perceive the loss as genuine because they believe it lacks certain elements. As Pauline Boss (1991) has indicated, with ambiguous loss a family member may be physically present and psychologically absent (as in the case of an Alzheimer's disease victim) or may be psychologically present and physically absent (as with a member of the armed forces declared missing in action). If the social network is unable to recognize the loss as real, it will not validate the grief felt by those who have experienced the loss.

Examples of ambiguous loss abound. Fetal and neonatal (during the first month of life) deaths are ambiguous losses, because of uncertainty over what (or who) exactly has been lost.[1] Following an automobile accident in which a family member is left in a persistent vegetative state, other members will cope with ambiguous loss. For children, the loss of a much-loved aunt, uncle, or stepparent through divorce could also be ambiguous.

Interminable loss.   A unique form of ambiguous loss is an interminable loss, one that is or seems to be never-ending. The uncertainty of an ambiguous loss is combined with the lack of control and helplessness of a traumatic loss. There may not even be a person to whom one's sense of loss can be tied, as in the case of infertility. For couples who are infertile, each month and each treatment brings a new sense of loss. Yet there is no public event to mark their loss, and limited support for their grief.[2]

Another example of interminable loss can be found among families of men still missing in action in South-

---

[1] Participants in my work on fetal and infant loss remarked during their interviews that they were astonished at the intensity of their grief. One man said he had always felt that it would be easy for a man to recover from a miscarriage, because "you don't really know the baby." He was amazed at the pain of the loss.

[2] In my current project on grief and coping after the termination of a wanted, but doomed, pregnancy, many of the participants have had fertility problems. One woman spoke of the "monthly death" symbolized by her menstrual period. Comments like "Oh, just adopt and you'll get pregnant right away" have not been helpful.

east Asia. Reports of sightings of Americans result in hopes that are later dashed when the reports cannot be confirmed or are discounted. Family members alternate between fearing that the serviceman is dead and fearing that he may be suffering and that they cannot help him (Figley, in press-b; Gilbert, in press-b).

Disenfranchised grief.   Disenfranchised grief occurs when a person or group experiences a loss but is not seen as having "a socially recognized right, role, or capacity to grieve" (Doka, 1989, p. 3). Although such people have suffered a loss, they are unable to mourn publicly. This may be seen in the hidden grief of grandparents when they lose a grandchild but then must "be strong" for their child, the bereaved parent. In many cases, men also experience a disenfranchisement of their grief because of gender expectations regarding appropriate male behavior after a loss.

Disenfranchised grief also takes place when the type of loss is not seen as deserving grief. Couples who have terminated pregnancies often feel this disenfranchisement quite strongly.[3] A combination of this sense of the loss not deserving grief and the griever not deserving to grieve can also be seen when a gay man dies of AIDS and his lover is prevented from participating in the funeral.

Stigmatized nature of grief.   Disenfranchised grief is often stigmatized grief; that is, it results from stigmatized losses. Such losses as those through suicide (Bouvard, 1988) or AIDS (Colburn & Malena, 1989) may serve to isolate family members from others outside the family. The members may also be isolated from one another, especially if they resort to blame as an explanation for the loss.

People who are grieving, in general, express at least some sense that their grief has been stigmatized (Arnold & Gemma, 1983; Frantz, 1984; Getzel & Masters, 1984; Helmrath & Steinitz, 1978; Schiff, 1977). This may be because the loss and the resulting grief make others uncomfortable, and they then need to distance themselves from the griever. By exerting social pressure, either

directly (through encouragement to "get on with your life") or indirectly (through shunning), they may be able to convince the person who is grieving to abandon his or her public expression of grief (Stephenson, 1985). There is some level of stigmatization for all grief. Even such losses as the death of a child to illness result in some level of stigmatized grief (Arnold & Gemma, 1983; Frantz, 1984; Getzel & Masters, 1984).

Men often face a unique form of stigmatization of grief (Cook, 1988). They are caught in a double bind in that they are taught to contain their emotions and "act like a man" while also being expected to express their emotions after a loss "like a woman." Regardless of how they respond to the loss, they will experience some form of censure for acting inappropriately.

Gender differences in grieving.   As indicated above, men commonly experience conflict in their grief. They tend to grieve differently from the traditional expectation of expressive, social grief. This traditional image of "healthy grief" was based on early grief studies, which utilized the most willing and available grievers, widows and mothers (Cook, 1988). Thus, what Cook has called "women's grief" has been presented as normal and healthy. The cognitive, solitary grief that predominated among the men in her study of fathers grieving the death of a child to cancer has been seen as unhealthy and counterproductive to grief resolution.

Other studies of grieving men have shown them to be more likely to avoid going through the grieving (emotional) process than women (Frantz, 1984), to be less willing to talk about the loss (DeFrain, 1991; Helmrath & Steinitz, 1978), or to experience a less intense grief that is resolved more quickly than women's grief (Benefield, Lieb, & Vollman, 1978; Helmrath & Steinitz, 1978; Osterweis, Solomon, & Green, 1984).

Reported emotions also are different (DeFrain, 1991), with women feeling more sorrow and depression and men feeling more anger, fear, and loss of control. Women have also expressed more guilt (Peppers & Knapp, 1980).

Cross-culturally, similar patterns of differences have been found in male and female grief, with women generally more expressive of their emotions and men more restrained (Haig, 1990). McGoldrick et al. (1991)

---

[3]A student at my university, upon being told that I was studying grief and coping among couples who had terminated a pregnancy following a diagnosis of lethal or serious fetal abnormalities, angrily said: "Why should they be allowed to grieve? They killed their kid!"

also found that expectations for men and women in mourning behavior differed dramatically.

Grief as an Active Process

Although the stage models of grief have been found to be problematic, they have been useful in promoting a sense of movement in the grief process. Here, another way of looking at the response to loss is explored. In this view, grief is seen as an active process, with grieving centered on regaining control and predictability in one's life while also working to integrate the loss into one's interpretive structures (Attig, 1991). These interpretive structures are a generalized set of beliefs within which the individual operates. They allow one to organize information encountered in the environment and to reasonably anticipate future events. These constructions have been referred to as the assumptive world (Parkes, 1972), the world of meaning (Marris, 1982), and one's personal construct theory (Hoagland, 1984). Grief is seen as the loss of meaning, and bereavement as the process of reconstructing the generalized belief structure (Fowlkes, 1991; Marris, 1982). According to Parkes (1972), the central task of bereavement is to fit the loss to existing assumptions or to modify one's assumptions so that the loss can be accepted as real.

Although seemingly easy, this acceptance of the loss as real is actually an arduous task. This is because the loss affects beliefs that are central to one's ability to make sense of reality. As Attig (1991) has written, "Grieving entails nothing less than a comprehensive reconstruction of personal integrity as the bereaved reweave the threads of caring involvement with all that matters to them" (p. 390).

Janoff-Bulman (1985, 1992) has proposed that the loss of a significant other affects three core beliefs held by almost everyone. She has identified these as a belief in personal invulnerability, a view of oneself in a positive light, and the perception of the world as orderly and predictable. These are demonstrated by the comments "I thought that things like this always happened to other people" (personal invulnerability), "But this can't be happening. Bad things don't happen to good people" (positive self-view), "It isn't fair! I saw the doctor every month. My baby can't have died" (orderly and predictable world).

Beliefs specific to the type of loss have also been found to be affected. In their study of parental grief, for example, Gilbert and Smart (1992) found that the core beliefs were also extended to the babies who had died. In addition, the parents questioned the meaning of the child, why he or she had come into existence only to die so young, or, in the case of pregnancy loss, if they had had a child to lose. The process of questioning these interconnected assumptions, assumptions that serve as the basis for other beliefs, results in some level of psychological upheaval (Janoff-Bulman, 1985, 1992). As will be discussed later in this chapter, it can also lead to disruption of interpersonal and systemic processes.

Making sense of the loss is complicated by the fact that throughout this process, the bereaved person experiences episodes of confusion with little opportunity to register a clear mental picture. Immediately following the loss, the bereaved may not be able to believe what has happened because they have had no similar loss experiences. Thus, they have no information in their belief structure with which to make sense of the loss. This could result in fragmented and disjointed images of the event; attributing meaning to these images would be difficult, at best (Holloway & Ursano, 1984; Horowitz, 1986; Janoff-Bulman, 1985, 1992; Loftus, 1979).

Building a Bridge between Old and New Assumptive Worlds

Thus far, the following has been proposed: In order to function, we must have assumptions about life upon which we can depend. Grief is a reaction to the disruption of those parts of our belief structure dependent on a continuing relationship with the person who has been lost. In order to continue to function after the loss, we must attribute meaning to the loss to allow us to regain a sense of order, control, and purpose in life. Accordingly, we must reconstruct those elements of the assumptive world that were disrupted by the loss.

Developing a healing theory.   In order to reconstruct the assumptive world, the bereaved must develop some sort of explanation, a personal or healing theory (Figley, 1983, 1985; Taylor, Lichtman, & Wood, 1987). They must explain the loss in such a way that the reality of the death can be integrated into their assumptive world so that it can be used again to explain reality as it is experienced (Hoagland, 1984).

The process of constructing a healing theory includes answering questions about the loss (Figley, 1983). Taylor et al.(1987) indicate that the central question is "Why me?" These questions of the bereaved can also be about what happened, how it happened, why it happened, why it happened to their loved one, why they responded as they did, and how they would respond if such a loss should occur again (Figley, 1983). Borg and Lasker (1988) have proposed that this search for an explanation for a loss is a normal part of bereaved parents' efforts to regain order in a situation that makes no sense.

Regardless of the specific questions, through the construction of a healing theory the bereaved modify their assumptive world to incorporate the loss, thereby achieving a new sense of normalcy and purpose. In this way, they are able to regain a sense of control and predictability, find some sort of understanding, and gain a sense of mastery with regard to the event (Taylor, 1983).

The drive to reestablish the assumptive world. The need to make sense of the loss is extremely strong. Yet the bereaved must cope throughout the grief process with often unbidden thoughts of the lost loved one, a strong urge to reunite with that person, and painful recollections of the loss experience itself (Parkes, 1972).

Often, thoughts of the lost loved one are too painful, and grieving persons attempt to block those thoughts out. Should they attempt to do this, they may experience unpredictable, repetitive, intrusive images of the loss. Strong emotions that result from the images will also be experienced (Raphael, 1983).

Raphael (1992) has referred to the typical grief response as a form of post-traumatic stress response, a normal response to extreme stress that is centered on the integration of disturbing memories. Horowitz (1979, 1986) has proposed that the inability to avoid distressing memories is powered by the completion tendency, a drive to integrate new information with one's existing assumptive world and to establish consistency between old and new world views. Until this consistency between world views is established, intrusive

thoughts about the loss will recur (Horowitz, 1982). Each time the bereaved actively consider the loss, it is adjusted in relation to their current assumptive world.

At the same time, the overwhelming nature of these thoughts often makes them difficult to consider, and the bereaved may attempt to suppress them. The result of these two diametrically opposed pressures, one to consider painful memories and the other to avoid them, is the experience of episodes of intrusive images followed by episodes of avoidant behavior. Theoretically, these will continue until the loss has been integrated and closure had been achieved (Horowitz, 1986).[4]

Such long-term recurrences of intense grief have been seen among family members. Grieving parents of homicide victims reported vivid, painful "aftershocks" many years after their child had been murdered (Rinear, 1985). A similar, although less intense, phenomenon has been seen among parents who have experienced fetal or infant loss (Gilbert & Smart, 1992, Peppers & Knapp, 1980; Rosenblatt & Burns, 1986).

Section Summary

Stage models that explain the progression through grief have been popular with lay people and professionals alike. Yet there are problems with these models. Grieving individuals appear to go through a more complicated experience, with recurrences of grief, episodes of intense grieving that alternate with relatively grief-free periods, and tremendous variance in the extent to which they are able to resolve their loss. Factors that may contribute to this complexity of grief include the relationship with the deceased, the ability to anticipate loss, the traumatic nature of loss, ambiguity surround-

---

[4]The dilemma in considering when closure occurs may never be completely resolved. Although the absence of recurrent images (for example, nightmares, daydreams about the lost loved one, memories being triggered by such ordinary experiences as seeing someone who looks like one's deceased mother, smelling one's late wife's perfume) may signal that the loss has been integrated, the reality is that one can never be sure if one has fully integrated it. While working on an early project on long-term effects of traumatic stress, I was told by a therapist about a client of his who, upon suffering a serious heart attack, began to have recurrent nightmares about the death of a close friend and fellow serviceman during World War II, over 40 years before. In between his return from war and his heart attack, he had no recollection of thinking about his friend. At the time he was being treated by my colleague, he was dreaming nightly about his wartime loss.

ing the loss, losses that are interminable, grief that is disenfranchised, the stigmatized nature of grief, and gender differences in grieving. In considering the extent of impact of a loss and the character of grief, these and other factors must be considered.

As an alternative to the notion of grief as a passive, linear process, grief can be viewed as active coping with a loss. To gain understanding of the loss and meaning in life as well as a sense of order and predictability in life, the bereaved person must consider and attribute meaning to the loss by creating a healing theory about it. At the same time, this process is painful and, as a result, may be avoided, thus resulting in cycles of grief. Rather than thinking of normal grief as a move from one point to another, we can see it as a long-term process of reconsideration and organization of perceptual inputs with the ultimate goal of integration in the assumptive world of grievers.

Grief as a Family Process

Most often, grief is conceptualized as an individual response to loss with little attention paid to family processes (Gelcer, 1986; Raphael, 1983; Walsh & McGoldrick, 1991a). Walsh and McGoldrick (1991b) reviewed clinical and research literature on loss and were amazed at the lack of family-focused bereavement scholarship. But loss and grief are not simply intrapsychic in nature. They are embedded in a social and relational context (Fowlkes, 1991), and the course of grief is affected by the context in which it takes place. Indeed, the sense of loss felt by individuals following a death is partly the result of aspects of the family that have been lost and must be grieved over (Walsh & McGoldrick, 1991b). At the same time, a supportive family environment is critical to resolving grief, as it may be the most important social context for doing so (Figley, 1985, 1989).

The Effects of Loss on the Family System

When a family member dies, the family system must be adapted to the loss. Family structure changes as a result of the loss, and the system must be reorganized (Detmer & Lamberti, 1991; Walsh & McGoldrick, 1991b). If the deceased has played a central role in the functioning of the family and the family is relatively rigid in identifying that specific individual in that role, adaptation to the loss will be made more difficult. The family may be resistant to change and may either abandon the activities related to that particular role or may attempt to require that the person who takes over that role carry it out in exactly the same way (Rosenblatt, 1983).

The impact may not be restricted to the generations that directly experience the loss. "Legacies of loss find expression in continuing patterns of interaction and mutual influence among survivors and across the generations" (Walsh & McGoldrick, 1991b, p. 3). Grief has an effect across multiple generations and within the extended family culture (Detmer & Lamberti, 1991). Although these familial effects are often thought of as negative, they need not be. A previous successful experience with a loss can provide families with shared coping resources as well as perceptions of family efficacy (Walsh & McGoldrick, 1991b).

Family Tasks of Grief

In order to successfully adapt to a loss, the family must achieve three tasks: recognize the loss, reorganize the family system, and move ahead.

Recognizing the loss as real.   In order to begin the process of grieving, the family must acknowledge the loss as real, and each family member must share the experience of grief (Jordan, 1990). The ability to communicate openly is essential to this process. Emotions and thoughts of family members are shared; at the same time, flexibility and tolerance for differences in response to the loss facilitate a sense of acceptance among members (Walsh & McGoldrick, 1991b).

Unfortunately, at the time when family members need one another to be communicative and supportive, they are least capable of doing so. Each family member has strong needs and limited resources (reduced flexibility, patience, energy, and ability to concentrate) at this time (Rosenblatt et al., 1991). Differing grief styles accompanied by each member's heightened emotional state can make this flexibility and tolerance extremely difficult to achieve (Jordan, 1990). Their views of the deceased will differ, they may have different belief systems (as with a newly married couple), and they may not be grieving the same relationship with the deceased (Rosenblatt, 1988). Funeral rituals serve an important purpose as an initial step toward the recognition of loss (Bowen, 1991; Imber-Black, 1991). Ultimately, the family members must recognize that their lives are changed forever by the loss and that they will never be the same (Jordan, 1990).

Reorganizing the family system.   The loss of a family member disrupts and destabilizes the family system. This necessitates that members reconstruct what the family means to them (family identity, membership, boundaries, and roles). Behaviors carried out by the deceased must be reassigned or abandoned (Jordan, 1990). Family life may seem chaotic, and family members may feel a strong need to regain order and control (Walsh & McGoldrick, 1991b).

Since they have each experienced a somewhat different loss, family members may feel "out of synch" with each other. In order to feel in synch, families need to work to reframe their differences as strengths rather than weaknesses (for example, seeing differences in coping approaches as skills to be learned.) They must also reorganize the way in which those aspects of family affected by the loss are carried out. Again, ritual serves a useful purpose in this reorganization, with roles ritually "passed down," or distributed, among other family members (Imber-Black, 1991). For example, responsibility for the traditional family dinners, previously organized by the deceased mother, may be passed to the eldest daughter or rotated through the homes of various family members. This allows the family to maintain a sense of connection and continuity.

Reinvesting the family.   The final task of the family is to reinvest itself in movement along its developmental path, while appropriately memorializing the deceased member (Jordan, 1990). The idea of reinvesting the family in relationships and becoming reintegrated in the social world is often thought to mean that the deceased must be left behind. The reality is that the family is forever changed by the loss and that attempting to abandon that family member's memory may contribute to restricted communication and increased secrecy in the family (Walsh & McGoldrick, 1991b). The

healthier approach is not to abandon the memory of the deceased but to find new ways to hold on to the memory until the letting go feels voluntary (Jordan, 1990).

The Importance of the Family Belief System for Grief Resolution

As discussed previously in this chapter, individuals who experience a loss feel a sense of uncertainty and ambiguity about what has happened, is happening, and will happen. Their loss may result in their questioning much about their life as they attempt to develop a healing theory. This theory will serve as a bridge between their previous assumptive world to their reconstructed one, incorporating information about the loss.

Ideally, family members interact to confirm the reality of the loss, legitimate one another's reactions, and initiate the healing process (Fowlkes, 1991). They also facilitate one another's construction of personal healing theories and, as a result, mutually generate an overlapping family healing theory. At the same time, they facilitate the return of a sense of order and help with basic tasks while providing goods and services (Cobb, 1982).

Although the family often serves as the primary source of support during times of great stress (Caplan, 1976), the reality is that providing such support is difficult, at best. More often than not, the ideal picture of the family is tempered by pressures on it and its members. Support frequently does not come easily, it may be positive or negative in its impact, and it may not come at all. Here, we first look at the interactive development of a healing theory and how the family acts as a resource in its genesis. Next, we explore how this interactive healing theory becomes a family healing theory that fits into the family's belief system. Finally, family-based meanings may be difficult to achieve, and possible explanations for this problem are given.

Reconstruction of meaning in a family context. The family's involvement in constructing reality is continuous. In their daily interactions, family members can consider and validate one another's view of what has happened, is happening, and will happen (Reiss, 1981). As they encounter new information in their environment, they compare and attempt to confirm beliefs, opinions, hunches, and theories.

Reiss and Oliveri (1980) have referred to the set of beliefs, assumptions, and orientations shared by family members as a *family paradigm*. It is within the context of the family paradigm that members recognize the loss as a group and reorganize the way in which the family functions and reinvests toward the future. The family paradigm is far more complex than the individual's assumptive world, encompassing each individual member's perceptions as well as their expectations and perceptions of one another. Thus, the family paradigm is not seen as a unitary view of the situation.

The family paradigm is continually being modified and built upon as the family experiences different events and integrates them into its shared view of the world. The emphasis is on the closeness of the family members' views of the situation and their ability to work as a problem-solving group (Reiss & Oliveri, 1980).

If family members confirm their subjective views of one another and the situation, these views are given objective reality; that is, what they perceive comes to be seen as reality because significant others also see it that way (Berger & Luckman, 1966; Fowlkes, 1991; Patterson & Gawick, 1992); if not, they question their own or the others' perceptions, and formation of an objective reality is made more difficult. Families at an early stage in their evolution may experience problems related to not having had an opportunity to develop a shared paradigm that would incorporate an appropriate family response to such an event.

In the case of loss, the family's shared view serves the purpose of reducing ambiguity and uncertainty about what has been lost, how the members are to cope with that loss, and how they are to go on with their lives. In this way, the meaning of a particular death and the individual responses to it are shaped by the family belief system. In addition, mutually validated definitions (shared meaning) facilitate communication, provide structure and meaning to interactions, and serve as the basis for familial coping behavior (McCubbin & Patterson, 1983; Patterson & Gawick, 1992; Reiss, 1981; Reiss & Oliveri, 1980).

Family healing theory. Just as it has been suggested that individuals form a theory to explain the loss, Figley (1989) has proposed that the family forms a healing theory after a catastrophic event. In this proc-

ess, family members exchange information about their personal theories. These personal theories eventually coalesce into a single, unifying family healing theory that explains the event and the behavior of members in relation to it. As the personal healing theory of each family member fits into the modified assumptive world of the individual, the family healing theory fits into the modified family paradigm.[5]

Differential grief—why it is difficult to grieve together. In discussing family response to loss, Bowlby (1980) has suggested that successful completion of the grief process among family members requires above all else that marital partners grieve in tandem. That is, the partners must grieve together and provide support and comfort to each other. The logical extension of this view is that all family members should grieve together and provide mutual support and comfort. Yet the reality of grief is often in conflict with this desired picture. Dissimilar, or incongruent, grief appears to be the norm (Peppers & Knapp, 1980). Rosenblatt et al. (1991) indicate that two people who experience a mutual loss are the least likely to be able to help each other. Rather than helping them grieve together, the "baggage" of their relationship with each other and with the deceased impedes mutual grief resolution. At the same time, various family members may *not* expect mutual grief but may expect that their grief should take precedence and that others should be supportive of them. Ultimately, it appears that conflict over expectations of appropriate behavior surrounds grief within the family system.

Thus, within the family the form of grief taken by each member will have its own unique character. The definition of the severity of the loss may vary. Some individuals in the family may define the loss as disappointing, while others may define it as devastating; family members may change their definition of severity and importance over time. The end result is that a great

---

[5]The family healing theory was originally developed by Figley for use in therapy to help families who had members at extremely different points in their resolution of a trauma. As with the family paradigm, it is intended to be very broad and is not expected to be as detailed as an individual healing theory. In addition, family members may also find that they are unable to agree totally on the family healing theory and may only "buy into"certain aspects while indicating that they agree to disagree on the rest.

deal is occurring simultaneously, as each family member attempts to come to grips with his or her loss. Intense emotions may be experienced as the reality of a future without this lost person is faced, accepted, and integrated into the assumptive world. The symbolic significance of the loss is different for each individual (Arnold & Gemma, 1983; Rando, 1984). Emotional reactions to the loss vary. The interaction of these differences and related conflicts may place tremendous strain on the family (Miles, 1984). Given that family members have only one another's behavior and imperfectly communicated information on which to base their interpretation of their grief states, it is not surprising that such conflicts occur.

These ineffective efforts are often interpreted as negative or absent social support (Gilbert & Smart, 1992). They can act as a "second wound" (Symonds, 1980), adding to the pain of the loss. Being told: "Stop dwelling on it" or "You used to be so much fun. Now you're a real downer" within weeks or months of the death of a beloved family member may be seen as helpful by the person offering the comment. Such statements are not helpful.

Studies on loss in the family indicate that several factors contribute to such negative social support. For example, the quality of the relationships among supporter, bereaved, and deceased that preceded the death may contribute to the situation. If the loss is a mutual one, as when parents lose a child or siblings lose a parent, each of them is directly affected by the loss and may be unable to provide much support to the other (Bugan, 1983; Rosenblatt et al., 1991).

Nervousness or discomfort, rather than ignorance, may be to blame for hurtful remarks made to the bereaved (Lehman, Ellard, & Wortman, 1986). Such comments are widely cited in the literature (Borg & Lasker, 1988; Gilbert & Smart, 1992; Klass, 1988; Peppers & Knapp, 1980). Uncertainty about the effect of one's comments may contribute to unfortunate and inappropriate remarks (Lehman et al., 1986).

Another possible reason for hurtful comments is that the deceased may be seen as responsible for his or her death (Janoff-Bulman, 1985, 1992). As noted earlier in this chapter, people need to feel that life is orderly and just and that bad things are unlikely to happen to them. Therefore, if something bad happens to someone,

it becomes logical to assume that that person somehow brought it on. If potential supporters hold to this belief, the death may serve as a reminder that they are not invulnerable. Should this be too frightening to consider, they may avoid the bereaved or may attempt to differentiate themselves by hurtful comments.

Family members may avoid sharing feelings because of role expectations about appropriate behavior (Cook, 1988; Gilbert & Smart, 1992) or as an effort to protect one another (Lopata, 1979). They may also avoid one another or use hurtful comments to create distance, because they feel overwhelmed by their own grief and unable to provide support (Schiff, 1977) or because the grief of others triggers their own (Cornwell, Nurcombe, & Stevens, 1977). This is especially true when their own movement through grief is at a different point and they either do not want to be "pulled back" into grief or resent others' "abandonment" of grief (Gilbert & Smart, 1992). Finally, seeing the loss as stigmatized or ambiguous may prohibit the family members from reaching out to one another. Their inability to talk about the loss would inhibit reconstruction.

Section Summary

In order to recover from a loss as a group, a family must recognize the loss, reorganize the family, and reinvest the family in the future. Underlying all of these essential tasks is the idea of a common meaning for the loss. Yet given that loss and grief can take many forms and result in a complex set of possible results, it should not be surprising that attributing a common, consistent meaning to the loss in the family is an arduous task and can affect the family in many ways. Defining the loss as devastating can overwhelm the family system, but it may also inspire the members to support one another. Defining the loss differentially within the family (incongruent perceptions) may lead to conflicts and interfere with the ability to support. For example, it may result in problems if the more intense grief of one person is seen as pathology while less intense grief is seen as a lack of caring. If the loss, the resulting grief, or both are seen as stigmatized, family members may feel uncomfortable about reaching out to one another. Their inability to talk about loss and discuss their developing healing theory will inhibit reconstruction. Finally, differential grief may lead to complications as family members experience and reexperience episodes of grief.

Conclusions and Implications for Family-Science Students

In order to help families as they cope with loss, the student of family science needs to understand how the family responds as an interactive, living system to a loss, with conflicting pressures on members to support and be supported. Concepts developed by family-stress scholars aid in understanding the process of grieving and grief resolution in a family context.

Any investigation or intervention in families in which a loss has occurred must not only focus on the individual but also take into account the family. This information has implications for those interested in family intervention in many areas. Students planning to become teachers of family science, family therapists, family counselors, medical personnel, funeral-home directors, support-group moderators, and those who will serve as informal supporters to family and friends will benefit from this knowledge.

Clearly, the family's experience following loss is far more complex than one might think at first, with each member attempting to come to terms with the loss and its resulting effects on the family as a whole. At the same time, they may be attempting to act as supporters to other family members as they grieve over the loss. To simply view one person as the aggrieved party and others in the family as potential supporters is not enough.

In addition, awareness of the intensity of grief and the importance of meaning will reduce the extent to which the griever feels disenfranchised or stigmatized. As Symonds (1980) suggests, this will reduce the "second wound" of the loss.

A loss can serve to shape family meanings and family interactions in ways that extend beyond the loss itself. Thus, such a loss must be taken in account in any intervention with families. Losses do not go away. Rather, they are embedded in the assumptive worlds of individuals and in the family paradigm.

Chapter Summary

The following are several important principles from the chapter:

1. Loss and the resultant grief are normative elements of family life.
2. Grief is a response to loss and involves the reconstruction of meaning. Some theorists hold that individuals progress through "stages" of grief as they reconstruct a sense of what is meaningful in life. This simplistic stage approach is probably not accurate and may, in fact, hinder the grief resolution of individuals. Seen as a process, grief involves the reconstruction of the "assumptive world," a set of beliefs about the way the world should behave.
3. The way in which people grieve is influenced by a number of factors. The centrality of the relationship of each family member with the lost individual will affect his or her response as well as the ability to understand the grief of others. The view of the loss is important. The degree of anticipation and the extent to which the loss is seen as traumatic influence grief. Ambiguous losses, particularly those that are interminable losses, result in grief that cannot easily be foreclosed. An inability to grieve publicly, as when grief is stigmatized, can impede grief resolution. Finally, gender, cultural, and age differences can add to grief if family members are not prepared for these differences.
4. Grief as a family process incorporates recognition of the loss as real, reorganization of the family system to adapt to changed membership in the family, and reinvestment of the family in movement along its developmental path.
5. Grief also involves reconstruction of meaning in the family system. An important influence in how well the family survives the loss is how each member influences the others in their efforts to redefine the situation. As the assumptive world is reconstructed, other family members serve as a source of validation of the revised world view of the bereaved. Grief work also involves the reconstruction of that part of the family paradigm affected by the loss. The family healing theory

serves the purpose of bridging between old and new family paradigms.

6. The response of family members varies greatly and affects their ability to confirm one another's view of the loss. Differential movement toward resolution may also complicate the ability of family members to work together to resolve their grief. The family's response to the recurrent grief of individual members may also add to the pain of loss.

Discussion Questions

1. Grief has often been depicted as occurring in a series of stages. What is the value of using the stage model to understand the grief process? What are the drawbacks of this approach?

2. The process of grief is extremely complex and individual. What factors discussed in the chapter contribute to this complexity? In what ways do they do this? How might they interact in the family to increase this complexity?

3. Grief is an active process of reestablishing a revised sense of normalcy. Describe the process of developing a healing theory to reclaim the normalcy of family functioning.

4. What tasks are necessary for the family to reestablish order and to maintain itself as a functional unit? How do these tasks relate to the formation of a family healing theory?

5. What is differential grief? How does it affect the grief process of individual family members? How does it affect the family's ability to carry out grief tasks?

Additional Resources

Bouvard, M. (1988). *The path through grief: A practical guide.* Portland, OR: Breitenbush Books.

Deits, B. (1992). *Life after loss: A personal guide dealing with death, divorce, job change and relocation.* Tucson, AZ: Fisher Books.

James, J. W., & Cherry, F. (1988). *The grief recovery handbook: A step-by-step program for moving beyond loss.* New York: Harper & Row.

Viorst, J. (1986). *Unnecessary losses: The loves, illusions, dependencies and impossible expectations that all of us have to give up in order to grow.* New York: Fawcett Gold Medal.

References

Arnold, J. H., & Gemma, P. G. (1983). *A child dies: A portrait of family grief.* Rockville, MD: Aspen.

Attig, T. (1991). The importance of conceiving of grief as an active process. *Death Studies, 15,* 385–393.

Benefield, D. G., Lieb, S. A., & Vollman, J. H. (1978). Grief response of parents to neonatal death and parent participation in deciding care. *Pediatrics, 62*(2), 171–177.

Berger, P., & Luckman, T. (1966). *The social construction of reality.* New York: Doubleday.

Borg, S., & Lasker, J. (1988). *When pregnancy fails: Families coping with miscarriage, stillbirth and infant death* (2nd ed.). New York: Bantam Books.

Boss, P. (1991). Ambiguous loss. In F. Walsh & M. McGoldrick (Eds.), *Living beyond loss: Death in the family* (pp. 164–175). New York: Norton.

Bouvard, M. (1988). *The path through grief: A practical guide.* Portland, OR: Breitenbush Books.

Bowen, M. (1991). Family reactions to death. In F. Walsh & M. McGoldrick (Eds.), *Living beyond loss: Death in the family* (pp. 79–92). New York: Norton.

Bowlby, J. (1961). Process of mourning. *International Journal of Psycho-Analysis, 42,* 317–340.

Bowlby, J. (1980). *Attachment and loss, Vol. 3.* New York: Basic Books.

Bugan, L. A. (1983). Childhood bereavement: Preventability and the coping process. In J. E. Schowalter, P. R. Patterson, M. Tallmer, A. H. Kutscher, S. V. Gallo, & D. Peretz (Eds.), *The child and death* (pp. 357–366). New York: Columbia University Press.

Caplan, G. (1976). The family as a support system. In G. Caplan & M. Killilea (Eds.), *Support systems and mutual help: Multidisciplinary explorations.* New York: Grune & Stratton.

Cobb, S. (1982). Social support and health through the life course. In H. I. McCubbin, A. E. Cauble, & J. M. Patterson (Eds.), *Family stress, coping, and social support* (pp. 189–199). Springfield IL: Charles C Thomas.

Colburn, K., & Malena, D. (1989). Bereavement issues for survivors of persons with AIDS: Coping with society's pressures. *Advances in Thanatology, 1,* 126–131.

Cook, J. A. (1988). Dads' double binds: Rethinking fathers' bereavement from a men's studies perspective. *Journal of Contemporary Ethnography, 17,* 285–308.

Cornwell, J., Nurcombe, B., & Stevens, L. (1977). Family response to the loss of a child by sudden infant death syndrome. *Medical Journal of Australia, 1,* 656–658.

Davidson, G. W. (1979). *Understanding the death of the wished-for child.* Springfield, IL: ORG Service Corp.

DeFrain, J. (1991). Learning about grief from normal families: SIDS, stillbirth, and miscarriage. *Journal of Marital and Family Therapy, 17,* 215–232.

Detmer, C. M., & Lamberti, J. W. (1991). Family grief. *Death Studies, 15,* 363–374.

Doka, K. (1989). *Disenfranchised grief: Recognizing hidden sorrow.* Lexington, MA: Lexington Books.

Edelstein, L. (1984). *Maternal bereavement: Coping with the unexpected death of a child.* New York: Praeger.

Figley, C. R. (1983). Catastrophes: An overview of family reactions. In C. R. Figley & H. I. McCubbin (Eds.), *Stress and the family: Volume 2. Coping with catastrophe* (pp. 3 20). New York: Brunner/Mazel.

Figley, C. R. (1985). From victim to survivor: Social responsibility in the wake of a catastrophe. In C. R. Figley (Ed.), *Trauma and its wake: The study and treatment of post-traumatic stress disorder* (pp. 398–417). New York: Brunner/Mazel.

Figley, C. R. (1989). Post-traumatic family therapy. In F. Ochberg (Ed.), *Post-traumatic therapy* (pp. 83–109). New York: Brunner/Mazel.

Figley, C. R. (in press-a). Death-related traumatic stress. In C. R. Figley (Ed.), *Death and trauma.* New York: Brunner/Mazel.

Figley, C. R. (Ed.) (in press-b). *Compassion fatigue: Secondary traumatic stress disorder for helping the traumatized.* New York: Brunner/Mazel.

Fowlkes, M. R. (1991). The morality of loss: The social construction of mourning and melancholia. *Contemporary Psychoanalysis, 27,* 529–551.

Frantz, T. T. (1984). Helping parents whose child has died. In T. T. Frantz (Ed.), *Death and grief in the family* (pp. 11–26). Rockville, MD: Aspen.

Gelcer, E. (1986). Dealing with loss in the family context. *Journal of Family Issues, 7,* 315–335.

Getzel, G. S., & Masters, R. (1984). Serving families who survive homicide victims. *Journal of Contemporary Social Work, 65*(3), 138–144.

Gilbert, K. R. (in press-a). Loss of a child—couple coping. In C. R. Figley (Ed.), *Death and trauma.* New York: Brunner/Mazel.

Gilbert, K. R. (in press-b). Spouses. In C. R. Figley (Ed.), *Compassion fatigue: Secondary traumatic stress disorder for helping the traumatized.* New York: Brunner/Mazel.

Gilbert, K., & Smart, L. (1992). *Coping with infant or fetal loss: The couple's healing process.* New York: Brunner/Mazel.

Haig, R. A. (1990). *The anatomy of grief: Biopsychosocial and therapeutic perspectives.* Springfield, IL: Charles C Thomas.

Helmrath, T. A., & Steinitz, E. M. (1978). Death of an infant: Parental grieving and the failure of social support. *Journal of Family Practice, 6,* 785–790.

Hoagland, A. C. (1984). Bereavement and personal constructs: Old theories and new concepts. In F. R. Epting & R. A. Neimeyer (Eds.), *Personal meanings of death: Application of personal construct theory to clinical practice* (pp. 89–109). Washington, DC: Hemisphere Pub. Co.

Holloway, H. C., & Ursano, R. J. (1984). The Vietnam veteran: Memory, social context and metaphor. *Psychiatry, 47,* 103–108.

Horowitz, M. (1979). Psychosocial response to serious life events. In V. Hamilton & D. M. Warburton (Eds.), *Human stress and cognition* (pp. 237–264). New York: Wiley.

Horowitz, M. (1982). Stress response syndromes and their treatment. In L. Goldberger & S. Breznitz (Eds.), *Handbook of stress: Theoretical and clinical aspects* (pp. 711–732). New York: Free Press.

Horowitz, M. (1986). *Stress response syndrome* (2nd ed.). New York: Aronson.

Imber-Black, E. (1991). Rituals and the healing process. In F. Walsh & M. McGoldrick (Eds.), *Living beyond loss: Death in the family* (pp. 207–223). New York: Norton.

Janoff-Bulman, R. (1985). The aftermath of victimization: Rebuilding shattered assumptions. In C. R. Figley (Ed.), *Trauma and its wake* (pp. 15–35). New York: Brunner-Mazel.

Janoff-Bulman, R. (1992). *Shattered assumptions: Towards a new psychology of trauma.* New York: Free Press.

Jordan, J. (1990, August). *Loss and family development: Clinical implications.* Paper presented at the 98th annual convention of the American Psychological Association, Boston.

Klass, D. (1988). *Parental grief: Solace and resolution.* New York: Springer.

Koocher, G. P. (1985). Talking with children about death. In S. G. Wilcox & M. Sutton (Eds.), *Understanding death and dying: An interdisciplinary approach* (3rd ed.) (pp. 259–268). Palo Alto, CA: Mayfield.

Kübler-Ross, E. (1969). *On death and dying.* New York: Macmillan.

Lehman, R. L., Ellard, J. H., & Wortman, B. W. (1986). Social support for the bereaved: Recipients' and providers' perspectives on what is helpful. *Journal of Consulting and Clinical Psychology, 54*(4), 438–446.

Lindemann, E. (1944). Symptomatology and management of acute grief. *American Journal of Psychiatry, 101,* 141–148.

Loftus, E. F. (1979). The malleability of human memory. *American Scientist, 67,* 312–320.

Lopata, H. Z. (1979). *Women as widows: Support systems.* New York: Elsevier.

Marris, P. (1982). Attachment and society. In C. M. Parkes & J. Stevenson-Hinde (Eds.), *The place of attachment in human behavior* (pp. 185–204). New York: Basic Books.

McCubbin, H. I., & Patterson, J. M. (1983). The family stress process: The Double ABCX model of adjustment and adaptation. *Marriage and Family Review, 6*(1/2), 2–38.

McGoldrick, M., Almeida, R., Hines, P. M., Rosen, E., Garcia-Preto, N., & Lee, E. (1991). Mourning in different cultures. In F. Walsh & M. McGoldrick (Eds.), *Living beyond loss: Death in the family* (pp. 176–205). New York: Norton.

Miles, M. S. (1984). Helping adults mourn the death of a child. In H. Wass & C. A. Corr (Eds.), *Childhood and death* (pp. 219–239). Washington, DC: Hemisphere.

Osterweis, M., Solomon, F., & Green, M. (1984). *Bereavement: Reactions, consequences and care.* Washington, DC: National Academy Press.

Parkes, C. M. (1972). *Bereavement: Studies of grief in adult life.* New York: International Universities Press.

Patterson, J. M., & Gawick, A. W. (1992, November). *Family meanings in family stress theory: The "C" factor.* Paper presented at the annual meeting of the National Council on Family Relations, Orlando, FL.

Peppers, L. G., & Knapp, R. J. (1980). *Motherhood and mourning: Perinatal death.* New York: Praeger.

Rando, T. A. (1983). An investigation of grief and adaptation in parents whose children have died from cancer. *Journal of Pediatric Psychology, 8*(1), 3–20.

Rando, T. A. (1984). *Grief, dying, and death: Clinical interventions for caregivers.* Champaign, IL: Research Press.

Rando, T. A. (1986). A comprehensive analysis of anticipatory grief: Perspectives, processes, promises, and problems. In T. A. Rando (Ed.), *Loss and anticipatory grief* (pp. 3–38). Lexington, MA: Lexington Books.

Rando, T. A. (1989, April 20). *Anniversary issues and reactions to the death of a child.* The eighth annual Kristen Hovda Lecture, Evanston Hospital, Evanston, IL.

Raphael, B. (1983). *The anatomy of bereavement.* New York: Basic Books.

Raphael, B. (1992, April). *Counseling after a catastrophic loss.* Keynote address given at the annual meeting of the Association for Death Educators and Counselors, Boston.

Reiss, D. (1981). *The family's construction of reality.* Cambridge, MA: Harvard University Press.

Reiss, D., & Oliveri, M. E. (1980). Family's intrinsic adaptive capacities to its responses to stress. *Family Relations, 29,* 431–444.

Rinear, E. (1985). *Signs and symptoms of post-traumatic stress disorder among surviving parents of child homicide victims.* Paper presented at the 62nd annual meeting of the American Orthopsychiatric Association, New York.

Roland, J. S. (1991). Helping families with anticipatory loss. In F. Walsh & M. McGoldrick (Eds.), *Living beyond loss: Death in the family* (pp. 145–163). New York: Norton.

Rosenblatt, P. C. (1983). *Nineteenth-century diarists and twentieth-century grief theories.* Minneapolis: University of Minnesota Press.

Rosenblatt, P. C. (1988). Grief: The social context of private feelings. *Journal of Social Issues, 44,* 67–78.

Rosenblatt, P. C., & Burns, L. H. (1986). Long-term effects of perinatal loss. *Journal of Family Issues, 7,* 237–253.

Rosenblatt, P. C., Spoentgen, P., Karis, T. A., Dahl, C., Kaiser, T., & Elde, C. (1991). Difficulties in supporting the bereaved. *Omega, 23,* 119–128.

Schiff, H. S. (1977). *The bereaved parent.* New York: Crown.

Silver, R. L., & Wortman, C. B. (1980). Coping with undesirable life events. In J. Garber & M. E. P. Seligman (Eds.), *Human helplessness: Theory and applications* (pp. 279–340). New York: Academic Press.

Stephenson, J. S. (1985). *Death, grief and mourning: Individual and social realities.* New York: Free Press.

Symonds, M. (1980). The "second injury" to victims. *Evaluation and Change,* special issue, 36–38.

Taylor, S. E. (1983). Adjustment to threatening events: A theory of cognitive adaptation. *American Psychologist, 38,* 1161–1173.

Taylor, S. E., Lichtman, R. R., & Wood, J. V. (1984). Attribution, beliefs about control and adjustment to breast cancer. *Journal of Personality and Social Psychology, 46,* 489–502.

Walsh, F., & McGoldrick, M. (1991a). Introduction. In F. Walsh & M. McGoldrick (Eds.), *Living beyond loss: Death in the family* (pp. xv–xix). New York: Norton.

Walsh, F., & McGoldrick, M. (1991b). Loss and the family: A systemic perspective. In F. Walsh & M. McGoldrick (Eds.), *Living beyond loss: Death in the family* (pp. 1–29). New York: Norton.

Wortman, C. B., & Silver, R. C. (1989). The myths of coping with loss. *Journal of Consulting and Clinical Psychology, 57,* 349–357.

PART V

Family Science at Work

This is a short but important part of this book. As the field of family science continues to grow and mature, a key element to its survival will be where family-science students find employment. Many would agree that in our complex and difficult world, it is no longer sufficient to *study* the family as one would an ancient archaeological find. Instead, we must learn how to help families meet their goals and survive the pressures and strains that confront them.

In Chapter 20, Philip Osborne presents an overview of information currently being promoted by parenting experts. As students of family science move out into the job market, it is critical that they understand the types of programs being presented in the communities in which they will work. Most communities have professionals and paraprofessionals who design and implement intervention strategies for families. Sometimes these programs are part of court services, and parents in trouble may be assigned to a parenting class or support group. In other cases, parents seek out these types of groups and classes on their own for self-improvement. Most of these programs are based on an educational model. That is, we believe that parents can improve the ways they interact with their children. Courts hope that these programs will provide an intermediate step when abuse or neglect occurs, something to try before a child is taken out of the home. In any case, most who work in family science will encounter a variety of these community-based programs.

In this book's final chapter, Robert Keim presents an overview of where family-science students find a place to intervene. Keim has directed the internship program at Northern Illinois University for many years. During this time he has collected and catalogued the places where his students have done internships and where they have found employment. As in most of the social sciences, employers do not usually come to university campuses and compete for family-science students as they do in other fields. Most students find employment as they perform internships and become connected in the network of professionals within a given state or region. Keim's chapter is an excellent starting place for such searches.

CHAPTER 20

The Parenting Experts

Philip Osborne
Hesston College

In this chapter, we will examine the models for parent education. The chapter is not a summary of the advice that is given but a kind of parent educator's guide to this advice, offering theoretical perspectives and a way of analyzing the strengths and weaknesses of various parent-education programs.

Five theoretical schools of thought will be examined, each of which has had a major impact on parenting advice. The five perspectives are traditional authoritarianism, humanistic psychology, behavioral psychology, developmental psychology, and family-systems theory. In each case I will discuss the most popular parenting experts and parent-education programs. For each model of thought, the historical development, assumptions, and impact on parent education will be summarized. In addition, the strengths and weaknesses of each approach will be assessed.

We will look first at the traditional, authoritarian model of parenting. This is the pattern on which less-educated parents have relied through the years. It has been a constant counterpoint to the changing theories of parenting experts who follow the trends in psychological thought.

Traditional Authoritarianism: Childhood as Evil and Parent as Disciplinarian

Parenting Expert A returned from a trip to find that the family's dachshund, named Sigmund Freud (Siggy), had become boss of the house in his absence. That evening when A told Siggy to go to his usual spot for the night, the dog flattened his ears and growled, refusing to budge. A got a small belt to help him "reason" with Siggy. When the dog still would not obey the command a fight between man and beast took place, with the man swinging the belt and the beast trying to bite the belt and the man. The struggle moved through the house, with Siggy growling but retreating until finally he was in the intended spot.

The following night Siggy complied immediately with the command and has not taken such a defiant stand since. "Just as surely as a dog will occasionally challenge the authority of his leaders," A concluded, "a little child is inclined to do the same thing, only more so."[1]

Background

The first philosophy of parenting, represented by Dobson, has roots that go back through the conservative Christians of this century to the Puritans, who emigrated to the New England colonies in the 17th century. They brought with them an austere moral code to combat the depraved human condition and a stiff determination to carry it out. Children were expected to stand when adults entered the room and to remain silent until given permission to speak. They were to obey commands promptly and without protest, especially those of the father, the primary authority.

[1]This story is told by James Dobson in one of his films about parenting and also at the beginning of his book *The Strong-Willed Child* (1978, pp. 1–14).

When they made mistakes or showed lack of deference, children were beaten on the hands, back, buttocks, or head. Beatings took place at home, in the school, or at work and were often severe.

The punitive treatment of children in former years, harsh by today's standards, was not due solely to the parenting philosophy summarized here. Child abuse and neglect also occurred because of ignorance and poverty. Life itself was harsh.

Nevertheless, this first parenting philosophy is still an important force in parenting advice today. The abusive techniques have been lessened, for the most part, but the assumptions about human nature that compel parents to correct their children remain.

Assumptions about Human Nature

More than the other theoretical perspectives summarized in this chapter, this position has a theological rationale, resting heavily on the doctrine of original sin formulated in the third century by Augustine. The doctrine is derived from Paul in the New Testament, who wrote that everyone shares with Adam and Eve the fall from perfection.

John Wesley (1703–1791), the English preacher who founded Methodism, held this view of the nature of children. In a "Sermon on the Education of Children" (about 1783), he exhorted parents to:

> teach your children, as soon as possibly you can, that they are fallen spirits; that they are fallen short of that glorious image of God, wherein they were first created. . . . Shew them that, in pride, passion, and revenge, they are now like the devil. (1783/ 1973, pp. 61–62)

Dobson's parenting philosophy begins with the belief that children are evil by nature. In *Dr. Dobson Answers Your Questions* (1982), he responds to the question "Many people believe that children are basically 'good.' . . . Do you agree?":

> If they mean that all children are worthy and deserving of our love and respect, I certainly do agree. But if they believe that children are by nature unselfish, giving, and sinless before God, I must disagree. I wish that assessment of human nature were accurate, but it contradicts scriptural understandings. Jeremiah wrote: "The heart is deceitful above all things, and desperately wicked: who can know it?" (Jer. 17:9) [p. 44].

Assumptions about the Causes of Problems in the Home

From this point of view, the misbehavior of children is caused by their sinful nature. They naturally want to go their own way. Willful disobedience is evidence of this, so the child's will is a focus of attention.

Goals of Parent Education

Since willfulness is the problem, the goal of parenting is to overcome defiance and gain submissiveness and trust. Wesley's (1783/1973) sermon illustrates this:

> A wise parent . . . should begin to break their will, the first moment it appears. In the whole art of Christian education there is nothing more important than this. The will of a parent is to a little child in the place of the will of God. Therefore, studiously teach them to submit to this while they are children, that they may be ready to submit to his will, when they are men. (pp. 59–60)

Dobson speaks of shaping the will, rather than breaking the will, but otherwise his message is similar to Wesley's: "I am recommending a simple principle: when you are defiantly challenged, win decisively. When the child asks, 'Who's in charge?' tell him" (1970, p. 50) Dobson's tough stance on this issue is revealed in the titles of some of his books: *Dare to Discipline* (1970), *The Strong-Willed Child* (1978), and *Parenting Isn't for Cowards* (1987).

According to Dobson's view, the reason it is so important to win in the contest of wills is that the parent/child relationship is based on the respect that winning engenders. "Nothing brings a parent and child closer together than for the mother or father to win decisively after being defiantly challenged" (Dobson, 1970, p. 35).

View of Punishment

In the struggle to subdue the child's will, physical punishment is sometimes levied. Scriptures about the use of the "rod" are used to justify the punishment of those who fail to meet parental demands.

Dobson does not recommend that parents use techniques that are harsh and oppressive in their resolve to correct their children. But he does recommend physical punishment:

> The parent should have some means of making the child want to cooperate, other than simply obeying because he was told to do so. For those who can think of no such device, I will suggest one: there is a muscle, lying snugly against the base of the neck. Anatomy books list it as the trapezius muscle, and when firmly squeezed, it sends little messengers to the brain saying, "This hurts; avoid recurrence at all costs." (1970, p. 38)

He recommends spanking under certain circumstances:

> In my opinion, spankings should be reserved for the moment a child (age ten or less) expresses a defiant "I will not!" or "You shut up!" When a youngster tries this kind of stiff-necked rebellion, you had better take it out of him, and pain is a marvelous purifier. (1970, p. 27)

Dobson (1982) suggests that parents use a switch or belt to end defiance, to preserve the hand as an "object of love" rather than using it as an "instrument of punishment" (p. 159).

Impact on Parent Education

For generations, the traditional authoritarian philosophy of parenting has been the basic blueprint for assembling parenting skills. Its most recent advocate, Dobson, has had enormous influence in recent years, especially with politically and religiously conservative families. His first book, *Dare to Discipline,* which appeared in 1970, has gone through several editions and over 40 printings, sold over 2.5 million copies, and been translated into more than a dozen other languages; a revision titled *The New Dare to Discipline* was recently released. Several other Dobson books were best-sellers, and his films, in which he lectures to live audiences, have been widely viewed.

Critique

The strengths of the traditional authoritarian philosophy represented by Dobson include his motivating talks, which prod parents to place parenting responsibilities high on their list of priorities, persuading them that there is no more important task than molding a child's identity and character.

Parents who are weak in the skills necessary to correct misbehavior need the courage and firmness that Dobson recommends. Some parents, for example, are so afraid of the children's displeasure that they are unable to take any kind of corrective action. They want so badly to make the children happy that the children are allowed to make everybody around them miserable.

But the emphasis that is Dobson's strength becomes its weakness when it is overemphasized. Shaping the will through demands for obedience and punishment for disobedience is but one small slice of the discipline pie. To make obedience such a major emphasis leads parents to power struggles that are not necessary; they become so focused on the child's willfulness that they are not able to perceive other means of gaining compliance. And too many parents cross the fine line from punishment to child abuse in responding to misbehavior, compelled by their belief that the evil nature of children requires that kind of response.

Humanistic Psychology: Childhood as Good and Parent as Communicator

On a rainy morning, Parenting Expert noticed that his daughter was leaving for school in the rain without her raincoat. He pointed this out to her, and she said she didn't need a raincoat. He explained that without a raincoat her clothes would get wet and she might catch cold, which concerned him. She insisted that she didn't want to wear her raincoat.

In the discussion that ensued, B found out that she didn't object to raincoats in general but that she didn't want to wear her raincoat because it was plaid; other kids were wearing plain-colored raincoats.

B still wasn't willing for her to be without a raincoat, so he asked her if she could think of a solution to the problem. The daughter suggested that she wear her mother's raincoat instead of her own. After gaining her mother's consent, she left for school that morning wearing a rain-

coat. The sleeves were rolled up because it was too large, but it was plain-colored.

The conflict with his daughter was resolved, B concluded, in a mutually satisfying manner, without using power and with both of them walking away from the incident feeling warm toward the other.[2]

Background

The second parenting philosophy is traced to Jean-Jacques Rousseau (1712–1778), whose 1762 book, *Emile*, emphasized the natural goodness of children. The premise of the book is that a young tutor takes a child, Emile, into the country to get him away from the corrupting influences of his family and society. There the child learns from nature, following his natural curiosity, and is protected from formal training for the first 12 years of life. "Train him gradually to prolonged attention to a given object; but this attention should never be the result of constraint, but of interest or desire" (Rousseau, 1762/1965, p. 90)

Emile outraged philosophers because it elevates feeling above reason, and it outraged the church because it barely recognizes religion. Nevertheless, its radical thesis was influential: children are different from adults, and they deserve to be valued and understood for what they *are* rather than what they will *become*.

A century later this point of view resulted in the child-study movement, in which children began to be studied with scientific methods. Its influence was felt also in the creation of programs to protect children: orphanages, shelters for street children, and various other asylums for children; laws that set the minimum age and maximum number of hours per day for child labor; and compulsory-education laws.

In the 20th century this philosophy found expression in the humanistic-psychology movement about 1950. One of the leaders of this movement, Carl Rogers (1951), developed the techniques of "client-centered therapy," which revolutionized individual counseling.

In the 1950s Thomas Gordon was working as a clinical psychologist, using the techniques of his colleague, Rogers. It occurred to him that the children he was seeing were not necessarily psychologically disturbed, nor were their parents. They were experiencing problems in their relationships because they were misinformed about what goes on in human relationships.

Gordon decided that parents could relate to their children in a healthier, more therapeutic manner if they were taught to use the communication skills employed in counseling. He began such a program, Parent Effectiveness Training (PET) (Gordon, 1980).

Assumptions about Human Nature

Rousseau (1762/1965) asserts that all of nature, including human nature, is good.

> God makes all things good; man meddles with them and they become evil. He forces one soil to yield the products of another, one tree to bear another's fruit. He confuses and confounds time, place, and natural condition. He mutilates his dog, his horse, and his slave. He destroys and defaces all things; he loves all that is deformed and monstrous; he will have nothing as nature made it, not even man himself, who must learn his paces like a saddlehorse, and be shaped to his master's taste like the trees in his garden. (p. 221)

Under Rogers (1980), this natural goodness came to mean a trust in self. One's feelings generated in the course of life are to be valued and not denied:

> I have moved a long way from some of the beliefs with which I started: that man was essentially evil . . . [and] that the expert could advise, manipulate, and mold the individual to produce the desired. . . . I have come to prize each emerging facet of my experience, of myself. . . . the feelings of anger and tenderness and shame and hurt and love and anxiety and giving and fear—all the positive and negative reactions that crop up. . . . I don't expect to act on all of them, but when I accept them all, I can be more real. (p. 43)

Obviously, Rogers believes that being "real" is a good thing to be. He trusts human nature to unfold in a positive way, if it is provided an accepting environment.

---

[2]This story is used by Thomas Gordon in Parent Effectivness Training classes and also in the book by the same title (Gordon, 1970, pp. 196–197).

Assumptions about the Causes of Problems in the Home

From this point of view, problems are caused by "nontherapeutic" messages in the home. These messages tend to "make people feel judged or guilty; they restrict expression of honest feelings, threaten the person, foster feelings of unworthiness or low self-esteem, [and] block growth and constructive change by making the person defend more strongly the way he is" (Gordon, 1970, p. 35). When children hear these messages, they become defensive and resistant to efforts to change them. Parents then become more coercive to bring about change, which creates resentment, and the problems worsen.

Goals of Parent Education

In programs based on this philosophy, parents are taught skills of communication: to listen accurately and empathically, to provide feedback in nonthreatening ways, and to resolve conflict to the point of mutual satisfaction. These skills enable parent and child "to relate to each other with mutual respect, love, and peace" (Gordon, 1970, p. 306).

View of Punishment

Gordon argues against the use of punishment for philosophical reasons. He rejects the notion that parents need to rely on their superior power to influence children:

> My own conclusion is that as more people begin to understand power and authority more completely and accept its use as unethical, more parents will apply those understandings to adult-child relationships . . . and then will be forced to search for creative new nonpower methods that all adults can use with children and youth. (1970, p. 191)

Not all parent educators of this philosophical bent take the radical position that Gordon does. Some accept brief, nonabusive physical punishment as a means of communicating a message that has not gotten through in other ways.

Impact on Parent Education

Gordon's first book, *Parent Effectiveness Training*, has sold widely (over 2 million copies) and has been translated into more than a dozen languages. With his daughter, Judy (the subject of the raincoat story), Gordon wrote a sequel, *P.E.T. in Action* (1976). He also adapted his parenting program to fit teachers (*Teacher Effectiveness Training*, (1974) and leaders (*Leader Effectiveness Training*, 1978). These books were used widely in public school and the education departments of churches and synagogues.

Few of today's young parents and college students have read Parent Effectiveness Training, and in fact most have not heard of it. Yet those who read about parenting inevitably are influenced by Gordon's ideas, because the techniques of PET (identification of problem ownership, active listening, I-statements, and mutual problem solving) have become standard in parenting advice.

Critique

Parent Effectiveness Training is still one of the best books for helping parents gain the skills they need to be supportive when their children are struggling. Unless parents have had some training in how to listen, they tend to rely on such old methods as lecturing, scolding, and blaming, which drive their children away.

PET is weak in helping parents correct the misbehavior of children. Gordon teaches the use of the I-statement, which is an important technique, but not enough by itself. The I-statement requires mutual respect to be effective, and some children do not respect their parents to the extent required. Used excessively, it becomes emotionally manipulative and personally irresponsible, in that parents demand that their children be responsible for their emotions.

The six-step problem-solving process that Gordon recommends is an important tool for mutual problems. By itself it is inadequate, however; additional parenting tools are needed when children (or parents) are not able to sit down and follow such a neat recipe for resolving conflict.

Behavioral Psychology: Childhood as Neutral and Parent as Environmental Engineer

Parenting Expert C built a closed compartment about the size of a crib for his infant daughter. One side of the compartment, which could be raised and lowered like a window, was made of glass. The temperature and humidity inside the box could be controlled. Through experimentation C discovered settings so comfortable that his daughter rarely cried.

The infant wore no clothing, except for a diaper, so that she would be more comfortable and less restricted in her movement. The mattress was a tightly stretched canvas, kept dry by warm air. A single bottom sheet operated like a roller towel; it was stored on a spool outside the compartment at one end and passed into a wire hamper at the other. A clean section of sheet could be pulled into place in seconds; the roll of sheet was 10 yards long and lasted a week.

The walls of the box were insulated to keep out unwanted noise, and a curtain could be drawn over the window to reduce light and other visual distractions so that the infant could sleep undisturbed.

The baby was removed from the box for feeding and changing, and also each afternoon for a play period. The play period was extended as she grew older, and eventually the box was used only as sleeping quarters.

C recommends that other parents use a box like the one he designed, using scientific principles to ease their job as parents and to improve the environment of babies.[3]

Background

The third philosophy of parenting looks on the child not as a soul to be saved or as a partner in communication but as an organism responding to its environment. John Locke (1632–1704) is credited with laying the foundation for this philosophy. He argues against the notion that children are born with innate ideas. Instead, they are born like a *tabula rasa* (blank slate), which is filled in by experience.

Differences among children, Locke (1690/1973) maintains, are due to differences in upbringing:

[3]This story is from an article written for *Ladies Home Journal* by B. F. Skinner (1945/1972a).

I have seen children at a table, who, whatever was there, never asked for any thing, but contentedly took what was given them: and at another place I have seen others cry for every thing they saw, must be served out of every dish, and that first too. What made this vast difference but this, that one was accustomed to have what they called or cried for, the other to go without it? (p. 25)

This emphasis on the environment was carried in the 20th century by the behaviorist branch of American psychology. John Watson, known as the founder of behaviorism, is famous for this claim made in 1914:

Give me a dozen healthy infants, well-formed, and my own specified world to bring them up in and I'll guarantee to take any one at random and train him to become any type of specialist I might select— doctor, lawyer, artist, merchant-chief, and yes, even beggar-man and thief, regardless of his talents, penchants, tendencies, abilities, vocations, and race of his ancestors. (1914/1958, p. 104)

B. F. Skinner (1904–1990) devoted a lifetime to studying the effects of environmental conditions on behavior, and he led behaviorism to such prominence that it was the major force within American psychology from the 1940s to the 1960s.

To solve specific problems of the home or school, Skinner advocated an experimental analysis of behavior to find out what works. The procedures for altering behavior, based on Skinnerian principles of reinforcement, came to be called behavior modification. Behavior modification has been applied to a wide variety of situations, and it is the basis for numerous parent-education programs.

Assumptions about Human Nature

In this third philosophy, the natural condition of childhood is seen not as evil or good but as neutral. Children are capable of doing bad or good things; what they do is what they have learned to do.

The radical form of behaviorism espoused by Skinner is not concerned with the issue of human nature. Humans, like other animals, are regarded as products of their environments. Skinner refers to such concepts as the human will, wishes, emotions, and attitudes as "mentalist" ideas, which if properly understood would be unnecessary. For example, of free will, he writes:

> A sense of freedom is another of those inner attributes which lose their force as we more clearly understand man's relation to his environment. Freedom—or, rather, behavior which "feels free"— is also the product of a history of conditioning. (1964/1972b, p. 53)

Assumptions about the Causes of Problems in the Home

Today's behaviorists would still agree with Locke's (1690/1973) statement regarding parental responsibility for the manners and abilities of their children:

> We have reason to conclude, that great care is to be had of the forming children's minds, and giving them that seasoning early, which shall influence their lives always after. For when they do well or ill, the praise or blame will be laid there: and when any thing is done awkwardly . . . it is suitable to their breeding. (p. 19)

From this point of view, parents train children to behave. If their behavior is judged to be inappropriate, it is because the home environment (or society in general) failed to provide the conditions necessary for them to learn the appropriate behavior.

Goals of Parent Education

Since parents are the most significant part of the child's environment, behavioral models of parent education focus on increasing parental skills in shaping desirable behavior in their children. Parents are taught to view learning as the problem, and also as the solution. Behavior that is inappropriate can be unlearned; behavior that is appropriate can be learned to take its place. The techniques that parents are taught deal with observing the specific behavior in question and altering the consequences of the child's behavior to bring about the desired behavior.

View of Punishment

This philosophy tends to oppose punishment for empirical reasons. The data of experimental research reveal that punishment is not as effective as parents commonly think it is. *Positive* reinforcement so powerfully shapes the desired behavior that punishing the misbehavior is not necessary. Furthermore, punishment has undesirable side effects (for example, escape, aggression, and depression).

Impact on Parent Education

Behaviorism's insistence that much of the misbehavior of children is learned had a great impact on parenting advice. It came at a time when family genes were assumed to be far more important than the family social environment. Behavioral psychology also provided a model for using objective research to test the effectiveness of parenting techniques, which was in itself an important contribution to parent education. Several programs for teaching parents to be more assertive have been developed. These programs are based in part on a behavioral model of parenting, with roots in the learning theory of Skinner.

In the 1970s behaviorism began to fade from public consciousness, and it was never adopted by ordinary American families to the extent that Dobson's and Gordon's concepts were. Most people today have heard of "behavior mod" and reject it for philosophical reasons, although they do not understand it. Their image of behavior modification tends to be the image portrayed by the mass media, which is inaccurate: punitive and inescapable control by a totalitarian government.

In professional settings behavior modification remains the strategy most frequently employed for such problems as autism, hyperactivity, self-injurious behavior, enuresis (bed wetting), phobias, language deficits, aggressiveness, withdrawal, and tantrums.

Critique

Behavior modification has become an essential tool for parent educators who work with children lagging in intellectual and social development. Many parents of mentally and socially handicapped children have been taught to use reinforcement systematically to regain control of their households and to train their children to behave in desirable ways.

Parents who are weak in the skills needed for correcting misbehavior can benefit from the training to be more assertive with children that the behavioral branch of psychology provides. It also informs parents of the various effects of punishment, enabling them to use punishment selectively or avoid it altogether.

The applications of the behaviorist approach to parenting, as important as they have been, form only one small part of discipline. For example, parents of normal children can get by without using behavior modification, since there are many other methods for dealing with misbehavior that are less contrived and less complicated.

The behaviorist approach contributes very little to the listening and encouraging cluster of parental skills because it pays scant attention to the child's feelings. And because it tends to reduce human behavior to mechanistic responses to environmental stimuli, the behavioral model overlooks the way family members affect one another in a dynamic, interlocking system of relationships.

Life-Span Developmental Psychology: Childhood as Journey and Parent as Fellow Traveler and Guide

In describing the interactions between a newborn and her first-time parents, Parenting Expert D wrote: "New developments in Anna's behavior began to appear rapidly. By four weeks of age she began to have a brief, transient smile in the midst of each play session. . . . The first time she smiled, they laughed out loud. She startled and began to cry. . . .

"Finally, they found that a low-keyed, rhythmic approach had the best results. . . . In the quiet intervals Anna would come out with a slow, tentative smile or an attempt to gurgle or coo. She worked so hard to produce these minimal responses that they could tell that she 'knew' what she wanted to do. . . . If they kept to her rhythm, adapting the quality of their responses to hers, they gradually began to prolong these 'play' periods from a few minutes to 15 or more."[4]

[4]This description of parent and child development is from *On Becoming a Family,* by the pediatrician T. Berry Brazelton (1981, pp. 151–152).

Background

The developmental perspective unfolded as a field of study beginning about 1900. For the first half of the 20th century, it was devoted to child and adolescent development; in the second half of the century, as interest in adulthood expanded, it became the field of life-span human development.

G. Stanley Hall (1844–1924) is regarded as the founder of developmental psychology. Under his influence (from approximately 1900 to 1925), new journals of child and adolescent psychology sprang up, child study labs were established, children were studied with more objective methods, longitudinal tracking of subjects began, and scientific interest in middle and old age was sparked.

Another pioneer of developmental research, the Swiss psychologist Jean Piaget (1896–1980), published dozens of books and hundreds of articles about children's mental constructions of the world. He wrote in French, however, and was not "discovered" by American educators until the 1960s when the research climate was ready for a turn in the direction of cognitive concerns.

Since 1970, the most significant shift within the developmental perspective has been the increased emphasis on adulthood. In the perspective of the life span, development does not end with the passage from childhood to adulthood, nor do individuals stop developing when they become parents. This emphasis on adult development is based on the longitudinal research of such individuals as Bernice Neugarten and Daniel Goleman and on the theoretical writings of Erik Erikson.

Erikson's influence is traced principally to a short chapter entitled "Eight Ages of Man" in his 1950 book *Childhood and Society.* Erikson conceptualizes eight stages of life, each with its own "issue" to be resolved. Since that time, numerous books for parents based on Erikson's "psychosocial" stages have appeared.

Assumptions about Human Nature

From this theoretical point of view, children are not naturally malevolent, naturally benevolent, or even "neutral" but simply children: humans who are not fully mature. Their immaturity means that compared with adults they have poorer memories, have weaker impulse control, are less insightful, and are less able to exercise good judgment. It is not surprising that they misbehave sometimes—even adults misbehave sometimes.

In addition, this perspective insists that each person is unique; each child is born with a temperament and other unique characteristics that cannot be overlooked. This view contrasts sharply with the behaviorist view, illustrated best by Watson's claim that any child can be trained to become whatever the behavioral engineer wants the child to become.

It contrasts just as sharply with the conservative Christian view of childhood, represented by Dobson, which views children as sinners. From the developmental perspective, there is no reason to interpret the misbehavior of children as a struggle between good and evil. Children are developmentally immature and respond to the world within the limits of their capabilities.

Children do misbehave at times and need to be corrected. But the will that sometimes leads them to misbehave also leads them to do what is desired, as when they greet a parent with a hug. This, too, is willful; it is voluntary, not automatic. Children are not puppets or trained seals, but individual *humans*, with wills of their own to be nurtured to maturity.

Assumptions about the Causes of Problems in the Home

The primary emphasis of the developmental perspective is that misbehavior often results from inappropriate parental expectations. A second assumption is that misbehavior occurs in predictable patterns; certain problems show up at certain stages of development and usually self-correct in time (for example, the "fear of strangers" that occurs near the end of the first year of life).

A third assumption of the developmental perspective is that problems are sometimes created by the parents' own developmental struggles. How they meet their own needs at these times affects their parenting.

A fourth assumption is that children are ultimately responsible for themselves and sometimes disappoint their parents. Parents do not have control over the disposition the child is born with, some of the choices the child makes, or many of life's circumstances.

From this point of view, parents need not take all the blame (or all the credit) for how their children turn out. The decisions parents make for themselves as they travel the journey of life with children by their sides do influence their children, and parents *are* responsible for *their* choices.

Goals of Parent Education

The primary goal of parent educators, from this perspective, is to teach parents about development. Parents need to know what to expect of their children and set their demands accordingly, neither too high nor too low. Much of parent education, therefore, is simply child-development education.

Children's "readiness" to do something is emphasized. The Russian developmental psychologist Lev Vygotsky suggests that there is a "zone of proximal development" where parental guidance, like scaffolding in the construction of a building, is most useful. The importance of helping children to stay "on schedule" developmentally is also emphasized. Whether this involves the first night away from home in childhood or getting a job in young adulthood, staying with the statistically normal pace of development is advantageous to both children and their parents.

In recent years, as psychologists became more concerned with adult development, the goal of parent education began to include teaching parents about parent development as well as child development. The research of Ellen Galinsky at the Bank Street College in New York, summarized in her book *Between Generations: The Six Stages of Parenthood* (1981), is a good example.

View of Punishment

Over the years, developmentalists have consistently recommended that parents not use physical punishment with children. Just as consistently, parents have tended to punish. In one study of 150 families, 148 reported having spanked their children at least once (Baumrind, 1973). The advice of parenting experts seeking a middle ground, therefore, tends to be: "Don't spank; but if you do, follow such and such guidelines to minimize the unwanted side effects" (see Dodson, 1970; Osborne, 1989).

With empirical data to support their position, developmentalists argue against "power-assertive" techniques (primarily, physical punishment) in favor of "inductive" techniques (especially, reasoning, empathy, and restitution to the victim of the misbehavior). Asserting power has several shortcomings; most important is that it calls children's attention to what happens to *them* when they misbehave. Induction, on the other hand, calls children's attention to how *others* are affected by their misbehavior and to what they need to do to undue the damage they have done.

Impact on Parent Education

For educated parents, the impact of this theoretical and research perspective has been the most important of all the schools of thought reviewed in this chapter. Its contributions are so widespread and its proponents so numerous that any attempt to summarize them is certain to leave out many who should be mentioned. Nevertheless, a few will be highlighted.

Arnold Gesell was one of the early developmentalists who made important contributions to parenting advice. Through 50 years of research at the Yale Clinic of Child Development, Gesell and his colleagues (most notably, Frances Ilg and Louise Bates Ames) published a series of books about child development (from which such expressions as "the terrible 2s" and "the trusting 3s" became household expressions). Gesell was the most trusted "baby doctor" until Benjamin Spock, another developmentalist, published the first edition of his famous book *The Common Sense Book of Baby and Child Care* in 1946.

In recent years, Brazelton has been dominant among developmental parenting experts. Through his books, public lectures, magazine advice columns, and even a television show, millions of parents have learned more about what to expect of their children (and themselves).

Burton White's 20 years of research on what parents do to develop competence in their children (White, Kaban, & Attanucci, 1979) is the basis of the Parents as Teachers parent-education program. With empirical data to support its effectiveness, PAT now operates through the welfare departments and public school systems of over 35 states and continues to expand. PAT is one of the most important employers of parent educators today.

Critique

Knowledge of normal child development enables parents to be appropriately supportive and encouraging with their children. In addition, the emphasis on the life span is helpful to parents in coping with their own development.

The most important limitation of the developmental perspective is that information about developmental stages and developmental influences does not necessarily result in good parenting. Some parents excuse their inability to correct their children's misbehavior by saying it is "just a stage" that their children are going through. Still other parents excuse their inabilities by laying blame on their past experiences—because they acquired "codependent" personalities, for example, as children of alcoholics. Parents also need skills to *do* what needs to be done.

Another criticism of the developmental approach is that parents become anxious when their children's development doesn't keep up with or exceed the norms. Parental concern about children's achievement is very strong, especially among educated, upwardly mobile professional parents who attempt to maximize their children's development (even prenatally) with "educational toys" and other gadgets. In the 1980s, David Elkind began to caution parents to respect the natural timing of children's development and not to be so concerned with achievement. This is the message of his books *The Hurried Child* (1981) and *All Grown Up and No Place to Go* (Elkind, 1984).

A final criticism of the developmental perspective is that it too often assumes normal children, normal parents, and normal circumstances, which excludes the concerns of many parents and children.

Family-Systems Theory: Childhood as Electrical Forces and Parent as Electrical Engineer

A mother sought the help of Parenting Expert E because she was anxious about her son's problems at school. She herself felt emotionally insecure and traced this to her mother's neglect of her as a child. In order to do better with her own child, she was determined to raise a child who did not feel as insecure and neglected as she had felt. Her efforts worked well until her son became an adolescent. At that time he began to get into trouble at school, and his academic performance deteriorated. She reacted to his problems by trying even harder to be loving and understanding. However, the more she tried to make him feel secure, the more he complained about being aimless and insecure. He believed that she did not love him because she did not let him be himself. Since he felt uncomfortable with her, he began to spend more time with his peers. This increased the stress in their relationship even more, as she believed his friends were leading him astray. The more she criticized his friends, the more he distanced himself from her. Finally, her concern about his problems led her to the therapist for help.[5]

Background

Since the 1950s a revolution in family counseling has taken place. Problems of individuals, in this last theoretical perspective, are traced to the emotional limitations of members of the individual's family and the members' patterns of interaction. This view of family relationships sees individual behavior in its social context. Instead of seeing problems as residing within the individual ("son is insecure" or "son is rebellious"), this view sees problems as residing in relationships ("mother is anxious about the poor school performance of her son, who distances himself from her and her goals for his life").

The movement began in the 1950s when a group of pioneers (most notably, Gregory Bateson, Jay Haley, Virginia Satir, Salvador Minuchin, and Murry Bowen) led family counselors away from individual psychology into the previously unmapped territory that today is called family science. Today, the field has its own heroes (the "master therapists"), its own theories and research literature, its unique techniques for working with families, and its own professional organizations (principally, the American Association for Marriage and Family Therapy and the National Council of Family Relations).

[5]This case is used by the master family therapist Murray Bowen and his colleague Michael Kerr in their book *Family Evaluation* (Kerr & Bowen, 1988, pp. 203–204) as a means of showing, from the perspective of family-systems theory, how the misbehavior of children is linked to the emotional limitations of parents, a key concept.

Only in recent years has the mainstream American Psychological Association (APA) added a division for members interested in family science (Division 43, Family Psychology).

Assumptions about Human Nature

In the systems perspective, individuals are seen as feeling and thinking beings who are both attracted to and repelled by one another. In the terms of family science, these emotional tugs and pushes are called *family process*. Humans interact in dynamic, circular patterns that are not adequately described by the behaviorists' laws of learning, the developmentalists' stages, or the good/evil dichotomy of the traditional authoritarians.

Assumptions about the Causes of Problems in the Home

In family-systems theory, such problems as academic failure, obesity, heart disease, teenage pregnancy, delinquency, alcoholism, depression, and phobias are regarded as symptoms of problems in the patterns of relationships in the family. The theory suggests that a family "gets" something from the problems of individual members. Sometimes it gets a distraction, so that a worse problem is avoided. Anxiety about a more basic relationship issue (the marital relationship, for example) may be redirected to a problem of one of the children, and a crisis is averted. As long as the individual's problem is the focus of anxiety, the family system will keep the problem and the child will continue to be symptomatic.

Goals of Parent Education

From a family-systems point of view, the goal of parenting is to create an emotionally healthy family, a group of unique individuals who relate well and enjoy one another's company but do not think and react emotionally as one.

From the perspective of this theory, the ideal parent/child relationship is one of closeness without fusion. Communication flows between the two, but the parent does not pressure the child to think or react emotionally in the same way, as if they were yoked to one set of perceptions and feelings. Therefore, increasing the levels of differentiation of family members and helping them maintain a comfortable closeness are the goals of family-systems-oriented parenting advice.

View of Punishment

Parents who are less differentiated, according to this perspective, tend to be more coercive and are more likely to punish. They make choices based on the flow of emotion in the moment of encounter with a misbehaving child. They tend to blame, induce guilt, obligate the other, persuade, intimidate, feel victimized and helpless, get silent, complain—and punish.

Therefore, parent educators using the systems perspective attempt to get parents to think calmly about what choices they have in dealing with their children, and not just to react emotionally and automatically.

Impact on Parent Education

The family-systems perspective dominates the field of *family therapy* today, but it has had less impact on *parent education* and even less impact on *parents* themselves. One reason is that it is still so new that few parent education programs with a systems perspective have been developed.

Several parenting books specifically based on systems thought have appeared in recent years. They include *How to Discipline without Feeling Guilty*, by Melvin Silberman and Susan Wheelan (1980); *Taming Monsters, Slaying Dragons*, by Joel Feiner and Graham Yost (1988); *Parenting for the 90s* by Philip Osborne (1989); and *Parenting by Heart*, by Ron Taffel (1991). The intellectual excitement about family-systems theory can be expected to be channeled into more such books and parent-education programs in the future.

Critique

The strength of the systems perspective is that it offers parents a way to *think* about children's behavior and the choices the parents have, which has potential for calming them down and guiding them to a different way of parenting. The systems perspective provides a way of thinking about balance—balance between too much closeness and too much distance, between over-involvement and under-involvement, as well as between thought and feeling. Finally, it enables parents to understand the part they play in conflicts and how to manage conflict better.

A limitation of family-systems theory is that it seems to be too complicated for the average parent to understand. This is partly because it represents a new way of thinking that requires some time to be accommodated. But it is also because very little written material addressed to parents is available. Most is written by professionals for other professionals.

Another limitation of systems theory is that it offers *insight* but not *skills* for parenting. Parents looking for techniques to "fix" their problem children do not find what they are looking for. Perhaps the major obstacle to applying family-systems concepts to parent education is the emotional limitations of parents themselves. What are parents to do when told they need to "deintensify" an issue or be more "nonanxiously present" with a child? To what extent can parents become more differentiated (that is, become more emotionally mature)?

While systems theory has revolutionized family counseling and can be expected to have an increasing impact on parent education, it will not make other approaches to parent education unnecessary. Thinking about family relationships isn't enough; parents also need training in *doing* what needs to be done to reduce dysfunctional patterns and establish healthier patterns for living together as members of a family.

The two parent-education programs that are now the most popular, Systematic Training for Effective Parenting (STEP) and Active Parenting, move the field of parent education a bit closer to the systems perspective. Both are based on the work of Rudolf Dreikurs, whose ideas about parenting, in turn, were based on the work of the personality theorist Alfred Adler, a contemporary of Freud. (Thus, the branch of parent education based on Dreikurs's work is called "Adlerian.")

Dreikurs's book *Children: The Challenge*, which he coauthored with Virginia Soltz (1964), sold widely and established his influence in parent education. He recommended that parents recognize the goals of misbehavior, use natural and logical consequences, avoid power struggles, offer encouragement, and establish a home atmosphere of mutual respect. He pioneered the use of parent discussion groups.

Donald Dinkmeyer coauthored with Dreikurs a book about encouragement (Dinkmeyer & Dreikurs, 1963), and later wrote with Gary McKay *Systematic Training for Effective Parenting Parent's Handbook* (Dinkmeyer & McKay, 1976).

Although the content of the STEP program comes primarily from Adler and Dreikurs, it also incorporates the concepts of problem ownership, active (or reflective) listening, and I-statements from the Parent Effectiveness Training program.

The parent-education program now the most popular is *Active Parenting*, Michael Popkin's (1983) adaptation of STEP. Popkin added his own stories and other teaching devices, and most importantly, produced videotapes to accompany the program.

For both STEP and Active Parenting, the parent handbooks are attractive, lessons are brief and well-illustrated, and leaders are provided many suggestions for guiding parent-discussion groups. The video format has been significant, especially for Active Parenting. In addition, both programs have been promoted successfully by their publishers.

STEP and Active Parenting best fit the systems perspective because both emphasize circular thinking rather than linear thinking: parents are taught to think about the possibility of altering the misbehavior of their children by altering their *own* behavior. They are taught that they are responsible for their feelings, thoughts, and behaviors and that they have control and choice in these matters. Parents are taught the importance of "family atmosphere" and the "family constellation" (birth-order roles). Family meetings are recommended for discussion of issues of concern to members.

Although the STEP and Active Parenting programs move parent education closer to a systems perspective, neither goes far in that direction. Concepts central to systems theory (misbehavior viewed as symptoms linked to the emotional processes of the family, differentiation, fusion, anxiety, reactivity, triangulation, distance/closeness) are not covered at all. The field of parent education still awaits a program that makes central the concepts of family emotional process.

There is a need today for parent educators who are sufficiently eclectic in theory and technique to be able to guide parents toward a balanced set of parenting skills and attitudes. This chapter is intended to serve as a guide to that end. (For additional information about a simple conceptual parent-education framework for developing a balanced set of parenting skills and attitudes, see Osborne, 1989.)

Chapter Summary

Discussion Questions

1. What exposure have you had to these five theories? What books about parenting have you read? Which of the perspectives do they fit best?
2. Which aspects of each of the theoretical perspectives appeal to you, and which aspects do not?
3. Which parent-education programs are you familiar with? What is your assessment of their various strengths and weaknesses? Which would you most be most comfortable with as a parent educator?
4. Do some parents not have a parenting philosophy? Do some have one without being aware of it, or without being able to articulate it? Does it make any difference?
5. To what extent were your parents influenced by these theoretical bases for parenting?
6. To the extent that you have one and can articulate it, what is your basis for parenting?

Additional Resources

Clarke, J. I., & Dawson, C. (1989). *Growing up again: Parenting ourselves, parenting our children.* New York: Harper & Row.

Elkind, D. (1984). *All grown up and no place to go.* Reading, MA: Addison-Wesley.

References

Baumrind, D. (1973). The development of instrumental competence through socialization. *Minnesota Symposia on Child Psychology, 7,* 3–46.

Brazelton, T. B. (1981). *On becoming a family.* New York: Dell.

Clarke, J. I., & Dawson, C. (1989). *Growing up again: Parenting ourselves, parenting our children.* New York: Harper & Row.

Dinkmeyer, D., & Dreikurs, R. (1963). *Encouraging children to learn: The encouragement process.* Englewood Cliffs, NJ: Prentice-Hall.

Dinkmeyer, D., & McKay, G. (1976). *Systematic training for effective parenting: Parent's handbook.* Circle Pines, MN: American Guidance Service.

Dobson, J. (1970). *Dare to discipline.* Wheaton, IL: Tyndale House.

Dobson, J. (1978). *The strong-willed child.* Wheaton, IL: Tyndale House.

Dobson, J. (1982). *Dr. Dobson answers your questions.* Minneapolis: Grason.

Dobson, J. (1987). *Parenting isn't for cowards.* Waco, TX: Word.

Dodson, F. (1970). *How to parent.* New York: Signet.

Dreikurs, R., with Soltz, V. (1964). *Children: The challenge.* New York: Hawthorn Books.

Elkind, D. (1981). *The hurried child.* Reading, MA: Addison-Wesley.

Elkind, D. (1984). *All grown up and no place to go.* Reading, MA: Addison-Wesley.

Feiner, J., & Yost, G. (1988). *Taming monsters, slaying dragons: The revolutionary family approach to overcoming childhood fears and anxieties.* New York: Arbor House.

Galinsky, E. (1981). *Between generations: The six stages of parenthood.* New York: Times Books.

Gordon, T. (1970). *Parent Effectiveness Training.* New York: Wyden.

Gordon, T. (1974). *Teacher Effectiveness Training.* New York: Wyden.

Gordon, T. (1976) *P. E. T. in action.* New York: Wyden.

Gordon, T. (1978). *Leader effectiveness training.* New York: Wyden.

Gordon, T. (1980). Parent effectiveness training: A preventive program and its effects on families. In M. J. Fine (Ed.), *Handbook on parent education* (pp. 101–121). New York: Academic Press.

Kerr, M. E., & Bowen, M. (1988). *Family evaluation.* New York: Norton.

Locke, J. (1973). Some thoughts concerning education. In P. J. Grever, Jr. (Ed.), *Child-rearing concepts, 1628–1861* (pp. 18–41). Itasca, IL: F. E. Peacock. (Originally published 1690)

Osborne, P. (1989). *Parenting for the 90s.* Intercourse. PA: Good Books.

Popkin, M. (1983). *Active Parenting handbook.* Atlanta: Active Parenting.

Rogers, C. (1980). *My philosophy of interpersonal relationships and how it grew.* In C. Rogers, A way of being (pp. 27–45). Boston: Houghton Mifflin.

Rousseau, J. (1965). The child in nature (excerpts from *Emile*). In W. Kessen (Ed.), *The child* (pp. 76–97). New York: Wiley. (Originally published 1762)

Silberman, M. L., & Wheelan, S. A. (1980). *How to discipline without feeling guilty: Assertive relationships with children.* Champaign, IL: Research Press.

Skinner, B. F. (1972a). Baby in a box. In B. F. Skinner, *Cumulative record: A selection of papers* (3rd ed.) (pp. 567–573). New York: Appleton-Century-Crofts. (Originally published in *Ladies Home Journal*, October 1945)

Skinner, B. F. (1972b). Man. In B. F. Skinner, *Cumulative record: A selection of papers* (3rd ed.) (pp. 51–57). New York: Appleton-Century-Crofts. (Originally published in *Proceedings of the American Philosophical Society*, 1964, 108, pp. 482–485)

Taffel, R. (1991). *Parenting by heart.* New York: Addison-Wesley.

Watson, J. B. (1958). *Behavior: An introduction to comparative psychology.* New York: Holt. (Originally published 1914)

Wesley, J. (1973). Sermon on the education of children. In P. J. Greven, Jr. (Ed.), *Child-rearing concepts, 1628–1861* (pp. 52–66). Itasca, IL: F. E. Peacock. (Originally published 1783)

White, B. L., Kaban, B., & Attanucci, J. (1979). *The origins of human competence.* Lexington, MA: Heath.

CHAPTER 21

Careers in Family Science

Robert Keim
Northern Illinois University

The study of family science prepares students to work with individuals and families in unique ways. As emerging professionals, students of family science are decidedly more informed about family development and its influence upon individuals than are many other professionals in the field of human and social services. As noted by Wesley Burr (Moore, 1987), family science "is a new field in the social sciences" (p. 1348).

Burr acknowledges that the various disciplines such as psychology, anthropology, economics, sociology, biology, and history provide much of the knowledge base. Before the discipline of family science emerged, however, this knowledge was fragmented and disconnected, he adds. Family science has now "integrated these fragments into a coherent body of knowledge" and has focused research upon "the internal dynamics of the family and the way families interact with the ecosystems" (p. 1348).

Burr cites the newer professionals who have emerged in the application phase of family science. These include marriage and family therapists, family-life educators, family extension agents, divorce mediators, teachers in public schools and colleges, and family researchers. He further notes that the family-enrichment movement has been a recent development, with its focus upon structured retreats and workshop programs. Family-science students should recognize that some of these endeavors may require more advanced graduate preparation, although many positions are available to baccalaureate graduates.

In addition, as college graduates enter the career search, they are likely to discover that they are very well prepared for many positions in the human and social services. Many social-service positions provide excellent opportunities to perform many of the activities cited by Burr, such as marriage and family therapy, family-life education, and family-enrichment programs.

The review of career opportunities that follows will incorporate the career areas cited by Burr in addition to others in the human and social services that directly involve individuals in the family context. The family-science student, through a breadth of studies, becomes alert and sensitive to recognizing developmental stages and strategies of interpersonal interactions and conflicts. You should clearly recognize this singularly important quality as you approach agencies for staff positions.

The Maze of Opportunities

In spite of their thorough preparation, or because of it, family-science students are often perplexed when it comes to narrowing down the specific area in which they wish to work. In being exposed to such a wide range of information and issues, students may be uncertain about or torn between competing interests. Generally, through their own life experiences, from faculty advice, and by selecting elective courses, most students begin to crystallize their interests toward certain populations or problem issues. Further exploration of the following factors related to the workplace can be helpful, and we will look at them in this section:

client populations or service categories

types of service (areas of work, job titles, and other characteristics)

services—agencies and organizations

Client Populations or Service Categories

When students are asked what they want to be doing in three to five years, they often respond, "Helping people." The time comes when this response needs to be more refined. Granted, "working with the elderly" or "working with youths" is more focused, but there are still wide areas of opportunity within these goals.

A review of client populations and service categories is important to help one realize the wide range of options. Table 21.1 is a revision of a list by Keim and Cassidy (1989).

In narrowing the field of interest, students should be cautioned not merely to select the one field in which they have had personal experience. Also, it is often easy to select a field because of age similarity to the popula-

tion. With experience, one discovers the enjoyment or challenge of working with other age groups. Volunteer experiences in the community can help broaden one's experiences, avoiding the dangers of having a limited exposure in only one or two areas.

Even within the populations or service areas noted above, there is a variety of settings for work. The following two subsections will provide information pertaining to more specific services and job settings as well as identifying numerous agencies and organizations that serve these client populations.

Types of Service

Work with a given client population may vary significantly. Each type of service listed below should be studied carefully in order to explore and discover your own (1) interests, (2) abilities, and (3) possible tolerance levels for particular work. Realize that volunteer work can help you discover some of these. When reviewing the types of service listing below, recognize that the services delivered by one given agency may be limited or broad. Some agencies may provide only one type of service; others may incorporate several services in their mission. An expansion of the services cited by Keim and Cassidy (1989) follows in Table 21.2.

In the following discussion of types of work, some job titles will be given. Such titles are taken from known positions that graduates have obtained as well as from published career-reference guides (Career Associates, 1986; Hopke, 1987; Norback, 1988; Snelling & Snelling, 1985; Visual Education Center Staff, 1992; Wright, 1991).

TABLE 21.1   Client Populations or Service Categories

Children's services
Cooperative extension
Elderly services—gerontology
Family-life education
Family violence
Financial assistance—consumer credit or public aid
Handicapped services
Hospitals—medical services
Marriage and family therapy—individual counseling
Military families
Mental health
Personnel work—employee-assistance programs
Religious work
Research and planning
Teaching family science in public schools and colleges
Student activities
Social services—specific and multiple
Substance-abuse services
Vocational guidance—counseling
Voluntary Action Centers
Women's and men's programs
Youth work

TABLE 21.2   Types of Service

1. Case management
2. Community outreach
3. Community social services (including family therapy)
4. Coordination or administrative work
5. Crisis or hot-line services
6. Day care—various populations
7. Education—community, public schools, colleges
8. Research and planning
9. Residential care
10. Vocational and professional guidance and training

1. Case management.   Case management often involves developing or overseeing the treatment plans of the individual client or family. The worker may "seek and monitor services from a variety of agencies" (Barker, 1991, p. 29). More prominent services involving case management include:

- casework, a generic term used in many situations
- protective services for abused and neglected children
- employee-assistance programming
- foster care for children and youths
- hospital social services for patients
- probation and parole services
- rehabilitation services for the handicapped
- residential care of a wide variety of populations
- vocational guidance or job-training activities
- welfare assistance with low-income families or the homeless

Individuals seem to vary in their attraction to and tolerance for this type of work. A professional worker may feel a strong sense of achievement. Others may feel a high level of frustration due either to heavy caseloads, changes occurring only slowly, or no recognizable changes appearing at all. One's motivation and interest in the type of service may be an important factor contributing to work satisfaction.

2. Community outreach.   A second type of work involves going to where the clients are, either where they commonly meet in a community or to their homes, as in the case with the elderly or others with physical needs. When working with youths, the location is often in schools or areas where they "hang out." In the schools, there may be informal meetings in the cafeteria or more formal support sessions in meeting rooms. Work with low-income families is often in their homes or in community centers. The goal is "to bring services and information about the availability of services to people in their homes or usual environments" (Barker, 1991, p. 164). The more common forms of outreach are:

- homemaker services for those with physical or household needs
- public-health services, especially with young mothers
- religious work, usually among teenagers and college students

- student activities in higher education
- visiting the elderly for need assessments
- youth work

Outreach services are typically provided by councils on aging, mental-health centers, and youth-service bureaus. Characteristics desirable for outreach work include flexibility, initiative, assertiveness, and the ability to work alone as well as with others. Clearly, the nature of work varies, and it depends upon the population being served. Books that could be helpful for those interested in religious outreach work are *Opportunities in Religious Service* (Nelson, 1980) and *Where to Start: An Annotated Career Planning Bibliography* (Rockcastle, 1985).

3. Community Social Services.   Social services, broadly speaking, involve many of the services cited among these ten types of work, especially including those cited under case management. As will be discussed later, numerous agencies provide multiple services to diverse populations. Agencies should be visited and carefully studied in order to discover opportunities of employment with them.

Keim and Cassidy (1989) cite community services as including services pertaining to "adoption, children of single parents, foster care, financial assistance, general welfare, the handicapped, homemaker services, parent support, substance abuse, and coordination of volunteer services" (p. 7). Barker (1991) defines social services as "promoting the health and well-being of people and . . . helping people to become more self-sufficient; preventing dependency; strengthening family relationships; and restoring individuals, families, groups, or communities to successful social functioning" (p. 221).

Many social services focus upon specific problems or issues. Awareness of some of the primary ones may assist you in recognizing areas of opportunity. A broad array of typical social services not directly included within other categories are:

- adoption and foster care for children and youth
- community centers maintained for varied activities
- domestic violence victims' assistance
- employee assistance programming
- family and individual therapy

- food assistance
- handicapped services
- homemaker services for various needs of new parents or the physically disabled
- hospital social services by a local agency for patients where neighboring hospitals are too small to provide a full-time staff member
- immigrant/migrant services, where larger populations warrant them
- investigative work and follow-up services for state child-protective units
- probation and parole units of counties or parishes
- rehabilitation services for the handicapped
- development and coordination of support groups for various stress issues
- substance-abuse counseling and services
- transportation needs for the disabled
- volunteer services
- vocational guidance or job-training activities
- welfare assistance for low-income families and the homeless by public aid offices, organizations such as the Salvation Army, and governmental and private agencies
- welfare assistance for the poor or homeless
- youth work and youth services

Titles for such positions obviously are numerous, including caseworker, counselor, chemical-dependency therapist, foster-care worker, homemaker, hospital social-worker, probation or parole officer, program coordinator, rehabilitation worker, social service worker, vocational counselor, and youth worker.

4. Coordination or Administrative Work. For most types of work cited in this chapter, needs exist for coordinating the activities of staff members and volunteers. Specific administrative functions include goal setting and implementation, program development and assessment, coordination of activities, supervision of staff, fund raising or grant-proposal writing, and overseeing other recording keeping, business, and resource activities. These functions need to be fulfilled at local, regional, state, and national levels. Other administrative functions might include in-service training and educational programs for volunteers and paraprofessionals as well as for the professional staff. Entry positions for recent college graduates may involve such functions as:

- activities coordinator in nursing or retirement homes
- coordinator of big brother/sister programs
- coordinator of drop-in center activities
- coordinator of numerous other programs

Titles for such positions are often as simple as center coordinator, program coordinator, or coordinator of (the activity). Higher levels of administrative supervision are usually held by persons with more extensive experience and possibly, though not necessarily, with advanced graduate degrees.

5. Crisis or hot-line services. Crisis services involve coordination of volunteers, training, and the development of resource and referral listings. The location of crisis lines tends to be associated with mental-health centers and women's support or shelter services. They are often independently established in larger metropolitan areas. The more common hot-line services include help for:

- child abuse
- rape or sexual assault
- runaways
- spouse abuse
- suicide
- general crises

Typical titles for positions may be crisis-line coordinator or assistant coordinator. Principal characteristics desirable for this type of work include counseling skills, a calm disposition, and the ability to quickly assess conditions and consider alternative referral services. Coordinating positions usually involve overseeing all functions as well as training volunteers.

6. Day care. Day-care work generally involves coordinating services to meet a wide spectrum of needs: (1) planning and leadership of activities for the clients, (2) planning for facility needs and layout, and (3) planning and providing for the daytime physical needs of clients. More common setting involving day care include:

- after-school programs
- child care and nursery-schools
- care for the elderly
- care for the handicapped
- care for the mentally disabled

The title of such positions may be child-care worker, day-treatment therapist, activities coordinator, or assistant director. Day-care work tends to have a more relaxed atmosphere than casework. In such settings, there is a place for the more outgoing, leadership type of professional as well as the more laid back, quieter, and calmer personality. Different clients also tend to relate to different personality types, so a varied staff can be beneficial.

7. Education.   First, community education covers a wide spectrum of family and individual needs, from abuse-awareness programs to programs for young mothers. Activities involve "providing relevant information . . . to the client, offering advice and suggestions, identifying alternatives and their probable consequences, modeling behaviors, teaching problem-solving techniques, and clarifying perceptions" (Barker, 1991, p. 71). Community education may be located in several settings, including:

- community college auxiliary educational services
- agency educational programs for parents and others
- public-awareness presentations for agencies
- workplace educational programs

Positions are less numerous than in most of the other services and may vary from part-time to full-time opportunities; or such educational functions may be performed in conjunction with other responsibilities of a staff member. Organizations typically hiring family-related educators include general social-service agencies, child-care programs, community colleges, large hospitals, mental-health centers, parenting centers, public-health departments, school districts, and state cooperative extension services. The more common subjects for community education include:

- child care, including birth-disorder education, nutritional health, parent education, pregnancy programs, and teenage parenting
- coping with various crises and stresses, such as death, divorce, single parenting, and stepparenting
- family-life education and family-enrichment programs
- health-awareness issues and related education
- parent education

- sexuality education
- substance-abuse education

Many of these opportunities are most suited for professionals who have had special training or experience in order to establish expertise in the subject. Nevertheless, some positions lend themselves to younger professionals with some entry-level experience. Also, activities may involve mostly coordination of peer-teaching programs such as MELD of Minneapolis (Payne, n.d.).

Second, family-life education may be practiced in more formal settings such as in public schools and at colleges. Those anticipating teaching in the public schools, usually at the high school level, should be enrolled in a teacher-certification program associated with a college or university. Graduation from such a program would qualify one to seek teaching positions in public schools.

College teaching, either in community colleges or other institutions of higher education, usually requires a least a master's degree in the subject area. A helpful discussion of this career focus is presented by Barbara Vance (1989) in her article "The Family Professional: Inside and Outside Academia." At the community college level, related courses may be found in several units, such as child development, human services, psychology, and sociology. For reviewing opportunities in other institutions of higher education, a booklet by John Touliatos (1994) could be useful: *Graduate Study in Marriage and the Family: A Guide to Master's and Doctoral Programs in the United States and Canada* (2nd ed.).

8. Research and planning.   Although most opportunities for research and planning are limited to persons with advanced graduate education, there are some opportunities for baccalaureate graduates to assist with projects. As Barker (1991) notes, planning includes "the process of specifying future objectives, evaluating the means for achieving them, and making deliberate choices about appropriate courses of action" (p. 174). Research may involve evaluating the outcome of such activities as well as studying other factors about individuals or family behavior. Such opportunities for research and planning related to families are associated with:

- cooperative extension services at land-grant universities
- county or urban planning offices, often with community-services units
- state and federal agencies and offices of elected officials
- university research associated with family-science departments and family centers

Title of positions might be research assistant, research associate, cooperative extension specialist, or community planner. As noted, most positions would be open to those with advanced education. Such opportunities are best suited for people with interest in extensive analysis of and strategic planning for family needs and services.

9. Residential care. Residential care is provided for numerous populations, usually involving some form of treatment. Barker (1991) defines it as "treatment intervention processes for people who cannot or do not function satisfactorily in their own homes" (p. 200). Residential care may include the following settings:

- assisting children to adjust to hospitalization (see Thompson, 1981)
- care for the elderly, especially those with special medical needs
- foster-care homes for abused children, orphans, and other minors in need of supervision and care
- homes for the handicapped
- shelters for abused women and their children
- short- and long-term delinquent care
- temporary shelters for the homeless
- treatment programs for psychiatric care and substance abuse

Titles for such work include activities coordinator, child-care worker (a generic term applied to settings for youths as well as younger children), director or assistant director of social services, or program coordinator. Besides planning and supervision of activities, work may involve issues related to intake and discharge planning, treatment planning, and general supervision of routine living activities.

10. Vocational and professional guidance and training. Vocational work covers a wide range of activities. In the social-service field, it often involves assistance to people with special needs due to mental or physical disabilities. It may include vocational guidance through helping them seek needed training and appropriate job placements. Other opportunities are in the area of employee-assistance programs, usually associated with personnel or human-resource departments of businesses. Guidance and training activities may involve positions related to:

- employee-assistance programs
- federal Job Training Partnership Act (JTPA)
- human-resource-development training
- numerous rehabilitation programs

Of the types of work associated with personnel departments, position titles may be adult retrainer, career counselor, program-coordinator trainee, and vocational counselor. In other positions, professionals may be working with youths and adults who need job training, with the handicapped, or with workers who can benefit from on-the-job training. Other activities may include in-service training and human-resource-development training of various types.

For persons interested in working with the blind or vision-impaired, a helpful book is the *American Foundation for the Blind Directory of Agencies Serving the Visually Handicapped in the U.S.* (1984). Agencies serving this population are listed by state.

Services—Agencies and Organizations

In some respects, it appears that there is no clear and consistent pattern in the delivery of services from one community to the next. Each community or general region should be studied to determine which agencies deliver which services. In one community, for example, a Big Brothers/Big Sisters program may be managed by a Family Service Agency, in another, by a mental-health center, and in a third, by itself.

Directory of Services. There are some aids to help determine which services are offered within a given community or neighboring region. A directory of services is usually published locally or regionally. A listing revealing most agencies and services can be found in a "Volunteer Opportunities Directory." Ideally, some organization will have published such a listing titled "Community Directory," "Community Organization," "Community Services," or a "Directory of Social Services."

A local newspaper or weekly shopper often publishes such a list on an annual basis. A Cooperative Extension Office, the United Way, the Voluntary Action Council, or the local Chamber of Commerce might have assisted in such a project. In any case, you should inquire about such a listing. A local reference librarian would probably know of its existence. If such a listing does not exist, you might consult local agencies or crisis-line services to review informal listings that they use for making referrals.

Local and regional agencies and organizations. After considering various populations to serve and the types of work noted above, it can now be helpful to review typical services and agencies commonly located in a community or region. The above categories of work may be performed by more than one agency. Likewise, one agency may perform a variety of services, while the same agency in another community may perform somewhat different services. For example, a senior citizens' center may be "sponsored" by a Family Service Agency in one area, while in another region a local municipality, township, parish, or county may "sponsor" the program. The more typical agencies and services in most regions are listed in Table 21.3.

Other services often may be provided. Whether they exist in a particular region may depend upon the availability of funding and perceived or actual needs. In the larger population or metropolitan centers, more services are likely to be provided. Examples of more limited services are listed in Table 21.4.

As mentioned earlier, services of agencies vary. One must become acquainted with the agencies and services of a specific region in order to learn about career opportunities.

Numerous nationwide social-service organizations should not be overlooked. For a detailed description of many of the agencies, one can consult a library's latest edition of the *Encyclopedia of Associations* (Bured, 1991) or *Social Service Organizations and Agencies: Directory* (Kruzas, 1982). Some religious groups sponsor social-service agencies, such as Catholic Social Services, Jewish Federations, LDS Social Services, Lutheran Social Services, the Lutheran Welfare League, and the Salvation Army. Except for administrative positions in the Salvation Army, most hiring practices are unrelated to one's own practicing faith.

Family-related social services are also provided throughout the nation by agencies affiliated with the Children's Home and Aid Society and Family Service America, the latter often being called locally a "Family Service Agency." Also, YMCA and YWCA centers often provide a variety of social services. Again, their services may vary widely from region to region.

Numerous other nationwide social-service organizations include various U.S and state governmental offices, such as the American Red Cross and the March of Dimes, Florence Crittenton units (usually serving women), Goodwill Industries helping the handicapped, legal aid societies, Planned Parenthood offices, regional representatives for scouting and other youth organizations, and Travelers Aid. One advantage of positions with some of these organizations is the opportunity for internal promotions, which may be better than in smaller local agencies. However, relocation may be necessary to take advantage of openings.

Factors Influencing Employment Choice

Once one has located agencies of interest, the next step my be to seek volunteer work with them or submit a résumé for possible employment or an internship. Several factors involved in their choice are:

- previous experience and the résumé
- educational prerequisites
- tests, certifications, registrations, and licensing
- salaries and other benefits
- future graduate school plans

Previous Experience

When seeking a position, you should recognize that apart from personal contacts, much of the initial screening of applicants depends upon your résumé and subsequent interview. You should not overlook gaining types of experiences noted in Table 21.5 and listing them on a résumé.

TABLE 21.3   Agencies, Organizations, and Services Found in Regions

Big Brothers/Big Sisters

Child-care programs (and after-school care)

Child-life programs for hospitalized children

Child and family services (state protective units)

Community colleges (adult and continuing-educational services)

Cooperative Extension Service—4H, home economics

Crisis lines

Food assistance (for example, meals on wheels for the handicapped or elderly; food banks

Foster care (contracted via court services and child-protective services; in private placements in homes and in group settings)

Head Start (preschool enrichment services for low-income families)

Health-promotion organizations (such as the March of Dimes)

Homemakers (services for people in need; connected with nonprofit agencies)

Hospitals (maternity and prenatal services; community support and education units; social services; addiction and psychiatric units)

Housing authorities (for public housing assistance to low-income families and seniors; housing and programming activities)

Job-training programs (including displaced homemakers and services connected with the JPTA)

Juvenile and adult court services (probation and parole services)

Mental-health centers (general therapy, substance-abuse treatment services; community education)

Nursing homes (public or private)

Park district (adult or youth activities and education)

Police department (youth divisions or services)

Public-aid offices (state, local, and nonprofit)

Public-health offices (county and state; teenage parent services)

Pupil personnel services (connected with school districts, includes counselors, psychologists, social workers, nurses, and special-education staff)

Rehabilitation services (state, private)

Residential care (group homes for youths, correctional facilities for youths and adults, elder care, handicapped care, substance-abuse treatment)

Senior-citizen centers and area agencies on aging

Scouting groups (area representatives)

Sheltered workshops/residential care (job training for the handicapped)

Shelters for abused women and children

Social Security office

Social-service agency (multiservice agencies, usually one or several in a general area such as Family Service Agency, Catholic Social Services, Jewish Federation, Latter-Day Saints Social Services, Lutheran Social Services, or Salvation Army)

Special-education services (for individuals and family support, conducted by independent districts, joint agreements, or cooperatives with school districts)

State employment office (and unemployment assistance)

State's Attorney's Office (victim/witness support services)

Teenage pregnancy programs (with public-health departments, nonprofit groups, hospitals, community centers)

Veterans' services (veterans' commissions, VA Hospitals, Department of Veterans Affairs)

Vocational-education units (vocational schools, public and private)

Voluntary Action Centers (volunteer coordination, transportation needs for the disabled)

WIC (Special Supplemental Food Program for Women, Infants, and Children)

Youth-service bureaus (nonprofit, public/governmental, occasionally with police departments)

TABLE 21.4   Limited Services, Depending on Regional Needs

Services for the blind
Camping programs (park districts, private, religious)
Child-care coordinating group (coordinating funding and
  educational programs; resources and referral services)
Community centers (typically offering social services and
  youth activities)
Day-care services (psychiatric care, disabled, and elderly)
Education (family-life education, health education, home
  economics, social science, special education)
Employee-assistance programs (associated with industries
  and institutions)
Holistic health centers
Homeless programs and services
Hospice programs
Immigrant services (relief services and assistance for refugees
  and others)
Legal aid societies and services
Migrant services (for farm workers)
Networking services
Parenting centers (associated with colleges and nonprofit
  service agencies)
Research and regional planning activities
Religious service organizations or groups
Substance-abuse treatment centers
Support groups or self-help groups (for numerous concerns)
Student services (housing staff; campus services and activities)
Women's services (displaced-homemaker services)
YMCA/YWCA (youth and family programs)

Not enough can be said about internships and extensive volunteer work. Supervisors often report that résumés are routinely discarded or set aside if they do not disclose some previous work-related experience. If one has no work experience, supervisors will usually consider the merits of internships or extensive volunteer work and keep such résumés in the pool of candidates to consider further. A few suggestions may be helpful regarding volunteer work and internships:

TABLE 21.5   Desirable Professionally Related Experience

Volunteer work, as varied and extensive as possible
Internships or cooperative-education experience
Appropriate summer employment
Other professionally related work experience, whether part-
  or full-time

1. If possible, it is advisable to do volunteer work with the agency, or one similar to it, that is a potential internship site or employer. Such experience serves several proposes: It helps you become more acquainted with and test your interest in the population served by the agency. You can become familiar with the structure and functions of the agency so that everything is not new when you begin as an intern or employee. And prospective employers can see that you are genuinely interested in the work of the agency and the population it serves. This "testing" helps reduce employee turnover rates; consequently, such experience is viewed very favorably by employers.

2. It is helpful if an intern can be full-time, serving a 40-hour week. Although most university internship programs provide only for part-time credit, such as three to six credit hours (Keim, 1990), there is nothing to stop you from offering more of your own time for the credit hours allowed. Serving full-time may take some planning to avoid conflicts with other needed courses or to dovetail with needed paid work hours at a part-time job. Summer may be an easier time to plan for it, if summer placements are allowed by your university program. If internships are only part time, Brock and Coufal (1989) suggest, students should extend the internship for two terms, if feasible. If students serve full-time or for an extended period, an agency staff is more likely to treat them like employees. This may strongly enhance the opportunities for being given greater responsibilities and for meaningful professional role modeling, and it may increase the chances of being offered a position with the agency should one become open. For a more extended discussion of the pros and cons of full-time placement, you might consult my article on internships (Keim, 1990).

3. It may help to serve an internship during the last term of your academic program. The reason is that it is common to be offered a position with the agency where an internship is being served. Having to return to school for a few courses can terminate the immediate connection or opportunity. In fact, some students begin assuming a full-time paid position prior to the completion of their formal internship.

4. When possible, it can be beneficial to serve an internship in the location where you wish later to become employed. By doing so, you can become per-

sonally knowledgeable about other agencies in the region and make acquaintances of other professionals whom you meet through networking contacts. Also, you can often become aware of open positions with other agencies, which otherwise are difficult to discover.

If internships are not available in a program, similar service opportunities are available in three other areas: extended volunteer work, a university cooperative-education program, or an informal internship. Some agencies will let a student serve with them on an extended volunteer basis comparable to an internship (often called an internship) without formally being linked with a university program. Many universities have a cooperative education program that serves students from all majors. Such programs offer off-campus work opportunities that are often similar to internships. For more information about volunteer opportunities, internships, or cooperative-education programs, consult a faculty adviser.

It is important for a résumé to reflect these experiences. Of equal importance is the wording of the résumé. The listing and clarification of extensive professionally related experiences, even through volunteer or part-time work or an internship, may help you secure a higher level position such as coordinator of a program. Or, as noted above, it may keep your résumé in the pool of applicants to be interviewed.

It is recommended that all such experiences be listed under one heading, "Professionally Related Experience" (Brock & Coufal, 1989). To list such entries under separate headings such as "Internship," "Volunteer Work," and "Work Experience" can make the résumé appear messy and fragmented. Listing the items together presents a greater continuity of experience. Seek guidance from a university career planning and placement office for résumé preparation, interview training, and other career resource materials. Likewise, seek suggestions from a faculty adviser, since properly highlighting one's education and related professional experiences can be critical.

You may plan to pursue a graduate degree immediately. Nevertheless, the above considerations can still be relevant in terms of gaining better insight into your career interests. Such experiences may be helpful in determining the type of graduate degree you wish to pursue.

Educational Prerequisites

To the surprise of many students, the details of one's transcript in the social-service field are often not of great interest to employers. Supervisors are usually more interested in (1) the kind of person the interviewee is, (2) how he or she relates to people, (3) signs of resourcefulness, creative thinking, appropriate assertiveness, and self-initiative, and (4) special experiences or interests that motivate the person toward the particular field of service.

In addition, two important special abilities are often looked for in an intern or a new employee: (1) the ability to speak "on one's feet" rather uninhibitedly and (2) the ability to be observant and easily relate to and lead others, especially in a small group. For a new professional in a family-science career, it is not at all uncommon to be quickly assigned the task of (1) leading or coleading a group of clients in some activity or (2) speaking to some outside group to describe the purposes of a proposed program or the services of the agency. Consequently, experience with small-group work and public speaking can be helpful in the majority of professional positions open to family scientists.

You can increase your skills in these two areas either by taking relevant academic courses in group process and public speaking or by assuming leadership positions in organizations or through relevant volunteer work. Useful training is available to students or new professionals by participation in Toastmasters International clubs, which meet weekly or biweekly. These clubs focus upon public speaking in a friendly and supportive atmosphere. This experience can also enhance one's awareness of small-group behavior. Membership is inexpensive and open to all. Guests are usually welcome in most clubs. Such clubs may be listed in the phone book or a community listing of clubs and organizations.

Other relevant academic education is appropriate and useful. Obviously, if you are applying for positions with the elderly, having courses in aging and gerontology are helpful. A child-abuse course would be appropriate for those seeking child-protection work. Courses in delinquency can be useful for probation work but are not essential. A course in medical terminology can aid those in hospital social services or nursing-home work, but many learn the basic terms on the job. One could go on listing specific courses for many different services. If relevant courses are available, you should take them. If in doubt, inquire from agencies about which specialized courses might be helpful.

If the career direction you are pursuing is very clear, an appropriately related concentration of courses, or minor, may be useful. You should realize that other liberal arts and sciences majors may be applying for similar professional positions. Therefore, you should recognize the unique qualifications you possess, as discussed in the opening pages of this chapter. It may be necessary to make prospective employers aware and appreciative of these unique qualifications. It is difficult to forget the statement a probation-office supervisor made regarding a family-science major, saying, in effect, "I can teach her the laws and regulations involved in probation work a lot quicker than I can teach a criminology student to be interpersonally sensitive, aware, and alert."

As for graduate work, as noted previously, many positions may require a master's degree or at least more experience. However, many positions are open to bachelor's degree graduates. In the rural areas or small towns, positions often reserved for the master's candidate in the city are open to baccalaureate graduates. You should not be discouraged by statements that a master's degree is required or preferred. With determination and effort, you can locate entry jobs.

Granted, some positions may require a master's or doctoral degree, such as marriage and family therapist, divorce mediator, college teachers, family researcher, and some administrative positions. In some cases, a bachelor's degree in addition to some special training or experience may qualify you for some of these positions. Also, in difficult employment times, the pool of candidates may be large. In such cases, the position may go to the best qualified or, possibly, to someone minimally qualified, in order to offer a lower salary and save money. If such tight employment times occur, you should realize the value of taking a less desired position, or even part-time or volunteer work, in order to gain the needed experience for job mobility.

Apart from special advanced educational needs, the availability of candidates and the rural/urban factor may have a greater influence upon which degree level is desired or required for a specific position. The career references cited earlier substantiate the point that numerous positions are open to one with a baccalaureate graduate (Career Associates, 1986; Hopke, 1987; Norback, 1988; Snelling & Snelling, 1985; Visual Education Center Staff, 1992; Wright, 1987).

Tests, Certifications, Registrations, and Licensing

Certification status or licensing is seldom required initially for positions open to baccalaureate graduates, except teaching in the public schools. Usually, one can obtain an entry position while still in pursuit of some certification, such as a Certified Family Life Educator, a certified chemical-dependency counselor, or some certified rehabilitation counseling positions.

Certified Family Life Educators have professional standing with the National Council on Family Relations. Certified Home Economists maintain standing with the American Home Economics Association. Certified Financial Counselors have training and standing with the National Foundation for Consumer Credit. Regulations for certification of abuse and for rehabilitation counselors vary from state to state. Therefore, local inquiry should be made with professionals in the field.

Civil-service testing may initially be required for some state and county positions. The nature of such testing is often very general knowledge of the field, along with the assessment of one's degree. Some test questions may relate to family and social-service issues as well as specific laws. Procedures may vary from state to state, so inquire at a state employment office or with established professionals about what is involved.

Licensing or registration is often similar to civil-service testing in which one is examined regarding general knowledge about the particular position. Advanced career positions and some entry ones may require certifications or licensing. For example, rehabilitation counselors often need to be registered social workers. For most entry positions, one can inquire soon after taking the position in a field about possible future expectations of licensing or registration.

Eventually, some graduates may wish to become clinical members of the Association of Marriage and

Family Therapy. Student status for this certification can be gained while still in graduate school. Others may wish to be licensed or registered social workers, a licensing procedure in many states. Majors from disciplines other than social work may qualify. Again, one should inquire about state regulations. Certified social workers are those having professional standing with the Academy of Certified Social Workers (Barker, 1991). This certification can be sought after one has more experience.

Salaries and Other Benefits

The most accurate information about beginning salaries for different types of work can be gained by asking agency staff members or supervisors. Although they may be reluctant to mention the salary of specific persons, administrators are usually willing to reveal the range of starting salaries.

Most career-guidance publications provide salary ranges in broad categories, such as mental-health work, handicapped services, and social work (Career Associates, 1986; Hopke, 1987; Norback, 1988; Snelling & Snelling, 1985; Visual Education Center Staff, 1992; Wright, 1987). Seldom does one find specific job titles and related beginning salaries as reported by Keim and Cassidy (1989). Also, salary data are often reported in dated publications. It is suggested by some that to determine the current level of salaries one should adjust the reported salary by adding 5% annually for each year from the reported date to the current year (Snelling & Snelling, 1985; Wright, 1987). In times of recession, this percentage for adjustment may be lower.

Various factors may influence what agencies consider a beginning salary. Factors reported by Keim and Cassidy (1989) are reviewed in Table 21.6.

The salaries in public agencies are generally better than those in private agencies, as reported by Wright

TABLE 21.6.   Factors Influencing Starting Salaries

Previous experience of the applicant
Funding level of the agency
Region of the country and urban versus rural locale
Salary levels of other professionals in the organization
Fringe benefits

(1991). He also notes that municipal departments usually pay more than county agencies, which tend to pay more than state agencies. Also, the range of salaries between different units of governments may be as much as $5,000 in the West, $1,000 in the central region, $3,000 in the South, and $1,500 on the East Coast. Salaries tend to be higher in metropolitan areas than in rural areas.

In agencies where there is hiring of diverse professionals, social-service workers tend to receive higher salaries. This is apparent in hospitals where doctors are employed and in probation work housed in the court system, with lawyers on the staff.

Fringe benefits should be considered when assessing the total salary package. Snelling and Snelling (1985) indicate that benefits account for as much as 30% of the base salary. More typical benefits may include health insurance, pension plans, paid vacation time, and sick leave. These benefits vary widely. Some small agencies may not provide medical insurance. Also, many beginning professionals wish to obtain a master's degree. Thus, it is important to realize that some agencies help finance the tuition of employees. The nature of these benefits should be carefully considered.

Future Graduate School Plans

By now, in the study of family science, the value of eventually obtaining a graduate degree has probably become apparent. For a review of possible graduate programs in family science, you could review the booklet by Touliatos (1994), *Graduate Study in Marriage and the Family: A Guide to Master's and Doctoral Programs in the U. S. and Canada* (2nd ed.). One hundred and four universities are listed, with information on program emphases, degree and admission requirements, tuition, financial assistance, deadlines, enrollment, and faculty.

For reviewing the diversity of future career paths that focus upon the family, review the article by Barbara Vance (1989), "The Family Professional: Inside and Outside Academia." She studied the careers of persons associated with the National Council on Family Relations, most of whom had advanced degrees. She cites 55 occupational specialties, most of which pertain to different degree emphases or preparation besides family science. Some of the other more typical specialties include alcoholism and drug abuse, clergy, counseling, gerontology, journalism, law, nursing, social work, and women's studies.

Typically, family-science graduates from Northern Illinois University, I have found, seek a similarly wide variety of advanced degrees, including adult continuing education, child development, communications disorders, community mental health, counselor education, early childhood education, family and child studies, family resource management, law, marriage and family therapy, public administration (in political science), and social work.

Although views differ, it is often recommended that one gain some work experience immediately after receiving a bachelor's degree. This can provide an opportunity to discover one's own latent interests. Other students may have a strong motivating direction, so that seeking an advanced degree immediately makes sense. Such issues should be carefully examined.

If you are planning to seek an advanced degree, of considerable importance during your junior or early senior year in college is to inquire about prerequisite courses that may be helpful. For seeking an advanced degree in marriage and family therapy, for instance, courses pertaining to personality theories and abnormal psychology would be useful. For any advanced degree, especially in social work, having a course in statistics, research methodology, and social policies or legislation would be helpful. In some cases, such courses may exempt one from taking certain graduate courses.

Seek to consider differences based upon varied local and regional societal needs.

2. By different client populations (elderly, abused women, children), share experiences and knowledge of (1) different local and regional organizations that provide services to families, (2) staff positions for which family-science graduates might qualify, and (3) any special prerequisite knowledge, skill, or talents that would be desirable for specific settings.

3. Discuss the various career goals of those in your class or group, and seek to identify different unique qualifications that each person possesses. Based upon his or her career goal, discuss what specific additional courses, experiences, personality traits, or skills might be helpful or needed.

4. Secure a "Directory of Social Services," possibly called "Community Directory," "Community Organizations," or "Community Services," or a comparable publication, and review it for agencies or services that relate to areas of your interest. In addition, review the various services and identify those that overlap as well as noting supplementary services that directly pertain to a client population of interest. Write a summary of the findings.

5. From the information in a social-services directory or from one's knowledge of a community, develop an alphabetical listing of agencies or organizations that perform various types of services cited in this chapter, or a listing of ones that pertain to your interests. Compare your listing with ones developed by others.

Chapter Summary

Discussion Questions

1. Based upon the awareness of family needs and crisis situations, develop through discussion a list of essential services that a community or region should provide. Assume that resources are limited and make a sincere attempt to prioritize the services from those most essential to those less urgently needed.

Additional Resources

Bolles, R. N. (1984). *What color is your parachute?* Berkeley, CA: Ten Speed Press.

Bured, D. M. (1991). *Encyclopedia of associations: Vol. 1, Parts 1–3* (26th ed.). Detroit: Gale Research.

Dictionary of Occupational Titles (4th ed.). (1991). U. S. Dept. of Labor, Employment and Training Administration, U. S. Employment Service. Washington, DC: U. S. Government Printing Office. (Section ranges beginning of 0.45.107–, 092.237–, 0.96.121–, 096.127–, 169.276–, 189.267–, 195.107–, 195.137–, 195.164–, 195.267–, and 195.367–.

Hopke, W. E. (1987). *The Encyclopedia of careers and vocational guidance: Vols. 1 and 2* (7th ed.). Chicago: T. G. Fergason.

Keim, R. E., & Myers, B. K. (1989). Professional organizations, associations, material resources, training programs, and other publications. *Family Science Review, 2,* 163–186.

Kipps, H. C. (Ed.). (1984). *Community resource directory: A guide to U. S. volunteer organizations.* Detroit: Gale Research.

Rockcastle, M. (Ed.). (1985). *Where to start: An annotated career planning bibliography.* Princeton, NJ: Peterson's Guides.

Sher, B. (1979). *Wishcraft: How to get what you really want.* New York: Ballantine.

Visual Center Staff. (1992). *Career Information Center* (13 vols.). New York: Macmillan.

References

American Foundation for the Blind. (1984). *American Foundation for the Blind directory of agencies serving the visually handicapped in the U. S.* (22nd ed.). New York: Author.

Barker, R. L. (1991). *The social work dictionary* (2nd ed.). Silver Spring, MD: NASW Press.

Bolles, R. N. (1984). *What color is your parachute?* Berkeley, CA: Ten Speed Press.

Brock, G. W., & Coufal, J. D. (1989). The résumé factor in seeking entry level family science positions. *Family Science Review, 2,* 117–124.

Bured, D. M. (Ed.). (1991). *Encyclopedia of associations: 1992: (Vol. 1, Parts 1–3)* (26th ed.). Detroit: Gale Research.

Career Associates. (1986). *Career choices encyclopedia: Guide to entry-level jobs.* New York: Walker & Co.

Hopke, W. E. (1987). *The encyclopedia of careers and vocational guidance: Vols. 1 and 2.* (7th ed.). Chicago: T. G. Ferguson.

Keim, R. E. (1990). Internships in family science: A model for development. *Family Science Review, 3,* 115–128.

Keim, R. E., & Cassidy, K. J. (1989). Careers for family scientists: Entry positions. *Family Science Review, 2,* 1–30.

Keim, R. E., & Myers, B. K. (1989). Professional organizations, associations, material resources, training programs, and other publications. *Family Science Review, 2,* 163–186.

Kipps, H. C. (Ed.). (1984). *Community resource directory: A guide to U. S. volunteer organizations.* (2nd ed.). Detroit: Gale Research.

Kruzas, A. T. (Ed.). (1982). *Social service organizations and agencies: Directory.* Detroit: Gale Research.

Moore, T. C. (Ed.). (1987). *Peterson's annual guides to graduate study: Book 2. Graduate programs in the humanities and social sciences 1988* (22nd ed.). Princeton, NJ: Peterson's Guides.

Nelson, J. O. (1980). *Opportunities in religious service.* New York: National Textbook.

Norback, C. T. (Ed.). (1988). *VGM's careers encyclopedia* (2nd ed.). Lincolnwood, IL: VGM Career Horizons.

Payne, C. (Ed.). (n.d.). *Programs to strengthen families: A resource guide.* Chicago: Family Resource Coalition.

Rockcastle, M. (Ed.). (1985). *Where to start: An annotated career planning bibliography.* Princeton, NJ: Peterson's Guides.

Sher, B. (1979). *Wishcraft: How to get what you really want.* New York: Ballantine.

Snelling, R. O., Sr., & Snelling, A. M. (1985). *Jobs! What they are . . . Where they are . . . What they pay.* New York: Simon & Schuster.

Thompson, R. (1981). *Child life in hospitals.* Springfield, IL: Charles C Thomas.

Touliatos, J. (1994). *Graduate study in marriage and the family: A guide to master's and doctoral programs in the United States and Canada* (2nd ed.). Forth Worth, TX: Human Sciences Publications.

Vance, B. (1989). The family professional: Inside and outside academia. *Family Science Review, 2,* 49–60.

Visual Education Center Staff. (1992). *Career Information Center* (Vols. 1–13). New York: Macmillan.

Wright, J. W. (1991). *The American almanac of jobs and salaries* (4th ed.). New York: Avon.

Name Index

Subject Index